SAS/GRAPH®
User's Guide,
Release 6.03 Edition

SAS Institute Inc.
SAS Circle □ Box 8000
Cary, NC 27512-8000

The correct bibliographic citation for this manual is as follows: SAS Institute Inc. *SAS/GRAPH® User's Guide, Release 6.03 Edition*. Cary, NC: SAS Institute Inc., 1988. 549 pp.

SAS/GRAPH® User's Guide, Release 6.03 Edition

Base SAS® software, the foundation of the SAS System, provides data retrieval and management, programming, statistical, and reporting capabilities. Also in the SAS System are SAS/GRAPH® SAS/FSP® SAS/ETS® SAS/IMS-DL/I® SAS/OR® SAS/AF® SAS/REPLAY-CICS® SAS/DMI® SAS/QC® SAS/SHARE® SAS/IML™ SAS/STAT™ SAS/DB2™ SAS/SQL-DS™ and SAS/ACCESS™ software. Other products include SYSTEM 2000® Data Management Software, with basic SYSTEM 2000® QueX™ Multi-User™ Screen Writer™ CREATE™ and CICS interface software; SAS/RTERM® software; and SAS/C™ and SAS/CX™ compilers. *SAS Communications® SAS Training® SAS Views®* and SASware Ballot® are published by SAS Institute Inc. The Institute is a private company devoted to the support and further development of the software and related services.

Contents

APPENDICES

Illustrations

Tables

Credits

Documentation

Composition	Blanche W. Phillips, Craig R. Sampson
Graphics and Graphic Design	Jesse C. Chavis, Jennifer A. Davis, Ginny Matsey, Michael J. Pezzoni
Proofreading	Bruce Calvin Brown, Rebecca A. Fritz, Reid J. Hardin, Molly M. Munro, Michael H. Smith
Technical Review	Roger Chenoweth, Mike Kalt, Doug Walker, Carl Zeigler
Writing and Editing	Betsy S. Corning, Ottis R. Cowper, Susan Cross, Gretel Easter, John Gough, Marla Z. Hudnell, Kathryn P. Ingraham, Mike Kalt, Gary R. Meek

Software Development

Program authorship includes design, programming, debugging, support, and preliminary documentation. The SAS Institute staff member whose name is followed by an asterisk has primary responsibility for the procedure; others give (or have given, in previous versions of SAS/GRAPH software) specific assistance.

GANNO	Anthony Friebel*
GCHART	Jack Bulkley*, J. H. Goodnight
GCONTOUR	Anthony Friebel, J. H. Goodnight, Jim Lee, Jade Walker*
GDEVICE	Jade Walker*
GFONT	Dale D. Ingold, Jim Lee, Doug Walker*
GMAP	J. H. Goodnight, Jim Lee*
GOPTIONS	Dale D. Ingold, Doug Walker*
GPLOT	David M. DeLong, Anthony Friebel*, J. H. Goodnight, Jane Pierce
GPRINT	Jack Bulkley*, J. H. Goodnight
GPROJECT	Dale D. Ingold, Jade Walker*
GREDUCE	David M. DeLong, Dave Jeffreys*
GREMOVE	Jack Bulkley, J. H. Goodnight, Dave Jeffreys*
GREPLAY	Rick Edwards*
GSLIDE	Dale D. Ingold, Jade Walker*
GTESTIT	Craige Hales, Jade Walker*
G3D	Craige Hales, Jim Lee, Jade Walker*
G3GRID	David M. DeLong, Jane Pierce*

Type Styles and Fonts	Anthony Friebel, Jim Lee, Doug Walker*
Map Data Sets	Jack Bulkley, Dave Jeffreys*
SAS/GRAPH Device Drivers	Jack Bulkley, Rob Dolan, Anthony Friebel, Howard Houston*, Mike Kalt, Jack Lin, Woody Middleton, Jade Walker
Annotate Facility	Anthony Friebel*
Global Statements	Dale D. Ingold, Doug Walker*
GSUBLIB	Valerie Blettner, Jack Bulkley, Rick Edwards, Howard Houston, Jim Lee*, Doug Walker, Jade Walker

Software Support

Color Graphics Production	Rob Dolan
Testing and Program Debugging	Art Barnes, Rob Dolan, Ken Ellis, Sheila Fitzgerald Evans, Stuart Nisbet, John Scott
Quality Assurance Testing	Shearin Bizzell, Roger Chenoweth, Brad L. Chisholm, John W. DeBoskey, Himesh G. Patel
Technical Support	Donna Bravo, Sarah Darden, Tom Dickey, Mike Kalt, Lelia McConnell, Martin Mincey, Peter Ruzsa

(If you have questions or encounter problems, call SAS Institute and ask for the Technical Support department rather than an individual staff member.)

We at SAS Institute are grateful for the support we have received from the vendors of the hardware that supports SAS/GRAPH software. Their contributions of time and technical expertise have helped immensely in the development of SAS/GRAPH software.

We acknowledge the time and effort of A. V. Hershey, who designed and supplied some of the character fonts used in SAS/GRAPH software.

Preface

What Is the SAS System?

The SAS System is a software system for data analysis. The goal of SAS Institute is to provide data analysts with one system to meet all their computing needs. When your computing needs are met, you are free to concentrate on results rather than on the mechanics of getting them. Instead of learning programming languages, several statistical and graphics packages, and utility programs, you only need to learn the SAS System.

The SAS System is available on many mainframes, minicomputers, and personal computers under a variety of operating systems. Not all products in the SAS System are available for all operating systems. For more information about how to license products under your operating system, see **Licensing the SAS System** later in this section.

Base SAS Software

Base SAS software provides tools for

- information storage and retrieval
- data modification and programming
- report writing
- descriptive statistics
- file handling.

Each of these tools is briefly summarized in the paragraphs below.

Information storage and retrieval The SAS System reads data values in virtually any form and then organizes the values into a SAS data set. The data can be combined with other SAS data sets by using the file-handling operations described below. You can analyze the data and produce reports. SAS data sets are automatically self-documenting because they contain both the data values and their descriptions. The special structure of a SAS data library minimizes maintenance.

Data modification and programming A complete set of SAS statements and functions is available for modifying data. Some program statements perform standard operations such as creating new variables, accumulating totals, and checking for errors; others are powerful programming tools such as DO/END and IF-THEN/ELSE statements. The data-handling features are so valuable that many people use base SAS software as a data base management system.

Report writing Just as base SAS software reads data in almost any form, it can write data in almost any form. In addition to the preformatted reports that SAS procedures produce, you can design and produce printed reports in any form, including output files on disk.

Descriptive statistics Procedures available in base SAS software

- provide simple descriptive statistics, such as averages and standard deviations
- produce bar charts, pie charts, and plots
- produce and analyze contingency tables
- rank and standardize data.

File handling   Combining values and observations from several data sets is often necessary for data analysis. Base SAS software has tools for editing, subsetting, concatenating, merging, and updating data sets. Multiple input files can be processed simultaneously, and several reports can be produced in one pass of the data.

Other SAS System Products

To base SAS software, you can add tools for statistical analysis, graphics, forecasting, data entry, operations research, quality control, interactive matrix applications, data base management, and interfaces to other data bases to provide one total system. The other products currently available for Release 6.03 are

SAS/AF software   a full-screen, interactive applications facility

SAS/FSP software   interactive, menu-driven facilities for data entry, editing, retrieval of SAS files, and text processing

SAS/GRAPH software
device-intelligent color graphics for business and research applications

SAS/IML software   an interactive matrix facility for advanced mathematical, engineering, and statistical needs

SAS/STAT software
a powerful set of statistical analysis procedures.

Documentation for the SAS System

This book documents Release 6.03 of SAS/GRAPH software. For more information on how to use this book, read the section titled "Using This Book."

Other manuals and technical reports are available for base SAS software and for the other products available for Release 6.03. In addition, other versions of the SAS System are documented in other manuals not listed here. The following is a list of Release 6.03 manuals and technical reports:

SAS Introductory Guide, Release 6.03 Edition
SAS Language Guide, Release 6.03
SAS Procedures Guide, Release 6.03
SAS/AF User's Guide, Release 6.03 Edition
SAS/FSP User's Guide, Release 6.03 Edition
SAS/IML User's Guide, Release 6.03 Edition
SAS/STAT User's Guide, Release 6.03 Edition
SAS/GRAPH Hardware Interfaces Guide, Release 6.03 Edition
SAS Guide to Macro Processing, Version 6 Edition
SAS Guide to TABULATE Processing, 1987 Edition

You can write the Institute's Book Sales Department for a current publications catalog, which describes the manuals and technical reports and lists their prices.

SAS Institute Services to Users

Technical support   SAS Institute supports users through the Technical Support Department. If you have a problem running a SAS job, you should contact your site's SAS Software Consultant. If the problem cannot be resolved locally, your local support personnel should call the Institute's Technical Support Department at (919) 467-8000 on weekdays between 9:00 a.m. and 5:00 p.m. Eastern Time. A brochure describing the services provided by the Technical Support Department is available from SAS Institute.

Training   SAS Institute sponsors a comprehensive training program, including programs of study for novice data processors, statisticians, applications programmers, systems programmers, and local support personnel. *SAS Training*, a semi-annual training publication available from the Education Division, describes the total training program and each course currently being offered by SAS Institute.

News magazine   *SAS Communications* is the quarterly news magazine of SAS Institute. Each issue contains ideas for more effective use of the SAS System, information about research and development underway at SAS Institute, the current training schedule, new publications, and news of the SAS Users Group International (SUGI).

To subscribe to *SAS Communications*, send your name and complete address to

SAS Institute Mailing List
SAS Institute Inc.
SAS Circle, Box 8000
Cary, NC 27512-8000

Sample library   Both base SAS and SAS/GRAPH software contain a directory of sample SAS applications that illustrate features of base SAS and SAS/GRAPH procedures and demonstrate creative SAS programming techniques that can help you gain an in-depth knowledge of the capabilities of the software. Check with your SAS Software Consultant to find out how to access the sample library.

SAS Users Group International (SUGI)

The SAS Users Group International (SUGI) is a nonprofit association of professionals who are interested in how others are using the SAS System. Although SAS Institute provides administrative support, SUGI is independent from the Institute. Membership is open to all users at SAS sites, and there is no membership fee.

Annual conferences are structured to allow many avenues of discussion. Users present invited and contributed papers on various topics.

Proceedings of the annual conferences are distributed free to SUGI registrants. Extra copies can be purchased from SAS Institute.

SASware Ballot   SAS users provide valuable input toward the direction of future SAS development by ranking their priorities on the annual SASware Ballot. The top vote-getters are announced at the SUGI conference. Complete results of the SASware Ballot are also printed in the *SUGI Proceedings*.

Licensing the SAS System

The SAS System is licensed to customers in the Western Hemisphere from the Institute's headquarters in Cary, NC. To serve the needs of our international customers, the Institute maintains many international subsidiaries. In addition, agents in other countries are licensed distributors for the SAS System. For a complete list of offices, write or call

SAS Institute Inc.
SAS Circle, Box 8000
Cary, NC 27512-8000
(919) 467-8000

Using This Book

Purpose of This Book

This book documents all of the procedures available in Release 6.03 of SAS/GRAPH software. To find out which release of SAS/GRAPH software you are using, look at the notes at the beginning of the SAS log.

How This Book Is Organized

Chapters 1 through 7 of this book provide an overview and introduce you to some of the graphics capabilities of SAS/GRAPH software, such as the three types of graphics output from a procedure and how available colors can be used and defined. Chapters 4 and 5 describe how you can enhance your graphics output text and designs. Chapter 6 describes the SAS/GRAPH system options that you can specify in a GOPTIONS statement. If you want to control the final appearance of your output, you can use the GOPTIONS statement to set certain options at the system level. SAS/GRAPH software features the Annotate facility, and Chapter 7 describes how you can customize procedure output by using an ANNOTATE= data set.

Chapters 8 through 24 describe individual SAS/GRAPH procedures in alphabetical order. Each procedure description is self-contained; you need to be familiar with only the most basic features of the SAS System and SAS terminology to use most procedures. The statements and syntax necessary to run each procedure are presented in a uniform format throughout this book. All the examples in this book can be found in the sample library that is provided with SAS/GRAPH software. You can duplicate the examples by copying the statements and data from the sample library and running the SAS program. The examples are also useful as models for writing your own programs. Contact your SAS Software Consultant or system administrator for information on the availability of the sample library at your site.

Each procedure description is divided into the following major parts:

ABSTRACT	a short paragraph describing what the procedure does.
INTRODUCTION	introductory and background material, including definitions and occasional introductory examples.
SPECIFICATIONS	reference section for the syntax for the procedure. The statement syntax is summarized, then the PROC statement is described, and then all other statements are described in alphabetical order. Options for a statement are described in alphabetical order, or they are grouped and described in alphabetical order within each group.
DETAILS	expanded descriptions of features, internal operations, statistical background, treatment of missing values, computational methods, required computational resources, and input and output data sets.
EXAMPLES	examples using the procedure, including data, SAS statements, and printed output. You can reproduce these examples by copying the statements and data from the sample library and running the job.

REFERENCES   a selected bibliography.

Following the chapters that describe SAS/GRAPH procedures, there are four appendices. The first appendix shows samples of SAS/GRAPH type styles and fonts, and the second appendix describes special SAS/GRAPH data sets. The third appendix lists available SAS/GRAPH device drivers, and the fourth appendix summarizes changes and enhancements for Version 6 SAS/GRAPH software.

How to Use This Book

If you have not used the SAS System before, you should read the *SAS Introductory Guide, Release 6.03 Edition* and also refer to the *SAS Language Guide, Release 6.03 Edition* and the *SAS Procedures Guide, Release 6.03 Edition*. These guides will help you learn the basics of using the SAS System.

Next, read Chapter 1, "Introduction to SAS/GRAPH Software," and note the different types of graphics that you can produce with SAS/GRAPH software by choosing different procedures. Once you have chosen a procedure that will meet your graphics needs, you can turn to the chapter on the procedure. First, read the **ABSTRACT** and **INTRODUCTION** to get an overview of how the procedure works. Next, look at the first part of the **SPECIFICATIONS** section to get a summary of which statements can be used with the procedure and what each statement does. At this point, you may know exactly what statements you need to use for your situation. If not, there may be an example in the **EXAMPLES** section that closely matches your problem and can guide you in selecting statements to use. Otherwise, you may need to read the **SPECIFICATIONS** section in more detail. Finally, the **DETAILS** section contains information on advanced topics and details of analysis.

If you are familiar with the SAS System and with the procedures in SAS/GRAPH software, first turn to Appendix 4, which summarizes the changes and enhancements to the software. Next, review specific chapters to learn more about the changes to a particular procedure. Many procedures have expanded introductions, new or expanded details sections, and new examples, so even if the procedure has not changed very much, the chapter on the procedure may have new information.

Typographical Conventions

The following type styles are used in this book:

roman type   is the basic type style used for most text.

italic type   is used to define new terms and to indicate items in statement syntax that you need to supply.

bold type   is used in **SPECIFICATIONS** sections to indicate that you must use the exact spelling and form shown, to refer to matrices and vectors, and to refer you to other sections (either in the same or in other chapters). In addition, sentences of extreme importance are entirely in bold type.

`code`   is used to show examples of SAS statements.

SAS code   Examples of SAS code are shown in lowercase type. You can enter your own SAS code in lowercase, uppercase, or a mixture of the two. The SAS System always changes your variable names to uppercase, but character variable values remain in lowercase on printed or displayed output if you have entered them that way. Enter any titles and footnotes exactly as you want them to appear on your output.

Referring to Files and Directories

File and directory names are shown in lowercase type in examples of SAS code and in uppercase type in the text. For operating systems that do not distinguish between uppercase and lowercase type, this typographic convention poses no problem. However, if you are using a *case-sensitive* operating system, the convention may seem confusing. If your operating system is case-sensitive, you must always refer to a file or directory name exactly as it was created. Using a different case for even one letter results in a different name.

To find out if your operating system is case-sensitive, contact your SAS Software Consultant or your system administrator.

In addition, this book does not specify complete pathnames for directories and files referred to in most examples because different computing installations use different conventions for naming directories and files. Instead, most examples refer to files and subdirectories in your current directory. For example, the following LIBNAME statement assigns the libref STORE1 to the subdirectory INVENTRY in your current directory:

```
libname store1 'inventry';
```

Similarly, the following FILE statement directs output to a file named YEAR85.DAT in the MISC subdirectory of your current directory. The syntax of this file specification is appropriate for UNIX® operating systems and derivatives:

```
file 'misc/year85.dat';
```

If you want to refer to a file or directory that is not in your current directory, specify the complete pathname. For example, the following FILE statement directs output to a file named ACCOUNTS in the directory /USR/SMITH:

```
file '/usr/smith/accounts';
```

Again, this file specification is appropriate for UNIX operating systems and derivatives. Note that how you specify the complete pathname, for example, whether you use a forward slash (/) or a back slash (\) to separate directory and file names, depends on your operating system and the conventions used at your site. See your SAS Software Consultant for more information.

Using the ENTER and Control Keys

Because keyboards differ in the number, placement, and use of their keys, you are not told exactly which keys to press as you use SAS software. However, in some chapters you are asked to type a command and press ENTER. On your keyboard, this key may be labeled with the word ENTER or RETURN or with a bent arrow. In addition, you may be asked to press the CTRL key; this key may be labeled CNTL on your keyboard.

For more information on using SAS software with your keyboard, see Chapter 10, "SAS Display Manager System," in the *SAS Language Guide*.

How the Output Is Shown

Printed and plotted output from procedures is enclosed in boxes. Within a chapter, the output is numbered consecutively starting with 1, and each output is given a title.

Color graphics output is shown in screens. The output screens were produced using the PCR4XL device driver with a Matrix PCR color film recorder, on which

---

UNIX is a registered trademark of AT&T.

SAS/GRAPH can display 256 colors. If you run the example programs, the colors produced by your device may be different from these shown in this book.

Chapter 1

Introduction to SAS/GRAPH® Software

What is SAS/GRAPH Software?

SAS/GRAPH software is a computer graphics system for displaying data in the form of color plots, charts, maps, and slides on your screen and on hardcopy devices.

SAS/GRAPH programs are SAS procedures, and they require only a few statements to produce results. All retrieval, data management, analysis, and other capabilities of base SAS software are available with SAS/GRAPH software. You place your data into SAS data sets before SAS/GRAPH procedures use them.

Using SAS/GRAPH software, you can design displays showing information in meaningful pictures. Extensive title and footnote capabilities allow you to explain the nature of your data and enhance the display. If you are a new user, carefully chosen default values for SAS/GRAPH system and procedure options mean that you can produce pictures immediately. You simply decide how you want to present your data and let SAS/GRAPH software do the rest. As you become a more experienced user, you can supply your own values for these same options, and tailor displays to suit your needs.

What Types of Displays Can You Create?

SAS/GRAPH software offers a variety of procedures that enable you to create presentation and information graphics. In addition, the Annotate facility has the flexibility and power to help you design your own graphics. To help you decide the best form for displaying your data, read through the descriptions of the procedures below and see which styles suit your needs.

To introduce you to the versatility of SAS/GRAPH software, simple examples of code and output from the GSLIDE and GCHART procedures are provided below. To demonstrate the power of SAS/GRAPH software, an example of PROC GREPLAY output is also provided. These examples use data on housing starts from 1980-1986 for single-family, condominium, and duplex homes.

Suppose you want to create presentation graphics showing the growth of housing sales from 1980-1986. Your data are stored in a SAS data set called HOMES. (You can find the data used in this example and other examples in this guide in the SAS Sample Library. Ask your SAS Software Consultant how to access or copy files from the library.) As the first part of your presentation, you want to create a simple text slide. You specify a TITLE statement and a PROC GSLIDE statement, for example,

```
title1 font=swiss height=2 'Local Housing Starts';
proc gslide;
run;
```

to create a slide with text as shown in **Output 1.1**.

Next, you want to create vertical bar charts showing starts of each type of home over the years 1980-1986. First, be sure your data are in a SAS data set. Then use the GCHART procedure to create the charts. You can use a BY statement to request a separate chart for each TYPE of home. To see the starts for each year, request a chart that has a bar for each value of YEAR. You are interested in seeing the total number of homes sold, so the variable to be totaled or summed is NUMBER. You can add a few PATTERN statements to make each bar unique. The basic statements you need to produce the charts are

```
proc gchart data=homes;
   by type;
   vbar year / discrete
               sumvar=number;
run;
```

Output 1.2 shows one of the bar charts you requested.

To create another chart that combines the information of your previous charts, you specify a few more options. This chart has a bar for each year, but each bar contains the total sales for the year subdivided by type of home. The statements you need are

```
proc gchart data=homes;
   vbar year / discrete
               subgroup=type
               sumvar=number;
run;
```

The chart you produced is shown in **Output 1.3**.

Finally, you want to place some of your slides on one page so that you can present the information as concisely as possible. To place your charts on one page, use the template facility in PROC GREPLAY. You can produce output like that shown in **Output 1.4**.

Output 1.1   Simple Text Slide: PROC GSLIDE

Output 1.2   Vertical Bar Chart: PROC GCHART

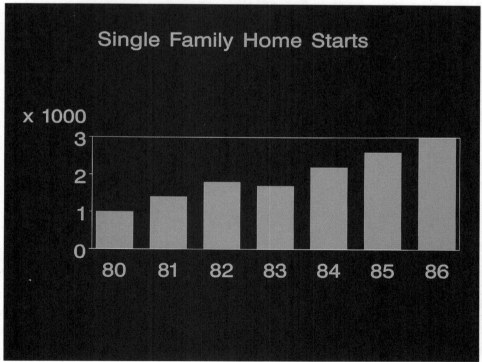

Output 1.3   Vertical Bar Chart with SUBGROUP= Option: PROC GCHART

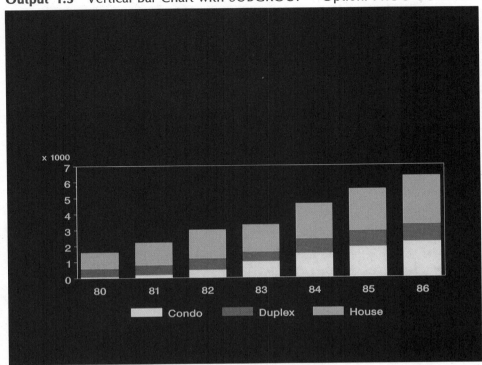

Output 1.4   Multiple Graphs on a Page: PROC GREPLAY

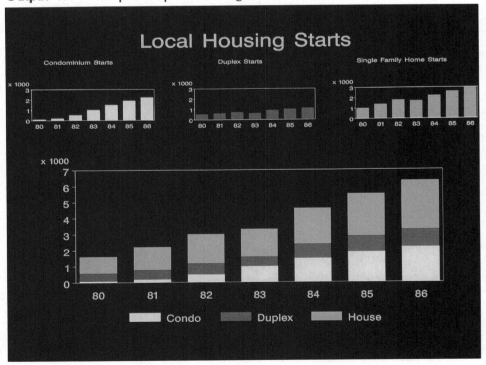

From these examples, you can see that SAS/GRAPH software can produce many types of output, from the simplest text slides to more complex graphic layouts that you design. The types of displays you can create are described briefly below. For complete information on the statements you need to create each type of display, read the appropriate chapter for each procedure.

Note that the colors shown in the output screens in this guide may be different from the colors you see on your device. The output screens were produced using the PCR4XL device driver with a Matrix PCR™color film recorder on which SAS/GRAPH can display 256 colors.

Color slides   The GSLIDE procedure displays lines of text. You specify options for colors, type fonts and sizes, and other attributes in TITLE, FOOTNOTE, and NOTE statements.

Bar charts, pies, stars, and block charts   The GCHART procedure draws vertical and horizontal bar charts (histograms), pies, stars, and block charts.

For bar and block charts, you can specify a different color for each bar, and you can produce subdivided bars where each subdivision has a different color and pattern. Up to sixty-four patterns are available; the number of colors depends on the graphics device you are using.

Graphs and plots   The GPLOT procedure graphs one variable against another. You can also produce plots for each value of a third variable on the same graph. Choose from among sixty-four plotting symbols to represent the points on your plot. You can connect the points on your plot by using either straight lines between the points or more sophisticated smoothing techniques. You can use regression routines to fit a line to the points, and confidence limits can also be drawn. If you want the points to fall on the plot line, you can use spline techniques to produce a smoothed line.

You can draw vertical needles from each point on the plot to a horizontal line and fill surfaces defined by plotted points. You can define different colors for the axis, points, and lines. Up to forty-six solid-line and dashed-line styles are available for plot lines.

Maps   The GMAP procedure produces choropleth, surface, prism, and block maps. Choropleth maps display responses within certain unit areas, such as states or counties. You select the patterns and colors with PATTERN statements. Surface maps, drawn in your choice of colors, give oblique perspective views of surfaces. Prism maps are three-dimensional graphics that use raised polygons to represent differences in magnitude. Block maps use blocks of varying heights to represent different values. You can create your own map data set containing geographical coordinates, or you can use one of the data sets provided with SAS/GRAPH software.

Special mapping-related procedures help you create maps more efficiently and accurately. The GPROJECT procedure applies one of several projection techniques to a map data set and creates a new map data set. The GREDUCE procedure processes a map data set so you can create subsets of the data that retain the overall appearance of the map. The GREMOVE procedure creates a new map by removing boundaries from an original map.

Contour plots   The GCONTOUR procedure produces contour plots, where values of three variables are represented in two dimensions. You can choose colors, line styles, and patterns for up to 100 levels of contour.

Three-dimensional plots   The G3D procedure plots the values of three variables, producing a three-dimensional surface graph (PLOT statement) or a three-dimensional scatter graph (SCATTER statement). You can specify options to tilt and rotate your surface plots and to select the size, shape, and color of plotting characters.

Processing graphics data   The G3GRID procedure interpolates values from an irregularly spaced set of points, generating a rectangular grid of values.

Enhancing any output   The GPRINT procedure lets you use the features of SAS/GRAPH TITLE and FOOTNOTE statements to enhance the appearance of any SAS output.

Customizing procedure output   The Annotate facility allows you to customize SAS/GRAPH procedure output or create your own custom graphics output. The GANNO procedure lets you plot the contents of an ANNOTATE= data set.

Storing, managing, and replaying graphics output   Use PROC GREPLAY to reconstruct pictures saved from previous SAS/GRAPH procedures. All SAS/GRAPH procedures allow you to save your pictures in a SAS catalog. PROC GREPLAY not only allows you to replay your graphs, but is a full-screen procedure with catalog management features. In addition, the procedure enables you to place several graphs on the same page with the template facility.

What Kinds of Utility Features are Available?

Special utility procedures allow you to perform functions that do not produce output.

Creating new type fonts   The GFONT procedure allows you to create new fonts and symbols to use in your SAS/GRAPH programs. You can also use PROC GFONT to display the fonts available with SAS/GRAPH software.

Listing system options   The GOPTIONS procedure lists the SAS/GRAPH system options currently in effect in your system. You can also list the current SYMBOL, PATTERN, TITLE, and FOOTNOTE statements.

Testing SAS/GRAPH installation   The GTESTIT procedure is a tool for testing the installation of SAS/GRAPH software. You can also use PROC GTESTIT to find out how the graphics options and some device settings are set on your output device.

How Can You Control Text, Design, and System Features?

You can use special statements to control your graphics output text and displays, regardless of the SAS/GRAPH procedure you are using. You can also control certain options at the system level, rather than at the procedure level.

Text control   You use FOOTNOTE, NOTE, and TITLE statements to place text on your graph. You can specify the color, type font, height, angle of rotation, spacing, and so on of lines of text.

Design control   The AXIS and LEGEND statements let you define exactly how your axes and legend will look in various procedures, including color, text, tick marks, and so on. PATTERN and SYMBOL statements let you determine the color, line types, and patterns of your charts, plots, and maps.

System control   The GOPTIONS statement lets you set options for color, type font, device information, and so on at the system level so you can concentrate your efforts on your SAS/GRAPH programs.

What Do You Need to Use SAS/GRAPH Software?

You need a device capable of producing graphics output. You will find a list of graphics output devices that can be used with SAS/GRAPH software in the appendix "SAS/GRAPH Device Drivers." The appendix contains descriptions of the devices supported by SAS/GRAPH software, including information on default settings for colors and system options.

If you are running the SAS System on a personal computer, you need an IBM Personal Computer (or a compatible device) with 640K memory and PC DOS 2.0 or greater to use the PC version of SAS/GRAPH software. A CGA (color graphics adapter), EGA (enhanced graphics adapter), or one of the other supported adapters will allow you to display graphics on the screen. An RS-232 serial port will allow you to attach one of the supported hardcopy devices.

You need a working knowledge of the SAS System to use SAS/GRAPH software. You should be able to read your data values into a SAS data set and perform any necessary data modifications. File-handling operations, such as subsetting and concatenating, are often useful when you want to improve a picture's information content.

If you are not familiar with the SAS System, the *SAS Introductory Guide, Release 6.03 Edition* will get you started. The *SAS Language Guide, Release 6.03 Edition*, and the *SAS Procedures Guide, Release 6.03 Edition* will help you prepare your data and give you more information on the types of applications you may want to perform.

We recommend that you read the other chapters in the OVERVIEW to find out what SAS/GRAPH software can do for you; then browse through the procedure chapters to decide what types of graphs you want to produce.

8

SAS/GRAPH®
Graphics Output

ABSTRACT

SAS/GRAPH software can produce several different types of graphics output from a procedure. Each type of output has its own special uses, and you can tailor the types of output produced to suit your application.

INTRODUCTION

Most SAS/GRAPH procedures produce graphics output. Output from these procedures can take one or more of the following forms:

- graphics displayed on a monitor, terminal, or workstation
- graphics sent to a peripheral device (usually a printer or plotter)
- device commands sent to a graphics stream file (GSF)
- graphics stored in a SAS catalog. The contents of a catalog can be replayed later on any supported device using PROC GREPLAY.

All SAS/GRAPH procedures that produce graphics output generate SAS catalog members, but they can create only one of the other types of output at a time. By specifying certain options in a GOPTIONS or PROC statement or in a device catalog entry, you can send your output to the desired destination. The next section of this chapter describes how to create different types of output using SAS/GRAPH software for personal computers. This is followed by a section describing how to create output using SAS/GRAPH software on UNIX operating systems and derivatives. You should read the appropriate section for the operating system you are using.

GRAPHICS OUTPUT FROM SAS/GRAPH SOFTWARE FOR PERSONAL COMPUTERS

Sending Output to the Monitor

If your personal computer has a supported graphics display adapter such as a CGA, EGA, or Hercules board, you can generate output on your video monitor by simply specifying the appropriate device driver for the adapter and monitor you have. You can specify the driver in either an OPTIONS statement or a GOPTIONS statement. If you have not already specified a driver when a SAS/GRAPH procedure is executed, you will be prompted to supply one at that time. For example, if you have an EGA board (with at least 128K of memory) and an EGA monitor, you can use the following statements to send PROC GSLIDE output to your monitor:

```
goptions device=egal;
title 'Output to the Monitor';
proc gslide;
run;
```

The appendix "SAS/GRAPH Device Drivers" provides details on choosing the appropriate driver for the hardware you have. Note that the drivers for display adapters send output directly to the screen and are incapable of producing a usable graphics stream file or of sending output to a communications or printer port.

SAS/GRAPH device drivers for some graphics adapters such as the Vectrix VXPC-4096 and Tektronix PC4100 make use of DOS device-driver software supplied with the boards. The SAS/GRAPH drivers for these devices behave like drivers for a communications port. See **Sending Output to a Device Attached to a Port** for details on using drivers for these adapters.

Sending Output to a Device Attached to a Port

Plotters, film recorders, and most laser printers are usually attached to one of the computer's serial ports (usually COM1:). When sending graphics output to one of these devices, you should select the appropriate driver for the device you are using and direct the output from the driver to the desired port. To do this, you can specify a path using the GACCESS field in the entry for the device in your device catalog or using the GACCESS= option in a GOPTIONS statement. (A device catalog contains entries that let you alter the attributes of each device driver. Refer to "The GDEVICE Procedure" for details on using PROC GDEVICE to modify catalog entries.)

In the Institute-supplied device catalog that accompanies SAS/GRAPH software, the GACCESS field for drivers for most hardcopy devices has the value SASGASTD>COM1:. This causes the driver to write a stream of graphics commands to the COM1: serial port. If you want to send output to a plotter attached to COM1:, specify the driver name in a GOPTIONS statement. The default values used by the driver then cause output to be sent to the plotter. For example, if you have a Hewlett-Packard 7475 plotter attached to COM1:, you can use these statements to send PROC GSLIDE output to the plotter:

```
goptions device=hp7475;
title 'Output to HP7475 Plotter Attached to COM1:';
proc gslide;
run;
```

The entries for Epson, Hewlett-Packard, and IBM printers in the Institute-supplied device catalog have a GACCESS value of SASGASTD>PRN:, which causes output to go to the printer port. If you are using one of these drivers and have the printer attached to your computer's parallel printer port, you need only specify the device name in a GOPTIONS statement to have output sent to the printer.

If your hardcopy device is attached to a port other than the one specified in the GACCESS field in your device catalog entry, you can modify the device catalog entry to direct output to the correct port. For example, if you have a laser printer attached to a printer port, and the default entry for the driver specifies a GACCESS value of SASGASTD>COM1:, you can modify the value to SASGASTD>PRN: or SASGASTD>LPT1:. You can also use the GACCESS= option in a GOPTIONS statement to override the value specified for GACCESS in the device catalog entry.

It is possible to display output on a supported graphics terminal (such as most Tektronix or Hewlett-Packard models) by attaching the terminal to a serial port with the proper cable. The standard device catalog entries for the drivers for these terminals contain a GACCESS value of SASGASTD>COM1:, so output from the driver is sent out to the terminal via COM1:.

If you are using a SAS/GRAPH driver for a device that uses a DOS device driver (such as the Vectrix VXPC-4096 or the Tektronix PC4100 graphics adapters), output is treated as though it is being sent to a communications port, and the GACCESS= option should specify a path to the driver. For example, the device catalog entry for the driver for the Vectrix adapter has a default GACCESS value of SASGASTD>VECTRIX, which sends output to the DOS driver supplied with the adapter.

You can find more detailed information on device drivers and hardware configuration in *SAS/GRAPH Hardware Interfaces for Personal Computers, Version 6 Edition*.

Sending Output to a Graphics Stream File (GSF)

You may occasionally want to send output from a driver to a graphics stream file instead of directly to the device. This type of output is typically used when the desired output device is not physically attached to your computer, or when the graphics output file must be transferred to another machine.

There are two ways of creating a graphics stream file. The first is to use a GOPTIONS statement to override the default output destination specified in device catalog entry fields so that the path points to a file instead of to a port. For example, output from the HP7475 driver usually goes to the COM1: port because the GACCESS value for the HP7475 entry in the Institute-supplied device catalog is SASGASTD>COM1:. Suppose instead you want to send the output to a file named HP7475.GSF in the directory MYDIR. To do this, you can use the GACCESS= option to specify the file as the destination for procedure output. You must also supply a GSFMODE value of APPEND or REPLACE to indicate whether the output is to be appended to or replace an existing file. (Refer to the description of the GSFMODE= option in "The GOPTIONS Statement" for details.) The complete GOPTIONS statement would be

```
goptions gaccess='sasgastd>\mydir\hp7475.gsf'
         gsfmode=append;
```

Alternatively, you can use PROC GDEVICE to change the values in the GACCESS and GSFMODE fields in the HP7475 entry in the device catalog.

A second way to create a graphics stream file is to use the GSFNAME= option in a GOPTIONS statement or to alter the GSFNAME field in the device catalog entry. This causes output to be written to a file with the specified fileref. (You must use a FILENAME statement to associate a filename with the fileref.) Here also, you must change the value of GSFMODE to APPEND or REPLACE. For example, to create the HP7475.GSF file as above, you can use the following statements:

```
filename grafout '\mydir\hp7475.gsf';
goptions gsfname=grafout
         gsfmode=append;
```

Note: the fileref used in the example, GRAFOUT, is arbitrary. Any valid SAS fileref can be used.

Alternatively, you can use PROC GDEVICE to modify the value in the GSFNAME and GSFMODE fields in the device catalog entry. In this case, you still must use a FILENAME statement to identify the name of the file associated with the fileref.

Note that the value in the GSFNAME field or the GSFNAME= option overrides any path specified with the GACCESS field or the GACCESS= option. For example, if you specify the following statements, the output is written to \MYDIR\HP7475.GSF:

```
filename grafout '\mydir\hp7475.gsf';
goptions gaccess='sasgastd>com1:'
         gsfname=grafout
         gsfmode=append;
```

You can use the GACCESS= option to control other attributes of the file (including whether or not carriage-return and line-feed characters are inserted). When creating a graphics stream file, you may need to change the value of the HANDSHAKE= option in order to provide for correct flow control when you actually send the output to the device. Refer to "The GOPTIONS Statement" for details on these options.

You should note the following points when generating a graphics stream file:

- You cannot generate a usable graphics stream file when using drivers for display adapters that do not have a data stream. (That is, such drivers cannot generate standard graphics stream files that can later be sent directly to the device to display the graph.) Examples include drivers for display adapters such as CGA or EGA.

- You should specify a value of APPEND or REPLACE for the GSFMODE field or the GSFMODE= option when writing to a file. (The default value for most drivers is PORT.) If you specify an option that is not appropriate for the destination of the output, your graph or file may be incorrect.
- If you specify the NODISPLAY option in a GOPTIONS statement and use the GACCESS= option (or the GACCESS field in the device catalog entry) to specify a path, no file is created. However, if you use the GSFNAME= option (or the GSFNAME field in the catalog entry) to specify the path and supply a value of APPEND or REPLACE in the GSFMODE= option (or the GSFMODE field), then a file *will* be created even if NODISPLAY is specified.

You can find further details on generating graphics stream files in *SAS/GRAPH Hardware Interfaces for Personal Computers, Version 6 Edition*.

Sending Output to a Catalog

Catalogs are members of SAS data libraries that can contain graphs created by SAS/GRAPH procedures. Each graph you produce with SAS/GRAPH software becomes an entry in a catalog. You can manage and later replay these entries using the GREPLAY procedure.

You can send graphs from a SAS/GRAPH procedure to a specific catalog by specifying the GOUT= option in a PROC statement. The general form is

```
proc procname gout=SAScatalog;
```

where *procname* is the name of a SAS/GRAPH procedure that produces graphics output and *SAScatalog* names the member in a SAS data library that is (or is to be) a SAS catalog. The catalog can later be referenced by specifying

```
proc greplay igout=SAScatalog;
```

All SAS/GRAPH procedures that produce graphics output create catalog entries, whether or not you specify GOUT= in the PROC statement. If you do not specify a catalog with the GOUT= option, catalog entries are written to the default catalog WORK.GSEG. Thus, you can run a SAS/GRAPH procedure without explicitly specifying the GOUT= option. To demonstrate this, create some graphics output and then specify the following statement to find the output from the procedure:

```
proc greplay igout=work.gseg;
```

Note, however, that GSEG is erased at the end of your SAS session (unless you specified the NOWORKINIT option at the invocation of the current SAS session).

You can specify a one- or a two-level name for the catalog. If you want to store the output from a procedure permanently, use a two-level name. If you specify a one-level name, the catalog will be in the WORK library.

By default, any graphs produced by the procedure are added to the end of the catalog. If the procedure produces multiple graphs, then multiple entries are made in the catalog. If you specify

```
goptions goutmode=replace;
```

when running a procedure that generates graphs for the catalog, those graphs replace *all* existing graphs in the catalog.

When your output is sent to a catalog, SAS/GRAPH automatically assigns a name and a description to each catalog entry so you can identify it. You can also use the NAME= and DESCRIPTION= options to supply a specific name and description when creating the graph. For example, suppose you run PROC GCHART and then PROC GMAP and each procedure step produces one graph.

When the output from the PROC steps is sent to a catalog, SAS/GRAPH assigns a name (usually the name of the procedure that produced the graph) and a description to each graph. If you do not supply a name and a description, the following entries are generated for the stated graphs:

GCHART   PIE CHART OF MONTH
GMAP   CHOROPLETH MAP OF REGION

Catalogs can contain both device-independent and device-dependent graphics output. The type of graph placed in the catalog can be specified using the GOUTTYPE= option in a GOPTIONS statement. The default is GOUTTYPE=INDEPENDENT, which causes only device-independent graphics data to be placed in the catalog. If GOUTTYPE=DEPENDENT is specified, both device-independent and device-dependent graphs are placed in the catalog.

Device-independent Graphics Output

Device-independent graphs can be replayed on any supported device. Independent graphs are also independent of many of the SAS/GRAPH options used to control size and orientation. The characteristics implied by these options (including CBACK=, HSIZE=, VSIZE=, and ROTATE) are not stored with the graph. If you want your graph to be drawn using these options, you should specify them when you replay the graph.

Independent graphs can be replayed with almost equal precision on all devices supported by SAS/GRAPH software. There are some limitations concerning colors and hardware characters because not all output devices have the same capabilities. Generally, as the resolution and number of available colors for the target device increase, problems when replaying independent graphics decrease. However, as you move down the scale of device capability, problems can arise with remapping colors and switching to software characters in order to preserve the same relative appearance of the graph.

For example, a graph generated for final viewing on your monitor can be replayed without problems on a 35mm slide camera, which has an extremely high degree of resolution. However, a graph generated for final viewing on the camera may not replay correctly on your monitor. There may be some remapping of colors because the monitor cannot display as many unique colors as the camera. In addition, SAS/GRAPH may use software characters because the monitor cannot vary its hardware character sizes. Despite these limitations, you can replay graphs on the less capable device, and it is possible to use a less capable device to preview graphs to be replayed on more capable devices.

Device-dependent Graphics Output

Device-dependent graphs are generated for a specific target device and will replay correctly only on the device for which they are generated. Usually, device-dependent graphs are used for executive graphics presentations, when you want to minimize replay execution time. Dependent graphs cannot be replayed in a template with the PROC GREPLAY template facility. Refer to *SAS/GRAPH Hardware Interfaces for Personal Computers, Version 6 Edition* for more information.

All graphs created by SAS/GRAPH are first stored in the independent form. If you specify GOUTTYPE=DEPENDENT in a GOPTIONS statement, the independent procedure output is translated via a device driver and placed as dependent output in the GOUT= catalog. The dependent output is placed in a catalog at the same time that the translated independent output is sent directly to a device. Therefore, you should note that for *one-time viewing* of a graph there is a higher cost, in terms of processing time, for specifying GOUTTYPE=DEPENDENT.

However, for executive presentations, you may find subsequent replays faster if you specify GOUTTYPE=DEPENDENT.

GRAPHICS OUTPUT FROM SAS/GRAPH SOFTWARE FOR UNIX OPERATING SYSTEMS AND DERIVATIVES

Displaying Graphs on Your Terminal or Workstation

If you are using a graphics terminal or workstation that is supported by SAS/GRAPH, you can display graphs on it by specifying the appropriate driver. You can specify the driver in either an OPTIONS statement or a GOPTIONS statement. If you have not already specified a driver when a SAS/GRAPH procedure is executed, you will be prompted to supply one at that time. For example, if you are using a Tektronix 4205 terminal, you can use the following SAS statements to produce PROC GSLIDE output on your terminal:

```
goptions device=tek4205;
title 'Output to the Terminal';
proc gslide;
run;
```

The appendix "SAS/GRAPH Device Drivers" contains a list of device drivers that are available with SAS/GRAPH. Consult the appendix to find out what driver name you should specify to display graphs on your terminal.

Sending Output to a Hardcopy Device

You can send output to a hardcopy device in one of three ways:

- The driver can pipe output to a UNIX command. Most frequently, the **lp** command is used to invoke the line printer daemon to send the output to the device.
- On multi-user systems, it is possible to attach certain hardcopy devices (usually pen plotters) in *eavesdrop* mode. In this configuration, the hardcopy device is attached to the line between your terminal and the host computer. When a device is in eavesdrop mode, you can have the driver send output back to your terminal (the file /DEV/TTY), and it will be intercepted by the device.
- If you have exclusive use of a device or are on a single-user system, you can have the SAS/GRAPH driver write to the file in the /DEV directory that is associated with the device. For example, if the device is recognized by the system as the file /DEV/TTYPLOT, the driver can write output directly to that file.

Your first step in sending output to a hardcopy device is to determine which of the above methods you want to use. The first method, with output piped to the UNIX lp command, is generally preferred when you are sending to a device that is defined as a system printer. If the device is attached to your terminal in eavesdrop mode, the second method is used. The third method is usually used only on single-user systems, or in cases where you have exclusive use of the output device.

To direct your output to the correct location, you should alter the GACCESS parameter in the device catalog entry for each driver you use. (A device catalog contains entries that let you alter the attributes of each device driver.) It is recommended that you create your own device catalog and modify only the entries in your personal catalog. On multi-user systems, only the system administrator may be able to modify entries in the standard catalog, SASHELP.DEVICES. Refer to "The GDEVICE Procedure" for details on using PROC GDEVICE to create a personal device catalog and to modify catalog entries.

You can also use the GACCESS= option in a GOPTIONS statement to direct output to the desired location for the duration of the current SAS session.

The GACCESS parameter has two parts. The first part specifies an access module that determines whether output is written to a file (usually a value of SASGASTD) or is piped to a UNIX command (a value of SASGACMD). The second part of the GACCESS parameter specifies the destination of the output: either the name of a file or a UNIX command and options. For example, a GACCESS value of SASGASTD>/DEV/TTY causes output to be written to the file /DEV/TTY (your terminal or workstation), whereas a value of SASGACMD>lp -dgoutput causes output to be piped through the UNIX command lp to the destination goutput. (Note: destination names are system-specific and are assigned by your system administrator.)

For hardcopy devices that can be accessed through the lp command, it is usually best to use the SASGACMD module to route output to that command. For example, suppose you are using a QMS 800 printer that has been assigned a system destination of qmsprn. You can use the following statements to produce output on the printer:

```
goptions device=qms800
         gaccess='sasgacmd>lp -dqmsprn';
title 'Hello World';
proc gslide;
run;
```

In this case, the GACCESS value invokes the lp command with the parameter -dqmsprn, which sends output to the destination qmsprn.

The example above uses a GOPTIONS statement to specify the GACCESS value. If you will be using this GACCESS value on a regular basis, you can modify the GACCESS field in the entry for the corresponding driver in your device catalog. Once you have modified the catalog entry, you will not have to specify the value in a GOPTIONS statement during each SAS session.

If you are using a terminal to access your host system and have a plotter attached in eavesdrop mode between your terminal and the host, you will want to specify a GACCESS value that sends output back to your terminal. When the output is sent to your terminal, it is intercepted by the plotter, which plots it. For example, if you have a Hewlett-Packard 7475 plotter that is configured this way, you can use the following SAS statements:

```
goptions device=hp7475
         gaccess='sasgastd>/dev/tty';
title 'Hello World';
proc gslide;
run;
```

On multi-user systems, graphics output devices such as printers and plotters are commonly shared by more than one user. While it is possible to send output directly to a shared device, this practice is not recommended. Problems may arise if two or more users try to access the device simultaneously. However, if you have a single-user system or have exclusive use of a particular hardcopy device on a multi-user system, you may at times want to route output directly to the destination device.

For example, suppose you are on a single-user system and you have a Post-Script printer that your system recognizes as a file named /DEV/TTYPOST. You can send output directly to the printer using the following SAS statements:

```
goptions device=ps
         gaccess='sasgastd>/dev/ttypost';
title 'Hello World';
proc gslide;
run;
```

In general, you should first determine how your hardcopy device is configured and how you want to direct output to it. Then use PROC GDEVICE to examine the catalog entry for the driver you will be using, and make any necessary changes to the GACCESS field.

The device catalog entries supplied with your version of SAS/GRAPH software contain GACCESS values that are appropriate for the most common configuration of the device on that system. When using a configuration that does not correspond with the default value, you will need to modify the GACCESS value in your catalog entry for the driver. For example, entries for plotter drivers may have a GACCESS value of SASGASTD>/DEV/TTY, which assumes an eavesdrop configuration. If you are using a plotter that is defined as a system printer, you may need to modify the GACCESS value in the catalog entry for the driver so that output is piped to the lp command. Most drivers for printers have a default GACCESS value of SASGACMD>lp -dgoutput. The first part of this value is correct if you want your output piped to the lp command, but you may need to change the -dgoutput destination specification to correspond to the actual destination name for your device.

Sending Output to a Graphics Stream File (GSF)

You may occasionally want to send output from a driver to a graphics stream file instead of directly to the device. You can then send the file to the device at a later time. This type of output is typically used when the desired output device is not directly connected to your host or workstation, or when the graphics output file must be transferred to another machine.

There are two ways of creating a graphics stream file. The first is to use a GOPTIONS statement to override the output destination specified in the device catalog entry so that the path points to a file instead of to the device. For example, output from the QMS800 driver is normally piped to the lp command because the GACCESS value for the QMS800 entry in the device catalog supplied by SAS Institute is SASGACMD>lp -dgoutput. Suppose you want to send the output to a file named QMSGSF in the directory /USERS/MYDIR instead of to the lp command. To do this, include the GACCESS= option in a GOPTIONS statement to direct output to /USERS/MYDIR/QMSGSF. You must also include the GSFMODE option with a value of APPEND or REPLACE to indicate whether the output is to be appended to or replace an existing graphics stream file. (Refer to the description of the GSFMODE= option in "The GOPTIONS Statement" for details.) The complete GOPTIONS statement would be

```
goptions gaccess='sasgastd>/users/mydir/qmsgsf'
         gsfmode=append;
```

Alternatively, you can use PROC GDEVICE to modify the values in the GACCESS and GSFMODE fields in the device catalog entry for the driver.

A second way to create a graphics stream file is to use the GSFNAME= option in a GOPTIONS statement or to modify the GSFNAME field in a device catalog entry. This causes output to be written to a file with the specified fileref. (You must use a FILENAME statement to associate a filename with the fileref.) Here also, you must change the value of the GSFMODE parameter to APPEND or REPLACE. For example, to create the /USERS/MYDIR/QMSGSF file as in the example above, you can use the following statements:

```
filename grafout '/users/mydir/qmsgsf';
goptions gsfname=grafout
         gsfmode=append;
```

Note: the fileref used in the example, GRAFOUT, is arbitrary. Any valid SAS fileref can be used.

Alternatively, you can use PROC GDEVICE to modify the values in the GSFNAME and GSFMODE fields in the device catalog entry for the driver. In this case, you still must use a FILENAME statement to identify the file associated with the fileref.

Note that a value in the GSFNAME field or GSFNAME= option overrides any path specified in the GACCESS field or GACCESS= option. For example, if you specify the following statements, output is written to /USERS/MYDIR/QMSGSF rather than to /DEV/TTY:

```
filename grafout '/users/mydir/qmsgsf';
goptions gaccess='sasgastd>/dev/tty'
         gsfname=grafout
         gsfmode=append;
```

You should note the following when generating a graphics stream file:

- You should specify a value of APPEND or REPLACE in the GSFMODE field or GSFMODE= option. (The default value for most drivers is PORT.) If you specify an option that is not appropriate for the destination of the output, your graph or file may be incorrect.
- If you specify the NODISPLAY option in a GOPTIONS statement and use the GACCESS parameter to specify a path, no file is created. However, if you use the GSFNAME parameter to specify the path and supply a GSFMODE parameter of either APPEND or REPLACE, then a file *will* be created even if you specify the NODISPLAY option.

You can find further details on generating graphics stream files in *SAS/GRAPH Guide to Hardware Interfaces, Release 6.03 Edition.*

Sending Output to a Catalog

Catalogs are members of SAS data libraries that can contain graphs created by SAS/GRAPH procedures. Each graph you produce with SAS/GRAPH software becomes an entry in a catalog. You can manage and later replay these entries using the GREPLAY procedure.

You can send graphs from a SAS/GRAPH procedure to specific a catalog by specifying the GOUT= option in a PROC statement. The general form is

```
proc procname gout=SAScatalog;
```

where *procname* is the name of a SAS/GRAPH procedure that produces graphics output and *SAScatalog* names the member in a SAS data library that is (or is to be) a SAS catalog. The catalog can later be referenced by specifying

```
proc greplay igout=SAScatalog;
```

All SAS/GRAPH procedures that produce graphics output create catalog entries, whether or not you specify GOUT= in a PROC statement. If you do not specify a catalog with the GOUT= option, catalog entries are written to the default catalog WORK.GSEG. Thus, you can run a SAS/GRAPH procedure without specifying the GOUT= option. To demonstrate this, create some graphics output and then specify the following statement to find the output from the procedure:

```
proc greplay igout=work.gseg;
```

Note, however, that GSEG is erased at the end of your SAS session.

You can specify a one- or a two-level name for the catalog. If you want to store the output from a procedure permanently, use a two-level name. If you specify a one-level name, the catalog will be in the WORK library.

By default, any graphs produced by the procedure are added to the end of the catalog. If the procedure produces multiple graphs, then multiple entries are made in the catalog. If you specify

```
goptions goutmode=replace;
```

when running a procedure that generates graphs for the catalog, those graphs replace *all* existing graphs in the catalog.

When your output is sent to a catalog, SAS/GRAPH automatically assigns a name and a description to each catalog entry so you can identify it. You can also use the NAME= and DESCRIPTION= options to supply a specific name and description when creating the graph. For example, suppose you run PROC GCHART and then PROC GMAP and each procedure step produces one graph. When the output from the PROC steps is sent to a catalog, SAS/GRAPH assigns a name (usually the name of the procedure that produced the graph) and a description to each graph. If you do not supply a name and a description, the following entries are generated for the stated graphs:

GCHART   PIE CHART OF MONTH
GMAP   CHOROPLETH MAP OF REGION

Catalogs can contain both device-independent and device-dependent graphics output. The type of graph placed in the catalog is specified using the GOUTTYPE= option in a GOPTIONS statement. The default is GOUTTYPE=INDEPENDENT, which causes only device-independent graphs to be placed in the catalog. If GOUTTYPE=DEPENDENT is specified, both device-independent and device-dependent graphs are placed in the catalog.

Device-independent Graphics Output

Device-independent graphs can be replayed on any supported device. Independent graphs are also independent of many of the SAS/GRAPH options used to control size and orientation. The characteristics implied by these options (including CBACK= HSIZE=, VSIZE=, and ROTATE) are not stored with the graph. If you want your graph to be drawn using these options, you should specify them when you replay the graph.

Independent graphs can be replayed with almost equal precision on all devices supported by SAS/GRAPH software. There are some limitations concerning colors and hardware characters because not all output devices have the same capabilities. Generally, as the resolution and number of available colors for the target device increase, problems when replaying independent graphs decrease. However, as you move down the scale of device capability, problems can arise with remapping colors and switching to software characters in order to preserve the same relative appearance of the graph.

For example, a graph generated for final viewing on your terminal can be replayed without problems on a 35mm slide camera, which has an extremely high degree of resolution. However, a graph generated for final viewing on the camera may not replay correctly on your terminal. There may be some remapping of colors because the terminal cannot display as many unique colors as the camera can. In addition, SAS/GRAPH may use software characters because some terminals cannot vary their hardware character sizes. Despite these limitations, you can replay graphs on the less capable device, and it is possible to use a less capable device to preview graphs to be replayed on more capable devices.

Device-dependent Graphics Output

Device-dependent graphs are generated for a specific target device and will replay correctly only on the device for which they are generated. Usually, device-dependent graphs are used for executive graphics presentations, when you want to minimize replay execution time. Dependent graphs cannot be replayed in a template with the PROC GREPLAY template facility.

All graphs created by SAS/GRAPH are first stored in the independent form. If you specify GOUTTYPE=DEPENDENT in a GOPTIONS statement, the independent procedure output is translated via a device driver and placed as dependent output in the GOUT= catalog. The dependent output is placed in a catalog at the same time that the translated independent output is sent directly to a device. Therefore, you should note that for *one-time viewing* of a graph there is a higher cost, in terms of processing time, for specifying GOUTTYPE=DEPENDENT. However, for executive presentations, you may find subsequent replays faster if you specify GOUTTYPE=DEPENDENT.

EXAMPLES

The examples below show how to create the various types of graphics output and illustrate the use of different graphics options in a SAS/GRAPH session.

Graphics Output on Personal Computer Systems

Example 1: Displaying Graphs on Your Monitor

If you want to display output from a SAS/GRAPH procedure on your monitor, you should specify the appropriate driver for the graphics adapter you are using. (Refer to the appendix "SAS/GRAPH Device Drivers" and to *SAS/GRAPH Hardware Interfaces for Personal Computers, Version 6 Edition* to determine what driver you should use with your adapter.) Suppose you have a CGA adapter and want to display a vertical bar chart of income. You can accomplish this with the following statements:

```
goptions device=cga;
proc gchart;
    vbar income;
run;
```

In this example, in addition to displaying the graph on your monitor, the procedure will place a picture in the catalog WORK.GSEG.

Example 2: Sending Output to a Device Attached to a Port

Suppose you want to produce a pie chart of the variable INCOME on a plotter, and the plotter is attached to the serial port designated COM1:. You can accomplish this with the following statements:

```
goptions device=drivername;
proc gchart;
    pie income;
run;
```

where *drivername* is the name of a SAS/GRAPH device driver for the plotter you are using. Refer to the appendix "SAS/GRAPH Device Drivers" and to *SAS/GRAPH Hardware Interfaces for Personal Computers, Version 6 Edition* for descriptions of drivers available for use with your graphics devices.

If you are using the standard entry for the driver as supplied with SAS/GRAPH software, then driver output will be directed to COM1:, and the graph is drawn on the plotter. If you have modified the standard device catalog entry for the driver, you may need to change it or use a GOPTIONS statement to route output to COM1:. Note that it may be necessary to issue a DOS MODE command before beginning the SAS session to properly configure the port to match the characteristics of the attached device.

Graphics Output on UNIX Operating Systems and Derivatives

Example 3: Displaying Graphs on a Plotter in Eavesdrop Mode

Suppose you are on a multi-user system and have a plotter that is attached between your terminal and the host in eavesdrop mode. (Some plotters may require a special Y cable.) If the plotter is connected in eavesdrop mode, it will intercept the output from the driver and use the commands to produce your plot. This means you can use the following statements to produce a graph:

```
goptions device=drivername
         gaccess='sasgastd>/dev/tty';
proc gchart;
    pie income;
run;
```

Note, however, that the GACCESS= option in the GOPTIONS statement is unnecessary if the device catalog entry for your device already has a value of SASGASTD>/DEV/TTY in the GACCESS field. If you regularly use the device in eavesdrop mode and the device catalog entry for the driver does not have a GACCESS value of SASGASTD>/DEV/TTY, you can modify the catalog entry to eliminate the need to issue the GOPTIONS statement in each SAS session.

Example 4: Sending Output to a Shared Printer or Plotter

Suppose you want to send graphics output to a QMS 800 laser printer, which is being used as a system printer. Assume in this case that the printer has a system destination of sysqms, so that printed output can be sent to the device with the UNIX command:

```
lp -dsysqms
```

To send SAS/GRAPH output to the printer, you must specify a GACCESS value that pipes output to the lp command and sends it to the correct destination. The following SAS statements can be used to send output to the printer:

```
goptions device=qms800
        gaccess='sasgacmd>lp -dsysqms';
proc gchart;
   pie income;
run;
```

The GACCESS value of SASGACMD>lp -dsysqms causes the driver to pipe output to the UNIX command lp and specifies a destination of sysqms. If you are using the printer on a regular basis, you can change the GACCESS value in the QMS800 entry in your device catalog to SASGACMD>lp -dsysqms. (Be sure to use the actual destination name your system has assigned to the printer).

If you are using a plotter that is defined to the system as a line printer, you should modify the GACCESS value in the same way. For example, if you have a Hewlett-Packard 7550 plotter that has a system destination of hpplot, you can use the following SAS statements to generate graphics output:

```
goptions device=hp7550 noprompt
        gaccess='sasgacmd>lp -dhpplot';
proc gchart;
   pie income;
run;
```

Graphics Output on All Systems

Example 5: Creating a Permanent Catalog

Suppose you want to create a series of graphs but not view them until later, when you will display them by using the GREPLAY procedure. The example below shows the steps you should follow to create a permanent catalog and store your graphs.

First, you must supply a SAS LIBNAME statement to identify the directory in which the permanent catalog is to be placed. With SAS/GRAPH software for personal computers, you can use the following statement to associate the libref MYLIB with the directory \MYDIR on drive C:

```
libname mylib 'c:\mydir\';
```

With SAS/GRAPH software on UNIX operating systems and derivatives, you can use the following statement to associate the libref MYLIB with the directory /USERS/MYDIR/:

```
libname mylib '/users/mydir/';
```

You can then use the following statements on either system to create a file named GRAPHS.SCT in the directory pointed to by the libref MYLIB. This file is the catalog containing your graphs.

```
goptions nodisplay
        device=drivername;
proc gchart gout=mylib.graphs;
   vbar month;
   pie year;
proc gplot gout=mylib.graphs;
   plot income*year;
proc g3d gout=mylib.graphs;
   plot y*x=z;
run;
```

where *drivername* is the name of a SAS/GRAPH device driver.

Once the statements have been processed, you can view the graphs by submitting the following statements:

```
goptions display
         device=drivername;
proc greplay igout=mylib.graphs;
```

where *drivername* is the name of a SAS/GRAPH device driver for the device on which you are replaying the graph.

When you invoke PROC GREPLAY, the names and descriptions of the graphs appear on a menu screen. Individual graphs can then be selected for replay. See "The GREPLAY Procedure" for further details.

Example 6: Creating a Graphics Stream File

Suppose you want to generate a plot of sales by month, but instead of having output go directly to the device, you want to create a file of the data stream as it would have been sent to the graphics device. Use the following statements to create the graphics stream file on a personal computer system:

```
filename grafout 'c:filename.ext';
goptions device=drivername
         gsfmode=replace
         gsfname=grafout;
proc gplot;
   plot sales*month;
run;
```

where *c:filename.ext* is the complete pathname for the target graphics stream file and *drivername* is the name of the SAS/GRAPH device driver for the plotter you are using.

The above SAS program causes a file of device-specific graphics commands to be written to the file pointed to by the fileref GRAFOUT. Any data previously in the file are replaced. An alternative method for creating the graphics stream file is to use the GACCESS parameter, as follows:

```
goptions device=drivername
         gsfmode=replace
         gaccess='sasgastd>c:filename.ext';
proc gplot;
   plot sales*month;
run;
```

where *c:filename.ext* is the complete pathname for the target graphics stream file and *drivername* is the name of the SAS/GRAPH device driver for the plotter you are using.

You can create the graphics stream file on UNIX operating systems and derivatives by using the following statements:

```
filename grafout '/users/mydir/filename';
goptions device=drivername
         gsfmode=replace
         gsfname=grafout;
proc gplot;
   plot sales*month;
run;
```

where */users/mydir/filename* is the complete pathname for the target graphics stream file and *drivername* is the name of the SAS/GRAPH device driver for the plotter you are using.

The statements above cause a file of graphics commands to be written to the file pointed to by the fileref GRAFOUT. Any data previously in the file are replaced.

Alternatively, you can use the GACCESS parameter to create the graphics stream file:

```
goptions device=drivername
         gsfmode=replace
         gaccess='sasgastd>/users/mydir/filename';
proc gplot;
   plot sales*month;
run;
```

where */users/mydir/filename* is the complete pathname for the target graphics stream and *drivername* is the name of the SAS/GRAPH device driver for the plotter you are using.

Note that you can also use PROC GDEVICE to modify the GACCESS, GSFNAME, and GSFMODE fields in the catalog entry for the driver you are using.

Example 7: Displaying Graphs and Creating Catalog Entries

Suppose you want to create a permanent catalog containing device-independent graphs, but you also want to see the graphs as the catalog is being created.

First, you must supply a LIBNAME statement to identify the directory in which the permanent catalog is to be placed. With SAS/GRAPH software for personal computers, you can use the following statement to associate the libref MYLIB with the directory \MYDIR on drive C:

```
libname mylib 'c:\mydir\';
```

On UNIX operating systems and derivatives, you can use the following statement to associate the libref MYLIB with the directory /USERS/MYDIR/:

```
libname mylib '/users/mydir/';
```

You can then use the following statements on either system to create the catalog and view the graph:

```
goptions display
         device=drivername
proc gchart gout=mylib.graphs;
   vbar month;
run;
```

where *drivername* is the name of a SAS/GRAPH device driver.

When this program is executed, the graph is drawn on your device and a device-independent graph is placed in the output catalog GRAPH.SCT.

Note that if the display device you are using is different from the target device and commands for the target device are sent to your display, device errors may occur. When the target device is different from the display device you are using when you create the graphs, and you want to use the driver for the target device, specify

```
goptions nodisplay;
```

to prevent the graph from being displayed as it is created.

Example 8: Creating Dependent Graphs from Independent Graphs

Suppose you have a catalog with several device-independent graphs, and you want to create device-dependent versions. You might want to do this to produce speedier replays for an interactive executive presentation using PROC GREPLAY. To store the dependent graphics in a permanent catalog PRES.SCT, you must first supply a LIBNAME statement to identify the directory in which the permanent catalog is to be placed. With SAS/GRAPH software for personal computers, you can use the following statement to associate the libref MYLIB with the directory \MYDIR on drive C:

```
libname mylib 'c:\mydir\';
```

On UNIX operating systems and derivatives, you can use the following statement to associate the libref MYLIB with the directory /USERS/MYDIR/:

```
libname mylib '/users/mydir/';
```

You can then use the following statements on either system to create device-dependent graphs and store them in the catalog PRES.SCT. (The example assumes that the device-independent graphs are in the catalog WORK.GSEG.)

```
goptions nodisplay
        goutttype=dependent
        device=drivername;
proc greplay igout=work.gseg
    gout=mylib.pres
    nofs;
   replay _all_;
   end;
```

where *drivername* is the name of a SAS/GRAPH device driver.

PROC GREPLAY replays each graph in the IGOUT= catalog using the device driver specified in the GOPTIONS statement. Because the NODISPLAY option is active, no graphics output comes to your device. Because you specified GOUTTYPE=DEPENDENT, the output from the device driver is placed in the permanent GOUT= catalog PRES.SCT in the directory you identified with the libref MYDIR.

Chapter 3

SAS/GRAPH®
Colors

Introduction

This chapter describes how colors can be defined and used with SAS/GRAPH software. The colors available to create your SAS/GRAPH output are determined by the graphics output device you have and by the program statements you use to generate or replay a graph. SAS/GRAPH allows you to define your own colors using RGB (red green blue), HLS (hue lightness saturation), and gray-scale color coding schemes, or you can use the named colors, which provide an intuitive method for specifying colors. You can also use names such as PEN1, PEN2, and PEN3 to define the pens you may have for your pen plotter.

To take full advantage of SAS/GRAPH capabilities and the various methods you can use to specify colors when creating color graphics with SAS/GRAPH, you first need to determine what type of device you are using and its color capabilities. Graphics devices used to display SAS/GRAPH output can be grouped into the following categories:

- devices that support user-defined colors
- devices that do not support user-defined colors
- pen plotters.

Devices That Support User-defined Colors

Devices that support user-defined colors are graphics devices that allow you to configure the device's color palette. A device in this category may be capable of generating as many as 16,000,000 colors, but it can only display 8, 16, 32, 64, 128, or 256 colors from the color palette at any one time. Devices that support user-defined colors are usually CRTs, but there are some ink jet printers and color copiers that fit into this category.

Devices That Do Not Support User-defined Colors

Devices that do not support user-defined colors are those that come with predefined nonalterable color palettes. These devices typically have between 8 and

256 predefined colors. The actual number of colors that can be displayed at one time may be less than the total number of predefined colors. Devices that do not support user-defined colors are usually CRTs, but there are several graphics printers that fit into this category.

Pen Plotters

Pen plotters can draw with up to 256 user-defined colors because you choose the color names (see **Color Names** below) and then place pens with those color names in the plotter when the message 'PLEASE MOUNT THE FOLLOWING PENS' appears. The assumption is that the colors you specify in your graph reflect the actual pens you have to put in your plotter.

Limitations

SAS/GRAPH can generate graphs with up to 256 unique colors including the background color (specified with CBACK= in a GOPTIONS statement) on each graph. The colors you want to display are specified with a color name. For example, if you create a graph with 257 unique color names, SAS/GRAPH issues a warning and remaps your colors because you exceeded the 256 color name maximum.

Use the PENMOUNTS= option in a GOPTIONS statement to indicate the number of foreground colors that can be displayed at one time on a given graphics output device. All graphs can be generated with up to 256 colors, but not all devices can display that many colors at one time. The PENMOUNTS= option defaults to the number of displayable colors on the basic model of each graphics device supported. If your graphics device can display more colors than the base model, use the PENMOUNTS= option in a GOPTIONS statement to specify the number of colors that can be displayed. For example, the base model Tektronix® 4115 terminal can display 16 colors (including the background color) and the top-of-the-line model can display 256 colors. To use all 256 colors on the higher capability device, specify

```
goptions penmounts=255;
```

For pen plotters, you use the PENMOUNTS= option to indicate the number of pen holders on the plotter. This does not limit the number of colors you can specify for a graph produced on a pen plotter. If you use more unique colors than the plotter has pens, you will be prompted to mount additional pens.

Getting Colors into the System

Before you can use the color capabilities of your graphics device, you must specify the colors you want to use to display your graphs. You can specify color names of up to eight characters in length in the following ways:

- in TITLE, FOOTNOTE, NOTE, SYMBOL, PATTERN, AXIS, and LEGEND statements
- as options in various SAS/GRAPH procedures
- in a GOPTIONS statement
- in the device catalog entry
- in the data set containing the graphics information to be plotted.

When you specify colors in an ANNOTATE= data set or a PROC G3D response data set, you should define the color variable with a LENGTH statement.

You can use three methods (singly or in combination) to give SAS/GRAPH a list of colors to use when generating graphics output.

Using the Device's Default Colors

The first method is not to specify any colors anywhere in your SAS program. If you do not specify any colors, a default list of colors is built from the colors list in the device catalog entry you have specified using the DEVICE= option in a GOPTIONS statement. Refer to "The GDEVICE Procedure" for details.

Specifying Colors in a GOPTIONS Statement

The second method is to specify your own default colors list using the COLORS= option in a GOPTIONS statement. This indicates that SAS/GRAPH is to ignore the device's default colors list and use your colors list as the default. For example, if you want to ensure that the colors red, green, and blue are available for use in creating your graphics output, you can specify this statement in your SAS program:

```
goptions colors=(red green blue);
```

Note that the COLORS= option only provides a default lookup table. Any time you explicitly reference any other colors in your SAS program, those colors are added to the internal colors list. For example, if you specify CTEXT=CYAN in a PLOT statement of PROC GPLOT and you have also specified GOPTIONS COLORS=(RED GREEN BLUE), the graph will have cyan text on its axis and red, green, and blue will be used in the places where you did not explicitly specify a color to be used.

Specifying Colors in Your SAS Program

The third method you can use to give SAS/GRAPH a list of colors is to have SAS/GRAPH software use only colors you specify in your SAS program. To use this method, specify COLORS=(NONE) in the GOPTIONS statement, and then colors are added to the colors list only as they are encountered in your SAS program. This is a useful feature if you want to generate graphics output with the maximum of 256 colors and you do not want to use any of the device's default colors. Allowing the system to use the device's default colors or the colors in your GOPTIONS statement uses slots in the internal colors list that could be used for colors you may want to define yourself. For example, the Tektronix 4115 device has fifteen colors in its default colors list. Suppose you want to create your own colors list and specify 256 colors for the list. If you omit the COLORS= option, the fifteen colors in the device's default colors list are placed in the first fifteen slots of the default colors list you are creating, and you can specify only 241 additional colors to be used on that device. If you want to define all 256 available colors, you must specify

```
goptions colors=(none);
```

and then specify the names of the colors you want to use in your programming statements. Alternatively, you can modify the colors list in the device catalog entry for the specified device to the colors list you want to use.

Color Names

You can specify color names using several common color coding schemes. These include RGB (red green blue), HLS (hue lightness saturation), gray scales, and named colors. Color name schemes can be intermixed freely in your programs, and SAS/GRAPH will translate the color name to the correct format for your output device. The color naming schemes recognized by SAS/GRAPH are discussed below.

RGB Color Coding Scheme

You can use the RGB color coding scheme to specify a color in terms of its red, green, and blue components. Color names are of the form CX*rrggbb*. The prefix CX indicates that this is an RGB color specification. The values *rr*, *gg*, and *bb* are the red, green, and blue components of the color you are defining. The components are given as hexadecimal numbers in the range 00–FF. This allows for up to 256 levels of each color component. For example, bright red is specified as CXFF0000, white as CXFFFFFF, and green as CX00FF00. Any combination of the color components is valid.

HLS Color Coding Scheme

You can use the HLS color coding scheme to specify colors in terms of hue, lightness, and saturation components. SAS/GRAPH uses an HLS color scheme modeled directly after the Tektronix Color Standard, which is shown in **Figure 3.1**. HLS color names are of the form H*hhhllss*. The prefix H indicates that this is an HLS color specification. The values *hhh*, *ll*, and *ss* are the hue, lightness, and saturation components of the color you are defining. The components are given as hexadecimal numbers. The hue component has the range 000–FFF. Valid values are 0–360 (168 base 16). Any values greater than 360 (168 base 16) will be taken modulo 360 (168 base 16). Both the lightness and saturation components are hexadecimal and have the range 00–FF. Thus, they provide all 256 levels for each component. For example, bright blue is specified as H14066FF, light gray as H000BB00, and so on.

Gray-scale Color Coding Scheme

You can use gray scales to specify colors in terms of gray components. Gray-scale color names are of the form GRAY*ll*. The value *ll* is the lightness of the gray and is given as a hexadecimal number in the range 00–FF. This allows for 256 levels on the gray scale. For example, GRAYFF is white, GRAY00 is black, and GRAY4C is one third of the way from black to white, or a dark gray.

Details

The trueness of the color produced when using a SAS/GRAPH user-defined color name is dependent upon the capabilities of your graphics output device. If you specify user-defined colors on a device that does not support this feature, the colors are mapped into the colors available for that device. No attempt is made when remapping the colors to match the user-defined color name with the colors available for the device. Therefore, when you replay a graph with user-defined colors on a device that does not support user-defined colors, you should use the device's default colors to avoid having incorrect colors in your graph.

Color resolution varies across graphics output devices, and the color resolution of your graphics device will affect the actual color displayed. Some devices can only generate 64, 1024, or 4096 different colors. For example, if your terminal can generate a maximum of 64 distinct colors and your graph contains 256 colors, many of the color specifications will appear as the same color.

The number of colors that can be displayed is limited by the type of graphics output device you have. If you produce a graph with more colors than the device can display, the colors that cannot be displayed are mapped back into the previously defined colors list or the device's default colors list. For best results when displaying colors used in SAS/GRAPH procedures, you should not try to produce graphics output with more colors than your graphics output device can display.

Because colors that cannot be displayed are remapped in color nondefinable devices, previewing complex graphs on lower capability devices is feasible.

Table 3.1 shows a list of colors and their SAS/GRAPH color names that you can use with SAS/GRAPH software.

Note that the colors shown in the output screens in this guide may be different from the colors you see on your device. The output screens were produced using the PCR4XL device driver with a Matrix PCR™ color film recorder, on which SAS/GRAPH can display 256 colors.

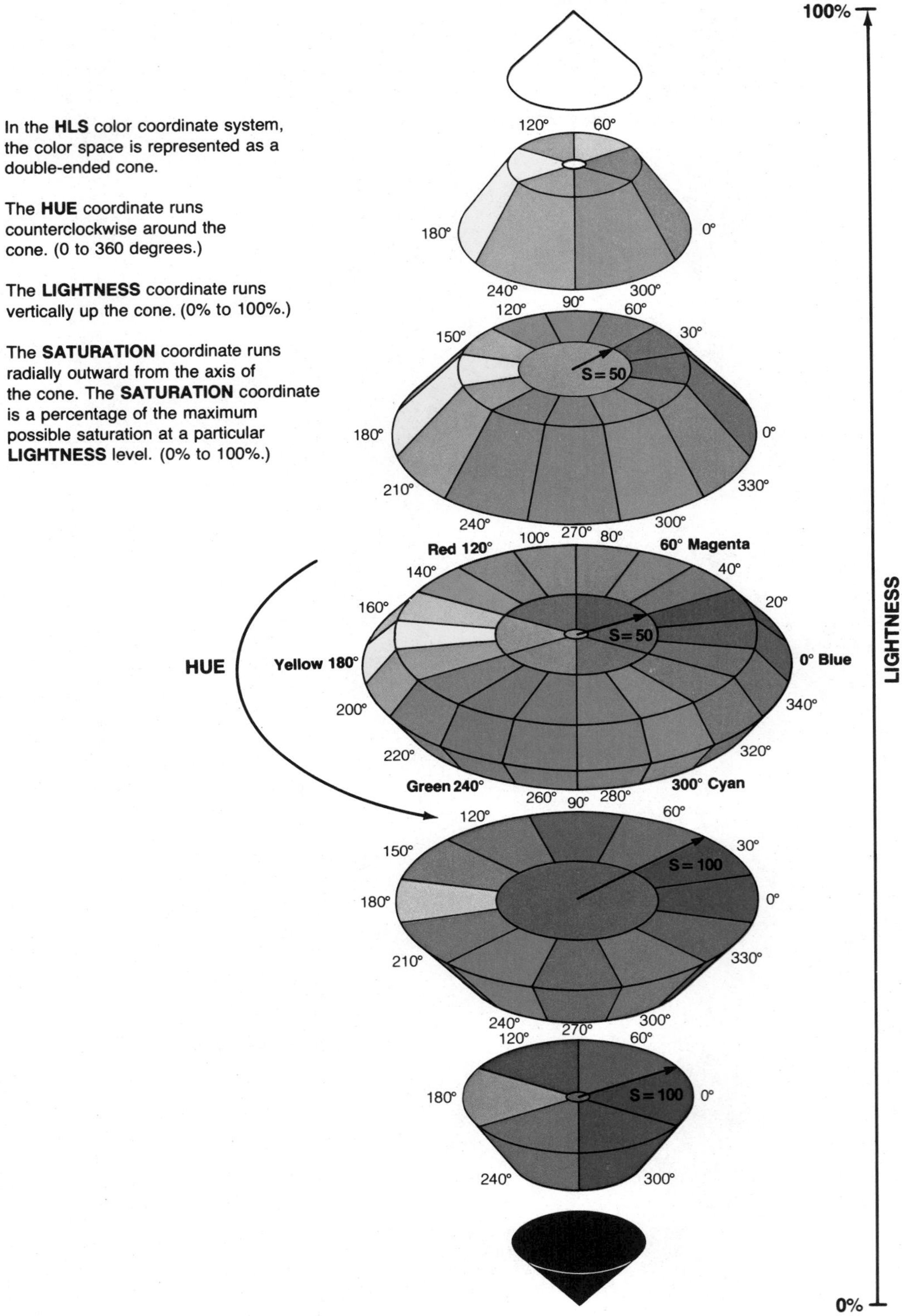
In the HLS color coordinate system, the color space is represented as a double-ended cone.
The HUE coordinate runs counterclockwise around the cone. (0 to 360 degrees.)
The LIGHTNESS coordinate runs vertically up the cone. (0% to 100%.)
The SATURATION coordinate runs radially outward from the axis of the cone. The SATURATION coordinate is a percentage of the maximum possible saturation at a particular LIGHTNESS level. (0% to 100%.)
100%
0%
LIGHTNESS
HUE
Red 120°
60° Magenta
Yellow 180°
0° Blue
Green 240°
300° Cyan
S=50
S=100

Figure 3.1 Tektronix Color Standard
Copyright © by Tektronix, Inc., Information Display Group.
Reprinted with permission.

Table 3.1 SAS/GRAPH Named Colors List

Name	Color	Name	Color
Basic Hues			
BLACK	black	OLIVE	olive
BLUE	blue	ORANGE	orange
BROWN	brown	PINK	pink
CHARCOAL	charcoal	PURPLE	purple
CREAM	cream	RED	red
CYAN	cyan	ROSE	rose
GOLD	gold	SALMON	salmon
GRAY	gray	STEEL	steel
GREEN	green	TAN	tan
LILAC	lilac	VIOLET	violet
LIME	lime	WHITE	white
MAGENTA	magenta	YELLOW	yellow
MAROON	maroon		
Blacks			
BL	black	OLBL	olive black
RBK	reddish black	PBL	purplish black
BRBL	brownish black	BBL	bluish black
GBL	greenish black		
Blues			
VIGB	vivid greenish blue	PAB	pale blue
BIGB	brilliant greenish blue	VPAB	very pale blue
STGB	strong greenish blue	GRB	grayish blue
DEGB	deep greenish blue	DAGRB	dark grayish blue
LIGB	light greenish blue	VIPB	vivid purplish blue
VLIGB	very light greenish blue	BIPB	brilliant purplish blue
MOGB	moderate greenish blue	STPB	strong purplish blue
DAGB	dark greenish blue	DEPB	deep purplish blue
VDAGB	very dark greenish blue	VLIPB	very light purplish blue
VIB	vivid blue	LIPB	light purplish blue
BIB	brilliant blue	MOPB	moderate purplish blue
STB	strong blue	DAPB	dark purplish blue
DEB	deep blue		

continued on next page

Table 3.1 *continued*

Name	Color	Name	Color
		Blues (*continued*)		
LIB	light blue	PAPB	pale purplish blue
VLIB	very light blue	VPAPB	very pale purplish blue
MOB	moderate blue	GRPB	grayish purplish blue
DAB	dark blue	BLB	blackish blue
		Browns		
LIBR	light brown	LIOLBR	light olive brown
MOBR	moderate brown	MOOLBR	moderate olive brown
DABR	dark brown	DAOLBR	dark olive brown
LIGRBR	light grayish brown	STB	strong brown
GRBR	grayish brown	STRBR	strong reddish brown
DAGRBR	dark grayish brown	DERBR	deep reddish brown
STYBR	strong yellowish brown	LIRBR	light reddish brown
DEYBR	deep yellowish brown	MORBR	moderate reddish brown
LIYBR	light yellowish brown	DARBR	dark reddish brown
MOYBR	moderate yellowish brown	LIGRRBR	light grayish reddish brown
DAYBR	dark yellowish brown	GRRBR	grayish reddish brown
LIGRYBR	light grayish yellowish brown	DAGRRBR	dark grayish reddish brown
GRYBR	grayish yellowish brown	DEBR	deep brown
DAGRYBR	dark grayish yellowish brown		
		Grays		
LIBRGR	light brownish gray	LIPGR	light purplish gray
BRGR	brownish gray	PGR	purplish gray
PKGR	pinkish gray	DAPGR	dark purplish gray
RGR	reddish gray	LIGR	light gray
DARGR	dark reddish gray	MEGR	medium gray
YGR	yellowish gray	DAGR	dark gray
LIGGR	light greenish gray	LTGRAY	light gray
GGR	greenish gray	DAGRAY	dark gray
DAGGR	dark greenish gray	LIBGR	light bluish gray
LIOLGR	light olive gray	BGR	bluish gray
OLGR	olive gray	DABGR	dark bluish gray

continued on next page

Table 3.1 *continued*

Name	Color	Name	Color
	Greens		
VIBG	vivid bluish green	BIYG	brilliant yellowish green
BIBG	brilliant bluish green	STYG	strong yellowish green
STBG	strong bluish green	DEYG	deep yellowish green
DEBG	deep bluish green	VDEYG	very deep yellowish green
LIBG	light bluish green	VLIYG	very light yellowish green
VLIBG	very light bluish green	LIYG	light yellowish green
MOBG	moderate bluish green	MOYG	moderate yellowish green
DABG	dark bluish green	DAYG	dark yellowish green
VDABG	very dark bluish green	VDAYG	very dark yellowish green
VILG	vivid yellow green	VIG	vivid green
BILG	brilliant yellow green	BIG	brilliant green
STLG	strong yellow green	STG	strong green
DELG	deep yellow green	DEG	deep green
LILG	light yellow green	LIG	light green
MOLG	moderate yellow green	VLIG	very light green
PALG	pale yellow green	MOG	moderate green
GRLG	grayish yellow green	DAG	dark green
STOLG	strong olive green	VDAG	very dark green
DEOLG	deep olive green	PAG	pale green
MOOLG	moderate olive green	VPAG	very pale green
DAOLG	dark olive green	GRG	grayish green
GROLG	grayish olive green	DAGRG	dark grayish green
DAGROLG	dark grayish olive green	BLG	blackish green
VIYG	vivid yellowish green		
	Olives		
LIOL	light olive	LIGROL	light grayish olive
MOOL	moderate olive	GROL	grayish olive
DAOL	dark olive	DAGROL	dark grayish olive
	Oranges		
VIRO	vivid reddish orange	BIO	brilliant orange

continued on next page

Table 3.1 *continued*

Name	Color	Name	Color
		Oranges *(continued)*		
STRO	strong reddish orange	STO	strong orange
DERO	deep reddish orange	DEO	deep orange
MORO	moderate reddish orange	LIO	light orange
DARO	dark reddish orange	MOO	moderate orange
GRRO	grayish reddish orange	BRO	brownish orange
VIO	vivid orange		
		Pinks		
VIPK	vivid pink	MOYPK	moderate yellowish pink
STPK	strong pink	DAYPK	dark yellowish pink
DEPK	deep pink	PAYPK	pale yellowish pink
LIPK	light pink	GRYPK	grayish yellowish pink
MOPK	moderate pink	BRPK	brownish pink
DAPK	dark pink	STPPK	strong purplish pink
GRPK	grayish pink	DEPPK	deep purplish pink
PAPK	pale pink	LIPPK	light purplish pink
VIYPK	vivid yellowish pink	MOPPK	moderate purplish pink
STYPK	strong yellowish pink	DAPPK	dark purplish pink
DEYPK	deep yellowish pink	PAPPK	pale purplish pink
LIYPK	light yellowish pink	GRPPK	grayish purplish pink
		BIPPK	brilliant purplish pink
		Purples		
VIP	vivid purple	DAGRP	dark grayish purple
BIP	brilliant purple	BLP	blackish purple
STP	strong purple	VIRP	vivid reddish purple
DEP	deep purple	STRP	strong reddish purple
VDEP	very deep purple	DERP	deep reddish purple
LIP	light purple	VDERP	very deep reddish purple
VLIP	very light purple	LIRP	light reddish purple
MOP	moderate purple	MORP	moderate reddish purple
DAP	dark purple	DARP	dark reddish purple
VDAP	very dark purple	VDARP	very dark reddish purple
PAP	pale purple	GRRP	grayish reddish purple
VPAP	very pale purple	PARP	pale reddish purple
GRP	grayish purple		

continued on next page

Table 3.1 *continued*

Name	Color	Name	Color
Reds			
VIR	vivid red	DAGRR	dark grayish red
STR	strong red	BLR	blackish red
DER	deep red	VIPR	vivid purplish red
VDER	very deep red	STPR	strong purplish red
MOR	moderate red	DEPR	deep purplish red
DAR	dark red	VDEPR	very deep purplish red
VDAR	very dark red	MOPR	moderate purplish red
LIGRR	light grayish red	DAPR	dark purplish red
GRR	grayish red	GRPR	grayish purplish red
LIGRPR	light grayish purplish red	VDAPR	very dark purplish red
Violets			
VIV	vivid violet	MOV	moderate violet
BIV	brilliant violet	DAV	dark violet
STV	strong violet	PAV	pale violet
DEV	deep violet	VPAV	very pale violet
LIV	light violet	GRV	grayish violet
VLIV	very light violet		
Whites			
WH	white	PKWH	pinkish white
YWH	yellowish white	PWH	purplish white
GWH	greenish white	BWH	bluish white
Yellows			
VIOY	vivid orange yellow	DAY	dark yellow
BIOY	brilliant orange yellow	PAY	pale yellow
STOY	strong orange yellow	GRY	grayish yellow
DEOY	deep orange yellow	DAGRY	dark grayish yellow
LIOY	light orange yellow	VIGY	vivid greenish yellow
MOOY	moderate orange yellow	BIGY	brilliant greenish yellow
DAOY	dark orange yellow	STGY	strong greenish yellow
PAOY	pale orange yellow	DEGY	deep greenish yellow

continued on next page

Table 3.1 *continued*

Name	Color	Name	Color
	Yellows (*continued*)		
VIY	vivid yellow	LIGY	light greenish yellow
BIY	brilliant yellow	MOGY	moderate greenish yellow
STY.	strong yellow	DAGY	dark greenish yellow
DEY	deep yellow	GRGY	grayish greenish yellow
LIY	light yellow	PAGY	pale greenish yellow
MOY	moderate yellow		

Chapter 4

Enhancing Your Graphics Output Text

INTRODUCTION

SAS/GRAPH software allows you to create graphics displays that range from simple text displays (such as slides and overheads) to highly sophisticated output (such as maps, charts, and plots). You can use TITLE, FOOTNOTE, and NOTE statements as the basis of text displays (with PROC GSLIDE) or as labels to enhance more complex graphics displays.

You can use TITLE and FOOTNOTE statements anywhere in your SAS/GRAPH programs. NOTE statements must be used within a procedure. The special rules that apply when you use these statements are discussed below. The options used with these statements allow you to specify the color, height, font, and placement of text in your output. The same options are available for TITLE, FOOTNOTE, and NOTE statements.

You can also use FORMAT and LABEL statements to prepare your data for processing by SAS/GRAPH procedures. For complete descriptions and examples of FORMAT and LABEL statements, see the *SAS Language Guide, Release 6.03 Edition*. For more detailed annotation of SAS/GRAPH output, you can use ANNOTATE= data sets. See "ANNOTATE= Data Sets" for more information.

TITLE Statement

You can use TITLE statements to specify lines of text to be drawn at the top of SAS/GRAPH displays. By specifying certain options in a TITLE statement, you can control the color, type font, type size, and position of lines of text in a title.

The general form of the TITLE statement is

TITLE*n options* **'text';**

where

n

is a number that represents the line to be occupied by the title. If you
do not specify a number following the keyword TITLE, TITLE1 is
assumed.

You can specify up to ten TITLE statements. If you specify a TITLE
statement with an *n* value greater than 10, you receive a warning
message in the SAS log and the TITLE statement is ignored. Once you
specify a TITLE statement for a line, the text of that statement is drawn
on all graphic displays until you specify another TITLE statement for that
line or cancel the TITLE statement. When a TITLE statement is specified
for a given line, it cancels all TITLE statements previously defined for
that line and for all lines below it.

For example, you can specify the following statements to produce a
display with five lines of text:

```
title1 c=red    f=centxi 'First line';
title2 c=green  f=centxi 'Second line';
title3 c=blue   f=centxi 'Third line';
title4 c=yellow f=centxi 'Fourth line';
title5 c=cyan   f=centxi 'Fifth line';
proc gslide;
run;
```

If you then specify the following statements, you produce a display in
which the first two lines remain the same, the third line contains the
new text in the new font and color, and the fourth and fifth lines have
been canceled:

```
title3 c=pink f=centx 'New third line';
proc gslide;
run;
```

If you then want to suppress the drawing of the second and third lines,
you can enter the following statements and only the text of the TITLE1
line is displayed:

```
title2;
proc gslide;
run;
```

To cancel all titles, specify

```
title;
```

options

allows you to specify the color, type font, type size, and position of the
text appearing in a TITLE statement. You can specify an option
anywhere within the TITLE statement. An option remains in effect until
that option is changed or until the end of the statement. You can specify
the values for many of the options globally in a GOPTIONS statement,
or you can use the defaults for these options. You can control as few or
as many of the options as you want. The options are described in
Options Specified in TITLE, FOOTNOTE, and NOTE Statements.

'text'

is the text displayed by your output device. The text **must** be enclosed in single or double quotes. The text appears exactly as it does in your TITLE, FOOTNOTE, or NOTE statement, including only the blanks within the quotes. All other blanks are ignored.

If your text is to contain quotes, they can be represented as a pair of single quotes; for example,

```
title 'All''s Well That Ends Well';
```

Specifying text is optional.

FOOTNOTE Statement

You can use FOOTNOTE statements to specify lines of text to be drawn at the bottom of SAS/GRAPH displays. By specifying certain options in a FOOTNOTE statement, you can control the color, type font, type size, and position of lines of text in a footnote.

The general form of the FOOTNOTE statement is

FOOTNOTE*n options* **'text';**

where

n

is a number that represents the line to be occupied by the footnote. You can specify up to ten FOOTNOTE statements. If you specify a FOOTNOTE statement with an *n* value greater than 10, you receive a warning message in the SAS log and the FOOTNOTE statement is ignored. Footnotes are pushed up from the bottom of the display area. Therefore, if you specify three FOOTNOTE statements, the text of the third footnote will appear on the bottom line of the display, the text of the second footnote will appear on a line above the third, and the text of the first footnote will appear on a line above the second and third footnotes. If you do not specify a number following the keyword FOOTNOTE, FOOTNOTE1 is assumed.

Once you specify a FOOTNOTE statement for a line, the text of that statement is drawn on all graphic displays until you specify another FOOTNOTE statement for that line or cancel the FOOTNOTE statement. When you specify a FOOTNOTE statement for a given line, it cancels all FOOTNOTE statements previously defined for that line and for all lines below it.

For example, the following statements produce a display with five lines of text drawn at the bottom:

```
footnote1 c=red    f=centx 'First footnote';
footnote2 c=green  f=centx 'Second footnote';
footnote3 c=blue   f=centx 'Third footnote';
footnote4 c=yellow f=centx 'Fourth footnote';
footnote5 c=cyan   f=centx 'Fifth footnote';
proc gslide;
run;
```

If you then specify the following statements, you produce a display in which the first three lines remain the same, the fourth line contains the new text in the new font and color, and the fifth line has been canceled:

```
footnote4 c=green f=centxi 'New fourth footnote';
proc gslide;
run;
```

If you then want to suppress the drawing of the second, third, and fourth lines, you can enter the following statements and the text of the first footnote line only is displayed:

```
footnote2;
proc gslide;
run;
```

To cancel all footnotes, specify

```
footnote;
```

options
> allows you to specify the color, type font, type size, and position of the text appearing in a FOOTNOTE statement. You can specify an option anywhere within the FOOTNOTE statement. An option remains in effect until that option is changed or until the end of the statement. You can specify the values for many of these options globally in a GOPTIONS statement, or you can use the defaults for these options. You can control as few or as many of these options as you want. The options are described in **Options Specified in TITLE, FOOTNOTE, and NOTE Statements**.

'text'
> is the text displayed by your output device. The text **must** be enclosed in single or double quotes. The text appears exactly as it does in your TITLE, FOOTNOTE, or NOTE statement, including only the blanks within the quotes. All other blanks are ignored.
>
> If your text is to contain quotes, they can be represented as a pair of single quotes; for example,

```
footnote 'All''s Well That Ends Well';
```

> Specifying text is optional.

NOTE Statement

You can use NOTE statements to specify lines of text to be drawn in the area remaining after titles and footnotes are drawn on SAS/GRAPH displays. By specifying certain options in a NOTE statement, you can control the color, type font, type size, and position of lines of text in a note.

The general form of the NOTE statement is

NOTE *options 'text'*;

where you can specify as many NOTE statements as you like in the order in which you want them to appear. **Unlike TITLE and FOOTNOTE statements, NOTE statements remain in effect only for the duration of the procedure step.**

options
> allows you to specify the color, type font, type size, and position of the text appearing in a NOTE statement. You can specify an option anywhere within the NOTE statement. An option remains in effect until that option is changed or until the end of the statement. You can specify

the values for many of these options globally in a GOPTIONS statement, or you can use the defaults for these options. You can control as few or as many of these options as you want. The options are described in **Options Specified in TITLE, FOOTNOTE, and NOTE Statements**.

'*text*'

is the text displayed by your output device. The text **must** be enclosed in single or double quotes. The text appears exactly as it does in your TITLE, FOOTNOTE, or NOTE statement, including only the blanks within the quotes. All other blanks are ignored.

If your text is to contain quotes, they can be represented as a pair of single quotes; for example,

```
note 'All''s Well That Ends Well';
```

Specifying text is optional.

Options Specified in TITLE, FOOTNOTE, and NOTE Statements

You can specify the following options in TITLE, FOOTNOTE, and NOTE statements:

ANGLE=*angle*
A=*angle*

specifies the angle at which to display lines of text. If you do not specify an angle, text is displayed horizontally (A=0) from the top of the page or screen down. When you specify an angle, it remains in effect until another angle is specified or until the end of the statement.

TITLE and NOTE statements Specifying A=−90 constitutes a special case. When you specify A=−90, titles and notes are rotated by −90 degrees (90 degrees clockwise) and are written vertically on the right side of the display. (See **Output 4.3** in the **EXAMPLES** section.)

Similarly, when you specify A=90, titles and notes are rotated 90 degrees counterclockwise and are written vertically on the left side of the display. (See **Output 4.3** in the **EXAMPLES** section.)

FOOTNOTE statements Specifying A=−90 constitutes a special case. When you specify A=−90, footnotes are rotated by −90 degrees (90 degrees clockwise) and are written vertically on the left side of the display. (See **Output 4.3** in the **EXAMPLES** section.)

Similarly, when you specify A=90, footnotes are rotated 90 degrees counterclockwise and are written vertically on the right side of the display. (See **Output 4.3** in the **EXAMPLES** section.)

BCOLOR=*color*
BC=*color*

specifies the color of the background within the box that is drawn around the text (see the BOX= option below). The BCOLOR= color can be different from the color of the outline of the box. By default, the background color of the box is the same as the background color for the entire display. If you do not specify the BOX= option, the BCOLOR= option is ignored.

Note: the BCOLOR= option is processed after all the text in a TITLE, FOOTNOTE, or NOTE statement has been processed. Therefore, if multiple commands are given, only the last one is processed. For example, if you specify the following TITLE statement, the background of the box will be green, and the BCOLOR=BLUE command is ignored:

```
title c=red box=1 bcolor=blue bcolor=green 'Draw a box';
```

BLANK=YES
BL=YES
>   specifies that nothing else should be drawn around the text in the box
>   after the text has been drawn. The BLANK= option allows you to
>   appear to overlay a line of text on top of a graph. The BLANK= option
>   is ignored if the BOX= option is not specified.
>
>   Note: the BLANK= option is processed after all the text in a TITLE,
>   FOOTNOTE, or NOTE statement has been processed. Therefore, if
>   multiple commands are given, only the last one is processed.

BOX=0, 1, 2, 3
BO=0, 1, 2, 3
>   specifies to draw a box around the text of the TITLE, FOOTNOTE, or
>   NOTE statement in which it appears. If you specify BOX=1, 2, or 3, the
>   box is drawn with an increasingly thicker line. Unlike the UNDERLINE=
>   option, the BOX= option does not rotate the lines used to draw the
>   box to match rotated text. The color of the box is the color value
>   currently in effect. For example, if you specify

```
title c=red box=1 c=blue 'Draw a box around this text';
```

>   the text of your TITLE statement will be blue and the box around it will
>   be a thin red line.
>
>   See "The GSLIDE Procedure" for an example using the BOX= option.
>
>   Note: the BOX= option is processed after all the text in a TITLE,
>   FOOTNOTE, or NOTE statement has been processed. Therefore, if
>   multiple commands are given, only the last one is processed. For
>   example, if you specify

```
title c=red box=1 c=blue box=3 'Draw a box';
```

>   the BOX=3 command is used to draw a single box with a thick blue
>   line, instead of two boxes.

BSPACE=positive number
BS=positive number
>   controls the amount of space reserved around the text that appears in a
>   box. You can set BSPACE equal to n CELLS (where n is expressed in
>   character cell units); n PCT (where n is expressed as a percentage of the
>   display area); n IN (where n is expressed in inches); or n CM (where n is
>   expressed in centimeters). If you do not specify a unit with n, the value
>   specified with the GUNIT= option in a GOPTIONS statement is used. If
>   you did not specify a GUNIT= value, the default value, character cells,
>   is used. The default BSPACE= value is 1.
>
>   When you specify a BSPACE= value, that value is reserved around
>   the text string enclosed in the box. For example, if you specify

```
title h=3 f=triplex box=1 bspace=2 cm 'Leave surrounding space';
```

>   the text of the TITLE statement will be enclosed in a box and will have
>   two centimeters of blank space before the first letter of the text, two
>   centimeters of blank space after the last letter of the text, two
>   centimeters of space above the text, and two centimeters of space
>   below the text.
>
>   See "The GSLIDE Procedure" for an example using the BSPACE=
>   option.
>
>   Note: the BSPACE= option is processed after all the text in a TITLE,
>   FOOTNOTE, or NOTE statement has been processed. Therefore, if

multiple commands are given, only the last one is processed. For example, if you specify

```
title1 c=red box=1 bspace=1.5 bspace=2 'Draw a box';
```

the BSPACE=2 command is used to place space within the box, and the BSPACE=1.5 command is ignored.

COLOR=*color*
C=*color*

names the color to use for the text that follows the specification. For example, the following statement specifies that the text GRAPHICS OUTPUT should be drawn in blue:

```
title1 c=blue 'GRAPHICS OUTPUT';
```

The following statement specifies to draw the word NEW in blue, GRAPHICS in red, and OUTPUT in green:

```
title2 c=blue 'NEW ' c=red 'GRAPHICS ' c=green 'OUTPUT';
```

Note: because none of the text strings above have embedded blanks, you must add a blank space to each string that precedes another. Otherwise, each text string will begin at the point where the preceding string stopped, and the strings will run together without spaces. In the TITLE2 statement above, the strings 'NEW ' and 'GRAPHICS ' each have a space at the end so that they will not run into the word that follows. (You could place a space at the beginning of the strings ' GRAPHICS' and ' OUTPUT' to achieve the same results.)

If you omit the C= option, the text of the TITLE, FOOTNOTE, and NOTE statements is displayed using the color specified by the CTITLE= option of your GOPTIONS statement. If you do not specify the CTITLE= option, the first color in the COLORS= list in the GOPTIONS statement is used. If you also omitted the COLORS= option, the first default color for your graphics device is used.

See the **EXAMPLES** section for statements that contain the C= option.

DRAW=*(coordinates)*
D=*(coordinates)*

enables you to draw lines on the display. You can use the D= option to underline text or draw a box around titles. The list of coordinates has the following form:

$$(x1, y1, x2, y2, x3, y3, . . . , xn, yn)$$

Commas between coordinates are optional. Each coordinate can be specified with or without a unit, and you can use various combinations of units. For example, you can set DRAW coordinates equal to (x,y) PCT, where (x,y) is expressed as a percentage of the display area; (x,y) IN, where (x,y) is expressed in inches; (x,y) CM, where (x,y) is expressed in centimeters; or (x,y) CELLS, where (x,y) is expressed in character cell units. If you do not specify a unit with (x,y), the value specified with the GUNIT= option in a GOPTIONS statement is used. If you did not specify a GUNIT= value, the default value, character cells, is used.

In addition, the following are both valid forms of specifying DRAW= values:

```
draw=(x cm, y pct)
draw=(x,y) in
```

The DRAW= option does not affect the position of text.

The values of x and y can be preceded by + or − symbols to indicate that the lines are to be displayed relative to the end of the preceding text. See **Output 4.4** in the **EXAMPLES** section for an example using the D= option.

FONT=*typefont*
F=*typefont*

names the type font to use for the text that follows the specification. For example, the statement

```
title f=swiss 'GRAPHICS OUTPUT';
```

specifies that the text GRAPHICS OUTPUT be drawn in the Swiss type font. See **Output 4.1** and the appendix "SAS/GRAPH Type Styles and Fonts" for examples of some available fonts.

A number of SAS/GRAPH type fonts are available when you specify the F= (or FTITLE= or FTEXT=) option. Refer to the appendix "SAS/GRAPH Type Styles and Fonts" for a complete list of the fonts available and a sample of each. You can also use PROC GFONT to display the character set for each font available with SAS/GRAPH software or to create your own font.

Most SAS/GRAPH fonts can be either proportionately or uniformly spaced. Proportionately spaced fonts contain characters that are spaced according to the width of the individual character; for example, the letter M may take up twice as much space as the letter I. (The text in this guide is proportionately spaced.) Uniformly spaced fonts, however, are spaced without regard to the actual width of the individual character; for example, the letter M takes up the same amount of space as the letter I. (Most typewriters use uniformly spaced fonts.) You should use a uniformly spaced font whenever you need to align characters vertically in text lines.

TITLE statements If you do not specify the F= option in the first TITLE statement, the type font specified in the FTITLE= option in the GOPTIONS statement is used. If you do not specify the FTITLE= option, SAS/GRAPH uses the font you specified with the FTEXT= option in a GOPTIONS statement. If you do not specify the FTITLE= or the FTEXT= option, the COMPLEX type font is used. If you want to use your device's hardware character set, specify F=NONE before the text in your first TITLE statement.

If you do not specify the F= option in TITLE statements after the first TITLE statement, SAS/GRAPH uses the font you specified with the FTEXT= option in a GOPTIONS statement. If you do not specify the FTEXT= option, then the hardware character set for your device is used to draw the text.

FOOTNOTE and NOTE statements If you do not specify the F= option in FOOTNOTE or NOTE statements, SAS/GRAPH uses the font you specified with the FTEXT= option in a GOPTIONS statement. If you do not specify the FTEXT= option, then the hardware character set for your device is used to draw the text.

HEIGHT=*n*
H=*n*

specifies the height of the characters. The height is the distance from the lowest point in the font to the capline. Ascenders may extend above the capline. You can set HEIGHT equal to *n* PCT (where *n* is expressed as a percentage of the display area); *n* IN (where *n* is expressed in inches); *n* CM (where *n* is expressed in centimeters); or *n* CELLS (where *n* is expressed in character cell units). If you do not specify a unit with *n*, the value specified with the GUNIT= option in a GOPTIONS statement is used. If you did not specify a GUNIT= value, the default value, character cells, is used.

For example, the following statement specifies that the second title line should be drawn in the Zapf font, in letters that are two inches tall:

```
title2 h=2 in f=zapf 'TALL TEXT';
```

See the **EXAMPLES** section for the use of different H= specifications.

If your text line is too long to be displayed in the character height specified in the H= option, the H= size is reduced so that the text can be displayed.

TITLE statements   If you do not specify the H= option in the first TITLE statement, SAS/GRAPH uses the value you specified with the HTEXT= option in a GOPTIONS statement. If you do not specify the HTEXT= option, then the default value of 2 is used. The unit used will be the one you specified with the GUNIT= option. If you did not specify a GUNIT= value, the default value, character cells, is used.

If you do not specify the H= option in TITLE statements after the first TITLE statement, SAS/GRAPH uses the value you specified with the HTEXT= option in a GOPTIONS statement. If you do not specify the HTEXT= option, then the default value of 1 is used. The unit used will be the one you specified with the GUNIT= option. If you did not specify a GUNIT= value, the default value, character cells, is used.

FOOTNOTE and NOTE statements   If you do not specify the H= option in a FOOTNOTE or NOTE statement, SAS/GRAPH uses the value you specified with the HTEXT= option in a GOPTIONS statement. If you do not specify the HTEXT= option, then the default value of 1 is used. The unit used will be the one you specified with the GUNIT= option. If you did not specify a GUNIT= value, the default value, character cells, is used.

J=LEFT | L
J=RIGHT | R
J=CENTER | C
controls the alignment on the page of the text specified in TITLE, FOOTNOTE, and NOTE statements. When you specify J=LEFT, all following text is aligned to the left of the graphic display. When you specify J=RIGHT, all following text is aligned to the right. J=CENTER is the default.

If you specify the same value for J= more than once in the same statement, the text appears on separate lines.

All titles, footnotes, and notes are displayed without regard to other text already on the graphic display. Thus, it is possible to overlay existing text.

See **Output 4.2** in the **EXAMPLES** section for an example using the J= option.

LANGLE=*angle*
LA=*angle*
specifies the number of degrees from the horizontal at which the text is to be rotated. The value of *angle* can be a positive or a negative number. The LANGLE= option differs from the ANGLE= option in that for LANGLE= there are no special cases (for specifications of ANGLE=+90 or −90 or 0 degrees).

See **Output 4.3** in the **EXAMPLES** section for an example using the LA= option.

LSPACE=*n*
LS=*n*

controls the spacing *above* lines of text specified in TITLE and NOTE statements. You can set LSPACE equal to *n* PCT (where *n* is expressed as a percentage of the display area); *n* IN (where *n* is expressed in inches); *n* CM (where *n* is expressed in centimeters); or *n* CELLS (where *n* is expressed in character cell units). If you do not specify a unit with *n*, the value specified with the GUNIT= option in a GOPTIONS statement is used. If you did not specify a GUNIT= value, the default value, character cells, is used. If you omit the LSPACE= option, the default value is used.

For example, if you specify the following statements, the TITLE1 text appears at the top of the display area, one line space (character cell) is skipped, and the TITLE2 text appears:

```
title1 f=swiss h=1 'How much space will be left?';
title2 f=swissi h=1 ls=1 'Allow space above this title';
```

The LSPACE= option controls the spacing *below* lines of text specified in FOOTNOTE statements.

For example, if you specify the following statements, the FOOTNOTE1 text appears at the top of the footnote area, one line space (character cell) is skipped, and the FOOTNOTE2 text appears:

```
footnote1 f=swiss  h=1 ls=1 'Leave space below this footnote';
footnote2 f=swissi h=1      'Draw this footnote';
```

The LSPACE= option remains in effect only for the duration of the statement in which you specify it, or until a J=, ANGLE=, or MOVE= option is encountered.

MOVE=(*x,y*)
M=(*x,y*)

allows you to move text by specifying the coordinates for the starting location. Commas between coordinates are optional. You can specify coordinates with or without a unit, and you can use various combinations of units in one specification.

For example, you can set MOVE equal to (*x,y*) PCT, where (*x,y*) is expressed as a percentage of the display area; (*x,y*) IN, where (*x,y*) is expressed in inches; (*x,y*) CM, where (*x,y*) is expressed in centimeters; or (*x,y*) CELLS, where (*x,y*) is expressed in character cell units. If you do not specify a unit with (*x,y*), the value specified with the GUNIT= option in a GOPTIONS statement is used. If you do not specify a GUNIT= value, the default value, character cells, is used.

In addition, the following are both valid forms of specifying MOVE= values:

```
move=(x cm, y pct)
move=(x,y) in
```

The values of *x* and *y* can be preceded by + or − symbols to indicate that the text is to be displayed relative to the end of the preceding text. See the **EXAMPLES** section for an example using positive and negative M= values.

J= is ignored for text positioned with the M= option.

See **Output 4.4** in the **EXAMPLES** section for an example using the M= option.

ROTATE=*angle*
R=*angle*

    specifies the degree at which to rotate each character of the text that follows the specification, relative to the baseline of the string. Normally, text is drawn in an upright position (R=0).

    You can specify both R= and A= values in a TITLE, FOOTNOTE, or NOTE statement. See **Output 4.3** in the **EXAMPLES** section for an example using the R= option.

UNDERLIN=0,1,2,3
U=0,1,2,3

    specifies to underline the text that follows. If you specify UNDERLIN=1, 2, or 3, text is underlined with an increasingly thicker line. If you want to stop underlining a portion of the text, specify UNDERLIN=0. If you specify an LANGLE= or ANGLE= option for the line of text, the underline is drawn at the same angle as the text. The color of the underline is the color value currently in effect. For example, if you specify

```
title c=cyan u=2 c=yellow 'Underline this text';
```

the text of your TITLE statement will be yellow and the underline will be a medium-thick cyan line.

    See **Output 4.4** in the **EXAMPLES** section for an example using the U= option.

EXAMPLES

The following examples illustrate the use of several options in TITLE, FOOTNOTE, and NOTE statements with PROC GSLIDE. See "The GSLIDE Procedure" for more examples using TITLE, FOOTNOTE, and NOTE statements.

Example 1: Selected SAS/GRAPH Fonts

In this example, various fonts are used with PROC GSLIDE to create a graphics display. The H= option is used to create characters of different heights.

    These statements produce **Output 4.1**.

```
goptions cback=black
         colors=(cyan);
title1 ls=3 f=swiss c=cyan 'SAS/GRAPH' f=special 'R  '
       f=gitalic 'Fonts';
title2 f=script c=cyan h=2
       'The title above this one used ls=3';
footnote1 f=oldeng c=cyan h=1.5
          'The footnote below this one used ls=1.5';
footnote2 h=1.2 f=brush ls=1.5 c=cyan 'BRUSH Font';

proc gslide ;
note j=l f=centxi h=2.5 c=cyan '      Font Examples';
note j=l f=centxi h=2   c=cyan '      Weather  ' f=weather 'K L J';
note j=l f=centxi h=2   c=cyan '      Cartog   ' f=cartog 'S K B';
note j=l f=centxi h=2   c=cyan '      Special  ' f=special 'B G N';
note j=l f=centxi h=2   c=cyan '      Music    ' f=music 'N G I';
note j=l f=centxi h=2   c=cyan '      Math     ' f=math 'I J M';
run;
```

Example 2: Using the J= Option to Position Text on a Page

In this example, the J= option is used to position text on the display area. This example also uses the BORDER option to draw a border around the display.
These statements produce **Output 4.2**.

```
goptions cback=black
        colors=(cyan);
title1 f=swiss c=cyan h=1
        j=l 'SAS Institute Inc.'
        j=l 'Run Date: 7/9/87'
        j=l 'Run Time: 16:05:23'
        j=c 'Text Positioning'
        j=r 'Page 1'
        j=r 'Version 6';
footnote1 f=centx c=cyan h=1 'D' h=1.1 'i'
          h=1.2 'f' h=1.3 'f' h=1.4 'e'
          h=1.5 'r' h=1.6 'e' h=1.7 'n' h=1.8 't' h=1.9 ' heights';
footnote2 h=1;

proc gslide border;
   note h=4 ' ';
   note j=l f=centxi h=2 c=cyan 'Left' j=c 'Center'
        j=r 'Right';
run;
```

Example 3: Rotating and Angling Text with the R= and A= Options

In the following example, the R= and A= options are used to rotate and angle text strings and individual characters.
These statements produce **Output 4.3**.

```
goptions cback=black
        colors=(cyan);
title1    h=2 f=swiss c=cyan 'Text Angles and Rotation';
footnote1 h=2 f=triplex c=cyan a=90 'Using A=90 option';

proc gslide border;
   note h=1 ' ';
   note f=complex h=1 c=cyan ' ' j=c
        'R ' r=30 'O ' r=45 'T ' r=60 'A ' r=90
        'T ' r=120 'I ' r=135 'O ' r=150 'N';
   note h=6 ' ';
   note f=duplex c=cyan ' ' m=(35,-45) pct
        la=30 '30 degrees    ' la=45 '45 degrees    '
        la=60 '60 degrees    ' la=90 '90 degrees    ';
run;
```

Example 4: Moving and Drawing Text with the M= and D= Options

This example illustrates the use of the M= and D= options, which allow you to place text at precise points on the display area. Note that a *y* coordinate of +0 causes succeeding text to be drawn in the same vertical location.

These statements produce **Output 4.4**.

```
goptions cback=black
         colors=(cyan);
title1 h=2 f=swiss c=cyan u=2 'VERTEBRATES';
title2 h=3 ' ';
title3 f=centx ' ' m=(25,+0) pct  h=1.5 c=cyan u=1 ' Birds    '
                  m=(45,+0) pct  h=1.5 c=cyan u=1 ' Reptiles '
                  m=(65,+0) pct  h=1.5 c=cyan u=1 ' Mammals  ';
footnote1 ' ' c=cyan d=(40,+5,40,90) pct  d=(60,+5,60,90) pct;
footnote2 h=1 f=centx c=cyan 'Selected Creatures';
footnote3 ' ';
proc gslide ;
   note h=1 ' ';
   note f=centx ' ' m=(27,+0) pct  h=1 c=cyan 'Turkey '
                    m=(47,+0) pct  h=1 c=cyan 'Snake  '
                    m=(67,+0) pct  h=1 c=cyan 'Mouse  ';
   note f=centx ' ' m=(27,+0) pct  h=1 c=cyan 'Buzzard'
                    m=(47,+0) pct  h=1 c=cyan 'Lizard '
                    m=(67,+0) pct  h=1 c=cyan 'Deer   ';
run;
```

Output 4.1   Displaying SAS/GRAPH Fonts: PROC GSLIDE

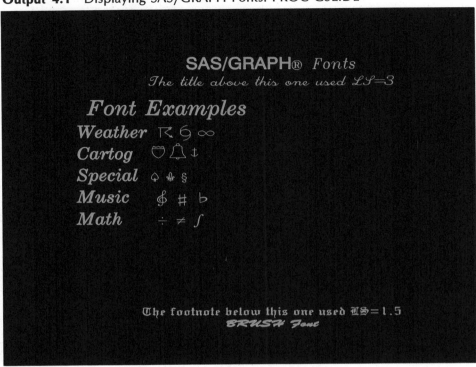

Output 4.2   Positioning Text on a Page: PROC GSLIDE

Output 4.3   Rotating and Angling Text: PROC GSLIDE

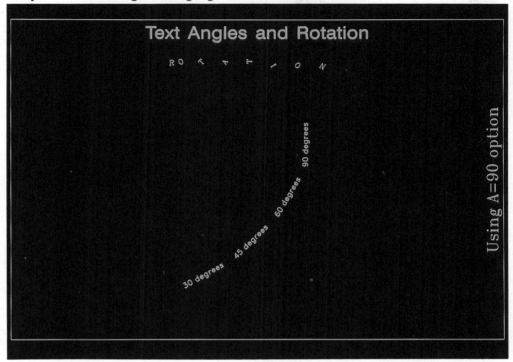

Output 4.4   Using the M= and D= Options: PROC GSLIDE

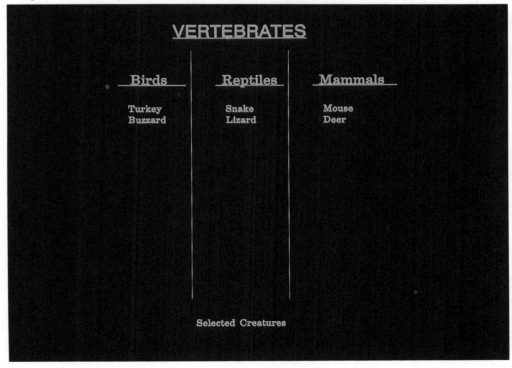

54

Chapter 5

Enhancing Your Graphics Output Designs

INTRODUCTION

You can use PATTERN, SYMBOL, AXIS, and LEGEND statements to alter the appearance of the plots, charts, maps, axes, and legends in your graphics displays.

Once you decide the best way to analyze and graphically represent data (using the GCHART, GMAP, GCONTOUR, GPLOT, or other graphics procedures), you can use special SAS/GRAPH statements to enhance the output you create with these procedures. PATTERN and SYMBOL statements allow you to specify the patterns and symbols used to draw, fill, and label the bars, pies, maps, and plots in your output. AXIS and LEGEND statements enable you to specify labels and values for your axes and legends. SAS/GRAPH software provides defaults for these features of your output. However, by specifying these statements and using some or all of the options available, you can tailor your output to fit your needs.

PATTERN Statement

You can use PATTERN statements to define colors and patterns in the GCHART, GCONTOUR, GMAP, and GPLOT procedures. You can use PATTERN statements anywhere in your SAS program. SAS/GRAPH software uses any PATTERN statements you specify. If more are needed, default PATTERN statements are used.

PATTERN Statements with PROC GCHART

If you do not specify the SUBGROUP= or PATTERNID= options when you use PROC GCHART, the color and pattern specified in your PATTERN1 statement are used for the bars or blocks produced by ᵖROC GCHART. You can specify a PATTERN statement for each value of the SᵁBGROUP= variable. The values of this variable are sorted, and the color and pattern specified in the PATTERN1 statement are assigned to the first value; the color and pattern in the PATTERN2 statement are assigned to the second value; and so on. If you are creating a pie or star chart, the pattern specified with the PATTERN1 statement is used for the first slice, the pattern specified with the PATTERN2 statement is used for the second slice, and so on.

See "The GCHART Procedure" for more information on how to use PATTERN statements.

PATTERN Statements with PROC GCONTOUR

If you want PROC GCONTOUR to fill each contour level with colors and patterns, specify the PATTERN option in the PLOT statement and a PATTERN statement for each level of contour. The procedure uses the PATTERN1 statement to fill the first contour level, the PATTERN2 statement to fill the second contour level, and so on.

See "The GCONTOUR Procedure" for more information on how to use PATTERN statements.

Pattern Statements with PROC GMAP

If you are producing a choropleth, block, or prism map, you can specify a PATTERN statement for each level of the response variable.

See "The GMAP Procedure" for more information on how to use PATTERN statements.

PATTERN Statements with PROC GPLOT

If you are plotting lines and want to fill the area under each curve, specify the AREAS= option in the PLOT statement and a PATTERN statement to fill each region (beginning at the horizontal axis).

See "The GPLOT Procedure" for more information on how to use PATTERN statements.

PATTERN Statement Specification

The general form of a PATTERN statement is

PATTERN*n options*;

where

n

is a number ranging from 1 to 255. If you do not specify a number after the keyword PATTERN, PATTERN1 is assumed.

options

allows you to specify the colors and patterns used to fill the bars, pies, maps, and other designs in your output.

PATTERN statements are additive; if you specify a C= or V= option in a PATTERN statement and then omit that option in a later PATTERN statement ending in the same number, the option remains in effect. To turn off options specified in a previous PATTERN*n* statement, either specify all options in a new PATTERN*n* statement, or use the keyword PATTERN*n* followed by a semicolon. For example, the following statement turns off any C= or V= option specified in previous PATTERN3 statements:

    pattern3;

You can reset options in PATTERN statements to their default values by specifying a null value. A comma can be used (but is not required) to separate a null parameter from the next option.

For example, the following statements both cause C= to have its default value (the value of the CPATTERN= option or the first color in the COLORS= list):

    pattern c=, v=solid;

or

    pattern c= v=solid;

In the following statement, both options are reset to their default values:

    pattern2 c= v=;

You can also turn off options by specifying the RESET= option in a GOPTIONS statement. Refer to "The GOPTIONS Statement" for details.

You can specify the following options in a PATTERN statement:

COLOR=*color*
C=*color*
> specifies the color to use for a bar or other area to be filled. If you do not specify C= in a PATTERN statement, the procedure uses the value you specified for the CPATTERN= option in a GOPTIONS statement. If you omitted the CPATTERN= option, the procedure uses the pattern specified by V= (below) with each color in the COLORS= list before it uses the next PATTERN statement.

REPEAT=*n*
R=*n*
> specifies the number of times the PATTERN statement is to be reused. For example, the following statement represents one pattern to be used by SAS/GRAPH software:

>   pattern1 v=x3 c=red;

> You can use the REPEAT= option in the statement to repeat the pattern before going to the next pattern. For example, if you specify the following statements, PATTERN1 is repeated ten times before PATTERN2 is used:

>   pattern1 v=x3 c=red   r=10;
>   pattern2 v=s   c=blue r=10;

> Remember that if you omit the COLOR= option from the PATTERN statement and you do not specify the CPATTERN= option, SAS/GRAPH software repeats the pattern for each color in the current COLORS= list. If you specify the R= option in a PATTERN statement from which the C= option is omitted, the statement cycles through the COLORS= list the number of times given by R=.

> For example, if the current device has seven colors, then the following statement results in seventy patterns because each group of seven patterns generated by cycling through the COLORS= list is repeated ten times:

>   pattern v=x3 r=10;

VALUE=*value*
V=*value*
> specifies the pattern to use for a bar or other area to be filled.

> The valid values you can use depend on what procedure you are using and the type of graph you are producing. If the procedure is being used to produce bars (for example, VBAR, HBAR, or BLOCK statements in PROC GCHART or the BLOCK statement in PROC GMAP), you must use one of the pattern values shown in **Figure 5.1**.

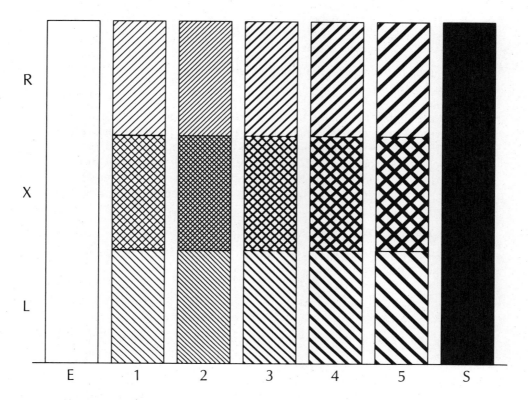

Figure 5.1 Pattern Selection Guide

If the procedure produces polygons (for example, any PROC GCONTOUR output; choropleth, prism, and surface maps produced with PROC GMAP; or area fills produced with PROC GPLOT), you should specify V=S and V=E or one of the Mxxxxx values.

Using the Mxxxxx values, you can specify several densities of filling, either single lines or crosshatched lines, and the angle of the lines.

```
M x x x x x
    1
    2
    3
    4
    5
      X or N
      N starting angle
```

Density of filling The value of the first character after the letter M determines the density of filling; specify 1 for the lightest shading, 5 for the heaviest. For example, if you specify the following statement, the pattern will be medium-thick red lines:

```
pattern1 c=red v=m3;
```

Crosshatching   For crosshatched lines, use an X *after* the shading density number. If you omit the X, parallel lines are used. For example, if you specify the following statement, the pattern will be dense, crosshatched green lines:

```
pattern2 c=green v=m5x;
```

Use an N for no crosshatching when you want to specify a starting angle for the single lines.

Starting angle   Normally, the lines are drawn horizontally. To request a different angle, give the angle at the end of the M*xxxxx* specification. If X is included in the specification, the crosshatch lines are drawn at a 90-degree angle from the first set of lines. The angle can range from 0 to 360 degrees. For example, if you specify the following statement, the pattern is thin single blue lines drawn at a 60-degree angle from the horizontal:

```
pattern4 c=blue v=m1n60;
```

Here are more examples of valid PATTERN statements with M*xxxxx* values:

`pattern2 c=red v=m3x;`	produces red crosshatch lines of medium density
`pattern2 c=blue v=m5n85;`	produces heavy blue lines at an 85-degree angle from the horizontal

In a PATTERN statement, if you specify a value for V= but not for C=, the procedure uses the value you specified for the CPATTERN= option in a GOPTIONS statement. If you omitted the CPATTERN= option, the procedure uses the pattern specified for V= with each color in the COLORS= list before it uses the next PATTERN statement. Thus, if you specify the following statements, the PATTERN1 statement is used for the first SUBGROUP= value in the bar:

```
pattern1 c=red    v=x3;
pattern2          v=s;
pattern3 c=blue   v=l3;
pattern4 c=green v=r4;
proc gchart data=sales;
    vbar year / subgroup=dept sumvar=sales discrete;
```

The PATTERN2 statement is used for the second SUBGROUP= value. Because a C= value is not specified in the PATTERN2 statement, SAS/GRAPH software uses the PATTERN2 statement and cycles through the colors in the COLORS= list for the device. If needed, the PATTERN3 and PATTERN4 values are then used for the remaining subgroup values.

If you are producing pie charts or star charts with PROC GCHART, you should specify V=E , V=S, or V=P*xxxxx*, where the *xxxxx* values correspond to those for the M*xxxxx* values described above.

If you specify a pattern value that is not appropriate for the type of graph you are generating (for example, if you specify V=L1 when drawing a choropleth map), default patterns are used.

SYMBOL Statement

You can specify a SYMBOL statement anywhere in your SAS program. SYMBOL statements give PROC GPLOT information about plot characters, plot lines, color, and interpolation (smoothing of lines). The information contained in a SYMBOL statement is used by PROC GPLOT in three different ways, as described below.

Overlaid Plot Explicitly Specified

Suppose you want to plot two pairs of variables and overlay them on one set of axes. You can specify the plot character, plot line, color, and interpolation for each pair of variables in the overlaid plot. Use a numbered SYMBOL statement for each pair of variables; then run PROC GPLOT and specify those numbers in a PLOT statement. Here is an example:

```
symbol1 c=red   v=square;
symbol2 c=blue v=triangle;
proc gplot;
   plot y*x=2 a*b=1 / overlay;
```

In the PLOT statement, A*B=1 tells PROC GPLOT to use the first SYMBOL statement characteristics; Y*X=2 tells PROC GPLOT to use the second SYMBOL statement characteristics. In the plot, the A*B points are represented by red squares, and the Y*X points are represented by blue triangles.

Overlaid Plot, Default Specification

When you omit the number following the plot request, PROC GPLOT uses information from the *n*th generated SYMBOL statement. For example, consider the statements above. If, instead, the PLOT statement were as follows, then the characteristics of the first SYMBOL statement would be used for the Y*X points, and the characteristics of the second SYMBOL statement would be used for the A*B points.

```
plot y*x  a*b / overlay;
```

Using a Third Variable in the Plot Request

You can plot several sets of data on the same graph when a third variable contains grouping levels. (The formatted values of the third variable are used.) For example, consider these statements:

```
symbol1 c=red   v=star;
symbol2 c=blue v=square;
proc gplot;
   plot weight*height=gender;
```

The points on the plot corresponding to observations with GENDER='F' appear as red stars; points for GENDER='M' appear as blue squares.

If you request interpolation in the SYMBOL statements (for example, I=SPLINE), PROC GPLOT connects the points for each value of the third variable. For example, consider these statements:

```
symbol1 c=red   v=star   i=spline;
symbol2 c=blue v=square i=spline;
proc gplot;
   plot weight*height=gender;
```

The points on the plot corresponding to observations with GENDER='F' appear as red stars and are connected with a red line; points for GENDER='M' appear as blue squares and are connected with a blue line.

SYMBOL Statement Specification

The general form of a SYMBOL statement is

SYMBOL*n options*;

where

n
>   is a number ranging from 1 to 255. Each SYMBOL statement remains in
>   effect until you specify another SYMBOL statement ending in the same
>   number. If you do not specify a number following the keyword
>   SYMBOL, SYMBOL1 is assumed.

options
>   allows you to specify the plot characters, plot lines, color, and
>   interpolation.

SYMBOL statements are additive; that is, if you specify a given option in a
SYMBOL statement and then omit that option in a later SYMBOL statement ending in the same number, the option remains in effect. To turn off all options specified in previous SYMBOL statements, you can specify all options in a new
SYMBOL*n* statement, use the keyword SYMBOL*n* followed by a semicolon, or
specify a null value. A comma can be used (but is not required) to separate a null
parameter from the next option.

For example, the following statements both cause C= to have its default value
(the value of the CSYMBOL= option or the first color in the COLORS= list):

```
symbol1 c=, v=plus;
```

and

```
symbol1 c= v=plus;
```

In the following statement, both options are reset to their default values:

```
symbol4 c= v=;
```

You can also turn off options by specifying the RESET= option in a GOPTIONS
statement. Refer to "The GOPTIONS Statement" for details.

You can specify the following options in the SYMBOL statement.

General Options

COLOR=*color*
C=*color*
>   specifies the color to use for the corresponding plot specification. Both
>   the points and the line will have this color.
>
>   If you do not specify the C= option in a SYMBOL statement, the
>   procedure uses the value you specified for the CSYMBOL= option in a
>   GOPTIONS statement. If you omit the CSYMBOL= option, the
>   procedure uses the value specified by the V= option with each color in
>   the COLORS= list before it uses the next SYMBOL statement.
>   Specifying the C= option is exactly the same as specifying both the
>   CI= and CV= options.

CV=*color*
CI=*color*
CO=*color*
>   CV= specifies the color of the symbol used at the plotted value. CI=
>   specifies the color of the interpolation line. CO= is a multipurpose
>   option that allows you to specify the outline color for map interpolation

(I=Mxxxxx), the color for confidence limit lines (I=Rxxx), and the color for staffs and bars (I=HILO | STD). These options allow you to produce symbols and lines of different colors without having to overlay multiple pairs when you are using PROC GPLOT.

Specifying the CV= and CI= options together gives exactly the same results as specifying the C= option alone. If CV= is specified and CI= is not, CI= assumes the value of CV=. If CI= is specified and CV= is not, CV= assumes the value of CI=.

F=*font*
W=*width*
H=*height*

F= specifies the font from which the value specified with V= is to be drawn. W= specifies the thickness, in pixels, of any interpolated lines. H= specifies the height of the characters. You can specify *height* as *n* PCT (where *n* is expressed as a percentage of the display area); *n* IN (where *n* is expressed in inches); *n* CM (where *n* is expressed in centimeters); or *n* CELLS (where *n* is expressed in character cell units). If you do not specify a unit for *height*, the value you specified with the GUNIT= option in a GOPTIONS statement is used. If you did not specify a GUNIT= value, the default value, character cells, is used.

For example, this SYMBOL statement

```
symbol1 c=green v=k f=special h=2 cm i=j w=2;
```

indicates that the symbol at each data point is the letter K from the SPECIAL font (a filled square), drawn in green two centimeters high. The points are to be connected by a double-width green straight line. The value given by V= can be up to eight characters long. The value is printed using the font specified by F=.

Note: if you use one of the special symbol values described in **Figure 5.2** (for example, PLUS) and also specify a font, the name PLUS is printed in the font rather than the plus sign (+).

L=*n*

allows you to specify the kind of line that is drawn on the plot. Possible values for *n* are

1   a solid line (the default value when L= is omitted)

2–46   various dashed lines. See **Figure 5.2**.

MODE=INCLUDE
MODE=EXCLUDE

specify that PROC GPLOT is to include or exclude observation values outside the axis range in interpolation calculations. The default value is EXCLUDE. Refer to **Values Out of Range** in "The GPLOT Procedure" for a discussion of the MODE= option.

REPEAT=*n*
R=*n*

specifies the number of times the SYMBOL statement is to be reused. See the description in **PATTERN Statement**.

V=*symbol*

gives the plot character for the corresponding plot specifications. Possible V= values are the letters A through W, the numbers 0 through 9, and the special symbols shown in **Figure 5.3**.

Note that if you use the special symbol comma (,) with V=, you must enclose the comma in quotes. Here is an example:

```
symbol1 v=',';
```

If you omit the V= value, V=NONE is used.

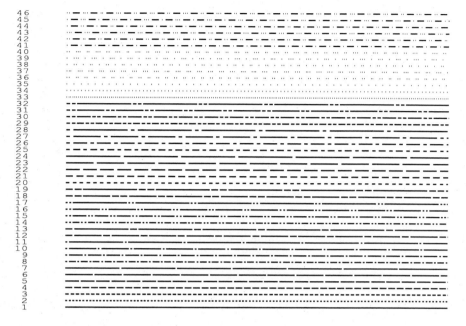

Figure 5.2   Values for the L= Option

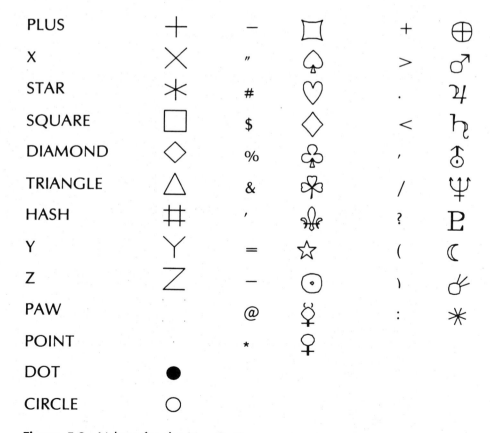

PLUS

X

STAR

SQUARE

DIAMOND

TRIANGLE

HASH

Y

Z

PAW

POINT

DOT

CIRCLE

Figure 5.3   Values for the V= Option

Interpolation Option

I=*interpolation*
> specifies whether to leave the plotted points unconnected or to connect the plotted points with either straight lines or a smoothed line; use regression to fit a line to the points; or draw vertical lines connecting the points and the zero horizontal.
>
> If you use the HAXIS= and VAXIS= options to control the range of values in a PLOT statement, any data points that lie outside of the range of the axes are discarded by default before the calculations are done for interpolation lines. Refer to the description of the MODE= option.
>
> Possible values for the I= option are given below.

Interpolation Values

I=NONE
> requests that the points on the plot be left unconnected. I=NONE is the default.

I=JOIN
> requests that the points on the plot be connected by a straight line.

I=NEEDLE
> draws a vertical line from each point on the plot to a horizontal line at zero on the Y axis.

I=STEP*xx*
> requests that a step function be used to plot the data. If you specify I=STEPL, the data point is on the left of the step; with I=STEPR, the data point is on the right; with I=STEPC, the data point is in the center of the step. If you do not specify L, R, or C, then L is assumed.
>
> Optionally, to join the steps with a vertical line, follow the I=STEP*x* specification with a J. For example, I=STEPRJ draws a step function with the data point on the right and joins the steps.
>
> You should sort your data before you specify the I=STEP option. Specify I=STEPS to sort your data internally if they are not ordered.

I=M*xxxxx*
> fills a figure that your plotted points define. See the V= option in **PATTERN Statement** for more information about the M*xxxxx* interpolation value.

I=STD*kxxx*
> is used when multiple Y values occur for each level of X and you want to join the mean Y value with (+ or −) 1, 2, or 3 standard deviations for each X. The value of *k* can be 1, 2, or 3. If you do not specify a value for *k*, the default value of two standard deviations is used. The *xxx* values can be M, P, J, B, T, or combinations of these letters (except B with T). The sample variance is computed about each mean, and from it, s_y, the standard deviation, is computed; or if you specify I=STDM, then $s_{\bar{y}}$, the standard error of the mean, is computed.
>
> If you specify I=STDP, sample variances are computed using a pooled estimate, as in a one-way ANOVA model.
>
> If you specify I=STDJ, the means are connected from bar to bar. Use B to request bars (rather than lines) to connect the points for each X. T specifies that tops and bottoms should be added to each line.
>
> B and T should not be used together, but other combinations of M, P, J, and B or T are acceptable.

Note that if you do not specify the VAXIS= option, the vertical axis ranges from the minimum to maximum Y value in the data. If the requested number of standard deviations from the mean covers a range of values that exceeds the maximum or is less than the minimum, the STD lines are cut off at the minimum and maximum Y values. When this cutoff occurs, you should rescale the axis using the VAXIS= specification.

I=HILOxxx

is used when multiple Y values occur for each level of X. The value of xxx can be T, B, C, or J, or combinations of these letters (except T with B). When you specify I=HILOxxx, the minimum and maximum Y values at each X level are connected by a solid line. For each X value, the mean Y value is marked with a tick, as shown in **Figure 5.4**.

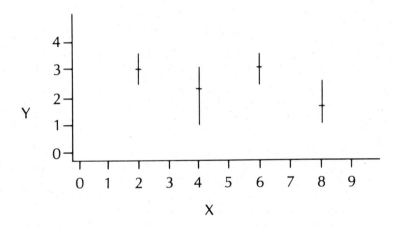

Figure 5.4   Specifying I=HILO

Specifying I=HILOT adds tops and bottoms to each line, as shown in **Figure 5.5**.

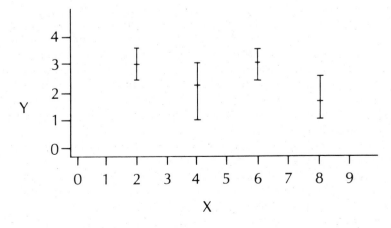

Figure 5.5   Specifying I=HILOT

Specifying I=HILOB produces bars instead of lines, as shown in **Figure 5.6**.

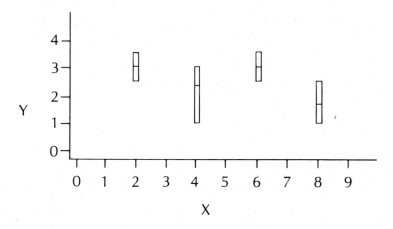

Figure 5.6   Specifying I=HILOB

Use I=HILOC (*high, low, close*) with stock market data so that a tick mark appears at the *close* value. If you do not give three Y values (*high, low, close*), the mean is ticked. The Y values can be in any order. See **Figure 5.7**.

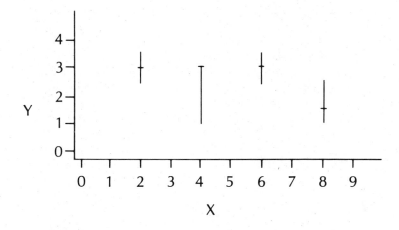

Figure 5.7   Specifying I=HILOC

The mean or *close* point can be joined from bar to bar by specifying I=HILOJ, as shown in **Figure 5.8**.

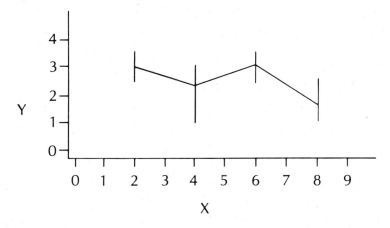

Figure 5.8   Specifying I=HILOJ

The mean or *close* point is not marked with a tick mark when you specify I=HILOJ.

Note: you cannot use the AREAS= option for area fill with I=HILOJ.

R-series Interpolation Value

I=Rxxxxxxx

specifies the characteristics of the regression analysis to use for fitting a line to the plotted points. The regression equations can be linear, quadratic, or cubic; confidence limits can be drawn at one of three levels. The points on the plot do not necessarily fall on the regression line.

The form of the Rxxxxxxx value determines whether linear, quadratic, or cubic regression is used to fit a plot line; whether the intercept is set to zero to force the line through the origin; whether additional lines representing confidence limits should be drawn and, if so, what confidence level should be used.

```
R x x x x x x x
  L
  Q
  C
    0
      C L I
      C L M
            9 0
            9 5
            9 9
```

As shown above, valid values for the first variable after the R include L, Q, and C.

Degree of regression equation   Use L as the first character after the R to request linear regression. For example, the statements

```
symbol1 v=star i=rl;
proc gplot;
   plot y*x;
```

produce a plot showing the points (stars) and a straight line representing the regression equation

$$Y = \beta_0 + \beta_1 X \quad .$$

Use Q as the first character after the R to request quadratic regression. The statements

```
symbol1 v=star i=rq;
proc gplot;
   plot y*x;
```

produce a plot showing the points and a curve representing the regression equation

$$Y = \beta_0 + \beta_1 X + \beta_2 X^2 \quad .$$

Use C as the first character after the R to request cubic regression. The statements

```
symbol1 v=star i=rc;
proc gplot;
   plot y*x;
```

produce a plot showing the points and a curve representing the regression equation

$$Y = \beta_0 + \beta_1 X + \beta_2 X^2 + \beta_3 X^3 \quad .$$

Intercept of zero   To eliminate the β_0 parameter, or intercept, from the regression equation and force the regression line through the origin, use a zero as the third character of the Rxxxxxx specification. For example, the statements

```
symbol1 i=rl0;
proc gplot;
   plot y*x;
```

produce a plot showing the points and a line representing the regression equation

$$Y = \beta_1 X \quad .$$

The line passes through the origin.

Confidence limits   When you request regression, you can ask that lines representing confidence limits for individual or mean predicted values be shown on the plot. Follow the L, Q, C, or zero in the Rxxxxxx specification with the characters CLM to show confidence limits for mean predicted values; use CLI to show confidence limits for individual predicted values.

To specify the confidence level, include the numbers 90, 95, or 99 after CLI or CLM. For example, the statements

```
symbol1 i=rl0cli95;
proc gplot;
    plot y*x;
```

produce a plot showing the points and a line that represents the regression equation $Y = \beta_1 X$. Two other lines are drawn to represent confidence limits at the 95th percentile.

The line style used for the confidence limit lines is determined by adding 1 to the L= value. For example, if the L= value were 1, line style 2 would be used to draw the confidence limit lines.

If the confidence level is omitted, a value of 95 is used.

Here are some examples of I=Rxxxxxxx values:

RC0CLI99
  requests cubic regression through the origin, with 99-percent confidence limits on individual predicted values.

RLCLM
  requests linear regression with 95-percent confidence limits on mean predicted values.

RQ
  requests quadratic regression.

Spline Interpolation Values

Several spline methods are available for smoothing points in a plot. SPLINE, which draws the smoothest line and is the least expensive of the nontrivial methods, is the method of choice for most plots. The Lagrange methods are useful chiefly when your data consist of tabulated, precise values. SM is the method to use for smoothing noisy data. Parametric forms of these methods are also available.

I=SPLINE
  specifies that the plot line be interpolated using a spline routine. The points on the plot fall on the line.
  When you use I=SPLINE, the plot line is smoothed using a cubic spline method with continuous second derivatives (Pizer 1975). This routine uses a piecewise third-degree polynomial for each set of two adjacent points. The polynomial passes through the plotted points and matches the first and second derivatives of neighboring segments at the points. For the two end segments, the curvature is set to zero. If the values of the horizontal variable are not strictly increasing, the parametric interpolation method SPLINEP (below) is used instead.

I=SPLINEP
  results in the use of a parametric spline method with continuous second derivatives. Using the method described above for the I=SPLINE option, a parametric spline is fitted to both the horizontal and vertical values. The parameter used is the distance between points

$$t = \sqrt{(x^2 + y^2)}$$

If two points are so close together that the computations overflow, the second point is not used.

I=Lx

specifies that the plot line be smoothed using a Lagrange interpolation.

When you specify I=L1, I=L3, or I=L5, the plot is smoothed using a Lagrange interpolation of degree 1, 3, or 5. A polynomial of the specified degree (1, 3, or 5) is fitted through the nearest 2, 4, or 6 points. In general, the first derivative is not continuous. If the values of the horizontal variable are not strictly increasing, the corresponding parametric method (L1P, L3P, or L5P) is used.

Specifying I=L1P, I=L3P, or I=L5P, results in a parametric Lagrange interpolation of degree 1, 3, or 5. The method described above for the L= option is used, but a parametric interpolation of degree 1, 3, or 5 is done on both the horizontal and vertical variables, using the distance between points as a parameter.

I=SMxx

specifies that a smooth line be fit to noisy data using a spline routine. The points on the plot do not necessarily fall on the line.

Specifying I=SMxx results in fitting a cubic spline that minimizes a linear combination of the sum of squares of the residuals of fit and the integral of the square of the second derivative (Reinsch 1967). The value xx can range from 01 to 99 and determines the relative importance of the two components: the larger the value, the smoother the fitted curve.

I=SMxxP

results in the use of a parametric cubic spline as described in I=SMxx.

Sorting by the x Variable

If you want the procedure to sort by the x axis variable before plotting, you add the letter S to the end of any of the spline interpolation methods described above. For example, suppose you want to overlay three plots (Y1*X1, Y2*X2, and Y3*X3) and for each plot, you want the x variable to be sorted in ascending order. You can use the following statements:

```
symbol1 i=splines c=red;
symbol2 i=splines c=blue;
symbol3 i=splines c=green;
proc gplot;
    plot y1*x1 y2*x2 y3*x3 / overlay;
run;
```

AXIS and LEGEND Statements

AXIS and LEGEND statements enable you to control the appearance of certain features in your graphs. These statements are used to describe axes or legends that are used later in a procedure, similar to the way TITLE or PATTERN statements are used. The difference in use is that the desired axis or legend is explicitly selected in the procedure.

The terms used to describe the parts of the axes and legends are defined below.

axis   the line, tick marks, values, and label associated with a variable in a plot or chart.

legend   the shapes, values, and label associated with a legend variable in a plot, chart, or map.

label   the text and attributes associated with a variable in a plot or chart.

value	the text and attributes associated with the values of a variable in a plot or chart.
item	in an axis, a major tick mark and the value associated with it. In a legend, a legend entry.
major tick mark	an axis tick mark that has a value associated with it.
minor tick mark	a tick mark between major tick marks.
offset	the distance from the axis origin to the first major tick mark or from the last major tick mark to the end of the axis line.

A simple example follows:

```
proc gplot;
   axis1 label=(c=yellow f=triplex) value=(c=blue);
   axis2 label=(c=yellow f=triplex) value=(c=green h=2);
   plot y*x / haxis=axis1 vaxis=axis2;
run;
```

The above statements produce a plot with a horizontal axis (in this case, X) that has a yellow label in TRIPLEX font with blue values. The vertical axis (in this case, Y) also has a yellow label in TRIPLEX font, but it has green values of height 2. This example shows the association between the AXIS statement and a graphics procedure. After you define an axis, you select it by specifying the appropriate option within a procedure. (See the chapters on the GCHART, GCONTOUR, and GPLOT procedures for more information.)

Although the two AXIS statements used here are simple and concise, you can have more control over the appearance of your axes by specifying more information in the AXIS statement.

AXIS Statement

The general form of the AXIS statement is

AXIS*n* *options;*

The AXIS statement allows you to control the appearance of the axes of your plots and charts. If you want to specify more than one AXIS statement, follow the keyword AXIS with a number, *n*. The value of *n* can range from 1 to 255.

You can use the following options in an AXIS statement:

COLOR=*color*
  specifies the color of the axis and text unless overridden by a more specific color option.

LABEL=NONE
LABEL=(*description*)
  specifies a label description. The LABEL= option gives the attributes or text of the variable label associated with the variable represented on this axis. If no text is specified, the variable label is used. If neither text nor a variable label is specified, the variable name is used. If you specify LABEL=NONE, the label is suppressed. If you specify LABEL=(*description*), *description* can take the parameters listed in the section **VALUE and LABEL Description Parameters for AXIS Statements**.

LENGTH=*n*
  specifies the length of the axis. You can set LENGTH equal to *n* CELLS (where *n* is expressed in character cell units); *n* PCT (where *n* is expressed as a percentage of the display area); *n* IN (where *n* is expressed in inches); or *n* CM (where *n* is expressed in centimeters).

If you do not specify a unit with *n*, the value you specified with the GUNIT= option in a GOPTIONS statement is used. If you did not specify a GUNIT= value, the default value, character cells, is used.

LOGBASE=*n*

LOGBASE=PI

LOGBASE=e

specify that the axis will be logarithmic and specify the base. The value you specify for *n* must be greater than 1.

LOGSTYLE=POWER

LOGSTYLE=EXPAND

specify the style for outputting the values on an axis when you use the LOGBASE= option. LOGSTYLE=POWER specifies that only the powers (for example, −1, 0, 1, 2, and so on) are displayed. LOGSTYLE=EXPAND specifies that the values should be expanded (for example, .1, 1, 10, 100, and so on). The default is LOGSTYLE=EXPAND.

MAJOR=NONE

MAJOR=(*description*)

specifies a major tick mark description. The MAJOR= option gives the attributes of the tick marks. If you specify MAJOR=NONE, no major tick marks appear on the axis; however, the values associated with those tick marks are not affected. If you specify MAJOR=(*description*), *description* can take the parameters listed in the section **Tick Description Parameters**.

MINOR=NONE

MINOR=(*description*)

specifies a minor tick mark description. The MINOR= option describes the minor tick marks in each major tick interval. This description is used between all major tick intervals. If you specify MINOR=NONE, no minor tick marks appear on the axis. If you specify MINOR=(*description*), *description* can take the parameters listed in **Tick Description Parameters**.

NOBRACKETS

suppresses the printing of group brackets. (See the description of the GAXIS= option in "The GCHART Procedure" for more information on group brackets.)

OFFSET=(*n,m*)

specifies the amount of space at which to offset the first major tick mark from the origin (*n*) and the amount of space at which to offset the last major tick mark from the end of the axis (*m*). If you do not specify *m*, *m* equals *n*.

You can set OFFSET equal to (*n,m*) PCT (where *n,m* is expressed as a percentage of the display area); (*n,m*) IN (where *n,m* is expressed in inches); (*n,m*) CM (where *n,m* is expressed in centimeters); or (*n,m*) CELLS (where *n,m* is expressed in character cell units).

If you do not specify a unit with *n,m*, the value you specified with the GUNIT= option in a GOPTIONS statement is used. If you did not specify a GUNIT= value, the default value, character cells, is used.

You can also use different units of measurement in a single specification to define *n* and *m*. For example, the following specification is valid:

```
offset=(n pct,m cm)
```

If you want to specify the length of only one of the offsets, you can supply a null value for the other offset. For example,

```
offset=(,3 cm)
```

If you specify only one offset without a null value, both offsets are set to that value. For example,

```
offset=(4 in)
```

ORDER=(*list*)

specifies the data values in the order they are to appear on the axis. This can imply clipping. (For example, if the data range is 1 to 10 and you specify ORDER=(3 to 5), then only the data in the range 3 to 5 appear on the plot.) See **Example 2** for a demonstration.

This option overrides the N= option described in **Tick Description Parameters** later in this chapter.

ORIGIN=(*x,y*)

specifies the x coordinate of the origin and the y coordinate of the origin on the screen or graphics display area. You can set each x,y pair equal to (x,y) PCT (where x,y is expressed as a percentage of the display area); (x,y) IN (where x,y is expressed in inches); (x,y) CM (where x,y is expressed in centimeters); or (x,y) CELLS (where x,y is expressed in character cell units). You can also specify units using the form x PCT,y PCT.

If you do not specify a unit with x,y, the value you specified with the GUNIT= option in a GOPTIONS statement is used. If you did not specify a GUNIT= value, the default value, character cells, is used.

You can use different units of measurement in a single specification to define the x and y coordinates For example,

```
origin=(45,55 pct)
```

places the origin 45 character cells from the left side and 55 percent of the way between the bottom and top of the graphics display area.

If you want to specify the location of only one of the coordinates, you can supply a null value for the other coordinate. For example,

```
origin=(,3 in)
```

If you specify only one coordinate without a null value, it is assumed to be the x coordinate. For example,

```
origin=(2 cm)
```

STYLE=*n*

specifies the line style of the axis line. If you specify STYLE=0, the axis line is not drawn. See **SYMBOL Statement** for a description of line styles.

VALUE=NONE

VALUE=(*description*)

specifies a value description. VALUE= gives the attributes or text of the values on the axis. A value is the text associated with a major tick mark. If no text is specified, the formatted variable values are used. If you specify VALUE=NONE, the values are suppressed. If you specify VALUE=(*description*), *description* can take the parameters listed in the section **VALUE and LABEL Description Parameters for AXIS Statements**.

WIDTH=*n*

specifies the width (in pixels) of the axis line, where *n* is a positive integer.

VALUE and LABEL Description Parameters for AXIS Statements

The VALUE and LABEL descriptions accept parameters much like TITLE, NOTE, or FOOTNOTE statements. The following parameters are valid:

ANGLE=n
A=n

> specifies the angle at which the baseline of the text is to be rotated with respect to the horizontal. The default value is 0.

COLOR=color
C=color

> specifies the color for the VALUE or LABEL descriptions. If you do not specify the COLOR= option, the color you specified in the CTEXT= option for the procedure is used. If you omitted the CTEXT= option, then the procedure uses either the first color in the COLORS= list or, if specified, the CTEXT= option in a GOPTIONS statement.

FONT=name
F=name

> specifies the font for the VALUE or LABEL descriptions. If you do not specify the FONT= option, the procedure uses the value specified for the FTEXT= option in a GOPTIONS statement. The default value is FONT=NONE.

HEIGHT=n [units]
H=n [units]

> specifies the height of characters from baseline to capline for the VALUE and LABEL descriptions. If you do not specify the HEIGHT= option, the default height of 1 is used.
>
> You can specify units as n PCT (where n is expressed as a percentage of the display area); n IN (where n is expressed in inches); n CM (where n is expressed in centimeters), or n CELLS (where n is expressed in character cell units).

JUSTIFY | J=l
JUSTIFY | J=r
JUSTIFY | J=c

> specifies the alignment of the VALUE and LABEL descriptions. JUSTIFY= can be used to obtain multiple lines of text for a single tick mark. Refer to **Example 12** for a demonstration of the J= option.

ROTATE=n
R=n

> specifies the angle at which each character is to be rotated with respect to the baseline. The default value is 0.

In addition to the values above, VALUE can take the following parameter:

T=n

> begins the definition for the nth tick mark. See **Example 7** and **Example 12** for demonstrations of the T= option.

For LABEL, the quoted string is the text of the label. For VALUE, each quoted string is associated with a tick mark unless the T= command appears at least once. Then the T= command(s) defines the association between the quoted strings and tick marks.

Tick Description Parameters

The tick description can contain the following parameters. Refer to the descriptions of the MAJOR= and MINOR= options, above, for more information.

COLOR=*color*
C=*color*
   specifies the color of the tick mark. The default is the color you
   specified in the CAXIS= option, or if you did not specify the CAXIS=
   option, the first color in the COLORS= list is used.

H=*n* [*units*]
   specifies the height of the tick mark.
      You can specify units as *n* PCT (where *n* is expressed as a percentage
   of the display area); *n* IN (where *n* is expressed in inches); *n* CM (where
   n is expressed in centimeters), or *n* CELLS (where *n* is expressed in
   character cell units).

N=*n*
   specifies the number of tick marks that are to be drawn. The default is a
   missing value.

W=*n*
   specifies the width (in pixels) of the tick marks, where *n* is a positive
   integer.

LEGEND Statement

LEGEND*n* *options*;

The LEGEND statement allows you to control the appearance of the legends for
your plots, charts, and maps. If you want to specify more than one LEGEND statement, follow the keyword LEGEND with a number, *n*. The value of *n* can range
from 1 to 255.
   The following options can appear in a LEGEND statement:

ACROSS=*n*
   specifies the number of shapes that appear in the legend's horizontal
   dimension.

DOWN=*n*
   specifies the number of shapes that appear in the legend's vertical
   dimension.

FRAME
   specifies to draw a frame around the legend window.

LABEL=NONE
LABEL=(*description*)
   specifies a label description. The LABEL= option gives the attributes or
   text of the variable label associated with the variable represented on this
   legend. If no text is specified, the variable label is used. If neither text
   nor a variable label is specified, the variable name is used. If you specify
   LABEL=NONE, the labels are suppressed. If you specify
   LABEL=(*description*), *description* can take the parameters listed in the
   section **VALUE and LABEL Description Parameters for LEGEND
   Statements**.

SHAPE=LINE(*length*) [*units*]
SHAPE=BAR(*width,height*) [*units*]
SHAPE=SYMBOL(*width,height*) [*units*]
   specifies the shape of legend entries. If you specify SHAPE=LINE, the
   legend entries will be straight lines of the length you specify. If you

specify SHAPE=BAR, the legend entries will be bars of the height and width you specify. If you specify SHAPE=SYMBOL, the legend entries will be the width and height of the symbols specified in the SYMBOL statement.

You can set each *width,height* pair equal to (*width,height*) PCT (where *width,height* is expressed as a percentage of the display area); (*width,height*) IN (where *width,height* is expressed in inches); (*width,height*) CM (where *width,height* is expressed in centimeters); or (*width,height*) CELLS (where *width,height* is expressed in character cell units).

If you do not specify a unit value, the value you specified with the GUNIT= option in a GOPTIONS statement is used. If you did not specify a GUNIT= value, the default value, character cells, is used.

You can also specify units using the form *width* PCT,*height* PCT.

VALUE=NONE
VALUE=(*description*)

specifies a value description. VALUE= gives the attributes or text of the values in the legend. A value is the text associated with a legend entry. If no text is specified, the formatted variable values are used. If you specify VALUE=NONE, the values are suppressed. If you specify VALUE=(*description*), *description* can take the parameters listed in the section **VALUE and LABEL Description Parameters for LEGEND Statements**.

VALUE and LABEL Description Parameters for LEGEND Statements

The VALUE and LABEL descriptions accept parameters much like TITLE, NOTE, or FOOTNOTE statements. The following parameters are valid:

ANGLE=*n*
A=*n*

specifies the angle at which the baseline of the text is rotated with respect to the horizontal. The default value is 0.

COLOR=*color*
C=*color*

specifies the color for the VALUE or LABEL descriptions. If you do not specify the COLOR= option, the color specified in the CTEXT= option for the procedure is used. If you do not specify the CTEXT= option, then the procedure uses either the first color in the COLORS= list or, if specified, the CTEXT= option in a GOPTIONS statement.

FONT=*name*
F=*name*

specifies the font for the VALUE or LABEL descriptions. If you do not specify the FONT= option, the procedure uses the value of the FTEXT= option in a GOPTIONS statement. The default value is FONT=NONE.

HEIGHT=*n* [*units*]
H=*n* [*units*]

specifies the height of characters from baseline to capline for the VALUE and LABEL descriptions. If you omit the HEIGHT= option, the default height of 1 is used.

You can specify units as *n* PCT (where *n* is expressed as a percentage of the display area); *n* IN (where *n* is expressed in inches); *n* CM (where *n* is expressed in centimeters); or *n* CELLS (where *n* is expressed in character cell units).

If you do not specify a unit value, the value you specified with the GUNIT= option in a GOPTIONS statement is used. If you did not specify a GUNIT= value, the default value, character cells, is used.

JUSTIFY | J=*l*
JUSTIFY | J=*r*
JUSTIFY | J=*c*

specifies the alignment of the VALUE and LABEL descriptions. JUSTIFY= can be used to obtain multiple lines of text for a single legend entry.

ROTATE=*n*
R=*n*

specifies the angle at which each character of text is rotated with respect to the baseline. The default is 0.

In addition to the values above, VALUE can take the following parameter:

T=*n*

begins the definition for the *n*th legend entry. See **Example 7** and **Example 12** for demonstrations of the T= option.

For LABEL, the quoted string is the text of the label. For VALUE, each quoted string is associated with a legend entry unless the T= command appears at least once. Then the T= command(s) defines the association between the quoted strings and legend entries.

EXAMPLES

Example 1: Color and Font of the Vertical Axis Labels and Values

This example shows how to control the color and font of the label and values on the vertical axis. The example also demonstrates how to combine an axis description for the vertical axis and a value list for the horizontal axis. The following statements produce **Output 5.1**.

```
title1 j=l a=90 h=2 ' ';
title2 j=l f=swiss 'Raleigh, NC Temperatures';
title3 j=l f=swiss 'in Degrees Fahrenheit';
footnote1 j=l 'Source:'
          m=(8,+0) '1984 American Express'
          m=(8,-1.12) 'Appointment Book';
footnote2 h=2 ' ';


axis1 label=none
      value=(c=cyan f=swiss h=2);
symbol i=j v=plus c=yellow;

proc gplot data=temps;
   plot f1*date / frame
                  vminor=1
                  hminor=0
                  vaxis=axis1
                  haxis='01jan83'd '01jul83'd '02dec83'd;
   format date monyy.;
run;
```

Example 2: Using More than One Axis Description

Example 2 illustrates how two different axis descriptions are used: one for the horizontal axis and one for the vertical axis. In the vertical axis description (AXIS1), a font and height for the values is specified, the label is suppressed, and the order of the values is specified.

In the horizontal axis description (AXIS2), the value and order of the values are specified differently, and the label is specified explicitly to be the string '1983' in the SWISS font, two character cells high. The following statements produce **Output 5.2**.

```
title1 j=l a=90 h=2 ' ';
title2 f=swiss j=l 'Seasonal Temperatures';
title3 f=swiss j=l 'Raleigh, NC';
title4 f=swiss j=l 'Degrees Fahrenheit';
footnote1 j=l 'Source:'
          m=(8,+0) '1984 American Express'
          m=(8,-1.12) 'Appointment Book';
footnote2 h=2 ' ';
symbol i=j v=square c=cyan;
axis1 value=(f=swiss h=2)
      label=none
      order=0 to 100 by 25
      minor=none;
axis2 value=(f=swiss h=2)
      label=(f=swiss h=2 '1983')
      order='01jan83'd '01may83'd '01sep83'd '02dec83'd;

proc gplot data=temps;
   plot f1*date / frame
                  vaxis=axis1
                  haxis=axis2;
   format date worddate3.;
run;
```

Example 3: Suppressing Tick Marks and the Axis Line

This example shows a vertical bar chart in which the major and minor tick marks, as well as the axis line itself, have been suppressed on the response axis (STYLE=0). Because the ORDER= value list and the REF= list are specified to be the same, the axis values are aligned with the reference lines. The A= option is used to rotate the vertical axis label. The following statements produce **Output 5.3**.

```
data citytemp;
   length city $12;
   set temps;
   city='RALEIGH';
   c=c1;
   output;
   city='MINNEAPOLIS';
   c=c2;
   output;
   city='PHOENIX';
   c=c3;
   output;
   keep city c;
```

```
run;
title1 j=l f=swiss 'Average Temperature';
footnote1 j=l 'Source:'
           m=(8,+0) '1984 American Express'
           m=(8,-1.12) 'Appointment Book';
footnote2 h=2 ' ';

axis3 label=(a=90 r=0 f=swiss)
      major=none
      minor=none
      style=0
      order=0 to 30 by 15;
pattern v=s c=vliyg;

proc gchart data=citytemp;
   label c='Degrees Celsius';
   vbar city / sumvar=c
               type=mean
               ref=0 to 30 by 10
               raxis=axis3;
   run;
```

Example 4: Specifying the Length of the Axis

This example shows how to specify the length of the axis. The offset for AXIS1 is set to zero, and the offset for AXIS2 is set to one character cell to allow plenty of room for the triangle symbols. In both cases, the length is specified as a percentage of the screen. The width of the axis line is set to two pixels for both AXIS1 and AXIS2. The following statements produce **Output 5.4**.

```
title1 j=l a=90 ' ';
title2 j=l f=swiss h=2 'Seasonal Temperatures';
title3 j=l f=swiss 'Raleigh, NC';
title4 j=l f=swiss 'Degrees Celsius';
footnote1 j=l 'Source:'
           m=(8,+0) '1984 American Express'
           m=(8,-1.12) 'Appointment Book';
footnote2 h=2 ' ';
axis1 length=50 pct
      label=none
      width=2
      offset=(0);
axis2 length=60 pct
      width=2
      offset=(1)
      minor=none
      order='01jan83'd '01jul83'd '02dec83'd;

symbol v=triangle i=needle c=yellow;

proc gplot data=temps;
   plot c1*date / vaxis=axis1
                  haxis=axis2;
   format date monyy.;
   run;
```

Example 5: Using the ORIGIN= Option

The example below uses the ORIGIN= option to place the axes away from the graph. The following statements produce **Output 5.5**.

```
title1 j=l a=90 h=1 ' ';
title2 j=l f=swiss h=2 '    Seasonal Temperatures';
title3 j=l f=swiss '       in Raleigh, NC';
footnote1 j=l 'Source:'
          m=(8,+0) '1984 American Express'
          m=(8,-1.12) 'Appointment Book';
footnote2 h=1 ' ';
axis1 origin=(10, 16)
      minor=(n=1)
      offset=(0);
axis2 origin=(11, 14)
      minor=none
      offset=(0)
      order='01jan83'd '01jul83'd '02dec83'd;

symbol i=sm05 ci=yellow cv=cyan v=diamond;

proc gplot data=temps;
   plot c1*date / vaxis=axis1
                  haxis=axis2;
   format date monyy.;
   label  c1='Degrees Celsius';
run;
```

Example 6: Specifying Text for the Axis Values

This example shows how to specify the text for the axis values. Each quoted string is a separate value along the axis because the T= option does not appear in the value description. The following statements produce **Output 5.6**.

```
data cars;
   input c units;
   units=units / 100000;
   cards;
1  372400
2  487100
3  551800
4  438700
;

title1 j=l a=90 ' ';
title2 j=l f=swiss h=2 '     Japanese Cars';
title3 j=l f=swiss '         Sold in US';
footnote1  j=l  'Source:'
           m=(8,+0) 'Industrial Review of Japan/1984'
           m=(8,-1.12) 'Nihon Keizai Shimbun, Inc.';
footnote2 h=2 ' ';

axis6 label=none
      value=('Honda' 'Nissan' 'Toyota' 'Others');
pattern v=s c=cyan;
```

```
proc gchart data=cars;
   label units='(x 100,000)';
   vbar c / discrete
             sumvar=units
             width=8
             maxis=axis6
             raxis=0 to 6 by 2;
run;
```

Example 7: Using the T= Option in a Value Description

Example 7 illustrates the use of the T= option in a value description. The color of the third tick value is changed for highlighting. The following statements produce **Output 5.7**.

```
data cars;
   input c units;
   units=units / 100000;
   cards;
1   372400
2   487100
3   551800
4   438700
;

title1 j=1 a=90 ' ';
title2 j=1 f=swiss h=2 '   Japanese Cars';
title3 j=1 f=swiss '      Sold in US';
title4 j=1 f=swiss '           (x 100,000)';
footnote1   j=1  'Source:'
             m=(8,+0) 'Industrial Review of Japan/1984'
             m=(8,-1.12) 'Nihon Keizai Shimbun, Inc.';
footnote2 h=2 ' ';
axis7 label=none
      value=(c=white
             t=1 'Honda'
             t=2 'Nissan'
             t=3 c=cyan 'Toyota'
             t=4 'Others');
axis8 label=none
      order=0 to 6 by 2;
pattern v=s c=cyan;

proc gchart data=cars;
   vbar c / discrete
             sumvar=units
             width=8
             maxis=axis7
             raxis=axis8;
run;
```

Example 8: Using the LOGBASE= Option

Example 8 illustrates the basic use of the LOGBASE= option. The vertical axis of the plot is represented in log base 10. Notice that the values appear as the expanded powers of 10 (LOGSTYLE=EXPAND is the default) and that the minor tick marks on the vertical axis are logarithmically spaced. The following statements produce **Output 5.8**.

```
data logs;
    do x=-5 to 5 by 0.5;
        a=2 ** (x - ranuni(54321) + 5.5);
        b=10 ** (abs (x) - ranuni(54321) + 0.5);
        c=2.7 ** (x - ranuni(54321) + 0.5);
        d=3.1 ** (x - ranuni(54321) + 0.5);
        output;
        end;
run;


title f=swiss 'Examples of Logarithmic Axis';
footnote1 f=swiss h=1.5 'LOGSTYLE=EXPAND';
footnote2 ' ';
symbol1 v=square i=sm20 ci=yellow cv=cyan;
axis2 logbase=10;


proc gplot data=logs;
    plot b*x / frame
               vaxis=axis2;
run;
```

Example 9: Using the LOGBASE= and LOGSTYLE= Options

Example 9 illustrates the use of the LOGSTYLE= option when combined with the LOGBASE= option. The vertical axis of the plot is represented in log base 2, the values appear as the powers of 2, and the default axis label has been modified. If you had specified a label for the axis, it would not have been modified. Notice also that there are no minor tick marks on the vertical axis. The following statements produce **Output 5.9**.

```
title f=swiss 'Examples of Logarithmic Axis';
footnote1 f=swiss h=1.5 'LOGSTYLE=POWER';
footnote2 ' ';
symbol1 v=square i=sm50 ci=yellow cv=cyan;
axis2 logbase=2 logstyle=power;


proc gplot data=logs;
    plot a*x / frame
               axis=axis2;
run;
```

Example 10: Specifying Special Values for the LOGBASE= Option

Example 10 illustrates the use of the LOGBASE=e and LOGBASE=PI options. The vertical axes show the default styles in which these values are displayed. If you had specified a format or LOGSTYLE=POWER option, these styles would not have been used. The following statements produce **Output 5.10**.

```
title f=swiss 'Examples of Logarithmic Axis';
footnote1 f=swiss h=1.5 'Base e and pi logs';
footnote2 ' ';
symbol1 v=square i=sm50 ci=yellow cv=cyan;
axis2 logbase=e;
```

```
axis3 logbase=pi;

proc gplot data=logs;
   plot1 c*x / frame
                vaxis=axis2;
   plot2 d*x / vaxis=axis3;
run;
```

Example 11: Using the ORDER= Option with LOGBASE= and LOGSTYLE= Options

Example 11 illustrates the interaction between the LOGBASE=, LOGSTYLE=, and ORDER= options. When you specify the LOGBASE= option, the numbers in the ORDER= option are assumed to be in the same form as they are in the LOGSTYLE= option.

By default, the ORDER= numbers are expected to be the expanded powers, as in the AXIS3 statement below. Note, however, that when you specify LOGSTYLE=POWER, the ORDER= numbers are assumed to be the powers or exponents of the log base, as in the AXIS2 statement below. The following statements produce **Output 5.11**.

```
title f=swiss 'Examples of Logarithmic Axis';
footnote1 f=swiss h=1.5
          'Using ORDER= with LOGSTYLE=POWER and EXPAND';
footnote2 ' ';
symbol1 v=square i=sm50 ci=yellow cv=cyan;
symbol2 v=none   i=none;                /* just add second axis */
axis1 order=1 to 3;
axis2 logbase=10 logstyle=power  order=0 1 2 3;
axis3 logbase=10 logstyle=expand order=1 10 100 1000;

proc gplot data=logs;
   plot1 b*x / frame
                haxis=axis1
                vaxis=axis2;
   plot2 b*x / vaxis=axis3;
run;
```

Example 12: Using the J= Option

Example 12 illustrates the use of J=, an option in the AXIS and LEGEND statements. In this case, the J= option is used in the LABEL= and VALUE= options of two different AXIS statements. In the VALUE= option, the label for the axis starts with the text "Quadrillion," then uses the J=R option to move to the next line and place the text "Btu." In the VALUE= option, the T= option is used to refer to a specific bar value in the vertical bar chart. The J=C option is then specified to center the multiple lines of text under the bars. The following statements produce **Output 5.12**.

```
data energy;
   input source $15. prod;
   cards;
coal           18.657
crude oil      18.357
natural gas    18.019
hydro           3.245
```

```
nuclear          3.084
ngpl             2.229
;


title f=swiss 'U. S. Energy Production';
footnote f=swiss h=1.5
         'Source: The World Almanac and Book of Facts: 1984';
footnote2 ' ';
pattern v=s c=cyan;
axis1 label=('Quadrillion' j=r 'Btu');
axis2 value=(t=1 'Coal'
             t=2 'Crude'   j=c 'Oil'
             t=3 'Natural' j=c 'Gas' j=c '(dry)'
             t=4 'Hydro-'  j=c 'Electric'
             t=5 'Nuclear' j=c 'Electric'
             t=6 'Natural' j=c 'Gas' j=c 'Plant' j=c 'Liquids');
label=none;
proc gchart data=energy;
   vbar source / descending
                 sumvar=prod
                 maxis=axis2
                 raxis=axis1
                 space=2
                 width=8
                 nolegend
                 frame;
run;
```

Example 13: Using a LEGEND Statement with PROC GCHART

Example 13 illustrates the use of the LEGEND statement to suppress the legend label and cause the characters to appear in the SWISS font, two character cells high. The following statements produce **Output 5.13**.

```
data disk;
/****************************************************************/
/*                                                            */
/*  Each input card will result in two observations in the    */
/*  DISK data set (one for the percentage of free disk space  */
/*  and one for the percentage of used disk space).           */
/*                                                            */
/****************************************************************/
   input volume used free;
   format volume words.;
   usage=100*free / (used+free);
   class='free';
   output;
   usage=100*used / (used+free);
   class='used';
   output;
   cards;
1  12000   32000
2  29000   32000
3  25000   64000
4  99000  128000
;
```

```
title1 f=swiss c=white 'Disk Usage';
title2 f=swiss c=white 'As of &sysdate';
footnote;

legend1 value=(f=swiss h=2)
        label=none;
pattern1 v=s c=cyan;
pattern2 v=s c=pink;

proc gchart data=disk;
    label usage='Percentage'  volume='Volume';
    hbar volume / sumvar=usage
                  discrete
                  nostats
                  subgroup=class
                  legend=legend1
                  cframe=black
                  raxis=0 to 100 by 25
                  minor=4
                  coutline=white;
run;
```

Example 14: Using the SHAPE= Option in a LEGEND Statement

Example 14 demonstrates the use of a LEGEND statement to make the bars and values larger. The following statements produce **Output 5.14**.

```
title1 f=swiss c=white 'Disk Usage';
title2 f=swiss c=white 'As of &sysdate';
footnote;
legend2 value=(f=swiss h=2)
        label=none
        shape=bar (4.3, 1.6);
pattern1 v=s c=cyan;
pattern2 v=s c=pink;

proc gchart data=disk;
    label usage='Percentage'  volume='Volume';
    hbar volume / sumvar=usage
                  discrete
                  nostats
                  subgroup=class
                  legend=legend2
                  raxis=0 to 100 by 25
                  minor=4
                  coutline=white;
run;
```

Example 15: Using the ACROSS= and FRAME Options in a LEGEND Statement

Example 15 uses a LEGEND statement to control the number of items across in the legend as well as the size of the values and bars. A frame is also placed around the legend. The following statements produce **Output 5.15**.

```
title1 f=swiss c=white 'Disk Usage';
title2 f=swiss c=white 'As of &sysdate';
footnote;
pattern1 v=s c=cyan;
pattern2 v=s c=pink;
legend2 value=(f=swiss h=2)
        label=none
        across=1
        frame
        shape=bar (4.3, 1.6);

proc gchart data=disk;
   label usage='Percentage'  volume='Volume';
   hbar volume / sumvar=usage
                 discrete
                 nostats
                 subgroup=class
                 legend=legend2
                 raxis=0 to 100 by 25
                 minor=4
                 coutline=whitel;
run;
```

Output 5.1   Controlling Color and Font of Vertical Axis Labels and Values: PROC GPLOT

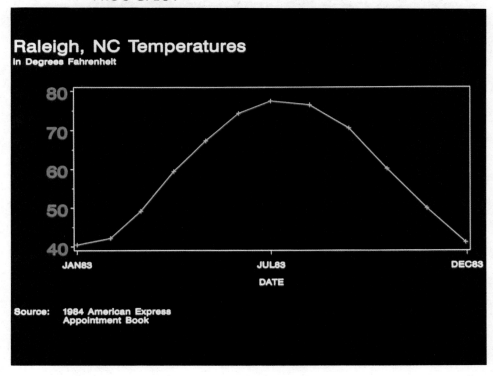

Output 5.2   Using Two Axis Descriptions: PROC GPLOT

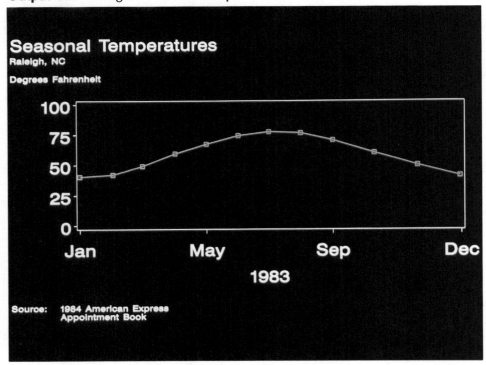

Output 5.3   Suppressing Tick Marks and the Axis: PROC GCHART

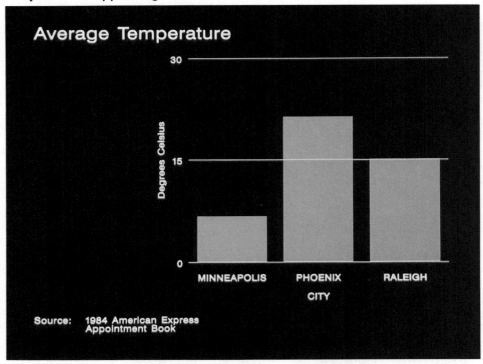

Output 5.4   Specifying the Length of the Axis: PROC GPLOT

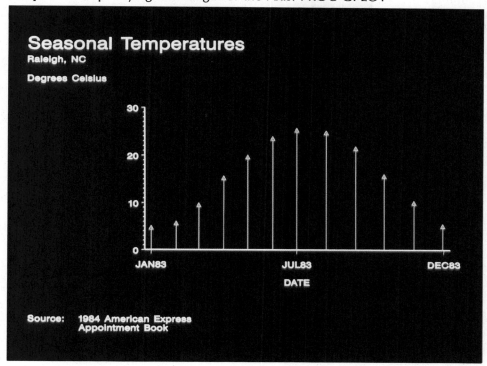

Output 5.5   Specifying the Origin of the Axis: PROC GPLOT

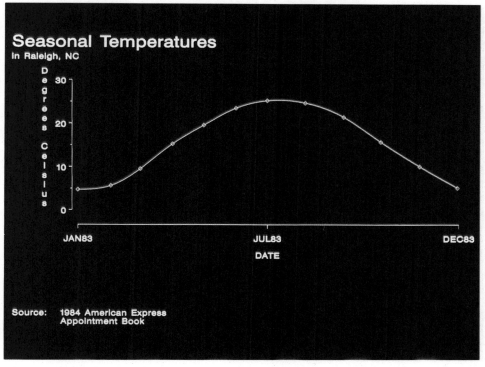

Output 5.6   Specifying Text for the Axis Values: PROC GCHART

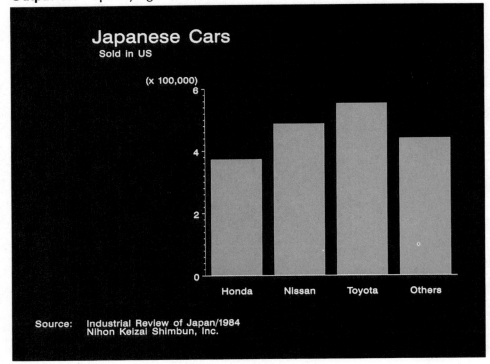

Output 5.7   Using the T= Option in a Value Description: PROC GCHART

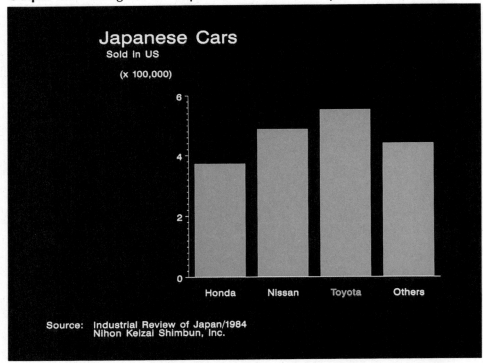

Output 5.8   Using the LOGBASE= Option: PROC GPLOT

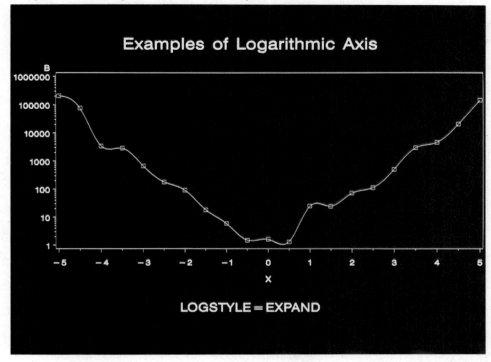

Output 5.9   Using the LOGBASE= and LOGSTYLE= Options: PROC GPLOT

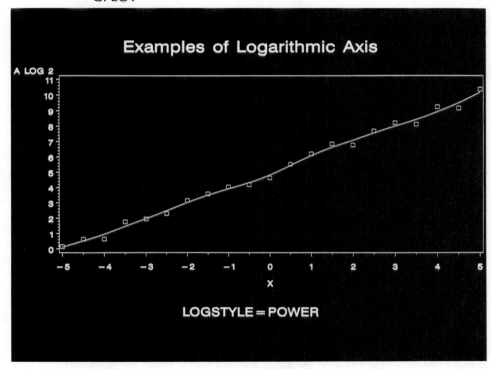

Output 5.10 Specifying Special Values for the LOGBASE= Option:
PROC GPLOT

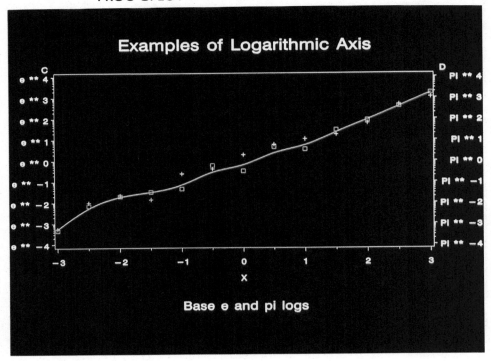

Output 5.11 Using the ORDER= Option with the LOGBASE= and
LOGSTYLE= Options: PROC GPLOT

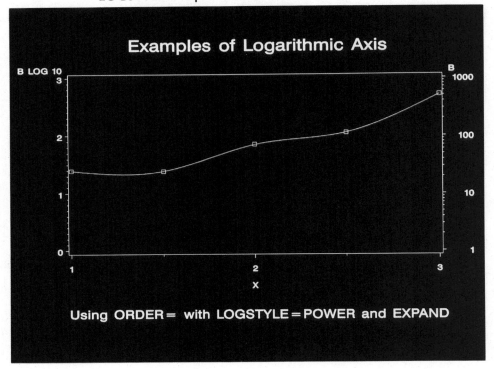

Output 5.12   Using the J= Option to Make Multiple Line Values:
PROC GCHART

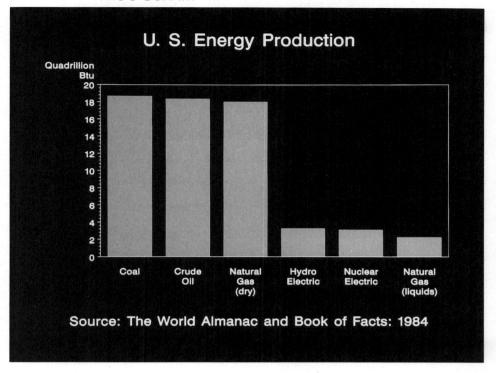

Output 5.13   Using a Basic LEGEND Statement: PROC GCHART

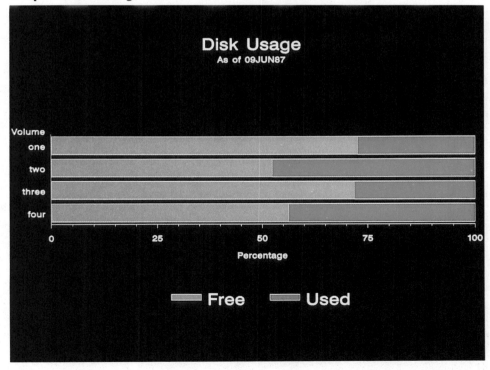

Output 5.14 Using the SHAPE= Option in a LEGEND Statement:
PROC GCHART

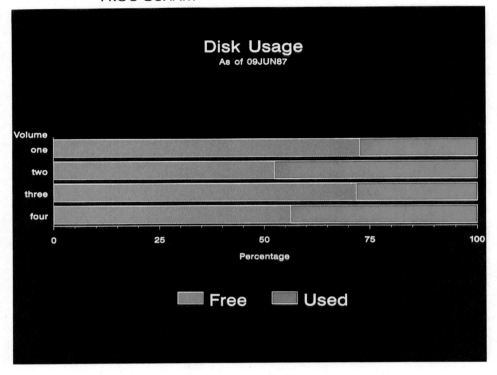

Output 5.15 Using the ACROSS= and FRAME Options in a LEGEND
Statement: PROC GCHART

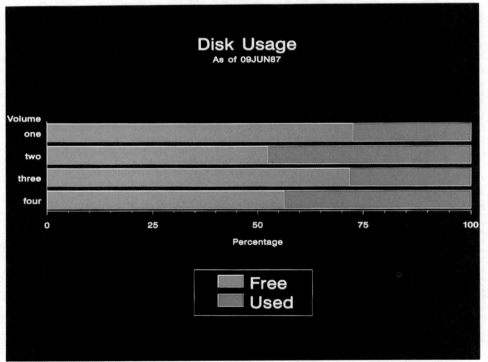

REFERENCES

Pizer, Stephen M. (1975), *Numerical Computing and Mathematical Analysis*, Chicago: Science Research Associates, Inc., Chapter 4.

Reinsch, C.H. (1967) "Smoothing by Spline Functions," *Numerische Mathematik*, 10, 177-183.

Chapter 6

The GOPTIONS Statement

INTRODUCTION

This chapter describes the SAS/GRAPH *system options* that you can specify in a GOPTIONS statement. You can run PROC GOPTIONS to find out the options currently in effect when you invoke the SAS System. (See the chapter "The GOPTIONS Procedure" for more information.)

A major benefit of SAS/GRAPH software is that it automatically uses built-in hardware and software commands to create and display graphics output from a procedure. Default colors, type fonts, and fill patterns allow you to create graphs with a minimum number of programming statements.

As you become more experienced using SAS/GRAPH software, you may want to have more control over the final appearance of your output. You can use a GOPTIONS statement to set certain options at the system level. These options remain in effect until you specify a new GOPTIONS statement or end the current SAS session.

You can also control your output by specifying options within procedures and statements. The values for these options remain in effect only for the duration of that procedure step. The advantage of using a GOPTIONS statement is that it enables you to override the default settings for certain options, to set options at the beginning of your session, and to concentrate your efforts on other programming statements.

GOPTIONS STATEMENT

The general form of the GOPTIONS statement is

GOPTIONS *options*;

The GOPTIONS statement can appear anywhere in your SAS program. Options that you specify in a GOPTIONS statement remain in effect until you use another GOPTIONS statement to change them or until you end the session.

The options you can specify in a GOPTIONS statement are listed alphabetically below.

Options marked with an asterisk (*) can be given defaults for a specific device in the device catalog entry for the corresponding device driver. Some options are supported for specific devices only. You can determine the default option values for a particular driver by running PROC GDEVICE. See the chapter "The GDEVICE Procedure" for details on device catalog entries.

Note that when you specify an option in a GOPTIONS statement, it overrides any corresponding value in a device catalog entry. If no value is specified for a device-related option in a GOPTIONS statement, then the value is taken from the catalog entry for the driver being used. Refer to "The GDEVICE Procedure" for further details.

*ASPECT=n

specifies the aspect ratio (width relative to height) for characters being displayed. The number given is the ratio of the horizontal to the vertical dimension. For example, if you specify ASPECT=1, each character has equal horizontal and vertical scaling factors; ASPECT=2 scales the character twice as wide horizontally as vertically; and so on. If the ASPECT= option is not specified or is set to zero or null, characters are displayed with the aspect ratio of the hardware device.

*AUTOCOPY | NOAUTOCOPY

specifies whether or not certain devices with attached hardcopy units will automatically generate hardcopy of your output.

*AUTOFEED | NOAUTOFEED

specifies whether or not certain devices with continuous paper or automatic paper feed will automatically roll or feed the paper for the next output display.

BAUD=baudrate

specifies the baud rate the device is using. This option is ignored by most device drivers but is used by some to control the timing of output to the device.

BORDER | NOBORDER

specifies whether or not a line (or border) is to be drawn around the display.

*CBACK=color

specifies the color of the background on certain graphics displays and hardcopy devices.

CBY=color
FBY=font
HBY=height [units]

specify the color, font, and height of any BY lines that appear. When you use a BY statement with a SAS/GRAPH procedure to process a data set in subgroups, each graph produced by that procedure is headed by a BY line giving values of the BY variables that define the current subgroup of observations.

If you do not specify the CBY= option, the color you specified in the CTEXT= option is used. If you do not specify the CTEXT= option, the first color in the COLORS= list is used. (See the COLORS= option.)

If you do not specify the FBY= option, then the font specified in the FTEXT= option is used. If you do not specify the FTEXT= option, then the output device's hardware character set is used to print BY lines. Refer to the appendix "SAS/GRAPH Type Styles and Fonts" for a complete list of the available fonts and a sample of each.

If you do not specify the HBY= option, the text height value specified in the HTEXT= option is used. If you do not specify the HTEXT= option, the default value of 1 is used. The optional units value can be CELLS (character cells), IN (inches), CM (centimeters), or PCT (percentage of the display area). If you omit units, the units value specified in the GUNIT= option is used. If you do not specify the

GUNIT= option, the default value, CELLS, is used. If you specify
HBY=0, the BY headings do not appear.

*CELL | NOCELL

invokes or disables cell alignment on your display. You can use the
NOCELL option if you want to preview a graph on a cell-aligned screen,
but intend to produce the final graph on a non-cell-aligned device such
as a pen plotter.

*CHARACTERS | NOCHARACTERS

specifies whether or not to use your device's hardware character set
when no font is specified. If you specify NOCHARACTERS, the
SIMULATE font is used to simulate hardware characters.

*CHARTYPE=*n*

specifies the number of the character set to use if the device has more
than one hardware character set. The value of *n* can range from 1 to
999 and should refer to the actual number for the hardware font you
want to use as listed on the CHARTYPE screen in the PROC GDEVICE
catalog entry for the selected device driver. Refer to *SAS/GRAPH Guide
to Hardware Interfaces, Release 6.03 Edition* or *SAS/GRAPH Hardware
Interfaces for Personal Computers, Version 6 Edition* for specific hardware
character sets that can be used with each supported device.

*CIRCLEARC | NOCIRCLEARC

invokes or disables your device's hardware circle-drawing command.

*COLORS=(*list*)

specifies the colors used to produce your displays if you do not want to
use the default colors for your device. If you omit the COLORS=
option, the default color list is taken from the PROC GDEVICE catalog
entry for the device driver you are using. Any colors you specify in
SAS/GRAPH statements (TITLE, FOOTNOTE, AXIS, and so on) are
added to the default list. See the chapter "SAS/GRAPH Colors" for more
information on specifying colors.

If you are using a pen plotter, SAS/GRAPH uses the colors in the
COLORS= list to define the order of pens for a multiple pen plotter or
to make a single pen plotter behave like a multiple pen plotter when it
chooses colors automatically.

For example, PROC G3D automatically chooses colors for the first title
line, axis, bottom surface, and top surface of the plot if none are
specified with the procedure. Suppose, however, that you are using a
single pen plotter and want to use four different colors. You can specify
the four colors in a COLORS= list; PROC G3D will then use the first
color for the title, the second for the axes, the third for the bottom
surface, and the fourth for the top surface, just as it would if you were
using a four-color pen plotter.

CPATTERN=*color*

specifies the default color to be used in PATTERN statements when a
color has not been specified. See the chapter "Enhancing Your Graphics
Output Designs" for more information on PATTERN statements.

CSYMBOL=*color*

specifies the default color to be used in SYMBOL statements when a
color has not been specified. See the chapter "Enhancing Your Graphics
Output Designs" for more information on SYMBOL statements.

CTEXT=*color*
FTEXT=*font*
HTEXT=*height* [*units*]
  specify the default color, font, and height for all text in the display.

CTITLE=*color*
FTITLE=*font*
HTITLE=*height* [*units*]
  specify default color, font, and height values. CTITLE= gives the default color to be used for *all* TITLE and FOOTNOTE lines.

    If you omit the CTITLE= option, the color you specified in the CTEXT= option is used. If you do not specify the CTEXT= option, the first color in the COLORS= list is used. (See the COLORS= option.)

    FTITLE= specifies the default font to be used for the *first* TITLE line. If you omit the FTITLE= option, then the font specified in the FTEXT= option is used. If you omit the FTEXT= option, then the COMPLEX font is used for the first TITLE line. See the chapter "Enhancing Your Graphics Output Text" for more information on TITLE statements. See the appendix "SAS/GRAPH Type Styles and Fonts" for a list of available fonts.

    HTITLE= specifies the default height to be used for the *first* TITLE line. If you omit the HTITLE= option, the height value specified in the HTEXT= option is used. If you omit the HTEXT= option, the default value of 2 is used. The optional *units* value can be CELLS (character cells), IN (inches), CM (centimeters), or PCT (percentage of the display area). If you omit the *units* value, the units value specified in the GUNIT= option is used. If you do not specify the GUNIT= option, the default value, CELLS, is used.

*DASH | NODASH
  invokes or disables your device's hardware dashed-line capability.

DEVICE=*drivername*
DEV=*drivername*
  indicate what graphics device you are using. If you have not previously specified a device driver name, SAS/GRAPH prompts you to enter a driver name when you execute a procedure that produces graphics output. The name you supply in the DEVICE= option actually refers to a driver entry in a device catalog. Refer to "The GDEVICE Procedure" for details on device catalogs.

    You can specify the DEVICE= option in either a GOPTIONS statement or an OPTIONS statement.

DISPLAY | NODISPLAY
  specifies whether output is produced on the graphics device. The option does not affect whether a graph is placed in a catalog. Usually, you should specify NODISPLAY in a GOPTIONS statement when you want to generate a graph in a catalog but do not want the graph to be displayed on your monitor or terminal or drawn on an attached device while the catalog entry is being produced.

    The effect of the NODISPLAY option depends on where graphics output is sent and what other options you have specified. If you are using a driver that usually sends output directly to the graphics device (or to your screen), then specifying NODISPLAY causes the graph not to be displayed. However, if you are creating a graphics stream file using the GSFNAME= option and you specify GSFMODE=REPLACE or GSFMODE=APPEND, then the NODISPLAY option is ignored, and the graphics stream file is created.

*ERASE | NOERASE

specifies whether or not to erase the graph after you have displayed it and pressed the RETURN key.

FCACHE=*n*

specifies how many software fonts to keep open at one time. Each font requires from 4K to 10K memory. The default is 4.

Graphs that use many fonts may run faster if you set the value of *n* to a higher number. However, graphs that use multiple fonts may require too much memory on personal computer systems if all the fonts are kept open. In such cases, you can set the value of *n* to a lower number to conserve memory. The minimum value is 0.

*FILL | NOFILL

invokes or disables your device's hardware rectangle-fill capability.

*GACCESS='*outputformat*'
*GACCESS='*outputformat*>*destination*'

specifies the format and, optionally, the destination of graphics data written to a device or graphics stream file (GSF). *Outputformat* specifies the format. SASGASTD, the default value for most drivers, specifies that a continuous stream of data is written. This is generally appropriate when output is to go directly to a device. If you specify SASGAEDT, new-line characters are inserted between each record of graphics data. If you specify SASGAFIX, fixed-length records are written, with the record length dictated by the GSFLEN= option. The records are padded (where necessary) with blanks. Usually, you should specify SASGAEDT or SASGAFIX if records are written to a file that is to be edited or transferred to another computer that requires a fixed-record format. If the records are to be sent to a file and later copied directly to a device, specify SASGASTD.

For SAS/GRAPH software on UNIX operating systems and derivatives, you can also use the value SASGACMD. This routes the graphics commands to the standard input of the specified *destination*, which should be a UNIX command. Note that SASGACMD is the only format for which the *destination* value can be a UNIX command.

Destination can be used to direct output to a device or file. For example, GACCESS='SASGASTD>MYFILE.GSF' would cause output from the driver to be written to the file MYFILE.GSF. In SAS/GRAPH software for personal computers, the default specification for many hardcopy devices is GACCESS='SASGASTD>COM1:'. This sends the graphics output to the COM1: serial port. Under UNIX operating systems and derivatives, the default specification for most display devices is GACCESS='SASGASTD>/DEV/TTY', which sends the graphics output to your controlling terminal or workstation. On these systems, GACCESS='SASGACMD>lp -dgoutput' is the default for many hardcopy devices. This sends the file of graphics data to the line printer daemon for your device.

If you specify both the GACCESS= and GSFNAME= options, the value of the GSFNAME= option overrides the *destination* specified in the GACCESS= option.

Note that the GACCESS= option cannot generate a usable graphics stream file when you are using a device driver that does not produce a graphics data stream. Examples include drivers for personal computer display adapters such as CGA, EGA, and Hercules. Graphics stream files created by such drivers cannot be displayed in the usual manner—by sending the file back to the device—because these devices cannot accept file input.

Refer to "SAS/GRAPH Graphics Output" and *SAS/GRAPH Guide to Hardware Interfaces, Release 6.03 Edition* or *SAS/GRAPH Hardware Interfaces for Personal Computers, Version 6 Edition* for additional details on using the GACCESS= option.

*GCOPIES=([d][,m])

specifies the current (d) and maximum (m) number of copies of each file to be printed or, for devices that support multiple copies, how many copies of a single graph are to be made. The d value can be from 0–255, but it cannot exceed the m value specified. The m value can be from 1–255. If you do not use the GCOPIES= option, the default values are 1 for current and 20 for maximum.

*GEND='string' ['string' . . .]

specifies a string of characters to be attached to the end of every graphics data record that is sent to a device or to a file. The string can be in character or hexadecimal format. If you specify more than one string, the strings are concatenated. The GSTART= option can be used in conjunction with GEND=.

*GEPILOG='string' ['string' . . .]

specifies a string to be sent to a device or to a file after all graphics commands have been sent. The string can be in character or hexadecimal format. If you specify more than one string, the strings are concatenated. The GPROLOG= option can be used in conjunction with GEPILOG=.

GOUTMODE=APPEND
GOUTMODE=REPLACE

specify whether graphs can be added to a GOUT= catalog (APPEND) or whether the entire contents of the catalog should be replaced (REPLACE). APPEND is the default.

Note that if you specify GOUTMODE=REPLACE, the entire contents of the catalog is replaced, not just graphs with the same name.

GOUTTYPE=INDEPENDENT
GOUTTYPE=DEPENDENT
GOUTTYPE=BOTH

specify whether or not device-dependent graphs are placed in GOUT= catalogs along with device-independent graphs.
GOUTTYPE=INDEPENDENT, the default, causes only device-independent graphs to be stored. GOUTTYPE=DEPENDENT and the equivalent GOUTTYPE=BOTH cause SAS/GRAPH procedures to store both a dependent and an independent version of each graph in the catalog.

See the chapter "SAS/GRAPH Graphics Output" for more information on device-dependent and device-independent graphics.

*GPROLOG='string' ['string' . . .]

specifies a string to be sent to a device or to a file before any graphics commands are sent. The string can be in character or hexadecimal format. You can use the GEPILOG= option in conjunction with GPROLOG=.

You can use GPROLOG= to place a device in a certain mode before a graph is produced. For example, suppose you are using a device that emulates a supported graphics device (such as a Tektronix 4010 terminal), and that a hexadecimal '7E' must be sent to the device to initialize emulation. You can specify

```
goptions gprolog='7e'x;
```

and a hexadecimal '7E' will be sent to the device, putting it in emulation mode before any SAS/GRAPH commands are sent to it.

*GPROTOCOL=*modulename*

specifies whether and how the graphics data generated by the SAS/GRAPH device driver are to be altered. Specifying GPROTOCOL=SASGPHEX causes the output from the driver to be written in hexadecimal format. (Some output devices may require this format.) The default value is GPROTOCOL=' ', which specifies that output from the driver is not to be written in hexadecimal format. Refer to *SAS/GRAPH Guide to Hardware Interfaces, Release 6.03 Edition* or *SAS/GRAPH Hardware Interfaces for Personal Computers, Version 6 Edition* for details.

*GSFLEN=*length*

specifies the length of the records written by the driver to a graphics stream file or to a port. GSFLEN= dictates the length of records whether they are generated by specifying a path with the GACCESS= option or with the GSFNAME= option.

*GSFMODE=APPEND
*GSFMODE=REPLACE
*GSFMODE=PORT

specify the disposition of records written to a graphics stream file or to a device or communications port by the device driver. If you specify GSFMODE=PORT, the driver performs output as if the records are going to a device or communications port. If you specify GSFMODE=APPEND, output is performed as if the records are being written to a graphics stream file and are being added to the end of the file. If you specify GSFMODE=REPLACE, output is performed as if records are being written to a graphics stream file and are replacing any output already placed in the file by a previous PROC step.

Note that the GSFMODE= option does not actually control where the output goes but simply controls the type of output that is done. (The GACCESS= and GSFNAME= options control where the output goes.) Therefore, you should specify GSFMODE=PORT if output is to go directly to a device or to a communications port and GSFMODE=APPEND or GSFMODE=REPLACE if it is to go to a file. If you specify a value that is inappropriate for the destination of the output, your file or graph may be incorrect.

*GSFNAME=*fileref*

specifies the fileref of the file to which graphics stream data are written. You must use a FILENAME statement to specify the name of that file associated with the fileref. (You cannot specify the name of a file in the GSFNAME= option.) Refer to the description of the FILENAME statement in the *SAS Language Guide, Release 6.03 Edition* for information on how to specify filerefs and filenames.

The GSFNAME= option overrides any file specification or path that is specified with the GACCESS= option. Refer to "SAS/GRAPH Graphics Output" for more information on graphics stream file output.

Note that the GSFNAME= option cannot generate a usable graphics stream file when you are using a device driver that does not generate a graphics data stream. Examples include drivers for personal computer display adapters such as CGA, EGA, and Hercules. Graphics stream files created by such drivers cannot be displayed in the usual manner—by sending the file back to the device—because these devices cannot accept file input.

*GSIZE=*lines*

defines the number of lines of the display to be used for graphics for certain devices whose screens can be divided into graphics and text areas. The line value specified can be larger or smaller than the number of lines the device can display at one time.

GSTART='string' ['string' . . .]

specifies a string of characters to be attached to the beginning of every record of graphics data that is sent to a device or to a file. The string can be in character or hexadecimal format. You can use the GEND= option in conjunction with GSTART=.

GUNIT=CELLS | IN | CM | PCT

specifies the unit of measurement to use with height specifications in TITLE, FOOTNOTE, NOTE, and SYMBOL statements, in the HBY= option, and in other graphics options. With these options, if you specify a value but do not specify an explicit unit, the value of GUNIT= is used. If you specify GUNIT=PCT, then the unit used is a percentage of the display area. If you specify GUNIT=IN, then the unit used is inches. If you specify GUNIT=CM, then the unit used is centimeters. If you specify GUNIT=CELLS, then the unit used is character cells. The default value is GUNIT=CELLS.

GWAIT=*n*

specifies, on certain devices, how much time to allow between displays when a series of graphs is to be generated. The value *n* is expressed in seconds. For example, if you specify GWAIT=5, then five seconds will elapse between the display of each graph in a series. The GWAIT= option allows you to view a series of graphs without having to press the RETURN key between each display. You should specify reasonable integer values for *n*. The default value is GWAIT=0, which means that you must press the RETURN key between each display in a series of graphs. If you specify a GWAIT= value less than 1, the default value is used.

*HANDSHAKE=SOFTWARE | SOFT
*HANDSHAKE=HARDWARE | HARD
*HANDSHAKE=XONXOFF
*HANDSHAKE=NONE

specify the type of *flow control* (often referred to as "handshaking") used to regulate the flow of data to a hardcopy device. Flow control is important because it is possible to send commands to a hardcopy device faster than they can be executed. If you specify HANDSHAKE=SOFTWARE or SOFT, SAS/GRAPH uses programmed flow control with most plotters. If you specify HANDSHAKE=HARDWARE or HARD, SAS/GRAPH uses the hardware CTS and RTS signals. (This is not appropriate for some plotters or computers.) If you specify HANDSHAKE=XONXOFF, SAS/GRAPH uses ASCII characters DC1 and DC3. (This is not appropriate for some plotters or computers.) You should specify HANDSHAKE=NONE only if the device driver you are using provides its own flow control.

If you do not specify a value for the HANDSHAKE= option, the value in the driver entry in the device catalog is used. (PROC GOPTIONS will show a default value of HANDSHAKE=NONE, but the GDEVICE default value is used instead.) When using SAS/GRAPH software on UNIX operating systems and derivatives, it is usually desirable to specify HANDSHAKE=XONXOFF for any device that supports that method of flow control.

Note that if you are creating a graphics stream file using a driver for a plotter and you specify HANDSHAKE=SOFTWARE, the software that you use to send the file to the plotter must be able to perform a software handshake. You will probably want to specify one of the alternative values if you route output to a file.

*HORIGIN=*n* (IN | CM)
*VORIGIN=*n* (IN | CM)

set the horizontal and vertical offsets from the lower-left corner of the display area to the lower-left corner of the graph. Default units are inches (IN). If you do not specify a value, the value is set by the driver.

These options are not valid for all devices. Refer to *SAS/GRAPH Guide to Hardware Interfaces, Release 6.03 Edition* or *SAS/GRAPH Hardware Interfaces for Personal Computers, Version 6 Edition* for details.

*HSIZE=*n* (IN | CM)
*VSIZE=*n* (IN | CM)

set the size of the area to be used on the device for the graphics display. If you specify HSIZE=0 and VSIZE=0 (the default), the full display area is used. Default units are inches (IN). If you do not specify a value, the value is set by the driver.

These options are not valid for all devices. Refer to *SAS/GRAPH Guide to Hardware Interfaces, Release 6.03 Edition* or *SAS/GRAPH Hardware Interfaces for Personal Computers, Version 6 Edition* for details.

HPOS=*columns*
VPOS=*rows*

specify the number of rows and columns in your graphics display area. Note that HPOS= and VPOS= do not affect the size of the graphics area but merely divide it into cells.

SAS/GRAPH determines the size of a character cell for the display based on the values specified in the VPOS= and HPOS= options. For example, if you specify GUNIT=CELLS and H=2 in a TITLE, NOTE, or FOOTNOTE statement, characters will be approximately 2 cells high. The width of the character is scaled to retain the normal aspect of the font.

The larger the size of your VPOS= and HPOS= values, the smaller the size of each character cell. For example, specifying VPOS=30 and HPOS=80 divides your display area into a grid with 30 rows and 80 columns. If you change the VPOS= value to 60, the graphics area is now divided into 60 rows, and the vertical dimension of each of the cells is now smaller. Setting HPOS=0 and VPOS=0 causes the driver to use the default hardware character cell size for the device.

For graphs with landscape orientation, you can set VPOS= values with the LROWS field in the device catalog entry. For graphs with portrait orientation, you can set VPOS= values with the PROWS field in the device catalog entry. Similarly, you can set HPOS= values with the LCOLS or PCOLS fields in the device catalog entry. Refer to "The GDEVICE Procedure" for more information on LROWS, LCOLS, PROWS, and PCOLS.

INTERPOL=*value*

specifies the default interpolation value for a SYMBOL statement when the I= option has not been specified. See the chapter "Enhancing Your

Graphics Output Designs" for more information on interpolation routine values in SYMBOL statements.

*PAPERFEED=n (IN | CM)
specifies the increment of paper that is ejected between graphs. The default value, PAPERFEED=8.5 IN, causes paper to be ejected in increments of 8.5 inches, measuring from the origin of the first graph.

The PAPERFEED= option specifies increments of paper ejection and not the total length of the ejection, so if you specify a value of 1, the driver will eject paper in one-inch increments until the total amount of paper ejected is at least half an inch greater than the size of the graph.

If you are using fanfold paper, you should specify a PAPERFEED= value that is equal to the distance between the perforations.

PENMOUNTS=n
specifies the number of active pens to use if you have a plotter with multiple pens. You are prompted to change the pens after the number of pens specified by PENMOUNTS= has been used. For other devices, PENMOUNTS= can be used to indicate the number of colors that can be displayed at one time.

*PIEFILL | NOPIEFILL
invokes or disables your device's hardware pie-fill capability.

*POLYGONFILL | NOPOLYGONFILL
invokes or disables your device's hardware polygon-fill capability.

*PROMPT | NOPROMPT
specifies whether or not prompts such as PLEASE PRESS RETURN or PLEASE CHANGE THE PAPER are issued.

*PROMPTCHARS='hexstring'
specifies the prompt characters to be used by SAS/GRAPH procedures. This option is most commonly used to specify parameters used in software handshaking (see the HANDSHAKE= option), but it can also be used to control the length of records written by most drivers. (You can also use the GSFLEN= option for this purpose.) The hexstring value specified for this option must be exactly 8 bytes specified as 16 hexadecimal digits, enclosed in single quotes, followed by an X; that is, a SAS hex character constant. See SAS/GRAPH Guide to Hardware Interfaces, Release 6.03 Edition or SAS/GRAPH Hardware Interfaces for Personal Computers, Version 6 Edition for further details.

*REPAINT=n
specifies how many times to redraw the graph. Use this option with printers that produce light images after only one pass.

This option is not valid for all devices. Refer to SAS/GRAPH Guide to Hardware Interfaces, Release 6.03 Edition or SAS/GRAPH Hardware Interfaces for Personal Computers, Version 6 Edition for details.

RESET=ALL
RESET=GLOBAL
RESET=statementname
RESET=(statementname, statementname, . . .)
set options to their default values and/or cancel any global statements (that is, TITLE, FOOTNOTE, AXIS, LEGEND, PATTERN, or SYMBOL statements) you have specified. If you specify the RESET= option, it must be the first option specified in a GOPTIONS statement; other options may follow it.

RESET=ALL sets all options to default values and cancels all global statements. RESET=GLOBAL cancels all global statements but does not reset options specified in GOPTIONS statements. RESET=*statementname* causes only the specified statement to be reset or canceled. For example, RESET=GOPTIONS sets all options to default values, and RESET=PATTERN cancels all PATTERN statements only. RESET=(*statementname, statementname, . . .*) resets or cancels several types of statements. For example, to cancel all TITLE, FOOTNOTE, and AXIS statements, specify RESET=(TITLE, FOOTNOTE, AXIS).

*ROTATE=(LANDSCAPE | PORTRAIT)
ROTATE
NOROTATE

specify whether and how to rotate the graph. If you specify NOROTATE, the graph is produced using the normal orientation of the device. The normal rotation is specified in the PROC GDEVICE catalog entry. See "The GDEVICE Procedure" for details.

If you specify ROTATE, the graph is rotated 90 degrees. If you specify ROTATE=LANDSCAPE, the graph is produced with the *longer* of the X and Y dimensions along the horizontal axis; if you specify ROTATE=PORTRAIT, the *shorter* of the X and Y dimensions will be along the horizontal axis.

*SPEED=*n*

indicates the pen speed for pen plotters with variable speed selection. You can specify a number from 1 to 100 to indicate a percentage of the maximum speed for the device being used. When the number specified is invalid, the maximum speed is used.

*SWAP | NOSWAP

specifies whether or not to reverse the areas shown in black and white on the screen when you print hardcopy. This option is useful when you want to preview a graph on a video device and send the final copy to a pen plotter that uses a white background.

*SYMBOL | NOSYMBOL

invokes or disables your device's hardware symbol-drawing capabilities.

DETAILS

Resetting GOPTIONS Values

You can reset options in a GOPTIONS statement to their default values by specifying the RESET= option, which is described above. Alternatively, you can reset options in a GOPTIONS statement by specifying a null value. A comma is required to separate a null parameter from the next option; commas are optional between parameters.

For example, the statement

```
goptions ctitle=,autocopy;
```

causes CTITLE= to have its default value (first color in COLORS= list). In this case, the comma is required after CTITLE= because you want to give it a null value. Without a comma, the AUTOCOPY option would be confused with a value for CTITLE=. In the statement

```
goptions csymbol= cpattern=;
```

both options are reset to their default values. No comma is required after CSYMBOL= because the keyword that follows is also followed by an equal sign.

Suppose you want to change the value of the COLORS= option back to the default value. You can specify COLORS= or COLORS=( ) to restore the default. You can also use commas to add colors to the existing list of colors in the COLORS= list. For example, suppose the COLORS= list contains the following colors:

```
goptions colors=(red,blue,green);
```

You can add colors to the existing list with this GOPTIONS statement:

```
goptions colors=(,,,pink,yellow,cyan);
```

Chapter 7

ANNOTATE= Data Sets

ABSTRACT

ANNOTATE= data sets are special SAS data sets that enable you to customize SAS/GRAPH procedure output or to create your own individualized graphics output.

INTRODUCTION

ANNOTATE= data sets contain the commands or *functions* that instruct SAS/GRAPH software on how to enhance your output. Two basic functions allow for moving and drawing. Other functions are used to position labels. More complex functions are used to create bars, pies, and polygons. In addition to the basic and advanced Annotate functions, several Annotate macros are available to simplify the process of creating an ANNOTATE= data set.

An ANNOTATE= data set consists of one observation per function, and predetermined variable names are used to define functions. You can use ANNOTATE= data sets to position text labels in a graph, to place symbols or city names on maps, to draw lines between points, and to compose special presentation graphics. You annotate graphs by using a DATA step to place commands into an ANNOTATE= data set and then specifying that data set with the ANNOTATE= option in any of the following SAS/GRAPH procedures: GANNO, GCHART, GCONTOUR, GMAP, GPLOT, GPRINT, GSLIDE, or G3D. For example, if you have a temporary ANNOTATE= data set named GDATA, you can specify

```
proc gplot data=plotdata annotate=gdata;
    more SAS statements
```

to customize the graphics output from PROC GPLOT. In addition, you can specify the ANNOTATE= option in the PLOT statement in PROC GPLOT, in the CHORO or PRISM statement in PROC GMAP, and so on. The PROC GPLOT example above could have been specified as follows:

```
proc gplot data=plotdata;
    plot x*y / annotate=gdata;
    more SAS statements
```

When you specify the ANNOTATE= option in a PROC statement, the option remains in effect until the end of the PROC step. This is especially useful when you want to repeat information in your ANNOTATE= data set (for example, a company logo on several pieces of output with one PROC step).

When you specify ANNOTATE= in a statement other than a PROC statement, the option is in effect only for that statement. The output from that statement is placed on the graph in addition to any Annotate output generated from the PROC statement specification. The ANNOTATE= option supports BY statement processing. Note that with statements other than PROC statements, the same BY variable must be present in the ANNOTATE= data set and in the procedure input data set.

If you are designing your own individualized graphics output without customizing output from a SAS/GRAPH procedure, you can use the ANNOTATE= option in a PROC GANNO statement. If you want to include TITLE, NOTE, or FOOTNOTE statements with your custom graphics output, use the ANNOTATE= option in a PROC GSLIDE statement. TITLE, NOTE, and FOOTNOTE statements are ignored in the GANNO procedure.

Introductory Example

ANNOTATE= data sets contain three basic variables: FUNCTION, X, and Y. The FUNCTION variable determines what action is going to be taken. The variables X and Y determine where the function is to be performed on the graphics output display area.

In the following example, suppose you want to create an ANNOTATE= data set to draw a box (rectangle) in the middle of the screen. To begin, use a SAS DATA step to define the variables to be included in the data set. The LENGTH statement specifies that the FUNCTION variable can be up to eight characters long. To create the box, move to a certain point on the display area (using the MOVE function) and then draw lines from that point to other points on the display area (using the DRAW function). Use the variables X and Y to define points (or x,y coordinates) on the display area.

The X and Y values can be interpreted in several different ways. For example, you can define an X or Y value as a percentage of the graphics display area (for instance, X=50 can be interpreted as 50 percent of the horizontal distance across the display area). You can define an X or Y value in terms of character cells (for instance, X=50 can be interpreted as 50 character cells across the display area).

By default, X and Y values are interpreted as screen cell values like those currently used by the NOTE statement. To change the default interpretation of X and Y values, you can specify values for the XSYS, YSYS, and ZSYS variables. See **XSYS, YSYS, ZSYS, and HSYS Variables** for more information.

The DATA step below creates the ANNOTATE= data set shown in **Output 7.1**.

```
data box;
    length function $ 8;
    function='move'; x=30; y=10; output;
    function='draw'; x=70; y=10; output;
    function='draw'; x=70; y=20; output;
    function='draw'; x=30; y=20; output;
    function='draw'; x=30; y=10; output;
run;
```

```
proc print;
run;
```

You can use PROC PRINT to print the data set BOX from the example above. **Output 7.1** shows that there is one observation for each function being defined.

Output 7.1   Printout of ANNOTATE= Data Set

```
OBS    FUNCTION    X     Y

1        move      30    10
2        draw      70    10
3        draw      70    20
4        draw      30    20
5        draw      30    10
```

You can then specify the ANNOTATE= option in a PROC GSLIDE statement. The statements below produce **Output 7.2**.

```
proc gslide annotate=box;
run;
```

Output 7.2   Using the ANNOTATE= Option

If you want to add the word ANNOTATE in the middle of the box, you need one additional observation to define the function that puts labels on the page.

This is the LABEL function. You must also specify the variables X and Y to determine where the label is placed on the page. Finally, you must add a new variable called TEXT. TEXT is a character variable whose value is the actual text string that will be placed on the page.

You can add your new observation containing the new variables to the data set in a DATA step, as shown below:

```
data boxt;
   length function  $ 8;
   function='move';  x=30; y=10; output;
   function='draw';  x=70; y=10; output;
   function='draw';  x=70; y=20; output;
   function='draw';  x=30; y=20; output;
   function='draw';  x=30; y=10; output;
   function='label'; x=50; y=15; text='ANNOTATE'; output;
run;

proc print;
run;
```

You can use PROC PRINT to print the data set BOX from the example above. **Output 7.3** shows the additional observation that has been added to place the word ANNOTATE in the middle of the box.

Output 7.3   Printout of ANNOTATE= Data Set with New Observation

OBS	FUNCTION	X	Y	TEXT
1	move	30	10	
2	draw	70	10	
3	draw	70	20	
4	draw	30	20	
5	draw	30	10	
6	label	50	15	ANNOTATE

You can then use the ANNOTATE= option in a PROC GSLIDE statement to draw a box in the middle of the screen and put the word ANNOTATE in the middle of the box. The statements below produce **Output 7.4**.

```
proc gslide annotate=boxt;
run;
```

Output 7.4 Using the LABEL Function in an ANNOTATE= Data Set

Next, you can add color to the ANNOTATE= data set using the COLOR variable with the DRAW and LABEL functions. If you want to outline the box in cyan and draw the text in salmon, you specify the following statements:

```
data boxtc;
   length function color $ 8;
   function='move';  x=30; y=10; output;
   function='draw';  x=70; y=10; color='cyan'; output;
   function='draw';  x=70; y=20; color='cyan'; output;
   function='draw';  x=30; y=20; color='cyan'; output;
   function='draw';  x=30; y=10; color='cyan'; output;
   function='label'; x=50; y=15; text='ANNOTATE'; color='salmon';
   output;
run;

proc print;
run;
```

If you use PROC PRINT to print the new data set containing the COLOR variable for the box and the label, your output looks like that shown in **Output 7.5**.

Output 7.5 Printout of ANNOTATE= Data Set with COLOR Variable

```
OBS    FUNCTION    COLOR      X     Y      TEXT
  1    move                   30    10
  2    draw        cyan       70    10
  3    draw        cyan       70    20
  4    draw        cyan       30    20
  5    draw        cyan       30    10
  6    label       salmon     50    15      ANNOTATE
```

You can then use the ANNOTATE= option in a PROC GSLIDE statement to color the box and the text. The statements below produce **Output 7.6**.

```
proc gslide annotate=boxtc;
run;
```

Output 7.6 Adding the COLOR Variable to an ANNOTATE= Data Set

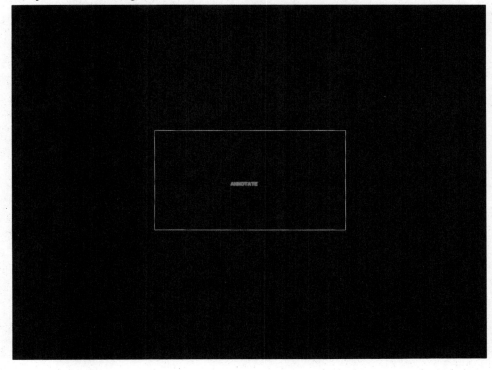

As a final enhancement, specify the line style used to draw the box with the LINE variable in the DRAW function. In this example, line style 4 (a dashed line) is used (see "Enhancing Your Graphics Output Designs" for a list of available line styles). You can use the following DATA step:

```
data boxtcl;
   length function color $ 8;
   function='move';   x=30; y=10; output;
   function='draw';   x=70; y=10; color='cyan'; line=4; output;
   function='draw';   x=70; y=20; color='cyan'; line=4; output;
   function='draw';   x=30; y=20; color='cyan'; line=4; output;
   function='draw';   x=30; y=10; color='cyan'; line=4; output;
   function='label'; x=50; y=15; text='ANNOTATE'; color='salmon';
   output;
run;

proc print;
run;
```

If you use PROC PRINT to print the new data set containing the LINE variable for the box, your output looks like that in **Output 7.7**.

Output 7.7   Printout of ANNOTATE= Data Set with LINE Variable

```
OBS    FUNCTION    COLOR     X     Y     LINE     TEXT

 1     move                 30    10      .
 2     draw        cyan     70    10      4
 3     draw        cyan     70    20      4
 4     draw        cyan     30    20      4
 5     draw        cyan     30    10      4
 6     label       salmon   50    15      4       ANNOTATE
```

You can then use the ANNOTATE= option in a PROC GSLIDE statement to see the new line style of the box. The statements below produce **Output 7.8**.

```
proc gslide annotate=boxtcl;
run;
```

Output 7.8 Specifying a LINE Variable in an ANNOTATE= Data Set

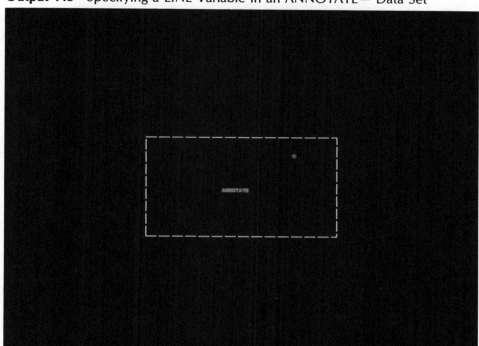

ANNOTATE= VARIABLES

The following variables are used to create an ANNOTATE= data set:

FUNCTION   the particular action you want to perform

X   the X or horizontal coordinate

Y   the Y or vertical coordinate.

In addition to FUNCTION, X, and Y, several other variables can be placed in an ANNOTATE= data set to control such attributes as color, font, line style, and so on. When you are creating an ANNOTATE= data set, you should also specify a LENGTH statement to indicate the length of the character variables to be included in the data set.

Table 7.1 lists all the variables in an ANNOTATE= data set and indicates the type, length, and default value for each variable.

Table 7.1   ANNOTATE= Variables

Name of Variable	Type	Length	Default
FUNCTION	character	8	'LABEL'
X	numeric	8	XLAST | XLSTT
Y	numeric	8	YLAST | YLSTT
Z*	numeric	8	(no default)
XC	character	16	XLAST | XLSTT
YC	character	16	YLAST | YLSTT
XSYS	character	1	'4'
YSYS	character	1	'4'
ZSYS *	character	1	'2'
HSYS	character	1	'4'
WHEN	character	1	'B'
POSITION	character	1	'5'
SIZE	numeric	8	1
ANGLE	numeric	8	0
ROTATE	numeric	8	0
STYLE	character	8	'NONE' | 'EMPTY'
COLOR	character	8	1st in device list
LINE	numeric	8	1
TEXT	character	to 200	blank string
MIDPOINT**	numeric	8	(no default)
	character	16	(no default)
GROUP**	numeric	8	(no default)
	character	16	(no default)
SUBGROUP**	numeric	8	(no default)
	character	16	(no default)

*Valid in PROC G3D only

**Valid in PROC GCHART only

FUNCTION Variable

The FUNCTION variable tells SAS/GRAPH what action to perform. When you create an ANNOTATE= data set in a DATA step, you specify the function you want to use like this:

FUNCTION='*functionname*';

Some basic functions need only the FUNCTION variable and the X and Y variables to perform an action. Other more advanced functions require additional variables but allow you more control over your output and more flexibility in use. The basic Annotate functions are listed and described briefly below. See **Outline of Use: Basic Functions** for a complete description of these functions and the variables you can use with them.

Basic Functions

FUNCTION='BAR'

constructs a fillable rectangle. You can define the color of the fill, the fill pattern, and the edge lines to be drawn.

FUNCTION='COMMENT'

places comments in your data set. The text of the comment is ignored when the data set is processed.

FUNCTION='DRAW'

draws a line on the display area. You can define the color, line style, and thickness of the lines to be drawn.

FUNCTION='FRAME'

draws a border around the outside of the defined display area. Optionally, you can specify a background color for the area of the display enclosed by the frame.

FUNCTION='LABEL'

places text on the display area. You can specify the color, size, font, base angle, and rotation of the characters displayed.

FUNCTION='MOVE'

allows you to move to a specific point on the display area without drawing a line. MOVE is most often used to prepare for a DRAW command or advanced text functions.

FUNCTION='PIE'

draws pie slices on the display area. You can specify the color, fill pattern, arc angle, radius, and edge lines of the slice being drawn.

FUNCTION='POINT'

places a single point at the (X,Y) coordinates using the specified color.

FUNCTION='POLY'

specifies the beginning of a polygon definition. You can define the fill pattern and color, as well as the line type for the outline. The POLY function is used with the POLYCONT function to define and fill areas on the display area.

FUNCTION='POLYCONT'

specifies successive points in the polygon definition in separate continuation observations. The color for the outline is specified in the first POLYCONT observation.

FUNCTION='SYMBOL'

places special symbols on the display area. You can specify the symbol, font, height, and color to be used.

X, Y, Z, and Related Variables

X, Y, and Z Variables

You can use the variables X, Y, and (in PROC G3D only) Z to specify the coordinates on the graph to which a function is applied. X, Y, and Z must be numeric. The X variable defines the horizontal coordinate, and the Y variable defines the vertical coordinate. The Z variable references the three-dimensional Z data values in PROC G3D. Some functions do not require or use the X and Y variables. If X and Y contain a missing value for a function that requires them, the default values shown in **Table 7.1** are used.

XC and YC Variables

XC and YC are character type equivalents of X and Y. They are used when you specify a coordinate system based on data values (see the XSYS and YSYS variables below), and a data axis is typed as character. The coordinate systems defined by XSYS and YSYS (for X and Y) are the same for XC and YC. XC and YC are ignored in *all procedures* if the axes are numeric.

X and Y Coordinate Systems

When you specify values for the X and Y variables (and Z variable in PROC G3D), you can also specify the coordinate system to use to place this information on the display area. A coordinate system defines the graphics area, units, and location for displaying Annotate information.

Defining the Graphics Area

Three types of area definition tell SAS/GRAPH software what portion of the display area to use to display the Annotate information: the DATA graphics area, the SCREEN graphics area, and the WINDOW graphics area.

The DATA graphics area is the area that is bordered by the horizontal and/or vertical axis (in PROC GMAP, the range of map coordinates) specified in a procedure step. For example, if you customize output from PROC GPLOT and specify the DATA coordinate system, the available area is the area enclosed by the axis lines.

The SCREEN graphics area is the entire area available for graphics on the device. When you specify the HSIZE= and VSIZE= options, these values set the physical limit of the SCREEN coordinate system.

The WINDOW graphics area is the same area defined by the SCREEN area minus the amount of space required by TITLE and FOOTNOTE statements.

Defining Units for X and Y

After defining the area to be used to display Annotate information, you can define the units used to interpret X and Y values and place information on the display. You can specify that X or Y be interpreted in character cells (for SCREEN and WINDOW areas), in data values (for DATA areas), or in percentage values (based on a scale ranging from 0 percent to 100 percent for DATA, SCREEN, and WINDOW areas).

For example, suppose you are running PROC GPLOT and your annotation is using a DATA graphics area and data units. If you specify X=10 and Y=20, the Annotate function is performed at the location (10,20) as defined by the values on your plot axis. If you had used percentage units, the function would have been performed at a location 10 percent of the way across the horizontal axis and 20 percent of the way up the vertical axis.

Defining Location

When you specify values for X and Y, you can also specify whether they are to be interpreted as absolute values (placed the specified distance from a fixed origin) or relative values (placed the specified distance from the last point referenced).

By combining values to define the area, unit, and location for the Annotate information, you can specify up to twelve coordinate systems. Each unique combination of area, unit, and location definition has been assigned a value that you specify with the XSYS, YSYS, ZSYS, and HSYS variables. See **Table 7.2** for a list of the coordinate systems available in the Annotate facility and the associated XSYS, YSYS, ZSYS, and HSYS values.

Figure 7.1 illustrates the coordinate systems available for displaying the information contained in ANNOTATE= data sets. The system values given are the values you specify for the XSYS, YSYS, ZSYS, and HSYS variables.

XSYS, YSYS, ZSYS, and HSYS Variables

XSYS, YSYS, and (in PROC G3D only) ZSYS are character variables that define the area and coordinate system used by the X, Y, and Z variables to display the Annotate information. Thus, the values for X, Y, and (in PROC G3D) Z can be interpreted in a variety of ways depending upon the coordinate system you specify with the XSYS, YSYS, and ZSYS variables.

For example, suppose you create an ANNOTATE= data set using the LABEL function to place text at various points on the display. You can specify

```
data anno;
   length function $ 8 text $ 11;
   function='label'; x=30; y=15;
   xsys='3'; ysys='3'; text='SCREEN PCT'; output;
   xsys='4'; ysys='4'; text='SCREEN CELL'; output;
   xsys='5'; ysys='5'; text='WINDOW PCT'; output;
   xsys='6'; ysys='6'; text='WINDOW CELL'; output;

proc gslide annotate=anno;
   title f=swiss h=2 'COORDINATE SYSTEMS';
   footnote f=swiss h=2 'USING X=30 AND Y=15';
run;
```

The interpretation of the X=30 and Y=15 values changes as you specify different values for XSYS and YSYS. The text is placed on the display area according to the values you specify with the XSYS and YSYS variables, as shown in **Output 7.9**.

Output 7.9   Using XSYS and YSYS to Interpret X and Y Values

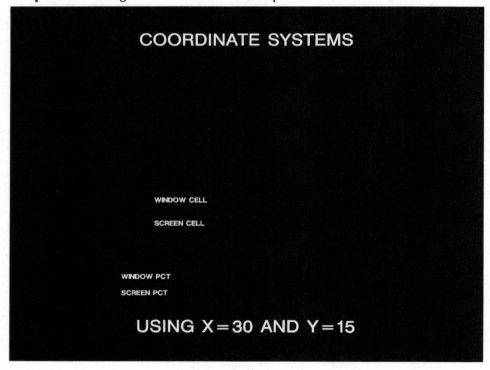

You can use these coordinate systems in any combination to specify display area locations in the ANNOTATE= data set. The X and Y variables need not be referenced with the same system value. X can be referenced as 'data value' and Y referenced as 'window percentage' in one observation, and both coordinates can be referenced as 'screen value' in the next.

The HSYS variable determines what coordinate system the variable SIZE uses. The coordinate system values specified with XSYS, YSYS, and ZSYS are valid with HSYS. **Table 7.2** lists the coordinate systems and the associated XSYS, YSYS, ZSYS, and HSYS system values available with the Annotate facility.

Table 7.2 Coordinate Systems

Location Definition	Unit Definition	Area Definition	System Values
ABSOLUTE	DATA %	0% to 100% of AXIS AREA	'1'
	DATA	AXIS MIN to AXIS MAX	'2'
	SCREEN %	0% to 100% of GRAPHICS PAGE	'3'
	SCREEN CELL	00 to EDGE of GRAPHICS PAGE	'4'
	WINDOW %	0% to 100% of PLOT WINDOW	'5'
	WINDOW CELL	00 to EDGE of PLOT WINDOW	'6'
RELATIVE	DATA %	0% to 100% of AXIS AREA	'7'
	DATA	AXIS MIN to AXIS MAX	'8'
	SCREEN %	0% to 100% of GRAPHICS PAGE	'9'
	SCREEN CELL	00 to EDGE of GRAPHICS PAGE	'A'
	WINDOW %	0% to 100% of PLOT WINDOW	'B'
	WINDOW CELL	00 to EDGE of PLOT WINDOW	'C'

Coordinate System Examples

As shown in **Table 7.2**, system numbers 1, 2, 7, and 8 are the DATA systems. The shading in **Figure 7.1** indicates the plot area referenced by these systems. Note that the data area is enclosed by the axis lines. For PROC GSLIDE and other procedures that do not support DATA systems, the DATA system is the same as the WINDOW system described below.

As shown in **Table 7.2**, system numbers 3, 4, 9, and A are the SCREEN systems. The shading in **Figure 7.1** indicates the plot area referenced by these systems.

As shown in **Table 7.2**, system numbers 5, 6, B, and C are the WINDOW systems. The shading in **Figure 7.1** indicates the plot area referenced by these systems. These systems are defined as the previously described SCREEN systems, minus the area required by TITLE and FOOTNOTE statements. If no TITLE or FOOTNOTE statements occur in a given procedure, then the WINDOW systems are identical to the SCREEN systems.

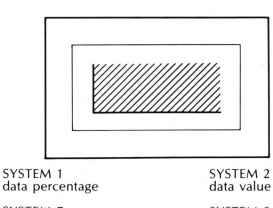

SYSTEM 1   SYSTEM 2
data percentage   data value

SYSTEM 7   SYSTEM 8
data relative percentage   data relative value

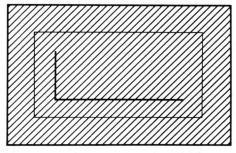

SYSTEM 3   SYSTEM 4
screen percentage   screen value

SYSTEM 9   SYSTEM A
screen relative percentage   screen relative value

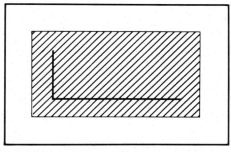

SYSTEM 5   SYSTEM 6
window percentage   window value

SYSTEM B   SYSTEM C
window relative percentage   window relative value

Figure 7.1   Available Coordinate Systems

Additional Variables

The following variables can be used in addition to the FUNCTION, X, Y, XSYS, YSYS, ZSYS, and HSYS variables in an ANNOTATE= data set. For a complete description of each variable's effect, see the FUNCTION descriptions in the sections **Outline of Use: Basic Functions** and **Outline of Use: Advanced Functions**.

ANGLE
> is a function-dependent numeric variable. ANGLE can be used with the functions LABEL and PIE. ANGLE is measured in degrees.

COLOR
> is a character variable of length eight that specifies the color used by the function (see "SAS/GRAPH Colors" for information on available colors). COLOR can be used with the functions BAR, DRAW, FRAME, LABEL, PIE, POLY, POLYCONT, and SYMBOL.

GROUP
> is a variable used to reference the GCHART group data value. GROUP should be of the same type (character or numeric) as the GCHART variable it references. GROUP is valid only with PROC GCHART. The use of the GROUP variable is similar to that of the X and Y variables when used for data-dependent placement. **Example 7** illustrates the use of the GROUP variable with PROC GCHART.

LINE
> is a function-dependent variable that usually specifies the line type (see "Enhancing Your Graphics Output Designs" for more information on the available line types). LINE can be used with the functions BAR, DRAW, FRAME, PIE, and POLY.

MIDPOINT
> is a variable used to reference the GCHART midpoint data value. MIDPOINT should be of the same type (character or numeric) as the GCHART variable it references. MIDPOINT is valid only with PROC GCHART. The use of the MIDPOINT variable is similar to that of the X and Y variables when used for data-dependent placement. **Example 7** illustrates the use of the MIDPOINT variable with PROC GCHART.

POSITION
> is a character variable used to control placement and alignment of a text string. POSITION can be used only with the text-handling functions.

ROTATE
> is a function-dependent numeric variable. ROTATE can be used with the functions LABEL and PIE. ROTATE can be used with the ANGLE variable and is measured in degrees.

SIZE
> is a function-dependent numeric variable. SIZE can be used with the functions DRAW, FRAME, LABEL, PIE, PIEXY, PIECNTR, and SYMBOL. The value of the variable SIZE defaults to 1.00 in all cases.

STYLE
> is a function-dependent character variable of length eight that normally specifies a font or pattern for the function. STYLE can be used with the functions BAR, FRAME, LABEL, PIE, POLY, and SYMBOL.

SUBGROUP
> is a variable used to reference the GCHART subgroup data value. SUBGROUP should be of the same type (character or numeric) as the GCHART variable it references. SUBGROUP is valid only with PROC

GCHART. The use of the SUBGROUP variable is similar to that of the X and Y variables when used for data-dependent placement. **Example 7** illustrates the use of the SUBGROUP variable with PROC GCHART.

WHEN
> is a sequencing variable that specifies when the function is performed in relation to generating graphics output for the procedure. WHEN can take the values 'A' (AFTER the graph is drawn) or 'B' (BEFORE the graph is drawn). 'B' is the default. A missing value is equivalent to specifying BEFORE. Normally, observations in an ANNOTATE= data set are processed sequentially. If the variable WHEN is used, all those observations with a WHEN value of 'B' are processed first, the graph is then processed (if one is to be produced), and finally the observations with a WHEN value of 'A' are processed. WHEN should always be a character variable of length 1. You should specify

> ```
> length when $ 1;
> ```

> in the SAS DATA step.

Table 7.3 lists the variables that can be used with the basic Annotate functions.

Utility Variables

The two utility pairs (XLAST,YLAST) and (XLSTT,YLSTT) are used to supply default values when X or Y contains a missing value. Both pairs are initially set to zero and remain zero until a valid function updates the values.

The variables XLAST and YLAST are an internal coordinate pair that track the last values specified for X and Y. Because the (XLAST,YLAST) coordinates are updated internally, you cannot specify values for them. However, these variables can be manipulated by the advanced functions documented in **ADVANCED FUNCTIONS**. The coordinate pair (XLAST,YLAST) is automatically updated by certain functions and is available for use by other functions that follow.

The coordinate pair (XLSTT,YLSTT) is similar to the (XLAST,YLAST) coordinate pair except that the (XLSTT,YLSTT) pair is only updated by the text-handling functions. Thus, it is possible to maintain two different coordinate pairs: one for text-handling functions and one for nontext handling functions. The (XLSTT,YLSTT) coordinates are updated automatically, and you cannot specify values for them. However, these values can be manipulated indirectly by the advanced functions described in **ADVANCED FUNCTIONS**.

Table 7.3 Annotate Variables Used with Basic Functions

	BAR	COMMENT	DRAW	FRAME	LABEL	MOVE	PIE	POINT	POLY	POLYCONT	SYMBOL
FUNCTION	X	X	X	X	X	X	X	X	X	X	X
X	X		X		X	X	X	X	X	X	X
XC	X		X		X	X	X	X	X	X	X
Y	X		X		X	X	X	X	X	X	X
YC	X		X		X	X	X	X	X	X	X
Z*	X		X		X	X	X	X	X	X	X
MIDPOINT**	X		X		X	X	X	X	X	X	X
GROUP**	X		X		X	X	X	X	X	X	X
SUBGROUP**	X		X		X	X	X	X	X	X	X
XSYS	X		X	X	X	X	X	X	X	X	X
YSYS	X		X	X	X	X	X	X	X	X	X
ZSYS*	X		X	X	X	X	X	X	X	X	X
HSYS			X	X	X		X				X
WHEN	X		X	X	X	X	X	X	X	X	X
POSITION					X						
SIZE			X	X	X		X				X
ANGLE					X		X				
ROTATE					X		X				
STYLE	X			X	X		X		X		X
COLOR	X		X	X	X		X	X	X	X	X
LINE	X		X	X			X		X		
TEXT		X			X						X

*Valid in PROC G3D only

**Valid in PROC GCHART only

Outline of Use: Basic Functions

The following section gives a detailed description of the basic functions and the Annotate variables that can be specified with each function. Although the additional variables can be used with many of the basic functions, they are function dependent and may be interpreted differently for each function.

FUNCTION='BAR'

The BAR function constructs a fillable rectangle whose lower-left corner is defined by (XLAST,YLAST) and whose upper-right corner is (X,Y). You can define the color of the fill, the fill pattern, and the edge lines being drawn. (For a complete list of available patterns, see "Enhancing Your Graphics Output Designs.") The BAR function updates the internal variables (XLAST,YLAST). You can use the following Annotate variables with this function:

X,Y,XC,YC   define the upper-right corner of a bar (rectangle) whose lower-left corner is (XLAST,YLAST). In addition, you can use MIDPOINT, GROUP, and SUBGROUP with PROC GCHART for this purpose, and you can use Z with PROC G3D. **Figure 7.2** shows a bar.

Figure 7.2   Points Used to Construct a Bar

XSYS   specifies the reference system to use for X and XC.

YSYS   specifies the reference system to use for Y and YC.

WHEN   specifies when to draw the bar in relation to generating the procedure output.

LINE   specifies in which direction to adjust the outline of the bar. LINE values 1 and 2 should be used to offset a particular bar from an axis or adjoining area. See **Figure 7.3** for the results of specifying the LINE values.

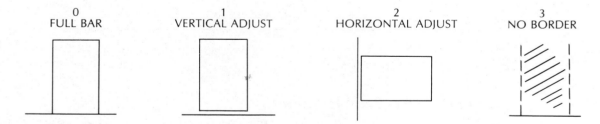

Figure 7.3   LINE Values for Bars

STYLE   specifies the fill pattern used to fill the bar. Valid values for STYLE are the fill patterns used for bars. For example, if STYLE='S' for the BAR function, a bar with solid fill is produced. If STYLE='X5', a bar with crosshatch fill is produced. (See the discussion of the PATTERN statement and **Figure 5.1** in "Enhancing Your Graphics Output Designs.")

COLOR   specifies the color used to fill the bar if a pattern is specified in the STYLE variable. For example, if you specify STYLE='S' and COLOR='RED' for a BAR function, a bar with red solid fill is produced.

FUNCTION='COMMENT'

The COMMENT function is a documentation aid. COMMENT allows you to specify comments within your data set. You can use the following Annotate variable with this function:

TEXT   specifies a comment. TEXT is ignored when the observation is processed and serves only as a documentation aid within the Annotate data stream.

FUNCTION='DRAW'

The DRAW function draws a line on the display area. The line is drawn from the (XLAST,YLAST) coordinates to the (X,Y) coordinates specified in the DRAW function. The DRAW function updates the (XLAST,YLAST) coordinates. You can use the following Annotate variables with this function:

X,Y,XC,YC   specify the endpoint of a line drawn from (XLAST,YLAST) to (X,Y). In addition, you can use MIDPOINT, GROUP, and SUBGROUP with PROC GCHART for this purpose, and you can use Z with PROC G3D.

XSYS   specifies the reference system to use for X and XC.

YSYS   specifies the reference system to use for Y and YC.

HSYS   specifies the reference system to be used for SIZE.

WHEN   specifies when to draw the line in relation to generating the procedure output.

LINE   specifies the line type used to draw the line. (See the list of available line types in "Enhancing Your Graphics Output Designs.")

SIZE   specifies the thickness of the line being drawn. As the thickness of the line increases, centering around a given coordinate may not be possible. For example, if you specify a thickness of value 2, the first line is drawn at the (X,Y) coordinates. The second is drawn slightly above the first. The exact amount varies by device, but it is always one pixel in width. A thickness of value 3 produces one line above, one line at, and one line below the (X,Y) coordinate position. See **Figure 7.4** for an example of line thickness.

1   2   3

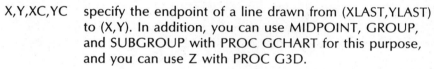

Figure 7.4   Line Thicknesses Used with SIZE Variable

COLOR   specifies the color used to draw the line. Its default value is the first color in the device's COLORS= list.

FUNCTION = 'FRAME'

The FRAME function allows you to create a border around and optionally specify a background color for the portion of the display area defined by the XSYS and YSYS variables. The FRAME function does not alter the (XLAST,YLAST) coordinates. The frame function works in addition to the CBACK= option. (See the description of the CBACK= option in "The GOPTIONS Statement" for details.) You can use the following Annotate variables with this function:

XSYS,YSYS   define the area to be enclosed by the frame.

HSYS   specifies the reference system to be used for SIZE.

WHEN   specifies when to draw the frame in relation to generating the procedure output.

LINE   specifies the line type used to draw the frame. (See the list of available line types in "Enhancing Your Graphics Output Designs.")

SIZE   specifies the thickness of the line used to draw the frame. See **FUNCTION = 'DRAW'** for details.

STYLE   specifies the fill pattern to be used. (See the discussion of the PATTERN statement and **Figure 5.1** in "Enhancing Your Graphics Output Designs.")

COLOR   specifies the color used for the frame and to fill the interior of the frame.

FUNCTION = 'LABEL'

The LABEL function places text on the display area. You can specify the color, size, font, base angle, and rotation of the characters displayed. The LABEL function updates the (XLSTT,YLSTT) coordinates. You can use the following Annotate variables with this function:

X,Y,XC,YC   specify the start point of the text string. In addition, you can use MIDPOINT, GROUP, and SUBGROUP with PROC GCHART for this purpose, and you can use Z with PROC G3D. Optionally, you can modify the placement of the text string with the POSITION variable (see the description below).

XSYS   specifies the reference system to use for X and XC.

YSYS   specifies the reference system to use for Y and YC.

HSYS   specifies the reference system to use for SIZE.

WHEN   specifies when to place the text strings of the display area in relation to generating the procedure output.

POSITION   controls placement and alignment of the text string. POSITION can take values from '0' to 'F' (hexadecimal numbering). Invalid or missing values default to POSITION='5'. POSITION should always be a character variable of length 1. You should specify

```
length position $ 1;
```

in a DATA step.

Figure 7.5 indicates the POSITION value's effect on the text string. The box represents the text string; the point represents (X,Y).

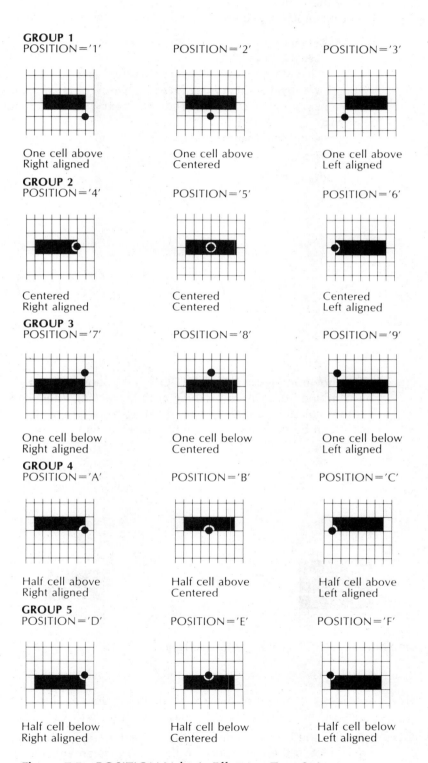

GROUP 1
POSITION='1'   POSITION='2'   POSITION='3'

One cell above   One cell above   One cell above
Right aligned   Centered   Left aligned

GROUP 2
POSITION='4'   POSITION='5'   POSITION='6'

Centered   Centered   Centered
Right aligned   Centered   Left aligned

GROUP 3
POSITION='7'   POSITION='8'   POSITION='9'

One cell below   One cell below   One cell below
Right aligned   Centered   Left aligned

GROUP 4
POSITION='A'   POSITION='B'   POSITION='C'

Half cell above   Half cell above   Half cell above
Right aligned   Centered   Left aligned

GROUP 5
POSITION='D'   POSITION='E'   POSITION='F'

Half cell below   Half cell below   Half cell below
Right aligned   Centered   Left aligned

Figure 7.5   POSITION Value's Effect on Text String

POSITION='0' is a special value to use when you want to pause and then continue a text string. With this value you can change colors, fonts, and so on in the middle of a line, while retaining the exact position of the text at the pause.

For example, if you specify,

```
data anno;
   length text $12;
   xsys='3'; ysys='3'; position='0'; size=3;
   x=5; y=50; style='triplex '; text='This is the'; output;
   x=.; y=.;  style='italic  '; text=' ITALIC font'; output;
run;
proc gslide annotate=anno;
run;
```

you produce the following:

This is the *ITALIC Font*

As shown in **Figure 7.6**, POSITIONs in groups 1–3 can be combined directly to produce a triple stacking effect without collision of text. Likewise, values from groups 4 and 5 can be combined for double stacking without collisions.

'2' '5' '8'   'B' 'E'

Figure 7.6   Combining POSITION Values to Stack Text

SIZE   specifies the height of the text string being drawn. The units for the SIZE variable are based on the HSYS value.

ANGLE   specifies the baseline angle of the character string. It is equivalent to the A= option in the NOTE statement (see "Enhancing Your Graphics Output Text").

ROTATE specifies the rotation angle of the character string. It is equivalent to the R= option in the NOTE statement (see "Enhancing Your Graphics Output Text").

STYLE specifies the character font used to draw the text. Specifying special characters is exactly as defined for the TITLE, NOTE, and FOOTNOTE statements. (See "Enhancing Your Graphics Output Text" for a complete discussion of character fonts.)

COLOR specifies the color used to draw the text.

TEXT specifies the character string to be written. You should define the TEXT variable with sufficient length to contain all the characters in your string. There is a maximum of 200 characters per string. If longer strings are needed, use separate observations and POSITION='0' to continue the text.

FUNCTION='MOVE'

The MOVE function allows movement to a specific point on the display area without drawing a line. MOVE is most often used to prepare for a DRAW command or advanced functions. MOVE updates the (XLAST,YLAST) coordinates. You can use the following Annotate variables with this function:

X,Y,XC,YC specify the coordinates to which the pen is to be moved. In addition, you can use MIDPOINT, GROUP, and SUBGROUP with PROC GCHART for this purpose, and you can use Z with PROC G3D. The (XLAST,YLAST) pair is updated by the MOVE function.

XSYS specifies the reference system to use for X and XC.

YSYS specifies the reference system to use for Y and YC.

WHEN specifies when to perform the move in relation to generating the procedure output.

FUNCTION='PIE'

The PIE function draws pie slices on the display area. You can specify the color, fill pattern, arc angle, radius, and edge lines of the slice being drawn. The PIE function maintains (XLAST,YLAST) as the center of the PIE defined. You can use the following Annotate variables with this function:

X,Y,XC,YC define the center of the PIE. All slices are referenced from that center. In addition, you can use MIDPOINT, GROUP, and SUBGROUP with PROC GCHART for this purpose, and you can use Z with PROC G3D. The first PIE command issued sets the center at the (X,Y) value. If subsequent values for X and Y are missing, the center points are assumed to be the defaults.

XSYS specifies the reference system to use for X and XC.

YSYS specifies the reference system to use for Y and YC.

HSYS specifies the reference system to use for SIZE.

WHEN specifies when to draw the pie slice in relation to generating the procedure output.

LINE   specifies which slice line(s) to draw. See **Figure 7.7** for values and their actions.

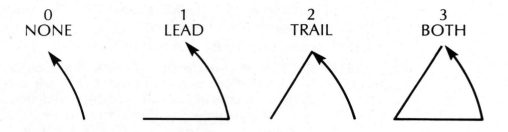

Figure 7.7 LINE Values

SIZE   specifies the RADIUS of the circle being drawn. SIZE is measured in the vertical direction in HSYS units.

ANGLE   specifies the starting angle of the slice arc. Its default value is 0.00 if ANGLE is not specified for the first slice. After the first slice, the default value is updated to the end of the slice arc just drawn. This allows you to specify an entire pie more easily by omitting the start and end calculations otherwise required.

ROTATE   specifies the angle of rotation or the delta angle of the slice arc. Its default value is 0.00.
For example, if you specify

```
. . . function='pie';
      angle=90;
      rotate=45;
      output;
```

the slice arc drawn begins at 90 degrees (vertical) and ends at 135 degrees (90+45). The ANGLE variable is internally updated to the end value, 135 degrees. The value is not modified in the input data set, only internally. If a second PIE command is used and ANGLE contains a missing value, the start angle is assumed to be the previous end, or 135 degrees. The arc is continued from that point.
For example, if you specify the statements above and then specify

```
. . . function='pie';
      angle=.;
      rotate=45;
      output;
```

the slice begins at 135 degrees (the end angle from the previous slice) and extends another 45 degrees to the end point, 180 degrees. This action is repeated for every missing angle in the sequence.

STYLE   specifies the value used to fill the pie slices. Valid values for STYLE are the PROC GCHART fill patterns.

COLOR   specifies the color used to fill the pie slice if a pattern is specified in the STYLE variable. COLOR also specifies the outline color of the pie slices if you specify STYLE='EMPTY'.

FUNCTION='POINT'

The POINT function places a single point at the (X,Y) coordinates using the color you specify. POINT updates the (XLAST,YLAST) coordinates. You can use the following Annotate variables with this function:

X,Y,XC,YC   specify the coordinates of the point to be drawn. In addition, you can use MIDPOINT, GROUP, and SUBGROUP with PROC GCHART for this purpose, and you can use Z with PROC G3D.

XSYS   specifies the reference system to use for X and XC.

YSYS   specifies the reference system to use for Y and YC.

WHEN   specifies when to draw the point in relation to generating the procedure output.

COLOR   specifies the color of the point drawn.

FUNCTION='POLY'

The POLY function specifies the beginning point of a polygon. You can define the fill pattern and color, as well as the line type used to outline the polygon. Use the POLY function with the POLYCONT function to define and fill areas on the display area. POLY and POLYCONT **do not** update the (XLAST,YLAST) coordinates. You can use the following Annotate variables with this function:

X,Y,XC,YC   specify the initial point of the polygon being created. In addition, you can use MIDPOINT, GROUP, and SUBGROUP with PROC GCHART for this purpose, and you can use Z with PROC G3D.

XSYS   specifies the reference system to use for X and XC.

YSYS   specifies the reference system to use for Y and YC.

WHEN   specifies when to draw the polygon in relation to generating the procedure output.

LINE   specifies the line type to use to outline the polygon. (See the list of available line types in "Enhancing Your Graphics Output Designs.")

STYLE   specifies the fill pattern used to fill the polygon. The value of STYLE must be a map fill pattern. (See the discussion of the PATTERN statement and **Figure 5.1** in "Enhancing Your Graphics Output Designs.")

COLOR   specifies the color used to fill the interior of the polygon if a pattern is specified in the STYLE parameter.

FUNCTION = 'POLYCONT'

The POLYCONT function specifies successive points in the polygon definition in separate continuation observations. The outline color is specified in the first POLYCONT observation. You cannot interrupt a polygon definition by specifying a basic function. A polygon definition is terminated by a new POLY command or by any other basic function. You can use the following Annotate variables with this function:

X,Y,XC,YC   specify a point on the outline of the polygon being created. In addition, you can use MIDPOINT, GROUP, and SUBGROUP with PROC GCHART for this purpose, and you can use Z with PROC G3D.

XSYS   specifies the reference system to use for X and XC.

YSYS   specifies the reference system to use for Y and YC.

WHEN   specifies when to draw the polygon in relation to generating the procedure output.

COLOR   specifies the outline color of the polygon. This is the color used when tracing the polygon perimeter. If you do not specify COLOR on the POLYCONT command, the interior color is used. You must specify an outline color on the first POLYCONT command; COLOR is ignored on all subsequent commands in the POLYCONT sequence.

Special considerations   The POLY and POLYCONT functions are used together to create a polygon. The first (X,Y) observation from the POLY function and the last (X,Y) observation from the POLYCONT function are assumed to connect. Thus, you are not required to respecify the first point. For example, the following are both valid ways to indicate the points used to draw the polygon:

Function	X	Y		Function	X	Y
POLY	0	0		POLY	0	0
POLYCONT	10	0	is the same as	POLYCONT	10	0
POLYCONT	10	10		POLYCONT	10	10
POLYCONT	0	10		POLYCONT	0	10
				POLYCONT	0	0

Missing values for the X and Y variables specified with the POLYCONT function are interpreted differently from the way they are interpreted with the other functions. Other functions use the missing values to request a default value. POLYCONT interprets a missing value as a discontinuity (that is, a hole) in the polygon. If you specify an X or Y value of −999 in a POLYCONT observation, the default of (XLAST,YLAST) is used. Note that if you specify −999 as the value in a POLYCONT observation, the active system cannot be a DATA system. Missing values to indicate holes are handled identically in the Annotate facility and PROC GMAP. (See "The GMAP Procedure" for more information on handling missing values.)

FUNCTION='SYMBOL'

The SYMBOL function places special symbols on the display area. You can specify the color, font, and height of the special symbols displayed. The SYMBOL function updates the (XLSTT,YLSTT) coordinates. You can use the following Annotate variables with this function:

X,Y,XC,YC specify the point at which the symbol is placed. In addition, you can use MIDPOINT, GROUP, and SUBGROUP with PROC GCHART for this purpose, and you can use Z with PROC G3D.

XSYS specifies the reference system to use for X and XC.

YSYS specifies the reference system to use for Y and YC.

HSYS specifies the reference system to use for SIZE.

WHEN specifies when to place the symbols on the display area in relation to generating the procedure output.

SIZE specifies the height of the symbol being drawn. The units for the SIZE variable are based on the HSYS value. (This is equivalent to the H= option in the SYMBOL statement.)

STYLE specifies the character font used to draw the symbol. Valid values are those described in the F= option in the SYMBOL statement. (See "Enhancing Your Graphics Output Designs" for a discussion of character fonts.)

COLOR specifies the color used to draw the symbol. (This is equivalent to the C= option in the SYMBOL statement.

TEXT specifies the symbol to be displayed. Valid values are those described in the V= option of the SYMBOL statement.

BASIC EXAMPLES

The following examples show you how to create ANNOTATE= data sets using the basic functions described in detail above. You can use these examples as models for creating your own ANNOTATE= data sets.

Example 1: Using XC and YC to Annotate Character-Valued Plots

In the following example, a SAS data set containing the variables X and Y is created for later use by PROC GPLOT. Next, an ANNOTATE= data set is created that contains the MOVE and BAR functions to place bars on the plot area. Finally, PROC GPLOT is used to create the plot, and the ANNOTATE= data set information is displayed on the plot, as shown in **Output 7.10**.

```
data one;
   input x $ ;
   y=x;
   cards;
A
B
C
D
```

```
       E
       F
       G
       H
       ;

       data two;
          length function color style $ 8;
          input function $ xc $ yc $ color $ style $ line;
          xsys='2';
          ysys='2';
          cards;
move      A A  .      .  .
bar       B B  salmon e  0
move      C A  .      .  .
bar       D D  cyan   e  1
move      E A  .      .  .
bar       F F  green  e  2
move      G A  .      .  .
bar       H H  yellow x1 3
       ;

       symbol v=none;

       proc gplot    data=one;
          plot y*x / ctext=white
                     caxis=white
                     annotate=two;
       run;
```

Example 2: Using the FRAME Function

The following example creates an ANNOTATE= data set containing the FRAME function to place a frame on the display area. The TITLE and FOOTNOTE statements place text on the display, and PROC GSLIDE is used to display the output, as shown in **Output 7.11**.

```
       data one;
          length function color $ 8;
          input function $ x y;
          xsys='6';
          ysys='6';
          color='white';
          cards;
frame     .  .
       ;

       title    c=cream f=swiss h=4 'FRAME';
       footnote c=cream f=swiss h=4 'FUNCTION';

       proc gslide  annotate=one;
       run;
```

Example 3: Using the POLY and POLYCONT Functions

The following example shows how to create an ANNOTATE= data set that contains the POLY and POLYCONT functions to draw three polygons. PROC GSLIDE is then used to display the polygons, as shown in **Output 7.12**.

```
data one;
   length function color style $ 8;
   input function $ x y color $ style $;
   xsys='4';
   ysys='4';
   cards;
poly       20  10  gold     solid
polycont   40  10  .        .
polycont   30  20  .        .
polycont   20  10  .        .
poly       40  10  yellow   x1
polycont   60  10  .        .
polycont   50  20  .        .
polycont   40  10  .        .
poly       30  20  cyan     l1
polycont   50  20  .        .
polycont   40  30  .        .
polycont   30  20  .        .
;

proc gslide annotate=one;
run;
```

Example 4: Using the PIE and PIEXY Functions

In this example, the PIE and PIEXY functions are used to place labels at various points on pie slices. The SIZE variable is used with the PIEXY function. (For a description of the PIEXY function, see **Outline of Use: Advanced Functions**.) These statements produce **Output 7.13**.

```
data one;
   length position $ 1;
   input function $ x y line color $ style $ size angle rotate position $
         text $ char30.;
   xsys='3';
   ysys='3';
   cards;
pie    75  75  0 yellow empty   4  0   360  .  .
piexy  .   .   .  .      .       1  45  .    .  .
swap   .   .   .  .      .       .  .   .    .  .
label  .   .   . gold    swiss   2  .   .    0  label
label  60  60  . white   triplex 1  .   .    0  PIEXY FUNCTION, SIZE=1.0
;

data two;
   length position $ 1;
   input function $ x y line color $ style $ size angle rotate position $
         text $ char30.;
   xsys='3';
   ysys='3';
   cards;
```

```
pie    25  75  0 yellow   empty    4    0    360  .  .
piexy   .    .   .   .          .    0.5  45   .  .  .
swap    .    .   .   .          .    .    .    .  .  .
label   .    .   . gold     swiss    2    .    .  0 label
label  10  60  . white    triplex   1    .    .  0 PIEXY FUNCTION, SIZE=0.5
;

data three;
   length position $ 1;
   input function $ x y line color $ style $ size angle rotate position $
         text $ char30.;
   xsys='3';
   ysys='3';
   cards;
pie    25  25  0 yellow   empty    4    0    360  .  .
piexy   .    .   .   .          .    1.5  45   .  .  .
swap    .    .   .   .          .    .    .    .  .  .
label   .    .   . gold     swiss    2    .    .  0 label
label  10  10  . white    triplex   1    .    .  0 PIEXY FUNCTION, SIZE=1.5
;

data four;
   length position $ 1;
   input function $ x y line color $ style $ size angle rotate position $
         text $ char30.;
   xsys='3';
   ysys='3';
   cards;
pie    75  25  0 yellow   solid    4    0    360  .  .
label  60  10  . white    triplex   1    .    .  0 PIE FUNCTION, SOLID FILL
;

data all;
   set one two three four;
run;

proc gslide annotate=all;
run;
```

Example 5: Using the PIE Function with the LINE Variable

The following example illustrates the LINE values' effect on the lines drawn with
the pie slices. These statements produce **Output 7.14**.

```
data one;
   length position $ 1;
   length function color style $ 8;
   input function $ x y color $ style $ size angle rotate line
         position $ text $ char30.;
   xsys='3';
   ysys='3';
   cards;
pie    75  75  yellow   empty    5    0    90   1  .  .
label  60  60  gold     triplex  1    .    .    .  0 EMPTY PIE, LINE=1
;
```

```
data two;
   length position $ 1;
   length function color style $ 8;
   input function $ x y color $ style $ size angle rotate line
         position $ text $ char30.;
   xsys='3';
   ysys='3';
   cards;
pie    25  25  yellow  empty    5   0   90   2  .  .
label  10  10  gold    triplex  1   .   .    .  0  EMPTY PIE, LINE=2
;

data three;
   length position $ 1;
   length function color style $ 8;
   input function $ x y color $ style $ size angle rotate line
         position $ text $ char30.;
   xsys='3';
   ysys='3';
   cards;
pie    75  25  yellow  empty    5   0   90   3  .  .
label  60  10  gold    triplex  1   .   .    .  0  EMPTY PIE, LINE=3
;

data four;
   length position $ 1;
   length function color style $ 8;
   input function $ x y color $ style $ size angle rotate line
         position $ text $ char30.;
   xsys='3';
   ysys='3';
   cards;
pie    25  75  yellow  empty    5   0   90   0  .  .
label  10  60  gold    triplex  1   .   .    .  0  EMPTY PIE, LINE=0
;

data all;
   set one two three four;
run;

proc gslide annotate=all;
run;
```

Example 6: Using the LABEL Function

The following example demonstrates the effect of the POSITION variable on the placement of text strings. The output produced is shown in **Output 7.15**.

```
data one;
   length position $ 1;
   input function $ x y color $ style $ size position $
         text $ char30.;
   cards;
move   10  18  .               .    .    .   .
draw   20  24  yellow          .    .    .   .
draw   30  18  yellow          .    .    .   .
```

```
label  20  24  gold     swiss    2   a LABEL
label   0  16  white    triplex  1   0 LABEL, POSITION=A
;

data two;
   length position $ 1;
   input function $ x y color $ style $ size position $
      text $ char30.;
   cards;
move   10   2  .        .        .   .   .
draw   20   8  yellow   .        .   .   .
draw   30   2  yellow   .        .   .   .
label  20   8  gold     swiss    2   c LABEL
label   0   1  white    triplex  1   0 LABEL, POSITION=C
;

data three;
   length position $ 1;
   input function $ x y color $ style $ size position $
      text $ char30.;
   cards;
move   50   2  .        .        .   .   .
draw   60   8  yellow   .        .   .   .
draw   70   2  yellow   .        .   .   .
label  60   8  gold     swiss    2   5 LABEL
label  40   1  white    triplex  1   0 LABEL, POSITION=5
;

data four;
   length position $ 1;
   input function $ x y color $ style $ size position $
      text $ char30.;
   cards;
move   50  18  .        .        .   .   .
draw   60  24  yellow   .        .   .   .
draw   70  18  yellow   .        .   .   .
label  60  24  gold     swiss    2   b LABEL
label  40  16  white    triplex  1   0 LABEL, POSITION=B
;

data all;
   set one two three four;
run;

proc gslide annotate=all;
run;
```

Example 7: Using the MIDPOINT, GROUP, and SUBGROUP Variables

The following example shows the use of the MIDPOINT, GROUP, and SUBGROUP variables to place labels on each subgroup value in a vertical bar chart. As shown in the example, the response can be specified by the Y value for a vertical bar chart, by the X value for a horizontal bar chart, or the appropriate SUBGROUP value if X and/or Y is missing. The output is shown in **Output 7.16**.

```
data food;
   do park=1 to 3;
      do location=1 to 3;
         do item=1 to 3;
            number=5+ranuni(98765)*10;
            output;
            end;
         end;
      end;
run;

proc format;
   value   stadium  1='CODGER'    2='CRANKY'    3='CANE';
   value   food     1='HOT DOG'   2='POP CORN'  3='BEVERAGE';
   value   where    1='1ST'       2='PLATE'     3='3RD';
run;

data labels;
   length function color $ 8;

   retain function 'label'   /* Place text on graph                  */
          position 'e'       /* 1/2 cell below and horizontal center */
          when     'a'       /* Place text after graph is drawn      */
          xsys     '2'       /* Horizontal values are data dependent */
          ysys     '2'       /* Vertical values are data dependent   */
          color    'black';  /* Text color                           */

   set food;                 /* Input data set                       */
   midpoint=location;        /* Locate the horizontal position       */
   group=park;               /*        within the appropriate group  */
   subgroup=item;            /* Locate the vertical position         */
   text=left(put(number,f2.0));
   output;
run;

pattern1 v=s c=gold;
pattern2 v=s c=yellow;
pattern3 v=s c=white;
title c=cream f=swiss ' PRE-GAME CONCESSIONS';

proc gchart data=food;
   label   park='00'x;               /* suppress group label    */
   label   location='00'x;           /* suppress midpoint label */
   label   number='UNITS SOLD';
   vbar    location   / midpoints=3 2 1
                        minor=0
                        sumvar=number
```

```
                       group=park
                       subgroup=ITEM
                       ctext=white
                       caxis=white
                       annotate=labels;
        format  park      stadium.
                item      food.
                location  where.;
      run;
```

Output 7.10   The XC and YC Annotate Variables and PROC GPLOT

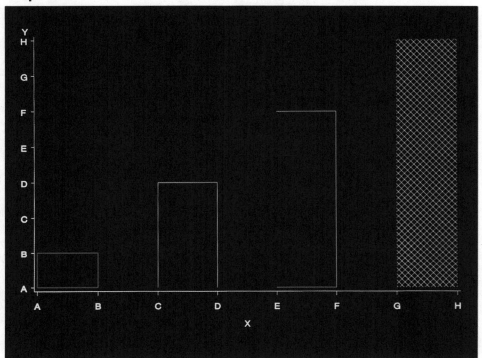

Output 7.11 The FRAME Function

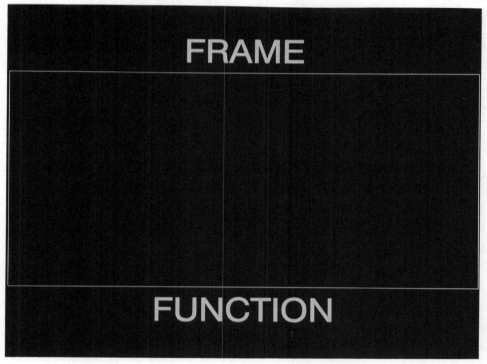

Output 7.12 The POLY and POLYCONT Functions

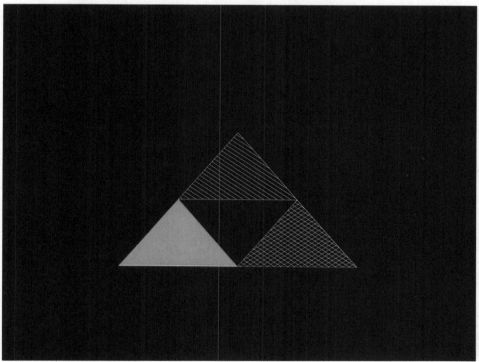

Output 7.13   Using the PIE and PIEXY Functions

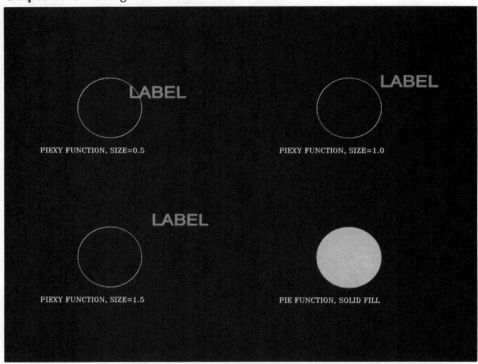

Output 7.14   Using the PIE Function with the LINE Variable

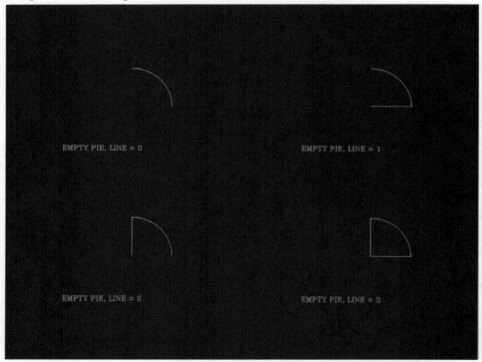

Output 7.15 Using the LABEL Function with the POSITION Variable

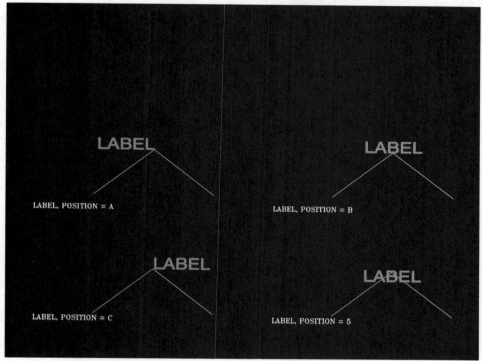

Output 7.16 Labeling SUBGROUP Values in a Vertical Bar Chart

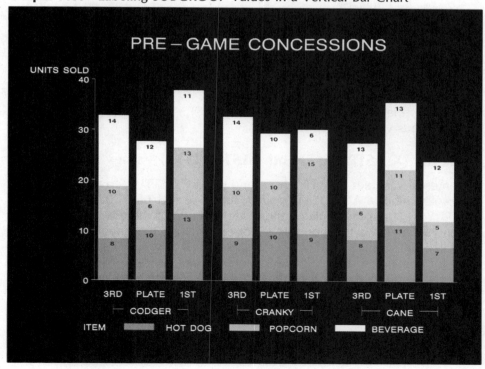

ADVANCED FUNCTIONS

The advanced Annotate functions take advantage of the utility features of the Annotate facility and give you greater control over your Annotate output. The advanced functions are listed and described briefly below. For a complete description of these functions and the variables you can use with them, see **Outline of Use: Advanced Functions**.

FUNCTION='CNTL2TXT'
  copies the values (XLAST,YLAST) to (XLSTT,YLSTT), replacing the previous values of (XLSTT,YLSTT).

FUNCTION='DEBUG'
  writes internal Annotate values to the SAS log before and after the next function is executed.

FUNCTION='DRAW2TXT'
  draws a line from (XLSTT,YLSTT) to (XLAST,YLAST).

FUNCTION='PIECNTR'
  sets new center and radius values for later use by the PIEXY function without drawing an arc as with the PIE function.

FUNCTION='PIEXY'
  returns a point on the outline of a pie so you can specify that point when adding a label.

FUNCTION='POP'
  removes the values for (XLAST,YLAST) and (XLSTT,YLSTT) from the LIFO (last in, first out) system stack and updates these pairs.

FUNCTION='PUSH'
  enters the values for (XLAST,YLAST) and (XLSTT,YLSTT) in the LIFO system stack.

FUNCTION='SWAP'
  exchanges the values (XLAST,YLAST) with (XLSTT,YLSTT) and vice versa.

FUNCTION='TXT2CNTL'
  copies the values (XLSTT,YLSTT) to (XLAST,YLAST), replacing the previous values of (XLAST,YLAST).

Updating (XLAST,YLAST) and (XLSTT,YLSTT) Values

The internal variables (XLAST,YLAST) and (XLSTT,YLSTT) keep track of X and Y values specified in ANNOTATE= data sets. The variables (XLAST,YLAST) and (XLSTT,YLSTT) are manipulated indirectly by most of the advanced functions. When you specify a function that is not text-related, the Annotate facility uses the values for X and Y (or the other variables used to specify coordinates) as the basis for updating the (XLAST,YLAST) internal pair. Text-handling functions are the only functions that update the (XLSTT,YLSTT) internal pair. The following example illustrates the importance of these variables in creating your ANNOTATE= data sets.

Suppose you want to draw a line from one point to another. You can use the MOVE and DRAW functions and specify X and Y values for the two points to be joined with a line. The following statements draw a line:

```
function='move'; x=10; y=10; output;
function='draw'; x=20; y=20; output;
```

You specified two points, but only one DRAW function. How were the points connected?

Based on the point you specified with the MOVE function, the internal values (XLAST,YLAST) were updated and became the starting point when the line was drawn. **Table 7.4** shows how the internal coordinate pair (XLAST,YLAST) is updated.

Table 7.4   Updating (XLAST,YLAST) with X and Y Values

FUNCTION	X	Y	XLAST	YLAST
			0	0
MOVE	10	10		
			10	10
DRAW	20	20		
			20	20

In **Table 7.4**, the (XLAST,YLAST) pair is initially set to (0,0) and is updated by the X and Y values specified with the first function. The updated (XLAST,YLAST) values are then available for use by the second function. Thus, in this example, the MOVE function causes the pen to move to coordinate position (10,10) and then the DRAW function draws a line from (XLAST,YLAST) to (X,Y). The result is a line drawn from coordinate position (10,10) to coordinate position (20,20).

Table 7.5 lists the variables that can be used with the advanced Annotate functions.

Table 7.5   Annotate Variables Used with Advanced Functions

	CNTL2TXT	DEBUG	DRAW2TXT	PIEXY	PIECNTR	POP	PUSH	SWAP	TXT2CNTL
FUNCTION	X	X	X	X	X	X	X	X	X
X					X				
XC									
Y					X				
YC									
Z*									
MIDPOINT**									
GROUP**									
SUBGROUP**									
XSYS									
YSYS									
ZSYS*									
HSYS			X						
WHEN	X	X	X	X	X	X	X	X	X
POSITION									
SIZE			X	X	X				
ANGLE			X						
ROTATE									
STYLE									
COLOR			X						
LINE			X						
TEXT									

*Valid for PROC G3D only

**Valid for PROC GCHART only

Outline of Use: Advanced Functions

The following section gives a detailed description of the advanced functions and the Annotate variables that can be specified with each function. Although you can use the additional variables with many of the advanced functions, they are function dependent and may be interpreted differently for each function.

FUNCTION='CNTL2TXT'

The CNTL2TXT function copies the values (XLAST,YLAST) to (XLSTT,YLSTT), replacing previous values of (XLSTT,YLSTT). You can use the following Annotate variable with this function:

WHEN   specifies when to copy the (XLAST,YLAST) values in relation to generating the procedure output.

FUNCTION='DEBUG'

The DEBUG function writes to the SAS log internal Annotate values before and after the execution of the next command, other than DEBUG, in the ANNOTATE= data set. You can use the following Annotate variable with this function:

WHEN   specifies when to write internal values to the log in relation to generating the procedure output.

FUNCTION='DRAW2TXT'

The DRAW2TXT function draws a line from (XLAST,YLAST) to (XLSTT,YLSTT). DRAW2TXT does not update the (XLAST,YLAST) or (XLSTT,YLSTT) variables. DRAW2TXT cannot interrupt a POLYCONT stream. You can use the following Annotate variables with this function:

HSYS   specifies the reference system to use for SIZE.

WHEN   specifies when to draw the line in relation to generating the procedure output.

LINE   specifies the line type to use to draw the line. (See the list of line types in "Enhancing Your Graphics Output Designs.")

SIZE   specifies the thickness of the line being drawn. See **FUNCTION='DRAW'** for details.

COLOR   specifies the color of the line being drawn. The default value is the first color in the device's COLORS= list.

FUNCTION='PIECNTR'

The PIECNTR function sets new center and radius values for later use by the PIEXY function but does not draw an arc. The PIECNTR function updates the (XLAST,YLAST) coordinates. You can use the following Annotate variables with this function:

X,Y,XC,YC   define the center and radius of the PIE. All slices are referenced from that center. In addition, you can use MIDPOINT, GROUP, and SUBGROUP with PROC GCHART for this purpose, and you can use Z with PROC G3D. The first PIE command issued sets the center at the (X,Y) value. If subsequent values for X and Y are missing, the center points are assumed to be the defaults.

XSYS   specifies the reference system to use for X and XC.

YSYS   specifies the reference system to use for Y and YC.

HSYS   specifies the reference system to use for SIZE.

WHEN   specifies when to draw the pie slice in relation to generating the procedure output.

SIZE   specifies the RADIUS of the circle being drawn. SIZE is measured in the vertical direction in HSYS units.

FUNCTION = 'PIEXY'

The PIEXY function calculates a point on the outline of the slice arc. The calculated coordinates of this point are placed in the internal coordinate pair (XLAST,YLAST). This is useful when you want to position text around a pie (circle). The PIEXY function assumes that a pie slice has previously been drawn. Erroneous results can occur if a slice has not been drawn and the PIEXY function is invoked. You can use the following Annotate variables with this function:

WHEN   specifies when to return the point in relation to generating the procedure output.

SIZE   specifies the radius multiplier. If you specify

```
size=1.5;  function='piexy'; output;
```

then the value of SIZE means 1.5 times the RADIUS (where the RADIUS is taken from the SIZE variable as listed in the **FUNCTION = 'PIE'** section).

ANGLE   specifies the angle of rotation when moving around the perimeter of a pie. The default value is 0.00.

FUNCTION = 'POP'

The POP function removes the coordinates (XLAST,YLAST) and (XLSTT,YLSTT) from the LIFO system stack and updates the internal coordinate pairs with these retrieved values. (See **FUNCTION = 'PUSH'** for a description of the stack.) You can use the following Annotate variable with this function:

WHEN   specifies when to remove and update coordinates in relation to generating the procedure output.

FUNCTION = 'PUSH'

The PUSH function enters the coordinates (XLAST,YLAST) and (XLSTT,YLSTT) in a LIFO system stack. The stack is a mechanism for saving previously calculated coordinates. It allows you to retain values for later use by utility functions without recalculating those values. When you specify FUNCTION = 'PUSH' to push coordinates on the stack, the coordinates occupy the space at the top of the stack. As you push more coordinates onto the stack, the previous coordinates are pushed down to occupy lower levels of the stack. When you specify FUNCTION = 'POP', the first coordinates are popped or removed, and coordinates at lower levels move up in the stack. You can use the following Annotate variable with this function:

WHEN   specifies when to enter the coordinates in the stack in relation to generating the procedure output.

FUNCTION = 'SWAP'

The SWAP function exchanges the values (XLAST,YLAST) with (XLSTT,YLSTT) and vice versa. You can use the following Annotate variable with this function:

WHEN   specifies when to exchange the values in relation to generating the procedure output.

FUNCTION = 'TXT2CNTL'

The TXT2CNTL function copies the values (XLSTT,YLSTT) to (XLAST,YLAST), replacing previous values of (XLAST,YLAST). You can use the following Annotate variable with this function:

> WHEN   specifies when to copy the values in relation to generating the procedure output.

ADVANCED EXAMPLES

The following examples use combinations of the basic and advanced Annotate functions to create ANNOTATE= data sets. Before recreating these examples or similar ones of your own, you should understand the basic and advanced functions, the utility variables (XLAST,YLAST) and (XLSTT,YLSTT), and the Annotate macros (see **Annotate Macros** in the **DETAILS** section) that are included in the SASMACRO subdirectory provided with SAS/GRAPH software.

Example 8: Annotating a Map of North Carolina

In the example below, the program takes city names and places them on an outline map of North Carolina. To do this, the locations of the cities must be in the same coordinate system used for the map.

The first step reads in city names from the SAS data set MAPS.USCITY, which is in the MAPS subdirectory provided with SAS/GRAPH software. If you need assistance accessing the MAPS subdirectory, see your SAS Software Consultant.

```
data cities;
   length text $ 40;
   length function color style  $ 8;
   set maps.uscity;                        /* Institute-supplied */
                                           /* data set           */

   if state=stfips('NC') then
   if upcase(city)='ASHEVILLE '  |
      upcase(city)='CHARLOTTE '  |
      upcase(city)='DURHAM    '  |
      upcase(city)='RALEIGH   '  |
      upcase(city)='WILMINGTON' then do;
      xsys='2'; ysys='2';                  /* data relative x,y  */
      text=city;
      function='label';                    /* place the text     */
      position='5';                        /* centered h/v       */
      when='a';                            /* after map is drawn */
      color='white';                       /* in white           */
      style='simplex';                     /* software font      */
      output;
      end;
   else delete;
run;
```

The next step creates a subset map of North Carolina:

```
data map;
   set maps.us;                            /* Institute-supplied */
                                           /* data set           */

   if state=stfips('NC');
run;
```

The last step produces the annotated map of North Carolina shown in **Output 7.17**.

```
title c=cream f=swiss h=2 'Cities of North Carolina';
pattern color=green v=empty;
proc gmap data=map map=map;
   id state;
   choro state / nolegend annotate=cities;
run;
```

Example 9: Placing Labels on a Plot

The example below places a descriptive character string at the termination of each of four plotted curves. First build a data set containing economic data to be plotted. The data are from Miller's *Economics Today, 4th Edition*.

```
data econ;
   retain  tcprev 0;
   input   q tvc;              /* Quantity & total variable cost */
   tfc=10;                     /* Total fixed cost               */
   tc=tfc+tvc;                 /* Total cost                     */
   afc=tfc / q;                /* Average fixed cost             */
   avc=tvc / q;                /* Average variable cost          */
   atc=tc / q;                 /* Average total cost             */
   costs=tc-tcprev;            /* Marginal cost                  */
   tcprev=tc;
   cards;
1        05
2        08
3        10
4        11
5        13
6        16
7        20
8        25
9        31
10       38
11       46
;
```

In the next step, create an ANNOTATE= data set using coordinates based on the values in the data being plotted. The coordinates for the placement of labels are determined by the values in the last observation.

```
data labels  (keep=x y xsys ysys text position style);
   set econ;
   if q=11 then do;                   /* Last observation in data set  */
      xsys='2';  ysys='2';  /* Coordinates in terms of data values     */
      position='3';         /* Labels up and to right of actual point */
      style='none';         /*    use hardware text                    */

      x=q; y=costs; text=' MC'; output;  /* Establish x and y values */
           y=atc;   text=' ATC'; output; /* based on values of the   */
           y=afc;   text=' AFC'; output; /* plotted variables.       */
           y=avc;   text=' AVC'; output; /* x remains constant (q)   */
   end;
run;
```

Next, produce the plot shown in **Output 7.18** using the ANNOTATE= option to specify the positions of the descriptive labels.

```
symbol1  c=cyan   v=plus    i=splines  l=2;
symbol2  c=yellow v=diamond i=splines;
symbol3  c=green  v=plus    i=splines  l=20;
symbol4  c=salmon v=diamond i=splines;
title1 c=cream f=swiss 'COST OF PRODUCTION';
title2 c=cream f=swiss "From Miller's Economics Today, 4th Edition";
footnote a=90 f=simplex h=3 ' ';
proc gplot data=econ;
    plot costs*q=1 atc*q=2 avc*q=3 afc*q=4 /  overlay
                                              vaxis=0 to 16 by 2
                                              haxis=0 to 11 by 1
                                              annotate=labels;
    label  q='OUTPUT (units per day)';
run;
```

Example 10: Adding a Customized Legend to PROC GPLOT Output

The following example demonstrates how to use the ANNOTATE= option to add a customized legend to PROC GPLOT.

```
data legend;
   length text  $ 16;
   length function style $ 8;
   length xsys $ 1 ysys $ 1;
   when='a'; position='0';
   input function $ x  y color $ xsys $ ysys $ text $ 16.;
   if function='bar' then do;
      line=3;                      /* Draw a full bar */
      style='solid';               /* solid fill.     */
      end;
   else do;
      style='simplex ';
      end;
   cards;
move     2   80   .       2 1  .
bar      1.5 0.8  gold     a a  .
move     1   -1   .        a a  .
cntl2txt .   .    .        . .  .
label    .   .    white    . . SALES
move     2   75   .       2 1  .
bar      1.5 0.8  green    a a  .
move     1   -1   .        a a  .
cntl2txt .   .    .        . .  .
label    .   .    white    . . PRODUCTION
label    2   90   white   2 1 LEGEND:
;
```

Now create a format for the displayed data.

```
proc format;
   value monfmt. 1='JAN'       2='FEB'       3='MAR'
                 4='APR'       5='MAY'       6='JUN'
                 7='JUL'       8='AUG'       9='SEP'
                10='OCT'      11='NOV'      12='DEC';
run;
```

In the next step, create the data set POINTS that contains the actual points to be plotted.

```
data points;
   input a m cost;
   q=m;
   cards;
 1 0 2
 2 2 3
 3 3 5
 4 4 6
 5 3 4
 6 2 4
 7 5 8
 8 6 9
 9 2 5
10 1 4
;
```

Finally, use PROC GPLOT to output the plot with the Annotate information, as shown in **Output 7.19**.

```
symbol1 c=green i=join v=none;
symbol2 c=gold  i=join v=none;
symbol3 c=green i=join v=none;
pattern1 v=s c=green;
pattern2 v=s c=gold;
title c=cream f=swiss 'Production vs. Sales';
proc gplot data=points;
   label a='Months';
   format a monfmt.;
   plot m*a cost*a / overlay
                     areas=2
                     haxis=1 to  12 by 1
                     hminor=0
                     vaxis=0 to  10 by 1
                     vminor=0
                     caxis=white
                     ctext=white
                     annotate=legend;
   plot2    q*a    / vaxis=0 to 100 by 10
                     vminor=0
                     caxis=white
                     ctext=white
                     frame;
run;
```

Example 11: Labeling a Pie Chart

This example demonstrates how to control the placement of text and lines on a pie chart. A single "slice" of a pie is drawn and text is stacked to the right. A line is drawn from the text to the center of the slice. The following statements produce **Output 7.20**.

Figure 7.8 displays coordinates referenced by each of the functions used to position the text and line. **Table 7.6** shows an execution trace of the functions and the contents of (XLAST,YLAST) and (XLSTT,YLSTT) before and after each function is executed.

```
data triple;
    length function color style    $ 8;
    length xsys ysys position when $ 1;
    retain xsys ysys '3' hsys '4' when 'a';
    x=30; y=50;
    angle=315; rotate=90; size=10;
    color='cyan'; style='empty'; line=3; function='pie';      output;
    angle=0; size=1.5;                     function='piexy';    output;
                                           function='cntl2txt'; output;
                                           function='push';     output;
                                           function='push';     output;
    x= .; y= .; text=' Triple';
    color='green'; angle=0; rotate=0;
    size=1; style='none'; position='3';    function='label';    output;
                                           function='pop';      output;
    x= .; y= .; text=' Stack ';
    color='green'; angle=0; rotate=0;
    size=1; style='none'; position='6';    function='label';    output;
                                           function='pop';      output;
    x= .; y= .; text=' Effect';
    color='green'; angle=0; rotate=0;
    size=1; style='none'; position='9';    function='label';    output;
                                           function='swap';     output;
    angle=0; size=0.6;                     function='piexy';    output;
    line=1; size=1; color='white';         function='draw2txt'; output;
    run;

    proc ganno annotate=triple
            name='ADVANCED'
            description='Using PIE/PIEXY to label slice';
    run;
```

Figure 7.8 Coordinates Used to Position Text and Line

Table 7.6 Execution Trace of Example 11

	Internal				Stack			
FUNCTION	XLAST	YLAST	XLSTT	YLSTT	XLAST	YLAST	XLSTT	YLSTT
(initial)	0.00	0.00	0.00	0.00	.	.	.	.
PIE	pcntr_x	pcntr_y	0.00	0.00	.	.	.	.
PIEXY	start_x	start_y	0.00	0.00	.	.	.	.
CNTL2TXT	start_x	start_y	start_x	start_y	.	.	.	.
PUSH	start_x	start_y	start_x	start_y	start_x	start_y	start_x	start_y
PUSH	start_x	start_y	start_x	start_y	start_x'	start_y'	start_x'	start_y'
					start_x	start_y	start_x	start_y
LABEL	start_x	start_y	end01_x	end01_y	start_x'	start_y'	start_x'	start_y'
					start_x	start_y	start_x	start_y
POP	start_x'	start_y'	start_x'	start_y'	start_x	start_y	start_x	start_y
LABEL	start_x'	start_y'	end02_x	end02_y	start_x	start_y	start_x	start_y
POP	start_x	start_y	start_x	start_y	.	.	.	.
LABEL	start_x	start_y	end03_x	end03_y	.	.	.	.
SWAP	end03_x	end03_y	start_x	start_y	.	.	.	.
PIEXY	line_x	line_y	start_x	start_y	.	.	.	.
DRAW2TXT	line_x	line_y	start_x	start_y	.	.	.	.

Example 12: Annotating Bars on a Spline

The example below shows how to annotate solid colored bars on a spline created with PROC GPLOT. This technique allows you to produce histograms with bars and interpolated curves on the same graph. The following statements produce **Output 7.21**.

Figure 7.9 shows how a bar is created, following the steps that are numbered in the DATA step. **Table 7.7** shows an execution trace of the functions and the contents of (XLAST,YLAST) and (XLSTT,YLSTT) before and after each function is executed.

```
data raw;
   input mid response;
   cards;
   1    23
   2    11
   3    19
   4    15
   5     7
   6     5
;
```

```
data gplbar;
   length function color style    $ 8;
   length xsys ysys position      $ 1;
   retain;
   retain position '2';
   set raw;

   /* generate a bar at each value    */
   width=3;
   color='green';
   style='solid';
❶ xsys='2'; ysys='2'; x=mid;      y=0;         function='move';      output;
❷ xsys='7'; ysys='7'; x=width;    y=0;         function='move';      output;
                                               function='push';      output;
❸ xsys='7'; ysys='2'; x=0; y=response; function='move';      output;
                                               function='push';      output;
❹ xsys='2'; ysys='7'; x=mid;      y=0;         function='move';      output;
❺ xsys='7'; ysys='7'; x=-width; y=0;         function='move';      output;
                                               function='push';      output;
❻ xsys='7'; ysys='2'; x=0;        y=0;         function='move';      output;
   xsys='4'; ysys='4'; x=.;        y=.;         function='poly';      output;
                                               function='pop';       output;
                       x=-999;    y=x;         function='polycont'; output;
                                               function='pop';       output;
                                               function='polycont'; output;
                                               function='pop';       output;
                                               function='polycont'; output;

   /* put the value on top of the bar */
   xsys='2'; ysys='2';
   function='label'; style='none'; color='white';
   x=mid; y=response;  text=left(put(response,f3.)); output;
run;

symbol i=spline v=none;
proc gplot data=raw;
   axis1 offset=(5,5);
   plot response*mid / frame hminor=0
                       vaxis=0 to 25 by 5
                       haxis=axis1
                       annotate=gplbar;
run;
```

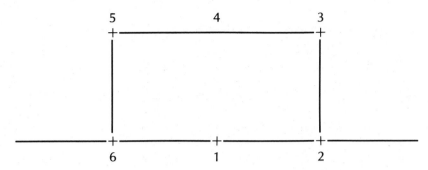

Figure 7.9   How a Bar is Created (Refer to Numbered Steps Above)

Table 7.7   Execution Trace of Example 12

FUNCTION	Internal				Stack			
	XLAST	YLAST	XLSTT	YLSTT	XLAST	YLAST	XLSTT	YLSTT
(initial)	0.00	0.00	0.00	0.00	.	.	.	.
MOVE	pos01_x	pos01_y	0.00	0.00	.	.	.	.
MOVE	pos02_x	pos02_y	0.00	0.00	.	.	.	.
PUSH	pos02_x	pos02_y	0.00	0.00	pos02_x	pos02_y	0.00	0.00
MOVE	pos03_x	pos03_y	0.00	0.00	pos02_x	pos02_y	0.00	0.00
PUSH	pos03_x	pos03_y	0.00	0.00	pos03_x	pos03_y	0.00	0.00
					pos02_x	pos02_y	0.00	0.00
MOVE	pos04_x	pos04_y	0.00	0.00	pos03_x	pos03_y	0.00	0.00
					pos02_x	pos02_y	0.00	0.00
MOVE	pos05_x	pos05_y	0.00	0.00	pos03_x	pos03_y	0.00	0.00
					pos02_x	pos02_y	0.00	0.00
PUSH	pos05_x	pos05_y	0.00	0.00	pos05_x	pos05_y	0.00	0.00
					pos03_x	pos03_y	0.00	0.00
					pos02_y	pos02_y	0.00	0.00
MOVE	pos06_x	pos06_y	0.00	0.00	pos05_x	pos05_y	0.00	0.00
					pos03_x	pos03_y	0.00	0.00
					pos02_y	pos02_y	0.00	0.00
POLY	pos06_x	pos06_y	0.00	0.00	pos05_x	pos05_y	0.00	0.00
					pos03_x	pos03_y	0.00	0.00
					pos02_y	pos02_y	0.00	0.00
POP	pos05_x	pos05_y	0.00	0.00	pos03_x	pos03_y	0.00	0.00
					pos02_x	pos02_y	0.00	0.00
POLYCONT	pos05_x	pos05_y	0.00	0.00	pos03_x	pos03_y	0.00	0.00
					pos02_x	pos02_y	0.00	0.00
POP	pos03_x	pos03_y	0.00	0.00	pos02_x	pos02_y	0.00	0.00
POLYCONT	pos03_x	pos03_y	0.00	0.00	pos02_x	pos02_y	0.00	0.00
POP	pos02_x	pos02_y	0.00	0.00	.	.	.	.
POLYCONT	pos02_x	pos02_y	0.00	0.00	.	.	.	.

Output 7.17 Annotated Map of North Carolina

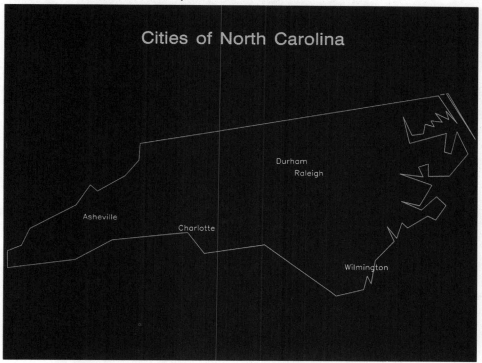

Output 7.18 Labeling the Curve on a Plot

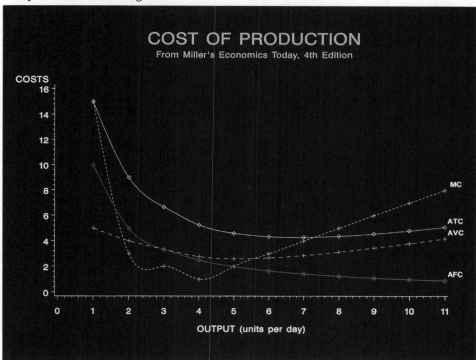

Output 7.19   Adding a Legend to a Plot

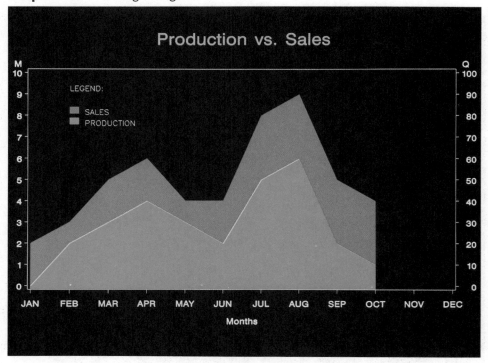

Output 7.20   Labeling a Pie Chart

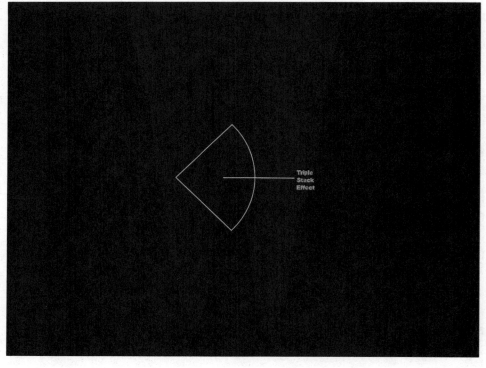

Output 7.21   Annotating Bars onto a Spline

DETAILS

Annotate Macros

The following Annotate macros can be used within a SAS DATA step to simplify the process of coding Annotate observations. You can find these macros in the SASMACRO subdirectory provided with SAS/GRAPH software. Each macro is described briefly below. See the function descriptions for more detailed information. See **Examples 13** and **14** for examples that use some of these macros to simplify programming steps.

%DCLANNO;
:   sets the length and data type specifications for Annotate variables.

%COMMENT(*txt*);
:   inserts a comment into an ANNOTATE= data set.

%SEQUENCE(*seq*);
:   defines the Annotate generation sequence. Valid *seq* values are AFTER (A) or BEFORE (B). The default is %SEQUENCE(BEFORE).

%SYSTEM(*xs, ys, hs*);
:   defines the Annotate reference systems. Valid system values are

ABSOLUTE SYSTEMS

1	data percentage	2	data value
3	screen percentage	4	screen value
5	window percentage	6	window value

RELATIVE SYSTEMS

7	data percentage	8	data value
9	screen percentage	A	screen value
B	window percentage	C	window value

The DEFAULT is %SYSTEM (4, 4, 4).

%MOVE(x1,y1);
specifies to move to the (x1,y1) coordinate.

%DRAW (x1, y1, color, linetype, linewidth);
specifies to draw a line to the (x1,y1) coordinate. You can use an asterisk (*) to indicate a previously defined value for color.

%LINE(x1, y1, x2, y2, color, linetype, linewidth);
specifies to draw a line from (x1,y1) to (x2,y2) coordinates. You can use an asterisk (*) to indicate a previously defined value for color.

%LABEL(x1, y1, text, color, ang, rot, ht, font, pos);
specifies to place a text label at the (x1,y1) coordinate. The text can be a variable name or a quoted string. You can use an asterisk (*) to indicate a previously defined value for color.

%RECT(x1, y1, x2, y2, color, linetype, linewidth);
specifies to draw a nonfillable rectangle with opposite corners at (x1,y1) and (x2,y2). You can use an asterisk (*) to indicate a previously defined value for color.

%BAR(x1, y1, x2, y2, color, bartype, pattern);
specifies to draw a fillable rectangle with opposing corners at (x1,y1) and (x2,y2). Valid bartype values are

0	draw all edges	1	vertical adjust
2	horizontal adjust	3	draw no edges

You can use an asterisk (*) to indicate a previously defined value for color.

%CIRCLE(x1, y1, rad, color);
specifies to draw an empty circle with the center at (x1,y1). You can use an asterisk (*) to indicate a previously defined value for color.

%SLICE(x1, y1, ang, rot, rad, color, pattern, slicetype);
specifies to draw an arc or section of a fillable circle with the center at (x1,y1). You can use an asterisk (*) to indicate a previously defined value for color. Valid slicetype values are

WHOLE	draws no radius lines
NONE	draws no radius lines
LEAD	draws a radius from lead point to center
TRAIL	draws a radius from trail point to center
BOTH	draws both lead and trail radii.

%PIEXY(ang, multiplier);
specifies to locate a point along a radius of multiplier length based on the previously drawn slice.

%POLY(x1, y1, color, pattern, linetype);
specifies to begin drawing a polygon at (x1,y1). The color value determines the fill color of the polygon being defined if pattern is not

empty. You can use an asterisk (*) to indicate a previously defined value for *color*.

%POLYCONT(*x1, y1, color*);
specifies to continue drawing the polygon. The first %POLYCONT value determines the outline color of the polygon being defined.

%SCALE(*ptx, pty, x0, y0, x1, y1, vx0, vy0, vx1, vy1*);
specifies to scale input coordinates (*ptx,pty*) from a range of the minima (*x0,y0*) and maxima (*x1,y1*) to a range of minima (*vx0,vy0*) and maxima (*vx1,vy1*).

%PUSH;
specifies to push control and text coordinates onto LIFO stack.

%POP;
specifies to pop control and text coordinates from LIFO stack.

%SWAP;
specifies to exchange control and text coordinates.

%TXT2CNTL;
specifies to assign the text coordinate to the control coordinate.

%CNTL2TXT;
specifies to assign the control coordinate to the text coordinate.

%DRAW2TXT(*color, linetype, linewidth*);
specifies to draw a line from the control coordinate to the text coordinate. You can use an asterisk (*) to indicate a previously defined value for *color*.

%FRAME(*color, linetype, linewidth, pattern*);
specifies to draw a fillable frame around the reference systems currently defined.

Example 13: Simple Population Tree Using Annotate Macros

This example creates a population tree chart (shown in **Output 7.22**) using some of the Annotate macros in the SASMACRO subdirectory provided with SAS/GRAPH software. In this example, macros are used to define variables, draw a frame, draw labels, and generate solid bars.

```
data poptree;
   %dclanno;                       /* length and type specification */
   length text $ 16;               /* set length of text variable   */
   %system(5,5,4);                 /* window percentage for x and y */

   %frame(white,1,1,empty);        /* draw frame around graph       */

   %move(5,5);                     /* draw axis lines for females   */
   %draw(40,5,yellow,1,1);
   %draw(40,90,yellow,1,1);

   %move(56,90);                   /* draw axis lines for males     */
   %draw(56,5,yellow,1,1);
   %draw(95,5,yellow,1,1);

   %label(75.0,97.0,'MALE',white,0,0,0.85,simplex,5);   /* label categories */
   %label(25.0,97.0,'FEMALE',white,0,0,0.85,simplex,5); /* at top  */
```

```
     %label(5.0,2.5,'100',white,0,0,0.70,simplex,5);   /* label bottom axes */
     %label(22.5,2.5,' 50',white,0,0,0.70,simplex,5);
     %label(40.0,2.5,' 00',white,0,0,0.70,simplex,5);
     %label(95.0,2.5,'100',white,0,0,0.70,simplex,5);
     %label(75.0,2.5,' 50',white,0,0,0.70,simplex,5);
     %label(56.0,2.5,' 00',white,0,0,0.70,simplex,5);

     %label(48.0,10.25,'UNDER 20',white,0,0,0.75,simplex,5); /* label age */
     %label(48.0,20.0,'20 - 29',white,0,0,0.75,simplex,5);
     %label(48.0,31.7,'30 - 39',white,0,0,0.75,simplex,5);
     %label(48.0,42.4,'40 - 49',white,0,0,0.75,simplex,5);
     %label(48.0,52.8,'50 - 59',white,0,0,0.75,simplex,5);
     %label(48.0,63.6,'60 - 69',white,0,0,0.75,simplex,5);
     %label(48.0,74.3,'70 - 79',white,0,0,0.75,simplex,5);
     %label(48.0,85.0,'over 79',white,0,0,0.75,simplex,5);

     %bar(56.2,5.5,95.0,15.0,gold,0,solid);        /* bars for male on right */
     %bar(56.2,15.71,90.0,25.71,cyan,0,solid);
     %bar(56.2,26.42,80.0,36.52,white,0,solid);
     %bar(56.2,37.14,62.0,47.14,magenta,0,solid);
     %bar(56.2,47.85,72.0,57.85,salmon,0,solid);
     %bar(56.2,58.57,60.0,68.57,yellow,0,solid);
     %bar(56.2,69.28,57.0,79.28,green,0,solid);
     %bar(56.2,80.0,59.0,90.0,gold,0,solid);

     %bar(39.8,5.5,25.0,15.0,gold,0,solid);        /* bars for female on left */
     %bar(39.8,15.71,15.0,25.7,cyan,0,solid);
     %bar(39.8,26.42,10.0,36.42,white,0,solid);
     %bar(39.8,37.14,32.0,47.14,magenta,0,solid);
     %bar(39.8,47.85,32.0,57.85,salmon,0,solid);
     %bar(39.8,58.57,38.0,68.57,yellow,0,solid);
     %bar(39.8,69.28,35.0,79.28,green,0,solid);
     %bar(39.8,80.0,37.0,90.0,gold,0,solid);
run;

   title1  c=cream h=2 f=swiss 'Population Tree';
   title2  c=cream h=1 f=swiss 'Distribution of Population by Sex';
   proc gslide annotate=poptree;
   run;
```

Example 14: Advanced Population Tree Using Annotate Macros

This example also creates a population tree chart. In addition, it demonstrates
the full range and flexibility of ANNOTATE= data sets because although it produces the same output as **Example 13**, it does so by calculating from the input
data set, rather than by hardcoding values. This version will change the output
as the input values change, so it is a better demonstration of using ANNOTATE=
data sets for generating custom graphics.

The statements below produce **Output 7.23**.

```
data pctdata;
******************************************************************;
**                                                              *;
** Text, as well as bar values, are ordered top to bottom.      *;
** The number of observations determines the number of bars.    *;
** Male/female response is assumed :     0<=resp<=100            *;
**                                                              *;
******************************************************************;

   input female male text $char20.;
   cards;
 9     9   over 79
14     1   70 - 79
 6    11   60 - 69
23    34   50 - 59
23    16   40 - 49
86    57   30 - 39
71    86   20 - 29
43   100   under 20
;


proc means data=pctdata noprint;
   var  male female;
   output out=stats(keep=nbars)
          n=nbars;
run;

data poptree (drop=col1-col7       colr_idx
              xxmin1 xxmin2  xxmax1 xxmax2
              mmin   mmax    fmin   fmax
              yaxmin yaxmax
              yaxlen ywidth ystart ybar    ymargn
              mscal1 fscal1
              xmid1  xmid2   xmid3
              male   female  xval1  xval2
              nbars  ncolors);

   %dclanno;
   %system( 5, 5, 4 );

   array colors(colr_idx) $ 8  col1-col7;

   retain  col1-col7       colr_idx
           xxmin1 xxmin2  xxmax1 xxmax2
           mmin   mmax    fmin   fmax
           yaxmin yaxmax
           yaxlen ywidth ystart ybar    ymargn
           mscal1 fscal1
           xmid1  xmid2   xmid3
           nbars  ncolors;
```

```
           if _n_=1 then do;
              set stats;

              ncolors=7;                        /* dimension of colors */

              colr_idx=1;    colors='gold';
              colr_idx=2;    colors='cyan';
              colr_idx=3;    colors='white';
              colr_idx=4;    colors='magenta';
              colr_idx=5;    colors='salmon';
           ymargn
                             mscal1 fscal1
                             xmid1   xmid2   xmid3
                             male    female  xval1 xval2
                             nbars   ncolors);
              xxmax1=40;        xxmax2=95;          yaxmax=95;

              mmin=0;        mmax=100;
              fmin=0;        fmax=100;

              yaxlen=yaxmax-yaxmin;
              ywidth=floor(yaxlen / (nbars+1));

              ymargn=(yaxlen-(ywidth*nbars)) / (nbars-1);

              mscal1=(xxmax2-xxmin2) / (mmax-mmin);
              fscal1=(xxmax1-xxmin1) / (fmax-fmin);

              when='a';
              %move(xxmin1, yaxmin);          /* draw axis lines for female */
              %draw(xxmax1, yaxmin, white, 1, 1);
              %draw(xxmax1, yaxmax, white, 1, 1);

              %move(xxmin2, yaxmax);          /* draw axis lines for male   */
              %draw(xxmin2, yaxmin, white, 1, 1);
              %draw(xxmax2, yaxmin, white, 1, 1);

              xmid1=(xxmin1+xxmax1) / 2;
              xmid2=(xxmin2+xxmax2) / 2;
              xmid3=(xxmin2+xxmax1) / 2;

              ystart=yaxmax;
              end;

         set pctdata;

              %label(xmid3, ystart-(ywidth/2),
                     text, white, 0, 0, 0.750, simplex, 5);

              ybar=ystart-ywidth;
              colr_idx=mod(_n_, ncolors)+1;
              color=colors;
```

```
          if male>mmax then male=mmax;
          if male<mmin then male=mmin;
          if female>fmax then female=fmax;
          if female<fmin then female=fmin;

          xval1=xxmax1-((female-fmin)*fscal1);
          xval2=xxmin2+((male-mmin)*mscal1);

          when='b';
          %bar(xval1,  ybar,    xxmax1, ystart, *, 2, solid);
          %bar(xxmin2, ystart, xval2,  ybar, *, 2, solid);
          when='a';

          ystart=ybar-ymargn;


      if _n_=nbars then do;
          %label(xxmin1, 2.5, '100', white, 0, 0, 0.700, simplex, 5);
          %label(xmid1,  2.5, '50 ', white, 0, 0, 0.700, simplex, 5);
          %label(xxmax1, 2.5, '00 ', white, 0, 0, 0.700, simplex, 5);
          %label(25.0, 98.0,'FEMALE',white, 0, 0, 0.850, simplex, 5);

          %label(xxmin2, 2.5, '00 ', white, 0, 0, 0.700, simplex, 5);
          %label(xmid2,  2.5, '50 ', white, 0, 0, 0.700, simplex, 5);
          %label(xxmax2, 2.5, '100', white, 0, 0, 0.700, simplex, 5);
          %label(75.0, 98.0,'MALE  ',white, 0, 0, 0.850, simplex, 5);

          end;
run;

goptions border;
title  j=l c=cream f=swiss ' Population Response';
title2 j=l c=cream f=swiss ' Question 3';

proc gslide annotate=poptree
            name='poptree'
            description='population response';
run;
```

Output 7.22   Creating a Population Tree with Annotate Macros

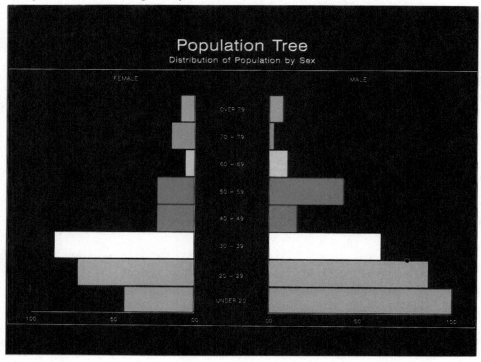

Output 7.23   Using All Annotate Macros to Create a Population Tree

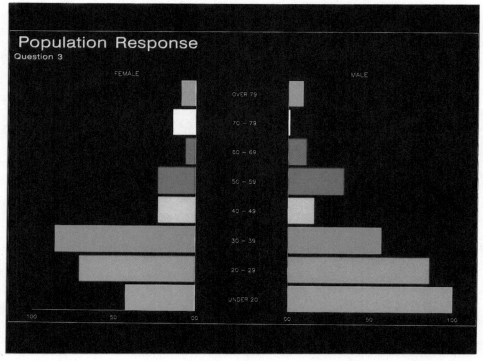

Error Messages

If you encounter errors when using Annotate macros, the ANNOTATE= option issues a series of diagnostic messages in the SAS log. A partial list of these messages is supplied below, in addition to suggested corrections for the problems or errors.

In the messages below, # indicates a value substitution when the message is issued.

If any irregularity is detected in the ANNOTATE= data set, the following message appears in the SAS log:

```
NOTE: ANNOTATE DETECTS ERROR IN DATA SET #.#
```

The line indicates the data set being processed. If the problem is encountered while processing an observation rather than in the pre-process data checking, the observation number is displayed in this format:

```
PROBLEM IN OBSERVATION # -
```

All relevant information for this observation will follow. If the error limit is reached in any pass of the data set, a termination message appears in the SAS log. The messages are similar to the example below:

```
ERROR LIMIT REACHED IN ANNOTATE PROCESS


        20 TOTAL ERRORS
```

Diagnostic messages and explanations follow.

ERROR: POSITION VALUE INVALID—MUST BE ONE OF "1234567890ABCDEF"

PROBLEM: Value of variable POSITION was not in range '0'–'9' or 'A'–'F' in a LABEL command.

CORRECTION: Check desired value in POSITION description and correct.

ERROR: VALUE SHOWN IS NOT A VALID FUNCTION

PROBLEM: Value supplied was not recognized as an available function.

CORRECTION: Check for misspellings or truncation of value. Truncation can be corrected by supplying a length of 8 in the LENGTH statement in the DATA step that generated the data set. For valid functions, see the FUNCTION description in **ANNOTATE= VARIABLES**.

ERROR: SYSTEM VALUE INVALID—MUST BE ONE OF "1234567890ABC"

PROBLEM: Value supplied for XSYS, YSYS, or HSYS is not within supported range.

CORRECTION: Check desired value for XSYS, YSYS, or HSYS description and correct.

ERROR: A CALCULATED COORDINATE LIES OUTSIDE THE
VISIBLE AREA

PROBLEM: The X or Y coordinate is outside the display area as defined
by the HPOS= and VPOS= values.

CORRECTION: Check for an invalid or misspecified SYSTEM value, or data
outside displayed range.

ERROR: INTERNAL SYSTEM STACK OVERFLOW—TOO MANY
"PUSH" FUNCTIONS

PROBLEM: The limit of 100 stack positions has been exhausted. Each
PUSH operation uses one position; each POP frees one
position for re-use.

CORRECTION: Decrease number of stack-stored values.

ERROR: INTERNAL SYSTEM STACK UNDERFLOW—TOO MANY
"POP" FUNCTIONS

PROBLEM: POP has been issued with no values on the LIFO stack.

CORRECTION: Check for unequal numbers of PUSHs vs. POPs. At least
one PUSH must occur *before* a POP can be issued.

ERROR: "POLYCONT" ENCOUNTERED BEFORE "POLY"

PROBLEM: POLYCONT was encountered with no POLY specification.

CORRECTION: Probable sequencing error. Check for missing POLY
command, improper ordering of polygon points, or
interruption of POLY type commands by other valued
FUNCTIONS.

ERROR: "POLYCONT" INTERRUPTED

PROBLEM: A POLYCONT definition has been interrupted and resumed
in the ANNOTATE= data set. Usually accompanies the
error message "POLYCONT ENCOUNTERED BEFORE
POLY."

CORRECTION: Check data stream for proper order.

ERROR: USE THE XC VARIABLE FOR DATA VALUES WHEN TYPE IS
CHARACTER

PROBLEM: X is character type in ANNOTATE= data set.

CORRECTION: If character data are being plotted, use the XC variable to specify any data-related points pertaining to character values. If not character data, omit quotes in X data value assignment.

ERROR: USE THE YC VARIABLE FOR DATA VALUES WHEN TYPE IS CHARACTER

PROBLEM: Y is character type in ANNOTATE= data set.

CORRECTION: If character data are being plotted, use the YC variable to specify any data-related points pertaining to character values. If not character data, omit quotes in Y data value assignment.

ERROR: VARIABLE SHOWN IS NOT OF THE PROPER DATA TYPE

PROBLEM: Data type does not match required type for variable listed. Either variable type is character where a numeric is required, or numeric where a character is required.

CORRECTION: Specify proper type for variable as described in **ANNOTATE= VARIABLES**.

ERROR: CHARACTER VALUE SHOWN IS NOT ON THE HORIZONTAL AXIS

PROBLEM: The specified value of the XC variable is not on the X axis of the graph or chart. The point will not be plotted.

CORRECTION: Check for misspelling, for upper- or lowercase conflict, or for exclusion in an axis specification.

ERROR: CHARACTER VALUE SHOWN IS NOT ON THE VERTICAL AXIS

PROBLEM: The specified value of the YC variable does not occur on the Y axis of the graph or chart. The point will not be plotted.

CORRECTION: Check for misspelling, for upper- or lowercase conflict, or for exclusion in an axis specification.

ERROR: REQUESTED POLYGON CONTAINS TOO MANY VERTICES (OBSERVATIONS)

PROBLEM: Maximum allocation for polygon points exhausted.

CORRECTION: Define polygon with fewer points or break polygon into sections.

ERROR: MINIMUM VARIABLES NOT MET—MUST HAVE X/XC, Y/YC IN DATA SET

PROBLEM: X/XC and/or Y/YC was not found in the ANNOTATE= data set.

CORRECTION: X/XC and Y/YC must be in the data set. In the extreme case of a GPLOT dual character axis plot, specify X=. and Y=. to avoid this error. This is instituted as a minimum validity check of the supplied ANNOTATE= data set.

ERROR: A CALCULATED WINDOW COORDINATE LIES OUTSIDE THE WINDOW AREA

PROBLEM: This message may accompany the message for invalid SYSTEM specification.

CORRECTION: Verify requested SYSTEM values.

ERROR: CONFLICT BETWEEN PROCEDURE AXIS TYPE AND ANNOTATE DATA TYPE

PROBLEM: Axis type is character and X/Y coordinates are numeric or vice versa.

CORRECTION: Check values for proper type matching.

ERROR: VARIABLE SHOWN HAS IMPROPER LENGTH IN ANNOTATE= DATA SET

PROBLEM: Length is incorrect for variable indicated.

CORRECTION: Supply a LENGTH statement in the DATA step.

ERROR: DATA SYSTEM REQUESTED, BUT POINT IS NOT ON GRAPH

PROBLEM: Point specified is not on displayed graph and DATA system placement was requested.

CORRECTION: Check for improper specification of data value or graph axis parameters.

ERROR: LINE VALUE SPECIFIED IS NOT WITHIN LIMITS—1<=L<=46

PROBLEM: LINE value specified was not in the range 1–46.

CORRECTION: Check for improper specification of data value. Valid LINE values can be found in "Enhancing Your Graphics Output Designs."

ERROR: CALCULATED COORDINATES LIE COMPLETELY OFF THE VISIBLE AREA

PROBLEM: Both the X and Y coordinates supplied are lying off the visible screen area.

CORRECTION: Check for improper/inappropriate SYSTEM specification.

ERROR: VALUE SHOWN IS NOT A VALID FONT OR PATTERN TYPE

PROBLEM: Value is not a valid font or pattern.

CORRECTION: Check the value supplied for misspelling, truncation, and support in the FUNCTION description. Character fonts are described in "Enhancing Your Graphics Output Text." Patterns are more fully described in "Enhancing Your Graphics Output Designs."

ERROR: VALUE SHOWN IS NOT A VALID SIZE FACTOR

PROBLEM: SIZE value is negative or excessive.

CORRECTION: Check request or calculation for positive value result.

ERROR: G3D DATA SYSTEM REQUESTED, VARIABLE CONTAINED MISSING VALUE

PROBLEM: X, Y, or Z contained a missing value.

CORRECTION: All values in G3D data placement requests must be specified. Remove the missing value from the request.

ERROR: G3D DATA SYSTEM REQUESTED, ALL SYSTEMS NOT DATA DEPENDENT

PROBLEM: All requested XSYS, YSYS, and ZSYS values were not DATA.

CORRECTION: If one variable in G3D annotation is data dependent, all variables must be data dependent. Either specify all points in the DATA system or use another reference system value.

ERROR: ANNOTATE MIDPOINT DATATYPE DOES NOT MATCH GCHART—INPUT WAS #

PROBLEM: MIDPOINT was character and GCHART midpoint was numeric or vice versa.

CORRECTION: Check for misspelling or wrong variable assignment, or check for quotes in the assignment statement.

ERROR: ANNOTATE GROUP DATATYPE DOES NOT MATCH GCHART—INPUT WAS #

PROBLEM: GROUP was character and GCHART group was numeric or vice versa.

CORRECTION: Check for misspelling or wrong variable assignment, or check for quotes in the assignment statement.

ERROR: ANNOTATE SUBGROUP DATATYPE DOES NOT MATCH GCHART—INPUT WAS #

PROBLEM: SUBGROUP was character and GCHART subgroup was numeric or vice versa.

CORRECTION: Check for misspelling or wrong variable assignment, or check for quotes in the assignment statement.

ERROR: CANNOT HAVE MISSING GROUP VALUE IF GROUPS ARE PRESENT

PROBLEM: GROUP variable contains a missing value in GCHART annotation.

CORRECTION: If GROUP= is specified in the PROC GCHART statement, the Annotate GROUP variable cannot contain missing values. Remove the missing value from the request. Check reference system for data dependent request.

ERROR: DATA SYSTEM NOT SUPPORTED FOR THIS STATEMENT

PROBLEM: SYSTEMS 1,2,7,8 are not permitted for this statement.

CORRECTION: Choose a different reference system for this observation.

ERROR: CANNOT HAVE SUBGROUP AND X/Y MISSING IN GCHART STREAM

PROBLEM: DATA coordinate system requested and X/Y and SUBGROUP contain missing values.

CORRECTION: Either X/Y or SUBGROUP must be specified if DATA coordinate system was requested. Check stream for improper request.

ERROR: TEXT STRING EXTENDS BEYOND BOUNDARY OF SYSTEM DEFINED

PROBLEM: Text string is too long.

CORRECTION: Check for excessive SIZE value or shorten the string.

ERROR: LINE VALUE SPECIFIED IS NOT WITHIN LIMITS—
0<=L<=3

PROBLEM: Invalid special line value.

CORRECTION: LINE value specified was not acceptable. Check function for definition of line values or previous value used in DATA step prior to this observation.

ERROR: A PERCENTAGE VALUE LIES OUTSIDE 0 TO 100 BOUNDARIES

PROBLEM: Value requested is negative or greater than 100 percent.

CORRECTION: Informational message. Check requested value for accuracy.

ERROR: LABEL FUNCTION REQUESTED, BUT TEXT VARIABLE NOT ON DATA SET

PROBLEM: Possibly invalid/incorrect ANNOTATE= data set.

CORRECTION: If FUNCTION=LABEL, then TEXT variable must contain the string to be placed in the display area. Check for misspelling of variable name or wrong ANNOTATE= data set specified.

ERROR: CANNOT OMIT GROUP VARIABLE IF GCHART GROUPS ARE PRESENT

PROBLEM: You specified the GROUP= variable in PROC GCHART, but the ANNOTATE= data set did not contain the variable GROUP.

CORRECTION: Supply the variable GROUP in the ANNOTATE= data set.

ERROR: BOTH OLD AND NEW VARIABLE NAMES ENCOUNTERED IN ANNOTATE= DATA SET

PROBLEM: Variables named both MIDPOINT and MIDPNT or
             SUBGROUP and SUBGRP were found in the ANNOTATE=
             data set. The old spellings (MIDPNT and SUBGRP) are
             obsolete in Version 6 of SAS/GRAPH software, but they are
             accepted if they are the only spellings encountered.
             Otherwise, MIDPOINT and SUBGROUP are used.

CORRECTION: Determine which variable has the proper values for the
             ANNOTATE= data set and either delete the other variable
             or rename MIDPNT to MIDPOINT and SUBGRP to
             SUBGROUP.

ERROR: MINIMUM VARIABLES NOT MET—AMBIGUITY PREVENTS
             SELECTION.

PROBLEM: Combinations of available X, Y, XC, YC, GROUP,
             MIDPOINT, and SUBGROUP variables did not identify the
             data dependent values uniquely.

CORRECTION: Check variable requirements and respecify. **Figure 7.10**
             illustrates the different ways you can specify the same
             coordinate location when annotating with GCHART data
             dependent values.

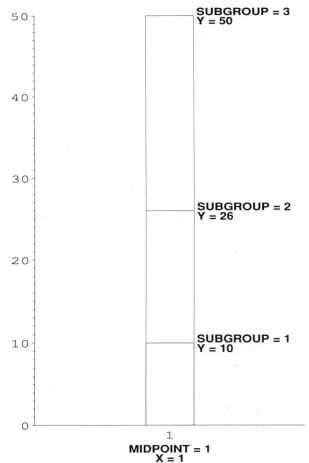

Figure 7.10   Specifying PROC GCHART Data Values in ANNOTATE=
                  Data Sets

Table 7.8 illustrates the possible specifications of data values in ANNOTATE= data sets and their corresponding PROC GCHART components. Note that DATA systems are not supported for STAR, PIE, and BLOCK statements in PROC GCHART.

Table 7.8   Data Values for ANNOTATE= and PROC GCHART Data Sets

STATEMENT	RESPONSE	GROUP		MIDPOINT		SUBGROUP	
	numeric	numeric	character	numeric	character	numeric	character
VBAR	Y	GROUP	GROUP	MIDPOINT X	MIDPOINT XC	SUBGROUP Y	SUBGROUP YC
HBAR	X	GROUP	GROUP	MIDPOINT Y	MIDPOINT YC	SUBGROUP X	SUBGROUP XC

The GANNO Procedure

ABSTRACT

The GANNO procedure displays graphs defined in ANNOTATE= data sets. It closely resembles PROC GSLIDE, but TITLE, FOOTNOTE, and NOTE statements are ignored.

INTRODUCTION

With PROC GANNO, you can produce separate graphs from the information contained in an ANNOTATE= data set. This capability is not available in other graphics procedures that support the ANNOTATE= option. For example, when you use the ANNOTATE= option in other procedures and specify the name of a SAS data set, the whole data set (rather than its separate parts) is reproduced. Because GANNO has no real data system, it is ideally suited for the WINDOW and SCREEN systems of the ANNOTATE= option.

SPECIFICATIONS

The only statement used is the PROC GANNO statement.

PROC GANNO ANNOTATE=*SASdataset options***;**

PROC GANNO Statement

PROC GANNO ANNOTATE=*SASdataset options;*

You can specify the following options in the PROC GANNO statement:

ANNOTATE=*SASdataset*
ANNO=*SASdataset*
   specifies a data set to be used for annotation. This data set must be an ANNOTATE= type data set containing the appropriate ANNOTATE= variables. See the chapter "ANNOTATE= Data Sets" for details. The ANNOTATE= option is required.

DATASYS
   indicates that Annotate data dependent coordinates occur in the input data set. PROC GANNO reads the input data set and creates a data

dependent environment based on the minimum and maximum values contained in the data set. You can save this extra pass of the data set by using data dependent values only in the procedures that currently support those system specifications. Annotate coordinate system '5', the WINDOW system, is recommended for use with PROC GANNO. (See the section on the XSYS/YSYS variables in the chapter "ANNOTATE= Data Sets.")

DESCRIPTION=*'string'*
DES=*'string'*

specifies a descriptive string, up to forty characters long, that appears in the Description field of PROC GREPLAY's master menu. If you omit the DESCRIPTION= option, the Description field of PROC GREPLAY's master menu reads "OUTPUT FROM PROC GANNO."

GOUT=*SAScatalog*

specifies the SAS catalog in which to place the output from the procedure. (See "SAS/GRAPH Graphics Output" for a complete description of SAS catalogs.) If you do not specify the GOUT= option, catalog entries are written to the default catalog GSEG, which is erased at the end of your session.

NAME=*'string'*

specifies a descriptive string, up to eight characters long, that appears in the Name field of PROC GREPLAY's master menu. If you omit the NAME= option, the Name field of PROC GREPLAY's master menu contains the procedure name.

NAME=*variable*

specifies that a separate graph is produced for each discrete value of the variable. This produces results similar to those of a BY statement. For more information, see "SAS Statements Used in the PROC Step" in the *SAS Language Guide, Release 6.03 Edition*. You should specify a character variable of length eight or less. No distinction is made between upper- and lowercase. Each value of the variable will appear on consecutive lines in the name field of PROC GREPLAY's master menu.

EXAMPLE

The following example illustrates the use of PROC GANNO. The data set SQUARES contains the commands needed to create four squares. The first PROC GANNO statement uses the ANNOTATE= option to display the entire contents of the ANNOTATE= data set. The NAME= option specifies the string SQUARES to be used with PROC GREPLAY. The second PROC GANNO statement uses the NAME= option to produce a separate graph for each color value.

These statements produce **Output 8.1**, **8.2a**, **8.2b**, **8.2c**, and **8.2d**.

```
data squares;
   length function style color $ 8;
   xsys='5'; ysys='5';
   style='solid';

   color='magenta';
   function='move'; x=10; y=10; output;
   function='bar';  x=30; y=40; output;
```

```
        color='cyan';
        function='move'; x=60; y=10; output;
        function='bar';  x=80; y=40; output;

        color='green';
        function='move'; x=10; y=60; output;
        function='bar';  x=30; y=90; output;

        color='white';
        function='move'; x=60; y=60; output;
        function='bar';  x=80; y=90; output;
run;

proc ganno anno=squares
        name='squares'
        gout=ganno1
        description='Four colored squares';
run;

proc ganno anno=squares
        name=color
        gout=ganno2
        description='Individual squares';
run;
```

Output 8.1   Four Colored Squares Generated by PROC GANNO

Output 8.2a   Cyan Square Generated by PROC GANNO with the
NAME= Option

Output 8.2b   Green Square Generated by PROC GANNO with the NAME= Option

Output 8.2c   Magenta Square Generated by PROC GANNO with the NAME= Option

Output 8.2d   White Square Generated by PROC GANNO with the
NAME= Option

Chapter 9

The GCHART
Procedure

ABSTRACT

The GCHART procedure produces vertical and horizontal bar charts (also called histograms), and block, pie, and star charts. You can use these charts to represent pictorially a given variable value or the relationship between two or more variables.

INTRODUCTION

The GCHART procedure is the SAS/GRAPH version of the CHART procedure described in *SAS Procedures Guide, Release 6.03 Edition*. PROC GCHART produces charts for both numeric and character variables. Character variables are truncated to a length of sixteen. For continuous numeric variables, PROC GCHART automatically selects display intervals, or you can explicitly define interval midpoints. For character variables and discrete numeric variables that contain several distinct values rather than a continuous range, the data values themselves define the intervals.

PROC GCHART can summarize several kinds of descriptive statistics. Data are collected into interval levels defined by the midpoints. You can specify midpoints with the MIDPOINTS= option (see below). Six types of statistics can be collected for each midpoint. Examples of charts summarizing these statistics are in the **EXAMPLES** section.

- Frequency counts: the number of observations contained in each midpoint level (see **Output 9.1**).
- Cumulative frequency counts: the number of observations at a specific midpoint level, including observations from all preceding midpoint levels (see **Output 9.4**).
- Percentages: the number obtained when you divide each interval level frequency by the total number of scores, and multiply the result by 100 (see **Output 9.3**).
- Cumulative percentages: the number obtained when you divide each interval level frequency by the total number of scores, multiply the result by 100, and include the percentages from all preceding midpoint levels (see **Output 9.5**).
- Sums: the midpoint value is derived from another variable in the data (specified by SUMVAR=) (see **Output 9.6**).
- Means: the number obtained when you sum a list of score values and divide by the number of scores used in the calculation (see **Output 9.7**).

Each of the above statistics is referred to as the *response value* in this chapter. **Figure 9.1** illustrates the terms *response axis* and *midpoint axis*.

PROC GCHART VBAR Terms

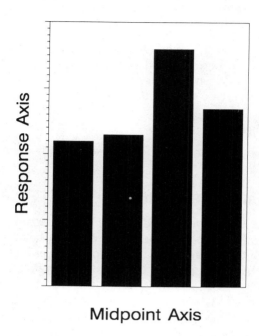

Figure 9.1 The Response Axis and the Midpoint Axis

Available Charts

You can produce bar, block, pie, and star charts with PROC GCHART. A brief description of each chart type is provided below.

Horizontal Bar Charts

Horizontal bar charts show relationships between various midpoint levels. The table of values drawn by default to the side of the bars (see **Output 9.2**) makes these charts very useful for exploratory data analysis. Each bar can also be divided into subgroups representing a variable other than the variable used with the midpoint levels. Each unique value of the subgroup variable is represented as a bar section (see **Output 9.20**). The bars can also be organized into groups according to a group variable. Each unique value of the group variable creates a group of bars containing one bar for each midpoint level (see **Output 9.19**).

Vertical Bar Charts

You can use vertical bar charts much like horizontal bar charts except that statistics are not included for each bar (see **Output 9.1**). The bars can be divided into subgroups and organized into groups just as in horizontal bar charts (see **Output 9.22**).

Block Charts

You can use block charts much like horizontal and vertical bar charts, but block charts add an extra visual dimension. Each midpoint level is represented by a column of blocks with the value of the statistic drawn at the bottom of each block (see **Output 9.23**). The blocks may be divided into subgroups similar to bar charts (see **Output 9.24**). If you use a group variable with a block chart, each unique value of the group variable is represented by a row of blocks (see **Output 9.25**).

Pie Charts

You can use pie charts when comparing the relationship between the parts and the whole, as in a market-share analysis. If a group variable is used with a pie chart, one pie is produced for each unique value of the group variable. (By default one pie is drawn per page.) Optionally, the group pies can be combined on a single page (see **Output 9.27**).

Star Charts

You can use star charts to represent multivariate data. See **Output 9.28** for an example of a star chart.

Introductory Examples

To give you an idea of PROC GCHART's capabilities, the kinds of charts that you can produce are described below. If you have a specific chart in mind, glance through the following examples for a similar one. Many other charts can be produced by combining the options. You can find more examples in the **EXAMPLES** section. All the examples and data are in the Sample Library provided with SAS/GRAPH software. Check with your SAS Software Consultant to find out how to access the Sample Library.

Frequency Bar Charts

When you want to divide your data into groups based on the values of a variable, frequency bar charts are useful. For example, perhaps you have a data set containing information about employees. You want to produce a bar chart comparing the total number of male employees with the total number of female employees. This chart is a frequency chart because it shows the number of employees (observations) of each gender. The following statements produce the vertical frequency bar chart shown in **Output 9.1**.

```
title 'Number of Male and Female Employees';
proc gchart;
   vbar gender;
```

At the bottom of the chart are the two values of GENDER, F and M. The vertical axis represents the number of observations in the data set containing the value; seventy-five of the employees are females and ninety-seven are males.

   If you prefer a horizontal bar chart, use the HBAR statement instead of the VBAR statement. You can use the keyword HBAR in any of the following examples instead of VBAR. The following statements produce the horizontal frequency bar chart shown in **Output 9.2**.

```
title 'Number of Male and Female Employees';
proc gchart;
   hbar gender;
```

Percentage Bar Charts

These charts are useful for showing what percentage of the observations falls into different groups. For example, you can show the percentage of employees of each gender. The TYPE=PERCENT option produces the percentage bar chart. The first two examples used the default pattern for the bars. In this example, a

PATTERN statement is specified to create graphs with solid bars in selected colors. The following examples also use the F= option of the TITLE statement so that the titles are drawn in the SWISS font. The following statements produce the percentage bar chart shown in **Output 9.3**.

```
title f=swiss 'Percent of Male and Female Employees';
pattern v=s c=gold;
proc gchart;
   vbar gender / type=percent;
```

Cumulative Frequency Charts

Sometimes you want a cumulative frequency chart where each bar represents the frequency of a given value plus the frequencies of all the values to its left in the chart. For example, using the data set containing employee information, you may want to show how many employees have not attended college. The TYPE=CFREQ option produces the cumulative frequency chart. Notice that the MIDPOINTS= option is used to order the bars (the default order for a character variable is alphabetical). The FRAME option is used to enclose the axis area. The last new part of this example is the use of two TITLE statements. In the TITLE2 statement, the H=2 option is used so that the titles will be the same height. (The default height for the first title is 2 units and for all others 1 unit.) The following statements produce the cumulative frequency bar chart shown in **Output 9.4**.

```
title1 f=swiss 'Number of Employees';
title2 f=swiss h=2 'in Increasing Education Levels';
pattern v=s c=gold;
proc gchart;
   vbar educ / type=cfreq frame
             midpoints='8TH' 'SOME HS' 'HS GRAD'
             'SOME COLL' 'COLL GRAD';
```

Cumulative Percentage Charts

The bars of a cumulative percentage chart represent the percentage of the observations having a given value plus the percentages of all the values appearing to the left in the chart.

For example, suppose you want to represent the educational attainments of the employees in terms of percentages rather than frequencies. The TYPE=CPERCENT option produces the cumulative percentage chart. Notice that when you have a long label such as CUMULATIVE PERCENT or CUMULATIVE FREQUENCY, PROC GCHART turns the label vertically. The following statements produce the cumulative percentage bar chart shown in **Output 9.5**.

```
title1 f=swiss 'Number of Employees';
title2 f=swiss h=2 'in Increasing Education Levels';
pattern v=s c=gold;
proc gchart;
   vbar educ / type=cpercent frame
             midpoints='8TH' 'SOME HS' 'HS GRAD'
                  'SOME COLL' 'COLL GRAD';
```

Bar Charts of Totals

These charts are similar to the frequency and percentage charts described above, but the vertical axis represents the totals for another variable in the data set instead of frequencies or percentages. This variable is usually a continuous variable, such as SALES.

Suppose you have a data set that consists of twelve observations for each department. Each observation contains DEPT, the chart variable that identifies the department, and the variable SALES, which gives each department's sales for one of the three years. Suppose you want to see the total sales for all the years for each department. You use the SUMVAR= option to specify SALES as the sum variable because you want the sum of each department's yearly sales for the chart. The following statements produce the bar chart of totals shown in **Output 9.6**.

```
title1 f=swiss 'Total Sales in Each Department';
title2 f=swiss h=2 'for the Years 1985-1987';
pattern v=s c=gold;
proc gchart;
   vbar dept / sumvar=sales frame;
```

Suppose you have one observation per department. You already have each department's total sales and want to display them. For example, say your data set consists of three observations, each giving the total sales for one of the three departments. You can use exactly the same statements as above:

```
proc gchart;
   vbar dept / sumvar=sales frame;
```

Although PROC GCHART does not need to total the SALES values, they do represent a sum, and so SUMVAR=SALES is the correct option to use. You can use this technique to present any value that has been entered as the value of a variable, such as a mean, standard deviation, or percentage.

Bar Charts of Means

Bar charts of means are like the bar chart of totals described above. However, the vertical axis represents the mean of another variable rather than the sum. For example, to show each department's average yearly sales, use these statements to produce a bar chart for means. The bar chart is shown in **Output 9.7**.

```
title1 f=swiss 'Average Sales in Each Department';
title2 f=swiss h=2 'for the Years 1985-1987';
pattern v=s c=gold;
proc gchart;
   vbar dept / type=mean sumvar=sales frame;
```

Subdividing the Bars

You can show the distribution of a second variable by using the SUBGROUP= option to divide the bars. For example, suppose you want to compare the number of males and females in each of the three departments. You can specify that PROC GCHART subdivide the bars by gender. You can also specify two PATTERN statements to distinguish between the two values of GENDER. The part of the bars representing F will be in the first pattern and the part representing M in the second pattern. See the **DETAILS** section for more information on how subgroups are selected and ordered. A vertical bar chart with the SUBGROUP= option produces a subdivided chart with the following statements. The bar chart is shown in **Output 9.8**.

```
title1 f=swiss 'Number of Males and Females';
title2 f=swiss h=2 'in Each Department';
pattern1 v=s c=gold;
pattern2 v=s c=cream;
```

```
proc gchart;
   vbar dept / subgroup=gender frame;
```

From **Output 9.8**, you can see that females represent about one-third of the PARTS employees, very few of the REPAIRS employees, and about one-fifth of the TOOLS employees.

You can use other options in addition to SUBGROUP= to produce more complicated charts. For example, suppose you want to compare the sales figures for each of the three departments over the past three years. Your data set contains nine observations, each having values of the variables YEAR, DEPT, and SALES. As shown in the following statements, use both the SUBGROUP= and SUMVAR= options to produce the chart shown in **Output 9.9**.

```
title f=swiss 'Department Sales for the Years 1985-1987';
pattern1 v=s c=gold;
pattern2 v=s c=cream;
pattern3 v=s c=styg;
proc gchart;
   vbar year / sumvar=sales subgroup=dept discrete frame;
```

You need the DISCRETE option to display three distinct YEAR values. When you omit the DISCRETE option for a numeric variable, the procedure divides the values into intervals. If YEAR had been a character variable, you could have omitted the DISCRETE option.

Side-by-side Charts

Another way to compare quantities is with side-by-side charts. You can show the same information as in the last example; that is, total sales for the three departments over the past three years, with the GROUP= option. In this example, YEAR has become the group variable and DEPT is now the midpoint variable instead of the subgroup variable. Compare **Output 9.9** with **Output 9.10** to see the difference between using the SUBGROUP= and the GROUP= options.

```
title f=swiss 'Department Sales for the Years 1985-1987';
pattern1 v=s c=gold;
proc gchart;
   vbar dept / sumvar=sales group=year;
```

Block Charts

You can also show the sales information by department for each year with a block chart. Block charts look like city blocks with a building drawn in each block. You can represent the frequency, mean, or sum by the height of the building. Use the following statements to produce the block chart shown in **Output 9.11**. The block chart displays the same total sales as the vertical bar charts shown in **Output 9.9** and **Output 9.10**.

```
title f=swiss 'Department Sales for the Years 1985-1987';
pattern1 v=s c=gold;
proc gchart;
   block dept / sumvar=sales group=year;
   format sales dollar6.0;
```

Pie Charts

You can use the GCHART procedure to draw a pie chart representing the distribution of a variable's values. In an example above, you wanted to show the total sales for each department over the three-year period. Use these statements to produce a pie chart that shows the same information. The pie chart is shown in **Output 9.12**.

```
title f=swiss 'Department Sales for the Years 1985-1987';
proc gchart;
   pie dept / sumvar=sales;
   format sales dollar7.0;
```

Star Charts

You can produce star charts showing group frequencies, totals, or means with PROC GCHART. See **Output 9.28** in the **EXAMPLES** section for an example of a star chart.

Output 9.1   A Vertical Frequency Bar Chart

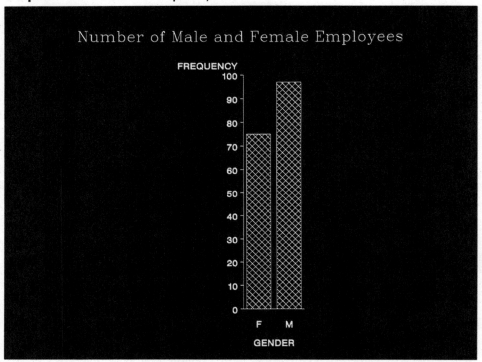

Output 9.2   A Horizontal Frequency Bar Chart

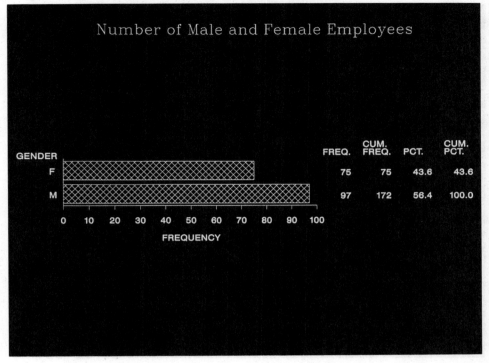

Output 9.3   A Percentage Bar Chart

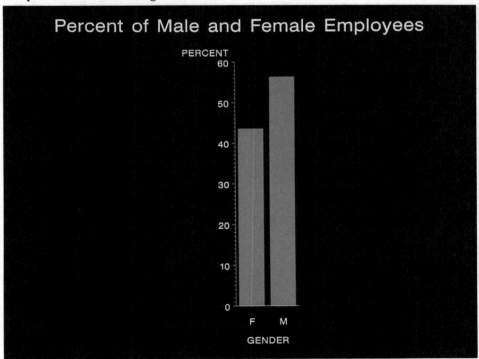

Output 9.4   A Cumulative Frequency Bar Chart

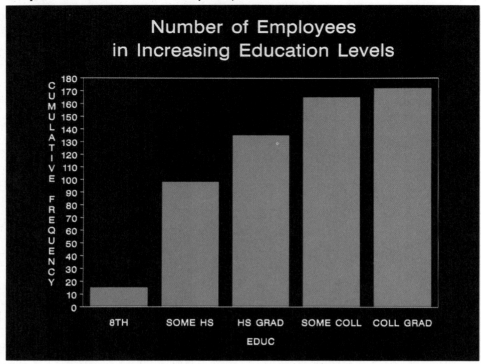

Output 9.5   A Cumulative Percentage Bar Chart

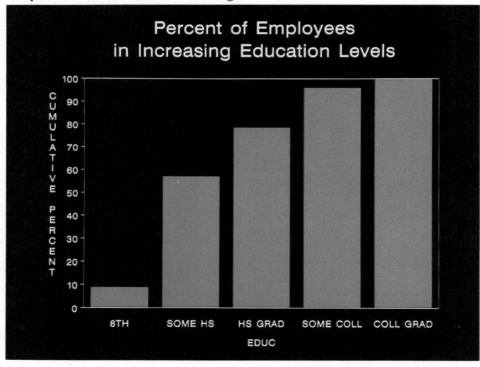

Output 9.6   A Bar Chart of Totals

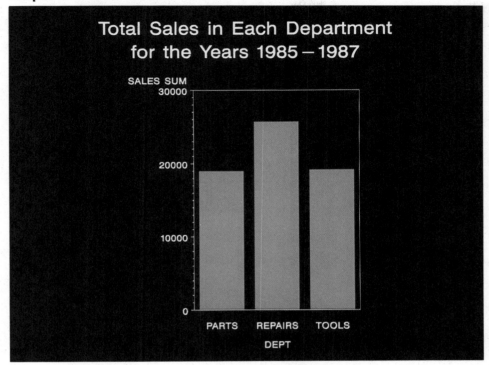

Output 9.7   A Bar Chart of Means

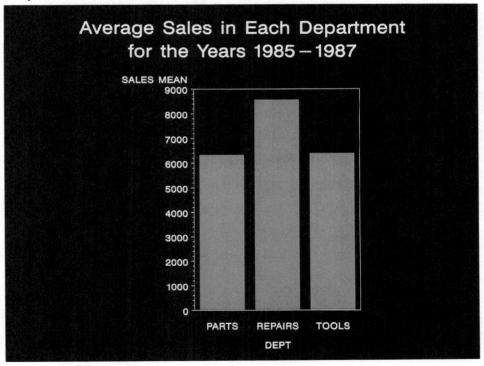

Output 9.8   A Subdivided Bar Chart

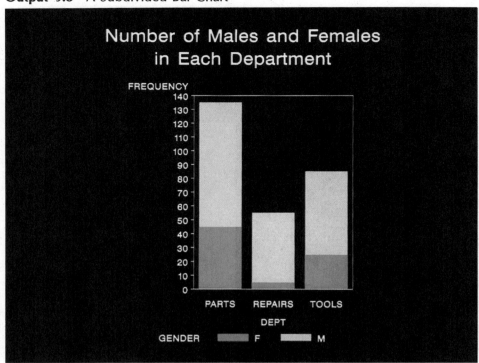

Output 9.9   Using the SUBGROUP= and SUMVAR= Options

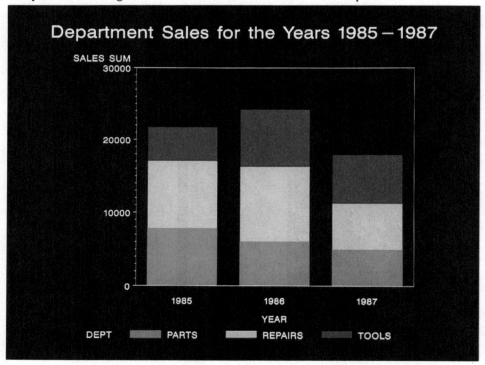

Output 9.10 A Side-by-side Bar Chart

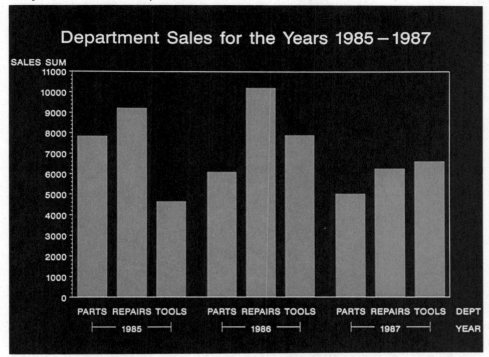

Output 9.11 A Block Chart

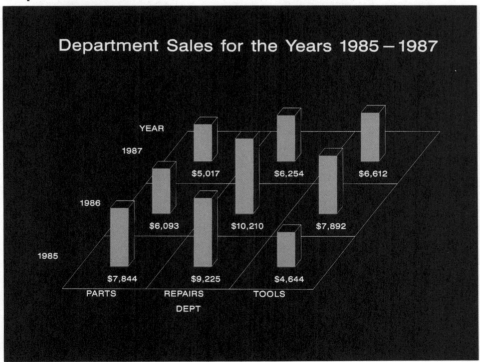

Output 9.12   A Pie Chart

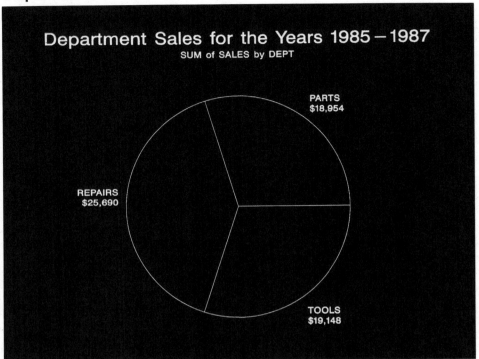

SPECIFICATIONS

The following statements are used with the GCHART procedure:

> **PROC GCHART** *options*;
>   **HBAR** *variables . . . / options*;
>   **VBAR** *variables . . . / options*;
>   **BLOCK** *variables / options*;
>   **PIE** *variables . . . / options*;
>   **STAR** *variables . . . / options*;
>   **AXIS***n options*;
>   **BY** *variables*;
>   **LEGEND***n options*;
>   **PATTERN***n options*;
>   **TITLE***n options 'text'*;
>   **FOOTNOTE***n options 'text'*;
>   **NOTE** *options 'text'*;

PROC GCHART Statement

PROC GCHART *options*;

You can specify the following options in the PROC GCHART statement:

ANNOTATE=*SASdataset*
> specifies the data set to be used for annotation. This data set must be an
> ANNOTATE= type data set containing the appropriate Annotate
> variables. (See "ANNOTATE= Data Sets" for details.)

DATA=*SASdataset*

gives the name of the SAS data set to be used by PROC GCHART. If you omit the DATA= option, PROC GCHART uses the most recently created SAS data set.

GOUT=*SAScatalog*

specifies the name of the SAS catalog used to save the output produced by PROC GCHART for later replay. See "The GREPLAY Procedure" for more details. If you do not specify the GOUT= option, catalog entries are written to the default catalog GSEG, which is erased at the end of your session.

AXIS Statement

AXIS*n options*;

You can use AXIS statements in PROC GCHART. For more information on AXIS statements, see "Enhancing Your Graphics Output Designs."

BLOCK Statement

BLOCK *variables / options*;

The BLOCK statement produces a chart that looks like a map divided into blocks. A three-dimensional building is drawn in each block for each variable listed. For example, the following statements produce a block chart for the variable CITY:

```
proc gchart;
    block city / sumvar=revenue;
```

For each value of CITY, PROC GCHART draws a three-dimensional building whose height represents the sum of the values of REVENUE.

The following options can appear in a BLOCK statement after a slash (/):

ANNOTATE=*SASdataset*

specifies the data set to be used for annotation. This data set must be an ANNOTATE= type data set containing the appropriate Annotate variables. (See "ANNOTATE= Data Sets" for details.)

BLOCKMAX=*n*

scales the blocks as if the tallest one had a value of *n*. If a BY statement also appears, uniform scaling is used over BY groups.

CAXIS=*color*

specifies the color to use for drawing the axes for block charts. If you do not specify CAXIS=, the first color in the COLORS= list is used to draw the axes. (See the description of the COLORS= option in "The GOPTIONS Statement.")

COUTLINE=*color*

specifies the color used to outline the front of the blocks.

CTEXT=*color*

specifies the color to use for drawing all text that appears on the chart. Variable names, labels, if any, and midpoint values are drawn using the color specified by the CTEXT= option. If you do not specify the CTEXT= option, the value you specified for the CTEXT= option in a GOPTIONS statement is used.

DESCRIPTION=*'string'*
DES=*'string'*

specifies a descriptive string, up to forty characters long, that appears in the Description field of PROC GREPLAY's master menu. If you omit the

DESCRIPTION= option, the Description field contains a description assigned by SAS/GRAPH.

DISCRETE

indicates that the numeric variables on the midpoint axis are discrete rather than continuous. This means that there will be a midpoint value for each unique value of the midpoint variable.

See **DETAILS** for more information on midpoint selection.

FREQ=_variable_

indicates that a variable in the data set represents a count (or weight) for each observation. Normally, each observation contributes a value of 1 to the frequency counts. When the FREQ= option appears, each observation contributes the FREQ= variable's value. If the FREQ= variable's values are not integers, they are truncated to integers. If the values are missing or negative, the contribution is zero.

G100

forces the bars to total 100 percent for each group and is used in conjunction with the GROUP= option.

GROUP=_variable_

specifies the variable used to break the data into groups. In a block chart, each group appears on its own row, one behind another. For example, the following statements produce a block chart for males and females in each department:

```
proc gchart;
    block gender / group=dept;
```

Missing values for a GROUP= variable are treated as a valid level, and a chart is produced.

LEGEND=LEGEND_n_

specifies the LEGEND statement to associate with the graph, where _n_ is the number of a LEGEND statement defined previously.

Use the LEGEND= option only if the graph requested normally produces a legend. A legend is drawn if you specify the SUBGROUP= option. Simply specifying LEGEND= in the HBAR statement does not cause a legend to be generated.

LEVELS=_n_

specifies the number of bars representing each variable when the variables given in the BLOCK statement are continuous. See **DETAILS** for more information.

MIDPOINTS=_values_
MIDPOINTS=OLD

defines the range each block represents by specifying the range midpoints. For example, the following statements produce a chart with five blocks: the first block represents the range of data values with a midpoint of 10; the second block represents the range of data values with a midpoint of 20; and so on.

```
proc gchart;
    block x / midpoints=10 20 30 40 50;
```

Numeric MIDPOINTS lists of the following form are also acceptable:

```
midpoints=10 to 100 by 5
```

For character variables, you can specify MIDPOINTS= values in any order. This is useful in ordering the blocks or in specifying a subset of the possible values. For example, a list of the following form can be used:

```
midpoints='jan' 'feb' 'mar'
```

If you specify MIDPOINTS=OLD, the midpoint selection algorithm used in Version 82.4 and Version 5 of SAS/GRAPH software is used. See the **DETAILS** section for more information.

MISSING
includes missing values as a valid level for the midpoint variable.

NAME='*string*'
where '*string*' specifies a descriptive string, up to eight characters long, that appears in the Name field of PROC GREPLAY's master menu. If you omit the NAME= option, the Name field of PROC GREPLAY's master menu contains the name of the procedure.

NOLEGEND
suppresses the drawing of the subgroup legend below block charts.

PATTERNID=*method*
specifies the chart variable that controls the change in pattern. Valid values for *method* are SUBGROUP, GROUP, MIDPOINT, and BY. If you specify PATTERNID=SUBGROUP, the pattern changes every time the SUBGROUP value changes. If you specify PATTERNID=GROUP, the pattern changes every time the GROUP value changes. If you specify PATTERNID=MIDPOINT, the pattern changes every time the MIDPOINT value changes. The default is PATTERNID=SUBGROUP. See the section **Controlling Patterns and Colors in Horizontal Bar, Vertical Bar, and Block Charts** for more information.

SUBGROUP=*variable*
specifies that the contribution of each value of the SUBGROUP= variable should be represented by a separate pattern. For example, the following statements produce a chart with one block for each department:

```
proc gchart;
   block dept / subgroup=gender;
```

Each block represents all the observations with a certain DEPT value. Each block is subdivided into as many parts as there are SUBGROUP= variable values.

The pattern and color used to shade each portion of the block are determined by the PATTERN statements given. (See "Enhancing Your Graphics Output Designs" for more information on PATTERN statements.) If no PATTERN statements are in effect when SUBGROUP= is specified, default patterns and colors are used to subdivide blocks.

SUMVAR=*variable*
represents sums or means of the specified variable. The SUMVAR= option is useful for producing bar charts showing variable means at each level of an experiment or for showing such quantities as total expenditures for each department. For example, the following

statements produce a chart showing the mean yield for each location:

```
proc gchart;
    block location / type=mean sumvar=yield;
```

In another example, the following statements chart total expenditures per department:

```
proc gchart;
    block dept / sumvar=expend;
```

TYPE=FREQ
TYPE=CFREQ
TYPE=PERCENT | PCT
TYPE=CPERCENT | CPCT
TYPE=SUM
TYPE=MEAN

specify the statistic that the blocks in the chart represent. If the TYPE= option is omitted, the default TYPE= value is FREQ except when SUMVAR= is specified, in which case the default TYPE= value is SUM. If you want to use a response variable with a TYPE= value other than SUM or MEAN, use the FREQ= option rather than the SUMVAR= option. If you specify TYPE=FREQ, each block represents the frequency with which a value (or range) occurs in the data. If you specify TYPE=CFREQ, each block represents the frequency of a value or range, plus the frequencies of the blocks before it. If you specify TYPE=PERCENT, each block represents the percentage of observations in the data having a given value (or falling into a given range). If you specify TYPE=CPERCENT, each block represents the percentage of observations in the data having a given value, plus the percentages of the blocks before it. If you specify TYPE=SUM, each block represents the sum of the SUMVAR= variable for observations having the block's value. The TYPE=SUM option is used in conjunction with the SUMVAR= option. For example, the following statements produce a chart with one block for each DEPT value.

```
proc gchart;
    block dept / sumvar=sales;
```

The block height for a given DEPT corresponds to the total of the SALES values for observations having that DEPT value. If you specify TYPE=MEAN, each block represents the mean of the SUMVAR= variable for observations having the block's value. See **Available Charts** for more information.

BY Statement

BY *variables*;

You can specify the BY statement with PROC GCHART to obtain separate analyses on observations defined by the BY variables. When a BY statement appears, the procedure expects the input data set to be sorted in order of the BY variables. If your input data set is not sorted in ascending order, use the SORT procedure with a similar BY statement to sort the data, or, if appropriate, use the BY statement options NOTSORTED or DESCENDING. For more information, see the discussion of the BY statement in the chapter "SAS Statements Used in the PROC Step" in the *SAS Language Guide, Release 6.03 Edition*.

FOOTNOTE Statement

FOOTNOTE*n options 'text'*;

You can use FOOTNOTE statements with PROC GCHART. They are described in detail in the chapter "Enhancing Your Graphics Output Text."

HBAR Statement

HBAR *variables . . . / options*;

You can use an HBAR statement to request a horizontal bar chart for each variable listed. For example, these statements produce three horizontal bar charts:

```
proc gchart;
   hbar a x1 x2;
```

Each chart occupies one page. Along the horizontal axis, PROC GCHART describes the kind of chart: frequency, cumulative frequency, percentage, cumulative percentage, sum, or mean. On the vertical axis beside each bar, PROC GCHART draws a value. For character variables or discrete numeric variables, these values are the actual values represented by the bar. For continuous numeric variables, the value gives the midrange of the interval represented by the bar.

PROC GCHART automatically scales the horizontal axis, determines the bar width, and chooses spacing between the bars. However, you can specify options to override the defaults and to choose bar intervals and the number of bars, to include missing values in the chart, and to subdivide the bars.

In addition, the HBAR statement writes the values of the statistics requested to the side of the chart. This is especially useful when you want to become more familiar with your data to determine the best way to analyze them.

The options below can appear in an HBAR statement following a slash (/):

ANNOTATE=*SASdataset*
   specifies the data set to be used for annotation. This data set must be an ANNOTATE= type data set containing the appropriate Annotate variables. (See "ANNOTATE= Data Sets" for details.)

ASCENDING
   draws the bars and any associated statistics in ascending order of response value within groups.

AUTOREF
   draws a reference line at each major tick mark on the response (horizontal) axis.

CAXIS=*color*
   specifies the color to use for drawing the axes for horizontal bar charts. If you do not specify CAXIS=, the first color in the COLORS= list is used to draw the axes. (See the description of the COLORS= option in "The GOPTIONS Statement.") If you do specify a color with the CAXIS= option, it overrides any axis color specified in an AXIS statement.

CFRAME=*color*
CFR=*color*
   specifies the color used to fill the axis area. If you specify the CFRAME= option, you do not need to specify the FRAME option.

COUTLINE=*color*
   specifies the color used to outline the bars.

CTEXT=*color*

specifies the color to use for drawing all text that appears on the chart. Variable names, labels (if any), and midpoint values are drawn using the color specified by the CTEXT= option. If you do not specify the CTEXT= option in the HBAR statement, the value you specified for CTEXT= in a GOPTIONS statement is used for drawing text. A color specified with the CTEXT= option overrides the AXIS statement COLOR= option, but not the C= option of the LABEL= or VALUE= options in an AXIS or LEGEND statement.

DESCENDING

draws the bars and any associated statistics in descending order of response value within groups.

DESCRIPTION=*'string'*
DES=*'string'*

specifies a descriptive string, up to forty characters long, that appears in the Description field of PROC GREPLAY's master menu. If you omit the DESCRIPTION= option, the Description field contains a description assigned by SAS/GRAPH.

DISCRETE

indicates that the numeric variables on the midpoint axes are discrete rather than continuous. This means that there will be a midpoint value for each unique value of the midpoint variable. See **DETAILS** for more information on midpoint selection.

FRAME
FR

specifies that the axis area be outlined in the color of the axis. If you do not specify FRAME, the axis area is not outlined.

FREQ=*variable*

indicates that a variable in the data set represents a count (or weight) for each observation. Normally, each observation contributes a value of 1 to the frequency counts. When the FREQ= option appears, each observation contributes the FREQ= variable's value. If the FREQ= variable's values are not integers, they are truncated to integers. If the values are missing or negative, the contribution is zero.

FREQ
CFREQ
PERCENT
CPERCENT
SUM
MEAN

specify the statistic you want drawn on a horizontal bar chart. You must specify the SUMVAR= option if you want the SUM or MEAN to be drawn.

G100

is used in conjunction with the GROUP= option and forces the bars to total 100 percent for each group.

GAXIS=AXIS*n*

specifies which axis description to use for the group axis, where *n* refers to an AXIS statement defined previously. The AXIS statement used for the group variable ignores the ORDER=, MAJOR=, and MINOR= options.

GROUP=*variable*

specifies the variable used to break the data into groups. In a horizontal bar chart, the groups appear one under another. For example, the following statements produce a frequency bar chart for males and females in each department:

```
proc gchart;
    hbar gender / group=dept;
```

Missing values for a GROUP= variable are treated as a valid level, and a chart is produced.

GSPACE=*n*

specifies the amount of extra space, in character cells, to leave between groups of bars in a horizontal bar chart. The GROUP= option must also be specified.

LEGEND=LEGEND*n*

specifies the LEGEND statement to associate with the graph, where *n* is the number of a LEGEND statement defined previously.

Use the LEGEND= option only if the graph requested normally produces a legend. A legend is drawn only if you specify the SUBGROUP= option. Simply specifying LEGEND= in the HBAR statement does not cause a legend to be generated.

LEVELS=*number*

specifies the number of bars representing each variable when the variables given in the HBAR statement are continuous. See **DETAILS** for additional information.

MAXIS=AXIS*n*

specifies which axis description to use for the midpoint axis, where *n* refers to an AXIS statement defined previously. The AXIS statement used for the midpoint variable ignores the MAJOR= and MINOR= options.

MIDPOINTS=*values*
MIDPOINTS=OLD

defines the range each bar represents by specifying the range midpoints. For example, the following statements produce a chart with five bars: the first bar represents the range of data values with a midpoint of 10; the second bar represents the range of data values with a midpoint of 20; and so on.

```
proc gchart;
    hbar x / midpoints=10 20 30 40 50;
```

Numeric MIDPOINTS lists of the following form are also acceptable:

```
midpoints=10 to 100 by 5
```

For character variables, MIDPOINTS= values can be specified in any order. This is useful in ordering the bars or in specifying a subset of the possible values. For example, a list of the following form can be used:

```
midpoints='jan' 'feb' 'mar'
```

If you specify MIDPOINTS=OLD, the midpoint selection algorithm used in Version 82.4 and Version 5 of SAS/GRAPH software is used. See **DETAILS** for more information.

MINOR=*n*

specifies the number of minor tick marks to be drawn between each major tick mark on the response axis.

MISSING
includes missing values as a valid level for the midpoint variable.

NAME='*string*'
where '*string*' specifies a descriptive string, up to eight characters long, that appears in the Name field of PROC GREPLAY's master menu. If you omit the NAME= option, the Name field of PROC GREPLAY's master menu contains the name of the procedure.

NOAXIS
NOAXES
suppresses the drawing of the axes.

NOSTATS
indicates that statistics are not to be included on your horizontal bar chart.

By default, when you specify TYPE= FREQ, CFREQ, PCT, or CPCT, the frequency, cumulative frequency, percent, and cumulative percent statistics, respectively, are included beside each bar. When TYPE=MEAN is requested, frequencies and means are included; when TYPE=SUM is requested, frequencies and sums are included unless the frequencies are all 1, in which case only the mean or sum is included.

NOSYMBOL
NOLEGEND
suppress the drawing of the subgroup symbol or legend below horizontal bar charts.

NOZEROS
specifies not to draw zero frequency midpoints.

PATTERNID=*method*
specifies the chart variable that controls the change in pattern. Valid values for *method* are SUBGROUP, GROUP, MIDPOINT, and BY. If you specify PATTERNID=SUBGROUP, the pattern changes every time the SUBGROUP value changes. If you specify PATTERNID=GROUP, the pattern changes every time the GROUP value changes. If you specify PATTERNID=MIDPOINT, the pattern changes every time the MIDPOINT value changes. If you specify PATTERNID=BY, the pattern changes every time the BY value changes. The default is PATTERNID=SUBGROUP. See **Controlling Patterns and Colors in Horizontal Bar, Vertical Bar, and Block Charts** for more information.

AXIS=*values*
AXIS=AXIS*n*
RAXIS=*values*
RAXIS=AXIS*n*
specifies the maximum value to use in constructing the response axis or an AXIS statement to be associated with the axis. If the horizontal bar chart is of TYPE=SUM or TYPE=MEAN, and if any of the sums or means are less than zero, then you can also specify a negative minimum value with the AXIS= option. Otherwise, a minimum value of zero is always assumed. Counts or percentages outside the maximum (or minimum) go only as far as the values specified in the AXIS= option. If you specify both the AXIS= option and a BY statement, uniform axes are produced over BY groups.

The AXIS= option can include a range of values to be used for tick marks on the response axis. Below are some examples of AXIS= specifications and the tick marks they produce.

Specification	Tick marks
`raxis=10 to 100 by 10`	10, 20, 30...100
`raxis=10,30,40`	10, 30, 40
`raxis=10,20,30 to 40 by 2`	10, 20, 30, 32...40
`raxis='01jan86'd to '01jan87'd by month`	01jan86 01feb86...01jan87
`raxis='01jan86'd to '01jan87'd by qtr`	01jan86 01apr86...01jan87

In the last two examples, the *from* and *to* values can be any of the valid SAS date, time, or datetime values described for the SAS functions INTCK and INTNX (see "SAS Functions" in the *SAS Language Guide, Release 6.03 Edition*). The BY value can be any of the valid values listed for the *interval* argument in the SAS functions INTCK and INTNX.

If you specify a range of tick marks that is not evenly divisible by the increment value, the highest value drawn on the axis is the highest value reached by incrementing.

For example,

```
raxis=5 to 100 by 10
```

yields a maximum tick mark at 95.

If values in the data set are larger than the highest tick mark, the bars are truncated at the highest tick mark.

You can also specify negative increment values. For example, you can specify the following values:

```
raxis=100 to -100 by -10
```

If you specify RAXIS=AXIS*n*, axis description *n* is used for the response axis. See "Enhancing Your Graphics Output Designs" for more information on AXIS statements, including logarithmic axes.

REF=*list*
    specifies a list of vertical reference lines to be drawn on the response axis. For TYPE=FREQ or TYPE=CFREQ, the REF= value should be one or more frequencies; for TYPE=PCT or TYPE=CPCT, the REF= value should be percents between 0 and 100. For TYPE=SUM or TYPE=MEAN, the REF= values should be sums or means.

SPACE=*n*
    specifies the space (in character cells) between the bars in a horizontal bar chart. If you do not want to leave any space between the bars, specify SPACE=0.

SUBGROUP=*variable*
    specifies that the contribution of each value of the SUBGROUP= variable should be represented by a separate pattern. For example, the following statements produce a chart with one bar for each department:

```
proc gchart;
    hbar dept / subgroup=gender;
```

Each bar represents all the observations with a certain DEPT value. Each bar is subdivided into as many parts as there are SUBGROUP= variable values.

The pattern and color used to shade each portion of the bar are determined by the PATTERN statements given. (See the chapter "Enhancing Your Graphics Output Designs" for more information on PATTERN statements.) If no PATTERN statements are in effect when SUBGROUP= is specified, default patterns and colors are used to subdivide bars.

SUMVAR=*variable*
> represents sums or means of the specified variable. The SUMVAR= option is useful for producing bar charts showing variable means at each level of an experiment or for showing such quantities as total expenditures for each department. For example, the following statements produce a chart showing the mean yield for each location:

```
proc gchart;
    hbar location / type=mean sumvar=yield;
```

In another example, the following statements chart total expenditures per department:

```
proc gchart;
    hbar dept / sumvar=expend;
```

TYPE=FREQ
TYPE=CFREQ
TYPE=PERCENT | PCT
TYPE=CPERCENT | CPCT
TYPE=SUM
TYPE=MEAN
> specify the statistic that the bars in the chart represent. If you omit the TYPE= option, the default TYPE= value is FREQ except when SUMVAR= is specified, in which case the default TYPE= value is SUM. If you want to use a response variable with a TYPE= value other than SUM or MEAN, use the FREQ= option rather than the SUMVAR= option.
>
> If you specify TYPE=FREQ, each bar represents the frequency with which a value (or range) occurs in the data. If you specify TYPE=CFREQ, each bar represents the frequency of a value or range, plus the frequencies of the bars before it. If you specify TYPE=PERCENT, each bar represents the percentage of observations in the data having a given value (or falling into a given range). If you specify TYPE=CPERCENT, each bar represents the percentage of observations in the data having a given value, plus the percentages of the bars before it. If you specify TYPE=SUM, each bar represents the sum of the SUMVAR= variable for observations having the bar's value. The TYPE=SUM option is used in conjunction with the SUMVAR= option. For example, the following statements produce a chart with one bar for each DEPT value:

```
proc gchart;
    hbar dept / sumvar=sales;
```

The bar length for a given DEPT corresponds to the total of the SALES values for observations having that DEPT value. If you specify TYPE=MEAN, each bar represents the mean of the SUMVAR= variable for observations having the bar's value. See **Available Charts** for more information.

WIDTH=*n*
specifies the width (in character cells) of horizontal bars.

LEGEND Statement

>LEGEND*n options*;

You can use LEGEND statements in PROC GCHART. For more information on LEGEND statements, see "Enhancing Your Graphics Output Designs."

NOTE Statement

>NOTE *options 'text'*;

You can use NOTE statements with PROC GCHART. They are described in detail in the chapter "Enhancing Your Graphics Output Text."

PATTERN Statement

>PATTERN*n options*;

You can specify colors and patterns for each SUBGROUP= category with PATTERN statements. (See "Enhancing Your Graphics Output Designs" for more information on PATTERN statements for bar and block charts.)

Special Patterns for Pie Slices

You can use three pattern specifications to fill pie slices:

- P*ntaaa*
- PEMPTY
- PSOLID.

These specifications are described below:

P*ntaaa*
>specifies the density of shading (*n*), single or crosshatched lines (*t*), and the angle of the lines (*aaa*).

>The *n* value can be a number from 1 through 5. The value *n* gives the density of filling; use 1 for the lightest shading, 5 for the darkest.

>Specify X for the *t* value to request crosshatched lines. If you omit X, parallel lines are used. Use an N for no crosshatching when you want to specify a starting angle for the lines.

>The angle *aaa* is the angle from the tangent to the center radius of the slice.

PEMPTY
PE
E
>requests empty slices.

PSOLID
PS
S
>requests solid-fill slices.

PIE Statement

>PIE *variables . . . / options*;

The PIE statement requests a pie chart for each variable listed. For example, the statements

```
proc gchart;
   pie a x1 x2;
```

produce three pie charts.

The following options can be used in a PIE statement after a slash (/):

ACROSS=*n*
specifies the number of pies to be displayed across each page. The default is 1. You must also specify the GROUP= option (see GROUP= below).

ANGLE=*n*
specifies the starting angle in degrees of the first pie slice. The pie slices proceed counterclockwise from the starting angle. The default starting angle is 0 (3:00).

ANNOTATE=*SASdataset*
specifies the data set to be used for annotation. This data set must be an ANNOTATE= type data set containing the appropriate Annotate variables. (See "ANNOTATE= Data Sets" for details.)

CFILL=*color*
specifies the color to be used for filling all slices of the pie. If you omit CFILL=, each slice is colored using the colors in the COLORS= list. (See the chapter "The GOPTIONS Statement" for more information on the COLORS= option.)

COUTLINE=*color*
specifies the color used to outline the pie slices.

CTEXT=*color*
specifies the color to use for drawing all text that appears on the chart. Variable names, labels, if any, and midpoint values are drawn using the color specified by the CTEXT= option. If you do not specify the CTEXT= option, the first color in the COLORS= list is used for drawing text. The MATCHCOLOR option (below) can override this option.

DESCRIPTION=*'string'*
DES=*'string'*
specifies a descriptive string, up to forty characters long, that appears in the Description field of PROC GREPLAY's master menu. If you omit the DESCRIPTION= option, the Description field contains a description assigned by SAS/GRAPH.

DISCRETE
indicates that the numeric variables included are discrete rather than continuous. This means that there will be a pie slice value for each unique value of the midpoint variable. See **DETAILS** for more information on midpoint selection.

DOWN=*n*
specifies the number of pies to be displayed vertically on each page. The default is 1. You must also specify the GROUP= option (see GROUP= below).

EXPLODE=*list*
uses the supplied values to define which slices are exploded (see the MIDPOINTS= option below). For numeric variables, *list* gives midpoints (or discrete values if DISCRETE is specified) to identify the slices; for character variables, *list* specifies the character levels.
When you specify the EXPLODE= option, the radii of the pie slices are reduced by 20 percent to allow room for exploding slices.

FILL=SOLID
FILL=X
specifies that each slice of the pie should be filled with a color or a crosshatch pattern. If FILL=SOLID, each slice of the pie is filled with

solid color. If FILL=X, each slice of the pie is filled with crossed lines. If you omit FILL=, the slices are not filled. In addition, you can use a PATTERN statement to specify special patterns. See the section on the **PATTERN Statement** for a description of these patterns.

FREQ=*variable*
indicates that a variable in the data set represents a count (or weight) for each observation. Normally, each observation contributes a value of 1 to the frequency counts. When the FREQ= option appears, each observation contributes the FREQ= variable's value. If the FREQ= variable's values are not integers, they are truncated to integers. If the values are missing or negative, the contribution is zero.

GROUP=*variable*
specifies that a separate pie should represent observations with each value of the GROUP= variable.

INVISIBLE=*list*
specifies values for which you do not want a slice to be drawn (see the MIDPOINTS= option below). For numeric variables, *list* gives midpoints (or discrete values if DISCRETE is specified) to identify the slices; for character variables, *list* specifies the character levels.

MATCHCOLOR
specifies that the slice text be the same color as the slice.

MIDPOINTS=*values*
MIDPOINTS=OLD
defines the range each pie slice represents by specifying the range midpoints. For example, the following statements produce a chart with five slices: the first slice represents the range of data values with a midpoint of 10; the second slice represents the range of data values with a midpoint of 20; and so on.

```
proc gchart;
    pie sales / midpoints=10 20 30 40 50;
```

Numeric MIDPOINTS lists of the following form are also acceptable:

```
midpoints=10 to 100 by 5
```

You can specify MIDPOINTS= values in any order. This is useful in ordering the pie slices or in specifying a subset of the possible values. For example, a list of the following form can be used:

```
midpoints='jan' 'feb' 'mar'
```

If you specify MIDPOINTS=OLD, the midpoint selection algorithm used in Version 82.4 and Version 5 of SAS/GRAPH software is used. See the **DETAILS** section for more information.

MISSING
includes missing values as a valid level for the pie variable.

NAME='*string*'
where '*string*' specifies a descriptive string, up to eight characters long, that appears in the Name field of PROC GREPLAY's master menu. If you omit the NAME= option, the Name field of PROC GREPLAY's master menu contains the name of the procedure.

NOGROUPHEADING
omits the automatic headings normally drawn when you specify the GROUP= option.

NOHEADING
  omits the automatic heading normally drawn on pie charts.

OTHER=*n*
  specifies the size of slices assigned to the OTHER group. The value *n* is a percent from 0 to 100. By default, any slice that is less than 4 percent of the circle is put in the OTHER category. If only one slice falls into OTHER, it is positioned as the last slice but is labeled with its actual label (that is, not as OTHER).

  PROC GCHART determines the number of slices for the pie in the same way that it determines the number of bars for vertical bar charts.

SUMVAR=*variable*
  represents sums or means of the specified variable. The SUMVAR= option is useful for producing pie charts showing variable means at each level of an experiment or for showing such quantities as total expenditures for each department. For example, the following statements produce a chart showing the mean yield for each location:

```
proc gchart;
   pie location / type=mean sumvar=yield;
```

  In another example, the following statements chart total expenditures per department:

```
proc gchart;
   pie dept / sumvar=expend;
```

TYPE=FREQ
TYPE=CFREQ
TYPE=PERCENT | PCT
TYPE=CPERCENT | CPCT
TYPE=SUM
TYPE=MEAN
  specify the statistic that the slices in the chart represent. If you omit the TYPE= option, the default TYPE= value is FREQ except when SUMVAR= is specified, in which case the default TYPE= value is SUM. If you want to use a response variable with a TYPE= value other than SUM or MEAN, use the FREQ= option rather than the SUMVAR= option. If you specify TYPE=FREQ or TYPE=CFREQ, each slice represents the frequency with which a value (or range) occurs in the data. If you specify TYPE=PERCENT or TYPE=CPERCENT, each slice represents the percentage of observations in the data having a given value (or falling into a given range). If you specify TYPE=SUM, each slice represents the sum of the SUMVAR= variable for observations having the slice's value. The TYPE=SUM option is used in conjunction with the SUMVAR= option. For example, the following statements produce a chart with one slice for each DEPT value:

```
proc gchart;
   pie dept / sumvar=sales;
```

  The slice size for a given DEPT corresponds to the total of the SALES values for observations having that DEPT value. If you specify TYPE=MEAN, each slice represents the mean of the SUMVAR= variable for observations having the slice's value. See **Available Charts** for more information.

PIE Statement Labeling Options

You can use the options below to label the slices of a pie. If you want to label the pie using the value of the midpoint associated with each slice, use the SLICE= option. If you want to label the pie using the percent of the pie each slice represents, use the PERCENT= option. If you want to label the pie using the value of each slice, use the VALUE= option. You can control the placement of the labels on the pie by specifying one of four methods after the PERCENT=, SLICE=, and VALUE= options.

PERCENT=*method*
: specifies the method used for labeling the percent of the pie the slice represents. See the description of the SLICE= option for valid values of *method*.

SLICE=*method*
: specifies the method used for labeling the value of the midpoint associated with each slice. Values for *method* are ARROW, INSIDE, NONE, and OUTSIDE:

SLICE=ARROW
: specifies that the value of the midpoint associated with each slice appears either flush left or flush right, depending on the side of the pie on which it is located. The text is connected to the slice with a line, and the connecting line is the same color as the text.

SLICE=INSIDE
: specifies that the value of the midpoint associated with each slice appears inside the slice.

SLICE=NONE
: specifies that the value of the midpoint associated with each slice does not appear.

SLICE=OUTSIDE
: specifies that the value of the midpoint associated with each slice appears outside the slice.

VALUE=*method*
: specifies the method used for labeling the value of each slice, such as FREQ, PCT, or SUM. See SLICE= above for valid values of *method*.

PIE Statement Labeling Methods: Example

In the following example, four pie charts are created, and the labeling methods described above are used to label the slices of the pies. PROC GREPLAY is then used to create a graph that places the separate pie charts on a single display using the template facility. (See "The GREPLAY Procedure" for more information on the template facility.) These statements produce **Output 9.13**.

```
proc gchart data=police gout=gchart13;
   pie officer / name='OUTSIDE'
                slice=outside
                value=outside
                percent=outside
                ctext=cream
                noheading;
```

```
            pie officer / name='INSIDE'
                           slice=inside
                           value=inside
                           percent=inside
                           ctext=cream
                           noheading;
            pie officer / name='ARROW'
                           slice=arrow
                           value=arrow
                           percent=arrow
                           noheading;
            pie officer / name='MIXED'
                           slice=outside
                           value=none
                           percent=inside
                           ctext=cream
                           noheading;
       run;

       proc greplay nofs gout=gchart;
          igout gchart13;
          tc     template;
          tc     template;
          tdef   t2x2  1 /  llx=0     ulx=0     urx=50    lrx=50
                            lly=50    uly=100   ury=100   lry=50
                        2 /  llx=50    ulx=50    urx=100   lrx=100
                            lly=50    uly=100   ury=100   lry=50
                        3 /  llx=0     ulx=0     urx=50    lrx=50
                            lly=0     uly=50    ury=50    lry=0
                        4 /  llx=50    ulx=50    urx=100   lrx=100
                            lly=0     uly=50    ury=50    lry=0   ;
          template t2x2;
          tplay 1:outside 2:inside 3:arrow 4:mixed;
       run;
```

Output 9.13 PIE Statement Labeling Methods

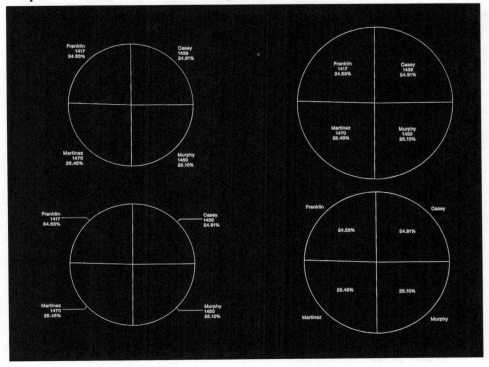

STAR Statement

   STAR *variables . . . / options*;

The STAR statement requests a star chart for each variable listed. For example, the statements

```
proc gchart;
   star z;
```

produce a one-page star chart for the variable Z.

   If all the data to be charted with the STAR statement are positive, the center of the star represents zero, and the outside circle represents the maximum value. If negative values occur in the data, the center represents the minimum.

   You can specify the center and outside circle values with the STARMIN= and STARMAX= options:

```
proc gchart;
   star a / sumvar=x type=sum starmin=100 starmax=200;
```

These statements produce a star chart for the sums of X, classified by A, and scaled from 100 at the center to 200 at the outside circle.

   If you want different variables to form the points of the star, use the OUTPUT statement in the DATA step. Here, you create new observations having one variable with values equal to the variables you want represented by the points.

   The number of points in the star is determined in the same way as the number of bars for vertical bar charts.

   The following options can be used with a STAR statement after a slash (/):

ACROSS=*n*
   specifies the number of star charts to be displayed across each page. The default is 1. You must also specify the GROUP= option.

ANGLE=*n*

    specifies the starting angle in degrees of the first section. The sections proceed counterclockwise from the starting angle. The default starting angle is such that the center of the first star segment is at 0 degrees (3:00).

ANNOTATE=*SASdataset*

    specifies the data set to be used for annotation. This data set must be an ANNOTATE= type data set containing the appropriate Annotate variables. (See "ANNOTATE= Data Sets" for details.)

CFILL=*color*

    specifies the color to be used for filling all sections of the star. If you omit CFILL=, each section is colored using the colors in the COLORS= list. (See "The GOPTIONS Statement" for more information on the COLORS= option.)

COUTLINE=*color*

    specifies the color used to outline the star.

CTEXT=*color*

    specifies the color to use for drawing all text that appears on the chart. Variable names, labels, if any, and midpoint values are drawn using the color specified by the CTEXT= option. If you do not specify CTEXT=, the CTEXT= option in a GOPTIONS statement is used for drawing text. The MATCHCOLOR option overrides this option.

DESCRIPTION=*'string'*

DES=*'string'*

    specifies a descriptive string, up to forty characters long, that appears in the Description field of PROC GREPLAY's master menu. If you omit the DESCRIPTION= option, the Description field contains a description assigned by SAS/GRAPH.

DISCRETE

    indicates that the numeric variables included are discrete rather than continuous. This means that there will be a midpoint value for each unique value of the midpoint variable. See **DETAILS** for more information.

DOWN=*n*

    specifies the number of star charts to be displayed vertically on each page. The default is 1. You must also specify the GROUP= option.

FILL=SOLID

FILL=X

    fills each section of the star with a solid color or crosshatch pattern. If FILL=SOLID, each section of the star is filled with solid color. If FILL=X, each section of the star is filled with crossed lines. If you omit FILL=, the sections are not filled. In addition, you can use a PATTERN statement to specify special patterns. See **PATTERN Statement** for a description of these patterns.

FREQ=*variable*

    indicates that a variable in the data set represents a count (or weight) for each observation. Normally, each observation contributes a value of 1 to the frequency counts. When you specify the FREQ= option, each observation contributes the FREQ= variable's value. If the FREQ= variable's values are not integers, they are truncated to integers. If the values are missing or negative, the contribution is zero.

GROUP=_variable_
　　specifies the variable used to break the data into groups. In a star chart,
　　each group appears in a separate chart (see ACROSS= and DOWN=
　　for more information on group stars).

MATCHCOLOR
　　specifies that the section text be the same color as the section.

MIDPOINTS=_values_
MIDPOINTS=OLD
　　defines the range each star point represents by specifying the range
　　midpoints. For example, the following statements produce a chart with
　　five sections: the first section represents the range of data values with a
　　midpoint of 10; the second section represents the range of data values
　　with a midpoint of 20; and so on.

```
proc gchart;
    star yield / midpoints=10 20 30 40 50;
```

　　Numeric MIDPOINTS= lists of the following form are also acceptable:

```
midpoints=10 to 100 by 5
```

　　For character variables, you can specify MIDPOINTS= values in any
　　order. This is useful in ordering the star points or in specifying a subset
　　of the possible values. For example, a list of the following form can be
　　used:

```
midpoints='jan' 'feb' 'mar'
```

　　If you specify MIDPOINTS=OLD, the midpoint selection algorithm used
　　in Version 82.4 and Version 5 of SAS/GRAPH software is used. See the
　　DETAILS section for more information.

MISSING
　　includes missing values as a valid level for the midpoint variable.

NAME=_'string'_
　　where _'string'_ specifies a descriptive string, up to eight characters long,
　　that appears in the Name field of PROC GREPLAY's master menu. If you
　　omit the NAME= option, the Name field of PROC GREPLAY's master
　　menu contains the name of the procedure.

NOCONNECT
　　specifies that lines connecting the ends of the star spines should not be
　　drawn. This has no effect if you specify the FILL= option or PATTERN
　　statements.

NOGROUPHEADING
　　omits the automatic headings normally drawn when you specify
　　GROUP=.

NOHEADING
　　omits the automatic heading normally drawn on star charts.

STARMAX=_n_
　　scales the spines of the stars so that the outside of the circle represents
　　_n_. Normally, the outside of the circle represents the largest response
　　value.

STARMIN=_n_
　　scales the spines of the stars so that the center of the circle represents
　　_n_. Normally, the center of the circle represents 0.

SUMVAR=*variable*

represents sums or means of the specified variable. The SUMVAR= option is useful for producing star charts showing variable means at each level of an experiment or for showing such quantities as total expenditures for each department. For example, the following statements produce a chart showing the mean yield for each location:

```
proc gchart;
    star location / type=mean sumvar=yield;
```

In another example, the following statements chart total expenditures per department:

```
proc gchart;
    star dept / sumvar=expend;
```

TYPE=FREQ
TYPE=CFREQ
TYPE=PERCENT | PCT
TYPE=CPERCENT | CPCT
TYPE=SUM
TYPE=MEAN

specify the statistic that the stars in the chart represent. If you omit the TYPE= option, the default TYPE= value is FREQ except when SUMVAR= is specified, in which case the default TYPE= value is SUM. If you want to use a response variable with a TYPE= value other than SUM or MEAN, use the FREQ= option rather than the SUMVAR= option. If you specify TYPE=FREQ or TYPE=CFREQ, each star represents the frequency with which a value (or range) occurs in the data. If you specify TYPE=PERCENT or TYPE=CPERCENT, each star represents the percentage of observations in the data having a given value (or falling into a given range). If you specify TYPE=SUM, each star represents the sum of the SUMVAR= variable for observations having the star's value. The TYPE=SUM option is used in conjunction with the SUMVAR= option. If you specify TYPE=MEAN, each star represents the mean of the SUMVAR= variable for observations having the star's value. See **Available Charts** for more information.

STAR Statement Labeling Options

You can use the options below to label the sections of a star chart. If you want to label the star chart using the value of the midpoint associated with each section, use the SLICE= option. If you want to label the star chart using the percent of the star each section represents, use the PERCENT= option. If you want to label the star chart using the value of each section, use the VALUE= option. You can control the placement of the labels on the star by specifying one of four methods after the PERCENT=, SLICE=, and VALUE= options.

PERCENT=*method*

specifies the method used for labeling the percent of the star the section represents. See SLICE= above for valid values of *method*.

SLICE=*method*

specifies the method used for labeling the value of the midpoint associated with each section. Values for *method* are ARROW, INSIDE, NONE, and OUTSIDE:

SLICE=ARROW

specifies that the value of the midpoint associated with each section appears either flush left or flush right, depending on the side of the star on which it is located. The text is connected to the section with a line, and the connecting line is the same color as the text.

SLICE=INSIDE

specifies that the value of the midpoint associated with each section appears inside the section.

SLICE=NONE

specifies that the value of the midpoint associated with each section does not appear.

SLICE=OUTSIDE

specifies that the value of the midpoint associated with each section appears outside the section.

VALUE=*method*

specifies the method used for labeling the value of each section, such as FREQ, PCT, or SUM. See SLICE= above for valid values of *method*.

See **PIE Statement Labeling Methods: Example** for an example that illustrates the use of the SLICE= option.

TITLE Statement

TITLE*n options* 'text';

You can use TITLE statements with PROC GCHART. They are described in detail in the chapter "Enhancing Your Graphics Output Text."

VBAR Statement

VBAR *variables* / *options*;

You can use a VBAR statement to list the variables that you want shown in vertical bar charts. Each occupies one page. Along the vertical axis, PROC GCHART describes the kind of chart: frequency, cumulative frequency, percentage, cumulative percentage, sum, or mean. At the bottom of each bar, PROC GCHART draws a value. For character variables or discrete numeric variables, these values are the actual value represented by the bar. For continuous numeric variables, the value gives the midrange of the interval represented by the bar.

PROC GCHART automatically scales the vertical axis, determines the bar width, and chooses spacing between the bars. However, you can specify options to override the defaults and to choose bar intervals and the number of bars, to include missing values in the chart, to produce side-by-side charts, and to subdivide the bars.

The options below can appear in the VBAR statement following a slash (/):

ANNOTATE=*SASdataset*

specifies the data set to be used for annotation. This data set must be an ANNOTATE= type data set containing the appropriate Annotate variables. (See "ANNOTATE= Data Sets" for details.)

ASCENDING

draws the bars and any associated statistics in ascending order of response value within groups.

AUTOREF

draws a reference line at each major tick mark on the response (vertical) axis.

CAXIS=*color*

specifies the color to use for drawing the axes for vertical bar charts. If you do not specify the CAXIS= option, the first color in the COLORS=

list is used to draw the axes. (See the description of the COLORS= option in "The GOPTIONS Statement.") If the color is specified with the CAXIS= option, it overrides any axis color specified in an AXIS statement.

CFRAME=*color*
CFR=*color*

specifies the color used to fill the axis area. If you specify the CFRAME= option, you do not need to specify the FRAME option.

COUTLINE=*color*

specifies the color used to outline the bars.

CTEXT=*color*

specifies the color to use for drawing all text that appears on the chart. Variable names, labels, if any, and midpoint values are drawn using the color specified by the CTEXT= option. If you do not specify the CTEXT= option in the HBAR statement, the value you specified for the CTEXT= option in a GOPTIONS statement is used for drawing text. If the color is specified with the CTEXT= option, it overrides the AXIS statement COLORS= option, but not the C= option of the LABEL= or VALUE= options on an AXIS or LEGEND statement.

DESCENDING

draws the bars and any associated statistics in descending order of response value within groups.

DESCRIPTION=*'string'*
DES=*'string'*

specifies a descriptive string, up to forty characters long, that appears in the Description field of PROC GREPLAY's master menu. If you omit the DESCRIPTION= option, the Description field contains a description assigned by SAS/GRAPH.

DISCRETE

indicates that the numeric variables on the midpoint axis are discrete rather than continuous. This means that there will be a midpoint value for each unique value of the midpoint variable.

See **DETAILS** for more information on midpoint selection.

FRAME
FR

specifies that the axis area be outlined in the color of the axis. If you do not specify FRAME, the axis area is not outlined.

FREQ=*variable*

indicates that a variable in the data set represents a count (or weight) for each observation. Normally, each observation contributes a value of 1 to the frequency counts. When the FREQ= option appears, each observation contributes the FREQ= variable's value. If the FREQ= variable's values are not integers, they are truncated to integers. If the values are missing or negative, the contribution is zero.

G100

forces the bars to total 100 percent for each group and is used in conjunction with the GROUP= option.

GAXIS=AXIS*n*

specifies which axis description to use for the group axis, where *n* refers to an AXIS statement defined previously. The AXIS statement used for the group variable ignores the ORDER=, MAJOR=, and MINOR= options.

GROUP=*variable*

specifies the variable used to break the data into groups. In a vertical bar chart, the groups appear side by side and share the same response axis. For example, the following statements produce a frequency bar chart for males and females in each department:

```
proc gchart;
    vbar gender / group=dept;
```

Missing values for a GROUP= variable are treated as a valid level, and a chart is produced.

GSPACE=*n*

specifies the amount of extra space, in character cells, to leave between groups of bars in a vertical bar chart. The GROUP= option must also be specified.

LEGEND=LEGEND*n*

specifies the LEGEND statement to associate with the graph, where *n* is the number of a LEGEND statement defined previously.

Use the LEGEND= option only if the graph requested normally produces a legend. A legend is drawn if you specify the SUBGROUP= option. Simply specifying LEGEND= in the VBAR statement does not cause a legend to be generated.

LEVELS=*n*

specifies the number of bars representing each variable when the variables given in the VBAR statement are continuous. See **DETAILS** for more information.

MAXIS=AXIS*n*

specifies which axis description to use for the midpoint axis, where *n* refers to an AXIS statement defined previously. The AXIS statement used for the midpoint variable ignores the MAJOR= and MINOR= options.

MIDPOINTS=*values*
MIDPOINTS=OLD

defines the range each bar represents by specifying the range midpoints. For example, the following statements produce a chart with five bars: the first bar represents the range of data values with a midpoint of 10; the second bar represents the range of data values with a midpoint of 20; and so on:

```
proc gchart;
    vbar x / midpoints=10 20 30 40 50;
```

Numeric MIDPOINTS lists of the following form are also acceptable:

```
midpoints=10 to 100 by 5
```

For character variables, MIDPOINTS= values can be specified in any order. This is useful in ordering the bars, or in specifying a subset of the possible values. For example, a list of the following form can be used:

```
midpoints='jan' 'feb' 'mar'
```

If you specify MIDPOINTS=OLD, the midpoint selection algorithm used in Version 82.4 and Version 5 of SAS/GRAPH software is used. See **DETAILS** for more information.

MINOR=*n*

specifies the number of minor tick marks to be drawn between each major tick mark on the response axis.

MISSING
> includes missing values as a valid level for the midpoint variable.

NAME='*string*'
> where '*string*' specifies a descriptive string, up to eight characters long, that appears in the Name field of PROC GREPLAY's master menu. If you omit the NAME= option, the Name field of PROC GREPLAY's master menu contains the name of the procedure.

NOAXIS
NOAXES
> suppresses the drawing of the axes.

NOLEGEND
> suppresses the drawing of the subgroup legend below vertical bar charts.

NOZEROS
> specifies not to draw zero frequency midpoints.

PATTERNID=*method*
> specifies the chart variable that controls the change in pattern. Valid values for *method* are SUBGROUP, GROUP, MIDPOINT, and BY. If you specify PATTERNID=SUBGROUP, the pattern changes every time the SUBGROUP value changes. If you specify PATTERNID=GROUP, the pattern changes every time the GROUP value changes. If you specify PATTERNID=MIDPOINT, the pattern changes every time the MIDPOINT value changes. If you specify PATTERNID=BY, the pattern changes every time the BY value changes. The default is PATTERNID=SUBGROUP. See **Controlling Patterns and Colors in Horizontal Bar, Vertical Bar, and Block Charts** for more information.

AXIS=*values*
AXIS=AXIS*n*
RAXIS=*values*
RAXIS=AXIS*n*
> specifies the maximum value to use in constructing the response axis or specifies the AXIS statement to use. If the vertical bar chart is of TYPE=SUM or TYPE=MEAN, and if any of the sums or means are less than zero, then you can also specify a negative minimum value with the AXIS= option. Otherwise, a minimum value of zero is always assumed. Counts or percentages outside the maximum (or minimum) go only as far as the values specified in the AXIS= option. If you specify both the AXIS= option and a BY statement, uniform axes are produced over BY groups.
>
> The AXIS= option can include a range of values to be used for tick marks on the response axis. Below are some examples of AXIS= specifications and the tick marks they produce.

Specification	Tick marks
`raxis=10 to 100 by 10`	10, 20, 30...100
`raxis=10,30,40`	10, 30, 40
`raxis=10,20,30 to 40 by 2`	10, 20, 30, 32...40
`raxis='01jan86'd to '01jan87'd by month`	01jan86 01feb86...01jan87
`raxis='01jan86'd to '01jan87'd by qtr`	01jan86 01apr86...01jan87

In the last two examples, the *from* and *to* values can be any of the valid SAS date, time, or datetime values described for the SAS functions INTCK and INTNX (see "SAS Functions" in the *SAS Language Guide*,

Release 6.03 Edition). The BY value can be any of the valid values listed for the *interval* argument in the SAS functions INTCK and INTNX.

If you specify a range of tick marks that is not evenly divisible by the increment value, the highest value drawn on the axis is the highest value reached by incrementing.

For example,

```
raxis=5 to 100 by 10
```

yields a maximum tick mark at 95.

If values in the data set are larger than the highest tick mark, the bars are truncated at the highest tick mark.

You can also specify negative increment values. For example, you can specify the following values:

```
raxis=100 to -100 by -10
```

If you specify RAXIS=AXIS*n*, axis description *n* is used for the response axis. Refer to "Enhancing Your Graphics Output Text" for more information on AXIS statements, including logarithmic axes.

REF=*list*
> specifies a list of horizontal reference lines to be drawn on the response axis. For TYPE=FREQ or TYPE=CFREQ, the REF= value should be one or more frequencies; for TYPE=PCT or TYPE=CPCT, the REF= value should be percents between 0 and 100. For TYPE=SUM or TYPE=MEAN, the REF= values should be sums or means.

SPACE=*n*
> specifies the space (in character cells) between the bars in a vertical bar chart. If you do not want to leave any space between the bars, specify SPACE=0.

SUBGROUP=*variable*
> specifies that the contribution of each value of the SUBGROUP= variable should be represented by a separate pattern. For example, the following statements produce a chart with one bar for each department:

```
proc gchart;
   vbar dept / subgroup=gender;
```

Each bar represents all the observations with a certain DEPT value. Each bar is subdivided into as many parts as there are SUBGROUP= variable values.

The pattern and color used to shade each portion of the bar are determined by the PATTERN statements given. (See "Enhancing Your Graphics Output Designs" for more information on PATTERN statements.) If no PATTERN statements are in effect when SUBGROUP= is specified, default patterns and colors are used to subdivide bars.

SUMVAR=*variable*
> represents sums or means of the specified variable. The SUMVAR= option is useful for producing bar charts showing variable means at each level of an experiment or for showing such quantities as total expenditures for each department. For example, the following statements produce a chart showing the mean yield for each location:

```
proc gchart;
   vbar location / type=mean sumvar=yield;
```

In another example, the statements

```
proc gchart;
    vbar dept / sumvar=expend;
```

chart total expenditures per department.

TYPE=FREQ
TYPE=CFREQ
TYPE=PERCENT | PCT
TYPE=CPERCENT | CPCT
TYPE=SUM
TYPE=MEAN

specify the statistic that the bars in the chart represent. If you omit the TYPE= option, the default TYPE= value is FREQ except when SUMVAR= is specified, in which case the default TYPE= value is SUM. If you want to use a response variable with a TYPE= value other than SUM or MEAN, use the FREQ= option rather than the SUMVAR= option. If you specify TYPE=FREQ, each bar represents the frequency with which a value (or range) occurs in the data. If you specify TYPE=CFREQ, each bar represents the frequency of a value or range, plus the frequencies of the bars before it. If you specify TYPE=PERCENT, each bar represents the percentage of observations in the data having a given value (or falling into a given range). If you specify TYPE=CPERCENT, each bar represents the percentage of observations in the data having a given value, plus the percentages of the bars before it. If you specify TYPE=SUM, each bar represents the sum of the SUMVAR= variable for observations having the bar's value. The TYPE=SUM option is used in conjunction with the SUMVAR= option. For example, the following statements produce a chart with one bar for each DEPT value:

```
proc gchart;
    vbar dept / sumvar=sales;
```

The bar height for a given DEPT corresponds to the total of the SALES values for observations having that DEPT value. If you specify TYPE=MEAN, each bar represents the mean of the SUMVAR= variable for observations having the bar's value. See **Available Charts** for more information.

WIDTH=n
specifies the width (in character cells) of vertical bars.

DETAILS

Selecting Midpoints

The method the GCHART procedure uses to choose the midpoint values depends on the type of variable, numeric or character, and the combination of specifying the following options: DISCRETE, MIDPOINTS=, and LEVELS=.

If the variable is a character variable, each unique value becomes a midpoint unless you specify the MIDPOINTS= option. For instance, if the variable has the values 'A', 'B', 'C', and 'D' and you specify MIDPOINTS='A' 'B' 'C', the data with the value 'D' are not included in the chart. The DISCRETE and LEVELS= options have no effect for character variables. If the character variable is formatted, then the bars or slices are drawn in formatted order.

If the variable is a numeric variable, and you omit the MIDPOINTS=, DISCRETE, and LEVELS= options, the GCHART procedure uses the algorithm described in Terrell and Scott (1985) to determine the number of midpoints. If you specify only MIDPOINTS=OLD, then the number of midpoints is determined by the algorithm described in Nelder (1976). If you specify the LEVELS= option, the number given is used for the number of midpoints. Specifying the DISCRETE option makes each unique formatted value a midpoint, but the midpoints are listed in the order of the original numeric value unless you use the ASCENDING or DESCENDING option. DISCRETE overrides LEVELS= and MIDPOINTS=OLD. Specifying MIDPOINTS=*numeric list* overrides the DISCRETE, LEVELS=, and MIDPOINTS=OLD options.

For both character and numeric variables, MIDPOINTS= generally controls the order in which the values appear, but the ASCENDING or DESCENDING option will override this order.

If you specify the SUBGROUP= or GROUP= option, then the subgroups or groups are determined in the same manner as are midpoints when you specify the DISCRETE option.

Controlling Patterns and Colors in Horizontal Bar, Vertical Bar, and Block Charts

By default, the pattern in horizontal bar, vertical bar, and block charts changes each time the subgroup changes. Thus, the SUBGROUP= option determines the colors and patterns in these charts. If you do not specify the SUBGROUP= option, all of the bars or blocks are assumed to have the same subgroup value. Rather than let the SUBGROUP= option determine when patterns change, you can use the PATTERNID= option to specify when the patterns should change.

The data used in the following examples are a fictional log of police calls. The data contain the time and date the calls were made, the name of the officer who answered the call, the time required to respond to the call, and the type of call. The edited output for the data analyzed appears in **Output 9.14**. (The data are included in the Sample Library provided with SAS/GRAPH software. Check with your SAS Software Consultant to find out how to access the Sample Library.)

Output 9.14   Contents of SAS Data Set POLICE

```
                              CONTENTS PROCEDURE

Data Set Name:  POLICE
Observations:   5776
Label:          PROC GCHART Examples, Version 6

                   -----Alphabetic List of Variables and Attributes-----

Variable  Type  Len    Format  Label
DATE      Num   8      DATE7.  Date
MERIDIAN  Char  2              Meridian
OFFICER   Char  8              Officer
RTIME     Num   8      TIME8.  Response Time
TIME      Num   8      TIME8.  Time
TYPE      Char  8              Type
```

The following examples show how patterns can be controlled in vertical bar charts. Pattern control works the same way in horizontal bar and block charts.

The following statements tell PROC GCHART to change the pattern of the bars when the SUBGROUP= value changes and produce **Output 9.15**.

```
pattern1 v=s c=cream;
pattern2 v=s c=gold;
pattern3 v=s c=styg;
pattern4 v=s c=vipk;
title1 f=swiss c=white 'PATTERNID=SUBGROUP';
title2 'Default';
footnote c=white 'GCHART Controlling Bar and Block Colors';
axis1 label=none;
proc gchart data=police;
   vbar type / group=meridian
               maxis=axis1
               gaxis=axis1
               subgroup=officer
               axis=0 to 2000 by 1000;
run;
```

The following statements tell SAS/GRAPH to change the pattern of the bars when the GROUP= value changes and produce **Output 9.16**.

```
pattern1 v=s c=cream;
pattern2 v=s c=gold;
title f=swiss c=white 'PATTERNID=GROUP';
footnote C=white 'GCHART Controlling Bar and Block Colors';
axis1 label=none;
proc gchart data=police;
   vbar type / group=meridian
               maxis=axis1
               gaxis=axis1
               patternid=group
               axis=0 to 2000 by 1000;
run;
```

The following statements tell SAS/GRAPH to change the pattern of the bars when the MIDPOINT= value changes and produce **Output 9.17**.

```
pattern1 v=s c=cream;
pattern2 v=s c=gold;
title f=swiss c=white 'PATTERNID=MIDPOINT';
footnote c=white 'GCHART Controlling Bar and Block Colors';
axis1 label=none;
proc gchart data=police;
   vbar type / group=meridian
               maxis=axis1
               gaxis=axis1
               patternid=midpoint
               axis=0 to 2000 by 1000;
run;
```

Controlling Patterns and Colors in Pie and Star Charts

By default, the pie and star slices are drawn with an empty pattern in the first color in the COLORS= list. To change this, specify pie patterns in the V= option of one or more PATTERN statements (see "Enhancing Your Graphics Output Designs") or by using the FILL= or CFILL= options. See **Special Patterns for Pie Slices** for details.

Output 9.15   Changing Patterns in Charts: PATTERNID=SUBGROUP

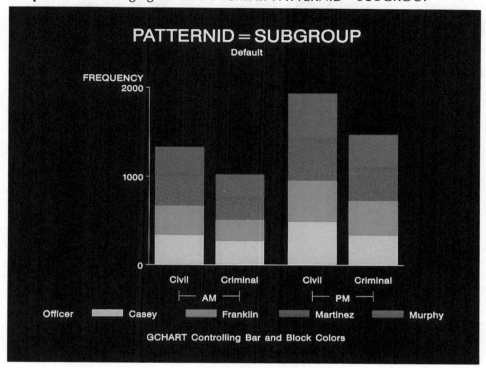

Output 9.16   Changing Patterns in Charts: PATTERNID=GROUP

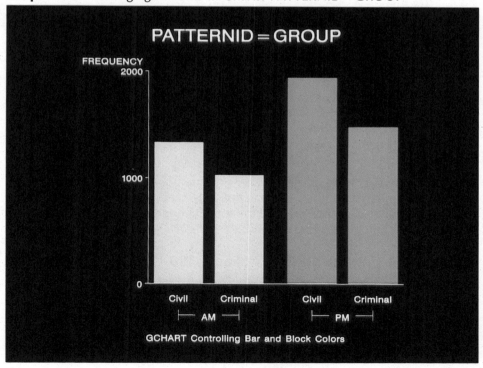

Output 9.17   Changing Patterns in Charts: PATTERNID=MIDPOINT

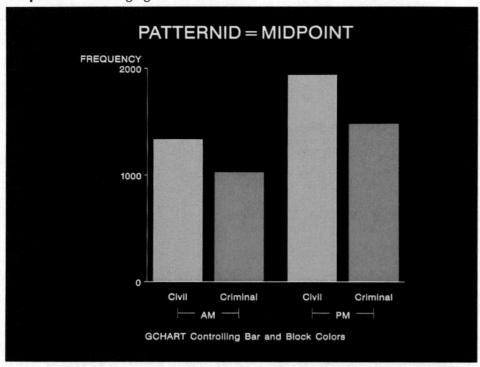

EXAMPLES

Example 1: Creating a Horizontal Bar Chart

To create a horizontal bar chart showing the number of calls handled by each officer, as shown in **Output 9.18**, specify the following statements:

```
pattern1 v=s c=gold;
title f=swiss c=white 'Calls Each Officer Made';
proc gchart data=police;
   hbar officer / frame;
run;
```

Although the bars were chosen to show the number of calls handled by each officer, you can also see the percentage of calls handled by each officer (in the column of numbers labeled PCT) and the total number of calls answered (the last number in the column labeled CFREQ).

Example 2: Using the GROUP= and G100 Options in an HBAR Statement

The following example shows how to create a horizontal bar chart and uses the GROUP= option to divide the bars. The G100 option makes the groups total 100 percent. The output is shown in **Output 9.19**.

```
pattern1 v=s c=cream;
pattern2 v=s c=gold;
title f=swiss c=white 'Types of Calls Handled';
proc gchart data=police;
   hbar type / discrete
```

```
            group=officer
            g100
            patternid=midpoint;
    run;
```

Example 3: Using the SUBGROUP=, FREQ, and PERCENT Options in an HBAR Statement

The following example creates a horizontal bar chart using the SUBGROUP= option. The FREQ and PERCENT options are used to print the statistics for frequency and percent to the right of the bar chart. The output is shown in **Output 9.20**.

```
    pattern1 v=s c=cream;
    pattern2 v=s c=gold;
    pattern3 v=s c=styg;
    pattern4 v=s c=vipk;
    title f=swiss c=white 'Time Spent Handling Calls';
    footnote ' ';
    proc gchart data=police;
       format time time6.;
       hbar time / midpoints='0:00't to '12:00't by '2:00't
                   type=cpct
                   freq
                   percent
                   frame
                   subgroup=officer;
    run;
```

Example 4: Creating a Vertical Bar Chart

The following statements produce **Output 9.21**, a vertical bar chart showing the number of calls answered in the morning and the afternoon. Notice that the MERIDIAN variable is used as both the midpoint and the subgroup variable.

```
    pattern1 v=s c=gold;
    pattern2 v=s c=vipk;
    title f=swiss c=white 'Morning and Afternoon Calls';
    footnote ' ';
    proc gchart data=police;
       vbar meridian / type=cfreq
                       subgroup=meridian;
    run;
```

Example 5: Creating a Vertical Bar Chart Showing Means

The following example shows how to use the SUBGROUP= and GROUP= options in a VBAR statement to create a vertical bar chart showing means. These statements produce **Output 9.22**.

```
    pattern1 v=s c=cream;
    pattern2 v=s c=gold;
    pattern3 v=s c=styg;
    pattern4 v=s c=vipk;
    title f=swiss c=white 'Time Spent Handling Calls';
    footnote ' ';
    proc gchart data=police;
```

```
      format rtime time5. time time5.;
      vbar time / midpoints='01:30't to '10:30't by '03:00't
                  raxis='00:00't to '01:30't by '00:30't
                  minor=1
                  type=mean
                  sumvar=rtime
                  subgroup=officer
                  group=meridian;
   run;
```

Example 6: Creating a Block Chart

To make a block chart showing the percent of calls each officer handled, specify the statements below, which produce **Output 9.23**.

```
   pattern v=s c=vipk;
   title f=swiss c=white 'Calls Each Officer Handled';
   proc gchart data=police;
      block officer / type=pct
                      noheading
                      coutline=white;
   run;
```

To make a block chart showing the percent of each type of call handled by each officer, specify the statements below, which produce **Output 9.24**.

```
   pattern1 v=s c=cream;
   pattern2 v=s c=gold;
   pattern3 v=s c=styg;
   pattern4 v=s c=vipk;
   title1 f=swiss 'Types of Calls Handled';
   footnote;
   proc gchart data=police;
      block type / discrete
                   type=pct
                   subgroup=officer
                   coutline=white
                   noheading;
   run;
```

To make a block chart showing the percent of each type of call handled by each officer using the GROUP= option, specify the following statements, which produce **Output 9.25**.

```
   pattern v=s c=gold;
   title f=swiss c=white 'Types of Calls Handled';
   proc gchart data=police;
      block officer / discrete
                      type=pct
                      group=type
                      g100
                      coutline=white;
      label type='00'x;
   run;
```

Example 7: Creating a Pie Chart

The pie chart in **Output 9.26** shows the relative number of calls handled by each officer as compared to the total number of calls handled. The percent is also shown. Specifying PCT=OUTSIDE overrides the default labeling method for the percent each slice represents of the whole pie.

```
goptions colors=(cream gold liyg stpk);
title f=swiss c=white 'Time Spent Handling Calls';
proc gchart data=police;
   format rtime time5.;
   pie officer / sumvar=rtime
                 pct=outside
                 fill=s        /* Colors from COLORS= list */
                 noheading
                 matchcolor;
run;
```

Example 8: Placing Two Pie Charts on a Page

The pie chart in **Output 9.27** uses the ACROSS= and GROUP= options to place two pies across the display area. The EXPLODE= option is used to offset pieces of the pie.

```
goptions colors=(cream gold styg vipk);
title f=swiss c=white 'Call Distribution';
proc gchart data=police;
   pie officer / group=meridian
                 across=2
                 fill=s        /* Colors from COLORS= list */
                 explode='Casey' 'Franklin' 'Martinez' 'Murphy'
                 coutline=white
                 ctext=white;
run;
```

Example 9: Creating a Star Chart

The following example uses two DATA steps. The first DATA step creates a SAS data set that is suitable for processing by many SAS procedures. The second DATA step shows how to get data into a form that PROC GCHART can use. PROC GCHART is then used to produce a star chart of the data. The following statements produce **Output 9.28**.

```
data paper;
   input total board contain box tissue wrap print news;
   cards;
126 92 86 97 130 76 142 122
;

data chart;  /* Modify PAPER data into a form suitable for PROC GCHART */
   length type $16;
   set paper;
   type='Paper Total';       amount=total;    output;
   type='Paper Board';       amount=board;    output;
   type='Containerboard';    amount=contain;  output;
   type='Boxboard';          amount=box;      output;
   type='Tissue';            amount=tissue;   output;
   type='Wrapping Paper';    amount=wrap;     output;
   type='Printing Paper';    amount=print;    output;
   type='Newsprint';         amount=news;     output;
 run;
```

```
goptions cback=black colors=(white tan);
title1 f=swiss   '1984 Japanese Paper Production';
title2           '(1973 production = 100)';
footnote1  'Source: Industrial Review of Japan/1984';
footnote2  'Nihon Keizai Shimbun, Inc.';
proc gchart data=chart;
   star type / sumvar=amount
               fill=s   /* Alternate between colors in COLORS= list */
               matchcolor
               noheading;
run;
```

Output 9.18 Horizontal Bar Chart

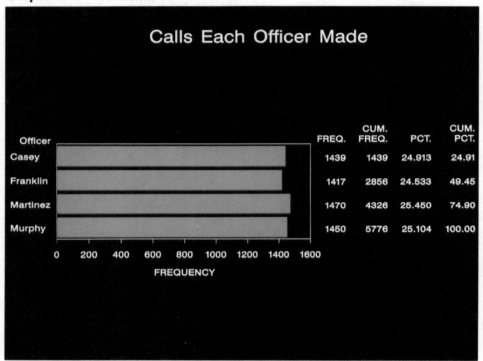

Output 9.19 Horizontal Bar Chart with GROUP= and G100 Options

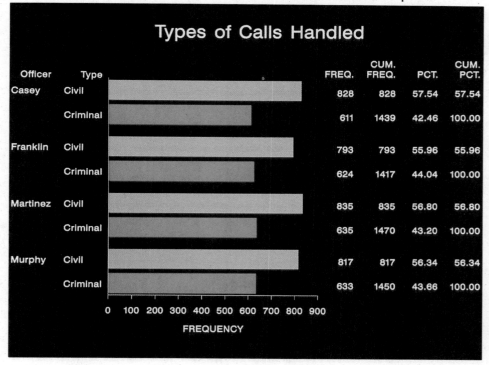

Output 9.20 Horizontal Bar Chart with SUBGROUP=, FREQ, and PERCENT Options

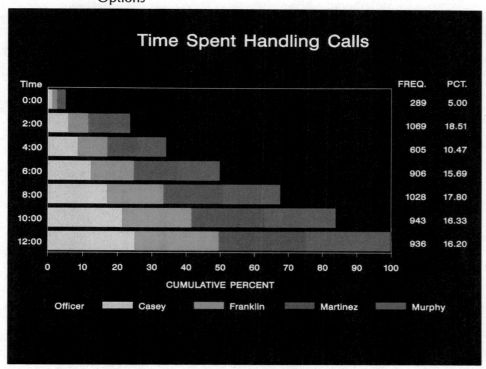

Output 9.21   Vertical Bar Chart

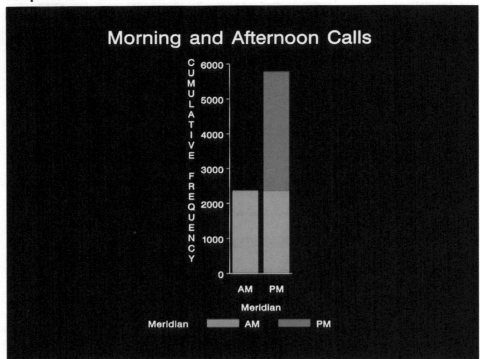

Output 9.22   Using the SUBGROUP= and GROUP= Options in a VBAR
Statement

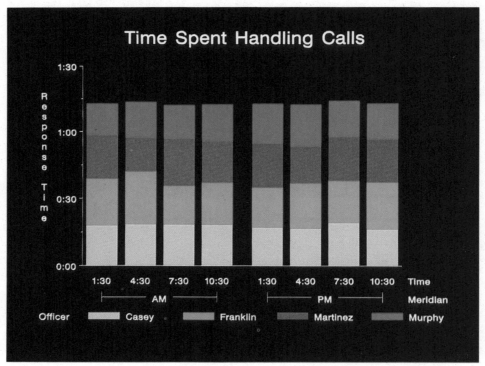

Output 9.23   Block Chart Showing Percent of Calls

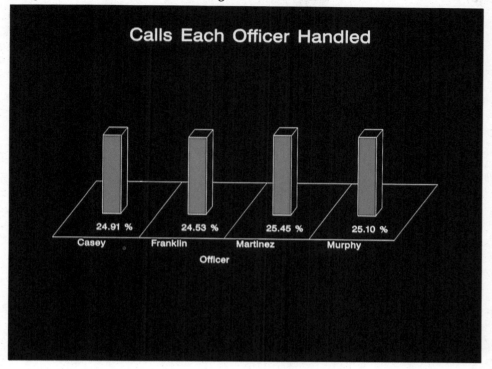

Output 9.24   Block Chart Showing Percent of Each Type of Call

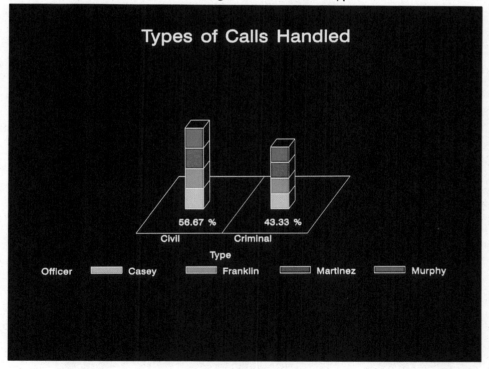

Output 9.25   Block Chart Showing Percentage of Types of Calls

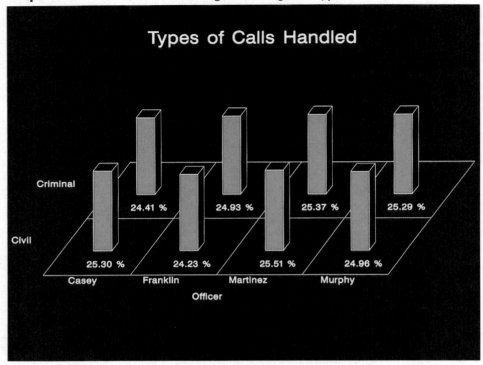

Output 9.26   Basic Pie Chart Using PERCENT=OUTSIDE and
MATCHCOLOR Options

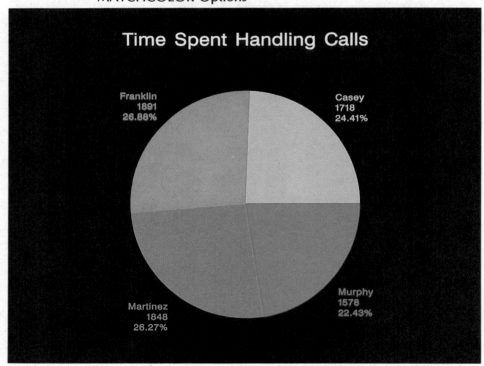

Output 9.27   Using the ACROSS=, GROUP=, and EXPLODE= Options in a
PIE Statement

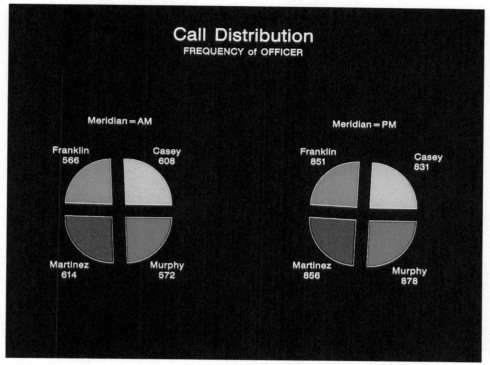

Output 9.28   A Star Chart

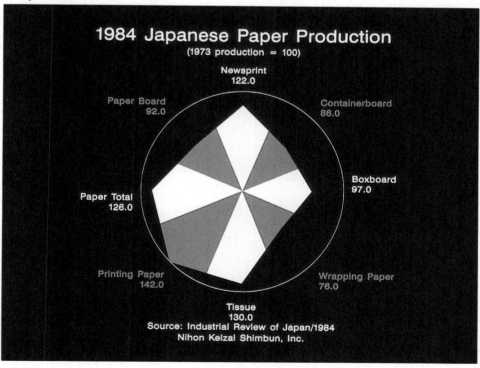

REFERENCES

Nelder, J. A. (1976), "A Simple Algorithm for Scaling Graphs" *Applied Statistics, Volume 25, Number 1*, London: The Royal Statistical Society.

Terrell, G.R. and Scott, D.W. (1985), "Oversmoothed Nonparametric Density Estimates," *Journal of the American Statistical Association*, 80.

Chapter 10

The GCONTOUR Procedure

ABSTRACT

The GCONTOUR procedure is the SAS/GRAPH version of the PLOT procedure's CONTOUR option. PROC GCONTOUR produces contour plots, in which values of three variables are represented in two dimensions. One of the variables is a contour variable; up to 100 levels of the contour variable can be represented on the plot. You can draw each contour level with a different color and line style, or you can specify patterns to fill each contour level. You can specify the variables you want plotted in a PLOT statement; PROC GCONTOUR automatically scales the vertical and horizontal axes. The algorithm used by PROC GCONTOUR is described in Snyder (1978).

INTRODUCTION

Below are some examples of plots produced by PROC GCONTOUR. The first plot, shown in **Output 10.1**, uses the default method for drawing contour levels; the second plot, shown in **Output 10.2**, uses the PATTERN option.

```
data area;
   do x=1 to 10;
      do y=1 to 10;
         z=sin(sqrt(x*x + y*y));
         output;
         end;
      end;

goptions cback=black
         colors=(white yellow rose cyan);
title1    j=l h=1.3 f=swiss c=white '    GCONTOUR Procedure          '
              h=3 f=simplex a= 90  ' '
              h=3 f=simplex a=-90  ' ';
footnote1 j=l h=1 f=none c=white '                                  ';
footnote2 j=l h=1 f=none c=white '     CONTOUR LINE          ';
footnote3 h=2 ' ';
proc gcontour  data=area;
   plot y*x=z;
run;

goptions cback=black
         colors=(white yellow vliyg cyan vibg vlipb pink);
title1    j=l h=1.3 f=swiss c=white '    GCONTOUR Procedure          '
              h=3 f=simplex a= 90  ' '
              h=3 f=simplex a=-90  ' ';
footnote1 j=l h=1 f=none c=white '                                  ';
footnote2 j=l h=1 f=none c=white '    PATTERN Option ';
footnote3 h=2 ' ';
pattern v=s;

proc gcontour data=area;
   plot y*x=z  /  pattern
                  ctext=white
                  caxis=white;
run;
```

Output 10.1   Contour Line: PROC GCONTOUR, Default Settings

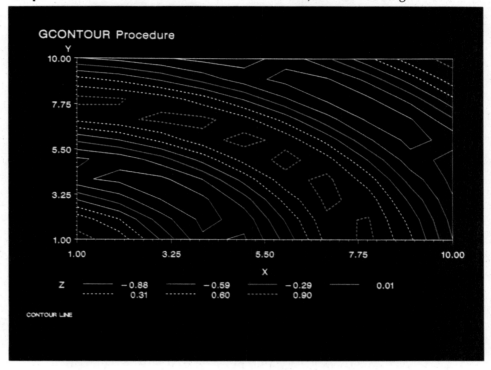

Output 10.2   Contour Line: PROC GCONTOUR with PATTERN Option

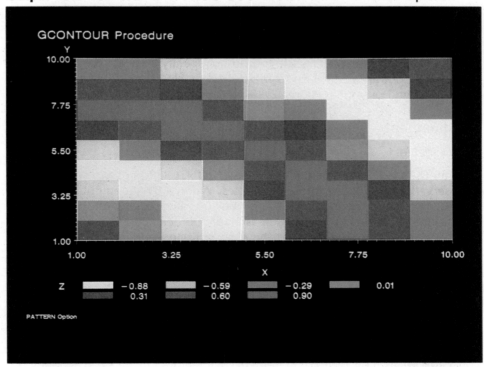

SPECIFICATIONS

The following statements can be used with PROC GCONTOUR:

PROC GCONTOUR *options*;
    PLOT *request / options*;
    BY *variables*;
    PATTERN*n options*;
    TITLE*n options 'text'*;
    FOOTNOTE*n options 'text'*;
    NOTE *options 'text'*;

The PLOT statement is required.

PROC GCONTOUR Statement

PROC GCONTOUR *options*;

You can specify the following options in the PROC GCONTOUR statement:

ANNOTATE=*SASdataset*
ANNO=*SASdataset*
    specifies a data set to be used for annotation. This data set must be an
    ANNOTATE= type data set containing the appropriate Annotate
    variables. (See "ANNOTATE= Data Sets" for details.)

DATA=*SASdataset*
    names the data set to be used by PROC GCONTOUR. When you omit
    the DATA= option, PROC GCONTOUR uses the most recently created
    SAS data set.

GOUT=*SAScatalog*
    specifies the name of the SAS catalog used to save the output produced
    by PROC GCONTOUR for later replay. (See "SAS/GRAPH Graphics
    Output" for more details.) If you do not specify the GOUT= option,
    catalog entries are written to the default catalog GSEG, which is erased
    at the end of your session.

BY Statement

BY *variables*;

You can use the BY statement with PROC GCONTOUR to obtain separate plots
of observations defined by the BY variables. When a BY statement appears, the
procedure expects the input data set to be sorted in order of the BY variables.
If your input data set is not sorted in ascending order, use the SORT procedure
with a similar BY statement to sort the data, or, if appropriate, use the BY statement options NOTSORTED or DESCENDING. For more information, see the discussion of the BY statement in "SAS Statements Used in the PROC Step" in the
SAS Language Guide, Release 6.03 Edition.

FOOTNOTE Statement

FOOTNOTE*n options 'text'*;

You can specify FOOTNOTE statements with PROC GCONTOUR. They are
described in "Enhancing Your Graphics Output Text."

NOTE Statement

NOTE *options 'text'*;

You can specify NOTE statements with PROC GCONTOUR. They are described in "Enhancing Your Graphics Output Text."

PATTERN Statement

PATTERN*n options*;

If you specify the PATTERN option in the PLOT statement, PROC GCONTOUR uses colors and patterns specified in PATTERN statements to fill each contour level. PATTERN statements are described in "Enhancing Your Graphics Output Designs." The only values for the V= option that you can specify are S, E, and M*xxxxx*.

PLOT Statement

PLOT *request / options*;

A PLOT statement must accompany the PROC GCONTOUR statement to request the plots to be produced. You can include any number of PLOT statements, but you can specify only one plot request with each PLOT statement. A *request* specifies the variables (vertical and horizontal) to be plotted and a numeric variable (in the data set) whose values determine the intensity of shading.
The options below can appear in the PLOT statement after a slash (/).

ANNOTATE=*SASdataset*
ANNO=*SASdataset*
   specifies a data set to be used for annotation. This data set must be an ANNOTATE= type data set containing the appropriate Annotate variables. (See "ANNOTATE= Data Sets" for details.)

CAXIS=*color*
   specifies the color to use for drawing the axes of the plot. If you omit the CAXIS= option, the second color in the COLORS= list is used to draw the axes. (See "The GOPTIONS Statement" for a description of the COLORS= option.)

COUTLINE=*color*
   specifies the outline color of filled areas. If you omit the COUTLINE= option, the outline color is the same as the color of the filled area.

CTEXT=*color*
   specifies the color to use for drawing all text that appears on the plot. Variable names, any labels, and tick mark values are drawn using the color specified by CTEXT=. If you omit the CTEXT= option, the first color in the COLORS= list is used for drawing text on the plot.

DESCRIPTION=*'string'*
DES=*'string'*
   specifies a descriptive string, up to forty characters long, that appears in the Description field of PROC GREPLAY's master menu. If you omit the DESCRIPTION= option, the Description field of PROC GREPLAY's master menu will contain a description assigned by SAS/GRAPH.

HAXIS=AXIS*n*
   specifies the axis description to use for the horizontal axis. Specify HAXIS=AXIS*n*, where *n* is the number of an AXIS statement previously defined. (See "Enhancing Your Graphics Output Designs" for more information about the AXIS statement.)

HMINOR=*n*
HM=*n*

gives the number of minor tick marks to draw between major tick marks on the horizontal axis. No values are drawn on the minor tick marks.

JOIN

tells SAS/GRAPH to combine grid cells of the same pattern, when possible, if you have also specified the PATTERN option. If you specify the PATTERN option but you do not specify JOIN, adjacent areas are not combined when drawn. See the **EXAMPLES** section for an illustration of the JOIN option.

LEGEND=LEGEND*n*

specifies the LEGEND statement to associate with the graph. Specify LEGEND=LEGEND*n*, where *n* is the number of a LEGEND statement you defined previously. Use LEGEND=LEGEND*n* only if the graph requested normally produces a legend (that is, it contains a request of the type Y*X=Z). Simply specifying LEGEND= in the PROC GCONTOUR statement does not cause a legend to be generated.

NAME=*'string'*

specifies a descriptive string, up to eight characters long, that appears in the Name field of PROC GREPLAY's master menu. If you omit the NAME= option, the Name field of PROC GREPLAY's master menu contains the procedure name.

NOAXES

requests that axes and axis labels not be drawn. The frame surrounding the plot is always printed.

NOLEGEND

requests that the legend showing contour levels and the type of line used to represent each level not appear at the bottom of the plot.

VAXIS=AXIS*n*

specifies the axis description to use for the vertical axis. Specify VAXIS=AXIS*n*, where *n* is the number of an AXIS statement previously defined. (See "Enhancing Your Graphics Output Designs" for more information about the AXIS statement.)

VMINOR=*n*
VM=*n*

specifies the number of minor tick marks to be drawn between major tick marks on the vertical axis. No values are drawn on the minor tick marks.

XTICKNUM=*n*

specifies the number of major tick marks to be drawn on the horizontal axis. The value of *n* must be 2 or greater.

YTICKNUM=*n*

specifies the number of major tick marks to be drawn on the vertical axis. The value of *n* must be 2 or greater.

Drawing Lines on the Plot

CHREF=*color*
CH=*color*

specifies the color to use for vertical lines requested by the HREF= option. If you do not specify a color, the axis color is used.

CVREF=*color*
CV=*color*

> specifies the color to use for horizontal lines requested by the VREF= option. If you do not specify a color, the axis color is used.

HREF=*values*

> specifies where vertical lines are to appear if you want them drawn on the plot. For example, the statements

```
proc gcontour;
    plot y*x=z / href=2 to 10 by 2;
```

> request a contour plot of Y by X, with Z as the contour variable. The plot has vertical lines at 2, 4, 6, 8, and 10 on the horizontal axis.

LHREF=*linetype*
LH=*linetype*

> specifies the line type (1–46, as shown in "Enhancing Your Graphics Output Designs") to use for drawing lines requested with HREF=. The default line type is 1, a solid line.

LVREF=*linetype*
LV=*linetype*

> specifies the line type (1–46, as shown in "Enhancing Your Graphics Output Designs") to use for drawing lines requested with VREF=. The default line type is 1, a solid line.

VREF=*values*

> specifies where horizontal lines are to appear if you want them drawn on the plot.

Specifying Contour Levels

The GCONTOUR procedure automatically selects seven contour levels for the range of values of the contour variable. PROC GCONTOUR chooses every 15th percentile between the 5th and the 95th, or you can specify contour levels using the LEVELS= option.

CLEVELS=*color1 color2 . . . colorn*

> specifies the list of colors to be used for drawing contour lines on the plot. One color is used to represent each level of contour; thus, the number of colors specified must correspond to the number of contour levels.

LEVELS=*values*

> specifies values to be used for contour levels on the plot. You can specify up to 100 values. For example, the statements

```
proc gcontour;
    plot y*x=z / levels=0 to 1 by .1;
```

> choose the eleven values, 0, 0.1, 0.2, . . . , 0.9, and 1, to represent the levels of the contour variable Z on the plot.
>
> PROC GCONTOUR normally selects colors and line types for the contour levels by rotating through the COLORS= list for each line type (1–46) until all the levels have been represented. (See "The GOPTIONS Statement" for a description of the COLORS= option; see "Enhancing Your Graphics Output Designs" for examples of the various line types.)
>
> You can specify the color and type of line to be used with the CLEVELS= and LLEVELS= options, or you can use the PATTERN option

to specify that each level be filled using colors and patterns specified in PATTERN statements.

LLEVELS=*linetypes*

specifies the line types to be used for drawing contour lines on the plot. The number of line types listed must correspond to the number of contour levels. The first contour level is drawn with the first color in the CLEVELS= color list and the first line type given by the LLEVELS= option; the second with the second color and the second line type, and so on.

PATTERN

requests that PROC GCONTOUR match each contour level with the patterns specified in PATTERN statements. PROC GCONTOUR determines the mean response of the four corners of each rectangle in the grid formed by the *x,y* axes. Then the procedure chooses the appropriate pattern for that contour level. When you omit the PATTERN option, each contour level is drawn with a different line type.

TITLE Statement

TITLE*n* options 'text';

You can specify TITLE statements with PROC GCONTOUR. They are described in "Enhancing Your Graphics Output Text."

EXAMPLES

Example 1: An Illustration of the JOIN Option

This example illustrates three plot statements: one with the JOIN and PATTERN options, one with the PATTERN option but without the JOIN option, and one with the JOIN option but without the PATTERN option. The graphics produced are in **Output 10.3–10.5.**

```
data rings;
   do x=-5 to 5 by 0.25;
      do y=-5 to 5 by 0.25;
         z=sin(x*x + y*y);
         output;
         end;
      end;


goptions cback=black
         colors=(yellow white cyan vliyg gold magenta salmon);
title1    j=l h=1.3 f=swiss c=white '     GCONTOUR Procedure            '
             h=3 f=simplex a= 90  ' '
             h=3 f=simplex a=-90  ' ';
footnote1 j=l h=1 f=none c=white '                                   ';
footnote2 j=l h=1 f=none c=white '     PATTERN / JOIN';
footnote3 h=2 ' ';
pattern v=s   r=99;
proc gcontour data=rings;
   plot y*x=z / pattern join
                ctext=white
                coutline=yellow;
run;
```

```
goptions cback=black
          colors=(yellow white cyan vliyg gold magenta salmon);
title1    j=l h=1.3 f=swiss c=white '   GCONTOUR Procedure       '
              h=3 f=simplex a= 90  ' '
              h=3 f=simplex a=-90  ' ';
footnote1 j=l h=1 f=none c=white '                             ';
footnote2 j=l h=1 f=none c=white '    PATTERN       ';
footnote3 h=2 ' ';
pattern v=s   r=99;

proc gcontour data=rings;
   plot y*x=z / pattern
               ctext=white
               coutline=yellow;
run;

goptions cback=black
          colors=(yellow white cyan rose gold magenta);
title1    j=l h=1.3 f=swiss c=white '   GCONTOUR Procedure       '
              h=3 f=simplex a= 90  ' '
              h=3 f=simplex a=-90  ' ';
footnote1 j=l h=1 f=none c=white '                            ';
footnote2 j=l h=1 f=none c=white '    JOIN         ';
footnote3 h=2 ' ';
proc gcontour data=rings;
   plot y*x=z / join
               ctext=white
               caxis=yellow;
run;
```

Output 10.3   PLOT Statement with Both JOIN and PATTERN Options:
                   PROC GCONTOUR

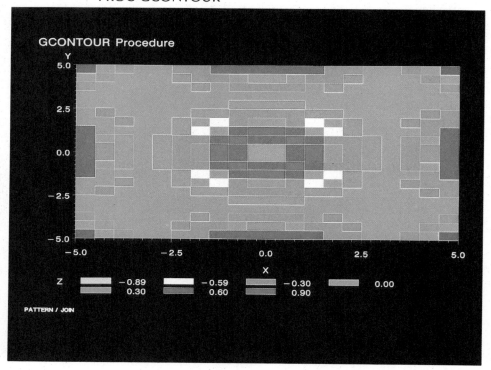

Output 10.4   PLOT Statement without JOIN: PROC GCONTOUR

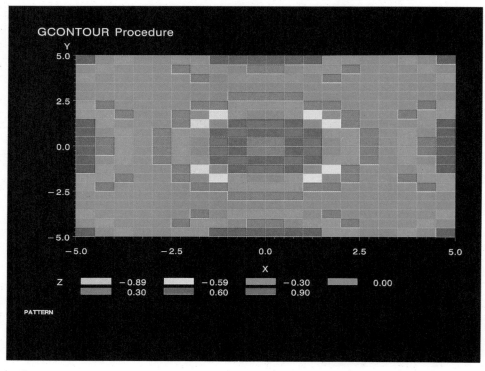

Output 10.5   PLOT Statement with JOIN Only: PROC GCONTOUR

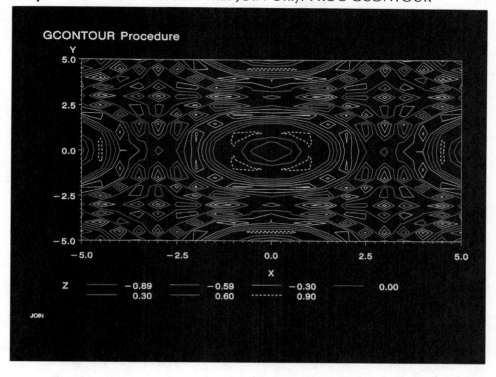

Example 2: An Illustration of the ANNOTATE= Option

This example illustrates the use of the ANNOTATE= option. A descriptive string is placed onto the picture generated by PROC GCONTOUR. See "ANNOTATE= Data Sets" for a detailed description of the ANNOTATE= option. The following statements produce **Output 10.6**.

```
goptions cback=black
         colors=(yellow white cyan);
title1    j=1 h=1.3 f=swiss c=white '      GCONTOUR Procedure            '
              h=3 f=simplex a= 90  ' '
              h=3 f=simplex a=-90  ' ';
footnote1 j=1 h=1 f=none c=white '                                        ';
footnote2 j=1 h=1 f=none c=white '     ANNOTATION           ';
footnote3 h=2 ' ';

data anno;
   length function color style $ 8;
   retain xsys '2' ysys '2';
   x=7; y=8.2; function='label';
              position='0';
              angle=-30;
              text='CAVITY';
              color='yellow';
              style='simplexu';
              output;
```

```
         x=3; y=3.5; position='5';
                     angle=-30;
                     output;
     run;

     proc gcontour data=area;
        plot y*x=z / ctext=white
                     caxis=yellow
                     annotate=anno;
     run;
```

Output 10.6 PLOT Statement Specifying ANNOTATE=: PROC GCONTOUR

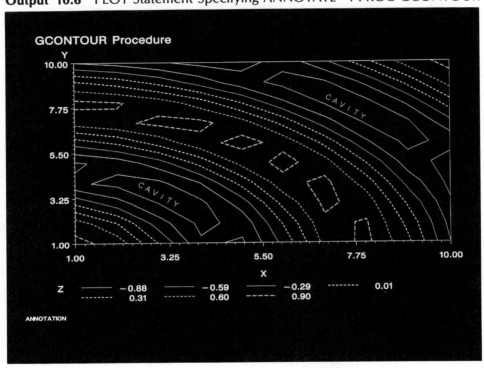

REFERENCE

Snyder, W.V. (1978), "Contour Plotting [J6]," *ACM Transactions on Mathematical Software*, 4, 290-294.

Chapter 11

The GDEVICE
Procedure

ABSTRACT

The GDEVICE procedure is a tool for examining and changing device driver parameters for graphics devices.

This chapter documents how to use PROC GDEVICE to change device driver parameters; it also lists all of the parameters that the procedure can change. You should follow the directions in this chapter down through **SETTING UP YOUR OWN DEVICE CATALOG**. Then, if you need to change parameters for your device driver, you should read the rest of the chapter.

With PROC GDEVICE, you can use full-screen menus or line-mode commands to

- list the device drivers available with your version of SAS/GRAPH software
- edit the options and parameters for Institute-supplied device drivers
- create new device drivers.

Use the GDEVICE procedure when you want to change system options for all of the graphs produced on a particular device. Use the GOPTIONS statement if you need to change system options for a particular graph or SAS session.

INTRODUCTION

When SAS/GRAPH software produces a graph on your device, it uses a *device driver*. The device driver takes the device-independent output generated by a SAS/GRAPH procedure and translates it into the particular graphics language required by your device.

You can control the way the device driver produces output for your device. The device driver uses the settings of a number of parameters to determine how it will draw a graph. The settings indicate, for example, how large to draw the graph, what default colors to use, and whether to send the graphics output directly to a device or to store it in a file. When a SAS/GRAPH procedure produces output, it looks in a *device catalog* to find the current parameter settings. A device catalog is a SAS catalog that contains *device entries*. Each device entry in the catalog stores the parameter settings for one device driver.

For example, when you specify DEVICE=HP7475 in a GOPTIONS statement, SAS/GRAPH software looks for an entry named HP7475 in the available device catalogs. It uses the information in that entry to determine the parameter settings to be used.

You can change the parameter settings in a device entry with the GDEVICE procedure. You can override the settings in a device entry with the GOPTIONS statement:

- Use PROC GDEVICE to set parameters for **all** SAS sessions.
- Use the GOPTIONS statement to modify parameters for **one** SAS session or in one SAS program (that is, to override the device entry settings for one session or graph).

USING THE DEFAULT DEVICE CATALOG

SASHELP.DEVICES, the device catalog supplied with SAS/GRAPH software, contains ready-to-use entries for many popular devices, including graphics terminals, plotters, printers, laser printers, and slide cameras.

To run SAS/GRAPH with your graphics device immediately, simply connect the hardware and use the DEVICE=*entryname* option in a GOPTIONS statement in your SAS session to identify which device entry to use. (See the appendix, "SAS/GRAPH Device Drivers," to determine the *entryname* to use for your device.) When you run SAS/GRAPH procedures, the software will automatically look for the specified device entry in SASHELP.DEVICES if no other device catalogs exist.

You should, however, set up your own device catalog, as described in the next section. Setting up your own device catalog will

- improve SAS/GRAPH performance by decreasing the number of entries that must be searched

- create personal copies of device entries that you can modify. (You should generally avoid changing the entries in SASHELP.DEVICES unless they contain values that are invalid for your system.)

SETTING UP YOUR OWN DEVICE CATALOG

SAS/GRAPH software looks only into catalogs with certain names to find device entries. Available names are given in **Device Catalog Precedence** below.

GDEVICE0.DEVICES is the first place that SAS/GRAPH software looks, so you should now

- identify the device entries for your devices by looking up the entry names in the appendix, "SAS/GRAPH Device Drivers"
- define the libref GDEVICE0
- copy the device entries for your devices from SASHELP.DEVICES into GDEVICE0.DEVICES.

The following examples define GDEVICE0 and copy two entries, one for a color graphics display (EGAL for personal computers, TEK4105 for UNIX operating systems and derivatives), and one for a plotter that uses standard paper (HP7550). See **EXAMPLES** at the end of this chapter for more detailed examples.

For SAS/GRAPH software on personal computers:

```
libname gdevice0 'c:\path';
proc gdevice catalog=gdevice0.devices nofs;
   copy egal   from=sashelp.devices
               newname=egal;
   copy hp7550 from=sashelp.devices
               newname=hp7550;
run;
```

For SAS/GRAPH software on UNIX operating systems and derivatives:

```
libname gdevice0 '~/path';
proc gdevice catalog=gdevice0.devices nofs;
   copy tek4105 from=sashelp.devices
               newname=tek4105;
   copy hp7550 from=sashelp.devices
               newname=hp7550;
run;
```

In either case, *path* is the complete pathname for the directory that will hold the device catalog.

Now include the LIBNAME statement defining GDEVICE0 in your AUTOEXEC.SAS file. If you usually use the same output device in all your SAS sessions, you can also put a GOPTIONS statement with the DEVICE=*entryname* option in the AUTOEXEC.SAS file to save you from having to submit it in every session.

Device Catalog Precedence

When you specify a device driver name (either with the DEVICE= option or when prompted), SAS/GRAPH software uses a device entry corresponding to the driver name you specify. The SAS System looks for device entries in this way:

If a catalog with libref GDEVICE0.DEVICES exists, then the SAS System looks there first for the entry. If the entry is not there, the SAS System looks for it next in a catalog with libref GDEVICE1.DEVICES and continues looking through GDEVICE9.DEVICES.

However, if the SAS System encounters an undefined libref in the sequence GDEVICE0.DEVICES to GDEVICE9.DEVICES **or** if it fails to find the specified entry in any of the catalogs in that sequence, then it searches for the entry in SASHELP.DEVICES. If it does not find the entry in SASHELP.DEVICES, then you are given an error message.

Options Precedence

When determining what value to use for a device parameter or option, the SAS System checks for the following, in order:

1. If a value for a device parameter or option is specified in a GOPTIONS statement, then the system uses that setting. If no value is specified, the corresponding device entry is checked.
2. If a value for the parameter or option is specified in the device entry, then the system uses that value.
3. If neither of the above conditions is met, then the system uses a default value. The system default for each field is given in the documentation in **USING FULL-SCREEN MENUS** below.

   Some parameters do not have default values; the corresponding fields in each device catalog entry *must* contain values. These parameters are identified as REQUIRED in the descriptions that follow.

CUSTOMIZING DEVICE ENTRIES

Adapting an Existing Entry

If you find it necessary to customize an entry, you should create your own device catalog and then copy the device drivers you need into it. You can then change your personal copies of the catalog entries without affecting the original drivers in SASHELP.DEVICES. (Use PROC GDEVICE, the CATALOG window, or PROC CATALOG to copy device entries).

If you try to change a field in an entry supplied by SAS Institute (either the original entry in SASHELP.DEVICES or a copy), the system will ask when you first try to modify it whether you really want to change the entry. Answer Y to continue or N to cancel the operation.

See **EXAMPLES** for a demonstration of how to create your own catalog and copy entries to it, both in full-screen mode and line mode.

Creating a New Device Entry

You can create an entry that is initialized with the system default values by using the ADD command in line mode. However, there is generally no need to do this because copying and adapting an existing entry is much easier.

Required Fields

Any device driver must have the following fields explicitly filled in (the fields have no system default but require a value): COLORS, MODULE, XMAX, XPIXELS, YMAX, YPIXELS. Additionally, at least one of the pairs LCOLS/LROWS or PCOLS/PROWS must be assigned positive nonzero values.

Metagraphics drivers require that additional fields be filled in; see **The METAGRAPHICS Screen** below.

THE PROC GDEVICE STATEMENT

The PROC GDEVICE statement has the general form

PROC GDEVICE [CATALOG=*catalog*] [BROWSE] [NOFS];

You can use the following options in the PROC GDEVICE statement:

BROWSE
: opens a catalog as read-only. You cannot make changes to catalog entries while in this mode. If you are in line mode, the only commands that are valid when you have specified BROWSE are FS | NOFS, LIST, QUIT, STOP, and END.

CATALOG=*catalog*
CAT=*catalog*
C=*catalog*
: names the catalog containing device information. If you do not specify a device catalog, the first catalog found in the search order of device catalogs is opened in browse mode. See **Device Catalog Precedence** above.

NOFS
: specifies line mode. Full-screen mode is the default, but you can switch between modes while you are running the procedure.

You can run PROC GDEVICE in line mode or in full-screen mode. In full-screen mode, you scroll through screens of fields and make changes by writing over field values. In line mode, the procedure is interactive: once you execute the PROC GDEVICE statement, you perform operations and change field values explicitly with line-mode commands.

USING FULL-SCREEN MENUS

In full-screen mode, you move through a set of menus, changing fields in them as appropriate. You view the menus one at a time, going through them in the following sequence:

CATALOG
: This screen is shown when you first enter the procedure. It lists the device drivers in the catalog you specified in the PROC GDEVICE statement. Here, you either work with entries (you can copy, rename, or delete them) or work with their contents (you can browse or edit the fields in one device entry).

  When you choose an entry to browse or edit, you are taken automatically to the DETAIL screen.

DETAIL
: This screen shows several basic characteristics of the device: display and graphics area size, where graphics output is sent by default, and how graphics data are written.

PARAMETERS
: This screen shows parameters that affect the way graphs are drawn. For example, you choose whether certain graphics primitives are drawn by your hardware or by SAS/GRAPH software, whether to feed paper to printers or plotters automatically, and whether to have the system prompt you with messages under certain conditions.

GCOLORS

> This screen lists the colors that the driver will use by default. When you do not explicitly specify the color of a graphics feature (for example, titles and axes) in your program, SAS/GRAPH software uses this list to determine what color to use.

CHARTYPE

> This screen lists the hardware fonts that the device can use, along with information about how much space the characters need.

METAGRAPHICS

> You probably will not use this screen. It is meaningful only if the device driver is a Metagraphics driver. Metagraphics drivers are essentially user-written device drivers; such drivers are needed in the instances when an Institute-supplied device driver cannot be adapted to run your graphics device.

GPROLOG

> This screen contains one field: a hex string that is sent to the device just before graphics commands are sent.

GEPILOG

> This screen contains one field: a hex string that is sent to the device just after graphics commands are sent.

GSTART

> This screen contains one field: a hex string that is put at the beginning of each record of graphics data.

GEND

> This screen contains one field: a hex string that is put at the end of each record of graphics data.

Common Commands

These commands can be issued from the command line in **all** screens:

CANCEL	prevents saving information to entry
END	saves current information to entry
NEXTSCR	saves any modified information and goes to the next screen
NOFS	exits full-screen mode and enters line mode
SAVE	saves current information to entry and remains in current screen.

There are additional commands that you can issue from the CATALOG and DETAIL screens. See the **Additional Commands** sections in **The CATALOG Screen** and **The DETAIL Screen** below.

The CATALOG Screen

Screen 11.1 is an example of the CATALOG screen.

```
┌─GDEVICE: DIRECTORY SASHELP.DEVICES (E) ──────────────────────────┐
│Command ===>                                                       │
│                                                                   │
│      Name      Type     Description                       Updated │
│                                                                   │
│   _  PS        DEV      PostScript Device                 05/19/87│
│   _  PS2EGA    DEV      PS/2 EGA with enhanced color display 05/19/87│
│   _  PS2EGAM   DEV      PS/2 EGA with monochrome display   05/19/87│
│   _  PSEPSF    DEV      PostScript Device- Encapsulated Files 05/19/87│
│   _  PSFIX     DEV      PostScript - fixed text spacing    05/19/87│
│   _  PSL       DEV      PostScript Device- thin lines      05/19/87│
│   _  PSLFIX    DEV      PostScript -fixed text space -thin line 05/19/87│
│   _  Q800PLUS  DEV      QMS PS-800 Plus Laser Printer      05/19/87│
│   _  QCR2X     DEV      QCR 2K Camera                      05/19/87│
│   _  QCR2XL    DEV      QCR 2K Camera with linear lookup table 05/19/87│
│   _  QCR4X     DEV      QCR 4K Camera                      05/19/87│
│   _  QCR4XL    DEV      QCR 4K Camera with linear lookup table 05/19/87│
│   _  QMS800    DEV      QMS Lasergrafix Printer- Portrait  05/19/87│
│   _  QMS800E   DEV      QMS Lasergrafix Printer- Portrait, Erase 05/19/87│
│   _  QMSPS800  DEV      QMS PS-800 Laser Printer           05/19/87│
│   _  QVP       DEV      Generic QVP SCODL file             05/19/87│
│   _  QVP2X     DEV      Generic QVP SCODL file - 2K resolution 05/19/87│
│   _  QVP4X     DEV      Generic QVP SCODL file - 4K resolution 05/19/87│
│   _  SER281    DEV      Servogor 281 Plotter               05/19/87│
│                                                                 ─R─┘
```

Screen 11.1   The CATALOG Screen

Note: the screens in this chapter are taken from various entries in SASHELP.DEVICES.

Additional Commands

In addition to the commands listed in **Common Commands**, the following commands can be used on the CATALOG screen command line:

BACKWARD *n*   goes backward *n* entries in the catalog.

BROWSE *entryname*

> shows the contents of the specified entry, beginning with the DETAIL screen. You cannot change information in the fields while viewing an entry in browse mode.

COPY *oldname newname*

> copies the information from the entry specified in *oldname* to a new entry, using the *newname* value as the name for the new entry.

DELETE *entryname*

> deletes the entry specified in *entryname*. When the DELETE command is executed, the entry and description are overwritten with a prompt to verify the deletion. Type v in the selection field and press RETURN to verify the deletion. Press RETURN alone to cancel the deletion. Use this command with care; there is no way to restore a catalog entry once it has been deleted.

EDIT *entryname*   shows contents of the entry specified in *entryname*, beginning with the DETAIL screen. If you are executing this command from the command line or in line mode, a new entry will be created if an entry with the name you specify does not already exist.

FORWARD *n*   goes forward *n* entries in the catalog.

RENAME *oldname newname* [*newdescription*]

changes the entry name and, optionally, the description of the entry specified in *oldname*. The entry is given the name specified in *newname*. If a *newdescription* value is also supplied, that value replaces the current description field for the entry. To change only the description, use the *oldname* value for *newname*.

SELECT *entryname*

shows detailed information on the entry specified in *entryname*, beginning with the DETAIL screen. This command is the same as BROWSE if the catalog was opened in browse mode; otherwise, it is equivalent to EDIT.

You can also issue global display manager commands from the command line of the CATALOG screen.

Using Selection Fields

You can also use one-letter commands in the CATALOG screen's selection fields to execute commands.

To use a selection field command, just move the cursor to the selection field of the entry that you want to use. Then type the command letter and press RETURN. These are the selection-field commands for the CATALOG screen:

b   browses the selected entry, beginning with the DETAIL screen. You cannot make changes to fields in any screen while in browse mode.

d   deletes the selected entry. When you press RETURN, a message will ask you if you really want to delete the entry. To verify, type v in the selection field and press RETURN. Press RETURN alone to cancel the deletion. Use this command with care; there is no way to restore a catalog entry once it has been deleted.

e   edits the selected entry, beginning with the DETAIL screen. You can make changes to fields in any screen while you are in edit mode.

r   renames the entry. When you press RETURN, the NAME and DESCRIPTION fields will be highlighted. Just type the new name or description over the old one; then press RETURN.

s   selects an entry. This command is the same as **b** if the catalog was opened in browse mode; otherwise, it is equivalent to **e**.

The DETAIL Screen

Screen 11.2 shows a DETAIL screen that is from the PSL entry in the SASHELP.DEVICES catalog. (The example screen shows the entry from the catalog supplied with SAS/GRAPH software for personal computers. The values for all fields except GACCESS are the same in the catalog supplied with SAS/GRAPH software for UNIX operating systems and derivatives.)

```
┌GDEVICE: Detail─────────────────────────────────────────────────────┐
│Command ===>                                                         │
│                                                                     │
│Catalog: SASHELP.DEVICES                               Entry:   PSL  │
│                                                                     │
│Orig Driver: PSL              Module:  SASGDPSL      Model:   1251   │
│Description: PostScript Device with thin lines        Type:   CRT    │
│Lrows:   75  Xmax:     8.500 IN  Hsize:      7.500 IN  Xpixels: 2550 │
│Lcols:  100  Ymax:    11.000 IN  Vsize:     10.000 IN  Ypixels: 3300 │
│Prows:  100                      Horigin:    0.500 IN               │
│Pcols:   75                      Vorigin:    0.500 IN               │
│Aspect:       0.000              Rotate:  _____                  │
│Driver query: _                  Queued messages: Y                │
│Gprotocol: _____              Paperfeed:     0.000 IN           │
│Gaccess: SASGASTD>COM1:                                            │
│Gsfname: _____                Gsfmode: PORT       Gsflen:     0  │
│Trantab: _____                Devmap:  _____                 │
│                                                                     │
│                                                                     │
│                                                                     │
│                                                                     │
└─────────────────────────────────────────────────────────────────────┘
```

Screen 11.2   The DETAIL Screen

Additional Commands

In addition to the commands listed in **Common Commands**, these commands can be issued from the DETAIL screen command line:

BACKWARD *n*   goes backward *n* entries in the catalog.

CHARTYPE   saves the current DETAIL information to the entry and goes to the CHARTYPE screen.

FORWARD *n*   goes forward *n* entries in the catalog.

GCOLORS   saves the current DETAIL information to the entry and goes to the GCOLORS screen.

GEND   saves the current DETAIL information to the entry and goes to the GEND screen.

GEPILOG   saves the current DETAIL information to the entry and goes to the GEPILOG screen.

GPROLOG   saves the current DETAIL information to the entry and goes to the GPROLOG screen.

GSTART   saves the current DETAIL information to the entry and goes to the GSTART screen.

META   saves the current DETAIL information to the entry and goes to the METAGRAPHICS screen.

PARAMETERS   saves the current DETAIL information to the entry and goes to the PARAMETERS screen.

You will find the following fields on the DETAIL screen. (Fields marked with an asterisk can be overridden by a similarly named option in a GOPTIONS statement.)

*ASPECT

Optional. Default is 0.0. Value must be a non-negative number. If the value is 0.0, then ASPECT is defined by the device.

Enter the aspect ratio for character cells (the ratio of cell width to cell height). For example, a value of 2 in the ASPECT field scales cells to be twice as wide as they are high. The character-cell aspect ratio affects many graphic characteristics, such as the shape of characters and the roundness of pie charts. Note that some graphics drivers do not produce correct output if the aspect ratio is anything other than the default. Be sure to inspect sample output if you change the value.

DESCRIPTION

Optional. Default is blank. Value is a string up to forty characters long, giving a description of the device. This is a comment field and does not affect the device output.

DEVMAP

Optional. Default is blank. Value is a string up to eight characters long designating the device map to be used when writing text with a hardware character set. See *SAS/GRAPH Guide to Hardware Interfaces, Release 6.03 Edition* or *SAS/GRAPH Hardware Interfaces for Personal Computers, Version 6 Edition* for more information on device maps.

DRIVER QUERY

Not used. Leave this field blank.

*GACCESS

Optional. Default is blank. Value is a character string designating *outputformat* [>*destination*]. *Outputformat* is SASGASTD, SASGAEDT, or SASGAFIX. In SAS/GRAPH software for UNIX operating systems and derivatives, the format SASGACMD is also available.

Enter the format and destination of graphics data written to a device or graphics stream file (GSF). SASGASTD, the default for most devices, specifies that a continuous stream of data is written. This is typically appropriate when the output file is to be sent directly to a device.

SASGAEDT specifies that new-line characters be inserted at the end of each record. In SAS/GRAPH software for personal computers, it also specifies that a CTRL-Z character be inserted at the end of the last record. SASGAEDT is typically used when the output file is to be edited later. Such use is rare and generally falls into two categories: debugging and file postprocessing (usually to convert characters that do not transfer across machine environments).

SASGAFIX specifies that fixed-length records be written (the record length is controlled by the value in the GSFLEN field). The records are padded with blanks where necessary. SASGAFIX is typically used when the output file is to be transferred to a computer that requires fixed-length records.

SASGACMD, valid only in SAS/GRAPH software for UNIX operating systems and derivatives, specifies that the graphics data stream is to be routed to the standard input of the UNIX command specified in the *destination* portion of the field.

Destination can be used to direct output to a particular device or to a file. For example, in SAS/GRAPH software for personal computers, SASGASTD>COM1: is the default for most plotters; it specifies that graphics data be sent to the COM1: serial port. The entries for some printers have the value SASGASTD>PRN:, which directs output to the parallel printer port. Under UNIX operating systems and derivatives, SASGASTD>/DEV/TTY is the default for most graphics terminals; it sends output to the standard terminal destination.

In SAS/GRAPH software for UNIX operating systems and derivatives, the *destination* value can also be a UNIX command, but only if the *outputformat* value is SASGACMD. This format routes the graphics data stream from the driver to the standard input of the specified UNIX command, usually **lp**. For example, the Institute-supplied device entries for most printers have the value SASGACMD>lp -dgoutput, which specifies that graphics data be sent to the line printer daemon for the device with the system destination goutput.

The *destination* value can also be a filename, in which case the stream of graphics data from the driver is written to the specified file. Such graphics stream files can later be replayed by sending the file to the device. For example, SASGAEDT>MYFILE.GSF causes output from the driver to be written to the file MYFILE.GSF in the current directory. You can use a full *pathname* for the file. In SAS/GRAPH software for personal computers the path can include a disk specification (for example, C:\MYDIR\MYFILE.GSF).

Note that the GACCESS specification cannot generate a usable graphics stream file when you are using a device driver that does not produce a graphics data stream. Examples include drivers for personal computer display adapters such as CGA, EGA, and Hercules. Graphics stream files created by such drivers cannot be displayed in the usual manner—by sending the file back to the device—because these devices cannot accept file input.

Refer to "SAS/GRAPH Graphics Output" in this guide and to *SAS/GRAPH Guide to Hardware Interfaces, Release 6.03 Edition* or *SAS/GRAPH Hardware Interfaces for Personal Computers, Version 6 Edition* for details on using the GACCESS field.

*GPROTOCOL

Optional; valid only for certain operating systems. Default is blank. Value is either blank (' ') or SASGPHEX.

Use this field to specify how the graphics data generated by the SAS/GRAPH device driver are to be altered. Most devices do not require that the data be altered; the default value is appropriate for such devices.

SASGPHEX will cause the output from the driver to be written in a printable hexadecimal format. Each character in the file is written as two printable ASCII characters. For example, a carriage return, which is a non-printable character ('0D'x), is translated into the two-character string, 0D. SASGPHEX is rarely used; however, you can use it to transfer files across machine environments when the graphics output contains characters that a file-transfer utility would not otherwise be able to send.

Refer to *SAS/GRAPH Guide to Hardware Interfaces, Release 6.03 Edition* or *SAS/GRAPH Hardware Interfaces for Personal Computers, Version 6 Edition* for details.

*GSFLEN

Optional. Default is 0. Value is a non-negative integer up to five digits long.

Enter the length of the records to be written by the driver to a graphics stream file or to a device.

*GSFMODE

Optional. Default is PORT. Value is a character string, either APPEND, PORT, or REPLACE.

Use this field to specify how the device driver will write graphics output records.

PORT is used when the records are to be sent to a device or communications port. The GACCESS or GSFNAME field value should point to the desired port or device.

APPEND is used when the records are to be added to the end of a graphics stream file. The GACCESS or GSFNAME field value should point to the file.

REPLACE is used when the records are to replace the existing contents of a graphics stream file. The GACCESS or GSFNAME field value should point to the file.

Note that the GSFMODE field does not specify whether records are actually written to a port or device or to a file but only specifies how to write the records. The GACCESS and GSFNAME fields specify the output destinations, and they must be set to match the GSFMODE value as stated above or else the output may be created incorrectly.

*GSFNAME

Optional. Default is blank. Value is a string up to eight characters long.

Enter the fileref for the file to which the device driver will write graphics stream files. You must use a FILENAME statement in your SAS program (or in AUTOEXEC.SAS) to assign the name of the desired file to the fileref. If you do not, you will get an error message and no graphics stream file will be generated when your program runs. Refer to the description of the FILENAME statement in "SAS Statements Used in the DATA Step" in the *SAS Language Guide, Release 6.03 Edition* for information on how to define filerefs.

The value in the GSFNAME field overrides any file specification or path in the GACCESS field.

Note that the GSFNAME specification cannot generate a usable graphics stream file when you are using a device driver that does not generate a graphics data stream. Examples include drivers for personal computer display adapters such as CGA, EGA, and Hercules. Graphics stream files created by such drivers cannot be displayed in the usual manner—by sending the file back to the device—because these devices cannot accept file input.

Refer to "SAS/GRAPH Graphics Output" for more information on graphics stream file output.

*HORIGIN

Optional. Default is 0.0. Value must be a non-negative number and may be followed by a units specification, either IN for inches (default) or CM for centimeters.

Enter the horizontal component of the graph origin. The graph origin is the lower-left corner of the area where graphs will be drawn; it is offset from the device origin (lower-left corner of the screen) by the values of the pair HORIGIN/VORIGIN.

This field is not supported on all devices. Refer to *SAS/GRAPH Guide to Hardware Interfaces, Release 6.03 Edition* or *SAS/GRAPH Hardware Interfaces for Personal Computers, Version 6 Edition* for details.

*HSIZE

Optional. No default, but XMAX (entire width of graphics area) is used if value is 0.0. Value must be positive and may be followed by a units specification, either IN for inches (default) or CM for centimeters.

Enter the desired width of the graphs that will be drawn.

*LCOLS

Optional. Default is 0. Value must be a non-negative integer up to three digits long. Either LROWS and LCOLS or PROWS and PCOLS must be nonzero.

Enter the width, in columns, of the display when it is in LANDSCAPE mode (when the image is wider than it is high), in columns. If you specify HPOS= in a GOPTIONS statement, it overrides the values in the LCOLS and PCOLS fields.

See also the ROTATE field description.

*LROWS

Optional. Default is 0. Value is a non-negative integer up to three digits long. Either LROWS and LCOLS or PROWS and PCOLS must be nonzero.

Enter the number of rows on the device when the device is in LANDSCAPE mode (when the image is wider than it is high). If you specify VPOS= in a GOPTIONS statement, it overrides the values in the LROWS and PROWS fields.

See also the ROTATE field description.

MODEL

Optional. Default is 0. Value is a non-negative integer up to five digits long.

Enter the Institute-designated model number for the corresponding device (it is not the same as a manufacturer's model number). See *SAS/GRAPH Guide to Hardware Interfaces, Release 6.03 Edition* or *SAS/GRAPH Hardware Interfaces for Personal Computers, Version 6 Edition* for the list of available model numbers.

Do not change this field in Institute-supplied drivers or in drivers that you copy from Institute-supplied drivers.

MODULE

REQUIRED. Enter the name of the corresponding driver file for the device. The *entryname* can be up to eight characters long. (All standard driver files begin with the characters SASGD.)

Do not change this field in Institute-supplied drivers or in drivers that you copy from Institute-supplied drivers.

ORIG DRIVER

Protected. This field reminds you what the driver was named in the Institute-supplied catalog, SASHELP.DEVICES. You can copy drivers from the one there and rename them (see **SETTING UP YOUR OWN DEVICE CATALOG**). The value is set to USER for new entries added to the catalog.

*PAPERFEED

Optional. Default is 0.0 IN. Value must be a non-negative number and may be followed by a units specification, either IN for inches (default) or CM for centimeters.

Enter the length of paper used for each graph (for fanfold paper, the distance between perforations). If PAPERFEED is a positive value and is less than the horizontal size of the graph (HSIZE or XMAX), the paper will perform PAPERFEED-size ejections until the graph is at least one half inch beyond the drawing area.

Not all device drivers use this field; it is provided mainly for plotters that use fanfold or roll paper.

*PCOLS

Optional. Default is 0. Value must be a non-negative integer up to three digits long. Either LROWS and LCOLS or PROWS and PCOLS must be nonzero.

Enter the number of columns on the display when it is in PORTRAIT mode (when the image is higher than it is wide). If you specify HPOS= in a GOPTIONS statement, it overrides the values in the LCOLS and PCOLS fields.

See also the ROTATE field description.

*PROWS

Optional. Default is 0. Value is a non-negative integer up to three digits long. Either LROWS and LCOLS or PROWS and PCOLS must be nonzero.

Enter the number of rows on the device when the device is in PORTRAIT mode (when the image is higher than it is wide). If you specify VPOS= in the GOPTIONS statement, it overrides the values in the LROWS and PROWS fields.

See also the ROTATE field description.

QUEUED MESSAGES

Optional. Default is blank (messages are not queued). Value is one character, either Y or N. (A blank field is equivalent to N.)

Enter Y to queue any messages issued by the procedure while it is in graphics mode and N to disable queuing. Message queuing is desirable on display devices that do not have a separate dialog and graphics area. Use N in this field for a plotter.

*ROTATE

Optional. Default is determined by whether XMAX is greater than YMAX if the field is blank. Value is a character string, either LANDSCAPE or PORTRAIT.

Enter LANDSCAPE if the display area is wider than it is high; enter PORTRAIT if it is higher than it is wide.

If the value of the ROTATE field is LANDSCAPE, the system uses the LROWS and LCOLS values to define the number of rows and columns on the device; if you specify PORTRAIT, it uses the PROWS and PCOLS values. However, in case of conflict between the ROTATE field and the row and column fields, the system will use the other row and column fields to set up the device. For example, if ROTATE is set to PORTRAIT and PROWS and PCOLS are set to zero, then the system will try to use the values for LROWS and LCOLS to set up the device.

Note that this field sets the **normal** orientation of graphs. You can use the ROTATE option in a GOPTIONS statement both to change the normal orientation (specified by values LANDSCAPE or PORTRAIT) and to rotate individual graphs on a one-time basis. (The ROTATE option causes graphs to be rotated 90 degrees from the normal orientation.

Not all devices support this option.

*TRANTAB

Optional. Default is blank. Value is a string up to eight characters long. Leave this field blank.

TYPE

Optional. Default is CRT. Value is either CRT or PLOTTER.

Enter CRT for a monitor, terminal, film-recording device, printer, or laser printer; enter PLOTTER for a plotter.

*VORIGIN

Optional. Default is 0.0. Value must be a non-negative number and may be followed by a units specification, either IN for inches (default) or CM for centimeters.

Enter the vertical component of the graph origin. The graph origin is the lower-left corner of the area where graphs will be drawn; it is offset from the device origin (lower-left corner of the screen) by the values of the pair HORIGIN/VORIGIN.

This field is not supported on all devices. Refer to *SAS/GRAPH Guide to Hardware Interfaces, Release 6.03 Edition* or *SAS/GRAPH Hardware Interfaces for Personal Computers, Version 6 Edition* for details.

*VSIZE

Optional. No default, but YMAX (entire height of the graphics area) is used if value is 0.0. Value must be positive and may be followed by a units specification, either IN for inches (default) or CM for centimeters.

Enter the desired height of the graphs that will be drawn.

XMAX

REQUIRED. No default. Value must be positive and may be followed by a units specification, either IN for inches (default) or CM for centimeters.

Enter the width of the graphics display area (the entire area that is addressable).

XPIXELS

REQUIRED. No default. Value must be a positive integer and may be up to five digits long. It corresponds to the XMAX field, but the width is in pixels rather than inches or centimeters.

Enter the width of the display in pixels.

YMAX

REQUIRED. No default. Value must be positive and may be followed by a units specification, either IN for inches (default) or CM for centimeters.

Enter the height of the graphics display area (the entire area that is addressable).

YPIXELS

REQUIRED. No default. Value must be a positive integer and may be up to five digits long. It corresponds to the YMAX field, but the height is in pixels rather than inches or centimeters.

Enter the height of the display in pixels.

The PARAMETERS Screen

Screen 11.3 shows the PARAMETERS screen from the HP7440 entry in SASHELP.DEVICES.

```
┌─GDEVICE: Parameters──────────────────────────────────────────────────────
│Command ===>
│
│Catalog: SASHELP.DEVICES                         Entry:     HP7440
│
│Erase:      _        Autofeed:    _       Chartype:    0
│Swap:       _        Cell:        _       Maxcolors:   9
│Autocopy:   _        Characters:  _       Repaint:     0
│Handshake: XONXOFF   Circlearc:   _       Gcopies:     0
│                     Dash:        _       Gsize:       0
│Prompt:  start up:      X  Fill:     _    Speed:       0
│         end of graph: _  Piefill:   _    Fillinc:     10
│         mount pens:   X  Polyfill:  _    Maxpoly:     128
│         change paper: X  Symbol:    _    Lfactor:     0
│Promptchars: 000A000D01460000      Dashline: _____
│Rectfill:    _____      Symbols:  _____
│Devopts:     _____
│UCC:         _____
│
│
│
│
│
│
└──────────────────────────────────────────────────────────────────────────
```

Screen 11.3 The PARAMETERS Screen

See **Common Commands** for a list of the commands you can use while on this screen.

You will find the following fields on the PARAMETERS screen. (Fields marked with an asterisk can be overridden by a similarly named option in a GOPTIONS statement.)

*AUTOCOPY

Optional. Default is blank (same as N). Value is Y, N, or blank.

Enter Y to automatically create a printed copy of graphs (applicable only to devices that have an appropriate hardcopy device attached), or enter N to suppress the printed copy.

*AUTOFEED

Optional. Default is blank (same as N). Value is Y, N, or blank.

Enter Y if you want the device to automatically feed new paper in for the next graph. (Not all devices are equipped to do so.) Enter N to suppress automatic feed.

*CELL

Optional. Default is blank (same as N). Value is Y, N, or blank.

Enter Y to enable cell alignment; N to suppress it. Some devices require this feature to align the hardware character set for the device. You use Y to display graphs on cell-aligned screens and N to display them on non-cell-aligned devices such as pen plotters.

*CHARACTERS

Optional. Default is blank (same as Y). Value is Y, N, or blank.

Enter Y if you want the device to use its hardware characters when a font is not specified in a SAS program. Enter N if you want the software to draw the characters.

*CHARTYPE

Optional. Default is 0 (use default character set for the device). Value is a non-negative integer up to five digits long.

Enter the number of the character set to use; the value can range from 1 to the total number of character sets available. The number corresponds to the number of the font in the CHARTYPE screen. See the CHARTYPE field description in **The CHARTYPE Screen**, below.

*CIRCLEARC

Optional. Default is blank (same as Y). Value is Y, N, or blank.

Enter Y to have the device use its built-in hardware circle- and arc-drawing capability in graphs. Enter N to have software draw circles and arcs. Hardware drawing is faster, but not all devices have the capability.

*DASH

Optional. Default is blank (same as Y). Value is Y, N, or blank.

Enter Y to have the device use its built-in hardware dashed-line-drawing capability in graphs. Enter N to have software draw dashed lines. Hardware drawing is faster, but not all devices have the capability.

DASHLINE

Optional. Default is blank. Value is a hex string sixteen characters long and completely filled.

Enter the hex string that represents which dashed lines should be generated by hardware means if possible. If the DASH field value is N, the hex string is ignored. For line style 1, turn on bit 1; for line style 2, turn on bit 2, and so on.

See *SAS/GRAPH Guide to Hardware Interfaces, Release 6.03 Edition* or *SAS/GRAPH Hardware Interfaces for Personal Computers, Version 6 Edition* for a table that shows what line style corresponds to each bit. Bit 1 should always be on because it corresponds to a solid line.

DEVOPTS

Optional. Default is blank. Value is a hex string sixteen characters long and completely filled.

Enter the hex string representing the hardware capabilities of the device. See *SAS/GRAPH Guide to Hardware Interfaces, Release 6.03 Edition* or *SAS/GRAPH Hardware Interfaces for Personal Computers, Version 6 Edition* for information on how to specify the string.

You can specify some options more easily by changing fields in the device entry with PROC GDEVICE. You should use DEVOPTS to change only those options that cannot be specified with PROC GDEVICE or the GOPTIONS statement.

*ERASE

Optional. Default is blank (no erase). Value is Y, N, or blank.

Enter Y if the graph is to be erased when you press RETURN after it has been completed or N if the graph is to remain. This option is useful for those devices that overlay the graphics area and the message area.

*FILL

Optional. Default is blank (same as Y). Value is Y, N, or blank.

Enter Y to have the device use its built-in hardware rectangle-filling capability. Enter N to have software fill rectangles. Hardware filling is faster, but not all devices have the capability.

FILLINC

Optional. Default is 0, which sets the system fill increment to 1. Value is a non-negative integer up to four digits long.

Enter the number of device coordinate units (pixels) to move before drawing the next line in a software fill of a solid area. If FILLINC is set to 0 or 1, adjacent lines are used (solid fill with no gaps). If FILLINC is set to 2, then a pixel-width line is skipped before drawing the next line of a fill. This option can be useful for keeping plotters from oversaturating a solid area. Some inks spread on paper (the type of paper used can also affect ink spread).

*GCOPIES

Optional. Default is 0 (1 copy). Value is a non-negative integer up to three digits long.

Enter the number of copies of each graph to print. Not all devices have the capability to print multiple copies. Both 0 and 1 specify that a single copy be printed.

*GSIZE

Optional. Default is 0. Value is a non-negative integer up to three digits long.

This field is used only with devices that can divide their display area into graphics and text areas. Enter the integer that specifies the number of lines to be used for graphics. The number can be larger or smaller than the total number of lines that can be displayed at one time. If the number is larger, you will have to scroll the graph to see it all.

*HANDSHAKE

Optional. Default is blank (same as S). Value is S[OFTWARE], H[ARDWARE], X[ONXOFF], or N[ONE].

You can enter just the first character of the value; the system automatically fills in the rest. This field specifies the type of *flow control* to be used. Flow control (often referred to as "handshaking") means controlling the flow of data to an output device; it is a way to keep your system from sending data faster than your output device can accept it. With flow control, your output device can tell your system either "Go ahead, send data" or "I'm busy; wait for a further signal before you send more data."

SOFTWARE tells SAS/GRAPH software to use programmed flow control.

HARDWARE tells SAS/GRAPH software to use the hardware CTS and RTS signals (this is not appropriate for some plotters and most modems).

XONXOFF tells SAS/GRAPH software to use ASCII characters DC1 and DC3. This is not appropriate for most personal computers but is used by many drivers in the Institute-supplied catalog for UNIX operating systems and derivatives.

NONE tells SAS/GRAPH software to send data without providing flow control. You should not use this option unless you are routing output through flow-control programs of your own. A situation where this can be used is in a multiple-machine personal computer environment where the graphics plotter is a shared resource. SAS/GRAPH software would send output to a server (the file transfer would not require flow control). The server would queue incoming graphs and send them to the plotter. The server, rather than SAS/GRAPH software, would be responsible for handling flow control.

Note that if you are creating a graphics stream file for a plotter and you specify the HANDSHAKE=SOFTWARE option, the software that later sends the file to the plotter must be able to perform software handshaking. You will probably want to specify one of the alternative values if you route output to a file.

LFACTOR

Optional. Default is 0 (same as 1). Value is a non-negative integer up to four digits long.

Enter the default line thickness for lines drawn on the device. Lines will be drawn LFACTOR times as thick as normal. Not all devices have the capability to vary line width.

MAXCOLORS

Optional. Default is 2. Value is an integer in the range 2 to 256.

Enter the total number of colors (foreground colors plus background color) that can be displayed at one time.

MAXPOLY

Optional. Default is 0 (unlimited vertices). Value is a non-negative integer up to four digits long.

Enter the maximum number of vertices that a hardware-generated polygon can have. A 0 means that there is no limit to the number of vertices that can be specified in the hardware's polygon-drawing command.

*PIEFILL

Optional. Default is blank (same as Y). Value is Y, N, or blank.

Enter Y to have the device use its built-in hardware capability to fill pies and pie sections; enter N to have the software do it. Hardware filling is faster, but not all devices have the capability.

*POLYGONFILL

Optional. Default is blank (same as Y). Value is Y, N, or blank.

Enter Y to have the device use its built-in hardware capability to fill polygons; enter N to have the software do it. Hardware filling is faster, but not all devices have the capability.

*PROMPT

Optional. Default is all blanks. Values consist of Xs in the fields.

This parameter is actually a series of action fields, each of which corresponds to having the system prompt you at a particular time. Fill in an X for each prompt that you want to be given.

Start up field

issues a message to turn the device on (if device is not running the SAS session) or the message "PLEASE PRESS RETURN AFTER EACH BELL TO CONTINUE." Exceptions: in SAS/GRAPH software for personal computers, display adapters (for example, CGA, EGA, and Hercules) never show this message when you are using the SAS Display Manager System.

End graph field

(valid for video terminals only) signals, usually by a bell, when the graph is complete.

Mount pens field

issues a message to mount pens in a certain order and (for certain devices only) to ask for pen priming strokes for plotters.

Change paper field

(valid for plotters only) prompts the user to change the paper.

If no Xs appear in these fields, no prompt messages are issued and the device will not wait for you to respond between graphs.

*PROMPTCHARS

Optional. Default is blank. Value is a sixteen character string that must be filled if used.

Enter a hex string to specify driver communication options. All bytes of this hex string are hexadecimal numbers representing ASCII symbols.

Byte 1   system prompt character (for software handshaking).

Byte 2   echo-terminator character (for software handshaking).

Byte 3   if '01', do not split commands across records.

Byte 4   line-end character (for software handshaking).

Byte 5   turnaround delay in tenths of a second (for software handshaking).

Byte 6   default record length in hex (00–FF).

Bytes 7–8   unused.

Use PROMPTCHARS='*hexstring*'x in line mode.

See also the discussion of PROMPTCHARS= in *SAS/GRAPH Guide to Hardware Interfaces, Release 6.03 Edition* or *SAS/GRAPH Hardware Interfaces for Personal Computers, Version 6 Edition.*

RECTFILL

Optional. Default is blank. Value is a string sixteen characters long and must be completely filled if used.

Enter the hex string representing which rectangle fills should be performed by hardware if possible. Not all devices support the capability. If the FILL field is N, this hex string is ignored.

The following table shows which bit position (left-to-right) within the value represented by the hex string controls each fill pattern. See the chapter "Enhancing Your Graphics Output Designs" for pictures of the patterns.

Fill pattern	Bit to turn on
E	0
R1	1
R2	2
R3	3
R4	4
R5	5
L1	6
L2	7
L3	8
L4	9
L5	10
X1	11
X2	12
X3	13
X4	14
X5	15
S	16

*REPAINT

Optional. Default is 0. Value is a non-negative integer up to three digits long.

Enter the number of times to redraw a graph to intensify the colors. Not all devices have this capability. This option is useful for producing transparencies; multiple passes make the colors more solid or more intense.

Refer to *SAS/GRAPH Guide to Hardware Interfaces, Release 6.03 Edition* or *SAS/GRAPH Hardware Interfaces for Personal Computers, Version 6 Edition* for details.

*SPEED

Optional. Default is 0 (normal speed). Value is a non-negative integer up to three digits long.

Enter the pen speed for pen plotters with a variable speed selection. The integer indicates a percentage of the maximum speed for the device. If the number is invalid, the maximum speed is used. In general, slowing the drawing speed will intensify colors.

*SWAP

Optional. Default is blank (no swap). Value is Y, N, or blank.

Enter Y if the color BLACK is to be substituted for the color WHITE or N if the colors are to remain the same. This is useful when you develop a graph on a video terminal (black background, white lines) and then produce a final copy on a printer (white background, black lines).

*SYMBOL

Optional. Default is blank (same as Y). Value is Y, N, or blank.

Enter Y to have the device use its built-in hardware capability to draw symbols or N to have software draw them.

SYMBOLS

Optional. Default is blank. Value is a string sixteen characters long that must be completely filled if used.

Enter the hex string representing which symbols should be generated by hardware. Note that not all devices are capable of drawing every symbol. If the SYMBOL field is N, the hex string is ignored.

The following table shows which bit position (left-to-right) within the value represented by the hex string controls each standard symbol. See "Enhancing Your Graphics Output Designs" for pictures of the symbols.

Symbol	Bit to turn on
PLUS	1
X	2
STAR	3
SQUARE	4
DIAMOND	5
TRIANGLE	6
HASH	7
Y	8
Z	9
PAW	10
POINT	11

DOT	12
CIRCLE	13

UCC

Optional. Default is blank. Value is a string sixty-four characters long and accepts only hexadecimal characters.

Enter the hex string that represents user-defined control characters for the device. Not all devices support this feature, and the meaning of each byte of the string varies from device to device. Refer to *SAS/GRAPH Guide to Hardware Interfaces, Release 6.03 Edition* or *SAS/GRAPH Hardware Interfaces for Personal Computers, Version 6 Edition*.

The GCOLORS Screen

Screen 11.4 shows the GCOLORS screen from the TEK4105 entry in SASHELP.DEVICES.

```
┌GDEVICE: Gcolors─────────────────────────────────────────────────────
Command ===>

Catalog: SASHELP.DEVICES                         Entry:    TEK4105

Cback: BLACK
Colors:

       WHITE          RED          GREEN         BLUE          CYAN
       MAGENTA        YELLOW       _____      _____      _____
       _____       _____     _____      _____      _____
       _____       _____     _____      _____      _____
       _____       _____     _____      _____      _____
       _____       _____     _____      _____      _____
       _____       _____     _____      _____      _____
       _____       _____     _____      _____      _____
       _____       _____     _____      _____      _____
       _____       _____     _____      _____      _____
       _____       _____     _____      _____      _____
       _____       _____     _____      _____      _____
       _____       _____     _____      _____      _____
       _____       _____     _____      _____      _____
```

Screen 11.4   The GCOLORS Screen

See **Common Commands** for a list of the commands you can use while in this screen.

You will find the following fields on the GCOLORS screen. (Fields marked with an asterisk can be overridden by a similarly named option in a GOPTIONS statement.)

*CBACK

Optional. Default is blank. Value is a string up to eight characters long.

Enter the name of the background color. Usually this field should be left blank. Foreground colors will then be presented against the dark background of a video device. If specified explicitly, the background color should contrast all foreground colors specified in the COLORS field. Do not specify a value in the CBACK field for plotters.

*COLORS

REQUIRED first field; others are optional. There is no default for the first field; blank is the default for other fields. Values are strings of up to eight characters.

Enter a list of foreground colors for the device. Colors must be specified consecutively (from left to right, top to bottom). WHITE is commonly the first foreground color for video devices; BLACK is commonly the first for plotters. All foreground colors should contrast with the background color (see the CBACK field above).

The order of the list is important when you are using default colors for parts of your graph. For example, if in PROC G3D you do not explicitly specify colors for titles, axes, the bottom surface, and the top surface, then PROC G3D will check the COLORS field. PROC G3D will assign the first color to titles, the second color to axes, the third color to the bottom surface, and the fourth color to the top surface.

The CHARTYPE Screen

Screen 11.5 shows a CHARTYPE screen that is taken from the PSL entry in SASHELP.DEVICES.

```
┌GDEVICE: Chartype─────────────────────────────────────────────────┐
│Command ===>                                                       │
│                                                                   │
│Catalog: SASHELP.DEVICES                        Entry:    PSL      │
│                                                                   │
│ Chartype  Rows   Cols                Font Name          Scalable  │
│                                                                   │
│      1     100    75   Courier                              Y     │
│      2     100    75   Courier-Oblique                      Y     │
│      3     100    75   Courier-Bold                         Y     │
│      4     100    75   Courier-BoldOblique                  Y     │
│      5     100    75   Times-Roman                          Y     │
│      6     100    75   Times-Italic                         Y     │
│      7     100    75   Times-Bold                           Y     │
│      8     100    75   Times-BoldItalic                     Y     │
│      9     100    75   Helvetica                            Y     │
│     10     100    75   Helvetica-Oblique                    Y     │
│     11     100    75   Helvetica-Bold                       Y     │
│     12     100    75   Helvetica-BoldOblique                Y     │
│     13     100    75   Symbol                               Y     │
│      0       0     0                                              │
│                                                                   │
│                                                                   │
│                                                                   │
└───────────────────────────────────────────────────────────────────┘
```

Screen 11.5 The CHARTYPE Screen

This screen is used to record the list of hardware fonts available on the device (for those devices that can produce multiple fonts). The CHARTYPE value on the PARAMETERS screen corresponds to the CHARTYPE number on this screen. The

ROWS and COLS fields here override the LROWS and LCOLS or PROWS and PCOLS fields on the DETAIL screen.

See **Common Commands** for a list of the commands you can use while in this screen.

You will find the following fields on the CHARTYPE screen:

CHARTYPE

Optional. Default is 0. Value is a non-negative integer up to four digits long.

Enter the integer that indicates which character set is desired for this device.

COLS

Optional. Default is 0. Value is a non-negative integer up to four digits long.

Enter the number of columns on the device for this font. Larger fonts will allow fewer columns; smaller fonts will allow more. You must specify a nonzero value. If you use 0, then the entire CHARTYPE record is deleted from the device entry.

FONT NAME

Optional. Default is blank. Value is a string up to forty characters long.

Enter the name of the font, making sure that it is in the form that the device driver expects. For example, a PostScript driver will expect a font name of *Times-Roman* for its Times Roman font. It will not recognize the font name unless you use the hyphen.

ROWS

Optional. Default is 0. Value is a non-negative integer up to four digits long.

Enter the number of rows on the device for this font. Larger fonts will allow fewer rows; smaller fonts will allow more. If you specify 0, the entire CHARTYPE record is deleted from the device entry.

SCALABLE

Optional. Default is blank (same as N). Value is Y, N, or blank.

Enter Y if the font is continuously scalable and N if it is not. A font is continuously scalable if it can be drawn at any given height without restrictions. If the font can only be drawn in a finite number of discrete sizes, then each size must be entered as though it were a different font (you will need a separate CHARTYPE record for each size).

To delete a CHARTYPE record already in the device entry, specify zeros for the ROWS or COLS fields.

The METAGRAPHICS Screen

Screen 11.6 shows a METAGRAPHICS screen that is from the GXTSLINK entry in SASHELP.DEVICES.

```
┌─GDEVICE: Metagraphics────────────────────────────────────────────────
│Command ===>
│
│Catalog: SASHELP.DEVICES                         Entry:    GXTSLINK
│
│Process: GXTSLINK
│Interactive:  PROC
│Processinput: METAFILE      Processoutput: _____
│Header:  _____
│Trailer: _____
│Headerfile:    _____     Trailerfile: _____
│Rotation:   0               Path:   0        Format: CHARACTER
│Colortype: NAME             Nak: _____
│Id: GXTSLINK
│
│
│
│
│
│
│
│
│
│
│
│
└──────────────────────────────────────────────────────────────────────
```

Screen 11.6   The METAGRAPHICS Screen

Do not alter the fields on the METAGRAPHICS screen unless you are building a Metagraphics driver. See *SAS/GRAPH Guide to Hardware Interfaces, Release 6.03 Edition* or *SAS/GRAPH Hardware Interfaces for Personal Computers, Version 6 Edition* for directions on building and using Metagraphics drivers.

See **Common Commands** for a list of the commands you can use while in this screen.

You will find the following fields on the METAGRAPHICS screen:

COLORTYPE
  Optional. Default is blank. Value can be NAME, RGB, HLS, or GRAY.
    Enter the type of color table used by the user-written part of the Metagraphics device driver. NAME means color names, RGB means RGB color specifications, HLS means HLS color specifications, and GRAY means gray-scale levels.

FORMAT
  Optional. Default is blank (same as CHARACTER). Value is either BINARY or CHARACTER.
    Enter the format of the file produced by the Institute-supplied part of the Metagraphics device driver.

HEADER
  Optional. Default is blank. Value is a string up to forty characters long.
    Enter the command that will create HEADER records for the driver. The command runs a user-written program; the program creates the HEADER file.

HEADERFILE
  Optional. Default is blank. Value is a string up to eight characters long.
    Enter the fileref (*not* the actual filename) for the file from which the Institute-supplied portion of the Metagraphics driver will read header records. You must use a FILENAME statement in the SAS session to

assign the name of the desired file to the fileref before running the Metagraphics driver.

ID

Optional. Default is blank. Value is a string up to seventy characters long.

Enter the description field to be used by the Metagraphics driver. If this field is blank, then the name and description of the graph as specified on the PROC GREPLAY master menu will be used.

INTERACTIVE

Optional. Default is USER. Value can be USER, PROC, or GRAPH.

Enter the level of interactivity that a Metagraphics driver will use. USER means that a postprocessing driver will be executed outside of SAS/GRAPH. PROC means that the user-written part of the Metagraphics driver will be invoked after the procedure is complete. GRAPH means that the user-written part will be invoked for each graph.

NAK

Optional. Default is blank. Value is character string up to sixteen characters long.

Enter the hex string that represents the negative handshake response for software handshaking in this device.

PATH

Optional. Default is 0 (no path angling is possible). Value is an integer in the range 0 to 360.

Enter the increment of the angle by which your device can rotate the text baseline (for example, every 5 degrees, every 45 degrees). Enter 0 if your device does not perform string angling in hardware.

PROCESS

REQUIRED if the value in the INTERACTIVE field is PROC or GRAPH. Default is blank. Value is a string up to forty characters long.

Enter the command that will translate the metafile into commands for the device. The command runs your program to produce the output.

PROCESSINPUT

REQUIRED for some Metagraphics drivers; otherwise optional. Default is blank. Value is a string up to eight characters long.

Enter the fileref (*not* the actual filename) for the file that contains the input for the user-written part of the Metagraphics driver. You must use a FILENAME statement in the SAS session to assign the name of the desired file to the fileref before running the Metagraphics driver.

PROCESSOUTPUT

Optional. Default is blank. Value is a string up to eight characters long.

Enter the fileref (*not* the actual filename) for the file that will receive output from the user-written part of the Metagraphics driver. You must use a FILENAME statement in the SAS session to assign the name of the desired file to the fileref before running the Metagraphics driver.

ROTATION

Optional. Default is 0 (no rotation allowed). Value is an integer in the range 0 to 360.

Enter the increment of the angle by which your device can rotate any given letter in a string of text (for example, every 5 degrees, every 45 degrees). Enter 0 if your device does not perform character rotation in hardware.

TRAILER
>   Optional. Default is blank. Value is a string up to forty characters long.
>   Enter the command that will create TRAILER records for the driver.
>   The command runs a user-written program; the program creates the
>   TRAILER file.

TRAILERFILE
>   Optional. Default is blank. Value is a string up to eight characters long.
>   Enter the fileref (*not* the actual filename) for the file from which the
>   Institute-supplied portion of the Metagraphics driver will read TRAILER
>   records. You must use a FILENAME statement in the SAS session to
>   assign the name of the desired file to the fileref before running the
>   Metagraphics driver.

The GPROLOG Screen

Screen 11.7 shows a GPROLOG screen.

```
┌─GDEVICE: Gprolog─────────────────────────────────────────────────┐
│Command ===>                                                       │
│                                                                   │
│Catalog: SASHELP.DEVICES                      Entry:     MYTEK     │
│                                                                   │
│   7E                                                              │
│   ─────────────────────────────────────────────────────────────  │
│   ─────────────────────────────────────────────────────────────  │
│   ─────────────────────────────────────────────────────────────  │
│   ─────────────────────────────────────────────────────────────  │
│   ─────────────────────────────────────────────────────────────  │
│   ─────────────────────────────────────────────────────────────  │
│   ─────────────────────────────────────────────────────────────  │
│   ─────────────────────────────────────────────────────────────  │
│   ─────────────────────────────────────────────────────────────  │
│   ─────────────────────────────────────────────────────────────  │
│   ─────────────────────────────────────────────────────────────  │
│   ─────────────────────────────────────────────────────────────  │
│   ─────────────────────────────────────────────────────────────  │
│   ─────────────────────────────────────────────────────────────  │
│   ─────────────────────────────────────────────────────────────  │
│   ─────────────────────────────────────────────────────────────  │
│   ─────────────────────────────────────────────────────────────  │
│   ─────────────────────────────────────────────────────────────  │
│   ─────────────────────────────────────────────────────────────  │
└───────────────────────────────────────────────────────────────────┘
```

Screen 11.7   The GPROLOG Screen

See **Common Commands** for a list of the commands you can use while in this
screen.

There is only one field on the GPROLOG screen, and it can be overridden by
a similarly named option in the GOPTIONS statement.

*GPROLOG
>   Optional. Default is blank. Value is a string of hexadecimal characters.
>   Enter the hexadecimal string that the driver should send the device
>   before any graphics commands are sent. Do not use quotes or a trailing
>   x in the field.
>   For example, assume you are using a display that will emulate a
>   Tektronix 4010 terminal, and it switches into the emulation mode when

it receives a hexadecimal 7E and back into native mode when it receives a hexadecimal 7F. You find that there is no device driver for your device in SASHELP.DEVICES, but there is one for the Tektronix 4010.

You can copy the TEK4010 device entry into your catalog, renaming it to MYTEK, for example. You then must fill in the GPROLOG field with 7E and the GEPILOG field with 7F. Now, when you use DEVICE=MYTEK, the device will automatically switch into emulation mode to draw your graphs, then switch back into native mode when the graph is complete.

Note: in line mode and in the GPROLOG= option in a GOPTIONS statement, you can express the string as a hex string, a character string, or a combination of several strings—some in hex format, some in character format. The strings are concatenated automatically. This feature makes it easier to specify the long and complicated initialization strings required by some devices (for example, PostScript printers). Thus, you may want to set the GPROLOG value using line mode rather than full-screen mode.

The GEPILOG Screen

Screen 11.8 shows a GEPILOG screen.

```
┌GDEVICE: Gepilog──────────────────────────────────────────────────────────┐
│Command ===>                                                                │
│                                                                            │
│Catalog: SASHELP.DEVICES                          Entry:    MYTEK           │
│                                                                            │
│  7F                                                                        │
│  _____ │
│  _____ │
│  _____ │
│  _____ │
│  _____ │
│  _____ │
│  _____ │
│  _____ │
│  _____ │
│  _____ │
│  _____ │
│  _____ │
│  _____ │
│  _____ │
│  _____ │
│  _____ │
│  _____ │
│  _____ │
│  _____ │
│                                                                            │
└────────────────────────────────────────────────────────────────────────────┘
```

Screen 11.8   The GEPILOG Screen

See **Common Commands** for a list of the commands you can use while in this screen.

There is only one field on the GEPILOG screen, and it can be overridden by a similarly named option in the GOPTIONS statement.

    *GEPILOG
        Optional. Default is blank. Value is a string of hexadecimal characters.

Enter the hexadecimal string that the driver should send the device before any graphics commands are sent. Do not use quotes or a trailing x in the field.

For example, assume you are using a display that will emulate a Tektronix 4010 terminal and it switches into the emulation mode when it receives a hexadecimal 7E and back into native mode when it receives a hexadecimal 7F. You find that there is no device driver for your device in SASHELP.DEVICES, but there is one for the Tektronix 4010.

You can copy the TEK4010 device entry into your catalog, renaming it to MYTEK, for example. You then must fill in the GPROLOG field with 7E and the GEPILOG field with 7F. Now, when you use DEVICE=MYTEK, the device will automatically switch into emulation mode to draw your graphs, then switch back into native mode when the graph is complete.

Note: in line mode and in the GEPILOG= option in a GOPTIONS statement, you may express the string as a hex string, a character string, or a combination of several strings—some in hex format, some in character format. The strings are concatenated automatically. Thus, you may find it easier to use line mode rather than full-screen mode to specify a long or complex GEPILOG string.

The GSTART Screen

Screen 11.9 shows a GSTART screen.

```
┌GDEVICE: Gstart───────────────────────────────────────────────────┐
│Command ===>                                                       │
│                                                                   │
│Catalog: SASHELP.DEVICES                        Entry:    PLOTTER  │
│                                                                   │
│ FFFFFF                                                            │
│ ───────────────────────────────────────────────────────────────  │
│ ───────────────────────────────────────────────────────────────  │
│ ───────────────────────────────────────────────────────────────  │
│ ───────────────────────────────────────────────────────────────  │
│ ───────────────────────────────────────────────────────────────  │
│ ───────────────────────────────────────────────────────────────  │
│ ───────────────────────────────────────────────────────────────  │
│ ───────────────────────────────────────────────────────────────  │
│ ───────────────────────────────────────────────────────────────  │
│ ───────────────────────────────────────────────────────────────  │
│ ───────────────────────────────────────────────────────────────  │
│ ───────────────────────────────────────────────────────────────  │
│ ───────────────────────────────────────────────────────────────  │
│ ───────────────────────────────────────────────────────────────  │
│ ───────────────────────────────────────────────────────────────  │
│ ───────────────────────────────────────────────────────────────  │
│ ───────────────────────────────────────────────────────────────  │
│ ───────────────────────────────────────────────────────────────  │
└───────────────────────────────────────────────────────────────────┘
```

Screen 11.9   The GSTART Screen

See **Common Commands** for a list of the commands you can use while in this screen.

There is only one field on the GSTART screen, and it can be overridden by a similarly named option in the GOPTIONS statement.

*GSTART

Optional. Default is blank. Value is a string of hexadecimal characters.

Enter the hexadecimal string to be attached to the beginning of every record of graphics data that is sent to the device. Do not use quotes or a trailing x in the field.

Note: in line mode and in the GSTART= option in a GOPTIONS statement, you can express the string as a hex string, a character string, or several strings—some in hex format, some in character format. The strings are concatenated automatically. Thus, you may find it easier to use line mode rather than full-screen mode to specify a long or complex GSTART string.

The GEND Screen

Screen 11.10 shows a GEND screen.

```
┌GDEVICE: Gend─────────────────────────────────────────────────────────┐
│Command ===>                                                           │
│                                                                       │
│Catalog: SASHELP.DEVICES                      Entry:    PLOTTER        │
│                                                                       │
│ 0D0A                                                                  │
│ ───────────────────────────────────────────────────────────────     │
│ ───────────────────────────────────────────────────────────────     │
│ ───────────────────────────────────────────────────────────────     │
│ ───────────────────────────────────────────────────────────────     │
│ ───────────────────────────────────────────────────────────────     │
│ ───────────────────────────────────────────────────────────────     │
│ ───────────────────────────────────────────────────────────────     │
│ ───────────────────────────────────────────────────────────────     │
│ ───────────────────────────────────────────────────────────────     │
│ ───────────────────────────────────────────────────────────────     │
│ ───────────────────────────────────────────────────────────────     │
│ ───────────────────────────────────────────────────────────────     │
│ ───────────────────────────────────────────────────────────────     │
│ ───────────────────────────────────────────────────────────────     │
│ ───────────────────────────────────────────────────────────────     │
│ ───────────────────────────────────────────────────────────────     │
│ ───────────────────────────────────────────────────────────────     │
│ ───────────────────────────────────────────────────────────────     │
│ ───────────────────────────────────────────────────────────────     │
│ ───────────────────────────────────────────────────────────────     │
└───────────────────────────────────────────────────────────────────────┘
```

Screen 11.10   The GEND Screen

See **Common Commands** for a list of the commands you can use while in this screen.

There is only one field on the GEND screen, and it can be overridden by a similarly named option in the GOPTIONS statement.

*GEND

Optional. Default is blank. Value is a string of hexadecimal characters.

Enter the hexadecimal string that is to be attached to the end of every record of graphics data that is sent to the device. Do not use quotes or a trailing x in the field.

Note: in line mode and in the GEND= option in a GOPTIONS statement, you can express the string as a hex string, a character string, or several strings—some in hex format, some in character format. The strings are concatenated automatically. Thus, you may find it easier to use line mode rather than full-screen mode to specify a long or complex GEND string.

USING LINE-MODE COMMANDS

The GDEVICE procedure is interactive; that is, once you enter the PROC GDEVICE statement, you can enter statements and run them without re-entering the PROC GDEVICE statement for each statement.

To exit PROC GDEVICE, you either enter the QUIT statement, exit your SAS session, or execute a PROC or DATA step.

These are the line-mode commands:

ADD *entryname driveroptions*;

adds a new device catalog entry with the driver name specified in *entryname. Driveroptions* can include any of the driver options described in **List of Driver Options** below. However, you **must** specify values for all of the following options: MODULE=, COLORS=, XMAX=, YMAX=, XPIXELS=, and YPIXELS=. Furthermore, you must provide positive nonzero values for either of the option pairs LCOLS=/LROWS= or PCOLS=/PROWS=.

COPY *entryname* [FROM=*SAScatalog*] NEWNAME=*entryname*;

copies information from *entryname* (from a different catalog if FROM= is specified) to a new entry specified with the NEWNAME= option. The catalog is checked to see that a driver with the name specified by the NEWNAME= option does not already exist in the catalog.

DELETE *entryname*;

deletes the entry with the specified *entryname*. You will be asked to verify that you really want to delete the entry.

END;   exits the GDEVICE procedure.

FS;   switches to full-screen mode.

LIST *entryname*;   lists the contents of the specified entry. You may use the following arguments in place of *entryname*:

NEXT   lists contents of next entry.

PREV   lists contents of previous entry.

ALL   lists brief information on all entries.

DUMP   lists detailed information on all entries. Warning: this option generates a large amount of output.

Using LIST with no arguments is the same as using LIST _ALL_.

MODIFY *entryname driveroptions*;

modifies the catalog entry with the specified *entryname. Driveroptions* should include at least one of the driver options described in **List of Driver Options** below).

When a field is specified as null, it sets the corresponding driver option to its default value.

QUIT;   exits the GDEVICE procedure.

RENAME *entryname* NEWNAME=*entryname*;
changes an entry's name to the one specified in NEWNAME=. The catalog is checked first to see that a driver with the new name does not already exist in the catalog.

STOP;   exits the GDEVICE procedure.

Specifying Driver Options

The list of driver options that you can use with the ADD and MODIFY commands appears below. Most of them correspond to fields that are filled in when the full-screen menus are used. If a full description does not appear here, then you are given a reference to the section on a screen in which the field is used. Just go to the section and look up the field in the list of fields given.

When a field is specified as null, it sets the option to its default value, as specified in the field's description. This is how you specify values in line mode:

- **Numbers:** SPEED=90
- **Keywords:** ROTATE=LANDSCAPE
- **Hex Strings:** GEND='0D0A'x

For hex strings, note the use of quotes and the terminating x.

The GPROLOG, GEPILOG, GSTART, and GEND fields can be filled by using multiple strings in the specification (they must be separated by blanks), for example,

```
GEND='04'x 'SAM' 'FF'x
```

The three values will be concatenated automatically. Note the use of the ASCII character string, 'SAM'. The value is in quotes but does not have a terminating x.

Using multiple fields can be more convenient when you are dealing with drivers that can require long values in the hex fields, like the PostScript driver.

List of Driver Options

Parameters and options use the same names in full-screen mode and line mode. The parameters and options below are listed with a reference to the screen that they appear on in full-screen mode. Refer to the list of fields for each screen in the sections above for a description. Where syntax is different for line mode, it is described below.

ASPECT=	DETAIL
AUTOCOPY=	PARAMETERS
AUTOFEED=	PARAMETERS
CBACK=	GCOLORS
CELL=	PARAMETERS
CHARACTERS=	PARAMETERS

CHARREC=(*charreclist*)
This parameter corresponds to the set of fields on the CHARTYPE screen. *Charreclist* is a list of *charrecs*. A charrec is of the form

```
type, rows, cols, 'fontname', 's'
```

where *type* is the CHARTYPE id, *rows* is the number of rows associated with that CHARTYPE, *cols* is the number of columns associated with that CHARTYPE, *fontname* is a quoted string containing the name of the font, and *s* is Y or N in quotes, depending on whether the font is scalable (Y) or not (N).

CHARTYPE=   PARAMETERS

CIRCLEARC=   PARAMETERS

COLORS=[(*colorslist*)]

Specify default colors for the device driver. Colors must be specified consecutively; at least one color must be specified. You leave a current color as it is in the list by using a null value in the list.

For example, an original list is specified COLORS=(RED,GREEN,BLUE). You can specify three new colors explicitly or leave no space between commas to leave one the same. COLORS=(WHITE,,BROWN) would keep GREEN in the list.

COLORTYPE=	METAGRAPHICS
DASH=	PARAMETERS
DASHLINE=	PARAMETERS
DES[CRIPTION]=	DETAIL
DEVMAP=	DETAIL
DEVOPTS=	PARAMETERS
ERASE=	PARAMETERS
FILL=	PARAMETERS
FILLINC=	PARAMETERS
FORMAT=	METAGRAPHICS
GACCESS=	DETAIL
GCOPIES=	PARAMETERS
GEND=	GEND
GEPILOG=	GEPILOG
GPROLOG=	GPROLOG
GPROTOCOL=	DETAIL
GSIZE=	PARAMETERS
GSFLEN=	DETAIL
GSFMODE=	DETAIL
GSFNAME=	DETAIL
GSTART=	GSTART
HANDSHAKE=	PARAMETERS
HEADER=	METAGRAPHICS
HEADERFILE=	METAGRAPHICS
HSIZE=	DETAIL

HORIGIN=	DETAIL
ID=	METAGRAPHICS
INTERACTIVE=	METAGRAPHICS
LCOLS=	DETAIL
LROWS=	DETAIL
MAXCOLORS=	PARAMETERS
MAXPOLY=	PARAMETERS
MODEL=	DETAIL
MODULE=	DETAIL
NAK=	METAGRAPHICS
PAPERFEED=	DETAIL
PATH=	METAGRAPHICS
PCOLS=	DETAIL
PIEFILL=	PARAMETERS
POLYGONFILL=	PARAMETERS
PROCESS=	METAGRAPHICS
PROCESSINPUT=	METAGRAPHICS
PROCESSOUTPUT=	METAGRAPHICS

PROMPT=*int* Specify an integer from 0 to 7 to represent the level of a prompt. A value of 0 means no prompting; 1 means startup messages only; 2 means signal end of graph if device is a video display or send message to change paper if device is a plotter; 3 combines the effects of 1 and 2; 4 means send a mount pens message if the device is a plotter; 5 combines the effects of 4 and 1; 6 combines the effects of 4 and 2; and 7 means send all prompts.

PROMPTCHARS=	PARAMETERS
PROWS=	DETAIL

QMSG | NOQMSG

use QMSG to queue driver messages while the device is in graphics mode and NOQMSG to prevent the queuing of messages. If not specified, it is true for video devices and false for plotters.

REPAINT=	PARAMETERS
RECTFILL=	PARAMETERS
ROTATE=	DETAIL
ROTATION=	METAGRAPHICS
SPEED=	PARAMETERS
SWAP=	PARAMETERS
SYMBOL=	PARAMETERS
SYMBOLS=	PARAMETERS
TRAILER=	METAGRAPHICS
TRAILERFILE=	METAGRAPHICS

TRANTAB=	DETAIL
TYPE=	DETAIL
VORIGIN=	DETAIL
VSIZE=	DETAIL
XMAX=	DETAIL
XPIXELS=	DETAIL
YMAX=	DETAIL
YPIXELS=	DETAIL

EXAMPLES

Example 1: Listing Catalog Entries

This example shows how to use PROC GDEVICE in line mode to list the entries in SASHELP.DEVICES. Submit these statements one at a time.

```
proc gdevice c=sashelp.devices nofs;
    list _all_;
```
(list of entries is displayed in the output window)

```
    list hp7475;
```
(contents of entry HP7475.DEV is displayed in the output window)

```
    quit;
```

Example 2: Creating A Personal Device Catalog Using Full-Screen Mode

This example walks you through the steps of copying and altering device drivers in full-screen mode.

1. Set up the GDEVICE0 library for your catalog. First create a directory named MYDEVICE under your main directory MYDIR, then enter and submit the appropriate LIBNAME statement to establish the libref for that directory:

   For SAS/GRAPH software on personal computers:

   ```
   libname gdevice0 'c:\mydir\mydevice\';
   ```

   For SAS/GRAPH software on UNIX operating systems and derivatives:

   ```
   libname gdevice0 '/users/mydir/mydevice/';
   ```

2. Execute PROC GDEVICE on GDEVICE0.DEVICES:

   ```
   proc gdevice catalog=gdevice0.devices;
   ```

3. You are now in the CATALOG screen. No entries are listed because you have not yet copied any into your catalog. Copy them now. At the command line, execute the COPY command to get entries for a graphics terminal and a plotter into GDEVICE0.DEVICES from the Institute-supplied catalog, SASHELP.DEVICES :

   ```
   copy sashelp.devices.tek4105.dev tek4105.dev
   copy sashelp.devices.hp7550.dev hp7550.dev
   ```

4. Now use the r command in the selection field to change the names and descriptions of the entries. You can also change the description to

reflect the fact that you have changed the entries from the way they were listed in SASHELP.DEVICES. Here is a sample name and description for the plotter device entry:

```
MYPLOT      HP plotter, modified. JG, 6-5-88
```

5. Now change a field in the terminal device entry. Enter e in the selection field next to the entry name; then press RETURN.
6. You are now in the DETAIL screen. Enter NEXTSCR on the command line; then press RETURN.
7. You are now in the PARAMETERS screen. Press RETURN repeatedly to position the cursor at the CIRCLEARC field. Enter N, then go back to the command line.
8. Enter CANCEL and press RETURN. The modification is not saved. If you want to save the change, you enter SAVE (instead of CANCEL) and press RETURN.
9. You are now viewing the DETAIL screen. Enter END and press RETURN.
10. You are now viewing the CATALOG screen. Enter END and press RETURN.
11. You are now viewing the display manager screen. The next time you use a SAS/GRAPH procedure, use the new entry name in the DEVICE= option. Even if the entry name remains the same as the one in SASHELP.DEVICES, SAS/GRAPH software will use the one in GDEVICE0.DEVICES.

Example 3: Creating a Personal Device Catalog Using Line Mode

This example walks you through the steps of copying and altering device drivers in line mode. (This example accomplishes the same task as the previous example.)

1. Set up the GDEVICE0 library for your own catalog. First you should create a directory named MYDEVICE under your main directory MYDIR, then enter and submit the appropriate LIBNAME statement to establish the libref for that directory:

   For SAS/GRAPH software on personal computers:

   ```
   libname gdevice0 'c:\mydir\mydevice\';
   ```

   For SAS/GRAPH software on UNIX operating systems and derivatives:

   ```
   libname gdevice0 '/users/mydir/mydevice/';
   ```

2. Submit PROC GDEVICE and specify the catalog GDEVICE0.DEVICES. Also specify the NOFS option:

   ```
   proc gdevice catalog=gdevice0.devices nofs;
   ```

3. List the entries by submitting the LIST command:

   ```
   list _all_;
   ```

4. Submit the COPY command to get entries for a graphics terminal and a plotter into GDEVICE0.DEVICES:

   ```
   copy tek4105 from=sashelp.devices newname=tek4105;
   copy hp7550  from=sashelp.devices newname=hp7550;
   ```

5. Now submit a RENAME command to change the descriptions of the entries. You can change the description to reflect the fact that you have changed the entries from how they are listed in SASHELP.DEVICES. Here is a sample description for the plotter device:

```
rename hp7550
        description='hp7550 plotter, modified.  jg, 6-5-88';
```

You can also change the names if you like (for example, to CRT and PLOT). Use NEWNAME= to specify the new name. If you do, remember to reference the entries by the new name whenever you use the DEVICE= option in a SAS/GRAPH procedure.

6. List the contents of HP7550 by submitting the LIST command:

```
list hp7550;
```

Examine the CIRCLEARC field (switch to the OUTPUT window and scroll until you find it).

7. Now change the CIRCLEARC field in the HP7550 entry. Submit the MODIFY command:

```
modify hp7550 circlearc=n;
```

8. Now change it back:

```
modify hp7550 circlearc=;
```

9. Exit the procedure by submitting the QUIT command:

```
quit;
```

Chapter 12

The GFONT Procedure

ABSTRACT

You can use the GFONT procedure to create your own character sets or *fonts* to use with SAS/GRAPH procedures and to display new or existing fonts created with PROC GFONT.

INTRODUCTION

To create your own fonts, you describe the shape of the characters by digitizing them either manually or with special digitizing equipment.

Once you have digitized the characters in the new font, you must read the data into a SAS data set with a special format. PROC GFONT then uses this data set to create the font. PROC GFONT stores fonts in the directory with libref GFONT0. Before the first occurrence of PROC GFONT in each SAS session, you must use a LIBNAME statement to associate the libref GFONT0 with a particular directory. Here is an example for UNIX operating systems and derivatives:

```
libname gfont0 '/mydir/fonts/';
```

For SAS/GRAPH software on personal computers, use a statement like the following:

```
libname gfont0 'c:\mydir\fonts\';
```

PROC GFONT can build or display filled or stroked fonts. A *filled font* has the open areas of the symbols shaded or colored as you request. A *stroked font* consists of characters drawn by discrete line segments or circular arcs. See the **EXAMPLES** section for a comparison of filled and stroked letters.

You can also control the resolution of the fonts. For example, you may want to specify a very dense set of points for each character so that the characters approximate smooth curved lines at very large sizes. PROC GFONT provides four resolution levels. **Table 12.1** shows the resolution number and the maximum number of distinct points that can be defined horizontally or vertically.

Table 12.1   Maximum Number of Distinct Points Corresponding to Each Resolution Level

Resolution	Number of Distinct Points
1	254
2	32,766
3	16,777,214
4	2,147,483,646

SPECIFICATIONS

The PROC GFONT statement is the only statement you use with this procedure:

PROC GFONT NAME=*font options***;**

PROC GFONT Statement

PROC GFONT NAME=*font options;*

You can specify various options to create and display fonts with PROC GFONT. The options that can be used to perform these tasks are described below.

Options Used to Create Fonts

BASELINE=*y*
B=*y*

specifies the vertical coordinate of the baseline of the characters in the input data set. This is the line on which all letters rest and below which the descenders of letters extend. If you do not specify the BASELINE= option, PROC GFONT uses the lowest vertical coordinate of the first character in the input data set.

CAPLINE=*y*
C=*y*

specifies the vertical coordinate of the capline of the characters in the input data set. This coordinate is the highest point of normal Roman capitals. If you do not specify the CAPLINE= option, PROC GFONT uses the highest vertical coordinate in the input data set. When PROC GFONT calculates the height of a character, any parts of the character that project beyond the capline are ignored. For example, if you specify two-inch characters, the height is measured from the font minimum to the capline, not from the font minimum to the font maximum.

CHARSPACETYPE=NONE | FIXED | DATA | UNIFORM
CSP=NONE | FIXED | DATA | UNIFORM

specifies the type of intercharacter spacing you want to use. Specify CHARSPACETYPE=NONE if you do not want any space between characters. This type of spacing is useful for script fonts, in which the characters should appear connected.

Specify CHARSPACETYPE=FIXED if you want to add a fixed amount of space, based on the font size.

Specify CHARSPACETYPE=DATA to indicate that the first observation of each character in the font should be the width of the character. Refer to **The PTYPE Variable** for details.

Specifying CHARSPACETYPE=UNIFORM is the same as specifying the UNIFORM Boolean option. The default value is FIXED.

DATA=*SASdataset*

gives the name of the SAS data set containing the coordinates of the digitized characters. If you do not specify the DATA= option, PROC GFONT uses the most recently created SAS data set.

FILLED
F

specifies that the characters are to be filled when displayed by PROC GFONT or any other SAS/GRAPH procedure. Note that the format for the input data set for FILLED fonts is different from the format for stroked fonts. The format for stroked fonts is the default.

GOUT=*SAScatalog*

specifies a SAS catalog to contain the pictures generated by the display of the font. This option is ignored if you specify NODISPLAY as an option in a PROC statement. If you do not specify the GOUT= option, catalog entries are written to the default catalog GSEG, which is erased at the end of your session.

KERNDATA=*SASdataset*
KERN=*SASdataset*

specifies the name of the SAS data set that contains kerning information. Refer to **The KERNDATA= Data Set** for details.

MWIDTH=*n*

specifies the width, in *font units*, of one lowercase Roman m. This printer's measure is used in conjunction with the CAPLINE= option to ensure that your characters have the correct aspect ratio. (Font units are the units that are used in the SAS data set you specify in the DATA= option.) You can correct characters that are too tall for their width by specifying a smaller MWIDTH= value. The default value is the width of the widest character in the font.

NAME=*font*
N=*font*

specifies the name of the font to be created or displayed. The NAME= option is required. The name must follow the requirements for SAS naming conventions, which are described in Chapter 1, "Introduction," in the *SAS Language Guide, Release 6.03 Edition*.

NODISPLAY
ND

specifies that PROC GFONT is not to display the font that you created.

RESOL=*bytes*
R=*bytes*
> specifies the number of bytes (1–4) for storing coordinates in the font. The higher the number, the closer together the points that define the character can be spaced. The default value is 1.
>
> See **Table 12.1** for the maximum number of distinct points corresponding to each resolution value.

SPACEDATA=*SASdataset*
SPACE=*SASdataset*
> specifies the name of the SAS data set containing track spacing information. Refer to **The SPACEDATA= Data Set** for details.

UNIFORM
U
> specifies that characters are to be spaced uniformly rather than proportionately.

Options Used to Display Fonts

CTEXT=*color*
CT=*color*
> specifies the color of the body of the characters to be displayed. If you do not specify the CTEXT= option, the first color in the COLORS= list is used for displaying the font. The CTEXT= value is not stored as part of the font.

HEIGHT=*characterheight* [*units*]
H=*characterheight* [*units*]
> specifies the size of the characters to be displayed. The size is measured from the minimum font measurement to the capline. (See the description of the REFLINES= option for information on how to determine the minimum font measurement and the capline.) You can specify the value of *units* as CELLS, PCT, IN, or CM. The default value is 2 cells.

NOBUILD
NB
> specifies that PROC GFONT is to display an existing font and that no new font is to be built.

REFCOL=*color*
> specifies the color to be used for the REFLINES option.

REFLINES
> specifies that PROC GFONT is to draw reference lines around each displayed character, showing the character width, the maximum and minimum font measurements, the baseline, and the capline. **Figure 12.1** demonstrates the placement of reference lines around the letter G.

Figure 12.1 Reference Lines Drawn for the Letter G

ROMCOL=*color*
RC=*color*
>   specifies for non-Roman fonts the color of the Roman character
>   equivalents. If you do not specify the ROMCOL= option, the first color
>   in the COLORS= list is used. The ROMCOL= value is not stored as
>   part of the font.

ROMFONT=*font*
RF=*font*
>   specifies for non-Roman fonts the font to be used to display the Roman
>   character equivalents. In addition to other fonts, you can specify
>   RF=NONE or RF=HARDWARE; the default is RF=NONE. The
>   ROMFONT= value is not stored as part of the font.

ROMHEX
HEX
>   specifies for non-Roman fonts that the hexadecimal values are to be
>   displayed below the non-Roman font characters.

ROMHT=*height* [*units*]
RH=*height* [*units*]
>   specifies for non-Roman fonts the height of the Roman character
>   equivalents and/or the hexadecimal values. You can specify the value of
>   *units* as CELLS, PCT, IN, or CM. The default value is 1 cell. The
>   ROMHT= value is not stored as part of the font.

SHOWALL
>   specifies that space is to be reserved for all definable character
>   positions. If no character has been defined for a position, that space is
>   skipped. This option can be used to show where undefined character
>   positions fall in the font. It can be used in conjunction with the
>   ROMHEX and SHOWROMAN options.

SHOWROMAN
SR
NOROMAN
NR
>   specify that the Roman character equivalents are to be displayed below
>   the non-Roman font characters. If you specify SHOWROMAN for a font,
>   you can later specify NOROMAN to suppress the display of the Roman
>   character equivalents.

DETAILS

Input Data Set

The format of the SAS data set input to PROC GFONT depends on whether the
font is filled or stroked. **Table 12.2** shows the variables that are required in the
input data set for the two types of fonts. An empty or outline version of a filled
font can be generated by running PROC GFONT on the same SAS data set without the FILLED option.

Table 12.2 Variables Required for Each Font

Variables	Fonts	
	Stroked	Filled
X	x	x
Y	x	x
CHAR	x	x
SEGMENT	x	x
LP		x
PTYPE		

X and Y Variables

The input data set contains a pair of variables whose values are the coordinates of the points for each character. These variables must be numeric and they must be named X and Y for the horizontal and vertical coordinates, respectively. Their values describe the position of the points of the character in any range you choose. Both variables must describe the character in the same scale or *font units*; in other words, ten horizontal units must be the same distance as ten vertical units.

Because the horizontal coordinates for one character are independent of the same coordinates for other characters, they may begin and end with any value without regard for where another character begins or ends. However, vertical coordinates for all characters must be defined on the same baseline. For example, suppose that the two characters A and B are defined. If character A has a range of horizontal values from 0 to 10 units, character B can have a range of horizontal values from 0 to 10 units, −5 to 5 units, or 125 to 135 units. But if character A's vertical values range from 5 to 15 units, then character B must also have the same range of vertical values.

Note that a character with a descender, such as the letter g, can have vertical values below that of the character A because an uppercase A rests on the baseline and the descender of a lowercase g extends below it.

The CHAR Variable

A character variable CHAR with a length of 1 is required in the input data set for stroked and filled fonts. CHAR contains the keyboard character that corresponds to the character you want to create. Usually, the keyboard character is the same as the character that is drawn; for example, CHAR='A' draws the uppercase Roman letter A. However, some fonts that contain only special characters (such as the SPECIAL font) or non-Roman letters (such as the HEBREW font) use the value of the CHAR variable to indicate another symbol to be drawn. For example, the letter G in the SPECIAL font causes SAS/GRAPH software to draw a fleur-de-lis.

The SEGMENT Variable

The numeric variable SEGMENT is required for filled and stroked fonts. SEGMENT values describe how a character or symbol is broken into several strokes. SEGMENT values for stroked fonts are different from SEGMENT values for filled fonts. For a stroked font, the SEGMENT variable must contain a unique value for each stroke of the character or symbol.

For example, the stroked letter O has two different SEGMENT values. The SEGMENT value of the inner circle is different from the SEGMENT value for the outer circle. In a filled font, however, the inner and outer circles both have the same SEGMENT value. An observation with missing X and Y values separates the coordinates of the inner circle from the outer circle. Because both circles are in the same segment, a single polygon with a hole is drawn.

Consider also this example: the stroked letter A has two or three strokes, depending upon how it is drawn. Usually, the two sides are drawn as one stroke, and the horizontal bar is drawn as a second stroke. Coordinates of the horizontal bar have SEGMENT values that are separate from the coordinates of the two sides.

The LP Variable

For filled fonts, the input data set must have a character variable of length 1 named LP. LP is optional for stroked fonts. LP values indicate to PROC GFONT whether the coordinates of each segment form a line or a polygon. This variable allows you to mix lines and polygons when creating characters in a font.

LP values are L for lines and P for polygons. When a character from the font is displayed, the polygons are filled in with whatever color you choose. When a polygon is defined around an empty space (for example, the top of the A in **Figure 12.3**), give X and Y variables a SAS missing value between the sets of coordinates. The observation with missing values for X and Y has the same SEGMENT value as the observations defining the rest of the polygon. Missing values in stroked fonts cause a break in the stroke, just as a new segment would.

The PTYPE Variable

PTYPE is a character variable of length 1 that is optional for both stroked and filled fonts. It tells PROC GFONT what type of data are in the observation. **Table 12.3** shows possible values for the PTYPE variable and their meanings.

Table 12.3   Values for the PTYPE Variable

PTYPE Value	Meaning
V	Normal point in the character outline
C	Center of a circular arc joining two V points
W	Width value for CHARSPACETYPE=DATA

V-type points are digitized points on the character outline connected by straight lines. If PROC GFONT encounters the sequence V-C-V in consecutive observations, a circular arc is drawn connecting the two V points with a center at the C point. If there is no circle centered at C and passing through both V points, the results will be unpredictable. Arcs are limited to 106 degrees or less. **Figure 12.4** shows a circular arc created using the PTYPE variable.

If you specify a W-type point, it must always be the first observation for a character. Instead of providing digitizing data to PROC GFONT, the W-type point gives the minimum and maximum X values for the character. Usually, these values include a little extra space for intercharacter spacing. Use W-type points only if you have specified CHARSPACETYPE=DATA; otherwise, they are ignored.

If you do not specify a PTYPE variable in an input data set, all points are assumed to be V-type points.

The KERNDATA= Data Set

Kerning is a method of adjusting intercharacter spacing so that part of one character extends over the body of the next. This is accomplished by adding or deleting space between the characters. Characters spaced in this way are termed "set tight."

Use the KERNDATA= data set to specify adjustments to normal intercharacter spacing for certain combinations of characters when they appear together. Examples of some combinations that should be kerned are AT, AV, AW, TA, VA, and WA. You can refine the kerning of your characters as little or as much as you like. Use of the KERNDATA= data set is optional.

The KERNDATA= data set contains the variables CHAR1, CHAR2, and XADJ. CHAR1 and CHAR2 are character variables with a length of 1, and XADJ is a numeric variable. XADJ specifies the adjustment in the direction of the X axis to be applied to CHAR2 whenever CHAR1 is followed immediately by CHAR2. XADJ uses the same unit type as the input data set for the font. Negative numbers *decrease* the spacing and positive numbers *increase* the spacing. Sort the KERNDATA= data set by CHAR1 CHAR2.

Example 4: Using the KERNDATA= and SPACEDATA= Data Sets shows an example of kerning data.

The SPACEDATA= Data Set

As the height of a font increases, less space is required between letters in relation to their height. The SPACEDATA= data set tells PROC GFONT how much space to allow for a given point size.

The variables in the SPACEDATA= data set are called SIZE and ADJ. Both of these variables are numeric. The SIZE variable specifies the point size of the font. The ADJ variable specifies the spacing adjustment for the point size in hundredths (1/100) of a point. (A point is equal to approximately 1/72 of an inch.) Sort the SPACEDATA= data set by SIZE.

Positive values for the ADJ variable result in greater spacing between characters. **Example 4: Using the KERNDATA= and SPACEDATA= Data Sets** shows an example of spacing data.

Values specified in the SPACEDATA= data set are added to the normal intercharacter spacing and any kerning data.

EXAMPLES

Example 1: The Letter A with a Stroked Font

These statements produce the letter A in a stroked font. Note that the stroked font is the default. The output produced is similar to **Figure 12.2**.

First, submit a LIBNAME statement to associate a directory with the font catalog libref, GFONT0. For UNIX operating systems and derivatives, use a statement of the form

```
libname gfont0 '/mydir/fonts/';
```

For SAS/GRAPH software on personal computers, use a statement like

```
libname gfont0 'c:\mydir\fonts\';
```

Then submit the following statements:

```
data a1;
   input char $ segment x y;
   cards;
```

```
a   1   45   40
a   1   50   50
a   1   55   40
a   2   47   45
a   2   53   45
;
proc gfont data=a1 name=font1;
```

Figure 12.2   Letter A with a Stroked Font

Example 2: The Letter A with a Filled Font

These statements produce the letter A in a filled font. The output produced is similar to **Figure 12.3**.

First, submit a LIBNAME statement to associate a directory with the font catalog libref, GFONT0. For UNIX operating systems and derivatives, use a statement of the form

```
libname gfont0 '/mydir/fonts/';
```

For SAS/GRAPH software on personal computers, use a statement like

```
libname gfont0 'c:\mydir\fonts\';
```

Then submit the following statements:

```
data a2;
   input char $ segment x y lp $;
   cards;
a   1   45   40   p
a   1   42   40   p
a   1   47   50   p
a   1   53   50   p
a   1   58   40   p
a   1   55   40   p
a   1   53   45   p
a   1   47   45   p
a   1    .    .   p
a   1   48   46   p
a   1   50   49   p
a   1   52   46   p
;
proc gfont data=a2 name=font2 filled;
```

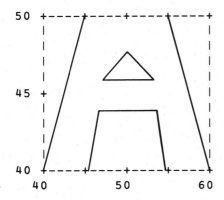

Figure 12.3   Letter A with Filled Font

Example 3: Using the PTYPE Variable

These statements produce output similar to **Figure 12.4**. In the first observation, the character has a PTYPE value of W, which indicates that the observation tells the width of the character. Remember that if you use a W-type point it *must* be the first observation for a character. A W-type point provides no digitizing data. Instead, it gives the minimum and maximum X values for the character.

The point with a PTYPE value of C is the center point for the circular arc.

First, submit a LIBNAME statement to associate a directory with the font catalog libref, GFONT0. For UNIX operating systems and derivatives, use a statement of the form

```
libname gfont0 '/mydir/fonts/';
```

For SAS/GRAPH software on personal computers, use a statement like

```
libname gfont0 'c:\mydir\fonts\';
```

Then submit the following statements:

```
data a3;
    input char $ segment x y lp $ ptype $;
    cards;
a 1 40 60 p w
a 1 45 40 p v
a 1 45 50 p v
a 1 45 40 p c
a 1 55 40 p v
;
proc gfont data=a3 name=font3 csp=data filled;
```

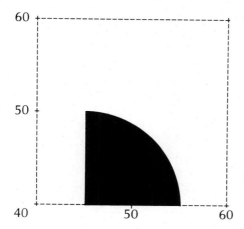

Figure 12.4   A Circular Arc Created Using the PTYPE Variable

Example 4: Using the KERNDATA= and SPACEDATA= Data Sets

The font described in this example consists of the letters A, D, and T only. The font is stroked and has a baseline of 41, an arbitrary value based on the input data. The width of each character is stored as the first observation; that is, the value of the PTYPE variable is W. First, enter the data for the font with the following statements:

```
data fontdat;
   input char $ x y segment ptype $;
   cards;
A  41  59  -1  W  /* Width record */
A  50  62   1  V
A  42  41   1  V
A  50  62   2  V
A  58  41   2  V
A  45  48   3  V
A  55  48   3  V
D  39  60  -1  W  /* Segment number does not matter on width records */
D  43  62   1  V
D  43  41   1  V
D  43  62   2  V
D  50  62   2  V
D  53  61   2  V
D  55  59   2  V
D  56  57   2  V
D  57  54   2  V
D  57  49   2  V
D  56  46   2  V
D  55  44   2  V
D  53  42   2  V
D  50  41   2  V
D  43  41   2  V
T  42  58  -1  W
T  50  62   1  V
T  50  41   1  V
T  43  62   2  V
T  57  62   2  V
;
```

Next, create the KERNDATA= data set. The variable XADJ specifies the amount of correction to be applied to CHAR2 when it follows CHAR1. Specify negative values for the XADJ variable to bring the two characters closer together.

```
data kern1;
   input char1 $ char2 $ xadj;
   cards;
A T -4
D A -3
T A -4
;
```

Next, create the SPACEDATA= data set. The SIZE variable specifies the size in points (one point is equal to approximately 1/72 of an inch). The ADJ variable specifies the adjustment to the intercharacter spacing based on the point size of the font and expressed in hundredths of a point. Specify negative values to bring the characters closer together.

```
data space1;
   input size adj;
   cards;
 6    40    /* Increase spacing on small sizes for better legibility */
12     0
18   -40    /* Decrease spacing as size increases */
24   -90
30  -150
36  -300
42  -620    /* Sizes greater than 42 points have an ADJ value of -620 */
;
```

Submit a LIBNAME statement to associate a libref with the name of the directory containing your font catalog. For personal computers, the LIBNAME statement should have the following form:

```
libname gfont0 'c:\mydir\fonts\';
```

For UNIX operating systems and derivatives, use a statement of this form:

```
libname gfont0 '/mydir/fonts/';
```

Although you can specify both a KERNDATA= and a SPACEDATA= data set, this example demonstrates how to generate separate fonts for each.
Submit the following statements to generate the font with kerning data:

```
proc gfont data=fontdat
           name=font3
           csp=data
           kerndata=kern1
           baseline=41;
run;
```

Now submit the following statements to generate the font with spacing data:

```
proc gfont data=fontdat
           name=font4
           csp=data
           spacedata=space1
           baseline=41;
run;
```

For comparison, you can generate another version, with no kerning or spacing, by submitting the following statements:

```
proc gfont data=fontdat
           name=font5
           csp=data
           baseline=41;
   run;
```

Now submit the following statements to compare kerned and unkerned text. The characters A, D, and T are shown as the word DATA in **Output 12.1** and **Output 12.2**.

```
title1 f=font3 h=10 j=l 'DATA';   /* Kerned     */
title2 f=font5 h=10 j=l 'DATA';   /* Not kerned */
proc gslide;
   run;
```

Submit the following statements to compare text with and without spacing adjustments.

```
title1 f=font4 h= 2 pct j=l 'DATA'; /* Spacing    */
title2 f=font5 h= 2 pct j=l 'DATA'; /* No spacing */
title4 f=font4 h= 4 pct j=l 'DATA';
title5 f=font5 h= 4 pct j=l 'DATA';
title6 f=font4 h= 6 pct j=l 'DATA';
title7 f=font5 h= 6 pct j=l 'DATA';
title8 f=font4 h=10 pct j=l 'DATA';
title9 f=font5 h=10 pct j=l 'DATA';
proc gslide;
   run;
```

Output 12.1   Kerned and Unkerned Text

Output 12.2   Text with and without Spacing Adjustments

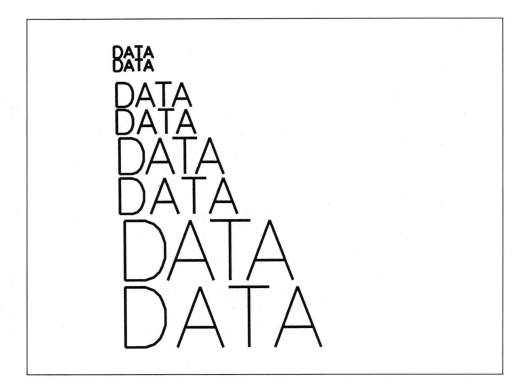

Chapter 13
The GMAP Procedure

ABSTRACT

You can use the GMAP procedure to produce color maps that are two-dimensional (choropleth) or three-dimensional (surface, block, and prism).

INTRODUCTION

For various applications, the best way to represent data is often in the form of a map that can immediately convey information on regional differences, extremes, and trends of data.

You can produce four types of maps with PROC GMAP:

choropleth two-dimensional graphics that use different color and pattern combinations to indicate levels of magnitude.

surface three-dimensional graphics that use spikes of varying heights to indicate levels of magnitude.

block   three-dimensional graphics that use blocks of varying heights, patterns, and colors to indicate levels of magnitude.

prism   three-dimensional graphics that use raised polygons or *prisms* of different heights, patterns, and colors to indicate levels of magnitude.

Output 13.1–13.4 shows examples of each of these map types. The statements used to produce this output are given in the section **Choropleth, Surface, Block, and Prism Maps**.

To produce a map with PROC GMAP you need two SAS data sets: a *map data set* and a *response data set*. The *map data set* contains points that are used to draw the map. The *response data set* contains the data to be evaluated and displayed on the map. In addition to other information, these two data sets **must** contain one or more ID variables that allow PROC GMAP to combine the information in both data sets and create a map. The ID variables identify the different *unit areas* (for example, counties, states, or provinces) that make up a map.

Output 13.1   Choropleth Map: PROC GMAP

Output 13.2   Surface Map: PROC GMAP

Output 13.3   Block Map: PROC GMAP

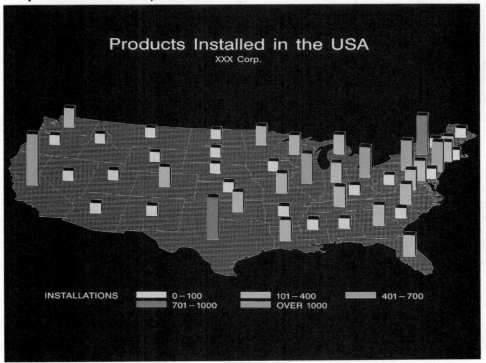

Output 13.4   Prism Map: PROC GMAP

Map Data Set

A map data set is a SAS data set containing coordinates for the boundaries of some unit area, such as states or counties. The map data set must contain the following variables:

- one or more ID variables that uniquely define the unit area, for example, STATE or COUNTY. ID variables can be character or numeric.
- a numeric variable named X containing the horizontal coordinates of the boundary points.
- a numeric variable named Y containing the vertical coordinates of the boundary points.

Optionally, the map data set can contain a variable named SEGMENT to identify segments of unit areas that are noncontiguous. For example, in a map of the United States, Hawaii would be represented as a single unit area (state) composed of multiple segments (its islands).

For each segment, observations in the map data set must occur in the order the points are to be joined. The GMAP procedure connects the points in each segment in the order they appear in the data set. The first and last points in each segment are joined.

The x and y values in the map data set should not be in any specific units because they will be rescaled by the procedure based on the minimum and maximum values in the data set. Note also that the minimum x and y values will be in the lower left corner of the map, and the maximum x and y values will be in the upper right corner. Map data set coordinates that are in latitude and longitude should be projected before being used with PROC GMAP. Refer to "The GPROJECT Procedure" for details.

SAS/GRAPH software includes several map data sets defining the United States and Canada. These data sets are described in the appendix "Special SAS/GRAPH

Data Sets." You can also create your own map data sets. For example, the statements below create a SAS data set containing coordinates for three unit areas: a square, a diamond, and a triangle.

```
data figures;
   input id $ 1-8 x y;
   cards;
square     3      5
square     7      5
square     7     10
square     3     10
diamond    8      8
diamond   10      5
diamond   12      8
diamond   10     11
triangle  12      5
triangle  15     10
triangle  18      5
;
```

Four observations are needed to define the square and the diamond; three observations are needed to define the triangle. Each unit area has a unique value for the variable ID.

The data set below defines a flower with twelve petals; each petal is a unique unit area. These statements generate the data:

```
data flower;
   pi2=3.14159265*2;
   delta=pi2/500;
   petal=1;
   rlast=1;
   do angle=0 to pi2 by delta;
      a=15*sin(6*angle);
      r=a+5*sign(a);
      if sign(r)+sign(rlast)=0 then do;
         petal+1;
         x=0;
         y=0;
         output;
         end;
      x=r*sin(angle);
      y=r*cos(angle);
      rlast=r;
      output;
      end;
   keep petal x y;
run;
```

Response Data Set

The response data set is also a SAS data set. For each unit area, the response data set contains one or more responses (for example, population) to be mapped. The response data set must contain ID variables with the same name, type, and length as those in the map data set. PROC GMAP matches these variables in the response data set to the same variables in the map data set to create a map.

Normally, the response data set includes one observation for each unique combination of ID variables. Each observation contains the response to be mapped for that unit area.

Response variables can be either character or numeric. For surface maps, the response variable must be positive numeric.

To produce a map from the FIGURES data set created above, a response data set named SHAPES can be matched to the map data set containing the three figures. The ID values in the response data set and the map data set are identical; each is a character variable with a length of eight. The response variable to be mapped is used to represent distinct responses to ensure that each figure is drawn in a different color. RESPONSE is a numeric variable; both numeric and character response variables can be used to draw choropleth maps.

The statements below produce **Output 13.5.**

```
data shapes;
   input id $ 1-8 response;
   cards;
square          1
diamond         2
triangle        3
;

pattern1 v=solid c=lioy;
pattern2 v=solid c=bioy;
pattern3 v=solid c=gold;
title f=swiss c=cream 'Simple Mapping Example: Figures';
footnote h=2 '  ';
proc gmap data=shapes map=figures;
   id      id;
   choro   response /  iscrete
                     coutline=cream
                     ctext=cream;
```

In the example below, a response data set to map the flower needs to contain only the ID variable PETAL. The following statements produce **Output 13.6.**

```
goptions cback=black
         colors=(cream lioy bioy vioy viypk gold vibg);
data resp;
   do petal=1 to 12;
      output;
      end;

pattern1 v=m1x;
pattern2 v=solid;
title f=swiss c=cream 'Simple Mapping Example: A Flower';
proc gmap data=resp
          map=flower;
   id      petal;
   choro   petal / discrete;
run;
```

Note that because no color value was specified in the PATTERN statements, PROC GMAP rotated through all of the colors in the colors list before going on to the next pattern.

Output 13.5   Simple Mapping Example for Figures: PROC GMAP

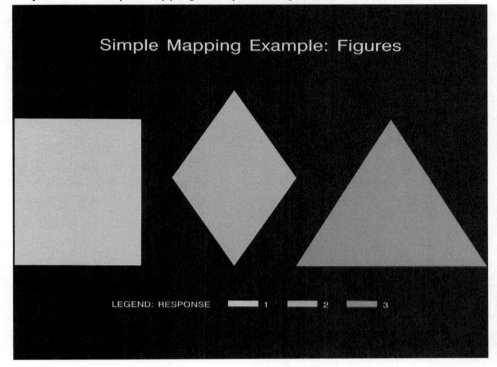

Output 13.6   Simple Mapping Example for a Flower: PROC GMAP

Other SAS/GRAPH Mapping Procedures

SAS/GRAPH software has other procedures that can be used to alter and enhance the output produced by PROC GMAP. With the GPROJECT procedure you can project the latitude and longitude coordinates of a map data set onto a two-dimensional plane. With the GREDUCE procedure you can reduce the number of points needed to draw a map, thus reducing processing time. With the GREMOVE procedure you can remove some of the boundaries in a map and create a subset of a map that combines the original areas.

United States Maps

SAS Institute provides the US map data set used in the examples that follow (see the appendix "Special SAS/GRAPH Data Sets"). When you use this or any other map data set supplied by SAS Institute, you must use a LIBNAME statement to point to the directory in which the maps are located.

Choropleth, Surface, Block, and Prism Maps

The statements below produce four maps showing the number of product installations in each state for the XXX Corporation, a fictitious company. A response data set containing the location for all products installed in the United States is matched to the US map data set. The DISCRETE option is needed because SITES is a numeric variable with discrete formatted values. See **Output 13.1–13.4** at the beginning of this chapter for the four maps (choropleth, surface, block, and prism) produced by these statements:

```
goptions cback=black;
pattern1  v=m5x c=lioy;
pattern2  v=ms  c=lioy;
pattern3  v=ms  c=bioy;
pattern4  v=ms  c=vioy;
pattern5  v=ms  c=viypk;
pattern6  v=ms  c=gold;
pattern7  v=s   c=lioy;
pattern8  v=s   c=bioy;
pattern9  v=s   c=vioy;
pattern10 v=s   c=viypk;
pattern11 v=s   c=gold;
title1 c=cream f=swiss 'Products Installed in the USA';
title2 c=cream f=swiss 'XXX Corp.';
proc gmap   data=sites
            map=maps.us;
    id      state;
    format  sites    sitesfmt.;
    label   sites='INSTALLATIONS';
    choro   sites / discrete
                    ctext=cream
                    coutline=cream;
    surface sites / cbody=viypk;
                    tilt=45
                    nlines=100;
    block   sites / discrete
                    ctext=cream
                    coutline=cream;
```

```
      prism   sites / discrete
                      ctext=cream
                      coutline=cream;
   run;
```

Combining Unit Areas

A character variable, REGION, is mapped in the next example. Six patterns are defined in PATTERN statements; one is used for each REGION value. The map data set is included with SAS/GRAPH software. The statements below produce the map shown in **Output 13.7**.

```
proc format;
   value regfmt
       0='Southwest'
       1='West'
       2='Central'
       3='South'
       4='Northeast'
       5='Midwest';

goptions cback=black;
pattern1 v=s c=lioy;
pattern2 v=s c=bioy;
pattern3 v=s c=vioy;
pattern4 v=s c=viro;
pattern5 v=s c=viypk;
pattern6 v=s c=gold;
title f=swiss c=cream 'Continental U.S. Regions';
footnote h=2 ' ';
proc gmap data=newus
          map=newus;
   id     state;
   choro  region / discrete
                    coutline=cream
                    ctext=cream;
   format region regfmt.;
run;
```

Separate Maps for Each Subgroup

When PROC GMAP is used with a BY statement, a map is produced for each value of the BY variable. The statements below produce a map for each REGION; the Northeastern region map is shown in **Output 13.8**.

```
data site4;
   set sites;
   if region=4;
goptions cback=black;
pattern1 v=s c=lioy;
pattern2 v=s c=bioy;
pattern3 v=s c=vioy;
pattern4 v=s c=viro;
pattern5 v=s c=viypk;
pattern6 v=s c=gold;
```

```
title1 c=cream f=swiss 'Products Installed';
title2 c=cream f=swiss 'By U.S. Region';
footnote h=2 '   ';
proc gmap data=site4
          map=newus;
   by      region;
   id      region  state;
   choro   sites / discrete
                   ctext=cream
                   coutline=cream;
   format region  regfmt.;
   format sites   sitesfmt.;
run;
```

Output 13.7   Combining Unit Areas: PROC GMAP

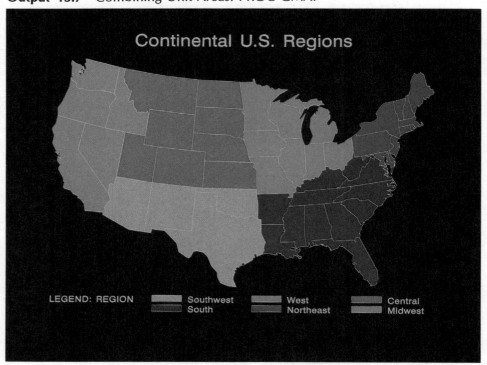

Output 13.8   Creating Separate Maps for Each Subgroup: PROC GMAP

County Maps

Another map data set available with SAS/GRAPH software defines the coordinates for counties within each state. The following examples use a subset of the data set containing only the coordinates for North Carolina counties. The response data set contains several statistics about North Carolina counties (U.S. Bureau of the Census, 1980).

The first North Carolina map shows credit union membership for North Carolina counties in 1980. The CTEXT= option specifies a color to use for printing all text on the map. The COUTLINE= option specifies the outline color. These statements produce the map shown in **Output 13.9**.

```
goptions cback=black;
pattern1 v=ms c=lioy;
pattern2 v=ms c=bioy;
pattern3 v=ms c=vioy;
pattern4 v=ms c=viypk;
pattern5 v=ms c=gold;
title1 f=swiss c=cream 'Credit Union Members';
title2 f=swiss c=cream 'North Carolina, 1980';
title3 f=swiss c=cream 'U.S. Census Data';
footnote h=2 '  ';
```

```
proc gmap data=ncdata
          map=ncmap;
   id     county;
   format members    memfmt.;
   choro  members / discrete
                    ctext=cream
                    coutline=cream;
   run;
```

Highlighting Areas

The next example shows a map drawn to highlight counties with more than 50,000 credit union members. The response data set is a subset of the original data set, but it includes only counties where membership falls in the desired range. The ALL option tells the procedure that all unit areas in the map data set are to be drawn, even those that do not appear in the response data set. The CEMPTY= option specifies a color to use for outlining the empty areas. The specification YSIZE=75 PCT tells PROC GMAP to use only 75 percent of the available screen space for the map. These statements produce the map shown in **Output 13.10**.

```
data highlite;
   set ncdata;
   if members > 50000;
   keep county members;

goptions cback=black;
pattern1 v=s c=gold;
title1 f=swiss c=cream 'Credit Union Members';
title2 f=swiss c=cream 'North Carolina, 1980';
title3 f=swiss c=cream 'Counties with More than 50,000 Members';
title4 f=swiss c=cream 'U.S. Census Data';
footnote h=2 '   ';

proc gmap data=highlite
          map=ncmap
          all;
   id     county;
   format members memfmt.;
   prism  members / discrete
                    cempty=lioy
                    coutline=lioy
                    ctext=cream
                    ysize=75 pct
                    nolegend;
   run;
```

Output 13.9   State Map: PROC GMAP

Output 13.10   Highlighting Sections of a Map: PROC GMAP

Displaying Empty Areas

The next example specifies V=E to represent missing or unavailable data in a unit area. The remaining formatted values for the response variable use solid fill with different colors. These statements produce the map shown in **Output 13.11**.

```
proc format;
   value memfmtm
       .='unavailable'
       0-1000='less than 1,000'
       1001-5000='1,001 to 5,000'
       5001-10000='5,001 to 10,000'
       10001-20000='10,001 to 20,000'
       20001-high='20,001 and up';
run;


pattern1 v=e c=cream;
pattern2 v=s c=lioy;
pattern3 v=s c=bioy;
pattern4 v=s c=vioy;
pattern5 v=s c=viypk;
pattern6 v=s c=gold;
title1 f=swiss c=cream 'Credit Union Members';
title2 f=swiss c=cream 'North Carolina, 1980';
title3 f=swiss c=cream 'U.S. Census Data';
footnote h=2 '  ';
proc gmap data=ncdata
          map=ncmap
          all;
   id      county;
   format members memfmtm.;
   choro   members / discrete
                     missing
                     ctext=cream
                     cempty=cream
                     coutline=cream;
run;
```

Other Maps

SAS/GRAPH software also includes a map data set defining the coordinates of Canadian provinces. In the next example, the response data set includes only the ID variables. Each unit area in the CANADA map data set is uniquely defined by two ID variables. These statements produce the map shown in **Output 13.12**.

```
pattern1  v=solid c=lioy;
pattern2  v=solid c=bioy;
pattern3  v=solid c=vioy;
pattern4  v=solid c=viro;
pattern5  v=solid c=viypk;
pattern6  v=solid c=gold;
pattern7  v=solid c=lioy;
pattern8  v=solid c=bioy;
pattern9  v=solid c=vioy;
pattern10 v=solid c=viro;
pattern11 v=solid c=viypk;
pattern12 v=solid c=gold;
```

```
title1 c=cream f=swiss 'Canadian Provinces';
title2 c=cream f=swiss 'Data from Statistics Canada';
footnote h=2 '   ';

proc gmap data=maps.canada
          map=maps.canada;
   id province cdcode;
   choro province / discrete
                    nolegend
                    coutline=cream;
run;
```

Output 13.11   Displaying Empty Areas Using the MISSING and CEMPTY=
Options and PATTERN Statements: PROC GMAP

Output 13.12   Using Other Map Data Sets: PROC GMAP

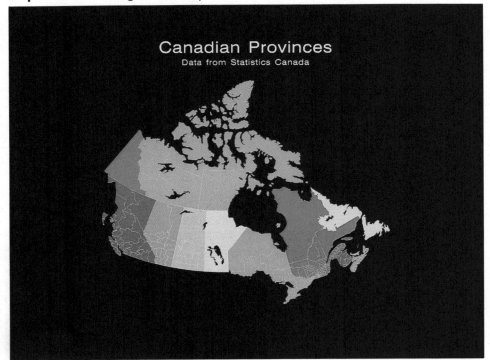

SPECIFICATIONS

The following statements can be used with PROC GMAP:

> **PROC GMAP MAP=** *mapdataset options*;
> **ID** *variables*;
> **CHORO** *variables / options*;
> **SURFACE** *variables / options*;
> **BLOCK** *responses / options*;
> **PRISM** *responses / options*;
> **BY** *variables*;
> **LEGEND***n options*;
> **PATTERN***n options*;
> **TITLE***n options 'text'*;
> **FOOTNOTE***n options 'text'*;
> **NOTE** *options 'text'*;

The ID statement is required. Any number of CHORO, SURFACE, BLOCK, and PRISM statements can be used.

PROC GMAP Statement

> PROC GMAP MAP=*mapdataset options*;

You can specify the following options in the PROC GMAP statement:

ALL
> specifies that the map include every unit area from the map data set (each distinct value of the ID variable(s)), even if there is no matching ID value in the response data set.

ANNOTATE=*SASdataset*
ANNO=*SASdataset*
> specifies a data set to be used for annotation. This data set must be an ANNOTATE= type data set containing the appropriate Annotate variables. (See "ANNOTATE= Data Sets" for details.)

DATA=*responsedataset*
> names the SAS data set that contains the response to be mapped. The data set should contain a variable with the same name, type (numeric or character), and length as each ID variable in the MAP= data set (see the MAP= option). Normally, the data set contains one observation for each value of the ID variable to be mapped, and one or more response variables for each observation. If you do not specify the DATA= option, PROC GMAP uses the most recently created SAS data set.

GOUT=*SAScatalog*
> names a SAS catalog used to save the output from the procedure. If you do not specify the GOUT= option, SAS catalog entries are written to the default catalog GSEG, which is erased at the end of your session. For more information on SAS catalogs, see "SAS/GRAPH Graphics Output."

MAP=*mapdataset*
> names a SAS data set containing the geographical coordinates for the boundaries of each unit area. For a more complete description of the map data set, see **Map Data Set**.
>> The MAP= option is required.

BLOCK Statement

> BLOCK *responses* / *options*;

The BLOCK statement creates a block map using the map and response data sets specified in the PROC GMAP statement. In the BLOCK statement, list the response variables for which you want a block map. You produce a map for each response variable listed. Response variables can be either numeric or character, and you can include any number of BLOCK statements.

The procedure draws a map with a block at the approximate center of each area. The height of the block represents an ordinal scale of the response variable.

You can specify the following options in the BLOCK statement:

ANNOTATE=*SASdataset*
ANNO=*SASdataset*
> specifies a data set to be used for annotation. This data set must be an ANNOTATE= type data set containing the appropriate Annotate variables. (See "ANNOTATE= Data Sets" for details.)

AREA=*position*
> specifies the position of the variable in the ID statement whose values determine groups distinguished by surface pattern. For example, if REGION is a variable in both the map and response data sets, then using these statements, the surface associated with each value of REGION is drawn with a different pattern:

```
data splitus;
   set newus;
   if region=0 then do;        /* Southwest */
      y=y-.05;
      end;
```

```
            else if region=1 then do;    /* West       */
               x=x-.05;
               y=y+.05;
               end;
            else if region=2 then do;    /* Central    */
               y=y+.05;
               end;
            else if region=3 then do;    /* Southeast */
               x=x+.05;
               y=y-.05;
               end;
            else if region=4 then do;    /* Northeast */
               x=x+.10;
               y=y+.10;
               end;
            else if region=5 then do;    /* Midwest    */
               x=x+.05;
               y=y+.05;
               end;

        goptions cback=black;
        pattern1  v=m5n  c=lioy;    /*patterns for surface areas*/
        pattern2  v=m5n  c=bioy;
        pattern3  v=m5n  c=vioy;
        pattern4  v=m5n  c=viro;
        pattern5  v=m5n  c=viypk;
        pattern6  v=m5n  c=gold;
        pattern7  v=s    c=lioy;    /*patterns for blocks*/
        pattern8  v=s    c=bioy;
        pattern9  v=s    c=vioy;
        pattern10 v=s    c=viro;
        pattern11 v=s    c=viypk;
        title1 c=cream f=swiss 'Products Installed in the USA';
        title2 c=cream f=swiss 'XXX Corp.';
        footnote h=2 '  ';
        proc gmap   data=sites
                    map=splitus;
           id       region  state;
           format   sites   sitesfmt.;
           label    sites='INSTALLATIONS';
           block    sites / discrete
                            area=1
                            coutline=cream;
        run;
```

AREA=1 tells the procedure to give each value of the first variable in the ID statement (REGION) a different pattern. **Output 13.13** was produced specifying AREA=1.

The following statements cause each state (the second variable in the ID list) to be drawn using a different pattern. **Output 13.14** was produced specifying AREA=2.

```
        pattern1 v=solid c=lioy;
        pattern2 v=solid c=bioy;
        pattern3 v=solid c=vioy;
        pattern4 v=solid c=viypk;
```

```
pattern5 v=solid c=gold;
pattern6 v=m5x   c=, r=10;   /* Rotate through colors with M5X */
                             /* pattern and repeat 10 times.   */
proc gmap  data=sites
           map=splitus;
    id     region  state;
    format sites   sitesfmt.;
    label  sites='INSTALLATIONS';
    block  sites / discrete
                   area=2
                   coutline=cream;
run;
```

When you specify the AREA= option, you should sort the map data set by the variables in the ID statement. If you omit the AREA= option from the BLOCK statement, the entire map is drawn using the same surface pattern.

If you use PATTERN statements with block maps, only mapping patterns (starting with the letter M) are used to fill the surface areas in the map; and the patterns L1 . . . L5, R1 . . . R5, X1 . . . X5, S, and E (that is, the patterns for PROC GCHART), are used to fill the blocks. You can specify solid and empty mapping patterns as MSOLID and MEMPTY, respectively.

Output 13.13   Determining Surface Pattern Groups: BLOCK Statement with AREA=1

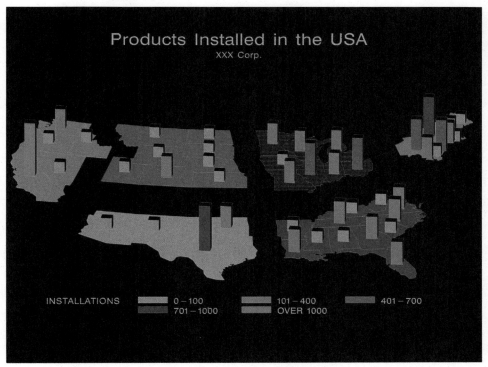

Output 13.14   Determining Surface Pattern Groups: BLOCK Statement with AREA=2

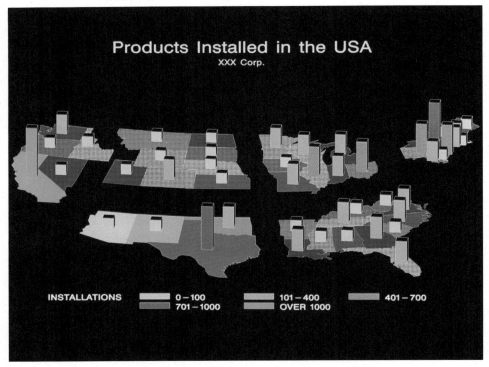

BLOCKSIZE=*size*
  specifies the size of the blocks. The unit of size is the width of a character cell of the particular output device. The default value is BLOCKSIZE=2.

CBLKOUT=*color*
  specifies the outline color for the block.

CEMPTY=*color*
  specifies the color used to outline empty unit areas on the map when ALL is specified in the PROC GMAP statement. If you specify the ALL option but omit the CEMPTY= option, PROC GMAP uses the first color in the COLORS= list to outline empty areas. (For more information on the COLORS= option, see "The GOPTIONS Statement.")

COUTLINE=*color*
  specifies the color used to outline nonempty unit areas. If you omit the COUTLINE= option, areas are outlined in the pattern color.

CTEXT=*color*
  specifies the color used to print the legend. If you do not specify the CTEXT= option, PROC GMAP uses the first color in the COLORS= list to print the text. (For more information on the COLORS= option, see "The GOPTIONS Statement.")

DESCRIPTION=*'string'*
DES=*'string'*
  specifies a descriptive string, up to forty characters long, that appears in the Description field of PROC GREPLAY's master menu. If you do not specify the DESCRIPTION= option, the Description field of PROC

GREPLAY's master menu contains a description assigned by
SAS/GRAPH.

DISCRETE
identifies the response variable as a numeric variable with discrete,
rather than continuous, values. If the response variable is continuous
and you do not specify the MIDPOINTS= or LEVELS= options, PROC
GMAP determines the number of intervals for the map using the formula
FLOOR(1+3.3log(N)), where N is the number of ID values.

LEGEND=LEGEND*n*
specifies the LEGEND statement to associate with the map, where n is
the number of a LEGEND statement defined previously. (For information
on LEGEND statements, see "Enhancing Your Graphics Output
Designs.")

LEVELS=*n*
specifies the number of midpoints to be used when the response
variables are continuous. PROC GMAP automatically generates
FLOOR(1+3.3log(N)) midpoints for the values of the response variable.

MIDPOINTS=*values*
allows you to define the range represented by each pattern by
specifying the midpoints of the ranges. For example, the following
statements produce a map with ten patterns: the first pattern represents
the range of RESPONSE values with a midpoint of 10; the second
pattern represents the range of values with a midpoint of 20; and so on.

```
proc gmap map=maps.us;
    id state;
    block response / midpoints=10 to 100 by 10;
```

For character variables, midpoints can be specified in any order. This
feature is useful in ordering the patterns listed or in subsetting the
values. For example, a list in the following form can be used:

```
midpoints='wheat' 'corn' 'soybeans' 'tobacco';
```

MISSING
requests that missing values be considered a valid level for the response
variable.

NAME=*'string'*
specifies a descriptive string, up to eight characters long, that appears in
the Name field of PROC GREPLAY's master menu. If you do not specify
the NAME= option, the Name field of PROC GREPLAY's master menu
contains the procedure name.

NOLEGEND
suppresses the printing, below the map, of the legend giving the range
of values and the corresponding pattern.

XSIZE=*n* PCT | *n* CM | *n* IN
YSIZE=*n* PCT | *n* CM | *n* IN
specify the physical size of the map you are creating. If a number
specified is larger than the default size, the default size is used. The
values PCT, CM, and IN refer to the specific unit in which size is
measured: percentage, centimeters, and inches, respectively. The default
size of the map graph area is 100 percent.

XVIEW | XV=*xcoordinate*
YVIEW | YV=*ycoordinate*
ZVIEW | ZV=*zcoordinate*

specify coordinates of the viewing position in the map coordinate system. You can position a block map on the *x,y* plane with the coordinates (0,0,0), (0,1,0), (1,1,0), and (1,0,0) as its four corners. (No axes are drawn on the maps produced by PROC GMAP, but imagine that the maps are drawn in an *x,y* plane as in **Figure 13.1**.) XVIEW=, YVIEW=, and ZVIEW= give the coordinates of your eye's position (your *viewing position*) in the map coordinate system. The *viewing reference point* of your eye is the center of the block map; that is, (0.5,0.5,0). Your viewing position cannot coincide with the viewing reference point. Note that you cannot give a negative value for the *z* coordinate (ZVIEW=).

If you do not specify XVIEW=, YVIEW=, and ZVIEW=, the viewing position is defined by the coordinates (0.5,−2,3). You can specify one, two, or all three of the VIEW coordinates; any that you do not specify are assigned the default values.

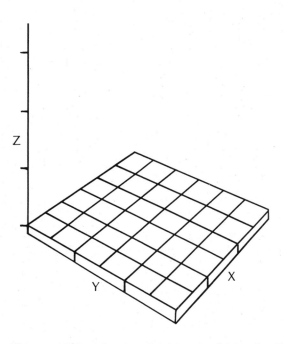

Figure 13.1   Viewing Position and Viewing Reference Point

BY Statement

BY *variables*;

You can use a BY statement with PROC GMAP to obtain separate maps on observations in groups defined by the BY variables. When a BY statement appears, the procedure expects the input data set to be sorted in order of the BY variables. If your input data set is not sorted in ascending order, use the SORT procedure with a similar BY statement to sort the data, or, if appropriate, use the BY statement options NOTSORTED or DESCENDING. For more information, see the discussion of the BY statement in "SAS Statements Used in the PROC Step" in the *SAS Language Guide, Release 6.03 Edition*. Each BY group in the response data set is processed with the entire map data set.

CHORO Statement

CHORO *variables* / *options*;

The CHORO statement creates a choropleth map using the map and response data sets specified in the PROC GMAP statement. In the CHORO statement, list the response variables for which you want choropleth maps. A map is produced for each response variable listed. You can specify any number of CHORO statements.

For each unique combination of ID values, PROC GMAP stores the first value of the response variable that it finds. This set of response variable values is used to determine the number of different patterns used in the map (unless the LEVELS= or MIDPOINTS= options are used).

You can specify the following options in the CHORO statement. Every option that you specify applies to all maps requested in the statement.

ANNOTATE=*SASdataset*
ANNO=*SASdataset*
   specifies a data set to be used for annotation. This data set must be an ANNOTATE= type data set containing the appropriate Annotate variables. (See "ANNOTATE= Data Sets" for details.)

CEMPTY=*color*
   specifies the color used to outline empty unit areas on the map when you have specified the ALL option in a PROC GMAP statement. If you specify the ALL option but omit the CEMPTY= option, PROC GMAP uses the first color in the COLORS= list to outline empty areas. (Empty unit areas are areas for which an ID value exists in the map data set, but not in the response data set.) For more information on the COLORS= option, see "The GOPTIONS Statement."

COUTLINE=*color*
   specifies the color used to outline nonempty unit areas. If you omit the COUTLINE= option, areas are outlined in the pattern color.

CTEXT=*color*
   specifies the color used to print the legend. If you omit the CTEXT= option, PROC GMAP uses the first color in the COLORS= list to print the text. (For more information on the COLORS= option, see "The GOPTIONS Statement.")

DESCRIPTION=*'string'*
DES=*'string'*
   specifies a descriptive string, up to forty characters long, that appears in the Description field of PROC GREPLAY's master menu. If you omit the DESCRIPTION= option, the Description field of PROC GREPLAY's master menu contains a description assigned by SAS/GRAPH.

DISCRETE
   identifies the response variable as a numeric variable with discrete, rather than continuous, values. If the response variable is continuous and you do not specify the MIDPOINTS= or LEVELS= options, PROC GMAP determines the number of intervals for the map using the formula FLOOR$(1+3.3\log(N))$, where N is the number of ID values.

   You should use this option if your response variable has a user-written format.

LEGEND=LEGEND*n*

specifies the LEGEND statement to associate with the map, where *n* is the number of a LEGEND statement defined previously. (For information on LEGEND statements, see "Enhancing Your Graphics Output Designs.")

LEVELS=*n*

specifies the number of midpoints to be used when the response variables are continuous. PROC GMAP automatically generates $FLOOR(1+3.3\log(N))$ midpoints for the values of the response variable.

MIDPOINTS=*values*

allows you to define the range represented by each pattern by specifying the midpoints of the ranges. For example, the following statements produce a map with ten patterns: the first pattern represents the range of RESPONSE values with a midpoint of 10; the second pattern represents the range of values with a midpoint of 20; and so on.

```
proc gmap map=maps.us;
   id state;
   choro response / midpoints=10 to 100 by 10;
```

For character variables, you can specify midpoints in any order. This feature is useful in ordering the patterns listed or in subsetting the values. For example, a list in the following form can be used:

```
midpoints='wheat' 'corn' 'soybeans' 'tobacco';
```

MISSING

requests that missing values be considered a valid level for the response variable.

NAME=*'string'*

specifies a descriptive string, up to eight characters long, that appears in the Name field of PROC GREPLAY's master menu. If you omit the NAME= option, the Name field of PROC GREPLAY's master menu contains the procedure name.

NOLEGEND

suppresses the printing, below the map, of the legend giving the range of values and the corresponding pattern.

XSIZE=*n* PCT | *n* CM | *n* IN
YSIZE=*n* PCT | *n* CM | *n* IN

specify the physical size of the map you are creating. If the number you have specified is larger than the default size, the default size is used. The values PCT, CM, and IN refer to the specific unit in which size is measured: percentage, centimeters, and inches, respectively. The default size of the map graph area is 100 percent.

FOOTNOTE Statement

FOOTNOTE*n* options *'text'*;

You can use FOOTNOTE statements with PROC GMAP. They are described in "Enhancing Your Graphics Output Text."

ID Statement

    ID *variables*;

The ID statement specifies the variable or variables that identify the unit areas. The ID variables must appear in both the map and the response data sets. ID variables can be either numeric or character, but their types and lengths must be the same in both data sets.

    The values of the ID variables in the response data set determine the unit areas to be included on the map unless you have specified the ALL option in the PROC GMAP statement. Thus, you do not need to subset your map data set if you are mapping only a small section of the map. However, if you map the same small section frequently, you should create a subset of the map data set for efficiency.

    The ID statement is required.

LEGEND Statement

    LEGEND*n options*;

You can use LEGEND statements with choro, block, and prism maps. For more information on LEGEND statements, see "Enhancing Your Graphics Output Designs."

NOTE Statement

    NOTE *options 'text'*;

You can use NOTE statements with PROC GMAP. They are described in "Enhancing Your Graphics Output Text."

PATTERN Statement

    PATTERN*n options*;

You can specify colors and patterns for each response category with PATTERN statements. PATTERN statements are described in "Enhancing Your Graphics Output Designs." For maps other than block maps, the only values for the V= option that can be specified with PROC GMAP are S, E, and M*xxxxx*. For block maps, you can specify L1 . . . L5, R1 . . . R5, and X1 . . . X5 for block patterns and S, E, and M*xxxxx* for surface patterns.

PRISM Statement

    PRISM *responses / options*;

The PRISM statement creates a prism map using the map and response data sets specified in the PROC GMAP statement. In the PRISM statement, list the response variables for which you want a prism map. You produce a map for each response variable listed. Response variables can be either numeric or character, and you can include any number of PRISM statements.

    When you specify the PRISM statement, each unit area is represented as a prism (a polyhedron with two parallel surfaces). The height of a prism represents an ordinal scale of the response variable.

    Note that the PRISM statement does not work well for maps containing intersecting polygons, polygons within polygons, extremely complicated maps, or maps containing line segments that cross. Use the GREDUCE procedure to reduce and simplify the map if necessary.

    The PRISM statement does not correctly draw polygons with common borders if the adjacent line segments of the polygons do not correspond exactly.

You can specify the following options in the PRISM statement:

ANNOTATE=*SASdataset*
ANNO=*SASdataset*

specifies a data set to be used for annotation. This data set must be an ANNOTATE= type data set containing the appropriate Annotate variables. (See "ANNOTATE= Data Sets" for details.)

CEMPTY=*color*

specifies the color used to outline empty unit areas on the map when ALL is specified in the PROC GMAP statement. If you specify the ALL option but omit the CEMPTY= option, PROC GMAP uses the first color in the COLORS= list to outline empty areas. (For more information on the COLORS= option, see "The GOPTIONS Statement.")

COUTLINE=*color*

specifies the color used to outline nonempty unit areas. If you omit the COUTLINE= option, areas are outlined in the pattern color. For some of the devices with hardware fill, white is always used to outline areas filled with solid patterns.

CTEXT=*color*

specifies the color used to print the legend. If you do not specify the CTEXT= option, PROC GMAP uses the first color in the COLORS= list to print the text. (For more information on the COLORS= option, see "The GOPTIONS Statement.")

DESCRIPTION=*'string'*
DES=*'string'*

specifies a descriptive string, up to forty characters long, that appears in the Description field of PROC GREPLAY's master menu. If you do not specify the DESCRIPTION= option, the Description field of PROC GREPLAY's master menu contains a description assigned by SAS/GRAPH.

DISCRETE

identifies the response variable as a numeric variable with discrete, rather than continuous, values. If the response variable is continuous and you do not specify the MIDPOINTS= or LEVELS= options, PROC GMAP determines the number of intervals for the map using the formula FLOOR($1+3.3$log(N)), where N is the number of ID values.

LEGEND=LEGEND*n*

specifies the LEGEND statement to associate with the map, where *n* is the number of a LEGEND statement defined previously. (For information on LEGEND statements, see "Enhancing Your Graphics Output Designs.")

LEVELS=*n*

specifies the number of midpoints to be used when the response variables are continuous. PROC GMAP automatically generates FLOOR($1+3.3$log(N)) midpoints for the values of the response variable.

MIDPOINTS=*values*

allows you to define the range represented by each pattern by specifying the midpoints of the ranges. For example, the following statements produce a map with ten patterns: the first pattern represents the range of RESPONSE values with a midpoint of 10; the second pattern represents the range of values with a midpoint of 20; and so on.

```
proc gmap map=maps.us;
   id state;
   prism response / midpoints=10 to 100 by 10;
```

For character variables, midpoints can be specified in any order. This feature is useful in ordering the patterns listed or in subsetting the values. For example, a list in the following form can be used:

```
midpoints='wheat' 'corn' 'soybeans' 'tobacco';
```

MISSING
   requests that missing values be considered a valid level for the response variable.

NAME=*'string'*
   specifies a descriptive string, up to eight characters long, that appears in the Name field of PROC GREPLAY's master menu. If you do not specify the NAME= option, the Name field of PROC GREPLAY's master menu contains the procedure name.

NOLEGEND
   suppresses the printing, below the map, of the legend giving the range of values and the corresponding pattern.

XSIZE=*n* PCT | *n* CM | *n* IN
YSIZE=*n* PCT | *n* CM | *n* IN
   specify the physical size of the map you are creating. If a number specified is larger than the default size, the default size is used. The values PCT, CM, and IN refer to the specific unit in which size is measured: percentage, centimeters, and inches, respectively. The default size of the map graph area is 100 percent.

XLIGHT=*xcoordinate*
YLIGHT=*ycoordinate*
   specify the coordinates of the imagined light source in the map coordinate system. Although you can specify any point for the light source, the points are actually simplified into only four positions.
   Assume that your eye's position (your *viewing position*) is point D (see **Figure 13.2**). If you specify a point that falls in quadrants I or II, or on the X or +Y axes, the light source is behind the map (point A), and all side polygons are shadowed. If you give a light source position that is on or within approximately 10 degrees of the −Y axis, the light source is at point D, and none of the side polygons are shadowed. When you give a point that is in quadrant III (except within 10 degrees of the Y axis), the light source is at the left of the map (point B), and the right-facing sides of the polygons are shadowed. When the light source coordinates are in quadrant IV (except within ten degrees of the Y axis), the source is at the right side of the map (point C), and the left-facing polygon sides are shadowed.
   If you specify none of these options, the light source position is the same as your eye's viewing position (point D), and none of the side polygons are shadowed.
   The light source position cannot coincide with the viewing reference point (0.5,0.5).

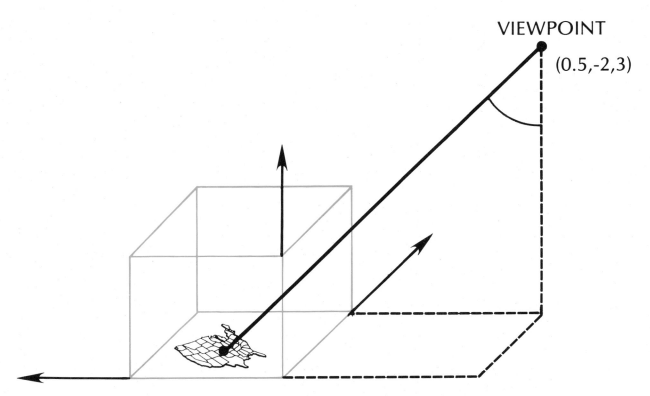

VIEWPOINT

(0.5,-2,3)

Figure 13.2   Coordinates of an Imagined Light Source in a Map Coordinate
System

XVIEW | XV=*xcoordinate*
YVIEW | YV=*ycoordinate*
ZVIEW | ZV=*zcoordinate*
   specify coordinates of the viewing position in the map coordinate
   system. You can position a prism map on the *x,y* plane with the
   coordinates (0,0,0), (0,1,0), (1,1,0), and (1,0,0) as its four corners. (No
   axes are drawn on the maps produced by PROC GMAP, but imagine
   that the maps are drawn in an *x,y* plane as in **Figure 13.1**.) XVIEW=,
   YVIEW=, and ZVIEW= give the coordinates of your eye's position
   (your *viewing position*) in the map coordinate system. The *viewing
   reference point* of your eye is the center of the prism map; that is,
   (0.5,0.5,0). Your viewing position cannot coincide with the viewing
   reference point. Note that you cannot give a negative value for the *z*
   coordinate (ZVIEW=).
      If you do not specify XVIEW=, YVIEW=, and ZVIEW=, the viewing
   position is defined by the coordinates (0.5,−2,3). You can specify one,
   two, or all three of the VIEW coordinates; any that you do not specify
   are assigned default values.
      Note: to ensure that the polygon edges are distinguishable, the angle
   from vertical (see **Figure 13.1**) must be less than or equal to 45 degrees.
   If you specify a ZVIEW= value such that this condition cannot be
   satisfied (that is, a very small value), PROC GMAP automatically
   increases the ZVIEW= value so that the angle is 45 degrees or less. The
   following statements produce the prism map shown in **Output 13.15**.

```
goptions cback=black;
pattern1 v=ms c=lioy;
pattern2 v=ms c=bioy;
pattern3 v=ms c=vioy;
pattern4 v=ms c=viypk;
pattern5 v=ms c=gold;
title1 c=cream f=swiss 'Products Installed in the USA';
title2 c=cream f=swiss 'XXX Corp.';
title3 c=cream f=swiss '(Viewed from Hawaii)';
title4;
footnote h=2 '  ';
proc gmap   data=sites
            map=maps.us;
   id       state;
   format   sites    sitesfmt.;
   label    sites='INSTALLATIONS';
   prism    sites / discrete
                    xview=-10
                    yview=-10
                    coutline=cream;
                    ctext=cream;
run;
```

Output 13.15 Prism Map of the United States as Seen from Hawaii

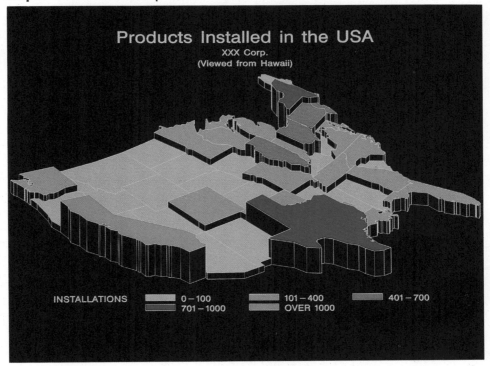

SURFACE Statement

> SURFACE *variables* / *options*;

The SURFACE statement creates a surface map using the map and response data sets specified in the PROC GMAP statement. In the SURFACE statement, list the response variables for which you want surface maps. The response variables must be positive numeric variables. You can include any number of SURFACE statements.

The procedure builds *spikes* at the approximate center of each unit area. The height of the spike corresponds to the relative value of the response variable.

You can specify the following options in the SURFACE statement. Every option you specify applies to each map requested in the statement.

ANNOTATE=*SASdataset*
ANNO=*SASdataset*
> specifies a data set to be used for annotation. This data set must be an ANNOTATE= type data set containing the appropriate Annotate variables. (See "ANNOTATE= Data Sets" for details.)

CBODY=*color*
> specifies the color used to draw the surface map. If you do not specify the CBODY= option, PROC GMAP uses the first color in the COLORS= list. (For more information on the COLORS= option, see "The GOPTIONS Statement.")

CONSTANT=*n*
> specifies a denominator to use in the distance decay function, described in the **DETAILS** section. The distance decay function is used to determine the height and base width of the spike drawn at each center. The denominator of this function is 10. Use the CONSTANT= option if you want to specify another denominator. If the CONSTANT= value is greater than 10, the spikes are taller and wider at the base. If the CONSTANT= value is less than 10, the spikes are shorter and narrower at the base.

DESCRIPTION=*'string'*
DES=*'string'*
> specifies a descriptive string, up to forty characters long, that appears in the Description field of PROC GREPLAY's master menu. If you do not specify the DESCRIPTION= option, the Description field of PROC GREPLAY's master menu contains a description assigned by SAS/GRAPH software.

NAME=*'string'*
> specifies a descriptive string, up to eight characters long, that appears in the Name field of PROC GREPLAY's master menu. If you do not specify the NAME= option, the Name field of PROC GREPLAY's master menu contains the procedure name.

NLINES=*n*
N=*n*
> specifies the number of lines used to draw the surface map. The number given should range from 50 to 100; the higher the value, the more solid the map appears. If you do not specify the NLINES= option, 50 lines are used to draw the map.

ROTATE=*angle*
> specifies the angle to rotate the map about the z axis. (See **Figure 13.3**.) The *angle* value can be any angle. If you do not specify the ROTATE= option, the default value of 70 degrees is used.

TILT=*angle*
> specifies the angle at which to tilt the map about the x axis. (Although no axes are actually drawn on the maps produced by PROC GMAP, imagine that the maps are drawn in the x,y plane as in **Figure 13.3**.)
>
> The angle values specified by TILT= can range from 0 to 90 degrees. As you increase the TILT= value, the map tilts down to make the spikes more prominent. As you decrease the TILT= value, the map is more distinguishable and the spikes less prominent. If you do not specify the TILT= option, the default value of 70 degrees is used.

XSIZE=*n* PCT | *n* CM | *n* IN
YSIZE=*n* PCT | *n* CM | *n* IN
> specify the physical size of the map you are creating. If you specify a number that is larger than the default size, the default size is used. The values PCT, CM, and IN refer to the specific unit in which size is measured: percentage, centimeters, and inches, respectively. The default size of the map graph area is 100 percent.

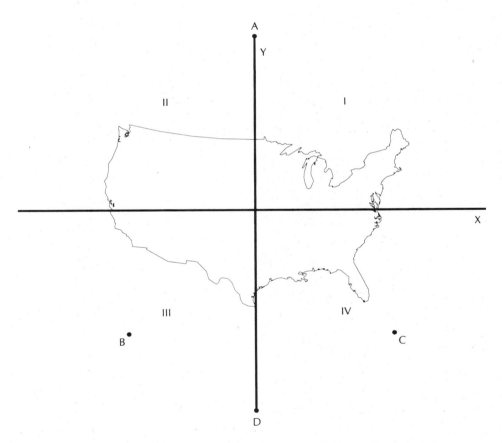

Figure 13.3 The x, y, and z Axes for a Three-Dimensional Surface Map

TITLE Statement

> TITLE*n* *options* 'text';

You can use TITLE statements with PROC GMAP. They are described in "Enhancing Your Graphics Output Text."

DETAILS

Map Data Set Processing with Surrounded Polygons

If one polygon is surrounded by another, the shading of the external polygon may be drawn over, instead of around, the shading for the internal one. This is illustrated in **Output 13.16**. The data and statements used to produce the output are as follows:

```
data hole1;
    input id x y segment;
    cards;
1   1   1     1
1   1   4     1
1   4   4     1
1   4   1     1
2   2   2     1
2   2   3     1
2   3   3     1
2   3   2     1
;
goptions cback=black;
pattern1 v=m1n45  c=viypk;
pattern2 v=m1n135 c=gold;
title1 c=cream f=swiss 'Polygon within a Polygon';
title2 c=cream f=swiss 'Without Special X Y Values';
footnote h=2 '  ';
proc gmap data=hole1
          map=hole1;
    id    id;
    choro id / discrete
              coutline=cream;
run;
```

You can avoid this problem by adding to the data an observation for the external polygon with missing values for X and Y, followed by the coordinates of the internal polygon with ID values for the external polygon. The data below include these extra observations. The output produced is shown in **Output 13.17**.

```
data hole2;
    input id x y segment;
    cards;
1   1   1     1
1   1   4     1
1   4   4     1
1   4   1     1
1   .   .     1
1   2   2     1
1   2   3     1
1   3   3     1
1   3   2     1
2   2   2     1
2   2   3     1
2   3   3     1
2   3   2     1
;
```

```
title1 c=cream f=swiss 'Polygon within a Polygon';
title2 c=cream f=swiss 'With Special X Y Values';
footnote h=2 '  ';
proc gmap data=hole2
          map=hole2;
    id      id;
    choro   id / discrete
                 coutline=cream;
run;
```

Output 13.16   A Polygon within a Polygon Using Ordinary X Y Values:
PROC GMAP

Output 13.17   A Polygon within a Polygon Using Special X Y Values:
PROC GMAP

Distance Decay Function

Let x_k and y_k represent the coordinates, and z_k the function value at the center of each unit area. The z_k values are scaled from 1 to 11. A square grid of (x,y) points (where the size of the grid is the NLINES= value) and the associated function value $f(x,y)$ is generated from the unit area center value using the following formula:

$$f(x,y) = \Sigma_k(1 - 1.5D_k + .5\ D_k^3)\ \Delta_k z_k$$

where

$$D_k = \sqrt{(((x - x_k)^2 + (y - y_k)^2)\ /\ \text{CONSTANT})}$$

and

$$\Delta_k = \begin{cases} 1 \text{ if } D_k < 1 \\ 0 \text{ otherwise} \end{cases}.$$

REFERENCE

U.S. Bureau of the Census (1982), *County and City Data Book, 1980*, U.S. Government Printing Office, Washington, D.C.

Chapter 14

The GOPTIONS Procedure

ABSTRACT

The GOPTIONS procedure lists the SAS/GRAPH system options currently in effect on your system.

INTRODUCTION

You can use PROC GOPTIONS to list the SAS/GRAPH system options that are in effect at any time during a session. The list includes the name and a brief description of each option. By specifying certain options in the PROC GOPTIONS statement, you can also request a list of all currently defined SYMBOL, PATTERN, TITLE, FOOTNOTE, AXIS, and LEGEND statements.

SPECIFICATIONS

The only statement used is the PROC GOPTIONS statement:

   PROC GOPTIONS *options*;

PROC GOPTIONS Statement

   PROC GOPTIONS *options*;

You can specify the following options in the PROC GOPTIONS statement:

AXIS
A
   requests a list of all currently defined AXIS statements.

LEGEND
L
   requests a list of all currently defined LEGEND statements.

NOLIST
N
   suppresses the printing of SAS/GRAPH system options. Use NOLIST when you want a listing of only the currently defined SYMBOL, PATTERN, TITLE, FOOTNOTE, AXIS, and LEGEND statements.

NOLOG
   causes output to appear in the procedure output stream instead of in the SAS log.

PATTERN
P
   requests a list of all currently defined PATTERN statements.

SHORT
   specifies a shortened listing so that several options without descriptions appear on one line. Normally, each option and a brief description are printed on a single line.

SYMBOL
S
   requests a list of all currently defined SYMBOL statements.

TITLE
T
   requests a list of all currently defined TITLE and FOOTNOTE statements, including any options defining height, type font, color, and other options specified in the statements when they were defined.

Chapter 15

The GPLOT
Procedure

ABSTRACT

The GPLOT procedure plots one variable against another. The coordinates of each point on the plot correspond to two variable values in an observation of the input data set.

INTRODUCTION

PROC GPLOT automatically scales the values on the axes of the plot, or you can explicitly specify *tick marks*, the marks on the axis representing specific values.

When you specify values for tick marks, PROC GPLOT spaces them equally on the axis. The values need not be uniformly distributed.

By specifying certain options in your PROC GPLOT program, you can

- draw horizontal or vertical reference lines on the plot
- superimpose two or more plots
- use any symbol to represent the points on the plot
- reverse the order of the values on the vertical axis so that they decrease rather than increase
- plot character variables (of length 16 or less) as well as numeric variables
- select colors, symbols, interpolation methods, and line styles for the plot
- produce circles of varying proportions (Z value) on the X-Y plane
- generate a second vertical axis
- produce logarithmic plots.

A variety of plots are shown in the **SYMBOL Statement** and **EXAMPLES** sections to give you an idea of PROC GPLOT's capabilities. You may find a plot among these examples that you want to produce to display your data.

SPECIFICATIONS

The following statements can be used with PROC GPLOT:

PROC GPLOT *options*;
    PLOT *yvariable*xvariable . . . / options*;
    BUBBLE *yvariable*xvariable=zvariable / options*;
    PLOT2 *yvariable*xvariable . . . / options*;
    BUBBLE2 *yvariable*xvariable=zvariable / options*;
    BY *variables*;
    SYMBOL*n options*;
    PATTERN*n options*;
    TITLE*n options 'text'*;
    FOOTNOTE*n options 'text'*;
    NOTE *options 'text'*;

PROC GPLOT Statement

PROC GPLOT *options*;

You can specify the following options in the PROC GPLOT statement:

ANNOTATE=*SASdataset*
ANNO=*SASdataset*
    specifies a data set to be used for annotation. The data set must be an ANNOTATE= type data set containing the appropriate Annotate variables. (See "ANNOTATE= Data Sets" for details.)

DATA=*SASdataset*
    gives the name of the SAS data set to be used by PROC GPLOT. If you do not specify the DATA= option, PROC GPLOT uses the most recently created SAS data set.

GOUT=*SAScatalog*
    specifies the SAS catalog used to store the output produced by PROC GPLOT for later replay. See "SAS/GRAPH Graphics Output" for further information on SAS catalogs. If you do not specify the GOUT= option, catalog entries are written to the default catalog GSEG, which is erased at the end of your session.

UNIFORM
  specifies that the same axis scaling should be used for all the plots produced. The UNIFORM option is helpful when you use a BY statement with PROC GPLOT because using the same scaling allows you to compare plots directly for each level.

BUBBLE Statement

  BUBBLE *yvariable*xvariable*=*zvariable* / *options*;

The BUBBLE statement produces a Y*X=Z type graph used mainly for market-share analysis (see the **PLOT Statement** section below for a description of Y*X=Z type graphs). You must specify either a BUBBLE statement or a PLOT statement with PROC GPLOT.

  The BUBBLE statement produces circles of varying proportion (Z value) on the X-Y plane rather than the lines or symbols used by the PLOT and PLOT2 statements. If a Z value causes a bubble to overlap the axis, the bubble will be clipped against the axis line. As with the PLOT statement, values that lie outside the axis area are not calculated, causing no part of the bubble to be visible. Ranges can be changed by specifying the axes. The size of the bubble depends on the numeric value of the Z observations. Thus, the bubble for a Z value of 3 is smaller than the bubble for a Z value of 10. Circles are drawn with a solid line if the Z value is positive and with a dashed line if the value is negative. For example, a Z-valued bubble of −5 is the same size as a Z-valued bubble of 5, but the negative-valued bubble is drawn with a dashed line.

  In a BUBBLE statement (as in a PLOT statement) values are plotted against the left vertical axis.

  In addition to the PLOT statement options, the options below can appear in a BUBBLE statement:

BCOLOR=*color*
  specifies the color to be used when producing bubbles. The default is the color specified with the CAXIS= option.

BFONT=*font*
  specifies the character font to be used when producing labels. (See the description of the BLABEL option.) The default font is SIMPLEX.

BLABEL
  produces formatted labels for the Z value around the bubbles on the graph. The default does NOT produce labels. Labels normally are placed directly outside the circle at 315 degrees rotation. If a label does not fit into the graph data area, other 45-degree placements (for example, 315, 135, 45, and 225 degrees) are attempted. If the label cannot be placed at any of the positions (315, 135, 45, or 225 degrees) without being clipped, the label is omitted. Labels are drawn in the color specified by the CTEXT= option.

BSCALE=AREA | RADIUS
  indicates whether the bubble scaling proportion is to be indicated by the area of the circles or the radius measure. The default value is AREA.

BSIZE=*multiplier*
  specifies an overall scaling factor of the bubbles being produced, where *multiplier* indicates the size of the largest bubble produced. You can increase or decrease the size of all bubbles produced by this factor. The default value is 5.

BUBBLE2 Statement

BUBBLE2 *yvariable*xvariable=zvariable / options*;

The BUBBLE2 statement allows you to generate a bubble plot against a right vertical axis, rather than the left vertical axis as with a BUBBLE statement. (See the **BUBBLE Statement** for a complete description of this statement's features.) You can specify the options available in the BUBBLE statement in the BUBBLE2 statement.

BY Statement

BY *variables*;

You can use a BY statement with PROC GPLOT to obtain separate analyses on observations in groups defined by the BY variables. When a BY statement appears, the procedure expects the input data set to be sorted in the order of the BY variables. If your input data set is not sorted in ascending order, use the SORT procedure with a similar BY statement to sort the data, or, if appropriate, use the BY statement options NOTSORTED or DESCENDING. For more information, see the discussion of the BY statement in "SAS Statements Used in the PROC Step," in the *SAS Language Guide, Release 6.03 Edition*.

FOOTNOTE Statement

FOOTNOTE*n options* 'text';

You can use FOOTNOTE statements with PROC GPLOT. They are described in "Enhancing Your Graphics Output Text."

NOTE Statement

NOTE *options* 'text';

You can use NOTE statements with PROC GPLOT. They are described in "Enhancing Your Graphics Output Text."

PATTERN Statement

PATTERN*n options*;

When you use the AREAS= option in a PLOT statement, PATTERN statements specify the colors and patterns to use for filling each area. (See "Enhancing Your Graphics Output Designs" for more information about PATTERN statements.)

PLOT Statement

PLOT *yvariable*xvariable* . . . / *options*;

The PLOT statement requests that plots be produced by PROC GPLOT. You can include any number of PLOT statements. You must specify either a PLOT statement or a BUBBLE statement with PROC GPLOT.

Each PLOT statement should include a request of the form *yvariable*xvariable*. For example, the statements

```
proc gplot;
   plot y*x;
```

request a plot of Y by X. Y appears on the vertical axis, X on the horizontal.

To request two or more plots, separate the plot requests by blanks:

```
proc gplot;
   plot a*b r*s;
```

You can request plots for combinations of several variables by enclosing each set of variables in parentheses and separating them with an asterisk (*). For example, the statements

```
proc gplot;
   plot (y x)*(a b);
```

request plots of Y by A, Y by B, X by A, and X by B.

A plot request of the form

```
plot a*b=c;
```

is used where C is a classification or nominal variable and produces a plot for each formatted value of C. All of the plots are drawn on the same graph, and a legend is automatically produced using the values of C. Values of C need not be in sorted order, but they cannot exceed a length of 16.

If you request a plot using the form

```
plot x*y=n;
```

the procedure uses the nth generated SYMBOL statement when it plots X and Y. Plot requests of this form are useful when you are producing overlaid plots and you want to specify the SYMBOL statement to use for each plot.

You can specify the options below in the PLOT statement after a slash (/).

General Options

ANNOTATE=*SASdataset*
ANNO=*SASdataset*
> specifies a data set to be used for annotation. The data set must be an ANNOTATE= type data set containing the appropriate Annotate variables. (See "ANNOTATE= Data Sets" for details.)

AREAS=*n*
> specifies that areas above or below plotted lines should be filled. Areas defined by lines on the plot are numbered from the bottom: the area below the first plotted line is area 1; the area above area 1 and below the second plotted line is area 2; and so on. If you specify AREAS=*n*, you can define *n* PATTERN statements to fill each area. The only valid values for V= in the PATTERN statement are M*xxxxx*, S, and E.
>
> When you use the AREAS= option, a line must be drawn in order for the area to be filled. Specify a value for the I= option in a SYMBOL statement to request a line. (I=NONE, I=HILO*xx*, and I=STD*kxxx* are not valid with the AREAS= option.) If you use the V= option in the SYMBOL statement, some symbols may be hidden.
>
> Refer to the PATTERN statement section in "Enhancing Your Graphics Output Designs" for more information.

DESCRIPTION=*'string'*
DES=*'string'*
> specifies a descriptive string, up to forty characters long, that appears in the Description field of PROC GREPLAY's master menu. If you do not specify the DESCRIPTION= option, the Description field of PROC GREPLAY's master menu contains a description assigned by SAS/GRAPH software.

LEGEND=LEGEND*n*

specifies the LEGEND statement to associate with the plot, where *n* is the number of a LEGEND statement you defined previously.

Specify the LEGEND= option only if the graph requested produces a legend (that is, it contains a request of the type Y*X=Z). Simply specifying the LEGEND= option in the PROC GPLOT statement does not cause a legend to be created.

NAME='*string*'

specifies a descriptive string, up to eight characters long, that appears in the Name field of PROC GREPLAY's master menu. If you do not specify the NAME= option, the Name field of PROC GREPLAY's master menu contains the procedure name.

NOLEGEND

suppresses drawing of the legend below the plot for plot requests of the form Y*X=Z.

OVERLAY

places all the plots requested by the PLOT statement on one set of axes. The axes are scaled to fit all the variables, and the variable labels (if any) associated with the first pair of variables are drawn next to the axes. For plots of the form Y*X=Z, OVERLAY cannot be specified.

You can create special effects by overlaying the same curves using different symbols, colors, and so on. Refer to **Output 15.10** and **15.13** for a demonstration of the OVERLAY option.

SKIPMISS

creates a gap in the simple JOIN line at occurrences of missing values or breaks an area fill if you also specify I=JOIN. Observations must be sorted by the variable on the horizontal axis.

Options to Draw Lines on the Plot

You can use the options below to draw vertical and horizontal reference lines on the plot, using whatever color and line type you choose.

AUTOHREF
AUTOVREF

automatically draws reference lines at major tick marks.

CHREF=*color*
CH=*color*

specifies the color used for vertical lines requested by the HREF= option. If you do not specify a color, the axis color is used.

CVREF=*color*
CV=*color*

specifies the color used for horizontal lines requested by the VREF= option. If you do not specify a color, the axis color is used.

GRID

produces the same results as using all of the following options together in a PLOT statement:

```
proc gplot;
   plot y*x / autovref lvref=34
              autohref lhref=34
              frame;
```

HREF=*values*
   specifies where vertical lines are to be drawn. For example, the
   following statements request a plot of Y by X with a vertical line at 5 on
   the horizontal axis:

```
proc gplot;
   plot y*x / href=5;
```

LHREF=*linetype*
LH=*linetype*
   specifies the line style (1–46) used for drawing reference lines specified
   with the HREF= option. (See "Enhancing Your Graphics Output
   Designs" for examples of the various line styles.) The default line style is
   1, a solid line.

LVREF=*linetype*
LV=*linetype*
   specifies the line style (1–46) used for drawing reference lines specified
   with the VREF= option. (See "Enhancing Your Graphics Output
   Designs" for examples of the various line styles.) The default line style is
   1, a solid line.

VREF=*values*
   specifies where horizontal lines are to be drawn.

Options to Define the Axes

PROC GPLOT automatically scales the axes, placing tick marks at even intervals.
However, you can use the options below to adjust the axes.

CAXIS=*color*
CA=*color*
   specifies the color used for the axis. If you do not specify the CAXIS=
   option, SAS/GRAPH uses the first color in the COLORS= list in the
   GOPTIONS statement.

CFRAME=*color*
CFR=*color*
   specifies the color used to fill the axis area. Specifying CFRAME=
   implies that you are also specifying the FRAME option.

CTEXT=*color*
CT=*color*
   specifies the color used for drawing text on the axes, including tick mark
   values and variable names or labels. If you do not specify the CTEXT=
   option, PROC GPLOT uses the first color in the COLORS= list in the
   GOPTIONS statement.

FRAME
FR
   specifies that the axis area be outlined in the color of the axis. If you do
   not specify the FRAME option, the axis area is not outlined.

HAXIS=*values*
HAXIS=AXIS*n*
   specifies tick mark values for the horizontal axis. The values are spaced
   equally along the horizontal axis.
      If you want to use a previously defined AXIS statement, specify
   HAXIS=AXIS*n* where AXIS*n* is the number of the AXIS statement you
   want to use. (See "Enhancing Your Graphics Output Designs" for more
   information concerning the AXIS statement.)

When the variable is numeric, the HAXIS= values must be given in either ascending or descending order. The values need not be uniformly distributed. For character variables, the values can be given in any order. Examples of axis specifications include:

Specification	Tick marks
haxis=10 to 100 by 10	10, 20, 30 . . . 100
haxis=10,30,40	10, 30, 40
haxis=10,20,30 to 40 by 2	10, 20, 30, 32 . . . 40
haxis='01jan85'd to '01jan86'd by month	01jan85, 01feb85 . . . 01jan86
haxis='01jan85'd to '01jan86'd by qtr	01jan85, 01apr85 . . . 01jan86

In the last two examples in the list above, the *from* and *to* values can be any of the valid SAS date, time, or datetime values described for the SAS functions INTCK and INTNX (see "SAS Functions" in the *SAS Language Guide, Release 6.03 Edition*). The BY value can be any of the valid values listed for the *interval* argument in the SAS functions INTCK and INTNX. When you use date or time values, you should use a FORMAT statement to draw the tick mark values in an understandable form.

Note that if a specified range in an HAXIS= or VAXIS= data list causes data values to fall outside the range extents, then by default, the outlying data values are *not* used in interpolation calculations for that axis. This will cause regression lines, hi-lo boxes, STD means, and so on to represent only part of the original data. You can specify options in a SYMBOL statement to include or exclude these data points in calculations. Refer to "Enhancing Your Graphics Output Designs" for information on the SYMBOL statement.

HMINOR=*n*
HM=*n*
specifies the number of minor tick marks between each major tick mark on the horizontal axis. No values are drawn on the minor tick marks.

HZERO
specifies that tick marks on the horizontal axis begin in the first position with a value of zero. The HZERO request is ignored if negative values are present for the horizontal variable or if the horizontal axis has been specified using the HAXIS= option.

NOAXES
suppresses drawing the axis lines, labels, and values.

VAXIS=*values*
VAXIS=AXIS*n*
specifies the tick mark values for the vertical axis. The values are spaced equally along the vertical axis. See the description of the HAXIS= option for details.

VMINOR=*n*

VM=*n*

specifies the number of minor tick marks to be drawn between each major tick mark on the vertical axis. No values are drawn on the minor tick marks.

VZERO

specifies that tick marks on the vertical axis begin in the first position with a zero. The VZERO request is ignored if negative values are present for the vertical variable or if the vertical axis has been specified using the VAXIS= option.

VREVERSE

specifies that the order of the values on the vertical axis be reversed. No option is available for reversing the values on the horizontal axis.

PLOT2 Statement

PLOT2 *yvariable*xvariable* . . . / *options*;

You can use a PLOT2 statement to generate a second vertical axis on the right side of the plot produced by PROC GPLOT.

When you use a PLOT2 statement, PROC GPLOT assumes that the second horizontal axis specified in the PLOT2 statement is identical to the PLOT statement's horizontal axis. If the PLOT2 statement's horizontal axis is not identical to the PLOT statement's horizontal axis, the axis is forced to be the same. Any PATTERN statements you specified in the PLOT statement are reused when the PLOT2 statement is executed, beginning with PATTERN1. The PLOT2 statement uses the SYMBOL statements not previously used in the PLOT statement.

When you use a PLOT2 statement with a PLOT statement, the plot pairs must be evenly matched on each statement. The examples below show correct and incorrect matching of plot pairs:

Correct   Incorrect

```
proc gplot;              proc plot;
   plot y*x y1*x;           plot y*x y1*x y3*x;
   plot2 y*x y2*x;          plot2 y*x y2*x;
   plot y3*x;           run;
run;
```

You can specify the options available with the PLOT statement in the PLOT2 statement.

SYMBOL Statement

SYMBOL*n options*;

You can use SYMBOL statements with PROC GPLOT to describe symbols, colors, interpolation methods, and line styles for the plots. See "Enhancing Your Graphics Output Designs" for a description of SYMBOL statements.

Plot of Points

If you do not specify a SYMBOL statement, SAS/GRAPH uses the default values for color, plotting symbol, and interpolation. The following statements produce the plot shown in **Output 15.1.**

Note that the DATA step that creates the TEMPS data set used in this example is contained in the SAS Sample Library that accompanies SAS/GRAPH software.

```
title1 j=1 h=2 f=swiss c=white '   Average Monthly Temperature'
          h=3 f=simplex a= 90  ' '
          h=3 f=simplex a=-90  ' ';
footnote1 j=1 ' Source:'
          m=(9,+0) '1984 American Express'
          m=(9,-1.12) 'Appointment Book';
footnote2 h=2 ' ';

proc gplot data=temps;
   plot f1*month / hminor=0
                   vminor=0;
run;
```

Joining Points

Using the same data as in the example above, the I= option in the SYMBOL1 statement joins the points with a gold line. (See "SAS/GRAPH Colors" for more detailed information on how to specify colors.)

By specifying PLOT F3*MONTH=2, you apply the second SYMBOL statement to define the color, symbol, and type of line drawn.

The following statements produce the plot shown in **Output 15.2**.

```
title1 j=1 h=2 f=swiss c=white '   Average Monthly Temperature'
          h=3 f=simplex a= 90  ' '
          h=3 f=simplex a=-90  ' ';
footnote1 j=1 ' Source:'
          m=(9,+0) '1984 American Express'
          m=(9,-1.12) 'Appointment Book';
footnote2 h=2 ' ';

symbol1 c=gold  i=join;
symbol2 c=cyan  i=join v=star;
symbol3 c=white i=join v=square;

proc gplot data=temps;
   plot f3*month=2 / hminor=0
                     vminor=0;
run;
```

Output 15.1 Using Default Colors, Plotting Symbol, and Interpolation

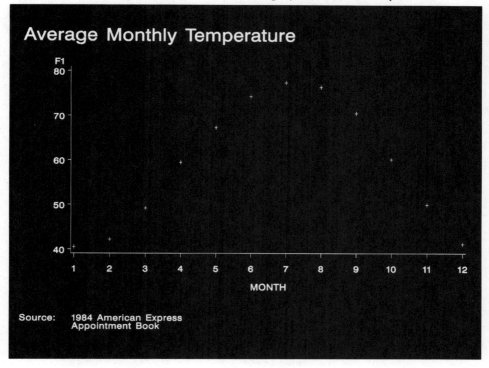

Output 15.2 Specifying a SYMBOL Statement: PROC GPLOT

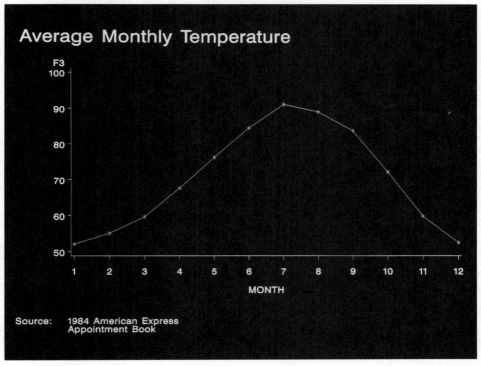

Regression Analysis—Plotting Points

Suppose you are investigating the relationship between the height and weight of a sample of elementary school students. You plot the raw data distribution with points using the following statements.

The SYMBOL1 statement is used by default because no SYMBOL statement is specified in the PLOT statement. Thus, statements SYMBOL2 and SYMBOL3 are not used here but will be used in the following examples. PROC GPLOT uses the labels associated with the variables for labeling the axes.

These statements produce the plot shown in **Output 15.3**.

```
title1 j=1 h=2 f=swiss c=white '   Study of Height vs Weight'
            h=3 f=simplex a= 90  ' '
            h=3 f=simplex a=-90  ' ';
footnote1 j=1 ' Source:'
            m=(9,+0) 'T. Lewis & L.R. Taylor'
            m=(9,-1.12) 'Introduction to Experimental Ecology';
footnote2 h=2 ' ';

symbol1 c=yellow           v=diamond;
symbol2 c=green i=rc       v=star;
symbol3 c=cyan  i=rcclm95 v=square;

proc gplot data=stats;
   plot height*weight / hminor=0
                        vminor=0;
run;
```

Drawing the Regression Line

You can request that PROC GPLOT fit a regression line to the data. The I=RC option requests that PROC GPLOT fit a cubic regression line to the data. (See the description of the I= option in "Enhancing Your Graphics Output Designs.")

Notice that PLOT HEIGHT*WEIGHT=2 identifies the second SYMBOL statement and requests the color, line, and symbol to be used.

These statements produce the plot shown in **Output 15.4**.

```
title1 j=1 h=2 f=swiss c=white '   Study of Height vs Weight'
            h=3 f=simplex a= 90  ' '
            h=3 f=simplex a=-90  ' ';
footnote1 j=1 ' Source:'
            m=(9,+0) 'T. Lewis & L.R. Taylor'
            m=(9,-1.12) 'Introduction to Experimental Ecology';
footnote2 h=2 ' ';

symbol1 c=yellow           v=diamond;
symbol2 c=green i=rc       v=star;
symbol3 c=cyan  i=rcclm95 v=square;

proc gplot data=stats;
   plot height*weight=2 / hminor=0
                          vminor=0;
run;
```

Output 15.3   Plotting Points in a Regression Analysis

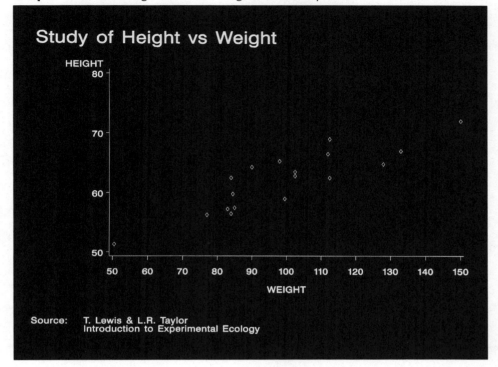

Output 15.4   Fitting a Regression Line to Your Data

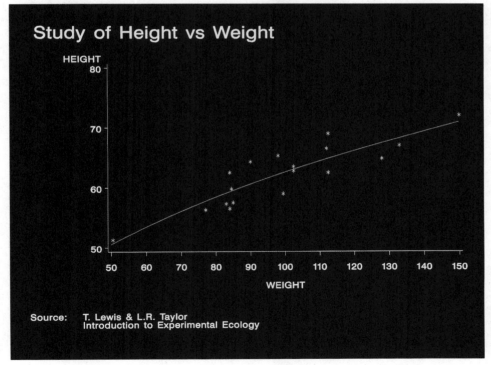

Drawing Confidence Limits

By specifying I=RCCLM95, the following statements request the 95 percent confidence limits for a mean predicted value.

When PROC GPLOT draws confidence limits, it adds 1 to the line style value in effect. In the statements below, the default line style L=1 is used to draw the regression line. Thus, L=2, a dashed line, is used to draw confidence limits.

These statements produce the plot shown in **Output 15.5**.

```
title1 j=l h=2 f=swiss c=white '    Study of Height vs Weight'
          h=3 f=simplex a= 90   ' '
          h=3 f=simplex a=-90   ' ';
footnote1 j=l ' Source:'
          m=(9,+0) 'T. Lewis & L.R. Taylor'
          m=(9,-1.12) 'Introduction to Experimental Ecology';
footnote2 h=2 ' ';

symbol1 c=yellow         v=diamond;
symbol2 c=green i=rc     v=star;
symbol3 c=cyan  i=rcclm95 v=square;

proc gplot data=stats;
   plot height*weight=3 / hminor=0
                          vminor=0;

run;
```

Changing Colors

You can use the CI=, CO=, and CV= options in SYMBOL statements to specify multiple colors for points and lines from a single curve request. You can use the same technique used with any I= value; the points drawn in one color, the lines joining the points in another.

The SYMBOL1 statement below marks the data points with yellow diamonds and draws a green regression line with cyan confidence limits. (SYMBOL and SYMBOL1 can be used interchangeably.)

These statements produce the plot shown in **Output 15.6**.

```
title1 j=l h=2 f=swiss c=white '    Study of Height vs Weight'
          h=3 f=simplex a= 90   ' '
          h=3 f=simplex a=-90   ' ';
footnote1 j=l ' Source:'
          m=(9,+0) 'T. Lewis & L.R. Taylor'
          m=(9,-1.12) 'Introduction to Experimental Ecology';
footnote2 h=2 ' ';

symbol1 cv=yellow v=diamond
        ci=green   i=rcclm95
        co=cyan;

proc gplot data=stats;
   plot height*weight=1 / hminor=0;
                          vminor=0;
run;
```

Output 15.5 Drawing Confidence Limits to the Plot

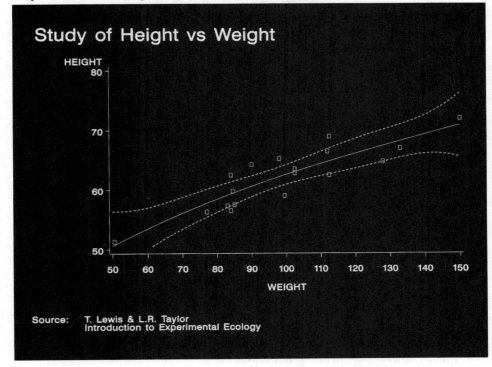

Output 15.6 Changing Colors

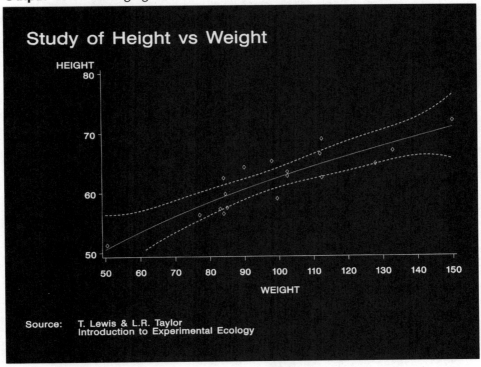

Plotting by a Third Variable

You can produce separate symbols and colors for each level of a classification variable on the same plot. Specify a different SYMBOL statement for each level of the classification variable.

The statements shown below produce **Output 15.7**. Note the following features of this plot:

- The formatted values are represented in a legend at the bottom of the plot, each with their individual symbols.
- Each season is represented by a different color as well as a different symbol, making the plot easier to read.
- SYMBOL statements access seasonally representative character fonts, such as leaves for autumn and snowflakes for winter.

```
title1 j=1 h=2 f=swiss c=white    '   Average Monthly Temperature'
           h=3 f=simplex a= 90  ' '
           h=3 f=simplex a=-90  ' ';
footnote1 j=1 ' Source:'
          m=(9,+0) '1984 American Express'
          m=(9,-1.12) 'Appointment Book';
footnote2 h=2 ' ';
symbol1 c=cyan   i=none v=star;
symbol2 c=green  i=none v=p f=cartog;
symbol3 c=salmon i=none v=i f=special;
symbol4 c=gold   i=none v=n f=cartog;
proc format;
   value sample   1='WINTER' 2='SPRING'
                  3='SUMMER' 4='AUTUMN';
run;

proc gplot data=temps;
   plot f2*month=season / hminor=0 vminor=0;
   format season sample.;
run;
```

NEEDLE Option

If you specify I=NEEDLE in a SYMBOL statement, a vertical line connects each point on the plot to the Y=0 line where Y is the variable on the vertical axis. The data generated in the example below have Y values between −20 and +30; thus, needles are drawn both up and down. If Y includes only positive values, needles are drawn from the horizontal axis to the points.

These statements produce the plot shown in **Output 15.8**.

```
title1 j=1 h=2 f=swiss c=white '   Average Monthly Temperature'
           h=3 f=simplex a= 90  ' '
           h=3 f=simplex a=-90  ' ';
footnote1 j=1 ' Source:'
          m=(9,+0) '1984 American Express'
          m=(9,-1.12) 'Appointment Book';
footnote2 h=2 ' ';
symbol c=cyan v=star i=needle;

proc gplot data=temps;
   plot c2*month / hminor=0 vminor=0;
run;
```

Output 15.7   Plotting by a Third Variable

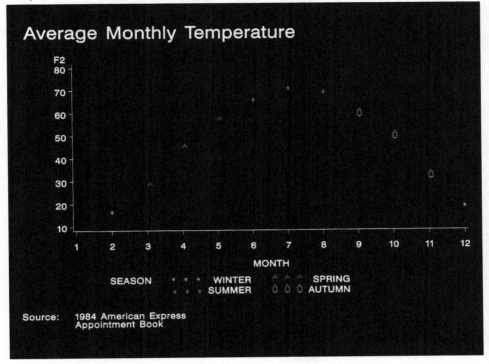

Output 15.8   Using the I=NEEDLE Option: PROC GPLOT

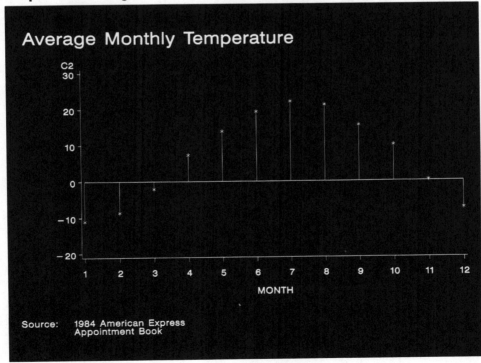

Mxxxxx Option

When the points that are plotted form a closed region, the M value of the I=
option in the SYMBOL statement requests that PROC GPLOT fill in the surface
drawn by the points. The example below generates data that form a surface when
plotted. I=M3X requests a medium grid (grid values range from 1 to 5), with lines
crossed (X) at a 90-degree angle (the default angle). For more information on the
I=Mxxxxx option, see the V= option in the PATTERN statement description in
"Enhancing Your Graphics Output Designs."

These statements produce the plot shown in **Output 15.9**.

```
title1 j=l h=2 f=swiss c=white '   Average Monthly Temperature'
          h=3 f=simplex a= 90  ' '
          h=3 f=simplex a=-90  ' ';
footnote1 j=l ' Source:'
          m=(9,+0) '1984 American Express'
          m=(9,-1.12) 'Appointment Book';
footnote2 h=2 ' ';

symbol c=gold v=none i=m3x;

data t1  (keep=f4 c4 month id)    /* Creates closed area */
     t2  (keep=f4 c4 month id);
   set temps;
   f4=f1;   c4=c1;   output t1;
   f4=f2;   c4=c2;   output t2;
run;

proc sort data=t2;
   by descending month;
run;

data new;
   set t1 t2;
run;

proc gplot data=new;
   plot f4*month / hminor=0
                   vminor=0;
run;
```

Filling Beneath Curves

If you specify the AREAS= option in the PLOT statement, PROC GPLOT numbers
each area defined by plotted lines: the area below the first plotted line is area
1; the area above area 1 and below the second plotted line is area 2; and so on.
The statements below produce a plot showing monthly temperature ranges for
three different cities. The plot defines three areas. Because AREAS=3 is specified,
three PATTERN statements are needed to fill the areas.

These statements produce the plot shown in **Output 15.10**.

```
title1 j=l h=2 f=swiss c=cream '   Average Monthly Temperature'
          h=3 f=simplex a= 90  ' '
          h=3 f=simplex a=-90  ' ';
footnote1 j=l ' Source:'
          m=(9,+0) '1984 American Express'
          m=(9,-1.12) 'Appointment Book';
```

```
footnote2 h=2 ' ';

symbol1 c=black i=join v=none;
symbol2 c=black i=join v=none;
symbol3 c=black i=join v=none;

pattern1 c=gold   v=solid;
pattern2 c=yellow v=solid;
pattern3 c=white  v=solid;

proc gplot data=temps;
   plot (f2 f1 f3)*month / overlay
                           areas=3
                           haxis=1 to 12
                           vaxis=0 to 100 by 10
                           hminor=0
                           vminor=0;
run;
```

Output 15.9   Using the I=Mxxxxx Option: PROC GPLOT

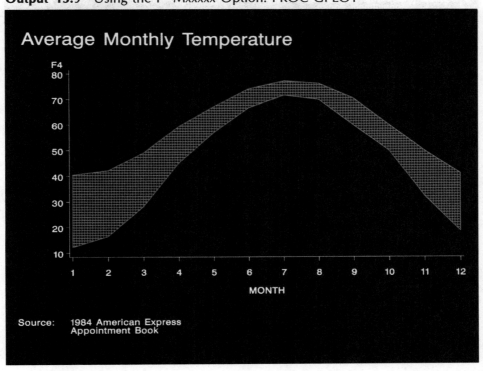

Output 15.10   Using the AREAS= Option: PROC GPLOT

TITLE Statement

   TITLE*n options 'text';*

You can use TITLE statements with PROC GPLOT. They are described in "En-hancing Your Graphics Output Text."

DETAILS

Missing Values

If either of the plot variables is missing, PROC GPLOT does not include the obser-vation in the plot.

Values Out of Range

It is possible to exclude data values from a graph by restricting the displayed axis range with the VAXIS= or HAXIS= options. When observations are encountered with values outside the displayed axis range, PROC GPLOT issues a message to the log and does not include the observation in the plot. Note that this exclusion of values may change interpolation values for the plot. The MODE=INCLUDE | EXCLUDE option in the SYMBOL statement modifies this behavior and permits the inclusion of observation values outside the axis range in interpolation calculations. The default (MODE=EXCLUDE) *omits* observations outside the axis range *from* interpolation calculations. MODE=INCLUDE *includes* observations outside the axis range *in* interpolation calculations.

   The following statements produce **Output 15.11–15.12**, which demonstrates the difference between using MODE=EXCLUDE and MODE=INCLUDE.

```
data hilo;
   input  x  y  @@;
   cards;
1 1   1 2   1 3   1 4   1 5
2 2   2 4   2 6   2 1   2 2
3 2   3 3   3 6   3 1   3 13
4 1   4 8   4 3   4 1   4 2
5 3   5 2   5 3   5 4   5 3
;

title2 j=l h=2 f=swiss 'SYMBOL MODE=EXCLUDE';
title3 j=l 'Observation at (3,13) is off the graph';
title4 j=l 'Calculated MEAN does not reflect omitted observation';

symbol1 mode=exclude ci=green i=hilotj cv=gold v=star;

proc gplot data=hilo;
   plot y*x / frame
              haxis=0 to 6
              vaxis=0 to 10;
run;

title2 j=l h=2 f=swiss 'SYMBOL MODE=INCLUDE';
title3 j=l 'Observation at (3,13) is off the graph';
title4 j=l 'Calculated MEAN reflects omitted observation';

symbol1 mode=include ci=green i=hilotj cv=gold v=star;

proc gplot data=hilo;
   plot y*x / frame
              haxis=0 to 6
              vaxis=0 to 10;
run;
```

Output 15.11   Using the MODE=EXCLUDE Option: PROC GPLOT

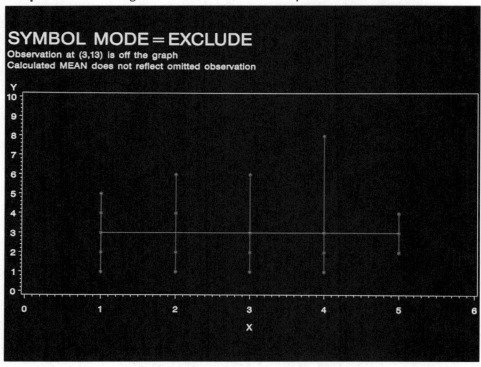

Output 15.12   Using the MODE=INCLUDE Option: PROC GPLOT

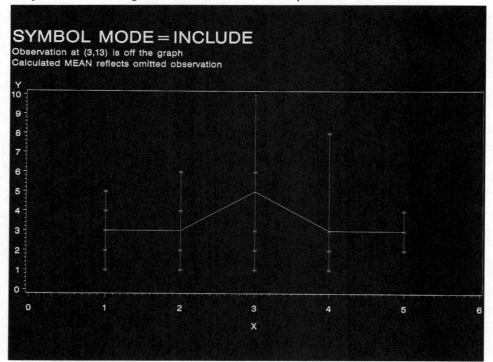

EXAMPLES

The following statements produce **Output 15.13**, which demonstrates the use of PROC GPLOT with an overlay.

```
title1 j=1 h=2 f=swiss c=white '   Average Monthly Temperature'
          h=3 f=simplex a= 90  ' '
          h=3 f=simplex a=-90  ' ';
footnote1 j=1 ' Source:'
          m=(9,+0) '1984 American Express'
          m=(9,-1.12) 'Appointment Book';
footnote2 h=2 ' ';

symbol1 c=yellow i=join;
symbol2 c=gold   i=join v=star;
symbol3 c=white  i=join v=square;

proc gplot data=temps;
   plot (f1 f2 f3)*month / overlay
                           haxis=1 to 12
                           vaxis=0 to 100 by 10
                           hminor=0
                           vminor=0;
run;
```

The following statements produce **Output 15.14**, which demonstrates the use of a second vertical axis, the left side depicting temperature in degrees centigrade, the right in degrees Fahrenheit.

```
title1 j=1 h=2 f=swiss c=white '   Average Monthly Temperature'
          h=3 f=simplex a= 90  ' '
          h=3 f=simplex a=-90  ' ';
footnote1 j=1 ' Source:'
          m=(9,+0) '1984 American Express'
          m=(9,-1.12) 'Appointment Book';
footnote2 h=2 ' ';

symbol1 c=green  i=spline v=none;
symbol2 c=yellow i=none v=diamond;

proc gplot data=temps;
   plot c1*date / haxis='01jan83'd to '01jan84'd by qtr
                  vaxis=0 to 30 by 10
                  hminor=0
                  vminor=0;

   plot2 f1*date / vaxis=32 to 86 by 18
                   hminor=0
                   vminor=0;

   label c1='centigrade';
   label f1='fahrenheit';
   label date='seasonally adjusted';
   format date date7.;
run;
```

The following statements produce **Output 15.15**, which shows the use of the BUBBLE statement.

```
title1 j=l h=2 f=swiss c=white '   Market Share Analysis
          h=3 f=simplex a= 90  ' '
          h=3 f=simplex a=-90  ' ';
footnote1 j=l c=white ' Source:'
        m=(9,+0) 'Strategic Market Planning'
        m=(9,-1.12) 'Abell & Hammond';
footnote2 ' ';

proc gplot data=bubbles;
   bubble rate*share=sales  / haxis=0 to 5
                             vaxis=-15 to 15 by 5
                             hminor=0
                             vminor=0
                             ctext=white
                             bsize=15
                             blabel
                             bcolor=yellow
                             bfont=none;

   format sales  dollar7. ;
   label share='RELATIVE MARKET SHARE';
run;
```

The following statements, which produce **Output 15.16**, demonstrate the use of the ANNOTATE= option to draw text on the plot.

```
data anno;
   length color $ 8;
   xsys='2';         /* data system */
   ysys='2';
   when='a';
   x=2; y=10; text='  BRRR '; position='3'; c='cyan'; output;
   x=7; y=75; text='COMFY  '; position='b'; c='magenta'; output;
run;

title1 j=l h=2 f=swiss c=white '   Average Monthly Temperature'
          h=3 f=simplex a= 90  ' '
          h=3 f=simplex a=-90  ' ';
footnote1 j=l ' Source:'
        m=(9,+0) '1948 American Express'
        m=(9,-1.12) 'Appointment Book';
footnote2 h=2 ' ';

symbol1 c=yellow i=join;
symbol2 c=salmon i=join v=star;
symbol3 c=green  i=join v=square;

proc gplot data=temps;
   plot f2*month / annotate=anno
                   hminor=0
                   vminor=0;
run;
```

The following examples use special formatting features to make three individual graphs showing the seasonal temperature of three cities. These statements produce the output shown in **Output 15.17–15.19**.

```
title1 j=l h=2 f=swiss c=white '   Average Monthly Temperature'
           h=3 f=simplex a= 90  ' '
           h=3 f=simplex a=-90  ' ';
title2 ' ';
footnote1 j=l c=white ' Source:'
           m=(9,+0) '1984 American Express'
           m=(9,-1.12) 'Appointment Book';
footnote2 h=2 ' ';

symbol1 c=cyan     i=none v=star;
symbol2 c=green    i=none v=p    f=cartog;
symbol3 c=magenta  i=none v=i    f=special;
symbol4 c=yellow   i=none v=n    f=cartog;

data new  (keep=month season temp city);
   set temps;
   temp=f1; city=1; output;
   temp=f2; city=2; output;
   temp=f3; city=3; output;
run;

proc sort;
   by city;
run;

proc format;
   value   sample   1='WINTER'
                    2='SPRING'
                    3='SUMMER'
                    4='AUTUMN';

   value   monfmt    1='JAN'     2='FEB'     3='MAR'
                     4='APR'     5='MAY'     6='JUN'
                     7='JUL'     8='AUG'     9='SEP'
                    10='OCT'    11='NOV'    12='DEC';

   value   citfmt    1='Raleigh, NC'
                     2='Minneapolis, MN'
                     3='Phoenix, AZ';
run;

proc gplot  data=new uniform;
   by city;
   plot temp*month=season / frame;
   format  season sample.  city citfmt.  month monfmt.;
   label city='00'x;
run;
```

The following statements produce **Output 15.20**, which demonstrates the use of the SKIPMISS and AREA= options with PROC GPLOT.

```
data units ;
   do month=1 to 12; input sales @@; output; end;
   cards;
100 80 35 . 50 51 66 75 90 85 95 117
;

pattern v=s c=green;

symbol i=join c=white v=none;
title f=swiss 'Quarterly Sales Projections';

proc gplot data=units;
   axis2 label=(c=white f=swiss j=c "Units"
                               j=c "Ordered")
         value=(c=white f=swiss);
   axis1 label=(c=white f=swiss "Quarterly Projections")
         order=(1 to 12 by 1)
         minor=none
         value=(c=white
               angle=0 rotate=0
         f=simplex j=r "|--" f=swiss j=c "First"  f=simplex j=l "--|"
         f=simplex j=r "|--" f=swiss j=c "Second" f=simplex j=l "--|"
         f=simplex j=r "|--" f=swiss j=c "Third"  f=simplex j=l "--|"
         f=simplex j=r "|--" f=swiss j=c "Fourth" f=simplex j=l "--|");

   plot sales * month / areas=1 frame
                        skipmiss
                        haxis=axis1 vaxis=axis2;
run;
```

Output 15.13   Using the OVERLAY Option: PROC GPLOT

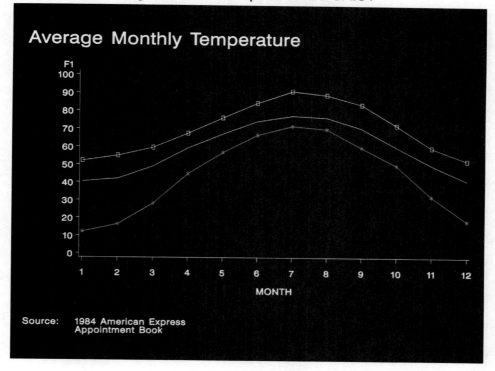

Output 15.14   Using a Second Vertical Axis: PROC GPLOT

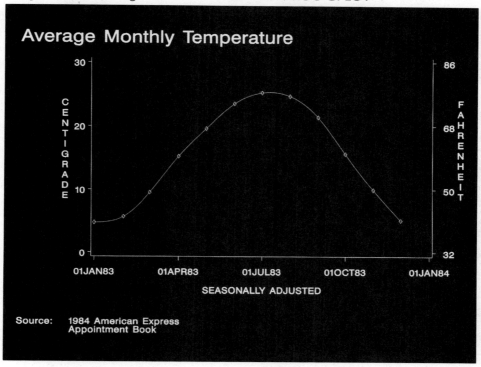

Output 15.15   Specifying a BUBBLE Statement: PROC GPLOT

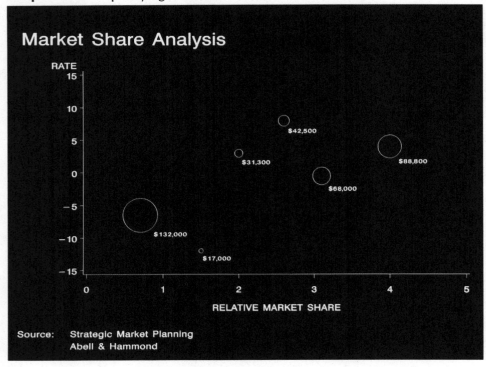

Output 15.16   Using the ANNOTATE= Option: PROC GPLOT

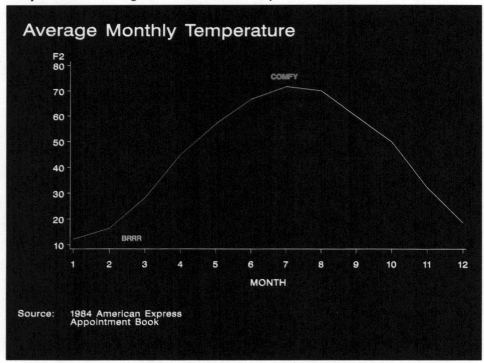

Output 15.17 Using a BY Variable (Raleigh): PROC GPLOT

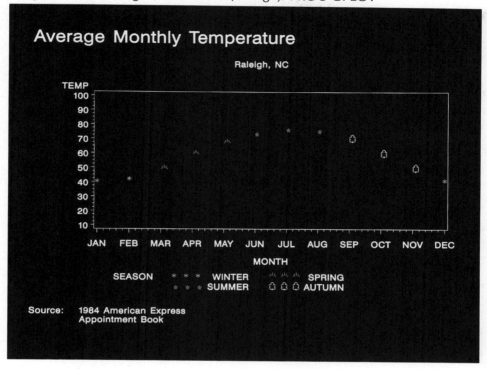

Output 15.18 Using a BY Variable (Minneapolis): PROC GPLOT

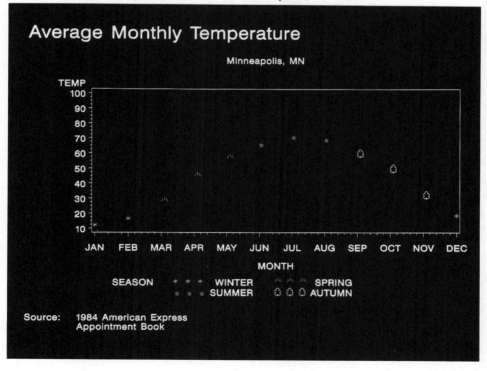

Output 15.19   Using a BY Variable (Phoenix): PROC GPLOT

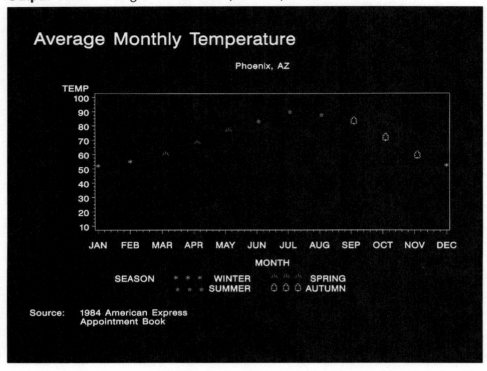

Output 15.20   Using the SKIPMISS and AREA= Options: PROC GPLOT

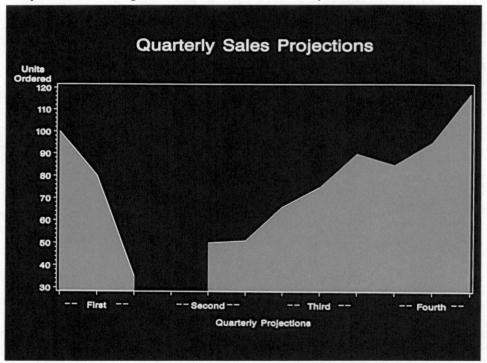

Chapter 16

The GPRINT Procedure

ABSTRACT

PROC GPRINT allows you to enhance the output of SAS procedures by adding titles and footnotes. For example, you can run a SAS procedure and then write the output to a disk. To enhance this output, invoke PROC GPRINT and specify TITLE, NOTE, and FOOTNOTE statements. The PROC GPRINT output is the original output plus the enhancements you specify.

INTRODUCTION

You can specify the input file for PROC GPRINT with the FILEREF= option. PROC GPRINT input can come from any external file in the proper format. (See Chapter 26, "The PRINTTO Procedure," in the *SAS Procedures Guide, Release 6.03 Edition* for more information on accessing and storing output in external files.)

SPECIFICATIONS

The following statements can be used with PROC GPRINT:

PROC GPRINT *options;*
   TITLE*n options 'text';*
   FOOTNOTE*n options 'text';*
   NOTE *options 'text';*

PROC GPRINT Statement

PROC GPRINT *options*;

You can specify the following options in the PROC GPRINT statement:

ANNOTATE=*SASdataset*
:   specifies the data set to be used for annotation. This data set must be an ANNOTATE= type data set containing the appropriate Annotate variables. (See "ANNOTATE= Data Sets" for details.)

CTEXT=*color*
:   specifies the color to use to print the output stored in the file.

DESCRIPTION=*'string'*
DES=*'string'*
:   specifies a descriptive string, up to forty characters long, that appears in the Description field of PROC GREPLAY's master menu. If you do not specify the DESCRIPTION= option, the Description field of PROC GREPLAY's master menu contains a description assigned by SAS/GRAPH.

FILEREF=*fileref*
:   specifies the fileref of the external file to be printed with PROC GPRINT.

GOUT=*SAScatalog*
:   specifies the name of the SAS catalog used to save the output produced by PROC GPRINT. See "SAS/GRAPH Graphics Output" for details. If you do not specify the GOUT= option, catalog entries are written to the default catalog GSEG, which is erased at the end of your session.

NAME=*'string'*
:   specifies a descriptive string, up to eight characters long, that appears in the Name field of PROC GREPLAY's master menu. If you do not specify the NAME= option, the Name field of PROC GREPLAY's master menu contains the procedure name.

O
:   causes a numeric zero to be converted to the letter "O" in the output. This option circumvents the use of a numeric zero with an interior slash that is present on some devices.

FOOTNOTE Statement

FOOTNOTE*n options* 'text';

You can use FOOTNOTE statements with PROC GPRINT. They are described in "Enhancing Your Graphics Output Text."

NOTE Statement

NOTE *options* 'text';

You can use NOTE statements with PROC GPRINT. They are described in "Enhancing Your Graphics Output Text."

TITLE Statement

TITLE*n options* 'text';

You can use TITLE statements with PROC GPRINT. They are described in "Enhancing Your Graphics Output Text."

DETAILS

PROC GPRINT determines the number of graphs produced by the input file by looking at three different sources of information concerning page size:

- the size of a page in the input file (as specified with the PS= and LS= options)
- the size of a page on the graphics device (as specified with the HPOS= and VPOS= options)
- the size of the page on the graphics device excluding the titles and footnotes (the *window*).

The size of a page in the input file is normally controlled by the PS= and LS= options when the file is created (see **The OPTIONS Statement** in the chapter "SAS Statements Used Anywhere" in the *SAS Language Guide, Release 6.03 Edition*). For PROC GPRINT to make the graphics output pages the same size as the input file pages, the *window* must be the same size as the input file page. There are two ways to accomplish this:

- Determine the number of horizontal (HPOS=) and vertical (VPOS=) positions on the graphics device you intend to use. Then determine the number of horizontal and vertical positions that you are going to use for titles and footnotes. Use the OPTIONS statement to set the PAGESIZE= option equal to the number of vertical positions on the graphics device minus the number of positions to be used by titles and footnotes; set the LINESIZE= option equal to the number of horizontal positions on the graphics device minus the number of positions used by titles and footnotes. Then create the file for PROC GPRINT to read. See the **EXAMPLE** section.
- Determine the number of horizontal (LS=) and vertical (PS=) positions used in the input file. Use the GOPTIONS statement to set the HPOS= option equal to the number of horizontal positions in the input file; set the VPOS= option equal to the number of vertical positions in the input file plus the number to be used by titles and footnotes. Note that changing the values of HPOS= and VPOS= changes the size of character output and, on some devices, may prevent the use of hardware characters.

You can specify the FTEXT= option in a GOPTIONS statement to indicate which font to use for the graphics output text. Be aware that if you use a proportionately spaced font (such as the SWISS font), the alignment of your output may be different from the original. Use a uniformly spaced font (such as the SWISSU font) to keep your output properly aligned. You can also specify the HTEXT= option in a GOPTIONS statement to specify the height of the text, but this will affect the calculations above. See "The GOPTIONS Statement" for more information on these two options.

EXAMPLE

Enhancing Output

The following example shows how to add a title and a footnote to otherwise standard output. A data set is created and is used as input to PROC TIMEPLOT; then a title and a footnote are added to the TIMEPLOT output using the GPRINT procedure. (For more information on the TIMEPLOT procedure, refer to the *SAS Procedures Guide, Release 6.03 Edition.*)

In this example, the name of the SAS fileref is OUT, and the name of the external file is GPRINT. (Refer to the chapter "Getting Your Data into a SAS Data Set" in the *SAS Introductory Guide, Release 6.03 Edition* for more information on the FILENAME statement.)

First, use a FILENAME statement to associate a SAS fileref with the external file:

```
filename out 'gprint';
```

Next, use PROC PRINTTO to direct the printed output into that file. Use PROC TIMEPLOT to create some printed output and run PROC PRINTTO to reset the printed output to the default. Finally, use PROC GPRINT to add a SAS/GRAPH title and footnote to the PROC TIMEPLOT output.

```
data dow;
   input date date7. volume high low close;
   format date date7.;
   cards;
07AUG81  3884.3  954.15  938.45  942.54
10AUG81  2937.7  948.82  935.88  943.68
11AUG81  5262.9  955.48  939.50  949.30
12AUG81  4005.2  955.86  942.26  945.21
13AUG81  3680.8  952.91  938.55  944.35
14AUG81  3714.1  947.77  933.79  936.93
17AUG81  3432.7  939.40  924.37  926.75
18AUG81  4396.7  932.74  916.38  924.37
19AUG81  3517.3  932.08  918.38  926.46
20AUG81  3811.9  935.31  923.52  928.37
21AUG81  2625.9  930.65  917.14  920.57
24AUG81  4736.1  917.43  896.97  900.11
25AUG81  4714.4  904.30  887.46  901.83
26AUG81  3279.6  908.39  893.65  899.26
27AUG81  3676.1  900.49  883.66  889.08
28AUG81  3024.2  898.78  884.80  892.22
;

proc printto print=out;
run;

proc timeplot data=dow;
   plot low close high / overlay
                         hiloc
                         ref=mean(low)
                         npp;
   id date volume;
   format volume 6.0 high low close 6.0;
run;

proc printto;
run;

title c=black f=swiss j=1 ' Dow-Jones Averages';
footnote c=black f=swiss j=1 ' High-Low-Close';
proc gprint fileref=out;
run;
```

The output from PROC TIMEPLOT is shown in **Output 16.1**. The output with a title and footnote produced by PROC GPRINT is shown in **Output 16.2**.

Output 16.1   PROC TIMEPLOT Output

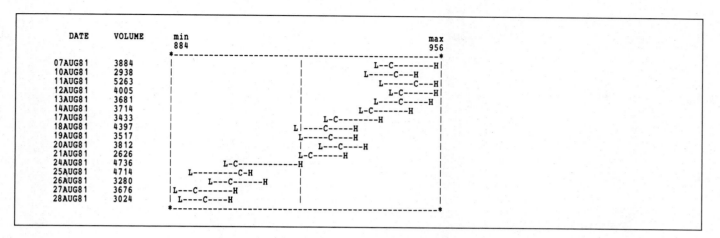

Output 16.2   PROC TIMEPLOT Output with PROC GPRINT Title and Footnote

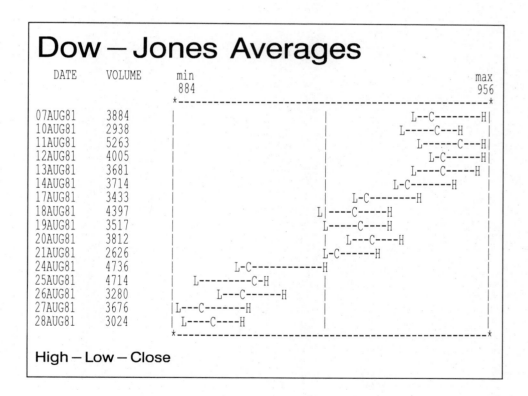

Chapter 17

The GPROJECT
Procedure

ABSTRACT

The GPROJECT procedure applies one of several map projection methods to a map data set containing coordinates expressed in latitude and longitude. You can use Albers' equal-area projection with two standard parallels, Lambert's conformal projection with two standard parallels, or the gnomonic projection (an azimuthal projection). Valid units of measure for these coordinates are radians and degrees.

INTRODUCTION

In a map data set, the observations used to draw a map are often stored as latitude and longitude coordinates of a sphere. Although the shape of the earth is not a sphere, no attempt is made by PROC GPROJECT to correct this small distortion. When the observations are plotted on a two-dimensional plane, the resulting map is often reversed and elongated as a result of forcing a curved map surface onto a flat plane. PROC GPROJECT allows you to project or transpose the coordinates onto an X-Y plane while preserving one or more properties of the original sphere (for example, area, distance, direction, or shape).

SPECIFICATIONS

The following statements are available in PROC GPROJECT:

PROC GPROJECT *options*;
  ID *variables*;

The ID statement is required.

PROC GPROJECT Statement

PROC GPROJECT *options*;

You can specify the following options in the PROC GPROJECT statement:

ASIS
DUPOK
  specify not to delete observations whose projected *x* and *y* values are identical to those in the last observation output. By default, successive identical observations are deleted.

DATA=*SASdataset*
  gives the name of the map data set to be used by PROC GPROJECT. If you omit the DATA= option, PROC GPROJECT applies the projection to the most recently created SAS data set.

DEGREE
DEG
  specifies that the units for the coordinates are in degrees of arc. The default units are radians.

EASTLONG
EAST
  specifies that the values of the longitude in the input data set increase to the east instead of to the west.

OUT=*SASdataset*
  gives the name of the new projected map data set. If you omit the OUT= option, the new data set is named with the DATA*n* naming convention.

PARADIV=*n*
  specifies the divisor used to compute the standard parallels chosen by default for ALBERS or LAMBERT projections. By default PARADIV=4; the parallels are set at 1/4 and 3/4 of the range in latitude of the input map data set. This option is ignored if you specify PARALEL1= or PARALEL2= (see the description below).
  Note: the standard parallels, whether specified or chosen by the procedure, must not lie on the equator. If they do, PROC GPROJECT prints an error message and stops.

PARALEL1=*latitude*
PARALEL2=*latitude*
  specify the latitude for each parallel in degrees of latitude. When you specify the ALBERS or LAMBERT projections, you can specify the standard parallels to be used. If you do not specify either PARALEL1= or PARALEL2=, the standard parallels are chosen by an algorithm to minimize the distortion inherent in the projection process. This algorithm is

$$PARALEL1 = R/P_D$$

$$PARALEL2 = R(1 - 1/P_D)$$

where

> R   is the range in latitude of the input map data set and P_D is he PARADIV divisor (see the PARADIV= option).

POLELAT=*latitude*
POLELONG=*longitude*

specify a map pole to use when you specify the GNOMON projection. POLELAT= gives the latitude of the map pole, and POLELONG= gives the longitude in degrees. If you do not specify the POLELAT= and POLELONG= options, the gnomonic projection uses the center of the unit area defined by the DATA= data set.

Note: the map defined by the DATA= data set should not be more than 85 degrees from the map pole; all points that exceed this value are deleted from the output data set.

PROJECT=ALBERS
PROJECT=LAMBERT
PROJECT=GNOMON

specifies the type of projection method to be applied to the map data set. PROJECT=ALBERS specifies Albers' equal-area projection with two standard parallels. PROJECT=LAMBERT specifies Lambert's conformal projection with two standard parallels. PROJECT=GNOMON specifies the gnomonic projection, an azimuthal projection.

Albers' and Lambert's projections are conical projections from the surface of a sphere (like the earth) to a cone sitting on the sphere. The line on which the cone touches the sphere is called a standard parallel. PROC GPROJECT uses two standard parallels for both Albers' and Lambert's projections. The cone goes below the sphere's surface at one parallel and emerges at the other.

The gnomonic projection method is a planar or azimuthal projection, a projection from the surface of a sphere directly to a plane. The map pole, or projection point, is the point at which the surface of the sphere touches the surface of the plane. If you do not specify the PROJECT= option, the Albers method is used.

ID Statement

ID *variables*;

The ID statement names the variable or variables whose values identify unit areas in the DATA= data set. The ID statement is required.

EXAMPLES

Example 1: Producing an Unprojected Map

In the following example, a data set called STATES is created from the MAPS.COUNTY data set that accompanies SAS/GRAPH software. PROC GMAP is used to display the map in its unprojected form as shown in **Output 17.1**.

```
data response;
  number=1;
  do state=1 to 56;
    if fipstate (state) ^= ''
      then output;
    end;
run;
```

```
proc gremove data=maps.county out=states;
   where state ^=2  and
         state ^=15 and
         state ^=72;
   id county;
   by state;
run;


pattern1 v=ms c=bioy;
title  f=swiss  c=white  'Unprojected';
footnote1 c=white  'Continental United States Map';
footnote2 ' ';
proc gmap map=states
         data=response;
   id state;
   choro number / nolegend
                  coutline=black;
run;
```

Example 2: Producing a Projected Map

In this example, the STATES data set created in the first example is projected with PROC GPROJECT. The default projection method, Albers, is used since the PROJECT= option is omitted. The statements below produce **Output 17.2**.

```
proc gproject data=states
              out=projst;
   id state;
run;


title  f=swiss  c=white 'Albers Projection';
proc gmap map=projst
         data=response;
   id state;
   choro number / nolegend
                  coutline=black;
run;
```

Output 17.1   Producing an Unprojected Map

Output 17.2   Producing a Projected Map

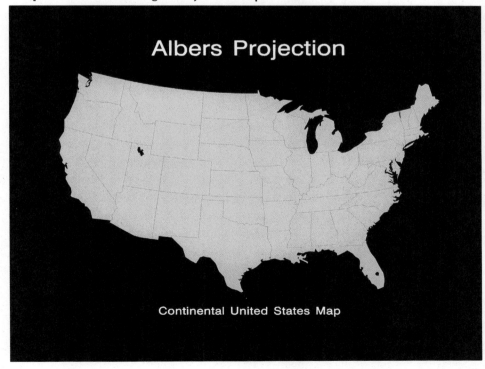

Example 3: Using PROC GPROJECT to Produce a State Map

The following example illustrates the use of PROC GPROJECT to project points for an ANNOTATE= data set using a map. The statements below produce **Output 17.3**.

```
data centers;
    /* the centers of selected southern California counties */
    length color function $8 text $25;
    d2r=atan(1) / 45;
    retain d2r;
    function='label';
    xsys='2';
    ysys='2';
    when='A';
    color='white ';
    input lond lonm lons latd latm lats text $char25.;
    x=d2r*(lond+lonm / 60+lons / 3600);
    y=d2r*(latd+latm / 60+lats / 3600);
    state=stfips ('CA');
    county=-1;
    drop d2r lond lonm lons latd latm lats;
    cards;
120 30 00   35 20 00 San Luis Obispo
118 40 00   35 20 00 Kern
120 00 00   34 45 00 Santa Barbara
119 05 20   34 30 00 Ventura
118 02 30   34 25 00 Los Angeles
116 15 00   34 50 00 San Bernadino
117 50 00   33 45 00 Orange
116 00 00   33 45 00 Riverside
116 40 00   33 00 00 San Diego
115 30 00   33 00 00 Imperial
;

data all;
    set maps.county centers;
    if state=stfips('CA') &
       ( county=-1 |
         county=25 |
         county=29 |
         county=37 |
         county=59 |
         county=65 |
         county=71 |
         county=73 |
         county=79 |
         county=83 |
         county=111);
run;

proc gproject data=all
              out=allproj;
    id county;
run;
```

```
data scalmap scalcity;
   set allproj;
   if county=-1
      then output scalcity;
   else output scalmap;
run;

data response;
   number=1;
   input county @@;
   cards;
25 29 37 59 65
71 73 79 83 111
;

pattern1 v=ms c=cream;
title  f=swiss  c=white 'Southern California Counties';
proc gmap map=scalmap
          data=response;
   id county;
   choro number / discrete
                  nolegend
                  annotate=scalcity
                  coutline=black;
run;
```

Output 17.3   Southern California Counties: PROC GPROJECT

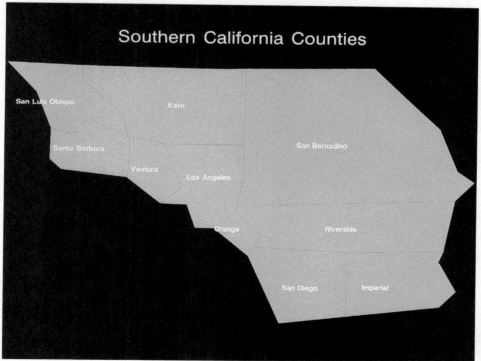

REFERENCES

Pearson, F., II (1977), "Map Projection Equations," Report Number TR-3624, Naval Surface Weapons Center, Dahlgren Laboratory, March, 1977.

Richardus, P., and Adler, R.K. (1972), *Map Projections*, Amsterdam: North-Holland Publishing Company; New York: American Elsevier Publishing Company.

Robinson, A.H. (1978), *Elements of Cartography*, New York: John Wiley & Sons, Inc.

Chapter 18

The GREDUCE Procedure

ABSTRACT

The GREDUCE procedure processes map coordinate data so you can reduce the number of points needed to draw a map.

INTRODUCTION

The degree of precision with which PROC GMAP draws a map is determined in part by the number of points (x,y coordinates or observations) it has to plot. The more points that are plotted, the more accurate each section of the map will be. If you are creating a map in which precise detail of the map points is not essential, you can use PROC GREDUCE to create a subset of an original map data set. The observations in this data set can then be used to draw a map that retains the overall appearance of your original map but contains fewer points and requires less computer resource to draw.

The GREDUCE procedure creates a map data set containing all the variables in the input map data set plus a new variable named DENSITY. For each observation in the original map data set, PROC GREDUCE determines the necessity of retaining that point in a new map drawn to resemble the original and gives the observation a corresponding DENSITY value. The values of DENSITY range from 0 to 6. A value of 6 corresponds to the original map density; 0 corresponds to a map of coarsest density, indicating points common to more than two line segments. The points with a DENSITY value of 0 are vertex points of the map.

Introductory Examples

The SAS data set MAPS.US (supplied with SAS/GRAPH software) is a map data set containing the variables STATE, SEGMENT, X, and Y. The statements below create a new map data set named NEWMAP, with all the variables from the original data set plus the variable DENSITY. The unreduced map is shown in **Output 18.1**.

```
goptions colors=(white);
pattern1 v=e r=100;
title f=swiss c=white 'Unreduced US Map';
proc gmap data=response map=maps.us;
   id state;
   choro number / discrete nolegend;
run;
```

The option N1=65 sets limits to the number of points that can appear in reduced polygons at density level one. A new data set, REDUCED, is created by selecting observations from NEWMAP with DENSITY values less than 2. Thus, maps produced from the data set REDUCED never have more than sixty-five points in a boundary unless there are more than sixty-five points of density 0 in a boundary. The reduced map is shown in **Output 18.2**.

```
proc greduce data=maps.us out=newmap n1=65;
   id state;
run;

data reduced;
   set newmap;
   if density < 2;
run;

title f=swiss c=white 'Reduced US Map';
proc gmap data=response map=reduced;
   id state;
   choro number / discrete nolegend;
run;
```

You can also reduce a data set by specifying the minimum distance that a point must lie from a straight line segment to be included at a given density level. The statements below specify a combination of criteria for defining density levels; density level 1 is set using the coarser of the two requirements, N1 and E1.

```
proc greduce data=maps.us out=newmap2 n1=40 e1=3e-1 n2=75;
   id state;
```

Output 18.1   Unreduced U.S. Map: PROC GMAP

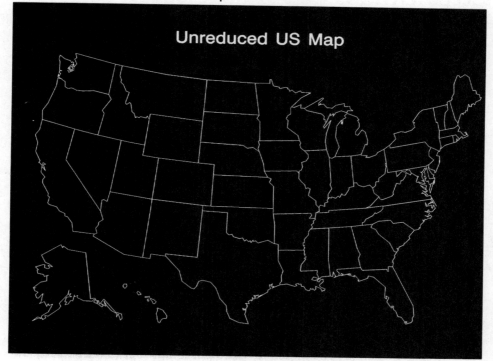

Output 18.2   Reduced U.S. Map: PROC GREDUCE and PROC GMAP

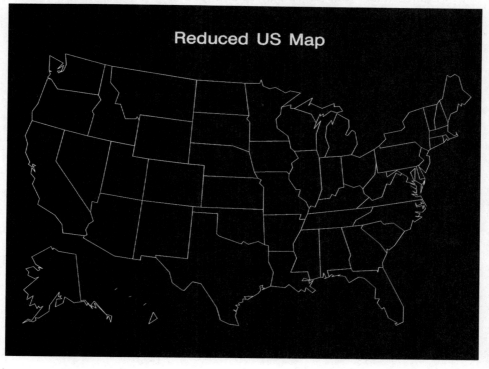

SPECIFICATIONS

The following statements can be used with PROC GREDUCE:

PROC GREDUCE *options*;
   ID *variables*;
   BY *variables*;

The ID statement is required.

PROC GREDUCE Statement

  PROC GREDUCE *options*;

You can specify the following options in the PROC GREDUCE statement:

DATA=*SASdataset*
   specifies the name of the map data set containing the map coordinates.
   If you omit the DATA= option, PROC GREDUCE uses the most recently
   created SAS data set.

E1=*value*
E2=*value*
E3=*value*
E4=*value*
E5=*value*
   specifies the minimum distance that a point must lie from a straight line
   segment to be included at density level 1, 2, 3, 4, or 5. That is, in a
   reduced curve of three points, the middle point will be at least a
   distance *value* from the straight line formed by the two outside points.
   The E*n*= values should be specified in *decreasing* order.

N1=*integer*
N2=*integer*
N3=*integer*
N4=*integer*
N5=*integer*
   specifies that for density level 1, 2, 3, 4, or 5 the boundary of a unit
   area should contain no more than *integer* points. The N*n*= values
   should be specified in *increasing* order.

OUT=*SASdataset*
   gives the name of the new map data set. The new data set contains all
   the observations and variables in the original map data set plus the new
   variable DENSITY. If you do not specify the OUT= option, the new
   data set is named with the DATA*n* naming convention.

Figure 18.1 shows a typical density value assignment given the distance parameter, E*n*. At density level *n*, only point C would remain between points A and
B. See Douglas and Peucker (1973).

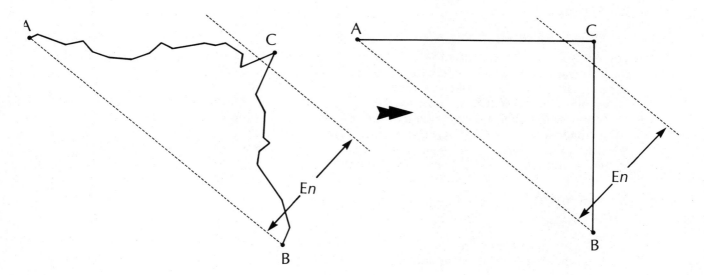

Figure 18.1   Typical Density Value Assignment

If you specify both Nn= and En= for the same density level, both criteria are met. However, the number of points is never reduced below the number of points corresponding to density level 0.

If you specify a combination of Nn= or En= values such that the resulting DENSITY values are not in order of increasing density, a note is printed in the SAS log, and the DENSITY values are listed in increasing order of density. If you do not specify Nn= or En= values, PROC GREDUCE sets the five Nx parameters to the values

$$Nx = (x^{**}2)^*NMAX / 36$$

where NMAX is the maximum number of points in any polygon in the input data set.

The procedure uses the usual Euclidean distance formula to determine the distance between points. For example, the distance between the points $(x\ 1, y\ 1)$ and $(x\ 0, y\ 0)$ is

$$d = \sqrt{((x\ 1 - x\ 0)^{**}2 + (y\ 1 - y\ 0)^{**}2)}\ .$$

If this distance function is not suitable, you should transform the (x,y) coordinates to an appropriate system of coordinates before using PROC GREDUCE. An example of inappropriate coordinates is latitude and longitude values around the North Pole. In this case the data should be projected before they are reduced.

BY Statement

BY *variables*;

You can specify a BY statement with PROC GREDUCE to obtain separate maps for observations in groups defined by the BY variables. When a BY statement appears, the procedure expects the input data set to be sorted in order of the BY variables. If your input data set is not sorted in ascending order, use the SORT procedure with a similar BY statement to sort the data, or, if appropriate, use the BY statement options NOTSORTED or DESCENDING. For more information, see the discussion of the BY statement in "SAS Statements Used in the PROC Step" in the *SAS Language Guide, Release 6.03 Edition*.

ID Statement

ID *variables*;

The ID statement names the variable or variables whose values label the unit areas on the map. The ID statement must be present.

DETAILS

If you are using maps in which area boundaries do not match precisely (for example, boundaries that were digitized with a different set of points) PROC GREDUCE may not be able to identify common boundaries properly, resulting in abnormalities in your output data set.

If the points in the area boundaries match up except for precision differences, round each *x,y* value in your map data set accordingly, using the DATA step function ROUND before using PROC GREDUCE. (Refer to "SAS Functions" in the *SAS Language Guide, Release 6.03 Edition* for information on the ROUND function.) For example, if the data set ANOMALY contains "equal" *x,y* values that are actually equal to three decimal places only, then the data set created with the statements shown below will be better suited for use with PROC GREDUCE:

```
data exact;
   set anomaly;
   if x^=. then
      x=round(x,.01);
   if y^=. then
      y=round(y,.01);
run;
```

Although it occurs infrequently, it is possible for the lines formed from a reduced polygon to intersect themselves. If this happens, it can cause difficulties for some types of subsequent plotting.

REFERENCE

Douglas, D.H. and Peucker, T.K. (1973), "Algorithms for the Reduction of the Number of Points Required to Represent a Digitized Line or Its Caricature," *The Canadian Cartographer*, 10, 112-122.

Chapter 19

The GREMOVE Procedure

ABSTRACT

The GREMOVE procedure allows you to remove map borders and combine the unit areas defined by a map data set into larger unit areas, producing a new map data set.

INTRODUCTION

The GREMOVE procedure is useful for producing regional maps from data sets containing state information. The original map data set must contain one or more variables that uniquely define new unit areas. Unit areas defined by the new data set have all interior line segments removed.

For example, the data set MAPS.US (supplied with SAS/GRAPH software) contains coordinates for the boundaries of the states. You can use a DATA step to add a variable REGION, identifying the geographical region of each state. (For the complete DATA step, see "The GMAP Procedure.") These statements create a new map data set called NEWMAP with geographical regions as unit areas:

```
proc gremove data=maps.us out=newmap;
   by region;
   id state;
```

The BY variable REGION uniquely defines unit areas in the new map data set NEWMAP. The new data set also contains the variables X, Y, and SEGMENT from the original data set. The ID variable from MAPS.US is dropped from the new data set.

SPECIFICATIONS

You must use the following statements with PROC GREMOVE:

PROC GREMOVE *options*;
    BY *variables*;
    ID *variables*;

The BY and ID statements are required.

PROC GREMOVE Statement

PROC GREMOVE DATA=*mapdataset* OUT=*newmapdataset*;

You can specify the following options in the PROC GREMOVE statement:

DATA=*mapdataset*
    gives the name of a map data set containing

- ID variables to define unit areas on the map
- BY variables to define new unit areas
- X and Y, the *x* and *y* coordinates of the boundary points
- optionally, the variable SEGMENT, defining noncontiguous segments.

    If you do not specify the DATA= option, PROC GREMOVE uses the most recently created SAS data set as the input map data set.

OUT=*newmapdataset*
    gives the name of the new map data set containing coordinates of the new unit areas. If you do not specify the OUT= option, PROC GREMOVE names the new data set using the DATA*n* naming convention.

BY Statement

BY *variables*;

The BY statement gives the variable or variables that identify the new unit areas. The map data set must be sorted by the variables in the BY statement. The BY variables become the ID variables for the new map data set. You must specify the BY statement.

ID Statement

ID *variables*;

The ID statement gives the variable or variables that identify unit areas in the original map data set. Variables specified in the ID statement do not appear in the new map data set. You must specify the ID statement.

DETAILS

Boundary Anomalies

If you are using maps in which area boundaries do not match precisely (for example, if the boundaries were digitized with a different set of points), PROC GREMOVE may not be able to identify common boundaries properly, resulting in abnormalities in your output data set.

If the points in the area boundaries match up except for precision differences, round each *x, y* value in your map data set accordingly, using the DATA step function ROUND before using PROC GREMOVE. (Refer to "SAS Functions" in the *SAS Language Guide, Release 6.03 Edition* for information on the ROUND function.) For example, if the data set ANOMALY contains "equal" *x,y* values that are actually equal to three decimal places only, then the data set created with the statements shown below will be better suited for use with PROC GREMOVE:

```
data exact;
   set anomaly;
   if x^=. then
      x= round(x,.01);
   if y^=. then
      y= round(y,.01);
run;
```

EXAMPLE

Subsetting a Map Data Set with PROC GREMOVE

The following example produces a regional map, REGIONS, from the US map supplied with SAS/GRAPH software. The data set NEWUS is created in a DATA step (not shown here) that illustrates one method for assigning states to regions. (The DATA step is contained in the SAS Sample Library.) Then PROC GREMOVE is used to create the map with the new regional boundaries instead of state boundaries. PROC GMAP is used to display the results, as shown in **Output 19.1**.

```
data newus;
   more SAS statements

proc gremove data=newus
             out=regions;
   id state;
   by region;
run;

data names;
   length name $14;
   input region name $char14.;
   cards;
0 Southwest
1 West
2 Central
3 South
4 Northeast
5 Midwest
;

pattern1 v=solid c=lilg;
pattern2 v=solid c=liyg;
pattern3 v=solid c=big;
pattern4 v=solid c=viyg;
pattern5 v=solid c=stg;
pattern6 v=solid c=vig;
```

```
title 'United States by Region';
footnote ' ';
proc gmap map=regions
          data=names;
   label name='Region:';
   id region;
   choro name / discrete
                ctext=white
                coutline=black;
run;
```

Output 19.1   Creating a Regional Map: PROC GREMOVE

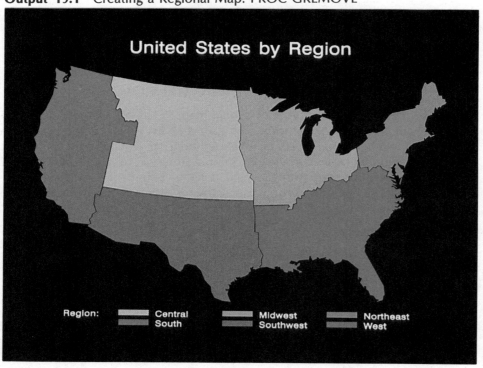

Chapter 20
The GREPLAY Procedure

ABSTRACT

The GREPLAY procedure is a full-screen or line mode presentation tool that manages catalogs of graphs produced by SAS/GRAPH procedures. Most of PROC GREPLAY's features are suited to interactive use, but the procedure can be used in either interactive or batch mode.

INTRODUCTION

All SAS/GRAPH procedures direct their graphics output to catalogs. A *catalog* is a special utility member of a SAS data library that contains information necessary to reconstruct graphs. You can use PROC GREPLAY to examine and modify these catalogs and select graphs for replay from the catalogs.

The GREPLAY procedure can interact with you in either full-screen or line mode, and you can change from full-screen to line mode and back as often as you like while running the procedure. When you are in full-screen mode, fill in the appropriate blanks on the screen, and use function keys to direct the procedure's operation. The available screens and functions are described in the section **USING PROC GREPLAY IN FULL-SCREEN MODE**.

When you are in line mode, PROC GREPLAY prompts you with the message

```
NOTE: ENTER GREPLAY COMMANDS OR STATEMENTS
```

and you use commands to direct the procedure's operation. The line-mode commands are explained in the section **USING PROC GREPLAY IN BATCH OR LINE MODE**.

PROC GREPLAY has a variety of graphics replay and catalog management functions. With PROC GREPLAY, you can

- replay graphs from a SAS catalog
- display multiple graphs on a single page using the template facility
- create a logical grouping of graphs within a catalog

- modify graph description fields
- copy graphs from one catalog to another
- delete graphs from a catalog
- route graphs to different devices, such as plotters and CRTs
- have access to a full-screen help facility.

Before using this procedure, you should know how to place your output in a catalog. (Read "SAS/GRAPH Graphics Output" for more information.) You should also be familiar with the device you are using to replay your graphs (see the appendix "SAS/GRAPH Device Drivers" for information on your device). If you plan to use the template facility, refer to the section **Example: Using the Template Facility in Full-Screen Mode** for a complete description of templates and template catalogs.

SPECIFICATIONS

The only statement used is the PROC GREPLAY statement:

PROC GREPLAY *options*;

PROC GREPLAY Statement

PROC GREPLAY *options*;

You can specify the following options in the PROC GREPLAY statement:

CC=*colormapcatalog*
specifies the color map catalog to use with the procedure. You can specify a two-level name. A color map catalog is a special catalog that contains color map definitions. Color maps allow you to change the colors in a graph by equating or *mapping* those colors to new colors.

CMAP=*colormapname*
specifies the name of a color map to use when replaying your graphs, where *colormapname* is any valid SAS name that you assign to the color map. *Colormapname* cannot contain underscore characters and cannot be used in full-screen mode.

    CMAP is the catalog entry type. If you omit this value, SAS/GRAPH software automatically assigns it to the color map.

    The CMAP= option is ignored if you do not specify a color map catalog. A color map is a list that contains up to 256 pairs of colors labeled FROM and TO. When you replay a graph and specify the CMAP= option, any color in your graph that appears in the FROM column is mapped to the corresponding color in the TO column of the color map list.

FS | NOFS
specifies whether you want to run PROC GREPLAY in full-screen or line mode. If the full-screen environment is available, the procedure begins execution in the full-screen mode unless you specify NOFS.

    If you specify FS, the procedure attempts to begin execution in full-screen mode and displays the PROC GREPLAY screen. If the full-screen environment is not available, the procedure begins execution with a line mode prompt.

    If you specify NOFS, the procedure begins execution in line mode, and you see the line mode prompt after entering the PROC GREPLAY statement.

GOUT=*SAScatalog*

specifies the SAS catalog that will receive output from the procedure. A catalog name that contains underscores cannot be used in full-screen mode. If the catalog does not already exist in the SAS data library, it will be created when you specify the GOUT= option in a PROC step. If you do not specify the GOUT= option, catalog entries are written to the default catalog GSEG, which is erased at the end of your session. You can use the same catalog as input to PROC GREPLAY or for output from PROC GREPLAY. See "SAS/GRAPH Graphics Output" for more information.

IGOUT=*SAScatalog*

names the SAS catalog to use as input to the procedure. A catalog contains information necessary to reconstruct graphs. The input catalog that you specify with IGOUT= should be a GOUT catalog created in an earlier PROC step. You can use the same catalog as input to PROC GREPLAY or for output from PROC GREPLAY. See "SAS/GRAPH Graphics Output" for more information.

NOBYLINE

specifies that BY statement information, which is normally displayed directly beneath the primary description of the graph, should not be displayed.

PRESENTATION

specifies that the procedure should begin execution in the full-screen environment and show the catalog denoted by IGOUT on the presentation screen. The presentation screen is different from the PROC GREPLAY screen in that it contains only parts of the catalog listing and function keys for scrolling through the catalog and exiting the procedure. This screen is intended for special presentations after the catalog has been defined on the PROC GREPLAY screen. Refer to **Accessing the Presentation Screen** for more information.

TC=*templatecatalog*

specifies the template catalog to use with the procedure. You can specify a two-level name. A template catalog contains template definitions. Templates are used to describe positioning for multiple graphs on a single page. Template catalogs can also contain color maps (see the CC= option). See **Example: Using the Template Facility in Full-Screen Mode** for more information on templates.

TEMPLATE=*templatename*

specifies the name of a template to use when displaying your graphs, where *templatename* is any valid SAS name that you assign to the template. A *templatename* that contains underscores cannot be used in full-screen mode. TEMPLATE is the catalog entry type (if you omit this value, it is automatically assigned to the template by SAS/GRAPH software). The TEMPLATE= option is ignored if you do not specify the name of a template catalog.

You can specify the options in the PROC GREPLAY statement, and the procedure will be invoked with a certain environment already established. You can alter the environment after the procedure has begun by specifying information on the screens (in full-screen mode) or by using the line-mode commands (in line mode). See **USING PROC GREPLAY IN BATCH OR LINE MODE** for information on line-mode commands.

USING PROC GREPLAY IN FULL-SCREEN MODE

You can use PROC GREPLAY in full-screen mode by entering information in the appropriate fields of the different screens and then pressing function keys to execute various commands. The screens available in full-screen mode are discussed in the section **Getting Started: PROC GREPLAY Screens**. All of the functions that are performed in full-screen mode can also be performed in line mode or in a batch job. See the section **USING PROC GREPLAY IN BATCH OR LINE MODE** for a complete description of the functions you can perform.

PROC GREPLAY Commands and Function Keys

Each screen has a set of function keys associated with it. Specify the KEYS command on the command line for information on default function key values. You can use function keys to scroll, replay and select graphs, and so on. Alternatively, you can specify the commands on the command line. Refer to "SAS Display Manager System" in the *SAS Language Guide, Release 6.03 Edition* for a list of global commands you can also specify in PROC GREPLAY. Note that you cannot use line mode commands in full-screen mode.

Getting Started: PROC GREPLAY Screens

From the PROC GREPLAY screen you can perform many of the replay and catalog management functions, and you can access the other screens available with the procedure. This section describes the functions you can perform from the PROC GREPLAY screen, tells you how to access the other screens, and describes the other screens and the functions you can perform from these screens.
The PROC GREPLAY screens are

- the PROC GREPLAY screen
- the presentation screen
- the color map directory screen
- the color mapping screen
- the template directory screen
- the template design screen.

To become more familiar with the screens available to you with PROC GREPLAY, you can run the procedure using a catalog that you created with another SAS/GRAPH procedure. As you read the screen descriptions in this chapter, access the screens and fill in the appropriate fields.
To begin using PROC GREPLAY in full-screen mode, you need to do three things:

1. Invoke SAS and create a catalog containing your graphs. You can run PROC GTESTIT, which generates two graphs that are test patterns of color and line-drawing capabilities of SAS/GRAPH software. These graphs are automatically stored in the temporary catalog GSEG, which is always available to you. You can direct output from the procedure to a permanent catalog by specifying the GOUT= option, but first you must submit a LIBNAME statement to associate a libref with the directory where the catalog will be located. For example, if the libref is MYLIB, UNIX operating systems and derivatives use a statement of the form

```
libname mylib '/mydir/';
```

For SAS/GRAPH software on personal computers, use a statement like

```
libname mylib 'c:\mydir\';
```

Then submit the following statements:

```
proc gtestit gout=mylib.grafcat;
run;
```

2. Specify the name of your device in a GOPTIONS statement. For example,

```
goptions device=xxxx;
```

where xxxx is the name of a SAS/GRAPH device driver for your output device. Refer to the appendix, "SAS/GRAPH Device Drivers," for details.

3. Invoke PROC GREPLAY with the following statement:

```
proc greplay;
```

When you press ENTER, the PROC GREPLAY screen is displayed.

PROC GREPLAY Screen

The PROC GREPLAY screen is the first screen to appear after you specify the PROC GREPLAY statement (without specifying any options) in full-screen mode. Depending upon the information you enter in the fields on this screen, you can access the other screens through the PROC GREPLAY screen. An example of a PROC GREPLAY screen is shown in **Screen 20.1**.

Listing the Graphs in an IGOUT Catalog

To see a list of the graphs in your IGOUT catalog, fill in the IGOUT field with either a one-level or a two-level name. In this example, the two-level name MYLIB.GRAFCAT is used. You must specify a LIBNAME statement before you invoke PROC GREPLAY if your graphs are stored in a permanent catalog. (You can also specify the name of a catalog with the IGOUT= option in a PROC GREPLAY statement, and the list of graphs appears when the screen is first displayed.) When you press ENTER, the PROC GREPLAY screen displays a list of the graphs in the catalog you specified, as shown in **Screen 20.2**.

```
┌ PROC GREPLAY ─────────────────────────────────────────────────┐
│ Command ===>                                                    │
│                                                                 │
│ IGOUT: _____      GOUT: _____   Device: PS2EGA │
│ TC:    _____      Template: _____      Scroll: PAGE   │
│ CC:    _____      Cmap: _____                      │
│                                                                 │
│                                                     0           │
│ Sel   Name    Type   Description                       Updated  │
│                                                                 │
│                                                                 │
│                                                                 │
│                                                                 │
│                                                                 │
│                                                                 │
│                                                                 │
│                                                                 │
│                                                                 │
│                                                                 │
│                                                            R    │
└─────────────────────────────────────────────────────────────────┘
```

Screen 20.1   PROC GREPLAY Screen

```
┌ PROC GREPLAY ─────────────────────────────────────────────────┐
│ Command ===>                                                    │
│                                                                 │
│ IGOUT: MYLIB.GRAFCAT        GOUT: _____   Device: PS2EGA │
│ TC:    _____      Template: _____      Scroll: PAGE   │
│ CC:    _____      Cmap: _____                      │
│                                                                 │
│                                                                 │
│ Sel   Name    Type   Description                       Updated  │
│                                                                 │
│ ____  PLOT1   I      1986 SALES by REGION             06/25/87  │
│ ____  PLOT2   I      1986 COST by REGION              06/25/87  │
│ ____  PLOT3   I      1986 REVENUE by REGION           06/25/87  │
│ ____  CHART1  I      Bar chart of SALES, COST, REVENUE 06/25/87 │
│ ____  G5      D      Dependent version of PLOT1       06/25/87  │
│ ____  G6      D      Dependent version of PLOT2       06/25/87  │
│ ____  G7      D      Dependent version of PLOT3       06/25/87  │
│ ____  G8      D      Dependent version of CHART1      06/25/87  │
│                                                                 │
│                                                                 │
│                                                            R    │
└─────────────────────────────────────────────────────────────────┘
```

Screen 20.2   Listing Graphs in an IGOUT Catalog

The information for each graph includes a name (eight characters or less), a description (forty characters or less), a type (D or I), and a date (that indicates when the graph was created or last modified). The name and description for each graph are those you specified with the NAME= and DESCRIPTION= options in the PROC step when you created the graph. If you did not specify the NAME= option or the DESCRIPTION= option, this information was generated by the procedure.

Notice the field labeled TYPE. This field indicates whether a graph is dependent (D) or independent (I). **Although either type of graph can be replayed with PROC GREPLAY, only independent graphs can be replayed using the template facility in PROC GREPLAY.** For more information on dependent and independent graphs, see "SAS/GRAPH Graphics Output."

Scrolling through the List of Graphs

If your list of graphs is too long to fit on one screen, you can submit the DOWN command or press the DOWN key to scroll the page forward. To scroll backward toward the beginning of the list of graphs, submit the UP command or press the UP key.

Replaying the Graphs in the List

You can replay any of the graphs in the list by placing an S or Sn in the SEL (for SELECT) field beside the graph name, where n is a one- or two-digit number that indicates the order in which the graphs should be replayed. This is shown in **Screen 20.3.**

```
┌ PROC GREPLAY ────────────────────────────────────────────────
│ Command ===>
│
│ IGOUT: MYLIB.GRAFCAT        GOUT: _____    Device: PS2EGA
│ TC:   _____       Template: _____      Scroll: PAGE
│ CC:   _____       Cmap: _____
│
│
│ Sel    Name      Type    Description                    Updated
│
│ s1_    PLOT1      I      1986 SALES by REGION           06/25/87
│ ___    PLOT2      I      1986 COST by REGION            06/25/87
│ s2_    PLOT3      I      1986 REVENUE by REGION         06/25/87
│ ___    CHART1     I      Bar chart of SALES, COST, REVENUE  06/25/87
│ ___    G5         D      Dependent version of PLOT1     06/25/87
│ ___    G6         D      Dependent version of PLOT2     06/25/87
│ ___    G7         D      Dependent version of PLOT3     06/25/87
│ ___    G8         D      Dependent version of CHART1    06/25/87
│
│
│
│
│
│                                                    R
└───────────────────────────────────────────────────────────────
```

Screen 20.3   Replaying Graphs with PROC GREPLAY

When you press ENTER, the graph you selected is displayed. If you want to replay more than one graph, place an S beside each graph you want displayed (or Sn if you want to specify the order in which the graphs are replayed). When you press ENTER, the first graph is shown. To see the remaining graphs you selected, press the END or ENTER key after each graph is displayed. You can use the system option GWAIT= to display graphs in a series without pressing ENTER between graphs. See "The GOPTIONS Statement" for more information on the GWAIT= option.

After the last graph has been displayed, press END or ENTER to return to the PROC GREPLAY screen. You can display graphs in another IGOUT catalog by entering the new name in the IGOUT field and pressing ENTER. Submit the END command or press the END key to exit the procedure.

Changing Information in the List of Graphs

If you want to change the names or descriptions of your graphs, submit the MODIFY command or press the MODIFY key and the NAME and DESCRIPTION fields change colors. You can then modify these fields by entering new information directly over the old information. When you have entered all your changes, submit the MODIFY command again, and your changes are saved. You can also perform any of the other functions while you are in modify mode.

Returning to Line Mode

You can return to line mode at any time by submitting the NOFS command or pressing the NOFS key.

Creating Groups within the List of Graphs

For presentations, you may find it useful to arrange the graphs in your catalog in groups that can be replayed later. To create groups of graphs, submit the GROUP command or press the GROUP key and you receive the following prompt:

```
SELECT GROUPS, PRESS ENTER TO STOP
```

You define the groups by entering characters in the SEL field beside the graphs. To specify groups, you can use letters, numbers, or a combination of both as prefixes (for example, A1 A2 A3 or 1A 1B 1C) and then order the graphs you select for the group with the appropriate letters or numbers.

In the example below, suppose you want to create one group that contains the graphs named PLOT1, CHART1, and G5 and another group that contains the graphs named PLOT2, PLOT3, and G6. You can use the letter A to denote the first group, and number your graphs in the order in which you want them to appear in the group. Thus, in this example, you should enter an A1 in the SEL field beside the graph PLOT1, an A2 beside the graph CHART1, and an A3 beside the graph G5. You can use the letter B to denote the second group and then order the graphs within the group. Because you do not want to include the graphs numbered G7 and G8 in either of the groups you created, leave the SEL field beside these graphs blank. After you fill in the grouping information, your screen should look like **Screen 20.4**.

When you press ENTER, the graphs have been placed in groups in the order in which you specified them, as shown in **Screen 20.5**.

```
┌ PROC GREPLAY ─────────────────────────────────────────────────────────
Command ===>

IGOUT: MYLIB.GRAFCAT      GOUT: _____      Device: PS2EGA
TC:    _____    Template: _____         Scroll: PAGE
CC:    _____     ∘   Cmap: _____

SELECT GROUPS; PRESS ENTER TO STOP.
Sel    Name     Type    Description                          Updated

a1_    PLOT1     I      1986 SALES by REGION                 06/25/87
b1_    PLOT2     I      1986 COST by REGION                  06/25/87
b2_    PLOT3     I      1986 REVENUE by REGION               06/25/87
a2_   ∘CHART1    I      Bar chart of SALES, COST, REVENUE    06/25/87
a3_    G5        D      Dependent version of PLOT1           06/25/87
b3_    G6        D      Dependent version of PLOT2           06/25/87
____   G7        D      Dependent version of PLOT3           06/25/87
____   G8        D      Dependent version of CHART1          06/25/87
```

Screen 20.4   Creating Groups of Graphs

```
┌ PROC GREPLAY ─────────────────────────────────────────────────────────
Command ===>

IGOUT: MYLIB.GRAFCAT      GOUT: _____      Device: PS2EGA
TC:    _____    Template: _____         Scroll: PAGE
CC:    _____         Cmap: _____

Sel    Name     Type    Description                          Updated

____   G7        D      Dependent version of PLOT3           06/25/87
____   G8        D      Dependent version of CHART1          06/25/87

____   ********         *** new group ***                    06/25/87
____   PLOT1     I      1986 SALES by REGION                 06/25/87
____   CHART1    I      Bar chart of SALES, COST, REVENUE    06/25/87
____   G5        D      Dependent version of PLOT1           06/25/87

____   ********         *** new group ***                    06/25/87
____   PLOT2     I      1986 COST by REGION                  06/25/87
____   PLOT3     I      1986 REVENUE by REGION               06/25/87
____   G6        D      Dependent version of PLOT2           06/25/87
```

Screen 20.5   PROC GREPLAY Screen after Selecting Groups

You can assign a new name and description to a group by submitting the
MODIFY command or pressing the MODIFY key, entering the group name and

description in the space provided, and submitting the MODIFY command again to save the changes you made. You can then replay a group of graphs by entering an S in the SEL field beside the group name, as shown in **Screen 20.6**.

When you press ENTER, the first graph in the group you selected is displayed. To see the rest of the graphs in the group, press ENTER after each graph is displayed. To return to the PROC GREPLAY screen, press ENTER after the last graph has been displayed.

Copying Graphs from an IGOUT to a GOUT Catalog

To copy a graph or group of graphs from an IGOUT catalog to a GOUT catalog, enter the name of one catalog in the IGOUT field and the name of a different catalog in the GOUT field in the PROC GREPLAY screen. When you press ENTER, a list of the graphics in your IGOUT catalog appears. Place a C in the SEL field beside the graph you want to copy and press ENTER.

You can have only one copy of a given graph in a catalog. You cannot use the COPY command to create a duplicate of a graph.

To copy a group of graphs from one catalog to another, place a C beside the group name or number. PROC GREPLAY also copies the group header so that the group retains its integrity in the new catalog.

Deleting Graphs from a Catalog

To delete a graph or group of graphs from a catalog, you must first enter the name of a catalog in the IGOUT field in the PROC GREPLAY screen. When you press ENTER, a list of the graphs in your IGOUT catalog appears. You can then place the letters DEL in the SEL field beside the graph you want to delete. To delete a group of graphs, place the letters DEL beside the group name or number.

Note: you are **not** prompted to confirm your request to delete a graph or group of graphs. Be careful when you delete graphs.

Suppressing or Displaying BYLINEs

Submit the NOBYLINE command to suppress the BY statement information, which is normally displayed, from the catalog listing. The BYLINE command causes the BY statement information to be displayed again.

Accessing the Presentation Screen

To access the presentation screen, enter the name of a catalog in the IGOUT field in the PROC GREPLAY screen, and submit the PRES command or press the PRES key. This takes you directly to the presentation screen, from which you can select graphs for replay. An example of a presentation screen is shown in **Screen 20.7**.

Refer to **Presentation Screen** for more information.

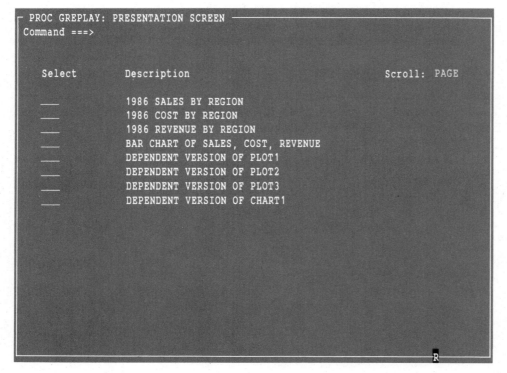

```
┌─ PROC GREPLAY ──────────────────────────────────────────────────┐
│ Command ===>                                                     │
│                                                                  │
│ IGOUT: MYLIB.GRAFCAT      GOUT: _____    Device: PS2EGA │
│ TC:    _____     Template: _____      Scroll: PAGE   │
│ CC:    _____     Cmap: _____                         │
│                                                                  │
│                                                                  │
│ Sel    Name      Type    Description                  Updated    │
│                                                                  │
│ ____   G7        D       Dependent version of PLOT3    06/25/87  │
│ ____   G8        D       Dependent version of CHART1   06/25/87  │
│                                                                  │
│ s___             Charts for June Meeting               06/25/87  │
│ ____   PLOT1     I       1986 SALES by REGION          06/25/87  │
│ ____   CHART1    I       Bar chart of SALES, COST, REVENUE 06/25/87│
│ ____   G5        D       Dependent version of PLOT1    06/25/87  │
│                                                                  │
│ ____             *** new group ***                     06/25/87  │
│ ____   PLOT2     I       1986 COST by REGION           06/25/87  │
│ ____   PLOT3     I       1986 REVENUE by REGION        06/25/87  │
│ ____   G6        D       Dependent version of PLOT2    06/25/87  │
│                                                              R   │
└──────────────────────────────────────────────────────────────────┘
```

Screen 20.6   Replaying Groups of Graphs

```
┌─ PROC GREPLAY: PRESENTATION SCREEN ─────────────────────────────┐
│ Command ===>                                                     │
│                                                                  │
│                                                                  │
│   Select        Description                    Scroll: PAGE      │
│                                                                  │
│   ____          1986 SALES BY REGION                             │
│   ____          1986 COST BY REGION                              │
│   ____          1986 REVENUE BY REGION                           │
│   ____          BAR CHART OF SALES, COST, REVENUE                │
│   ____          DEPENDENT VERSION OF PLOT1                       │
│   ____          DEPENDENT VERSION OF PLOT2                       │
│   ____          DEPENDENT VERSION OF PLOT3                       │
│   ____          DEPENDENT VERSION OF CHART1                      │
│                                                                  │
│                                                                  │
│                                                              R   │
└──────────────────────────────────────────────────────────────────┘
```

Screen 20.7   Presentation Screen

Accessing the Template Directory Screen

To access the template directory screen, enter the name of a template catalog in the TC field in the PROC GREPLAY screen and submit the TC command or press the TC key. In this example, the two-level name MYLIB.TEMPCAT is used. To use the template catalog provided by SAS Institute, specify SASHELP.TEMPLT in the TC field. An example of a template directory screen is shown in **Screen 20.8**.

Refer to **Template Directory Screen** for more information.

Accessing the Template Design Screen

To access the template design screen, enter the following command on the command line of the template directory screen, or place an S beside the name of an existing template in the template directory screen:

```
edit templatename.template
```

When you press ENTER, the template design screen is displayed, as shown in **Screen 20.9**. See **Template Design Screen** for more information on using this screen to design templates.

Accessing the Color Map Directory Screen

To access the color map directory screen, enter the name of a color map catalog in the CC field in the PROC GREPLAY screen and submit the CC command or press the CC key. In this example, the two-level name MYLIB.COLORCAT is used. This takes you directly to the color map directory screen, from which you can select color maps to use when replaying your graphs. An example of a color map directory screen is shown in **Screen 20.10**.

See **Color Map Directory Screen** for more information.

Accessing the Color Mapping Screen

To access the color mapping screen, enter the following command on the command line of the color map directory screen, or place an S beside the name of an existing color map in the color map directory screen:

```
edit colormap.cmap
```

When you press ENTER, the color mapping screen is displayed, as shown in **Screen 20.11**.

Exiting the Procedure

When you have completed all the operations you want to perform with PROC GREPLAY in full-screen mode, press the END key or enter END on the command line to exit the procedure and return to your SAS/GRAPH session.

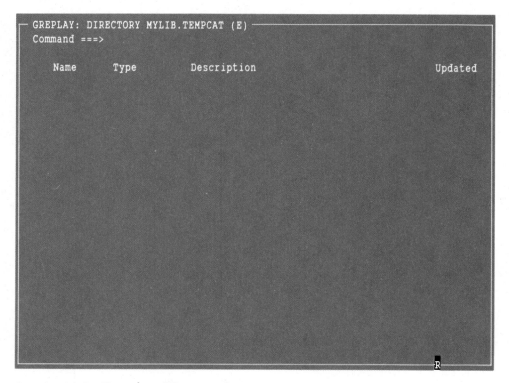

Screen 20.8   Template Directory Screen

```
┌─ PROC GREPLAY: TEMPLATE DESIGN ─────────────────────────────────────────┐
│ Command ===>                                                            │
│                                                                         │
│   TEMPLATE: TEMP1                              TC: MYLIB.TEMPCAT         │
│   DESC: *** new template ***                   Scroll: PAGE             │
│                                                Device: PS2EGA           │
│ Panel Clp Color    L-left U-left U-right L-right   Scale  Xlate  Rotate │
│                                                                         │
│ ____  _   _____  X: ____  ____   ____   ____   X: ____   ____   _____   │
│                  Y: ____  ____   ____   ____   Y: ____   ____           │
│                                                                         │
│ ____  _   _____  X: ____  ____   ____   ____   X: ____   ____   _____   │
│                  Y: ____  ____   ____   ____   Y: ____   ____           │
│                                                                         │
│ ____  _   _____  X: ____  ____   ____   ____   X: ____   ____   _____   │
│                  Y: ____  ____   ____   ____   Y: ____   ____           │
│                                                                         │
│ ____  _   _____  X: ____  ____   ____   ____   X: ____   ____   _____   │
│                  Y: ____  ____   ____   ____   Y: ____   ____           │
│                                                                         │
│ ____  _   _____  X: ____  ____   ____   ____   X: ____   ____   _____   │
│                  Y: ____  ____   ____   ____   Y: ____   ____           │
│                                                                      R  │
└─────────────────────────────────────────────────────────────────────────┘
```

Screen 20.9   Template Design Screen

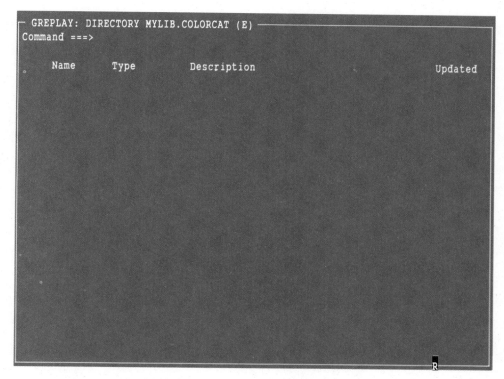

Screen 20.10   Color Map Directory Screen

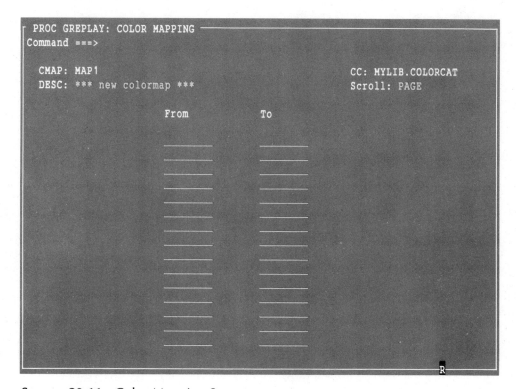

Screen 20.11   Color Mapping Screen

Presentation Screen

Once you have created your catalog, you can use the presentation screen to present the catalog. The presentation screen is a modified version of the PROC

GREPLAY screen and contains only the SELECT and DESCRIPTION fields. To access this screen from the PROC GREPLAY screen, you must enter the name of the IGOUT catalog containing your graphs and then submit the PRES command or press the PRES key. (You can go directly to the presentation screen if you specify the PRESENTATION option in a PROC GREPLAY statement that contains the name of your IGOUT catalog.) An example of a presentation screen is shown in **Screen 20.12**.

To use the presentation screen, enter an S (or S*n*, if you want to specify the order in which your graphs are replayed) beside the graph or group of graphs you want to display and press the ENTER key. Press the END or ENTER key after each graph is displayed to view any remaining graphs you have selected. When you have displayed all the graphs, press the END or ENTER key to return to the presentation screen, and press the END key to return to the PROC GREPLAY screen. If you entered the presentation screen using the PRESENTATION option in the PROC GREPLAY statement, submit the END command to return to your SAS session.

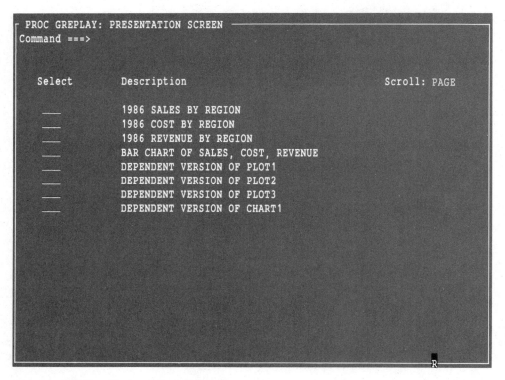

Screen 20.12 Presentation Screen

Color Map Directory Screen

The color map directory screen lists the color maps in the color map catalog you specified in the CC field of the PROC GREPLAY screen (or the color map catalog you specified with the CC= option in the PROC GREPLAY statement).

To access the color map directory screen, enter the name of a color map catalog in the CC field in the PROC GREPLAY screen and submit the CC command or press the CC key. In this example, the two-level name MYLIB.COLORCAT is used.

You can store any number of color maps in a color map catalog. The color map directory screen lists the names (any valid SAS name) of the available color maps and indicates the date on which a color map was created or last updated. An example of a color map directory screen is shown in **Screen 20.13**.

To create a color map or to change an existing one, enter the command

> `edit` *`colormapname`*

on the command line and press ENTER, or you can place an S in the SEL field beside an existing color map and press ENTER. This takes you to the color mapping screen, from which you can create or modify color maps to be used to display your graphs. An example of a color mapping screen is shown in **Screen 20.14**.

To browse a color map, enter a B in the field to the left of the appropriate NAME field and press ENTER. You cannot make changes when you work in browse mode. If the catalog was opened for update and you enter an S in the field, you are working in edit mode. Otherwise, you are working in browse mode. For more information, see **Color Mapping Screen**.

After creating a new color map, or after making changes to existing ones on the color mapping screen, you can submit the END command or press the END key to return to the color map directory screen. You can then select another color map for editing, create a new color map, or submit the END command again to return to the PROC GREPLAY screen to perform another function.

If you want to copy a color map from one catalog to another, go to the color map directory screen of the target catalog (the one into which the color map will be copied). On the command line enter

> `copy` *`libref.catalog.colormapname`*`.cmap`

where *libref* and *catalog* are the libref and catalog name of the source catalog, *colormapname* is the name of the color map to be copied, and CMAP is the catalog entry type (if you omit this value, it is automatically assigned to the color map by SAS/GRAPH software). For example, to copy a color map called ZETA887 from the catalog MYLIB.MYCAT to the catalog YOURLIB.YOURCAT, first access the color map directory screen for YOURLIB.YOURCAT by entering YOURLIB.YOURCAT in the CC field of the PROC GREPLAY screen and submitting the CC command or pressing the CC key. When the color map directory screen for YOURLIB.YOURCAT appears, enter the following command on the command line as shown in **Screen 20.15**.

> `copy mylib.mycat.zeta887.cmap`

When you press ENTER, the color map ZETA887 is copied to the target catalog, YOURLIB.YOURCAT. If a color map named ZETA887 already exists in the target catalog, the copy will fail.

If the source catalog is a temporary one, you must specify a libref of WORK for the catalog. For example, to copy the color map TEK4107 from a temporary catalog named TEMPTEMP, enter the following command on the command line of the color map directory screen for the target catalog.

> `copy work.temptemp.tek4107.cmap`

You can store both color maps and templates in a color map catalog. Use the color map directory screen to edit, browse, copy, or delete color maps or templates. If you specify the name only (and omit the type) in a line command, PROC GREPLAY searches for *colormapname*.CMAP. If *colormapname*.CMAP cannot be found, PROC GREPLAY searches for *colormapname*.TEMPLATE. If the search is unsuccessful and you specified the EDIT command, *colormapname*.CMAP is created. If *colormapname*.TEMPLATE is found, PROC GREPLAY takes you to the template design screen.

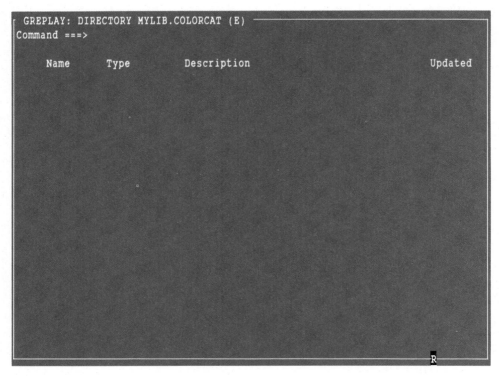

Screen 20.13   Color Map Directory Screen

```
┌ PROC GREPLAY: COLOR MAPPING ─────────────────
│Command ===>

   CMAP: MAP1                              CC: MYLIB.COLORCAT
   DESC: *** new colormap ***             Scroll: PAGE

              From              To
             _____         _____
             _____         _____
             _____         _____
             _____         _____
             _____         _____
             _____         _____
             _____         _____
             _____         _____
             _____         _____
             _____         _____
             _____         _____
             _____         _____
             _____         _____
             _____         _____
             _____         _____
             _____         _____
                                                        R
```

Screen 20.14   Color Mapping Screen

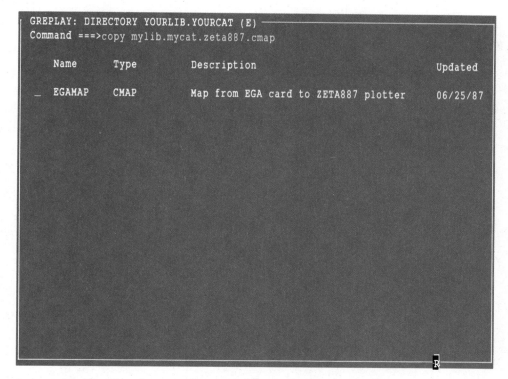

Screen 20.15   Copying a Color Map from One Catalog to Another

Color Mapping Screen

A color map is a list that contains up to 256 pairs of colors labeled FROM and TO. When you replay a graph and specify the CMAP= option, any color in your graph that appears in the FROM column is mapped to the corresponding color in the TO column of the color map list.

You can create or modify a color map by entering pairs of colors in the FROM and TO fields in the color mapping screen. You can access the color mapping screen by entering the following command on the command line of the color map directory screen:

```
edit colormapname
```

Alternatively, you can enter an S in the SEL field beside the name of a color map and press ENTER.

Suppose, for example, that you want to edit the color map TEKMAP2, which is in the color map catalog MYLIB.COLORCAT. Enter the following command on the command line of the color map directory screen:

```
edit tekmap2
```

Alternatively, you can place an S or an E next to the color map name. When you press ENTER, the color mapping screen for the color map TEKMAP2 is displayed, as shown in **Screen 20.16**.

For each color you enter in the FROM field, you must enter a color in the TO field. You can enter up to 256 pairs of colors in each color map. PROC GREPLAY accepts only valid color names in the TO fields (see "SAS/GRAPH Colors" for a list of valid colors). If you specify colors that are not valid, you receive a warning to that effect. When you run PROC GREPLAY and specify a color map catalog and a color map, any colors in your graph(s) are mapped to the new colors in the color map when the graph is replayed.

In this example, the FROM and TO fields already contain colors to be mapped. In addition to mapping white to black and yellow to orange, you want to map tan to brown and cyan to violet. You can enter these color pairs as shown in **Screen 20.17**.

Note that you can remove color pairs from the color map by entering blanks in the appropriate fields.

When you have made these changes to the color map, press the END key to return to the color map directory screen. If you want to return to the PROC GREPLAY screen, submit the END command again.

```
┌ PROC GREPLAY: COLOR MAPPING ─────────────────────────────────────────┐
│ Command ===>                                                          │
│                                                                       │
│   CMAP: TEKMAP2                              CC: MYLIB.COLORCAT        │
│   DESC: Map from TEK4107 CRT to Zeta887 plotter     Scroll: PAGE      │
│                                                                       │
│                      From           To                                │
│                                                                       │
│                      WHITE          BLACK                             │
│                      YELLOW         ORANGE                            │
│                      _____         _____                           │
│                      _____         _____                           │
│                      _____         _____                           │
│                      _____         _____                           │
│                      _____         _____                           │
│                      _____         _____                           │
│                      _____         _____                           │
│                      _____         _____                           │
│                      _____         _____                           │
│                      _____         _____                           │
│                      _____         _____                           │
│                      _____         _____                           │
│                                                                    R  │
└───────────────────────────────────────────────────────────────────────┘
```

Screen 20.16   Color Mapping Screen

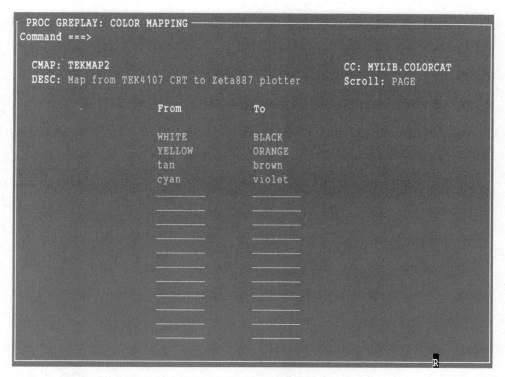

```
 PROC GREPLAY: COLOR MAPPING
Command ===>

  CMAP: TEKMAP2                                    CC: MYLIB.COLORCAT
  DESC: Map from TEK4107 CRT to Zeta887 plotter    Scroll: PAGE


                    From              To

                    WHITE             BLACK
                    YELLOW            ORANGE
                    tan               brown
                    cyan              violet

                    _____           _____

                    _____           _____

                    _____           _____

                    _____           _____

                    _____           _____

                    _____           _____

                    _____           _____

                    _____           _____

                    _____           _____
                                                            R
```

Screen 20.17   Adding Colors to a Color Mapping Screen

Template Directory Screen

Templates are used to describe positioning for multiple graphs on a single page. The template directory screen lists the templates in the template catalog you specified in the TC field of the PROC GREPLAY screen (or the template catalog you specified with the TC= option in the PROC GREPLAY statement). In this example, the two-level name MYLIB.TEMPCAT is used. The screen lists the names (up to eight characters long) of the available templates, gives a brief description (up to forty characters long) of each, and indicates the date on which a template was created or last updated.

To create a new template or to change an existing one, enter the following command on the command line and press ENTER:

    edit *templatename*

Alternatively, you can place an S in the SEL field beside an existing template and press ENTER. This takes you to the template design screen, from which you can design or modify templates to be used to display your graphs. An example of a template design screen is shown in **Screen 20.18**. For more information, see **Template Design Screen**.

After creating a new template or making changes to an existing one on the template design screen, you can press the END key to return to the template directory screen. You can then select another template for editing, create a new template, or press the END key again to return to the PROC GREPLAY screen to perform another function.

If you want to copy a template from one catalog to another, go to the template directory screen of the target catalog (the one into which the template will be copied). On the command line enter

    copy *libref.catalog.templatename*.template

where *libref* and *catalog* are the libref and catalog name of the source catalog, *templatename* is the name of the template to be copied, and TEMPLATE is the catalog entry type (if you omit this value, it is automatically assigned to the template by SAS/GRAPH software). For example, to copy a template called FOURBOX from the catalog MYLIB.MYCAT to the catalog YOURLIB.YOURCAT, first access the template directory screen for YOURLIB.YOURCAT by entering YOURLIB.YOURCAT in the TC field of the PROC GREPLAY screen and submitting the TEMPLATE command or pressing the TEMPLATE key. When the template directory screen for YOURLIB.YOURCAT appears, enter the following command on the command line as shown in **Screen 20.19**.

```
copy mylib.mycat.fourbox.template
```

When you press ENTER, the template FOURBOX is copied to the target catalog, YOURLIB.YOURCAT. If a template named FOURBOX already exists in the target catalog, the copy will fail.

If the source catalog is a temporary one, you must specify a libref of WORK for the catalog. For example, to copy the template TWOBOX from a temporary catalog named TEMPTEMP, enter the following command on the command line of the template directory screen for the target catalog:

```
copy work.temptemp.twobox.template
```

You can store both templates and color maps in a template catalog. Use the template directory screen to edit, browse, copy, or delete templates or color maps. If you specify the name only (and omit the type) in a line command, PROC GREPLAY searches for *templatename*.TEMPLATE. If *templatename*.TEMPLATE cannot be found, PROC GREPLAY searches for *templatename*.CMAP. If the search is unsuccessful and you have specified the EDIT command, then *templatename*.TEMPLATE is created. If *templatename*.CMAP is found, PROC GREPLAY takes you to the color mapping screen.

```
┌─ PROC GREPLAY: TEMPLATE DESIGN ─────────────────────────────
│Command ===>
│
│  TEMPLATE: TEMP1                              TC: MYLIB.TEMPCAT
│  DESC: *** new template ***                  Scroll: PAGE
│                                              Device: PS2EGA
│Panel Clp Color      L-left U-left U-right L-right  Scale  Xlate  Rotate
│
│ ___  _  _____   X: ____ _____ _____ _____  X: _____ _____ ____
│                 Y: ____ _____ _____ _____  Y: _____ _____
│
│ ___  _  _____   X: ____ _____ _____ _____  X: _____ _____ ____
│                 Y: ____ _____ _____ _____  Y: _____ _____
│
│ ___  _  _____   X: ____ _____ _____ _____  X: _____ _____ ____
│                 Y: ____ _____ _____ _____  Y: _____ _____
│
│ ___  _  _____   X: ____ _____ _____ _____  X: _____ _____ ____
│                 Y: ____ _____ _____ _____  Y: _____ _____
│
│ ___  _  _____   X: ____ _____ _____ _____  X: _____ _____ ____
│                 Y: ____ _____ _____ _____  Y: _____ _____
│                                                            R
└─────────────────────────────────────────────────────────────
```

Screen 20.18 Template Design Screen

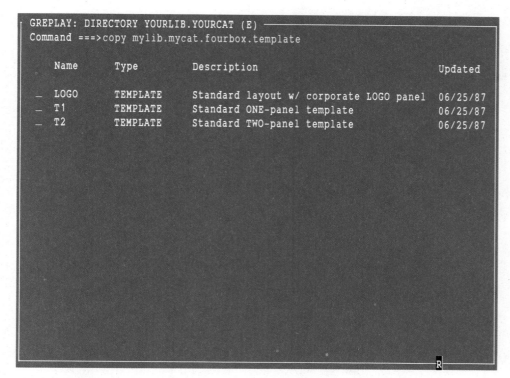

```
GREPLAY: DIRECTORY YOURLIB.YOURCAT (E)
Command ===>copy mylib.mycat.fourbox.template

     Name        Type        Description                         Updated

 _   LOGO        TEMPLATE    Standard layout w/ corporate LOGO panel  06/25/87
 _   T1          TEMPLATE    Standard ONE-panel template         06/25/87
 _   T2          TEMPLATE    Standard TWO-panel template         06/25/87
```

Screen 20.19   Copying a Template from One Catalog to Another

Template Design Screen

You can create or modify a template by entering values in the fields provided in the template design screen. To access the template design screen, enter the following command on the command line of the template directory screen:

>   edit *templatename*

Alternatively, you can enter an S in the SEL field beside the name of a template. An example of a template design screen is shown in **Screen 20.20**.

The fields displayed on the template design screen are defined below:

TC	gives the name of the template catalog in which this template is stored. (This field cannot be modified on the template design screen.)
TEMPLATE	names the template being created or modified. (This field cannot be modified on the template design screen.)
DESC	describes the template. This field can contain up to forty characters, including blank spaces.
DEVICE	displays the name of the current device.
SCROLL	displays the scroll value. Valid values are PAGE, MAX, HALF, or a number. The default value is PAGE.
PANEL	indicates the number of the panel being defined. Possible values are 0 through 999. Panels are drawn in order according to the number you specified in the PANEL field.
CLP	indicates whether or not clipping is in effect. If clipping is in effect for a panel, nothing other than the graph to be placed in that panel can appear in the space that the

panel occupies on the screen. Place any character in this field to invoke clipping.

Any subsequent panels are clipped if they overlap the clipping panel's area. Panels drawn before the clipping panel are *not* clipped. For example, if a template has four panels and you have specified clipping for panels 2 and 3, then panel 2 will clip panels 3 and 4. Panel 3 will clip panel 4. However, neither panel 2 nor panel 3 will clip panel 1.

COLOR   indicates the color used to draw the border around the graphic display. Possible values for this field are the colors that are valid for your device. If you leave this field blank, a border is not drawn around the graphs you display. However, in order for you to preview a template when you leave the COLOR field blank, your device chooses a color and displays a border when you press the DISPLAY key so that the outline of your template can be seen.

L-LEFT   specifies the x,y coordinates for the lower-left corner of the panel. Valid values are 0 through 100 and decimal values are accepted.

U-LEFT   specifies the x,y coordinates for the upper-left corner of the panel. Valid values are 0 through 100 and decimal values are accepted.

U-RIGHT   specifies the x,y coordinates for the upper-right corner of the panel. Valid values are 0 through 100 and decimal values are accepted.

L-RIGHT   specifies the x,y coordinates for the lower-right corner of the panel. Valid values are 0 through 100 and decimal values are accepted.

SCALE   specifies a value by which the length of the panel's edges should be increased or decreased. When you enter a value in this field and press ENTER, the x and y coordinates are recalculated at about the center of the panel. Possible values depend upon the size of the original panel. If the SCALE value is too large, the panel surpasses the size limits of the device and is clipped.

XLATE   moves the panel up, down, left, or right on the screen. The values you specify for x and y are added to the values that define the x and y coordinates for the panel.

ROTATE   indicates the angle at which the panel should be rotated. Values are interpreted in degrees. If you enter a value for the ROTATE field and press ENTER, the coordinates are recalculated.

Each template can be composed of multiple panels numbered from 0 through 999. For each panel within the template you design, designate the position of the template corners as an x,y coordinate pair. Because the display area of various output devices differs, template design should be based upon an imaginary screen that measures 100 percent in the x direction and 100 percent in the y direction. A coordinate pair of x=50,y=50 indicates the middle of the screen. A coordinate pair of x=0,y=0 indicates the lower-left corner; x=0,y=100 is the upper-right corner; and so on. You can specify the size and shape of each panel by entering the x,y coordinates for the corners of each panel.

After you have entered the values for the panel(s) in the template, submit the SAVE command or press the SAVE key if you want to save the template in an intermediate step. You can then view the template by submitting the PREVIEW command or pressing the PREVIEW key, and the panel(s) you have defined will appear on the screen. When you have finished viewing the panel(s) in the template, submit the END command or press ENTER to return to the template design screen. You can then modify the template, or, if you want to modify another template or create a new template, submit the END command again to return to the template directory screen. If you submit the END command, your template is automatically saved when you exit the procedure.

Several templates are provided by SAS Institute for use with the template facility of PROC GREPLAY. See the section **SAMPLE TEMPLATES** for illustrations.

Example: Using the Template Facility in Full-Screen Mode

Suppose you have four graphs that you want to display on one page. You have a template catalog called MYLIB.TEMPCAT that contains some templates; however, you want to create a new template to display your graphs, and you want to store the template for later use. The steps you must follow to create a new template, preview it, and display graphs in it are described below.

Previewing a template produces output, so remember that you must have the correct environment set for your device if you want to preview a template. See *SAS/GRAPH Hardware Interfaces for Personal Computers, Version 6 Edition* or the *SAS/GRAPH Guide to Hardware Interfaces, Release 6.03 Edition* for a description of how to configure the environment for your device.

Step 1. Accessing a Template Catalog

Enter a PROC GREPLAY statement in full-screen mode. When the PROC GREPLAY screen appears, enter the name of your template catalog, MYLIB.TEMPCAT (a two-level name so that your template will be permanently stored), in the TC field as shown in **Screen 20.21**. When you submit the TC command or press the TC key, the template catalog MYLIB.TEMPCAT is displayed as shown in **Screen 20.22**.

Step 2. Creating a New Template

If you want to create a new template called NEWFOUR, enter the following command on the command line:

```
edit newfour
```

When you press ENTER, the template design screen for the template NEWFOUR is displayed, as shown in **Screen 20.23**.

```
┌ PROC GREPLAY: TEMPLATE DESIGN ───────────────────────────────────────────
Command ===>


  TEMPLATE: TEMP1                                    TC: MYLIB.TEMPCAT
  DESC: *** new template ***                         Scroll: PAGE
                                                     Device: PS2EGA

Panel Clp Color      L-left U-left U-right L-right   Scale  Xlate  Rotate


____  _  _____  X: ____  ____  ____  ____   X: ____  ____  ____
                 Y: ____  ____  ____  ____   Y: ____  ____


____  _  _____  X: ____  ____  ____  ____   X: ____  ____  ____
                 Y: ____  ____  ____  ____   Y: ____  ____


____  _  _____  X: ____  ____  ____  ____   X: ____  ____  ____
                 Y: ____  ____  ____  ____   Y: ____  ____


____  _  _____  X: ____  ____  ____  ____   X: ____  ____  ____
                 Y: ____  ____  ____  ____   Y: ____  ____


____  _  _____  X: ____  ____  ____  ____   X: ____  ____  ____
                 Y: ____  ____  ____  ____   Y: ____  ____


                                                                      R
```

Screen 20.20 Template Design Screen

```
┌ PROC GREPLAY ────────────────────────────────────────────────────────────
Command ===>


IGOUT: _____      GOUT: _____      Device: PS2EGA
TC:    MYLIB.TEMPCAT        Template: _____        Scroll: PAGE
CC:    _____      Cmap: _____


Sel    Name     Type   Description                            Updated
```

(blank directory area)

```
                                                                      R
```

Screen 20.21 Accessing a Template Directory: the PROC GREPLAY Screen

```
┌─ GREPLAY: DIRECTORY MYLIB.TEMPCAT (E) ──────────────────────────────┐
│ Command ===>                                                        │
│                                                                     │
│      Name       Type        Description                  Updated    │
│                                                                     │
│   _  ADD2       TEMPLATE    Fancy layout, 12 graphs per page 06/25/87│
│   _  EOM        TEMPLATE    End-of-month cost reporting layout 06/25/87│
│   _  LOGO       TEMPLATE    Standard layout w/ corporate LOGO panel 06/25/87│
│   _  T1         TEMPLATE    Standard ONE-panel template   06/25/87  │
│   _  T2         TEMPLATE    Standard TWO-panel template   06/25/87  │
│   _  T4         TEMPLATE    Standard FOUR-panel template  06/25/87  │
│                                                                     │
│                                                                     │
│                                                                     │
│                                                                     │
│                                                                     │
│                                                                     │
│                                                                     │
│                                                                  R  │
└─────────────────────────────────────────────────────────────────────┘
```

Screen 20.22   Template Directory Screen

```
┌─ PROC GREPLAY: TEMPLATE DESIGN ─────────────────────────────────────┐
│ Command ===>                                                        │
│                                                                     │
│   TEMPLATE: NEWFOUR                          TC: MYLIB.TEMPCAT       │
│   DESC: *** new template ***                 Scroll: PAGE           │
│                                              Device: PS2EGA         │
│ Panel Clp Color     L-left U-left U-right L-right   Scale  Xlate  Rotate│
│                                                                     │
│ ___  _  _____  X: ____ ____ ____ ____   X: ____ ____ _____       │
│                 Y: ____ ____ ____ ____   Y: ____                    │
│                                                                     │
│ ___  _  _____  X: ____ ____ ____ ____   X: ____ ____ _____       │
│                 Y: ____ ____ ____ ____   Y: ____                    │
│                                                                     │
│ ___  _  _____  X: ____ ____ ____ ____   X: ____ ____ _____       │
│                 Y: ____ ____ ____ ____   Y: ____                    │
│                                                                     │
│ ___  _  _____  X: ____ ____ ____ ____   X: ____ ____ _____       │
│                 Y: ____ ____ ____ ____   Y: ____                    │
│                                                                     │
│ ___  _  _____  X: ____ ____ ____ ____   X: ____ ____ _____       │
│                 Y: ____ ____ ____ ____   Y: ____                    │
│                                                                  R  │
└─────────────────────────────────────────────────────────────────────┘
```

Screen 20.23   Creating a New Template: Template Design Screen

The names of the template catalog and the template you are creating have been filled in. You can add a description (up to forty characters) for the template by filling in the DESC field. In this example, the description is "Four squares of equal size." To create the template, you must specify values in the fields provided. Because you want to display four graphs on one screen (or page), you should define four panels for the template. Enter the numbers 1, 2, 3, and 4 in the spaces provided in the PANEL field, as shown in **Screen 20.24**.

You do not want to define the panels as overlapping, so leave the CLP field blank. (Note: using the CLP field when it is not needed uses a great deal of unnecessary processing time.) To enhance the appearance of the template, choose a color for the border to be drawn around each panel, and enter the color value for each panel in the fields provided. In this example, the colors for the borders of the panels are blue, cyan, red, and yellow as shown in **Screen 20.25**.

The template you are creating is divided into four squares of equal size, so you can specify the x,y coordinates of each panel easily. Because you want the entire display area used by the panels and you do not want to move or rotate the panels on the display area, leave the SCALE, XLATE, and ROTATE fields blank. The rest of the information needed to create the template is shown in **Screen 20.26**.

Step 3. Previewing the Template You Have Created

When you have entered the values necessary to create the template, you can preview the template to be sure that it appears the way you intended. To view the template NEWFOUR, submit the PREVIEW command or press the PREVIEW key and the template is displayed as shown in **Screen 20.27**. When you have finished viewing the template, press ENTER to return to the template design screen.

```
┌─ PROC GREPLAY: TEMPLATE DESIGN ──────────────────────────────
 Command ===>

   TEMPLATE: NEWFOUR                          TC: MYLIB.TEMPCAT
   DESC: Four squares of equal size           Scroll: PAGE
                                               Device: PS2EGA

 Panel Clp Color     L-left U-left U-right L-right  Scale  Xlate  Rotate

 1__   _   _____ X: _____ _____ _____ _____   X: _____ _____  ___
                   Y: _____ _____ _____ _____   Y: _____ _____


 2__   _   _____ X: _____ _____ _____ _____   X: _____ _____  ___
                   Y: _____ _____ _____ _____   Y: _____ _____


 3__   _   _____ X: _____ _____ _____ _____   X: _____ _____  ___
                   Y: _____ _____ _____ _____   Y: _____ _____


 4__   _   _____ X: _____ _____ _____ _____   X: _____ _____  ___
                   Y: _____ _____ _____ _____   Y: _____ _____


 __    _   _____ X: _____ _____ _____ _____   X: _____ _____  ___
                   Y: _____ _____ _____ _____   Y: _____ _____
                                                               R
```

Screen 20.24 Specifying Panels in a Template Design Screen

```
┌ PROC GREPLAY: TEMPLATE DESIGN ──────────────────────────
Command ===>


   TEMPLATE: NEWFOUR                           TC: MYLIB.TEMPCAT
   DESC: Four squares of equal size            Scroll: PAGE
                                               Device: PS2EGA

 Panel Clp Color      L-left U-left U-right L-right  Scale  Xlate  Rotate

 1___   _   blue___  X: _____  _____  _____  _____  X: _____  _____   ___
                     Y: _____  _____  _____  _____  Y: _____  _____


 2___   _   cyan___  X: _____  _____  _____  _____  X: _____  _____
                     Y: _____  _____  _____  _____  Y: _____  _____


 3___   _   red____  X: _____  _____  _____  _____  X: _____  _____
                     Y: _____  _____  _____  _____  Y: _____  _____


 4___   _   yellow_  X: _____  _____  _____  _____  X: _____  _____
                     Y: _____  _____  _____  _____  Y: _____  _____


 ___    _            X: _____  _____  _____  _____  X: _____  _____
                     Y: _____  _____  _____  _____  Y: _____  _____



                                                               R
```

Screen 20.25   Specifying Colors in a Template Design Screen

```
┌ PROC GREPLAY: TEMPLATE DESIGN ──────────────────────────
Command ===>


   TEMPLATE: NEWFOUR                           TC: MYLIB.TEMPCAT
   DESC: Four squares of equal size            Scroll: PAGE
                                               Device: PS2EGA

 Panel Clp Color      L-left U-left U-right L-right  Scale  Xlate  Rotate

 1     _   BLUE    X:   0.0    0.0   50.0   50.0  X: _____  _____   ___
                  Y:   0.0   50.0   50.0    0.0  Y: _____  _____


 2     _   CYAN    X:   0.0    0.0   50.0   50.0  X: _____  _____
                  Y:  50.0  100.0  100.0   50.0  Y: _____  _____


 3     _   RED     X:  50.0   50.0  100.0  100.0  X: _____  _____
                  Y:  50.0  100.0  100.0   50.0  Y: _____  _____


 4     _   YELLOW  X:  50.0   50.0  100.0  100.0  X: _____  _____
                  Y:   0.0   50.0   50.0    0.0  Y: _____  _____


 ___   _          X: _____  _____  _____  _____  X: _____  _____
                  Y: _____  _____  _____  _____  Y: _____  _____



                                                               R
```

Screen 20.26   Specifying Coordinates in a Template Design Screen

Screen 20.27   Previewing a Template

When you are satisfied with the appearance of the template, you can return to the template directory screen by pressing the END key. The template is automatically saved.

You can use the INI (initialize), C (copy), O (over), and D (delete) commands in the PANEL field of the template design screen as aids in template design.

Use the INI command to initialize a panel that is the size of the screen. You can then change the size and location of the panel using the SCALE and XLATE fields. If you enter values in these fields at the same time you enter INI in the SELECT field, the transformations are performed before the coordinate values are displayed.

You can also initialize a panel by entering a value in any field (or fields) in a new row. The default values are $x=1,y=1$ for SCALE, $x=0,y=0$ for XLATE, and 0 for ROTATE. These values are used for any unspecified coordinates or transformations.

You can use the C and O commands to duplicate the information for a panel. For example, suppose you want to create another template called CENTER and you have entered the coordinates for panel 1 in the appropriate fields of the template design screen. You have specified a blue panel that encompasses the entire screen and has the coordinates $llx=0,lly=0$, $ulx=0,uly=100$, $urx=100$, $ury=100$, and $lrx=100,lry=0$. When you submit the PREVIEW command or press the PREVIEW key, the template CENTER is displayed as shown in **Screen 20.28**.

Without recalculating any coordinates, you can create another panel that will be displayed on another part of the screen. First, duplicate the original panel information by placing a C in the PANEL field for the original panel and an O in the PANEL field where you want the panel duplicated as shown in **Screen 20.29**.

When you press ENTER, the information for the first panel is duplicated for the second panel as shown in **Screen 20.30**.

You can renumber panel 2 and change the color to cyan to add variety to the template. You can then use the SCALE, XLATE, and ROTATE fields to translate your original coordinates to new coordinates that will create a new panel at a different screen location.

To create a panel one-third the size of the original that is centered on the screen, specify .33 for the X and Y values in the SCALE field. (You do not have to specify the same SCALE value for X and Y.) When you press ENTER, the values for X and Y are multiplied by the SCALE value. The new values have been recalculated (or scaled) around the center based on the SCALE value you supplied; they are shown in **Screen 20.31**.

When you submit the PREVIEW command or press the PREVIEW key, the template CENTER with two panels is displayed as shown in **Screen 20.32**.

To create a new panel that has been moved up, down, left, or right on the screen, you can fill in the XLATE field on the PROC GREPLAY screen after copying the coordinates for a panel. To place a panel in the upper-right corner of the screen, specify .33 for the X and Y values in the SCALE field of the next panel, and specify 33 for the X and Y values in the XLATE field. (You can specify positive or negative values for X and Y, and you do not have to specify the same XLATE value for X and Y.) Number this panel 3, and enter the value RED in the COLOR field. When you press ENTER, the default coordinates are scaled as in panel 2, then 33 is added to each of the X and Y values as shown in **Screen 20.33**.

When you submit the PREVIEW command, the template CENTER with three panels is displayed, as shown in **Screen 20.34**.

To place a panel in the lower left corner of the screen, first copy the coordinates for panel 3 in a new panel field and renumber this panel 4. You can change the color to YELLOW to distinguish this panel from the others. Then translate the coordinates by entering negative X and Y values in the XLATE field. In this example, enter the value −65.5 for X and Y in the XLATE field. When you press ENTER, the value −65.5 has been added to each of the coordinates as shown in **Screen 20.35**.

When you submit the PREVIEW command, the template CENTER with four panels is displayed as shown in **Screen 20.36**.

Because panels 2, 3, and 4 overlap somewhat, you may want to rotate panel 2. You can specify an angle (for example, 90 degrees) at which to rotate the panel by entering 90 in the ROTATE field. When you press ENTER, the coordinates of the new panel are recalculated based on the degree of rotation you specified as shown in **Screen 20.37**.

The DEVICE field is important for rotations because the device's aspect ratio is used in the calculation to preserve the shape of a template after rotation. If you are rotating panels, be sure that you have entered the driver name for the device you are are using in the DEVICE field; otherwise, the rotation may not be accurate for the device you are using.

Screen 20.28   Template with One Panel in the Center

```
┌─ PROC GREPLAY: TEMPLATE DESIGN ────────────────────────────────┐
│ Command ===>                                                    │
│                                                                 │
│   TEMPLATE: CENTER                        TC: MYLIB.TEMPCAT      │
│   DESC: *** new template ***              Scroll: PAGE          │
│                                           Device: PS2EGA        │
│                                                                 │
│ Panel Clp Color    L-left U-left U-right L-right  Scale  Xlate  Rotate │
│                                                                 │
│ c 1  _  BLUE    X:    0.0    0.0  100.0  100.0  X: ____  ____   ____ │
│                 Y:    0.0  100.0  100.0    0.0  Y: ____  ____        │
│                                                                 │
│ o__  _          X: ____ ____ ____ ____           X: ____ ____  ____ │
│                 Y: ____ ____ ____ ____           Y: ____ ____        │
│                                                                 │
│ ____ _          X: ____ ____ ____ ____           X: ____ ____  ____ │
│                 Y: ____ ____ ____ ____           Y: ____ ____        │
│                                                                 │
│ ____ _          X: ____ ____ ____ ____           X: ____ ____  ____ │
│                 Y: ____ ____ ____ ____           Y: ____ ____        │
│                                                                 │
│ ____ _          X: ____ ____ ____ ____           X: ____ ____  ____ │
│                 Y: ____ ____ ____ ____           Y: ____ ____        │
│                                                            R    │
└─────────────────────────────────────────────────────────────────┘
```

Screen 20.29   Using the C and O Commands

```
┌─ PROC GREPLAY: TEMPLATE DESIGN ──────────────────────────────┐
│ Command ===>                                                 │
│                                                              │
│   TEMPLATE: CENTER                          TC: MYLIB.TEMPCAT│
│   DESC: *** new template ***                Scroll: PAGE     │
│                                             Device: PS2EGA   │
│ Panel Clp Color    L-left U-left U-right L-right  Scale Xlate Rotate│
│                                                              │
│   1    _  BLUE   X:  0.0    0.0   100.0  100.0  X: ____ ____ ___│
│                  Y:  0.0  100.0   100.0    0.0  Y: ____ ____    │
│                                                              │
│   1    _  BLUE   X:  0.0    0.0   100.0  100.0  X: ____ ____ ___│
│                  Y:  0.0  100.0   100.0    0.0  Y: ____ ____    │
│                                                              │
│   __   _         X:  ____  ____   ____   ____   X: ____ ____ ___│
│                  Y:  ____  ____   ____   ____   Y: ____ ____    │
│                                                              │
│   __   _         X:  ____  ____   ____   ____   X: ____ ____ ___│
│                  Y:  ____  ____   ____   ____   Y: ____ ____    │
│                                                              │
│   __   _         X:  ____  ____   ____   ____   X: ____ ____ ___│
│                  Y:  ____  ____   ____   ____   Y: ____ ____    │
│                                                          R   │
└──────────────────────────────────────────────────────────────┘
```

Screen 20.30   Duplicating the Coordinates for a Template Panel

```
┌─ PROC GREPLAY: TEMPLATE DESIGN ──────────────────────────────┐
│ Command ===>                                                 │
│                                                              │
│   TEMPLATE: CENTER                          TC: MYLIB.TEMPCAT│
│   DESC: *** new template ***                Scroll: PAGE     │
│                                             Device: PS2EGA   │
│ Panel Clp Color    L-left U-left U-right L-right  Scale Xlate Rotate│
│                                                              │
│   1    _  BLUE   X:  0.0    0.0   100.0  100.0  X: ____ ____ ___│
│                  Y:  0.0  100.0   100.0    0.0  Y: ____ ____    │
│                                                              │
│   2    _  CYAN   X: 33.5   33.5    66.5   66.5  X: ____ ____ ___│
│                  Y: 33.5   66.5    66.5   33.5  Y: ____ ____    │
│                                                              │
│   __   _         X:  ____  ____   ____   ____   X: ____ ____ ___│
│                  Y:  ____  ____   ____   ____   Y: ____ ____    │
│                                                              │
│   __   _         X:  ____  ____   ____   ____   X: ____ ____ ___│
│                  Y:  ____  ____   ____   ____   Y: ____ ____    │
│                                                              │
│   __   _         X:  ____  ____   ____   ____   X: ____ ____ ___│
│                  Y:  ____  ____   ____   ____   Y: ____ ____    │
│                                                          R   │
└──────────────────────────────────────────────────────────────┘
```

Screen 20.31   Scaling Coordinates in a Template Panel

Screen 20.32   Template with Two Panels

```
┌─ PROC GREPLAY: TEMPLATE DESIGN ────────────────────────────────┐
│ Command ===>                                                   │
│                                                                │
│   TEMPLATE: CENTER                        TC: MYLIB.TEMPCAT     │
│   DESC: *** new template ***              Scroll: PAGE          │
│                                           Device: PS2EGA        │
│                                                                │
│ Panel Clp Color      L-left U-left U-right L-right  Scale  Xlate  Rotate │
│                                                                │
│   1   _  BLUE    X:    0.0    0.0   100.0  100.0  X: ____  ____   ____ │
│                  Y:    0.0  100.0   100.0    0.0  Y: ____  ____   ____ │
│                                                                │
│   2   _  CYAN    X:   33.5   33.5    66.5   66.5  X: ____  ____   ____ │
│                  Y:   33.5   66.5    66.5   33.5  Y: ____  ____   ____ │
│                                                                │
│   3   _  RED     X:   66.5   66.5    99.5   99.5  X: ____  ____   ____ │
│                  Y:   66.5   99.5    99.5   66.5  Y: ____  ____   ____ │
│                                                                │
│  ____ _ _____  X: ____ ____ ____ ____            X: ____ ____   ____ │
│                 Y: ____ ____ ____ ____            Y: ____ ____   ____ │
│                                                                │
│  ____ _ _____  X: ____ ____ ____ ____            X: ____ ____   ____ │
│                 Y: ____ ____ ____ ____            Y: ____ ____   ____ │
│                                                            R   │
└────────────────────────────────────────────────────────────────┘
```

Screen 20.33   Translating Coordinates in a Template Panel

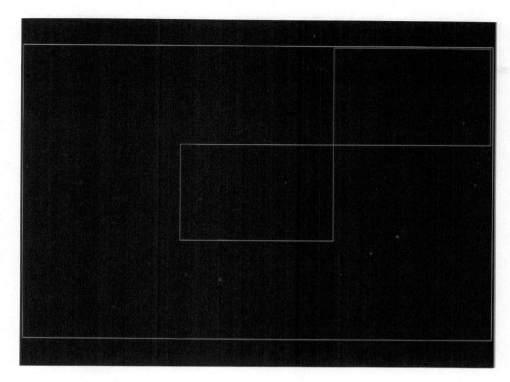

Screen 20.34   Template with Three Panels

```
┌─ PROC GREPLAY: TEMPLATE DESIGN ──────────────────────────────────┐
│ Command ===>                                                      │
│                                                                   │
│   TEMPLATE: CENTER                          TC: MYLIB.TEMPCAT     │
│   DESC: *** new template ***         ○      Scroll: PAGE          │
│                                             Device: PS2EGA        │
│ Panel Clp Color    L-left U-left U-right L-right  Scale  Xlate  Rotate │
│                                                                   │
│   1   _   BLUE    X:   0.0    0.0  100.0  100.0  X: ____  ____   ___ │
│                   Y:   0.0  100.0  100.0    0.0  Y: ____  ____       │
│                                                                   │
│   2   _   CYAN    X:  33.5   33.5   66.5   66.5  X: ____  ____   ___ │
│                   Y:  33.5   66.5   66.5   33.5  Y: ____  ____       │
│                                                                   │
│   3   _   RED     X:  66.5   66.5   99.5   99.5  X: ____  ____   ___ │
│                   Y:  66.5   99.5   99.5   66.5  Y: ____  ____       │
│                                                                   │
│   4   _   YELLOW  X:   1.0    1.0   34.0   34.0  X: ____  ____   ___ │
│                   Y:   1.0   34.0   34.0    1.0  Y: ____  ____       │
│                                                                   │
│  ___  _   ___     X: ____  ____  ____  ____     X: ____  ____       │
│                   Y: ____  ____  ____  ____     Y: ____  ____       │
│                                                            R      │
└──────────────────────────────────────────────────────────────────┘
```

Screen 20.35   Specifying Negative Values to Translate Coordinates

Screen 20.36 Template with Four Panels

```
┌─ PROC GREPLAY: TEMPLATE DESIGN ──────────────────────────────────┐
│ Command ===>                                                      │
│                                                                   │
│   TEMPLATE: CENTER                          TC: MYLIB.TEMPCAT     │
│   DESC: *** new template ***                Scroll: PAGE          │
│                                             Device: PS2EGA        │
│                                                                   │
│ Panel Clp Color    L-left U-left U-right L-right  Scale  Xlate  Rotate │
│                                                                   │
│   1    _   BLUE    X:   0.0    0.0  100.0  100.0  X: ____ ____  ___ │
│                    Y:   0.0  100.0  100.0    0.0  Y: ____ ____      │
│                                                                   │
│   2    _   CYAN    X:  61.4   38.6   38.6   61.4  X: ____ ____  ___ │
│                    Y:  26.2   26.2   73.8   73.8  Y: ____ ____      │
│                                                                   │
│   3    _   RED     X:  66.5   66.5   99.5   99.5  X: ____ ____  ___ │
│                    Y:  66.5   99.5   99.5   66.5  Y: ____ ____      │
│                                                                   │
│   4    _   YELLOW  X:   1.0    1.0   34.0   34.0  X: ____ ____  ___ │
│                    Y:   1.0   34.0   34.0    1.0  Y: ____ ____      │
│                                                                   │
│ ____   _           X: ____ ____ ____ ____       X: ____ ____      │
│                    Y: ____ ____ ____ ____       Y: ____ ____      │
│                                                                   │
│                                                            R      │
└───────────────────────────────────────────────────────────────────┘
```

Screen 20.37 Rotating Coordinates in a Template Panel

The template CENTER now contains four panels: the original panel, a panel one-third the size of the original rotated 90 degrees, a panel in the upper-right corner, and a panel in the lower-left corner. When you submit the PREVIEW command, the new template CENTER is displayed as shown in **Screen 20.38**.

After displaying the template, submit the END command to return to the template design screen. You may want to modify the DESC field to reflect the changes you made to the original template.

You can use the D line command to remove a panel from the template. Place a D in the PANEL field and press ENTER. The panel will be removed.

When you submit the END command again, you return to the template directory screen, shown in **Screen 20.39**, which contains the new entries for the templates NEWFOUR and CENTER.

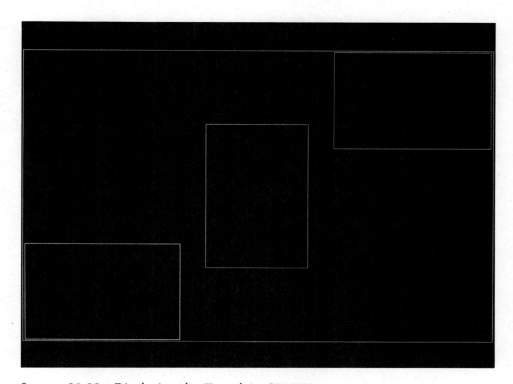

Screen 20.38   Displaying the Template CENTER

```
┌─ GREPLAY: DIRECTORY MYLIB.TEMPCAT (E) ──────────────────────────────┐
│ Command ===>                                                        │
│                                                                     │
│     Name      Type        Description                    Updated    │
│                                                                     │
│   _ ADD2      TEMPLATE     Fancy layout, 12 graphs per page 06/25/87 │
│   _ CENTER    TEMPLATE     4 panels scaled, titled, and rotated 06/25/87 │
│   _ EOM       TEMPLATE     End-of-month cost reporting layout 06/25/87 │
│   _ LOGO      TEMPLATE     Standard layout w/ corporate LOGO panel 06/25/87 │
│   _ NEWFOUR   TEMPLATE     Four squares of equal size      06/25/87 │
│   _ T1        TEMPLATE     Standard ONE-panel template      06/25/87 │
│   _ T2        TEMPLATE     Standard TWO-panel template      06/25/87 │
│   _ T4        TEMPLATE     Standard FOUR-panel template     06/25/87 │
│                                                                     │
│                                                                     │
│                                                                     │
│                                                                     │
│                                                                     │
│                                                                     │
│                                                                     │
│                                                                     │
│                                                                  R  │
└─────────────────────────────────────────────────────────────────────┘
```

Screen 20.39   Updated Template Directory Screen

Step 4. Displaying Graphs in Your Template

To display graphs in the template you have created, you must specify both a catalog that contains graphs and an entry in a template catalog. To do this, submit the END command to exit the template directory screen and return to the PROC GREPLAY screen. You can then fill in the IGOUT, TC, and TEMPLATE fields. In this example, the name of the catalog containing SAS/GRAPH output is MYLIB.GRAFCAT, the name of the template catalog containing templates is MYLIB.TEMPCAT, and the name of the template in which you want to display your graphs is the one you previously created, NEWFOUR.

After specifying this information on the PROC GREPLAY screen, you can select the graphs to be displayed in the template by placing a number in the SEL field beside each graph you want displayed. The number you enter corresponds to the number of the panel you defined in the template design screen. Thus, if you want to display only one graph and you want to display it in the area occupied by panel number 2 in the template, you can enter the number 2 beside the name of the graph you want displayed. If you want to display four graphs in the template you designed, place the numbers 1 through 4 beside the graphs you want displayed. When you press ENTER, your graphs are displayed in the template as shown in **Output 20.1**.

By displaying graphs in a template, you create a new graph. This graph is placed in the GOUT catalog or, if you have not specified a catalog, in the default catalog GSEG.

Output 20.1   Displaying Graphs in a Template

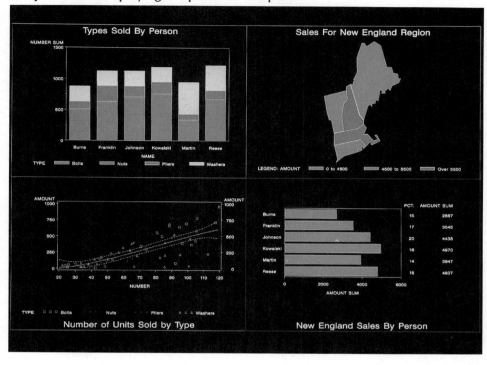

USING PROC GREPLAY IN BATCH OR LINE MODE

You can use PROC GREPLAY in batch or line mode by specifying the PROC GREPLAY statement with the NOFS option and, after receiving the line mode prompt, entering the line-mode command keyword and any required information, followed by a semicolon. The general form of a line-mode command is

   command specification;

The line-mode commands used with PROC GREPLAY are described in detail below.

PROC GREPLAY Line-Mode Commands

There are five types of PROC GREPLAY line-mode commands: specification commands, information commands, change commands, replay commands, and operation commands. The commands in each category are

specification
   IGOUT, GOUT, TC, TEMPLATE, CC, CMAP, DEVICE (or DEV)

information
   LIST, ?

replay
   REPLAY (or PLAY), TREPLAY (or TPLAY), PREVIEW

change
   GROUP, MODIFY, DELETE (or DEL), TDELETE (or TDEL), COPY,
   TCOPY, CCOPY, TDEF, CDEF, NOBYLINE

operation
   FS, QUIT | STOP | END

These functions can be performed in line mode and in full-screen mode. In line mode, you enter the command keyword and any required information followed by a semicolon. In full-screen mode you fill in the information in the appropriate field of the menu or directory screen. See the section **USING PROC GREPLAY IN FULL-SCREEN MODE** for a complete description of the functions you can perform.

Specification Commands

The specification commands are those in which you supply information necessary for the procedure to run. You can specify the name of a catalog containing graphs or in which graphs will be stored, a template or color catalog, a template, a color map, or a device to be used by PROC GREPLAY.

CC Command

   CC *colormapcatalog*;

The CC command specifies the color map catalog to be used with the procedure. A color map catalog contains color map definitions. Color maps allow you to change the colors in a graph by mapping those colors to a list of new colors.

To create a color map catalog or to use an existing color map catalog in line mode, specify the name of the color map catalog with the CC command. If you specify a one-level name, the color map catalog is in the WORK data library. If you specify a two-level name, the color map catalog is stored in a permanent SAS data library.

You can specify CC as both a line-mode command and an option in the PROC GREPLAY statement.

CMAP Command

   CMAP *colormapname*;

The CMAP command specifies the name of a color map to use when replaying your graphs. A color map is a list that contains up to 256 pairs of colors labeled FROM and TO. When you replay a graph and specify the CMAP command, any color in your graph that appears in the FROM column is mapped to the corresponding color(s) in the TO column of the color map list.

If you specify a color map that is not in the color map catalog, or if you specify a color before you have specified a color map catalog, PROC GREPLAY issues an error message.

You can specify CMAP as both a line-mode command and an option in the PROC GREPLAY statement.

DEVICE Command

   DEVICE *devicename*;
   DEV *devicename*;

The DEVICE (or DEV) command specifies the device driver to be used for replaying graphs. In line mode you can enter or change the device name with the DEVICE command. If you specify an unknown device name, PROC GREPLAY issues a message indicating that. Otherwise, the device you specify becomes the current device and is used for all subsequent replays. If you want to switch to another device, simply use the DEVICE command again to enter a different device name. This can be very useful if you have an interactive SAS/GRAPH session and are using both the display and a hardcopy device.

GOUT Command

GOUT *SAScatalog;*

In addition to (or instead of) displaying the contents of a catalog, you can create a new output catalog. Use the GOUT command in line mode to tell PROC GREPLAY which catalog to use as the output catalog or to change from one output catalog to another.

You can specify GOUT as both a line-mode command and as an option in the PROC GREPLAY statement.

When you use the PROC GREPLAY COPY command, graphs are copied from the current IGOUT catalog to the current GOUT catalog. If you specify a one-level name, the GOUT catalog is in the WORK data library. If you specify a two-level name, the catalog is stored in a permanent SAS data library. If you use the procedure to create device-dependent or device-independent graphics output, the output is stored in the GOUT catalog. For more information on device-dependent and device-independent output, see "SAS/GRAPH Graphics Output."

When you create templated graphs, they are placed in the GOUT catalog.

IGOUT Command

IGOUT *SAScatalog;*

Use the IGOUT command in line mode to tell PROC GREPLAY which catalog to use as the input catalog or to change from one input catalog to another. If you specify a one-level name, the IGOUT catalog is in the WORK data library. If you specify a two-level name, the catalog is assumed to be stored in a permanent SAS data library.

You can specify IGOUT as both a line-mode command and as an option in the PROC GREPLAY statement.

TC Command

TC *templatecatalog;*

The TC command specifies the template catalog to use with PROC GREPLAY. Template catalogs contain template definitions. Templates are used to describe positioning for multiple graphs on a single page. For more information about templates, see the section **Example: Using the Template Facility in Full-Screen Mode**. To create a template catalog or to use an existing template catalog in line mode, specify the name of the template catalog with the TC command. If you specify a one-level name, the template catalog is in the WORK data library. If you specify a two-level name, the template catalog is assumed to be stored in a permanent SAS data library. See the TDEF command for details on defining templates.

You can specify TC as a line-mode command and as an option in the PROC GREPLAY statement.

TEMPLATE Command

TEMPLATE *templatename;*

Use the TEMPLATE command in line mode to specify the name of a template from the current template catalog to use for template replays. If you specify a template that is not in the template catalog, PROC GREPLAY issues an error message. You must specify a template catalog before you specify the template. For more information on templates, see **Example: Using the Template Facility in Full-Screen Mode**. See the TDEF command for details on defining templates.

You can specify TEMPLATE as both a line-mode command and as an option in the PROC GREPLAY statement.

Information Commands

Information commands are those in which you get information about the current status of certain PROC GREPLAY option values.

LIST Command

LIST IGOUT | TC | TEMPLATE | CC | CMAP;

In line mode, the LIST command is used in conjunction with the IGOUT, TC, TEMPLATE, CC, and CMAP commands to list the graphs in the IGOUT catalog, the templates in the template catalog, the values of the current template, the color maps in a color map catalog, or the values of a color map.

To determine the contents of the current IGOUT catalog, you can enter the following command:

    list igout;

Output 20.2 shows an example of a list you can receive.

Output 20.2   Line Mode List of the Contents of the Current Catalog

```
NOTE: graphs on MYLIB.GRAFCAT

      NAME           DESCRIPTION

   1  PLOT1      I   1986 SALES by REGION
   2  PLOT2      I   1986 COST by REGION
   3  PLOT3      I   1986 REVENUE by REGION
   4  CHART1     I   Bar chart of SALES, COST, REVENUE
   5  G5         D   Dependent version of PLOT1
   6  G6         D   Dependent version of PLOT2
   7  G7         D   Dependent version of PLOT3
   8  G8         D   Dependent version of CHART1
```

The names and descriptions of the graphs in the catalog are listed. In addition, the type of each graph (dependent or independent) is shown. For more information on dependent and independent-type graphs, see "SAS/GRAPH Graphics Output." If the template catalog contains both templates and color maps, only templates are listed.

To determine the contents of the current template catalog, you can enter the following command:

    list tc;

Output 20.3 shows an example of a list you can receive.

Output 20.3   Line Mode List of the Contents of the Current Template
Catalog

```
NOTE: catalog members: MYLIB.TEMPCAT

   NAME              DESCRIPTION

   ADD2              Fancy layout, 12 graphs per page
   EOM               End-of-month cost reporting layout
   LOGO              Standard layout w/corporate LOGO panel
   T1                Standard ONE-panel template
   T2                Standard TWO-panel template
   T4                Standard FOUR-panel template
```

To determine the values of the variables in the current template, you can enter
the following command:

```
list template;
```

Output 20.4 shows an example of a list you can receive.

Output 20.4   Line Mode List of the Values for the Current Template

```
LOGO           Standard layout w/corporate LOGO panel

Pan Clp Color      Ll-x  Ll-y  Ul-x  Ul-y  Ur-x  Ur-y  Lr-x  Lr-y

0       WHITE       0.0   0.0   0.0 100.0 100.0 100.0 100.0    0.0
1       WHITE      70.0   0.0  70.0  20.0 100.0  20.0 100.0    0.0
```

To determine the contents of the current color map catalog, you can enter the
following command:

```
list cc;
```

Output 20.5 shows an example of a list you can receive.

Output 20.5   Line Mode List of the Contents of the Current Color Map
Catalog

```
NOTE: catalog members: MYLIB.COLORCAT

   NAME              DESCRIPTION

   CGAMAP            Map from CGA card to ZETA887 hardcopy
   EGAMAP            From standard names to MATRIX QCR
   EGAMAP1           From standard names to MATRIX QCR
   EGAMAP2           Map from EGA card to ZETA887 hardcopy
   EGAMAP3           Map from EGA card to MATRIX QCR
   QCRMAP            From standard names to MATRIX QCR
   QMSMAP            From standard names to QMS LASER
```

To determine the values of the variables in the current color map, you can enter the following command:

```
list cmap;
```

Output 20.6 shows an example of a list you can receive.

Output 20.6   Line Mode List of the Values for the Current Color Map

```
QCRMAP          From standard names to MATRIX QCR

        FROM            TO
    1   C1              CYAN
    2   C2              WHITE
    3   C3              MAGENTA
    4   C4              GRAY33
    5   C5              GRAY36
    6   C6              GRAY39
    7   C7              GRAY42
    8   C8              GRAY45
    9   C9              GRAY48
   10   C10             GRAY51
```

? Command

? options;

Use the ? command to inquire about the current values of certain PROC GREPLAY options. Valid values for *options* include IGOUT, GOUT, TC, CMAP, CC, TEMPLATE, and DEV. The following examples illustrate the use of the ? command in line mode:

```
? igout;        /* What is the current igout catalog?     */
? template;     /* What is the current template?          */
? device;       /* What device has been specified?        */
? cc;           /* What is the current color map catalog? */
? cmap;         /* What is the current color map?         */
```

The procedure returns the appropriate information or a message indicating that a value has not been specified for that option.

Replay Commands

Replay commands allow you to replay or preview graphs or templates in your template catalogs.

REPLAY Command

REPLAY *replay list* | _LAST_ | _ALL_;
PLAY *replay list* | _LAST_ | _ALL_;

You can use the REPLAY (or PLAY) command in line mode to tell GREPLAY which graphs from the current IGOUT catalog to select for replay. Use the IGOUT command to specify the IGOUT catalog.

When you use the REPLAY command in line mode, you specify the keyword REPLAY followed by items in a *replay list*. The replay list can contain graph numbers, graph names, or both. You can reference an individual graph by its name or number. If you want to replay all the graphs in the current IGOUT catalog, you can specify the keyword _ALL_ following the REPLAY command. If you want to replay the last graph in the current IGOUT catalog, you can specify the keyword _LAST_ following the REPLAY command.

Suppose your IGOUT catalog looks like the list in **Output 20.7**.

Output 20.7   Line Mode List of the Graphs in Catalog MYLIB.GRAFCAT

```
NOTE: graphs on MYLIB.GRAFCAT

    NAME          DESCRIPTION
 1  PLOT1    I    1986 SALES by REGION
 2  PLOT2    I    1986 COST by REGION
 3  PLOT3    I    1986 REVENUE by REGION
 4  CHART1   I    Bar chart of SALES, COST, REVENUE
 5  G5       D    Dependent version of PLOT1
 6  G6       D    Dependent version of PLOT2
 7  G7       D    Dependent version of PLOT3
 8  G8       D    Dependent version of CHART1
```

To select the first graph by number, you can use the command:

```
replay 1;
```

To select the third, first, and fourth graphs, in that order, you can use the command:

```
replay 3 1 4;
```

To select the first, second, and fourth graphs by name, you can specify the following statement and graphs PLOT1, PLOT2, and CHART1 will be replayed in that order:

```
replay plot1 plot2 chart1;
```

You can mix graph names and numbers within a command. For example, the following command is valid:

```
replay chart1 1 g5;
```

The REPLAY command can also be used to select all graphs in the IGOUT catalog for replay. Use the _ALL_ keyword for the replay list:

```
replay _all_;
```

If any graphs in the replay list are not found in the IGOUT catalog, PROC GREPLAY issues a message indicating that they are not found, and then replays the valid graph selections.

To select a range of graphs to be replayed, you can specify the following command:

```
replay 1 to 4;
```

To reverse the order of replay, specify

```
replay 4 to 1;
```

When you are replaying a range of graphs, the default increment is one. If you want to replay every third graph, for example, you can specify the increment as follows:

```
replay 10 to 40 by 3;
```

or

```
replay 40 to 10 by -3;
```

Note that if a group lies within a range and it is selected along with some or all of its members, then the selected members are replayed twice.

TREPLAY Command

TREPLAY *template replay list;*
TPLAY *template replay list;*

The TREPLAY (or TPLAY) command is used in line mode to select graphs for template replays. Use the TC and TEMPLATE commands to specify the template catalog and template to be used.

When you are in line mode and want to replay a template containing a graph, you specify the keyword TREPLAY followed by a template replay list. A *template replay list* is made up of one or more select pairs. A *select pair* has the form:

panel number:graph name

or

panel number:graph number

where

panel number
    indicates the panel on the current template in which to place the graph indicated by *graph name* or *graph number*.

graph name
    gives the name of the graph to be placed in the template panel.

graph number
    gives the number of the graph to be placed in the template panel.

The template replay list can contain any number of select pairs. A graph can appear in more than one panel. A panel can be referenced more than one time.
    If you specify the command

```
treplay 1:plot1 2:plot2 3:chart1;
```

PLOT1 will be placed in panel 1 of the current template, PLOT2 will be placed in panel 2, and CHART1 will be placed in panel 3. You can use graph numbers in place of graph names. The following command produces the same results:

```
treplay 1:1 2:2 3:chart1;
```

As shown above, you can mix graph names and graph numbers within the same command.
    To display the same graph in several panels of a template, you could use the command

```
treplay 1:plot1 2:plot1 3:plot1;
```

Graph PLOT1 appears three times on the page.
    To plot several graphs in the same template panel, you could use the following command:

```
treplay 1:plot1 1:plot2;
```

If you do not specify clipping for panel 1, then PLOT1 and PLOT2 both appear in panel 1 of the template. Otherwise, only the first graph specified, PLOT1, appears. See **Template Design Screen** for more information on clipping.

PREVIEW Command

PREVIEW *template list;*

Use the PREVIEW command to preview a template. The template is shown on the device currently active (see **DEVICE Command**). You can preview any template in the current template catalog. Use the TC and TEMPLATE commands to specify the template catalog and template. The template list can be made up of one or more template names from the current template catalog, or it can be the keyword _ALL_. For the above example of the LIST command, the following preview commands are valid:

```
preview logo;    /* Preview template named LOGO          */
preview t1 logo; /* Preview templates T1 and LOGO        */
preview _all_;   /* Preview all templates in the current */
                 /* template catalog                     */
```

Press END or ENTER to go from template to template.

Change Commands

Change commands are those you use to rearrange, rename, delete, or copy information in your template and color map catalogs.

GROUP Command

GROUP *replay list;*

Use the GROUP command in line mode to change the order of graphs in the current IGOUT catalog (previously specified with the IGOUT command). With the GROUP command, you can select and group graphic displays in a logical order and then replay several graphs at one time.

When you use the GROUP command in line mode, you specify the keyword GROUP followed by a replay list. A *replay list* contains one or more graphs. (See **REPLAY Command** for more information on specifying a replay list.) A group is created with this ordering, and only one group at a time can be created. For example, suppose your catalog looks like the one shown in **Output 20.8**.

Output 20.8   Line Mode List of the Graphs in MYLIB.GRAFCAT

```
NOTE: graphs on MYLIB.GRAFCAT

    NAME        DESCRIPTION

  1 PLOT1    I  1986 SALES by REGION
  2 PLOT2    I  1986 COST by REGION
  3 PLOT3    I  1986 REVENUE by REGION
  4 CHART1   I  Bar chart of SALES, COST, REVENUE
  5 G5       D  Dependent version of PLOT1
  6 G6       D  Dependent version of PLOT2
  7 G7       D  Dependent version of PLOT3
  8 G8       D  Dependent version of CHART1
```

If you specify

```
group plot1 plot2 plot3 chart1;
```

then your graphs will be grouped together. If you then specify the LIST IGOUT command, the catalog has been changed as shown in **Output 20.9**.

Output 20.9   Line Mode List of Graphs after Grouping

```
NOTE: graphs on MYLIB.GRAFCAT

    NAME          DESCRIPTION

  1 G5        D   Dependent version of PLOT1
  2 G6        D   Dependent version of PLOT2
  3 G7        D   Dependent version of PLOT3
  4 G8        D   Dependent version of CHART1

  5 ********      *** new group ***
  6 PLOT1     I   1986 SALES by REGION
  7 PLOT2     I   1986 COST by REGION
  8 PLOT3     I   1986 REVENUE by REGION
  9 CHART1    I   Bar chart of SALES, COST, REVENUE
```

Similarly, if your IGOUT catalog looks like the one shown in **Output 20.8** and you specify the GROUP command

```
group plot1 g5 plot2 g6;
```

then if you specify the LIST IGOUT command, your catalog will look like the one shown in **Output 20.10**.

Output 20.10   Line Mode List of Graphs after Grouping

```
NOTE: graphs on MYLIB.GRAFCAT

    NAME          DESCRIPTION

  1 PLOT3     I   1986 REVENUE by REGION
  2 CHART1    I   Bar chart of SALES, COST, REVENUE
  3 G7        D   Dependent version of PLOT3
  4 G8        D   Dependent version of CHART1

  5 ********      *** new group ***
  6 PLOT1     I   1986 SALES by REGION
  7 G5        D   Dependent version of PLOT1
  8 PLOT2     I   1986 COST by REGION
  9 G6        D   Dependent version of PLOT2
```

The graphs have been grouped according to your specifications, and you can replay each group later with the REPLAY command.

MODIFY Command

MODIFY *modify list;*

Use the MODIFY command in line mode to modify the names and descriptions of graphs in the current IGOUT catalog (previously specified with the IGOUT command).

When you use the MODIFY command in line mode, you specify the keyword MODIFY followed by a modify list. A *modify list* contains one or more modify pairs. A *modify pair* has the following format:

graph/NAME=*name* DES='*description*' BYLINE='*BYline information*'

where

graph
> is either a graph name or graph number in the current IGOUT catalog.

name
> specifies the new name for the graph.

'description'
> is a string that describes the graph that is created. The description can be forty characters or less and must be enclosed in quotes.

'BYline information'
> is a string that can be used for additional information. The string can be forty characters or less and must be enclosed in quotes.

You can specify NAME=, DES=, BYLINE=, or any combination, but you must specify at least one in each modify pair.

Suppose your catalog looks like the one shown in **Output 20.10**. You can specify a name and description for the first group, and new names for graphs 3 and 5 using the MODIFY command. For example, if you specify

```
modify 1/name=group1 des='This is the first group'
       3/name=plot1d
       5/name=plot2d;
```

the values in the catalog are changed. If you then specify a LIST IGOUT command, your list will look like the one shown in **Output 20.11**.

Output 20.11   Line Mode List of Graphs after Using the MODIFY Command

```
NOTE: graphs on MYLIB.GRAFCAT

      NAME            DESCRIPTION

  1  PLOT3     I     1986 REVENUE by REGION
  2  CHART1    I     Bar chart of SALES, COST, REVENUE
  3  G7        D     Dependent version of PLOT3
  4  G8        D     Dependent version of CHART1

  5  GROUP1          This is the first group
  6  PLOT1     I     1986 SALES by REGION
  7  PLOT1D    D     Dependent version of PLOT1
  8  PLOT2     I     1986 COST by REGION
  9  PLOT2D    D     Dependent version of PLOT2
```

The following MODIFY command renames graphs 8 and 9:

```
modify 8/name=plot3d 9/name=chart1d;
```

A subsequent LIST IGOUT command shows the list that appears in **Output 20.12**.

Output 20.12   Line Mode List of Graphs after Using the MODIFY Command

```
NOTE: graphs on MYLIB.GRAFCAT

    NAME            DESCRIPTION

  1  PLOT3    I    1986 REVENUE by REGION
  2  CHART1   I    Bar chart of SALES, COST, REVENUE
  3  PLOT3D   D    Dependent version of PLOT3
  4  CHART1D  D    Dependent version of CHART1

  5  GROUP1         This is the first group
  6  PLOT1    I    1986 SALES by REGION
  7  PLOT1D   D    Dependent version of PLOT1
  8  PLOT2    I    1986 COST by REGION
  9  PLOT2D   D    Dependent version of PLOT2
```

DELETE Command

> DELETE *replay list*;
> DEL *replay list*;

The DELETE (or DEL) command deletes graphs from the current IGOUT catalog (previously specified with the IGOUT command). When you use the DELETE command in line mode, you specify the keyword DELETE and specify a replay list. A *replay list* can contain graph names, graph numbers, or both. See **REPLAY Command** for more information on specifying a replay list. You can delete a group of graphs by specifying the keyword DELETE followed by the group name or group number. In addition, you can use the keyword _ALL_ to delete all graphs in a catalog.

Note: you are **not** prompted to confirm your request to delete graphs. You should be careful when using the DELETE command.

If the current IGOUT catalog looks like the one shown in **Output 20.12**, then each of the following examples is valid for the DELETE command:

```
delete plot1;      /* delete PLOT1 from the IGOUT catalog       */
delete 2 3;        /* delete the second and third graphs        */
delete group1      /* delete the graphs in GROUP1               */
delete _all_;      /* delete all graphs from the IGOUT catalog  */
```

TDELETE Command

> TDELETE *template list*;
> TDEL *template list*;

The TDELETE (or TDEL) command deletes templates from the current template catalog (previously specified with the TC command). To delete one or more templates from the template catalog, you specify the keyword TDELETE followed by the template names or the keyword _ALL_.

Note: you are **not** prompted to confirm your request to delete templates. You should be careful when using the TDELETE command.

Suppose your template catalog looks like the one shown in **Output 20.13**.

Output 20.13   Line Mode List of Templates in MYLIB.TEMPCAT

```
NOTE: catalog members: MYLIB.TEMPCAT

    NAME              DESCRIPTION

    ADD2              Fancy layout, 12 graphs per page
    EOM               End-of-month cost reporting layout
    LOGO              Standard layout w/corporate LOGO panel
    T1                Standard ONE-panel template
    T2                Standard TWO-panel template
    T4                Standard FOUR-panel template
```

Each of the following examples is a valid form of the TDELETE command:

```
tdelete add2;     /* delete ADD2 from the template catalog       */
tdelete add2 eom;/* delete ADD and EOM from the template catalog  */
tdelete _all_;    /* delete all templates from the template catalog */
```

COPY Command

COPY *replay list;*

The COPY command copies graphs from the current IGOUT catalog to the current GOUT catalog. Use the IGOUT and GOUT commands to specify these catalogs. You can copy individual graphs, entire groups, or the entire catalog. To copy graphs, groups of graphs, or catalogs from an IGOUT catalog to a GOUT catalog, specify the keyword COPY followed by a replay list. A replay list contains a name for each graph or group of graphs. See **REPLAY Command** for more information on specifying a replay list.

Suppose the current IGOUT catalog looks like the one shown in **Output 20.14**.

Output 20.14   Line Mode List of Graphs in MYLIB.GRAFCAT

```
NOTE: graphs on MYLIB.GRAFCAT

      NAME              DESCRIPTION

   1  PLOT3       I     1986 REVENUE by REGION
   2  CHART1      I     Bar chart of SALES, COST, REVENUE
   3  PLOT3D      D     Dependent version of PLOT3
   4  CHART1D     D     Dependent version of CHART1

   5  GROUP1            This is the first group
   6  PLOT1       I     1986 SALES by REGION
   7  PLOT1D      D     Dependent version of PLOT1
   8  PLOT2       I     1986 COST by REGION
   9  PLOT2D      D     Dependent version of PLOT2
```

Then each of the examples below is a valid form of the COPY command:

```
copy plot1;  /* copy PLOT1 from IGOUT catalog to GOUT catalog  */
copy group1; /* copy GROUP1 from IGOUT catalog to GOUT catalog */
copy _all_;  /* copy all graphs from IGOUT to GOUT catalog     */
```

The COPY command does not cause two copies of the same graph to be made in a catalog.

TCOPY Command

TCOPY *templatename;*
TCOPY *libref.catalog.templatename.*TEMPLATE;

The TCOPY command copies templates from one catalog to another. To copy a template, first use the TC command to define the target catalog (the one into which the template will be copied). Then specify the keyword TCOPY and the name of the template you want copied. For example, if you want to copy a template called FOURBOX from the template catalog MYLIB.MYCAT to the catalog YOURLIB.YOURCAT, first use the TC command to specify that the target catalog is YOURLIB.YOURCAT. Then enter the following command:

```
tcopy mylib.mycat.fourbox.template;
```

If you then use the LIST TC command to list the contents of the catalog YOURLIB.YOURCAT, you will see that the template FOURBOX has been copied into the catalog. If a template named FOURBOX already exists in the target catalog, a suffix will be added to the name of the new template to avoid duplication.

If the source catalog is a temporary one, you must specify a libref of WORK for the catalog. For example, to copy the template TWOBOX from a temporary catalog named TEMPTEMP, enter

```
tcopy work.temptemp.twobox.template;
```

To duplicate a template in an existing catalog, you can enter the command

TCOPY *templatename;*

where *templatename* is the name of the template to be duplicated. SAS/GRAPH adds a suffix to the name of the duplicated template to avoid a name conflict with the original template.

CCOPY Command

CCOPY *colormapname;*
CCOPY *libref.catalog.colormapname.*CMAP;

The CCOPY command copies color maps from one catalog to another. To copy a color map, first use the CC command to define the target catalog (the one into which the color map will be copied). Then specify the keyword CCOPY and the name of the color map you want copied. For example, to copy a color map called ZETA887 from the catalog MYLIB.MYCAT to the catalog YOURLIB.YOURCAT, first use the CC command to specify that the name of the target catalog is YOURLIB.YOURCAT. Then enter the following command:

```
ccopy mylib.mycat.zeta887.cmap;
```

If you then use the LIST CC command to list the contents of the catalog YOURLIB.YOURCAT, you will see that the color map ZETA887 has been copied into the catalog. If a color map named ZETA887 already exists in the target catalog, a suffix will be added to the name of the new color map to avoid duplication.

If the source catalog is a temporary one, you must specify a libref of WORK for the catalog. For example, to copy the color map TEK4107 from a temporary catalog named TEMPTEMP, enter

```
ccopy work.temptemp.tek4107.cmap;
```

To duplicate a color map in an existing catalog, you can enter the command

CCOPY *colormapname*;

where *colormapname* is the name of the color map to be duplicated. SAS/GRAPH adds a suffix to the name of the duplicated color map to avoid a name conflict with the original color map.

TDEF Command

TDEF *options*;

You can use the TDEF command to define or modify templates in line mode. Use the TC and TEMPLATE commands to specify the template catalog and template name. The general form of the TDEF command is as follows:

```
tdef templatename       /* template name           */
     des='description'   /* optional description    */

     /* The following section of the command shows
        options that are not required. This section
        may be repeated for each panel to be defined
        by this TDEF command */

     panel number /      /* panel number on template  */
     llx=                /* lower left corner x        */
     lly=                /* lower left corner y        */
     ulx=                /* upper left  corner x       */
     uly=                /* upper left  corner y       */
     urx=                /* upper right corner x       */
     ury=                /* upper right corner y       */
     lrx=                /* lower right corner x       */
     lry=                /* lower right corner y       */
     scalex=             /* scale amount for x coordinates */
     scaley=             /* scale amount for y coordinates */
     xlatex=             /* xlate amount for x coordinates */
     xlatey=             /* xlate amount for y coordinates */
     rotate=             /* rotate amount for panel    */
     color=              /* color for panel border     */
     clip                /* clip panel                 */
     delete(del)         /* delete panel specified     */
     copy=               /* panel to copy              */
     def;                /* set up default panel       */
```

The only required portion of this command is the template name. However, if you use the TDEF command and specify only the template name and none of the other options, nothing happens.

To use the TDEF command you must have previously specified the name of a template catalog in a PROC GREPLAY statement or with a TC command. If the template name you specify with the TDEF command is not in the current template catalog, then the template will be created. If the template name is already in the current template catalog, then you can use the TDEF command to modify or make additions to that template.

Suppose you want to modify the description of an existing template or create a new template that has a description and no other information. You can use the following TDEF command:

TDEF *templatename* DES=*'description string'*;

You can then use the LIST TC command to get a list of the templates in the template catalog. The list will reflect the changes or additions you made.

Suppose you want to create a template called TEMPL1 with the description "One panel in lower left corner." You want the template to contain one panel whose corners contain the coordinates 0,0 0,25 25,25 and 25,0 (as defined on the imaginary screen used to create templates). You also want the panel to be drawn with a blue border. You can use the following TDEF command to create TEMPL1:

```
tdef templ1 des='One panel in lower left corner'
     1/llx=0   lly=0
       ulx=0   uly=25
       urx=25  ury=25
       lrx=25  lry=0
       color=blue;
```

Now you want to see what the template panel looks like. Be sure that you have specified a device with the DEVICE command; then specify

```
preview templ1;
```

The template TEMPL1 is displayed as shown in **Screen 20.40**.

Screen 20.40   Displaying One Template with the PREVIEW Command

Alternatively, you could create the panel with the following TDEF command:

```
tdef templ1 des='One panel in lower left corner'
1/scalex=.5 scaley=.5 xlatex=-25 xlatey=-25
   color=blue;
```

If you do not specify all coordinates, PROC GREPLAY supplies a default value of 0.0 or 100.0, depending upon which points you did not specify, according to the following scheme:

llx=0.0   ulx=0.0   urx=100.0 lrx=100.0

lly=0.0   uly=100.0 ury=100.0 lry=0.0

This scheme produces a template the size of the screen that can be used to produce multiple copies of a graph in one catalog. These default values are supplied when TDEF is used with any of the options except DEL and COPY. If the SCALE, XLATE, or ROTATE options are used, the default values are supplied and the transformations applied in the following order: SCALE, XLATE, ROTATE. If you want to create a screen-size panel without clipping or a border, use the DEF option:

```
tdef templ1 1/def;
```

Now that you have created a template, suppose you want to add an additional panel. The panel will be of the same size as the last, but you want it shifted over to the lower right corner of the screen. You can specify the following TDEF command:

```
tdef templ1
    2/copy=1        /* to create panel 2, copy panel 1      */
      xlatex=75;    /* translate over to lower right corner */
```

To see what the template looks like with panels 1 and 2 in place, be sure that you have specified a device with the DEVICE command, then specify:

```
preview templ1;
```

The new template is shown in **Screen 20.41**.

If you want to add two panels between the two panels previously defined for a total of four panels along the bottom half of the screen, you can specify the following TDEF command:

```
tdef templ1
    3/copy=1     /* panel 3 like panel 1 but xlated right 25% */
      xlatex=25
    4/copy=1     /* panel 4 like panel 1 but xlated right 50% */
      xlatex=50;
```

To see what the template looks like, specify

```
preview templ1;
```

and the template shown in **Screen 20.42** is displayed.

Screen 20.41   Displaying Two Templates with the PREVIEW Command

Screen 20.42   Displaying Four Templates with the PREVIEW Command

If you decide to delete the fourth panel, you can specify the following TDEF command:

```
tdef templ1
     4/delete;
```

There is an order of precedence to the individual panel operations. If you specify DELETE for an individual panel, the panel is deleted, and any other operations for that panel are ignored. If you specify COPY, the source panel is copied to the target panel, and then the rest of the operations for that panel are performed. The panel coordinates are copied into the panel **after** any COPY operation and **before** any of the transformation operations are performed.

CDEF Command

CDEF *colormapname* DES='*description*'n / FROM:TO;

The CDEF command is used to define or modify color maps in line mode. The general format of the CDEF command is as shown above, where

colormapname
is the name of an existing or new color map (up to eight characters long).

'*description*'
is a description of the color map (up to forty characters long and enclosed in single quotes).

n
is the number of a color pair.

FROM
is the color to be mapped.

TO
is the new color that replaces the FROM color.

To use the CDEF command you must have previously specified the name of a color map catalog in a PROC GREPLAY statement or with the CC command. If the color map name you specify with the CDEF command is not in the current color map catalog, then the color map will be created. If the color map name is already in the current color map catalog, then you can use the CDEF command to modify or make additions to that color map.

Suppose you want to modify the description of an existing color map or create a new color map that has a description and no other information. You can use the following CDEF command:

CDEF *colormapname* DES='*description*';

You can then use the LIST CC command to get a list of the color maps in the color map catalog. The list will reflect the changes or additions you made.

Suppose you want to create a color map called MAP2. You can use the following commands to create the color map:

```
cdef map2 des='map of new colors'
     1/black:white
     2/red:green
     3/blue:cyan
     4/cx000000:yellow;
```

where the command CDEF is followed by the name of a new color map catalog; DES= is followed by a description of the new color map catalog;

1/BLACK:WHITE indicates that in the first color pair, black is mapped to white, in the second color pair, red is mapped to green; and so on. You can specify up to 256 color pairs in a color map. If you specify

```
list cmap;
```

the color map shown in **Output 20.15** is displayed.

Output 20.15   Color Map for MAP2

```
MAP2           map of new colors
     FROM      TO
1    BLACK     WHITE
2    RED       GREEN
3    BLUE      CYAN
4    CX000000  YELLOW
```

NOBYLINE Command

```
NOBYLINE;
```

Use the NOBYLINE command to specify that BY statement information, which is normally displayed directly beneath the primary description of a graph, should not be displayed.

BYLINE Command

```
BYLINE;
```

Use the BYLINE command to specify that BY statement information should be displayed.

Operation Commands

The operation commands direct the operation of PROC GREPLAY.

FS Command

```
FS;
```

Use the FS command to request that GREPLAY switch from line mode to full-screen mode. If full-screen mode is not available, PROC GREPLAY issues a message and remains in line mode. If full-screen mode is available, the PROC GREPLAY screen is displayed. If you are in full-screen mode and want to return to line mode, you can press the NOFS key and return to line mode.

QUIT, STOP, or END Commands

```
QUIT;
STOP;
END;
```

You can specify the QUIT, STOP, or END commands to terminate the GREPLAY procedure when you are in line mode. You can also terminate the procedure by specifying another PROC or DATA statement.

SAMPLE TEMPLATES

A library of sample templates is included with SAS/GRAPH software. Three of these sample templates are represented in **Figure 20.1**. To access the sample templates, specify SASHELP.TEMPLT as your catalog name in full-screen or line mode. To view the templates, refer to the section **Example: Using the Template Facility in Full-Screen Mode**, then issue a PROC GREPLAY statement and press ENTER. When the PROC GREPLAY screen is displayed, enter the template catalog name in the TC field (you can also specify the template catalog with the TC= option in the PROC GREPLAY statement in full-screen mode and with the TC command in line mode). When you press the TC key, the template catalog is displayed, listing the templates in the catalog. To view a template, place an S beside the template you want to see and submit the PREVIEW command or press the PREVIEW key. The template you selected will be displayed.

In line mode, specify the following:

```
proc greplay;
    tc yyyyyy.yyyyy;
run;
```

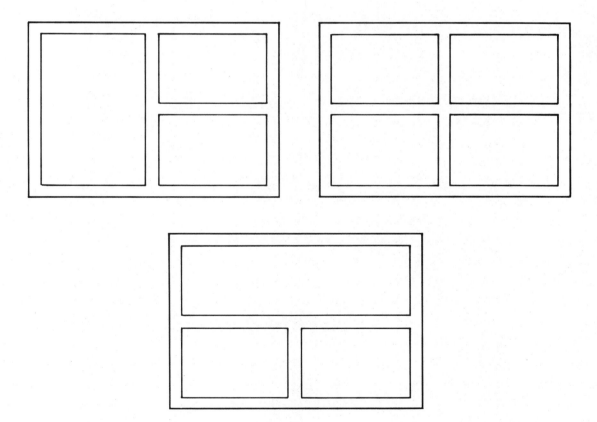

Figure 20.1   Sample Templates

454

The GSLIDE
Procedure

ABSTRACT

The GSLIDE procedure produces graphic output containing lines of text. You can specify TITLE, FOOTNOTE, and NOTE statements to produce the desired text. You can also use an ANNOTATE= data set as input to the procedure.

INTRODUCTION

The following TITLE, FOOTNOTE, and NOTE statements used with PROC GSLIDE illustrate the use of various options to place text on the display area. These statements produce **Output 21.1**.

```
title1 h=2 f=swiss c=white 'Use of FRAME and BOX= Options';
footnote1 ' ';
footnote2 h=1 f=none 'Footnotes are Below the Frame';
proc gslide cframe=white lframe=4 wframe=3;
   note h=1.5;
   note j=c h=1.5 c=white f=triplex box=1 c=white
        'Box without specified spacing';
   note h=1.5;
   note j=c h=1.5 c=white f=triplex box=1 bs=2
        'Box with specified spacing';
run;
```

SPECIFICATIONS

The following statements can be used with PROC GSLIDE:

> **PROC GSLIDE** *options;*
>   **TITLE***n options* 'text';
>   **FOOTNOTE***n options* 'text';
>   **NOTE** *options* 'text';

PROC GSLIDE Statement

> PROC GSLIDE *options;*

You can specify the following options in the PROC GSLIDE statement. If you specify CFRAME=, LFRAME=, or WFRAME=, you do not need to specify FRAME.

ANNOTATE=*SASdataset*
ANNO=*SASdataset*
> specifies the data set to be used for annotation. The data set must be an ANNOTATE= type data set containing the appropriate Annotate variables. (See "ANNOTATE= Data Sets" for details.)

BORDER
> draws a border around the display area, outside of titles and footnotes. Unlike the BORDER option in a GOPTIONS statement, the GSLIDE BORDER option remains in effect only for the duration of the procedure.

CFRAME=*color*
> specifies the color of the frame outline.

DESCRIPTION=*'string'*
DES=*'string'*
> specifies a descriptive string, up to forty characters long, that appears in the description field of PROC GREPLAY's master menu. If you omit the DESCRIPTION= option, the Description field of PROC GREPLAY's master menu will contain a description assigned by SAS/GRAPH.

FRAME
> causes a window on the screen to be outlined inside of titles and footnotes.

GOUT=*SAScatalog*
> specifies the name of a SAS catalog in which to save the output produced by PROC GSLIDE for later replay. If you want to create a permanent graphics catalog, you must specify a two-level name. If you do not specify the GOUT= option, catalog entries are written to the default catalog GSEG, which is erased at the end of your session. See "SAS/GRAPH Graphics Output" for more details.

LFRAME=*linetype*
> specifies the line type (1-46, as shown in "Enhancing Your Graphics Output Designs") to use for drawing the frame outline. The default line type is 1, a solid line.

NAME=*'string'*
> specifies a descriptive string, up to eight characters long, that appears in the Name field of PROC GREPLAY's master menu. If you omit the NAME= option, the Name field of PROC GREPLAY's master menu contains the procedure name.

WFRAME=*width*

specifies the width (in number of strokes) of the frame outline. Refer to "Enhancing Your Graphics Output Designs" for more information on line widths.

FOOTNOTE Statement

FOOTNOTE*n options 'text'*;

You can specify FOOTNOTE statements to produce up to ten specified lines at the bottom of the slide. You can use options in the FOOTNOTE statement to select color, type font, and height of the text. For a complete description of the FOOTNOTE statement, see "Enhancing Your Graphics Output Text."

NOTE Statement

NOTE *options 'text'*;

You can use NOTE statements with PROC GSLIDE to specify text to appear after any title lines and before any footnote lines. In a NOTE statement, you can specify the options described in "Enhancing Your Graphics Output Text." NOTE statements remain in effect only for the duration of the GSLIDE procedure. Text specified in a NOTE statement is left-aligned on the display (unless you specify the J= option to change the default alignment).

The keyword NOTE is not followed by a number. You must give your NOTE statements following the PROC GSLIDE statement in the order you want them to appear in the slide, unless you specify their placement with the MOVE= option. (Refer to "Enhancing Your Graphics Output Text" for more information on the MOVE= option.)

TITLE Statement

TITLE*n options 'text'*;

You can specify TITLE statements to produce up to ten specified lines at the top of the slide. You can use the options in the TITLE statement to select color, type font, and height of the text. For a complete description of the TITLE statement, see "Enhancing Your Graphics Output Text."

EXAMPLE

Using an ANNOTATE= Data Set with PROC GSLIDE

In the example below, an ANNOTATE= data set is created and used as input to PROC GSLIDE. The result is shown in **Output 21.2**. (See "ANNOTATE= Data Sets" for more information on creating ANNOTATE= data sets.)

```
goptions penmounts=255 colors=(none);
data back;
   length color $8.;
   xsys='3';
   ysys='3';
   do i=1 to 200;
      line=1;
      style='solid   ';
      color='cx0000' || put ((i - 1), hex2.);
      function='move     ';
```

```
            x=0;
            y=(201 - i) * 100 / 200;
            output;
            line=0;
            function='bar      ';
            x=100;
            y=(200 - i) * 100 / 200;
            output;
        end;
    run;

    title1 h=4 color=white f=swiss 'Shaded Backgrounds';
    title2 ' ';
    title3 h=2 color=white f=swiss 'Created with';
    title4 h=2 color=white f=swiss 'User-defined Colors';

    proc gslide annotate=back;
    run;
```

Output 21.1   Using FRAME and BOX= Options: PROC GSLIDE

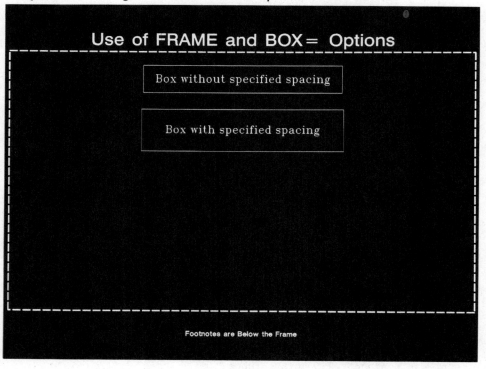

Output 21.2   Using an ANNOTATE= Data Set: PROC GSLIDE

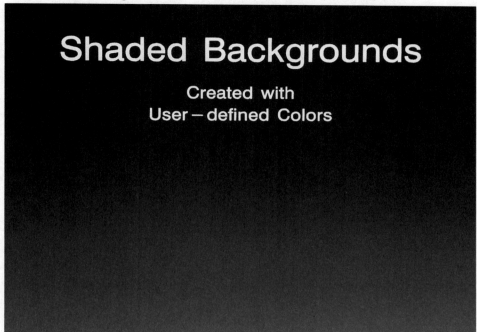

The GTESTIT
Procedure

ABSTRACT

The GTESTIT procedure is a diagnostic tool for testing the installation of SAS/GRAPH software.

INTRODUCTION

You can use PROC GTESTIT to generate a SAS/GRAPH test pattern on your device and to determine whether your device is correctly configured. You can also use PROC GTESTIT to find out how the graphics options (called GOPTIONS) and some device settings are set on your particular device.

SPECIFICATIONS

The only statement used is the PROC GTESTIT statement:

PROC GTESTIT *option*;

PROC GTESTIT Statement

PROC GTESTIT *option*;

You can specify the following option in the PROC GTESTIT statement:

PICTURE | PIC=1
PICTURE | PIC=2

> indicates the number of the test pattern to be displayed. If you specify PICTURE=1, then the test pattern displaying the available colors and patterns is shown. If you specify PICTURE=2, then the test pattern for continuous drawing ability is shown.

EXAMPLE

The following statements produce the log shown in **Output 22.1** and the sample
PROC GTESTIT output in **Output 22.2** and **Output 22.3**:

```
goptions device=pcr4xxl;
proc gtestit;
run;
```

Output 22.1   Log From GTESTIT Procedure

```
NOTE: Copyright(c) 1987 SAS Institute Inc., Cary, NC 27512, U.S.A.
NOTE: SAS (r) Proprietary Software Release 6.xx
      Licensed to SAS INSTITUTE INC., Site xxxxxxxx.

NOTE: AUTOEXEC processing completed.

      1? goptions device=pcr4xxl;
      2? proc gtestit;
      3? run;

D=PCR4XXL  B=1200    R= 40 C= 80 P=256
H=500 W=375 MAX=  0 D=0000000000000000
RF=0000800000000000 S=0000000000000000
OPTS=FD92300000000000 NCOLORS=  7
Background color = BLACK
Color 1 = WHITE
Color 2 = RED
Color 3 = GREEN
Color 4 = BLUE
Color 5 = YELLOW
Color 6 = MAGENTA
Color 7 = CYAN
Ratio = 0.66667
F=1

      4? endsas;

NOTE: SAS Institute Inc., SAS Circle, Box 8000, Cary, NC 27512-8000
```

Output 22.2   Options in Effect and Patterns Available: PROC GTESTIT

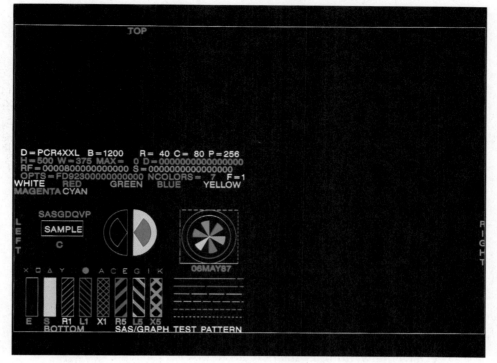

Output 22.3   Test of Line-Drawing Capabilities: PROC GTESTIT

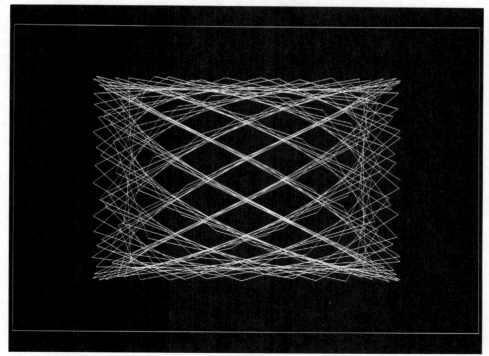

The first pattern (**Output 22.2**) displays device options in effect (by default, or as specified either in a GOPTIONS statement or by the current device entry) and draws a number of patterns. For most devices, the options and patterns appear in the lower left corner of the plot or screen. The second pattern (**Output 22.3**) tests line-drawing capabilities. The options that appear in the first pattern and a description of each are given below:

D=
    specifies the device driver you are using.

B=
    specifies the value of the BAUD= option.

R=
    specifies the number of rows (use the VPOS= option to change this value).

C=
    specifies the number of columns (use the HPOS= option to change this value).

P=
    specifies the total number of colors (foreground and background).

H=
    specifies the height of character cells in pixels.

W=
    specifies the width of character cells in pixels.

MAX=
    specifies the maximum number of vertices that can be processed by a hardware polygon command. If MAX=0, then the number of vertices is unbounded.

D=
    specifies the hardware dashed-line patterns available.

RF=
    specifies the hardware rectangle-fill patterns available.

S=
    specifies the hardware symbols available.

OPTS=
    specifies the other hardware options available.

NCOLORS=
    specifies the number of colors in the COLORS list or the number of foreground colors.

Ratio=
    specifies the aspect ratio of the device.

F=
    specifies the solid fill increment (the number of pixels between "strokes" when doing a solid fill).

An asterisk (*) after the P= or F= options indicates that the value for that option is greater than 999.

Chapter 23

The G3D Procedure

ABSTRACT

The G3D procedure produces three-dimensional graphs of the values of variables that you specify in PLOT or SCATTER statements. A three-dimensional surface graph is produced for the three variables in a PLOT statement. A three-dimensional scatter graph is produced for the three variables that are required in a SCATTER statement; you can also specify size, shape, and color variables for the scatter graph.

INTRODUCTION

Below are three graphs produced by PROC G3D. The first example uses generated data to produce a three-dimensional surface graph called the "cowboy hat." The first plot is drawn using the default value (70 degrees) for both the TILT= and ROTATE= options.

```
goptions cback=black
         colors=(white cyan magenta gold yellow);
data hat;
   do x=-5 to 5 by .25;
      do y=-5 to 5 by .25;
         z=sin(sqrt(x*x + y*y));
         output;
         end;
      end;

title1 c=white f=swiss 'The Cowboy Hat';
```

```
   title2 h=2  angle=90 ' ';
proc g3d data=hat;
   plot y*x=z / ctop=yellow ctext=white;
run;
```

The graph produced by these statements is shown in **Output 23.1**.

You can produce a second graph by specifying new values for the TILT= and ROTATE= options. For example, these statements produce the graph shown in **Output 23.2**.

```
title1 c=white f=swiss 'The Cowboy Hat';
title2 c=white f=swiss 'Tilted and Rotated at a 45-Degree Angle';
title3 h=2 angle=90 ' ';
proc g3d data=hat;
   plot y*x=z / ctop=yellow
                tilt=45
                rotate=45;
                ctext=white;
run;
```

In the next example, the SCATTER statement is used to produce a scatter graph (**Output 23.3**) of the iris species measurement data (Fisher 1936). The data used to produce the graphs are in the SAS Sample Library that is included with SAS/GRAPH software.

```
goptions cback=black
         colors=(white cyan yellow magenta gold);
title1 f=swiss c=white 'Iris Species Classification';
title2 f=swiss c=white 'by Physical Measurement';
title3 f=swiss c=white 'Source: Fisher (1936) Iris Data';
title4 h =2 angle=90 ' ';

footnote1 j=1 ' PETALLEN:'
          m=(11,+0) 'Petal length in MM.'
          m=(60 pct,+0) 'PETALWID:   Petal width in MM.';
footnote2 j=1 ' SEPALLEN:'
          m=(11,+0) 'Sepal length in MM.'
          m=(60 pct,+0) 'Sepal width is not shown';
footnote3 h=2 ' ';
proc g3d data = iris;
   note m=(60,32) c=white 'SPECIES:'
        m=(69,+0) c=yellow 'VIRGINICA'
        m=(69,-1) c=magenta 'VERSICOLOR'
        m=(69,-1) c=gold 'SETOSA';
   scatter petallen * petalwid=sepallen /
           color=colorval ctext=white;
run;
```

Output 23.1   The Cowboy Hat: PROC G3D

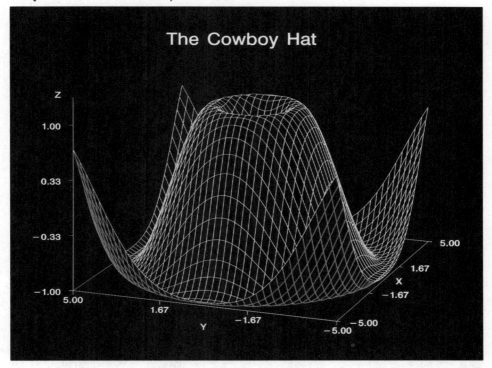

Output 23.2   The Cowboy Hat: PROC G3D Specifying the TILT= and
ROTATE= Options

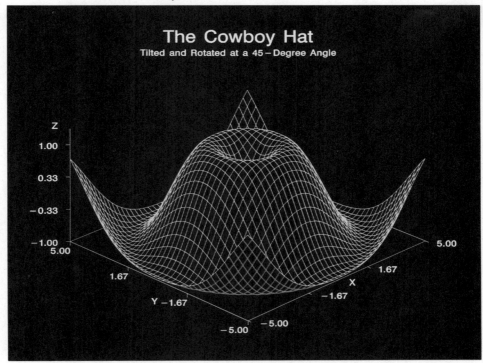

Output 23.3 Three-Dimensional Scatter Graph of Fisher's Iris Data:
PROC G3D

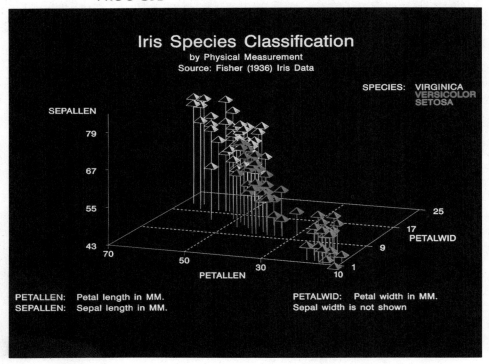

SPECIFICATIONS

The following statements can be used with PROC G3D:

PROC G3D *options*;
   PLOT *yvariable*xvariable*=*zvariable* / *options*;
   SCATTER | SCAT *yvariable*xvariable*=*zvariable* / *options*;
   BY *variables*;
   TITLE*n options 'text'*;
   FOOTNOTE*n options 'text'*;
   NOTE *options 'text'*;

At least one PLOT or SCATTER statement is required.

PROC G3D Statement

   PROC G3D *options*;

You can specify the following options in the PROC G3D statement:

   ANNOTATE=*SASdataset*
   ANNO=*SASdataset*
     specifies the data set to be used for annotation. The data set must be an
     ANNOTATE= type data set containing the appropriate Annotate
     variables. (See "ANNOTATE= Data Sets" for details.)

   DATA=*SASdataset*
     gives the name of the SAS data set to be used by PROC G3D. If you
     omit the DATA= option, PROC G3D uses the most recently created
     SAS data set.

GOUT=*SAScatalog*
> specifies the name of the SAS catalog used to save the output produced by PROC G3D for later replay. See "SAS/GRAPH Graphics Output" for more details. If you do not specify the GOUT= option, catalog entries are written to the default catalog GSEG, which is erased at the end of your session.

BY Statement

BY *variables*;

You can specify the BY statement with PROC G3D to obtain separate analyses on observations defined by the BY variables. When a BY statement appears, the procedure expects the input data set to be sorted in order of the BY variables. If your input data set is not sorted in ascending order, use the SORT procedure with a similar BY statement to sort the data, or, if appropriate, use the BY statement options NOTSORTED or DESCENDING. For more information, see the discussion of the BY statement in "SAS Statements Used in the PROC Step" in the *SAS Language Guide, Release 6.03 Edition*.

FOOTNOTE Statement

FOOTNOTE*n* *options* '*text*';

You can specify FOOTNOTE statements with PROC G3D. For a complete description of the FOOTNOTE statement, see "Enhancing Your Graphics Output Text."

NOTE Statement

NOTE *options* '*text*';

You can specify NOTE statements with PROC G3D. For a complete description of the NOTE statement, see "Enhancing Your Graphics Output Text."

PLOT Statement

PLOT *yvariable*xvariable*=*zvariable* / *options*;

The axis for each variable is shown in **Figure 23.1**.

A PLOT or a SCATTER statement must accompany the PROC G3D statement to request the graphs to be produced. You can include any number of PLOT statements.

You can specify the following options in the PLOT statement after a slash (/). If you do not specify any options, the slash is not needed.

ANNOTATE=*SASdataset*
ANNO=*SASdataset*
> specifies the data set to be used for annotation. The data set must be an ANNOTATE= type data set containing the appropriate Annotate variables. (See "ANNOTATE= Data Sets" for details.)

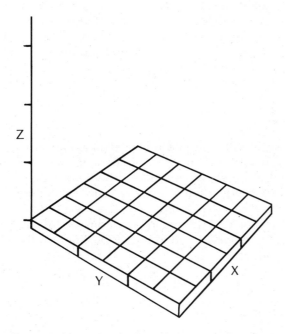

Figure 23.1   The *x*, *y*, and *z* Axes for a Three-Dimensional Surface Graph

CAXIS=*color*
    specifies the color used to draw the axes of the plot. If you do not
    specify the CAXIS= option, the second color in the COLORS= list is
    used to draw the axes. (See "The GOPTIONS Statement" for a
    description of the COLORS= option.)

CBOTTOM=*color*
    specifies the color used to draw the bottom surface of the plot. If you
    do not specify the CBOTTOM= option, the fourth color in the
    COLORS= list is used.

CTEXT=*color*
    specifies the color used to draw all text that appears on the plot.
    Variable names, labels (if any), and tick mark values are drawn using the
    color specified by CTEXT=. If you do not specify the CTEXT= option,
    the first color in the COLORS= list is used to draw text on the plot.
    (See "The GOPTIONS Statement" for a description of the COLORS=
    option.)

CTOP=*color*
    specifies the color used to draw the top surface of the three-dimensional
    plot. If you do not specify the CTOP= option, the third color in the
    COLORS= list is used.

DESCRIPTION=*'string'*
DES=*'string'*
    specifies a descriptive string, up to forty characters long, that appears in
    the Description field of PROC GREPLAY's master menu. If you omit the
    DESCRIPTION= option, the Description field of PROC GREPLAY's
    master menu contains a description assigned by SAS/GRAPH.

GRID
> draws grid lines at each tick mark on all axes.

NAME='*string*'
> specifies a descriptive string, up to eight characters long, that appears in the Name field of PROC GREPLAY's master menu. If you omit the NAME= option, the Name field of PROC GREPLAY's master menu contains the procedure name.

NOAXES
> requests that axes and axis labels not be drawn.

NOLABEL
> requests that tick labels and axis labels not be drawn. The axes and tick marks are still drawn. This is useful if you want to arrange your own tick labels and axis labels using the ANNOTATE= option.

ROTATE=*angle*
ROTATE=*angle1 angle2* . . .
ROTATE=*angle* TO *angle* BY *increment*
> specifies one or more angles at which to rotate the picture about the z axis. The value of *angle* can range from 0 to 90 degrees. The default ROTATE= value is 70 degrees.
>
> When you specify more than one ROTATE= angle, values are paired with TILT= values and several pictures are produced at various angles. See the description of the TILT= option.

SIDE
> produces a side wall for a surface graph.

TILT=*angle*
TILT=*angle1 angle2* . . .
TILT=*angle* TO *angle* BY *increment*
> specifies one or more angles at which to tilt the picture about the y axis. *Angle* values can range from 0 to 90 degrees. The default TILT= value is 70 degrees.
>
> When you specify more than one TILT= angle, values are paired with ROTATE= values (see the description of the ROTATE= option), and several pictures are produced at various angles as if you had specified several PLOT statements. If one list is shorter than the other, the last value in the shorter list is paired with the remaining values in the longer list.

XTICKNUM=*n*
YTICKNUM=*n*
ZTICKNUM=*n*
> specifies the number of tick marks to place on the axes. You should give reasonable values for *n*. The value for *n* cannot be less than 2. The default value is 4.

XYTYPE=1
XYTYPE=2
XYTYPE=3
> specifies the pattern used to draw the plot. If you specify XYTYPE=1, only those lines parallel to the x axis are drawn. If you specify XYTYPE=2, lines parallel to the y axis are drawn. If you specify XYTYPE=3 (the default), both sets of lines are drawn.

ZMAX=*value*
ZMIN=*value*
> specifies the minimum and maximum values of the Z variable to be drawn. The value of ZMAX= must be greater than ZMIN= . If you

specify the ZMAX= or ZMIN= value within the actual range of the Z variables, the data are clipped on the graph.

SCATTER Statement

SCATTER *yvariable*xvariable=zvariable / options;*
SCAT *yvariable*xvariable=zvariable / options;*

You can use a SCATTER (or SCAT) statement to produce a three-dimensional scatter graph using the shape, size, and color values you specify for each data value. A PLOT or a SCATTER statement must accompany the PROC G3D statement to request the graphs to be produced. You can include any number of SCATTER statements. Because a scatter graph does not form an exact grid, it is less sensitive to missing values than a surface graph produced by a PLOT statement. **Output 23.4** illustrates all of the possible shapes.

Output 23.4 Shapes That You Can Specify in a SCATTER Statement

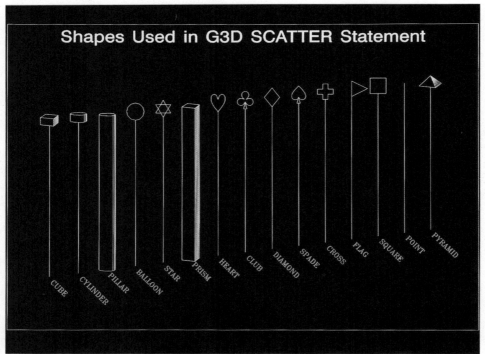

You can specify the following options in the SCATTER statement after a slash (/). If you do not specify any options, the slash is not needed.

ANNOTATE=*SASdataset*
ANNO=*SASdataset*
   specifies the data set to be used for annotation. The data set must be an ANNOTATE= type data set containing the appropriate Annotate variables. (See "ANNOTATE= Data Sets" for details.)

CAXIS=*color*
   specifies the color used to draw the axes of the plot. If you specify the CAXIS= option, the second color in the COLORS= list is used to draw

the axes. (See "The GOPTIONS Statement" for a description of the
COLORS= option.)

COLOR=*colorname*
COLOR='*string*'

specifies the color of the shapes that are drawn on the scatter graph.
The color variable is a character variable in the data set. Color values
must be valid color names for the device used. If you do not specify the
COLOR= option, or if an invalid value is specified, the default is used.
The default value is the third color in the COLORS= list.

CTEXT=*color*

specifies the color used to draw all text that appears on the plot.
Variable names, labels (if any), and tick mark values are drawn using the
color specified by CTEXT=. If you do not specify the CTEXT= option,
the first color in the COLORS= list is used to draw text on the plot.
(See "The GOPTIONS Statement" for a description of the COLORS=
option.)

DESCRIPTION='*string*'
DES='*string*'

specifies a descriptive string, up to forty characters long, that appears in
the Description field of PROC GREPLAY's master menu. If you omit the
DESCRIPTION= option, the Description field of PROC GREPLAY's
master menu contains a name and description assigned by SAS/GRAPH.

GRID

draws grid lines at each tick mark on all axes.

NAME='*string*'

specifies a descriptive string, up to eight characters long, that appears in
the Name field of PROC GREPLAY's master menu. If you omit the
NAME= option, the Name field of PROC GREPLAY's master menu
contains the procedure name.

NOAXES

requests that axes and axis labels not be drawn.

NOLABEL

requests that tick labels and axis labels not be drawn. The axes and tick
marks are still drawn. This is useful if you want to arrange your own tick
labels and axis labels using the ANNOTATE= option.

NONEEDLE

specifies that the line connecting the base plane to the suspended shape
should not be drawn.

ROTATE=*angle*
ROTATE=*angle1 angle2* . . .
ROTATE=*angle* TO *angle* BY *increment*

specifies one or more angles at which to rotate the picture about the z
axis. The value of *angle* can range from 0 to 90 degrees. The default
ROTATE= value is 70 degrees.

When you specify more than one ROTATE= angle, values are paired
with TILT= values and several pictures are produced at various angles.
See the description of the TILT= option.

SHAPE=*shapename*
SHAPE='*string*'

specifies which shapes to use in the scatter graph. There are fifteen valid
shape names: CUBE, CYLINDER, PILLAR, BALLOON, STAR, PRISM,

HEART, CLUB, DIAMOND, SPADE, CROSS, FLAG, SQUARE, POINT, and PYRAMID. The default shape is PYRAMID. If you specify SHAPE='xxx' for an unknown shape, then PYRAMID is used. The shape variable is a character variable in the input data set, and only the first four characters are significant.

SIZE=*sizevariable*
SIZE=*value*

specifies the size of the shapes that are drawn on the scatter graph. The size variable is a numeric variable in the data set. The default value is 1.0.

TILT=*angle*
TILT=*angle1 angle2 . . .*
TILT=*angle* TO *angle* BY *increment*

specifies one or more angles at which to tilt the picture about the y axis. *Angle* values can range from 0 to 90 degrees. The default TILT= value is 70 degrees.

When you specify more than one TILT= angle, values are paired with ROTATE= values (see the description of the ROTATE= option), and several pictures are produced at various angles as if you had specified several PLOT statements. If one list is shorter than the other, the last value in the shorter list is paired with the remaining values in the longer list.

XTICKNUM=*n*
YTICKNUM=*n*
ZTICKNUM=*n*

specifies the number of tick marks to place on the axes. You should give reasonable values for *n*. The value for *n* cannot be less than 2. The default value is 4.

ZMAX=*value*
ZMIN=*value*

specifies the minimum and maximum values of the Z variable to be drawn. The value of ZMAX= must be greater than ZMIN=. If you specify the ZMAX= or ZMIN= value within the actual range of the Z variables, the data are clipped on the graph.

TITLE Statement

TITLE*n options* 'text';

You can specify TITLE statements with PROC G3D. For a complete description of the TITLE statement, see "Enhancing Your Graphics Output Text."

DETAILS

Missing Values

For the PLOT statement, the x,y data should form a rectangular grid with a z value present for every possible (x,y) combination. In other words, if you have five distinct values for x in your data and ten distinct values of y, your data set should contain fifty observations, each containing values for x, y, and z. PROC G3D can produce the best three-dimensional surface plots if your data contain no "holes." Note that you may need to use the G3GRID procedure to shape your data into a rectangular grid.

EXAMPLES

Example 1: PROC G3D Options and Parameters

This example illustrates the use of the SIDE, GRID, YTICKNUM=, ZTICKNUM=, ZMIN=, and ZMAX= options. The graph produced by these statements is shown in **Output 23.5**.

```
goptions cback=black
         colors=(white cyan yellow magenta gold);
data plot3;
   do x=-5 to 5 by 0.25;
      do y=-10 to 10 by 0.25;
         z=-sin(sqrt(x*x + y*y));
         output;
         end;
      end;

title1 f=swiss c=white 'PROC G3D Options and Parameters';
title2 h=2 angle=90 ' ';
footnote1 f=swiss
   'SIDE, GRID, YTICKNUM=, ZTICKNUM=, ZMIN=, AND ZMAX= are Specified.';
footnote2 h=2 ' ';
proc g3d data=plot3;
   plot y*x=z / side
                grid
                yticknum=5
                zticknum=5
                zmin=-3
                zmax=1
                ctop=yellow
                cbottom=gold;
run;
```

Example 2: Scatter Graphs of Fisher Iris Data

This example illustrates the use of options with the SCATTER statement. In the first graph, COLOR= and SIZE= refer to variables in the input data set. The SHAPE= value is '*string*'. The NONEEDLE option is also specified. See **Output 23.6**.

```
goptions cback=black
         colors=(white cyan yellow magenta gold);
title1 f=swiss c=white 'Iris Species Classification';
title2 f=swiss c=white 'by Physical Measurement';
title3 f=swiss c=white 'Source: Fisher (1936) Iris Data';
title4 h=2 angle=90 ' ';
footnote1 j=l ' PETALLEN:'
          m=(11,+0) 'Petal length in MM.'
          m=(60 pct,+0) 'PETALWID:   Petal width in MM.';
footnote2 j=l ' SEPALLEN:'
          m=(11,+0) 'Sepal length in MM.'
          m=(60 pct,+0) 'Size of balloons is sepal width';
footnote3 h=2 ' ';
proc g3d data=iris;
   note m=(60,32) c=white 'SPECIES:'
        m=(69,+0) c=yellow 'VIRGINICA'
        m=(69,-1) c=magenta 'VERSICOLOR'
        m=(69,-1) c=gold 'SETOSA';
   scatter petallen * petalwid=sepallen /
           shape='BALLOON'
           color=colorval
           size=sizeval
           zmin=0
           zmax=80
           zticknum=5
           noneedle;
run;
```

In the second graph, SHAPE= and COLOR= refer to variables in the input data set.

Output 23.7 was produced by the following statements:

```
footnote1 j=l ' PETALLEN:'
          m=(11,+0) 'Petal length in MM.'
          m=(60 pct,+0) 'PETALWID:  Petal width in MM.'
footnote2 j=l ' SEPALLEN:'
          m=(11,+0) 'Sepal length in MM.'
          m=(60 pct,+0) 'Sepal width is not shown';
footnote3 h=2 ' ';
proc g3d data=iris;
   note m=(60,32) c=white 'SPECIES:'
        m=(69,+0) c=yellow 'VIRGINICA'
        m=(69,-1) c=magenta 'VERSICOLOR'
        m=(69,-1) c=gold 'SETOSA';
   scatter petallen * petalwid=sepallen /
           shape=shapeval
           color=colorval
           zmin=0
           zmax=80
           zticknum=5;
run;
```

Output 23.5   Surface Graph: PROC G3D

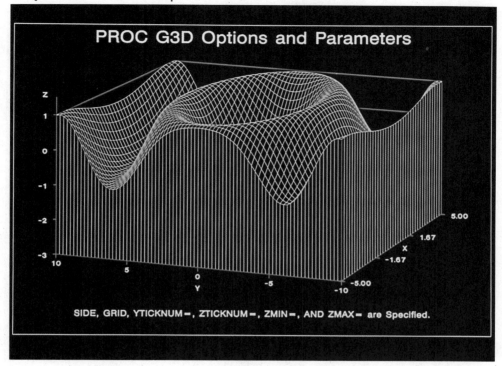

Output 23.6   Scatter Graph: PROC G3D with COLOR= and SIZE= Denoting Variables in the Data Set

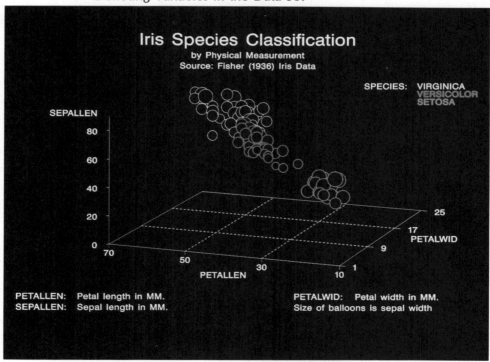

Output 23.7 Scatter Graph: PROC G3D with SHAPE= and COLOR=
 Denoting Variables in the Data Set

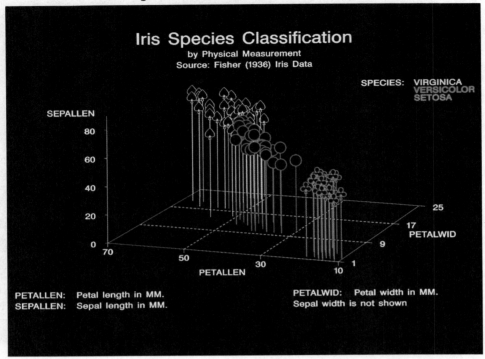

REFERENCES

Fisher, R.A. (1936), "The Use of Multiple Measurements in Taxonomic Problems,"
 Annals of Eugenics, *7*, 179-188.

Watkins, Steven L. (1974), "Algorithm 483, Masked Three-Dimensional Plot Program with Rotations (J6)," Collected Algorithms from ACM.

The G3GRID Procedure

ABSTRACT

The G3GRID procedure interpolates or smoothes values from an irregularly spaced set of points, generating a rectangular grid of interpolated or smoothed values. PROC G3GRID produces no graphics output. The output data set from PROC G3GRID is normally used as input to PROC G3D or PROC GCONTOUR.

INTRODUCTION

PROC G3GRID interpolates a function of two variables onto a rectangular grid, given a set of values for the function and the variables.

Bivariate Interpolation

The default method used for interpolation is a modification of that described by Akima (1978). This method consists of first dividing the plane into nonoverlapping triangles using the positions of the available points and then fitting a bivariate fifth degree polynomial within each triangle. The interpolated values are given by evaluating the polynomial at each grid point that falls in the triangle.

The coefficients for the polynomial are computed using the values of the function at the vertices of the triangle and the estimated values for the first and second derivatives of the function at the vertices. The estimates of the first and second derivatives are computed using the n nearest neighbors of the point, where n is an option that can be specified. This method works best for fairly smooth functions with values given at uniformly distributed points in the plane.

An alternative method is available that produces an interpolation that is optimally smooth in a certain sense (Harder and Desmarais 1972, Meinguet 1979). The surface generated can be thought of as the one that would be formed if a stiff, thin metal plate were forced through the given data points. For large data sets, this method is substantially more expensive than the default method.

SPECIFICATIONS

The following statements can be used with PROC G3GRID:

> **PROC G3GRID** *options*;
>   **GRID** *variable1*variable2=variable3* . . . / *options*;
>   **BY** *variables*;

The GRID statement is required.

PROC G3GRID Statement

> PROC G3GRID *options*;

You can specify the following options in the PROC G3GRID statement:

DATA=*SASdataset*
> names the SAS data set containing the initial values of the function to be interpolated and the coordinates of the points at which it is evaluated. If you do not specify the DATA= option, the most recently created SAS data set is used.

OUT=*SASdataset*
> names the output SAS data set that will contain any BY variables specified, the interpolated values, and the coordinates of the grid points. If smoothing has been requested (see GRID statement options), the output data set also contains a variable named _SMTH_, whose value is that of the smoothing parameter.

OUTTRI=*SASdataset*
> names an additional SAS data set that will contain any BY variables specified, the two variables giving the planar coordinates of the input points, and a variable named TRIANGLE that takes on integer values and labels the triangles.
>
> There are three observations for each value of the variable TRIANGLE. The three observations yield the coordinates of the three vertices of the triangle. Points on the convex hull of the input set of points are also assumed to lie in degenerate triangles whose other vertices are at infinity. The points in the convex hull can be recovered by keeping only those triangles with exactly two missing vertices.
>
> The OUTTRI= option is not valid when you specify the SPLINE option in the GRID statement.

BY Statement

> BY *variables*;

You can use the BY statement with PROC G3GRID to obtain separate analyses on observations in groups defined by the BY variables. When a BY statement appears, the procedure expects the input data set to be sorted in order of the BY variables. If your input data set is not sorted in ascending order, use the SORT procedure with a similar BY statement to sort the data, or, if appropriate, use the BY statement options NOTSORTED or DESCENDING. For more information, see the discussion of the BY statement in "SAS Statements Used in the PROC Step" in the *SAS Language Guide, Release 6.03 Edition*.

GRID Statement

GRID *variable1*variable2=variable3* . . . / *options*;

In the GRID statement, *variable1* and *variable2* are variables containing the available points, and *variable3* is the name of the variable containing the function values.

The names of the variables containing the available points must follow the word GRID in the form *variable1*variable2*. These are followed by =*variable3* for the function variable. More than one function variable can follow the equal sign.

The GRID statement must accompany the PROC G3GRID statement. You can specify the following options with the GRID statement:

AXIS1 =*list of ascending numbers*
gives a list of values to use for the first variable (*variable1*) on the grid. Use the following form to give an abbreviated list:

    `axis1=a to b by c;`

These values override any specified values for NAXIS1 =.

AXIS2 =*list of ascending numbers*
gives a list of values to use for the second variable (*variable2*) on the grid. Use the following form to give an abbreviated list:

    `axis2=a to b by c;`

These values override any specified values for NAXIS2 =.

JOIN
requests that a linear interpolation be done within a set of triangular regions formed from the input data set. This interpolation method creates values in the range of the original response variable, but the resulting interpolated surface may not be very smooth.

NAXIS1 =*number*
specifies the number of values of the first variable (*variable1*) to use on the grid. The default is 11.

NAXIS2 =*number*
gives the number of values of the second variable (*variable2*) to use on the grid. The default is 11.

NEAR =*number*
specifies the number of nearest neighbors to use in computing the estimates of the first and second derivatives. If an insufficient number of input data points are given, fewer nearest neighbors than requested are used. The default is 3.

NOSCALE
requests that the independent variables not be scaled to the same range before interpolation. Because the interpolation methods assume that the scale of both independent variables is comparable, the default is to perform the interpolation after scaling both independent variables to have the same range. If this is not desirable, then you can specify the NOSCALE option.

PARTIAL
requests the use of the spline to estimate the derivatives for the biquintic polynomial interpolation. A bivariate spline is fit to the nearest neighbors and used to estimate the needed derivatives. This option produces results that are less smooth than those produced by the

SPLINE option, but smoother than those produced by the default. If you specify both PARTIAL and SPLINE, SPLINE overrides PARTIAL.

SMOOTH=*list of ascending numbers*
gives a list of ascending numbers. Use this option only when you have specified the SPLINE option. For each value λ of the smoothing parameter, a function $\mathbf{u}(x,y)$ is formed that minimizes

$$\frac{1}{n} \Sigma_{j=1}^{n}(\mathbf{u}(x_j,y_j) - z_j)^2 + \lambda \Sigma_{j=0}^{2} \int_{-\infty}^{\infty} \int_{-\infty}^{\infty} \binom{2}{j} \left(\frac{\partial^2 \mathbf{u}}{\partial x^j \partial y^{2-j}}\right)^2 dxdy$$

where n is the number of data points and the pairs (x_j, y_j) are the available points, with corresponding function values z_j (Wahba 1979). For further discussion, see the **DETAILS** section.

The procedure is repeated for each value of the smoothing parameter. The output data set will contain the interpolated values, the values of the grid points, and the values of the smoothing parameter. The default value, 0, yields an interpolated surface.

SPLINE
requests the use of a bivariate spline (Harder and Desmarais 1972, Meinguet 1979) to interpolate or, if SMOOTH is requested, to form a smoothed estimate. This option results in an order n^3 algorithm being used, where n is the number of input data points. Consequently, this method can be time-consuming. If you use fewer than 100 input points, the time spent should be acceptable.

DETAILS

Computational Method

A Delaunay triangulation (Ripley 1981, p. 38) is used for the default method. The coordinates of the triangles are available in an output data set (OUTTRI=) if requested.

The function $\mathbf{u}$, formed when you specify the SPLINE option, is determined as follows. Letting

$$t_j = (x_j, y_j),$$

$$t = (x,y)$$

and

$$|t - t_j| = ((x - x_j)^2 + (y - y_j)^2)^{1/2},$$

$$\mathbf{u}(x,y) = \Sigma_{j=1}^{n} c_j E(t,t_j) + d_0 + d_1 x + d_2 y,$$

where

$$E(s,t) = |s - t| \log(|s - t|) .$$

The coefficients $c_1, c_2, \ldots, c_n$ and d_1, d_2, d_3 of this polynomial are determined by the following equations:

$$(\mathbf{E} + n\lambda \mathbf{I}) \mathbf{c} + \mathbf{T} \mathbf{d} = \mathbf{z}$$

and

$$T'c = 0$$

where

E   is the $n \times n$ matrix $E(t_i, t_j)$

I   is the $n \times n$ identity matrix

c $= (c_1, \ldots, c_n)'$

z $= (z_1, \ldots, z_n)'$

d $= (d_1, d_2, d_3)'$

T   is the $n \times 3$ matrix whose ith row is $(1, x_i, y_i)$.

See Wahba (1979) for more detail.

Except when smoothing is done with the SPLINE option, PROC G3GRID is an interpolation procedure. In these cases, the surface, from which the interpolated data are sampled, must pass precisely through the data points in the input data set. If the data points are very erratic, an interpolated surface can be very erratic. A smoothed spline, however, will trade closeness to the original data points for smoothness. If feasible, you should try several values of the smoothing parameter to see which seems to give the best balance between smoothness and fit.

If the points generated by the independent variables tend to lie along a nonlinear curve, a poor interpolation or spline may result. In such cases, both the response and one of the independent variables should be modeled as a function of the remaining independent variable. A scatter plot of the two independent variables can be helpful in such cases.

Input Data Set

If more than one observation in the input data set has the same values for the independent variables, a warning message is printed and only the first such point is used. If the independent variable points are collinear, the function is interpolated as constant along lines perpendicular to the line in the plane generated by the input data points.

EXAMPLE

In the DATA step of the following example, a data set HAT with variables X, Y, and Z is created using several SAS functions. Because the data do not form a grid, PROC G3GRID is used for interpolation. First the default method of PROC G3GRID is invoked, then PROC G3GRID with the SPLINE option in effect, and then PROC G3GRID with the PARTIAL option in effect. The results of each execution of PROC G3GRID are plotted using PROC G3D and are shown in **Output 24.1–24.5.**

Reconstruction of the "Cowboy Hat"

```
     /*----------------------------------------------------------*/
     /*  G3GRID Example: Reconstruction of the "Cowboy Hat" from  */
     /*                  a randomly sampled set of points.        */
     /*----------------------------------------------------------*/
data hat;
   keep x y z;
   do i=1 to 30;
      x=10*ranuni(33)-5;
      y=10*ranuni(35)-5;
      z=sin(sqrt(x*x + y*y));
      output;
      end;
run;


     /*----------------------------------------------------------*/
     /*   Use the default method with 3 nearest neighbor points.  */
     /*----------------------------------------------------------*/
proc g3grid data=hat out=gridhat outtri=tri;
   grid x*y=z /
   axis1=-5 to 5 by .5
   axis2=-5 to 5 by .5;
run;


     /*----------------------------------------------------------*/
     /*   Do a plot of the triangles.  The X Y pairs will        */
     /*      be the vertices of the triangles.                   */
     /*----------------------------------------------------------*/
proc means noprint data=tri;
   output out=out n=n;
   by triangle;
run;


pattern1 v=e r=100;
title  f=swiss  'Triangularization of Initial Data';
footnote;
proc gmap data=out map=tri;
   id triangle;
   choro n / discrete nolegend
            ctext=white
            coutline=white;
run;


pattern;
title1  f=swiss  'Default Interpolation';
title2  f=swiss  'Using 30 sample points';

proc g3d data=gridhat;
   plot x*y=z / caxis=white
                ctext=white
                ctop=yellow
                cbottom=cyan;
run;
```

```
     /*-------------------------------------------------------------*/
     /* Use the SPLINE option to get the smoothest interpolation.  */
     /*-------------------------------------------------------------*/
proc g3grid data=hat out=gridhat;
   grid x*y=z / spline
                axis1=-5 to 5 by .5
                axis2=-5 to 5 by .5;
run;

title1  f=swiss  'Spline Interpolation';
title2  f=swiss  'Using 30 sample points';
proc g3d data=gridhat;
   plot x*y=z / caxis=white
                ctext=white
                ctop=yellow
                cbottom=cyan;
run;


     /*-------------------------------------------------------------*/
     /* Use the smoothed SPLINE option to get a smoother surface.  */
     /*-------------------------------------------------------------*/

proc g3grid data=hat out=gridhat;
   grid x*y=z / spline smooth=.05
                axis1=-5 to 5 by .5
                axis2=-5 to 5 by .5;
run;

title1  f=swiss  'Smoothed Spline Estimation';
title2  f=swiss  'Using 30 sample points';
proc g3d data=gridhat;
   plot x*y=z / caxis=white
                ctext=white
                ctop=yellow
                cbottom=cyan;
run;


     /*-------------------------------------------------------------*/
     /* Use the PARTIAL option with 8 nearest neighbors.           */
     /*-------------------------------------------------------------*/
proc g3grid data=hat out=gridhat;
   grid x*y=z / partial
                near=8
                axis1=-5 to 5 by .5
                axis2=-5 to 5 by .5;

title1  f=swiss  'Partial Spline Interpolation';
title2  f=swiss  'Using 30 sample points';
proc g3d data=gridhat;
   plot x*y=z / caxis=white
                ctext=white
                ctop=yellow
                cbottom=cyan;
run;
```

Output 24.1   A Plot of Triangles: PROC G3GRID

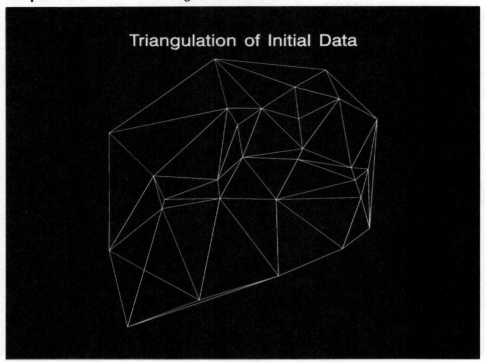

Output 24.2   Default Interpolation

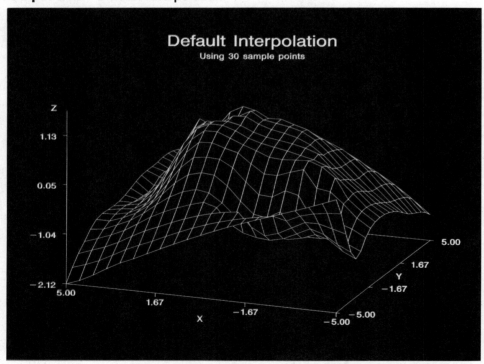

Output 24.3 Spline Interpolation

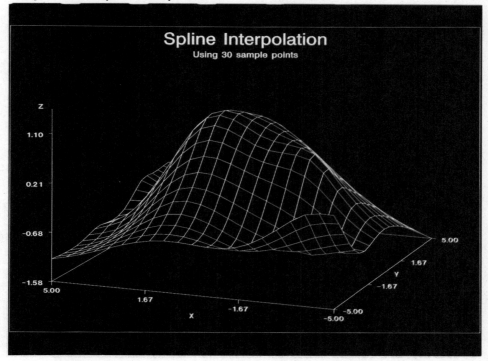

Output 24.4 Spline Interpolation with Smoothing

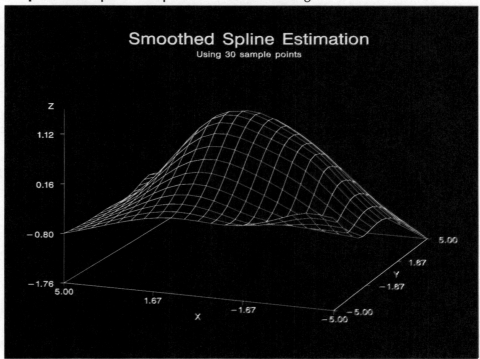

Output 24.5   Partial Spline Interpolation

REFERENCES

Akima, Hiroshi (1978) "A Method of Bivariate Interpolation and Smooth Surface Fitting for Irregularly Distributed Data Points," *ACM Transaction on Mathematical Software* 4, 148-159.

Harder, R.L. and Desmarais, R.N. (1972) "Interpolation Using Surface Splines," *Journal of Aircraft* 9, 189-191.

Meinguet, Jean (1979) "Multivariate Interpolation at Arbitrary Points Made Simple," *Journal of Applied Mathematics and Physics* 30, 292-304.

Ripley, B.D. (1981), *Spatial Statistics*, New York: John Wiley & Sons, Inc.

Wahba, Grace (1979) "How to Smooth Curves and Surfaces with Splines and Cross-validation," *Proceedings of the 24th Conference on the Design of Experiments*, U.S. Army Research Office Report 79-2.

SAS/GRAPH®
Type Styles and Fonts

SAS/GRAPH software has a variety of fonts that you can use to display text and special characters in your procedure output. Samples of the type styles and fonts you can use with SAS/GRAPH software are included in this appendix.

Use the F= option to specify a font to display text. You can also use the FBY= and FTEXT= options. The F= option is described in the chapter "Enhancing Your Graphics Output Text"; the FBY= and FTEXT= options are described in the chapter "The GOPTICNS Statement." To display a font's character set on your output device, you can use PROC GFONT to specify the name of a SAS/GRAPH font or a font you designed as shown in the following example:

```
proc gfont name=math
           nobuild;
run;
```

By default, SAS/GRAPH first searches for all fonts in the catalog SASHELP.FONTS. If you want to use fonts you have designed, you must change the default order that SAS/GRAPH uses to search for fonts. First, use a LIBNAME statement to associate a libref with the name of the directory containing your font catalog. Refer to "The GFONT Procedure" for information on creating your own font catalog. SAS/GRAPH will search GFONT0 first, then GFONT1, and so on up to GFONT9 or the first undefined libref.

For example, suppose you have a personal font called MYFONT in a working directory, but you also want to use system fonts such as SWISS or COMPLEX. You should use a LIBNAME statement to identify the directory that contains your personal font. For UNIX operating systems and derivatives, use a statement of the form

```
libname gfont0 '/mydir/fonts/';
```

For SAS/GRAPH software on personal computers, use a statement of the form

```
libname gfont0 'c:\mydir\fonts\';
```

SAS/GRAPH searches the catalog GFONT0.FONTS first, then searches SASHELP.FONTS to find any of the fonts you requested.

The fonts listed below are available for use with SAS/GRAPH software. These fonts are shown in their entirety in SAS Technical Report P-170, "Typestyles and Fonts for Use with SAS/GRAPH Software."

SAS/GRAPH fonts that do not end in the letter U are proportionately spaced; fonts ending in the letter U are uniformly spaced versions of their counterparts. For example, the CGREEK font draws characters that are proportionately spaced; the CGREEKU font draws characters that are uniformly spaced.

Similarly, fonts ending in the letter I are italic, and fonts ending in the letter B are bold. Fonts ending in the letter E are empty (not filled) versions of their counterparts, and fonts ending in the letter L are light.

You can use PROC GFONT to display the character set for each font available with SAS/GRAPH software.

Table A1.1 shows which of the fonts are available in empty versions and which are available in uniform versions.

Table A1.1   Fonts Available in Empty and Uniform Versions

	Empty	Uniform
BRUSH		
CARTOG		x
CENTB	x	x
CENTBI	x	x
CENTX	x	x
CENTXI	x	x
CGREEK		x
COMPLEX		x
CSCRIPT		
CYRILLIC		x
DUPLEX		x
ELECTRON		x
GERMAN		x
GITALIC		x
GREEK		x
HEBREW	x	x
ITALIC		x
MARKER	x	
MATH		x
MUSIC		x
OLDENG		x
SCRIPT		
SIMPLEX		x
SPECIAL		x
SWISS	x	x
SWISSB	x	x
SWISSBI	x	x
SWISSI	x	x
SWISSL	x	x
SWISSX	x	x
SWISSXB	x	x
TITALIC		x
TRIPLEX		x
WEATHER		x
ZAPF	x	x
ZAPFB	x	x
ZAPFBI	x	x
ZAPFI	x	x

BRUSH

ABCabc123

CENTB

ABCabc123

CENTBI

ABCabc123

CENTX

ABCabc123

CENTXI

ABCabc123

COMPLEX

ABCabc123

CSCRIPT

ABCabc123

DUPLEX

ABCabc123

GITALIC

ABCabc123

ITALIC

ABCabc123

OLDENG

ABCabc123

SCRIPT

ABCabc123

SIMPLEX

ABCabc123

SWISS

ABCabc123

SWISSB

ABCabc123

SWISSBI

ABCabc123

SWISSI

ABCabc123

SWISSL

ABCabc123

SWISSX

ABCabc123

SWISSXB

ABCabc123

TITALIC

ABCabc123

TRIPLEX

ABCabc123

ZAPF

ABCabc123

ZAPFB

ABCabc123

ZAPFBI

ABCabc123

ZAPFI

ABCabc123

CARTOG

⚑	⚓	⊥	⚒	⌂	🔔	🌴	🎄	♣	🌳
A	B	C	D	E	K	L	M	N	O

⛵	◿	✚	☾	✡	☀	○	⬯	⛨
F	G	H	I	J	P	Q	R	S

CGREEK

.	φ	(	+	!	&	|	$	*	)	;	—	/
.	<	(	+	!	&	]	$	*	)	;	-	/

,	ϑ	＿	ς	?	:	#	@	'	=	"	α	β
,	%	_	>	?	:	#	@	'	=	"	a	b

ξ	δ	ε	φ	γ	η	ι	ε	κ	λ	μ	ν	o
c	d	e	f	g	h	i	j	k	l	m	n	o

π	θ	ρ	σ	τ	υ	∂	ω	χ	ψ	ζ	{	Α
p	q	r	s	t	u	v	w	x	y	z	{	A

Β	Ξ	Δ	Ε	Φ	Γ	Η	Ι	}	Ε	Κ	Λ	Μ
B	C	D	E	F	G	H	I	}	J	K	L	M

Ν	Ο	Π	Θ	Ρ	Σ	Τ	Υ	∇	Ω	Χ	Ψ	Ζ
N	O	P	Q	R	S	T	U	V	W	X	Y	Z

0	1	2	3	4	5	6	7	8	9
0	1	2	3	4	5	6	7	8	9

CYRILLIC

.	<	(	+	!	&	|	$	*	)	;	—	/
.	<	(	+	!	&	]	$	*	)	;	-	/

,	%	_	>	?	:	#	@	'	=	"	а	б
,	%	_	>	?	:	#	@	'	=	"	a	b

ц	д	е	ф	г	ж	и	й	к	л	м	н	о
c	d	e	f	g	h	i	j	k	l	m	n	o

п	ш	р	с	т	у	в	щ	х	ы	з	{	А
p	q	r	s	t	u	v	w	x	y	z	{	A

Б	Ц	Д	Е	Ф	Г	Ж	И	}	Й	К	Л	М
B	C	D	E	F	G	H	I	}	J	K	L	M

Н	О	П	Ш	Р	С	Т	У	В	Щ	Х	Ы	З
N	O	P	Q	R	S	T	U	V	W	X	Y	Z

0	1	2	3	4	5	6	7	8	9
0	1	2	3	4	5	6	7	8	9

ELECTRON

A	B	C	D	E	F

GERMAN

.	<	(	+	!	&	|	$	*	)	;	–	/
.	<	(	+	!	&	]	$	*	)	;	-	/

,	%	__	>	?	:	#	@	'	=	''	a	b
,	%	_	>	?	:	#	@	'	=	"	a	b

c	d	e	f	g	h	i	j	k	l	m	n	o
c	d	e	f	g	h	i	j	k	l	m	n	o

p	q	r	s	t	u	v	w	x	y	z	{	A
p	q	r	s	t	u	v	w	x	y	z	{	A

B	C	D	E	F	G	H	I	}	J	K	L	M
B	C	D	E	F	G	H	I	}	J	K	L	M

N	O	P	Q	R	S	T	U	V	W	X	Y	Z
N	O	P	Q	R	S	T	U	V	W	X	Y	Z

0	1	2	3	4	5	6	7	8	9
0	1	2	3	4	5	6	7	8	9

MUSIC

·	♪	⌐	○	○	—	✗	⌐	𝄞	⊚:
A	B	C	D	E	K	L	M	N	O

●	#	♮	♭	—	‖	⅄	⊃:	𝄢
F	G	H	I	J	P	Q	R	S

GREEK

∅	(	+	!	&	|	$	*	)	;	—	/
<	(	+	!	&	]	$	*	)	;	-	/

,	ϑ	＿	ς	?	:	#	@	'	=	''	α	β
,	%	_	>	?	:	#	@	'	=	"	a	b

ξ	δ	ε	φ	γ	η	ι	ϵ	κ	λ	μ	ν	ο
c	d	e	f	g	h	i	j	k	l	m	n	o

π	θ	ρ	σ	τ	υ	∂	ω	χ	ψ	ζ	{	A
p	q	r	s	t	u	v	w	x	y	z	{	A

B	Ξ	Δ	E	Φ	Γ	H	I	}	E	K	Λ	M
B	C	D	E	F	G	H	I	}	J	K	L	M

N	O	Π	Θ	P	Σ	T	Υ	∇	Ω	X	Ψ	Z
N	O	P	Q	R	S	T	U	V	W	X	Y	Z

0	1	2	3	4	5	6	7	8	9
0	1	2	3	4	5	6	7	8	9

WEATHER

A	B	C	D	E	F	G	H	I	J

K	L	M	N

HEBREW

א ב ג ד ה ה ו ז ח ט י ך כ ל
& a b c d e f g h i j k l

מ ם ן נ ס ע פ ף צ ק ר ש
m n o p q r s t u v w x y

ת ס ו 1 2 3 4 5 6 7 8 9
z 0 1 2 3 4 5 6 7 8 9

MATH

√ ⊂ ∪ ⊃ ∩   ‖ ⊥ ∠ ∴ <
a b c d e   A B C D E

∈ → ↑ ← ↓   > ± ∓ ÷ ≠
f g h i j   F G H I J

∂ ∇ ∫ ∮ ∞   ≡ ≦ ≧ ∝ ∼
k l m n o   K L M N O

∃ ∏ ∑
p q r

MARKER

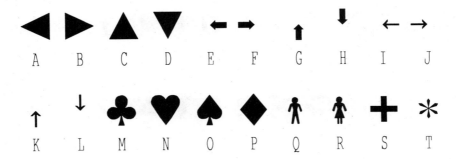

| A | B | C | D | E | F | G | H | I | J |

| K | L | M | N | O | P | Q | R | S | T |

SPECIAL

| ♈ | [| ≋ | ♌ | ↗ | | ▢ | ♤ | ♡ | ◇ | ♧ |
| . | < | (| ! | $ | | A | B | C | D | E |

| ✳ | ♋ | ♑ | ♉ |] | | ☘ | ⚜ | ○ | ☆ | ● |
|) | ; | / | , | > | | F | G | H | I | J |

| ♍ | ♊ | ♎ | ♏ | ☉ | | ■ | ▲ | ★ | § | † |
| ? | : | ' | " | a | | K | L | M | N | O |

| ☿ | ♀ | ⊕ | ♂ | ♃ | | ‡ | ff | ® | fi | fl |
| b | c | d | e | f | | P | Q | R | S | T |

| ♄ | ♅ | ♆ | ♇ | ☾ | | ffi | ffl | © | ° | ˆ |
| g | h | i | j | k | | U | V | W | 0 | 1 |

| ☌ | ✳ | ☋ | ☊ | ff | | ´ | ` | ˘ | ' | ' |
| l | m | n | o | q | | 2 | 3 | 4 | 5 | 6 |

| fi | fl | ffi | ffl | | | ' | ' | | | |
| s | t | u | v | | | 7 | 8 | | | |

Special
SAS/GRAPH®
Data Sets

MAP DATA SETS

Notes on Using Map Data Sets

This chapter discusses the map data sets that are available with SAS/GRAPH software. Be sure the SAS/GRAPH map data sets are installed before you run any SAS programs that request information from a map data set.

You should contact your SAS Software Consultant to verify the name and location of the map data sets file before you use the map data sets. As shipped, the maps for SAS/GRAPH software Release 6.03 for personal computers are stored in a file called \SAS\MAPS; the default location for maps for UNIX operating systems and derivatives is in /USER/LIB/SAS/MAPS. However, you can change the storage location.

We recommend that you put a LIBNAME statement to reference the maps in your AUTOEXEC.SAS file. Refer to the *SAS Language Guide, Release 6.03 Edition* for information on the LIBNAME statement. Here is an example of a LIBNAME statement for SAS/GRAPH software on personal computers:

```
libname maplib 'c:\sas\maps\';
```

For UNIX operating systems and derivatives, you could use a statement like the following if the maps are in their default location:

```
libname maplib '/user/lib/sas/maps/';
```

Because some of these data sets are large, you can shorten jobs that use only a few states or provinces by using the FIRSTOBS= and OBS= data set options to select the states or provinces you want. For example, to create a data set containing only the data for Quebec, you first access the CANADA data set, and then you can use a DATA step in the following form:

```
data quebec;
    set libref.canada (firstobs=1376  obs=3182);
```

The following example shows you how to find the first and last observations for each state in the USCOUNTY data set. You can use a similar job to create a list for any map data set. This example shows the fastest technique for selecting one area from a map data set. First, produce a list of the first and last observations for each state in the USCOUNTY data set provided with SAS/GRAPH software. You can keep the list for future reference when creating a map containing only one state. A California county map is created as an example. This example assumes that the libref MAPS has already been defined in a LIBNAME statement. Be aware that the observation numbers may change in future releases of SAS/GRAPH software.

```
data _null_;
    set maps.uscounty;
    by state;
    file numbers;    /* A permanent file named numbers is created.*/
    stname=fipnamel (state);
    if first.state then put a5 stname a30 _n_ comma7.0 aa;
    else if last.state then put a40 _n_ comma7.0;
run;

data ca;
    /* These observation numbers are only an example. */
    /* Use the DATA step above to obtain the correct values. */
    set maps.uscounty (firstobs=1643 obs=2226);
run;
```

Map Data Set Descriptions

Release 6.03 of SAS/GRAPH software contains several useful data sets. For information on variable names in these data sets, use PROC CONTENTS or PROC DATASETS (refer to the *SAS Procedures Guide, Release 6.03 Edition*) or any other procedure that allows you to examine the contents of a data set. You can also use the VAR command to receive information on variable names (see "SAS Display Manager System" in the *SAS Introductory Guide, Release 6.03 Edition*).

ANOMALY data set   The ANOMALY data set contains information about known changes or differences in the other map data sets. This includes counties that have been created or dissolved since the boundaries delineated in the map data sets were created. If you have questions about some of the values in the maps, you should examine the ANOMALY data set before you contact your SAS Software Representative.

CANADA data set   The CANADA data set contains a projected and reduced regional boundary map of Canadian provinces and census districts.

CANADA2 data set   The CANADA2 data set contains a projected and reduced regional boundary map of Canadian provinces.

CANCENS data set   The CANCENS data set lists the names (up to 30 characters) of the Canadian census divisions.

CNTYNAME data set   The CNTYNAME data set contains county names (up to 25 characters) of the counties in the COUNTY and USCOUNTY data sets. The COUNTY number in the CNTYNAME data set can be used to match county names with county boundaries in the COUNTY and USCOUNTY data sets.

COUNTY data set   The COUNTY data set contains the unprojected but reduced county boundaries for the United States. There are no county boundaries for Alaska, so only the state boundaries are provided for that state.

US data set   The US data set contains the projected and reduced coordinates of the state boundaries for all 50 states in the U.S. with Alaska and Hawaii rescaled to appear under California and Arizona. This data set has been projected to match the USCENTER and USCITY data sets described below.

USCENTER data set   This data set contains coordinates for the visual centers of the 50 states of the U.S. and Washington, D.C., as well as points in the ocean for states often too small to contain a label. There are two pairs of variables for locating labels using ANNOTATE= data sets. The X and Y variables are projected to match the US data set provided with SAS/GRAPH software (see above). The LAT and LONG variables contain unprojected coordinates and can be used with the COUNTY data set provided with SAS/GRAPH software.

Some of the smaller states have two observations in the USCENTER data set. One of the observations gives a location in the visual center of the state. However, the centers of some states are too close together and the labels will overlap. The second observation gives an "ocean" location for labeling. The points are distinguished by the value of the OCEAN variable. A value of 'Y' indicates that the point is the "ocean" location.

The following example shows how to use the "ocean" points for labeling and moving to the beginning of a line that is drawn to the interior point of the state. This example produces **Output A2.1**.

```
data center;
   length color function $ 8;
   set maps.uscenter;
   retain flag 0;
   xsys='2';   /* X and Y use the map data coordinate system.*/
   ysys='2';
   when='a';              /* Annotate after the map is drawn.*/
   color='white';
   if fipstate (state)='dc'
      then delete;                      /* Do not label D.C. */
   else do;
      text=fipstate (state);  /* Convert FIPS to postal code.*/
      function='label';
      if flag=1 then do;     /* Draw a line to the interior point.*/
         function='draw';
         flag=0;
         end;
      if ocean='y' then do;   /* Place text in the ocean. Move to */
         position='6';              /* beginning of line to be drawn.*/
         output;
         function='move';
         flag=1;
         end;
      output;
      end;
```

```
      keep x y xsys ysys function when color position text;
                   /* Keep only the variables needed by Annotate.*/
   run;


   title f=swiss c=white 'USCENTER Data Set with Annotate';
   pattern  v=s  c=vlib  r=66;
   proc gmap data=maps.us
             map=maps.us;

      id state;
      choro  state / nolegend
                     coutline=white
                     annotate=center;
      run;
```

USCITY data set   This data set contains the locations of some cities in the U.S. There are two pairs of variables for locating labels using ANNOTATE= data sets. The X and Y variables are projected to match the US data set provided with SAS/GRAPH software (see above). The LAT and LONG variables contain unprojected coordinates and can be used with the COUNTY data set provided with SAS/GRAPH software.

The following example shows one way to use the USCITY data set to annotate a map; this example produces **Output A2.2.**

```
   data flcity;            /* Subset the Florida cities.        */
      length color $ 8;
      set maps.uscity;
      where state=12;
      xsys='2';            /* Set the coordinate system to data. */
      ysys='2';
      color='white';
      when='a';
      rename city=text;    /* The Annotate text is the city name. */

                           /* Some of the cities are too close   */
                           /* together, so delete a few.         */

      if _n_=02 |          /* Delete Clearwater.                */
         _n_=04 |          /* Delete Fort Lauderdale.           */
         _n_=06 |          /* Delete Hialeah.                   */
         _n_=09 |          /* Delete Largo.                     */
         _n_=10 |          /* Delete Miami.                     */
         _n_=14 |          /* Delete Pompano Beach.             */
         _n_=16           /* Delete St. Petersburg.            */
         then delete;
   run;

   data flmap;             /* Subset the Florida map.           */
      set maps.us;
      if state=stfips ('fl');
   run;

   title 'USCITY Data Set with Annotate';
   footnote;
   pattern  v=s  c=vlib;
```

```
proc gmap data=flcity
         map=flmap;
   id state;
   choro  state / nolegend
                    annotate=flcity;
run;
```

For an example of how to project an ANNOTATE= data set along with a map data set, see "The GPROJECT Procedure."

USCOUNTY data set The USCOUNTY data set contains the projected and reduced county boundaries for the United States. There are no county boundaries for Alaska, so only the state boundaries are provided for that state. Alaska and Hawaii have been repositioned to appear in the lower left corner of the map.

Using FIPS and Province Codes with Mapping Procedures

Many of the map data sets included with SAS/GRAPH software contain a variable whose values are FIPS codes or province codes (standardized numeric codes that identify geographic locations). When you use the SAS/GRAPH mapping procedures, the ID variables defining unit areas in your response data set must have the same values as the ID variables in your map data set. If you have state or province names in your response data set, you must convert them to FIPS codes or province codes before using them with Institute-supplied map data sets. **Table A2.1** lists the FIPS codes for the United States (by state) and the Canadian province codes. Several functions allow you to convert state names to FIPS codes. See "SAS Functions" in the *SAS Language Guide, Release 6.03 Edition* if you need to convert state names to FIPS codes.

The CNTYNAME data set contains names and FIPS codes for all counties in the United States. The CANCENS data set contains census district names and codes for the Canadian provinces.

Table A2.1   United States FIPS Codes and Canadian Province Codes

UNITED STATES			
FIPS code	**State**	**FIPS code**	**State**
01	Alabama	30	Montana
02	Alaska	31	Nebraska
04	Arizona	32	Nevada
05	Arkansas	33	New Hampshire
06	California	34	New Jersey
08	Colorado	35	New Mexico
09	Connecticut	36	New York
10	Delaware	37	North Carolina
11	District of Columbia	38	North Dakota
12	Florida	39	Ohio
13	Georgia	40	Oklahoma
15	Hawaii	41	Oregon
16	Idaho	42	Pennsylvania
17	Illinois	44	Rhode Island
18	Indiana	45	South Carolina

(continued on next page)

(continued from previous page)

UNITED STATES

FIPS code	State	FIPS code	State
19	Iowa	46	South Dakota
20	Kansas	47	Tennessee
21	Kentucky	48	Texas
22	Louisiana	49	Utah
23	Maine	50	Vermont
24	Maryland	51	Virginia
25	Massachusetts	53	Washington
26	Michigan	54	West Virginia
27	Minnesota	55	Wisconsin
28	Mississippi	56	Wyoming
29	Missouri	72	Puerto Rico

CANADIAN PROVINCES

Province Code	Province Name
10	Newfoundland
11	Prince Edward Island
12	Nova Scotia
13	New Brunswick
24	Quebec
35	Ontario
46	Manitoba
47	Saskatchewan
48	Alberta
59	British Columbia
60	Yukon
61	Northwest Territories

Data Library Series

The SAS Data Library Series contains additional data sets that may be useful when you are running SAS/GRAPH procedures. You can order these data sets from the SAS Institute Book Sales Department, Box 8000, Cary, North Carolina 27512-8000.

You can also create your own map data sets. Refer to SAS Technical Report A-107, "Creating Your Own SAS/GRAPH Map Data Sets with a Digitizer." This report can also be ordered from Book Sales.

Note that because of size limitations the map data sets for SAS/GRAPH software Release 6.03 for personal computers do not include the CANADA3, CANADA4, COUNTIES, and STATES map data sets supplied with Version 5 SAS/GRAPH software.

Output A2.1   USCENTER Data Set Using the ANNOTATE= Option

Output A2.2   USCITY Data Set Using the ANNOTATE= Option

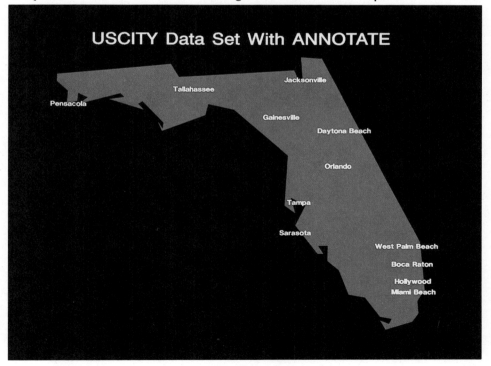

SAS/GRAPH®
Device Drivers

SAS/GRAPH DEVICE DRIVERS

This appendix describes how to generate output on graphics devices supported by SAS/GRAPH software. The first two parts describe basic configuration requirements and usage instructions for devices on personal computers and under UNIX operating systems and derivatives. The last part is a table listing many of the device drivers that are included with the release of SAS/GRAPH software you are using.

USING DEVICE DRIVERS WITH SAS/GRAPH SOFTWARE FOR PERSONAL COMPUTERS

Graphics Display Adapters

To display SAS/GRAPH output on your personal computer monitor, you must have a supported graphics display adapter. These include IBM's CGA and EGA adapters, the Hercules monochrome adapter, or other adapters that are compatible with these. (Note that if your personal computer does not have graphics capabilities, you can still generate graphics output on a supported printer, plotter, or camera, but you cannot display it on your monitor. See the section **Hardcopy Devices** for information on hardcopy device support.)

The particular SAS/GRAPH device driver you use to display output on your monitor depends on the type of adapter you have, the type of monitor you have, and (for certain adapters) the amount of memory available on your adapter. It is important that you use the correct driver for the equipment you have. While the driver attempts to check for the type of adapter you have and to respond accordingly, it may not always be able to correctly determine what you have installed because of variations between different manufacturers' hardware. Therefore, you must know what type of adapter you have in your personal computer before specifying a driver. If you are unsure about your hardware, check with your hardware support personnel.

CGA Adapters

If you have a CGA adapter, the driver you choose will depend on whether you have a monochrome or color monitor and whether you want to use high-intensity colors. The CGA, CGA0, and CGA1 drivers display colors with normal intensity and are designed to be used with color monitors. The only difference between these drivers is the color palette supported. (The CGA driver is the same as the CGA0 driver.) The CGAH0 and CGAH1 drivers use high-intensity colors. (Some monitors may not show any difference between normal- and high-intensity colors.) Driver selection is summarized in **Table A3.1**.

Table A3.1   Drivers for CGA Adapters

Driver	Resolution	Rows	Columns	Colors
CGA	320 x 200	25	64	green, red, yellow
CGA0	320 x 200	25	64	green, red, yellow
CGA1	320 x 200	25	64	cyan, magenta, white
CGAH0	320 x 200	25	64	green, red, yellow (high intensity)
CGAH1	320 x 200	25	64	cyan, magenta, white (high intensity)
CGAM	640 x 200	25	80	white

Note: depending on your adapter or monitor, yellow may appear as brown.

EGA Adapters

Choosing a driver for EGA devices is more complicated because EGA adapters can have 64K, 128K, or 256K of memory installed and can be attached to monochrome, CGA, or EGA monitors. The type of monitor with which your EGA adapter is used, the amount of memory installed on the EGA adapter, and how the switches on the adapter have been set determine the maximum resolution and number of colors you can display. Almost all third-party EGA-compatible adapters have 256K of memory, but IBM EGA adapters may come with as little as 64K memory. Find out from your hardware support personnel how much memory your adapter has before referring to **Table A3.2**.

Table A3.2   Drivers for EGA Adapters

Driver	Minimum Required Memory	Monitor	Resolution	Rows	Columns	Number of Colors
EGAM	64K	MONO	640 x 350	43	80	1
EGAC	64K	CGA	640 x 200	25	80	15
EGA	64K	CGA	640 x 200	25	80	15
EGACX	64K	CGA	320 x 200	25	64	15
EGAS	64K	EGA	640 x 350	43	80	3
EGAL	128K	EGA	640 x 350	43	80	15

Note that the EGA and EGAC drivers are the same. Consult the entry for each driver in the device catalog for a list of default colors. (Refer to "The GDEVICE Procedure" for instructions on how to browse the device catalog.)

Hercules Adapters

To use SAS/GRAPH software with Hercules and Hercules-compatible monochrome graphics adapters, specify

```
goptions device=hercules;
```

The driver uses one foreground color (white) and has a resolution of 348 x 720 pixels, with 43 rows and 90 columns for text.

IBM PS/2

IBM PS/2 models have a built-in graphics display adapter. The driver to use depends on what model of monitor you are using. For IBM color monitors (models 8512, 8513, and 8514), use the PS2EGA driver. For the IBM monochrome monitor (model 8503), use the PS2EGAM driver.

Other Displays and Adapters

Finally, SAS/GRAPH software supports a number of other monitors and graphics display adapters, including the IBM 3270 Personal Computer with APA card and the Vectrix VXPC-4096 graphics board. Browse the device catalog in PROC GDEVICE to determine if support for your hardware is in the release of SAS/GRAPH software you are using. Submit the following statements to list a short description of the available device support:

```
proc gdevice nofs;
   list;
   quit;
run;
```

Hardcopy Devices

It is not necessary for you to have a graphics display adapter installed in your personal computer in order to generate output on hardcopy devices. In general, to produce a graph on a plotter, printer, or film recorder attached to a personal computer, you need only attach the device to a serial or printer port and ensure that the driver sends graphics commands out through that port.

Plotters

Plotters supported by SAS/GRAPH software are usually connected to the serial port of the personal computer using an appropriate cable. By default, SAS/GRAPH drivers for plotters direct output to COM1:, so all you need to do is attach the plotter to the COM1: port and specify the appropriate driver. If you want to attach the plotter to another port—COM2: instead of COM1:, for example—you can use PROC GDEVICE to change the GACCESS field for the device from SASGASTD>COM1: to SASGASTD>COM2:. You can also use the GACCESS= option in a GOPTIONS statement to override the GACCESS value specified in the device catalog entry.

In addition to making sure that SAS/GRAPH software directs output through the appropriate port, you must also make sure that the communications parameters for the port match the switch settings of the output device for such items as baud rate and parity. It may be necessary to use the MODE command from DOS to set port parameters before beginning the SAS session.

Dot-matrix and Inkjet Printers

A series of drivers (FX85, FX185, LQ800, LQ1000) can produce output on Epson and Epson-compatible dot-matrix printers. The IBM Graphics Printer can be driven with the IBMGPRT driver. Hewlett-Packard PaintJet printers can be driven with the HPPJ90 and HPPJ180 drivers. All these printers are usually attached to the personal computer with a standard printer cable, so the drivers for these devices route output to the printer port (PRN: or LPT1:). You can route output from the driver to a serial port by using PROC GDEVICE to change the GACCESS field for the device from SASGASTD>PRN: to SASGASTD>COM1:. You can also use the GACCESS= option in a GOPTIONS statement to override the GACCESS value specified in the device catalog entry.

Laser Printers

Output from SAS/GRAPH drivers for most laser printers (except Hewlett-Packard LaserJet models) is usually routed through COM1:. When output is sent through COM1:, the printer should be attached to the personal computer with a null modem cable. If your laser printer is attached to the printer port of your personal computer, you can use PROC GDEVICE to change the GACCESS field for the device from SASGASTD>COM1: to SASGASTD>PRN: or to SASGASTD>LPT1:. (For Hewlett-Packard LaserJet models, the standard drivers send output to the printer port.) You can also use the GACCESS= option in a GOPTIONS statement to override the GACCESS value specified in the device catalog entry.

Terminals

You can display SAS/GRAPH output on the screens of supported graphics terminals (including most Tektronix models) by connecting an appropriate cable from the serial port of the personal computer to the RS-232 port on the terminal. Output from these drivers is sent by default to COM1:. You will need to change the GACCESS setting if you want to use a different port.

Output to a File

One way to route output to a disk file is by using the GSFNAME= option (either in a GOPTIONS statement or in a GDEVICE entry). For example, to route output from the HP7475 driver to a graphics stream file named HP7475.GSF on a disk in drive A:, you can use the following statements:

```
filename grafout 'a:hp7475.gsf';
goptions gsfname=grafout
         gsfmode=replace
         device=hp7475;
title 'Test Output';
proc gslide;
run;
```

You must provide a FILENAME statement for the fileref. (Note that GRAFOUT is an arbitrary fileref; any valid SAS name is acceptable.) You must also specify either GSFMODE=REPLACE or GSFMODE=APPEND so that the driver performs the appropriate file output.

You can also specify a pathname using the GACCESS parameter (either in the device catalog entry or with the GACCESS= option in a GOPTIONS statement). If you use this method, you do not have to use the GSFNAME= option, but you still must specify GSFMODE=REPLACE or GSFMODE=APPEND. The following statements illustrate using a GOPTIONS statement to create the graphics stream file:

```
goptions gaccess='sasgastd>a:hp7475.gsf'
         gsfmode=replace;
title 'Test Output';
proc gslide;
run;
```

If you are sending output to a file that is later to be sent to a plotter, you may have to use the HANDSHAKE= option to specify how flow control is to be handled when the output is sent to the plotter. In SAS/GRAPH software for personal computers, drivers for some plotters use a software handshake (HANDSHAKE=SOFT), which is not appropriate when copying a file directly from disk to a plotter. If you intend to use a plotter in this manner, you should specify HANDSHAKE=NONE or HANDSHAKE=HARD.

Refer to "SAS/GRAPH Graphics Output" and "The GOPTIONS Statement" for details on using the GSFNAME=, GSFMODE=, and GACCESS= options.

USING DEVICE DRIVERS WITH SAS/GRAPH SOFTWARE FOR UNIX OPERATING SYSTEMS AND DERIVATIVES

SAS/GRAPH device drivers use the value of the GACCESS parameter to determine how to send output to a device. The GACCESS parameter is usually specified in the device catalog entry for the driver but can also be specified in the GACCESS= option in a GOPTIONS statement.

The GACCESS parameter value has the form

outputformat>destination

where *outputformat* indicates whether output is written to a file (usually a value of SASGASTD), or is piped to a UNIX command (a value of SASGACMD). The meaning of the *destination* portion of the parameter depends on the *outputformat* value.

If SASGASTD is specified, then the *destination* value is the name of the file to which the output is written. When the file is associated with a device, output is written directly to that device. For example, a GACCESS value of

SASGASTD>/DEV/TTY causes output to be written to /DEV/TTY (your terminal or workstation).

If SASGACMD is used as the *outputformat* value, then the *destination* value is the name of the UNIX command to which output is piped. Usually the **lp** command is used to invoke the line printer daemon to manage output. For example, the GACCESS value in standard device catalog entries for most printers is SASGACMD>lp -dgoutput, which causes output to be piped to the UNIX command 'lp -dgoutput'. This command uses the line printer daemon to send the output to the system destination defined as goutput.

The device catalog entries supplied with your release of SAS/GRAPH software contain GACCESS values that are appropriate for the most common configuration of the device on that system. When using a configuration that does not correspond with the default value, you will need to modify the driver to suit your needs. We recommend that before using a driver you use PROC GDEVICE to check the value of the GACCESS parameter in the device catalog entry for your driver. The following sections illustrate GACCESS values that can be used for different types of devices and configurations.

Terminals and Workstations

SAS/GRAPH software can be used with almost all graphics terminals from major manufacturers. To display a graph on your terminal, just specify the appropriate driver name in a GOPTIONS statement or when prompted by the SAS/GRAPH procedure. By default, SAS/GRAPH drivers for terminals and workstations use a GACCESS value of SASGASTD>/DEV/TTY, which causes output to be displayed on your screen. For example, if you are using a Hewlett-Packard 2697 terminal, you can use the following statements to produce a test graph on the terminal:

```
goptions device=hp2697;
proc gtestit;
run;
```

Hardcopy Devices

SAS/GRAPH drivers for hardcopy devices can send their output to the device in one of three ways:

- Output can be piped to a UNIX command (usually **lp**), which can then send the output to the device. This is usually used in cases where the hardcopy device is defined as a system output device that is shared by multiple users.
- On multi-user systems, some types of plotters can be attached in *eavesdrop* mode, between your terminal and the host computer. In these cases, output is sent back to your terminal but is intercepted and processed by the plotter.
- Output can be written directly to the file in the /DEV directory that is associated with the device. This sends the output directly to the device. This method should be used only if you have a single-user system or if you have exclusive access to the device.

Piping Output

In many cases you will want to pipe graphics output to one or more UNIX commands. This is especially useful when you are using a device that is shared by many users and you want to invoke a line printer daemon to manage the output.

To pipe output, use a GACCESS value of the form

SASGACMD>*commandname*

where *commandname* is the command to which output is to be piped. Most commonly, the **lp** command is used to invoke the line printer daemon to manage output to the device. For example, if you are using a Hewlett-Packard 7550 plotter that can be accessed by having the line printer daemon send output to a destination of hpplot, you can use the following SAS program to send output to it:

```
goptions device=hp7550
         gaccess='sasgacmd>lp -dhpplot';
title 'Hello World';
proc gslide;
run;
```

The Institute-supplied catalog entries for many printer drivers have a default GACCESS value of SASGACMD>lp -dgoutput. The first part of the value is correct for situations in which you want to pipe output to the lp command, but you will probably need to modify the destination to match what is used on your system.

If you are using a line printer daemon to send output to your device, an interface program should be used by the daemon to transmit the file. Your system administrator should refer to SAS Technical Report P-177, *System Administrator's Guide to the SAS System under UNIX Operating Systems and Derivatives* for details on writing an interface program.

Using Plotters in Eavesdrop Mode

If you are using a terminal to connect with a host computer and you have a plotter attached between the terminal and host, you should specify a GACCESS value of SASGASTD>/DEV/TTY. This value causes the driver to send its output back to your terminal. If the plotter is connected between the terminal and host, it will intercept the output and plot it. For example, if you have a Hewlett-Packard 7550 plotter attached in eavesdrop mode, you can use the following SAS statements:

```
goptions device=hp7550
         gaccess='sasgastd>/dev/tty';
title 'Hello World';
proc gslide;
run;
```

The Institute-supplied catalog entries for many plotter drivers have a default GACCESS value of sasgastd>/DEV/TTY, which assumes that the plotter will be attached in an eavesdrop configuration. You will need to modify the GACCESS value if your plotter is accessed through the lp command.

Output Directly to the Device

To send output directly to a hardcopy device, you can specify a GACCESS value that causes the driver to write output to the file in the /DEV directory that is associated with the device. For example, suppose you have a Hewlett-Packard 7550 plotter that your system recognizes as /DEV/TTY08. You can send output directly to the plotter with the following SAS statements:

```
goptions device=hp7550
         gaccess='sasgastd>/dev/tty08';
title 'Hello World';
proc gslide;
run;
```

Note that if you have specified the desired GACCESS value in the HP7550 entry in your device catalog, you do not have to specify it in a GOPTIONS statement.

You should send output directly to the device only when you have a single-user system or have exclusive access to the device. If more that one person tries to directly access the device at the same time, results may be unpredictable. Even if you do have a single-user system or exclusive access to the device, you may still find it preferable to send output through the lp command rather than directly to the device since writing directly to the device will tie up your SAS session while the graph is being drawn.

Output to a File

In some cases, you may want to send driver output to a disk file rather than directly to the device. You can then send the graphics stream file to the device at a later time. This is commonly done when the device is not directly attached to the host computer or workstation.

One way to route output to a disk file is by using the GSFNAME= option (either in a GOPTIONS statement or in a GDEVICE entry). For example, to route output from the HP7475 driver to a file named /USERS/MYDIR/HPGSF, you can use the following statements:

```
filename grafout '/users/mydir/hpgsf';
goptions gsfname=grafout
         gsfmode=replace
         device=hp7475;
title 'Test Output';
proc gslide;
run;
```

You must provide a FILENAME statement to associate a filename with the fileref. (Note that GRAFOUT is an arbitrary fileref; you can use any valid SAS name.) You must also specify either GSFMODE=REPLACE or GSFMODE=APPEND so that the driver performs the appropriate file output.

Another way of creating a graphics stream file is to specify a pathname using the GACCESS= option (either in a GOPTIONS statement or in a GDEVICE catalog entry). If you use this method, you do not have to use the GSFNAME= option, but you still must specify GSFMODE=REPLACE or GSFMODE=APPEND. The following statements illustrate this approach using a GOPTIONS statement:

```
goptions gaccess='sasgastd>/users/mydir/hpgsf'
         gsfmode=replace;
title 'Test Output';
proc gslide;
run;
```

MODIFYING OR CREATING DEVICE DRIVERS

If you have a device for which there is not an Institute-supplied driver, you may be able to modify an existing driver to use with your device. This can be done by copying an entry from the Institute-supplied device catalog and modifying options using PROC GDEVICE. See "The GDEVICE Procedure" for details on modifying entries in a device catalog.

If this approach is not suitable for your device, you can write your own driver using the Metagraphics driver facility. Details on creating a Metagraphics driver can be found in *SAS/GRAPH Guide to Hardware Interfaces, Release 6.03 Edition* or in *SAS/GRAPH Hardware Interfaces for Personal Computers, Version 6 Edition*.

LIST OF SAS/GRAPH DEVICE DRIVERS

Table A3.3 lists most of the device drivers that are available with SAS/GRAPH software. This may not be a complete list of all of the drivers available to you. For a complete list of drivers available with the release of SAS/GRAPH software you are using, run PROC GDEVICE using the LIST command. (See "The GDEVICE Procedure" for details on using PROC GDEVICE.)

When using the table below, you should be aware of the following:

- You can determine additional attributes for all drivers (such as default colors, graph size, HPOS= and VPOS= values, and so on) by running PROC GDEVICE.
- Many devices that are not listed below can be used with drivers for other devices. For example, the PS driver can be used with any device that uses the PostScript page description language. The drivers for Hewlett-Packard plotters (HP7475 and others) can be used for devices that support HPGL plotter graphics language.
- You can use PROC GDEVICE to create new entries in your device catalog by modifying existing drivers. This is useful if you want to change such attributes as default colors, size, resolution, or orientation for a driver. In many cases, if the device you are using is not listed below, you may be able to create one for it by modifying one of the catalog entries for an existing driver.
- For some devices, dimensions are listed that reflect the size of the paper that the driver assumes is being used, not the size of the graph. The graph itself allows for a border and will be somewhat smaller than the paper.

Drivers for most personal computer display adapaters are available only with SAS/GRAPH software for personal computers. Devices that are supported only for personal computers are indicated by an asterisk (*).

Table A3.3 SAS/GRAPH Device Drivers

Device	Driver Name
Apple LaserWriter (PostScript device)	APPLELW
Apple LaserWriter Plus (PostScript device)	APLPLUS
ACT inkjet printer with Lasergraphics UI-100 rasterizer	UI100A
AGS 1000 terminal	AGS1000
*AT&T PC6300 (high-resolution monochrome)	PC6300
*AT&T PC6300 (low-resolution color)	PC6300L
*AT&T PC6300 (medium-resolution monochrome)	PC6300M
CalComp 81 plotter	CAL81
CalComp 84 plotter	CAL84
*CGA card: high intensity, palette 0 (green, red, yellow)	CGAH0

(continued on next page)

Table A3.3 (continued)

Device	Driver Name
*CGA card: high intensity, palette 1 (cyan, magenta, white)	CGAH1
*CGA card: monochrome monitor	CGAM
*CGA card: palette 0 (green, red, yellow)	CGA
*CGA card: palette 0 (green, red, yellow)	CGA0
*CGA card: palette 1 (cyan, magenta, white)	CGA1
*COMPAQ Portable III and IV	COMPAQ3
Digital LCP01 printer	LCP01
Digital LN01 printer, Tektronix 4014 emulation	TEKLN01
Digital VT125 terminal	VT125
Digital VT240 terminal	VT240
Digital VT241 terminal	VT241
Digital VT241A terminal	VT241A
Digital VT330 terminal	VT330
Digital VT340 terminal	VT340
*EGA card: color monitor display 320 x 200 resolution (16 colors)	EGACX
*EGA card: color monitor display 640 x 200 resolution (16 colors)	EGA
*EGA card: color monitor display 640 x 200 resolution (16 colors)	EGAC
*EGA card: monochrome display	EGAM
*EGA card: 128K, enhanced color display (16 colors from palette of 64)	EGAL
*EGA card: 64K, monitor with two bit planes (3 colors)	EGAS
Epson FX-85 printer	FX85
Epson FX-185 printer	FX185
Epson LQ-800 printer	LQ800
Epson LQ-1000 printer	LQ1000
*Hercules monochrome graphics board	HERCULES
Hewlett-Packard COLORPRO plotter	COLORPRO
Hewlett-Packard 2393 terminal	HP2393
Hewlett-Packard 2397A terminal	HP2397
Hewlett-Packard 2623 terminal	HP2623
Hewlett-Packard 2627 terminal	HP2627
Hewlett-Packard 2647 terminal	HP2647
Hewlett-Packard 2648 terminal	HP2648
Hewlett-Packard 7220 plotter A model, 4 pens	HP7220

(continued on next page)

Table A3.3   (*continued*)

Device	Driver Name
Hewlett-Packard 7220 plotter C model, 8 pens	HP7220C
Hewlett-Packard 7220 plotter S model, 4 pens, autofeed	HP7220S
Hewlett-Packard 7220 plotter T model, 8 pens, autofeed	HP7220T
Hewlett-Packard 7225 plotter	HP7225
Hewlett-Packard 7440 plotter	HP7440
Hewlett-Packard 7440 plotter with GEC cartridge	HP7440E
Hewlett-Packard 7470 plotter	HP7470
Hewlett-Packard 7475 plotter A size paper (8.5″ x 11″)	HP7475
Hewlett-Packard 7475 plotter A size paper (8.5″ x 11″)	HP7475A
Hewlett-Packard 7475 plotter B size paper (17″ x 22″)	HP7475B
Hewlett-Packard 7510 film recorder	HP7510
Hewlett-Packard 7550 plotter A size paper (8.5″ x 11″)	HP7550
Hewlett-Packard 7550 plotter A size paper (8.5″ x 11″)	HP7550A
Hewlett-Packard 7550 plotter B size paper (11″ x 17″)	HP7550B
Hewlett-Packard 7570 plotter C size paper (17″ x 22″)	HP7570
Hewlett-Packard 7570 plotter D size paper (22″ x 34″)	HP7570D
Hewlett-Packard 7580 plotter A size paper (8.5″ x 11″)	HP7580A
Hewlett-Packard 7580 plotter B size paper (22″ x 34″)	HP7580B
Hewlett-Packard 7580 plotter C size paper (17″ x 22″)	HP7580C
Hewlett-Packard 7580 plotter D size paper (22″ x 34″)	HP7580D
Hewlett-Packard 7585 plotter C size paper (17″ x 22″)	HP7585C
Hewlett-Packard 7585 plotter D size paper (22″ x 34″)	HP7585D
Hewlett-Packard 7585 plotter E size paper (34″ x 44″)	HP7585E

(*continued on next page*)

Table A3.3   (*continued*)

Device	Driver Name
Hewlett-Packard 7586 plotter C size paper (17″ x 22″)	HP7586C
Hewlett-Packard 7586 plotter E size paper (34″ x 44″)	HP7586E
Hewlett-Packard LaserJet Printer (75 dpi resolution)	HPLJ0
Hewlett-Packard LaserJet Plus Printer (150 dpi resolution)	HPLJ5P2
Hewlett-Packard LaserJet 500 Plus Printer (300 dpi resolution)	HPLJ5P3
Hewlett-Packard LaserJet Series II Printer (300 dpi resolution)	HPLJS2
Hewlett-Packard PaintJet Printer (180 dpi resolution)	HPPJ180
Hewlett-Packard PaintJet Printer (90 dpi resolution)	HPPJ90
Houston Instrument DMP-3 plotter, 1 pen	DMP3B
Houston Instrument DMP-3 plotter, 6 pens	DMP3
Houston Instrument DMP-4 plotter, 1 pen	DMP4B
Houston Instrument DMP-4 plotter, 6 pens	DMP4
Houston Instrument DMP-6 plotter, 1 pen	DMP6B
Houston Instrument DMP-6 plotter, 8 pens	DMP6
Houston Instrument DMP-7 plotter, 1 pen	DMP7B
Houston Instrument DMP-7 plotter, 8 pens	DMP7
Houston Instrument DMP-29 plotter A3 paper (11″ x 17″)	DMP29
Houston Instrument DMP-29 plotter A4 paper (8.5″ x 11″)	DMP29A4
Houston Instrument DMP-40 plotter A size paper (8.5″ x 11″)	DMP40A
Houston Instrument DMP-40 plotter B size paper (11″ x 17″)	DMP40
Houston Instrument DMP-41 plotter C size paper (17″ x 22″)	DMP41C
Houston Instrument DMP-41 plotter D size paper (22″ x 34″)	DMP41
Houston Instrument DMP-42 plotter A1 size paper (24″ x 34″)	DMP42
Houston Instrument DMP-42 plotter A2 size paper (17″ x 24″)	DMP42A2
Houston Instrument DMP-50 plotter A size paper (8.5″ x 11″)	DMP50A

(*continued on next page*)

Table A3.3 (*continued*)

Device	Driver Name
Houston Instrument DMP-50 plotter B size paper (11″ x 17″)	DMP50
Houston Instrument DMP-51 plotter C size paper (17″ x 22″)	DMP51C
Houston Instrument DMP-51 plotter D size paper (22″ x 34″)	DMP51
Houston Instrument DMP-52 plotter Architectural paper (24″ x 36″)	DMP52AR
Houston Instrument DMP-52 plotter A1 size paper (24″ x 34″)	DMP52
Houston Instrument DMP-52 plotter A2 size paper (17″ x 24″)	DMP52A2
Houston Instrument DMP-56A plotter DIN A0 paper	DMP56A0
Houston Instrument DMP-56A plotter DIN A1 paper	DMP56A1
Houston Instrument DMP-56A plotter DIN A2 paper	DMP56A2
Houston Instrument DMP-56A plotter DIN A3 paper	DMP56A3
Houston Instrument DMP-56A plotter DIN A4 paper	DMP56A4
Houston Instrument DMP-56A plotter Architectural C paper	DMP56ARC
Houston Instrument DMP-56A plotter Architectural D paper	DMP56ARD
Houston Instrument DMP-56A plotter Architectural E paper	DMP56ARE
Houston Instrument DMP-56A plotter Engineering A paper	DMP56ENA
Houston Instrument DMP-56A plotter Engineering B paper	DMP56ENB
Houston Instrument DMP-56A plotter Engineering C paper	DMP56ENC
Houston Instrument DMP-56A plotter Engineering D paper	DMP56END
Houston Instrument DMP-56A plotter Engineering E paper	DMP56ENE
Houston Instrument DMP-56A plotter Oversize A0 paper	DMP56OA0
Houston Instrument DMP-56A plotter Oversize A1 paper	DMP56OA1

(*continued on next page*)

Table A3.3   (*continued*)

Device	Driver Name
Houston Instrument DMP-56A plotter Oversize A2 paper	DMP56OA2
Houston Instrument DMP-56A plotter Oversize A3 paper	DMP56OA3
Houston Instrument DMP-56A plotter Oversize A4 paper	DMP56OA4
Imagen graphics printer, black only	IMPRESS
Imagen graphics printer, 7 gray shades	IMPRESSC
IBM 3852-2 printer (100 x 96 DPI resolution)	IBM3852
IBM 3852-2 printer (100 x 72 DPI resolution)	IBM3852L
IBM 80 CPS graphics printer	IBMGPRT
IBM Colorjet printer	COLORJET
IBM Instruments XY/749 plotter	IBMXY749
IBM Instruments XY/750 plotter	IBMXY750
*IBM 3270 PC with APA card high intensity palette 0 (green, red, brown)	PC3270D
*IBM 3270 PC with APA card high intensity palette 1 (cyan, magenta, white)	PC3270C
*IBM 3270 PC with APA card, monochrome	PC3270M
*IBM 3270 PC with APA card palette 0 (green, red, brown)	PC3270
*IBM 3270 PC with APA card palette 0 (green, red, brown)	PC3270B
*IBM 3270 PC with APA card palette 1 (cyan, magenta, white)	PC3270A
IBM Proprinter	PROPRINT
Lasergraphics UI-100 rasterizer	UI100
Matrix Instruments PCR film recorder linear lookup table, 2K x 2K resolution	PCR2XL
Matrix Instruments PCR film recorder linear lookup table, 4K x 4K resolution	PCR4XL
Matrix Instruments PCR film recorder log lookup table, 2K x 2K resolution	PCR2X
Matrix Instruments PCR film recorder log lookup table, 4K x 4K resolution	PCR4X
Matrix Instruments QCR film recorder linear lookup table, 2K x 2K resolution	QCR2XL
Matrix Instruments QCR film recorder linear lookup table, 4K x 4K resolution	QCR4XL
Matrix Instruments QCR film recorder log lookup table, 2K x 2K resolution	QCR2X
Matrix Instruments QCR film recorder log lookup table, 4K x 4K resolution	QCR4X

(*continued on next page*)

Table A3.3 (continued)

Device	Driver Name
Matrix Instruments QCR 2K film recorder with Lasergraphics UI-100 rasterizer	UI100Q
Matrix Instruments QCR 35mm 2K film recorder with Lasergraphics UI-100 rasterizer	UI100Q35
Matrix Instruments QCR 35mm 4K film recorder with Lasergraphics UI-100 rasterizer	UI200Q35
Matrix Instruments QCR 4K film recorder with Lasergraphics UI-100 rasterizer	UI200Q
Matrix Instruments TT200 printer: QVP/SA or MVP/SA	TT200
Matrix Instruments TT200 printer: QVP/PC or MVP/PC	TT200PC
Metagraphics driver calling CalComp routines	GXTSLINK
PostScript Devices	PS
PostScript Devices: IBM encapsulated files	PSEPSF
PostScript Devices: 1-pixel-width lines	PSL
PostScript Devices: fixed text spacing	PSFIX
PostScript Devices: fixed text spacing, 1-pixel-width lines	PSLFIX
Printacolor inkjet printer with Lasergraphics UI-100 rasterizer	UI100P
*PS/2 with 8503 monochrome monitor	PS2EGAM
*PS/2 with 8512, 8513, or 8514 monitors (16 colors of palette of 64)	PS2EGA
QMS printer, Tektronix 4014 emulation	TEKQMS
QMS PS-800 laser printer (PostScript device)	QMSPS800
QMS PS-800+ laser printer (PostScript device)	Q800PLUS
QMS 800 printer, QUIC controller	QMS800
QMS 800 printer, QUIC controller, erase vectors	QMS800E
QVP SCODL file (generic)	QVP
QVP SCODL file (generic), 2K resolution	QVP2X
QVP SCODL file (generic), 4K resolution	QVP4X
Seiko D-SCAN inkjet printer with Lasergraphics UI-100 rasterizer	UI100S
Servogor 281 plotter	SER281
Tektronix PC-4100 system	PC4100
Tektronix 4010 terminal	TEK4010
Tektronix 4014 terminal	TEK4014
Tektronix 4015 terminal	TEK4015
Tektronix 4104 terminal	TEK4104
Tektronix 4104A terminal	TEK4104A

(continued on next page)

Table A3.3   (*continued*)

Device	Driver Name
Tektronix 4105 terminal	TEK4105
Tektronix 4105A terminal	TEK4105A
Tektronix 4106 terminal	TEK4106
Tektronix 4106A terminal	TEK4106A
Tektronix 4107 terminal	TEK4107
Tektronix 4107A terminal	TEK4107A
Tektronix 4109 terminal	TEK4109
Tektronix 4109A terminal	TEK4109A
Tektronix 4111 terminal	TEK4111
Tektronix 4112 terminal	TEK4112
Tektronix 4113 terminal	TEK4113
Tektronix 4113 terminal, 4 bit planes	TEK4113X
Tektronix 4115 terminal	TEK4115
Tektronix 4125 terminal, 2 bit planes	TEK4125
Tektronix 4125 terminal, 4 bit planes	TEK4125X
Tektronix 4125 terminal, 6 bit planes	TEK4125Y
Tektronix 4125 terminal, 8 bit planes	TEK4125Z
Tektronix 4128 terminal, 4 bit planes	TEK4128X
Tektronix 4128 terminal, 6 bit planes	TEK4128Y
Tektronix 4128 terminal, 8 bit planes	TEK4128Z
Tektronix 4129 terminal	TEK4129
Tektronix 4205 terminal	TEK4205
Tektronix 4207 terminal	TEK4207
Tektronix 4208 terminal	TEK4208
Tektronix 4209 terminal	TEK4209
Tektronix 4510 rasterizer with 4691/4692 inkjet printer	TEK4510
Tektronix 4691/4692 inkjet printer with Lasergraphics UI-100 rasterizer	UI100T
Vectrix VXPC-4096 graphics board	VECTRIX
Vectrix VXPC-4096 graphics board, hex mode	VECTRIXX
Xerox 2700 printer 300 dpi resolution (4" x 4" image)	X2700
Xerox 2700 printer 150 dpi resolution (10" x 7.5" image)	X2700B
Xerox 2700 printer 75 dpi resolution (10" x 13" image)	X2700C
Xerox 3700 printer, 300 dpi resolution	X3700

(*continued on next page*)

Table A3.3   (*continued*)

Device	Driver Name
Xerox 4045 printer 512K memory (5" x 7.5" picture at 300 dpi)	X4045
Xerox 4045 printer, 150 dpi resolution	X4045B
Xerox 4045 printer, 150/300 dpi resolution	X4045AB
Xerox 4045 printer, 150/75 dpi resolution	X4045BC
Xerox 4045 printer, 300/75 dpi resolution	X4045AC
Xerox 4045 printer, 75 dpi resolution	X4045C
Xerox 4045 printer 300 dpi resolution—landscape	X4045L
Xerox 4045 printer 300 dpi resolution—portrait	X4045P
Xerox 6500 color copier with Lasergraphics UI-100 rasterizer	UI100X
ZETA 1453 plotter	ZETA1453
ZETA 8 or 887 plotter, film roll	ZETA8F
ZETA 8 or 887 plotter, Kromecote roll	ZETA8K
ZETA 8 or 887 plotter, Mylar roll	ZETA8M
ZETA 8 or 887 plotter, translucent roll	ZETA8T
ZETA 8 or 887 plotter, vellum roll	ZETA8V
ZETA 8 plotter, Kromecote roll	ZETA8
ZETA 887 plotter, Kromecote roll	ZETA887
ZETAVUE film recorder	ZETAVUE
ZETA8 plotter, 5.3z level firmware	OLDZETA8

Changes and Enhancements to SAS/GRAPH® Software

Listed below are brief summaries of the changes and enhancements to SAS/GRAPH software for Version 6. Version 5 SAS/GRAPH software users should note that the basic operation of procedures is the same in Version 5 and Version 6. However, several options have been added to enhance the capabilities of various statements and procedures. Refer to the appropriate chapter(s) in this guide for complete descriptions.

GOPTIONS Statement

New options allow you more control over your graphics environment and output.

- The CTEXT=, FTEXT=, and HTEXT= options allow you to specify the default color, font, and height for all text in the display. This is especially useful with PROC GCHART, PROC GPRINT, and PROC G3D.
- The REPAINT option allows you to overdraw graphs on hardcopy devices that produce light images.
- The RESET= option allows you to easily reset options previously specified to their default values. You can also cancel the values of any global statements (including TITLE, NOTE, FOOTNOTE, PATTERN, SYMBOL, and so on) using the RESET= option.
- The ROTATE= option allows you to specify landscape or portrait orientation for your graphs.

CHANGES TO PROCEDURES

GCHART Procedure

One option has changed and a new option has been added to the GCHART procedure.

- The MIDPOINTS= option now provides two different algorithms for selecting numeric midpoints. You can specify the method to be used.
- A new option, NOGROUPHEADING, is available in PIE and STAR statements to omit the headings normally drawn on pie and star charts when you specify the GROUP= option.

GCONTOUR Procedure

In the GCONTOUR procedure, legends are now calculated with a method that is also used in the GCHART and GPLOT procedures. Therefore, legends in graphs produced with the GCONTOUR procedure have a greater precision than in previous releases.

GDEVICE Procedure

A new procedure, GDEVICE, allows you to examine and change device driver parameters for graphics devices. The GDEVICE procedure can be used in full-screen or line mode to

- list the device drivers available with your version of SAS/GRAPH software
- edit the options and parameters for Institute-supplied device drivers
- create new device drivers.

Unlike the GOPTIONS statement, which allows you to change system options for a particular graph or session, the GDEVICE procedure allows you to change system options for all graphs produced on your graphics device.

GFONT Procedure

The GFONT procedure now supports the following features:

- kerning and spacing of characters
- proportional characters
- circular arcs.

GOPTIONS Procedure

Two new options are available in the GOPTIONS procedure:

- The AXIS option lists all currently defined AXIS statements.
- The LEGEND option lists all currently defined LEGEND statements.

GREPLAY Procedure

Several new features are available in the GREPLAY procedure:

- The REPLAY, TPLAY, COPY, DELETE, and GROUP commands now accept a range of graphs for processing.
- The SAS Display Manager System global commands can be used in PROC GREPLAY screens.
- When you enter a value for any field in a template design screen for a new template and press RETURN, the remaining fields are filled with default values.

- The TDEF (template definition) command now requires only one option (you can specify more than one). Any unspecified options are assigned default values.

GTESTIT Procedure

The following new features are available in the GTESTIT procedure:

- The driver load module is displayed in picture 1 (for example, SASGDEGA).
- If the device specifies more than fifteen colors, only fifteen colors are displayed in picture 1 but the log lists all available colors.
- The background color is listed in the log.
- The MAX= option refers to MAXPOLY, the maximum number of vertices a hardware polygon command can have.

ADDITIONAL CHANGES

SAS/GRAPH Type Styles and Fonts

In addition to the fonts available in Version 5 SAS/GRAPH software, fifteen new fonts are available in Release 6.03 SAS/GRAPH software.

SAS/GRAPH Map Data Sets

The COUNTY and USCOUNTY data sets have been substituted for the COUNTIES data set available in Version 5 SAS/GRAPH software. The COUNTY data set contains unprojected but reduced coordinates for county boundaries. The USCOUNTY data set contains projected and reduced coordinates for county boundaries. No equivalent for the COUNTIES data set, which provided unprojected and unreduced coordinates for county boundaries, has been provided.

Index

G

Q

R

Z

Your Turn

If you have comments or suggestions about the *SAS/GRAPH User's Guide, Release 6.03 Edition* or SAS/GRAPH software, please send them to us on a photocopy of this page.

Please return the photocopy to the Publications Division (for comments about this book) or the Technical Support Department (for suggestions about the software) at SAS Institute Inc., SAS Circle, Box 8000, Cary, NC 27512-8000.